LITERACY RESEARCH METHODOLOGIES

Also from the Editors

Best Practices in Early Literacy Instruction
Edited by Diane M. Barone and Marla H. Mallette

Handbook of Effective Literacy Instruction:
Research-Based Practice K–8
Edited by Barbara M. Taylor and Nell K. Duke

Literacy
Research
Methodologies

THIRD EDITION

edited by
Marla H. Mallette
Nell K. Duke

Foreword by Seth A. Parsons

THE GUILFORD PRESS
New York   London

Library of Congress Cataloging-in-Publication Data

Names: Mallette, Marla H., editor. | Duke, Nell K., editor.
Title: Literacy research methodologies / edited by Marla H. Mallette,
    Nell K. Duke.
Description: Third edition. | New York : The Guilford Press, 2021. |
    Includes bibliographical references and index.
Identifiers: LCCN 2020006178 | ISBN 9781462544318 (paperback) |
    ISBN 9781462544325 (cloth)
Subjects: LCSH: Reading—Research—Methodology.
Classification: LCC LB1050.6 .L58 2021 | DDC 428.407/2—dc23
LC record available at *https://lccn.loc.gov/2020006178*

About the Editors

Marla H. Mallette, PhD, is Associate Professor in the Department of Teaching, Learning and Educational Leadership at Binghamton University, State University of New York, where she also serves as Doctoral Program Coordinator. Her research focuses on early literacy, research methodologies, and mixed methods research in literacy. Dr. Mallette has published and presented on literacy research methodologies and the preparation of literacy researchers, and has used various methodologies in her own work.

Nell K. Duke, EdD, is Professor in Language, Literacy, and Culture and in the Combined Program in Education and Psychology at the University of Michigan. Her work focuses on early literacy development, particularly among children living in economic poverty. She has a strong interest in bridging gaps between educational research, policy, and practice. Dr. Duke is a recipient of the William S. Gray Citation of Merit from the International Literacy Association. She has used a variety of research methodologies in her own research and has taught courses on research design.

Contributors

Gwynne Ellen Ash, PhD, is Professor in the Department of Curriculum and Instruction at Texas State University, where she teaches undergraduate and graduate courses in literacy methods, literacy assessment and intervention, and children's and young adult literature. Her work has been published in books and leading journals in the fields of literacy research and instruction.

James J. Bason, PhD, is Associate Research Scientist and Director of the Survey Research Center at the University of Georgia, Athens. He is also a fellow at the University's Institute for Behavioral Research. Dr. Bason is the author of several publications based on data collected by the Center and is an active member of the American Association for Public Opinion Research, a past president of the Southern Association for Public Opinion Research, and a current executive committee member of the National Network of State Polls. His research interests include survey methodology, elections, and electoral behavior.

James F. Baumann, PhD, holds the Chancellor's Chair for Excellence in Literacy Education emeritus at the University of Missouri. Formerly, he was the Wyoming Excellence Chair of Literacy Education at the University of Wyoming and was a professor of reading education at the University of Georgia and Purdue University. Dr. Baumann has served as editor of *The Reading Teacher* and on the Boards of Directors for the International Literacy Association and the Literacy Research Association. An elected member of the Reading Hall of Fame, Dr. Baumann has conducted survey research and published on elementary teachers' perspectives on reading instruction and materials.

Adriana G. Bus, PhD, is Professor in Early Childhood Education at the University of Stavanger, Norway; honorary professor at ELTE Eötvös Loránd University, Budapest, Hungary; and an emeritus professor of Leiden University, Netherlands. She has carried out experimental research and meta-analyses of both paper book reading and digital book reading, with a special interest in early childhood. Dr. Bus aims at designing new digital book formats that benefit not only children's meaning-making of narratives but also their enjoyment of literature.

Byeong-Young Cho, PhD, is Associate Professor in the College of Education at Hanyang University in Seoul, South Korea. Previously he taught at the University of Pittsburgh, where he was also a Research Scientist at the Learning Research and Development Center. His major research interests are in the area of reading comprehension, new literacies, higher-order thinking, and reading assessment. Dr. Cho has published journal articles and book chapters on how to support and engage students with multiple sources in complex literacy tasks.

Jessica A. Church, PhD, is an Associate Professor in the Department of Psychology at the University of Texas at Austin, and a member of the Psychiatry Department, Institute for Neuroscience, and Biomedical Imaging Center. Dr. Church heads the Austin neuroimaging team that evaluates functional brain data collected as part of the Texas Center for Learning Disabilities. Her lab investigates how academic learning and learning change interacts with the brain's control networks, and how control abilities are impacted by different developmental disorders.

Catherine Compton-Lilly, EdD, holds the John C. Hungerpiller Chair in the College of Education at the University of South Carolina. She engages in longitudinal research projects. Her interests include examining how time operates as a contextual factor in children's lives as they progress through school and construct their identities as students and readers. In an ongoing study, Dr. Compton-Lilly is following children from immigrant families from primary school through high school.

Samuel DeJulio, PhD, is Assistant Professor of Literacy in the Department of Interdisciplinary Learning and Teaching at the University of Texas at San Antonio. His work is focused on literacy teacher preparation, particularly on experiences within field-based courses and partnerships with local schools, teachers, and families. Recently, he has collaborated with literacy teachers in Colombia to explore inquiry-based teaching and learning across international contexts.

Nell K. Duke, EdD (see "About the Editors").

Jack M. Fletcher, PhD, is a Hugh Roy and Lillie Cranz Cullen Distinguished Professor and Chair, Department of Psychology, at the University of Houston. A board-certified child neuropsychologist, Dr. Fletcher completed research on many issues related to learning disabilities and dyslexia, including definition and classification, neurobiological correlates, and intervention. He is a recipient of the Samuel T. Orton Award from the International Dyslexia Association, a co-recipient of the Albert J. Harris Award from the International Literacy Association, and a past president of the International Neuropsychological Society.

Sarah Galvin is a doctoral student in the Educational Psychology and Educational Technology Program at Michigan State University. Her research focuses on the intersection of social media, literacies, and identity development in adolescent and young adult learning. More specifically, she is interested in how students' identities as writers differ on social media compared to in the classroom and what implications this might have for writing pedagogy.

Christine Greenhow, EdD, is Associate Professor of Educational Psychology and Educational Technology at Michigan State University. Her research focuses on the study and design of technologies, such as social media, for teaching and learning and new forms of digital, open, and social scholarship. She is currently exploring young people's social media practices within various educational settings and uneven technology infrastructures. She serves on the editorial boards of various journals.

Douglas K. Hartman, PhD, is Professor of Literacy and Technology in the College of Education at Michigan State University. He has served as co-lead editor of the *Journal of Literacy Research,* codirector and principal investigator in the Literacy Achievement Research Center, and research fellow with the Center for Health Intervention and Prevention. Dr. Hartman's research focuses on the use of technologies for human learning in a number of domains.

James V. Hoffman, PhD, is Professor of Language and Literacy Studies at the University of North Texas, where he holds the Meadows Endowed Chair for Excellence in Literacy. Dr. Hoffman is a former editor of *The Reading Research Quarterly* and *The Yearbook of the National Reading Conference.* He has served as president of the National Reading Conference and as a member of the Board of Directors of the International Literacy Association. His research interests focus on initial teacher preparation in literacy.

Gay Ivey, PhD, is the William E. Moran Distinguished Professor in Literacy at the University of North Carolina at Greensboro. Her research focuses on the processes and consequences of school reading and writing experiences that children and young adults find meaningful and on co-designing with teachers instruction that prioritizes student engagement. She is a past president of the Literacy Research Association and an elected member of the Reading Hall of Fame.

Michael J. Kieffer, EdD, is Associate Professor of Literacy Education at the Steinhardt School of Culture, Education, and Human Development at New York University. His research focuses on the language and literacy development of students from linguistically diverse backgrounds. He uses a variety of longitudinal, experimental, quasi-experimental, and correlational methods to shed light on the complexities of students' reading and language learning. Dr. Kieffer's work has been published in journals of education, reading research, applied linguistics, and applied psychology. He has received awards from the Spencer Foundation, the American Educational Research Association, and the International Literacy Association.

Alice Y. Lee, PhD, is Assistant Professor of Critical Literacy in the Graduate School of Education at the University of California, Riverside. Her research focuses on the raciolinguistic life experiences of teachers, and how such experiences are embodied into pedagogy. She employs this lens to interrogate the continued maltreatment of African American Black Language speakers in schooling. Dr. Lee also applies her work toward teacher selection, recruitment, and education in efforts to diversify the teacher workforce. Her work has been supported by the Spencer Foundation; published in *The Reading Teacher, Language Arts Journal of Michigan*, and *Talking Points*; and she currently serves on the editorial board of the *Journal of Literacy Research.*

Amos J. Lee, PhD, is Assistant Professor of Teaching in the Graduate School of Education at the University of California, Riverside. His research uses critical race methodology and critical race spatial analysis in deconstructing the ways that school-of-choice models fall short in promoting racial equity in public schools. Dr. Lee applies this work in consulting school districts about desegregating schools.

Julia Lindsey is a doctoral candidate at the University of Michigan School of Education. Her research interests focus on phonics, early reading instruction, and developing early reading programs and materials that can impact reading outcomes while also engaging children in meaningful, culturally relevant instruction. She is currently exploring the implementation of research-aligned texts on early reading outcomes and the implementation of a culturally responsive summer literacy program.

Marla H. Mallette, PhD (see "About the Editors").

Ramón A. Martínez, PhD, is Assistant Professor in the Graduate School of Education and the Center for Comparative Studies in Race and Ethnicity at Stanford University. His research explores language and literacy among students of color in urban schools, with a particular focus on the learning experiences of bi/multilingual Chicana/o/x and Latina/o/x children and youth.

Sarah J. McCarthey, PhD, is Professor of Language and Literacy and Department Head of Curriculum and Instruction at the University of Illinois at Urbana–Champaign. Her research focuses on students' literate identities and use of online writing environments, classroom writing instruction, and the role of professional development in teachers' understandings of writing. Dr. McCarthey is a member of the Board of Directors for the Literacy Research Association and Co-Director of the University of Illinois Writing Project. She is President of the McCarthey Dressman Education Foundation, which provides grants for innovative teaching and enhancing student learning.

Suzanne E. Mol, PhD, is Assistant Professor in the Institute of Education and Child Studies at Leiden University, Netherlands. Her research interests focus on reading development, reading motivation, parental involvement, and inclusive education. Dr. Mol has experience with conducting meta-analyses, surveys, and experimental research.

M. Kristiina Montero, PhD, is Associate Professor in the Faculty of Education at Wilfrid Laurier University, Waterloo, Canada. Her research and practice are framed in community-engaged scholarship that aims to use the space of research to engage with practical problems defined by community stakeholders and to give voice to marginalized individuals and communities. Dr. Montero's work examines the impact of culturally responsive early literacy instructional practices on the language and literacy development of adolescent English language learners with limited prior schooling, and exploring the use of decolonizing pedagogies in teacher education.

Susan B. Neuman, EdD, is Professor and Chair of the Teaching and Learning Department at the Steinhardt School of Culture, Education, and Human Development at New York University. Previously, she served on the faculty in Educational Studies at the University of Michigan and also as the U.S. Assistant Secretary of Elementary and Secondary Education. Dr. Neuman helped to establish the Early Reading First program and the Early Childhood Educator Professional

Development Education Program. Her work focuses on interventions that change the odds for children at risk and on bringing content-rich instruction to children through shared books and media experiences.

Anthony J. Onwuegbuzie, PhD, is a Senior Research Associate at the University of Cambridge. In addition, he is Distinguished Visiting Professor at the University of Johannesburg and Honorary Professor at the University of South Africa. Dr. Onwuegbuzie is a former editor of *Educational Researcher* and currently serves as editor-in-chief of the *International Journal of Multiple Research Approaches* and as editor of *Research in the Schools.* He is a past president of the Mixed Methods International Research Association.

Misty Sailors, PhD, is Professor and Chair of the Department of Teacher Education and Administration in the College of Education at the University of North Texas. A literacy researcher, reading specialist, and teacher educator, her scholarly work focuses on literacy tools found in classrooms, the professional development of reading teachers and literacy coaches, literacy program development, and literacy research methodologies. Dr. Sailors's work has appeared in leading journals, and she is coeditor or coauthor of several books.

Melissa Schieble, PhD, is Associate Professor of English Education at Hunter College of the City University of New York. Her research interests focus on the intersections of critical literacies, literature-based instruction, and classroom discourse. She is currently exploring the ways that discourse analysis methodologies can be used as a tool for critical reflexive practice and teacher learning.

Anna Shapiro, PhD, is a Postdoctoral Research Associate at the Curry School of Education and Human Development, University of Virginia. Her research interests include access to high-quality early learning environments for preschool-age children, early intervention services for children with or at risk for developing disabilities, and special education policies in early elementary grades.

Norman A. Stahl, PhD, is Professor Emeritus of Literacy Education at Northern Illinois University. He has been the president of the Literacy Research Association, the Association of Literacy Educators and Researchers, and the College Reading and Learning Association, and chair of the American Reading Forum. He is a CLADEA National Fellow and a member of the Reading Hall of Fame. Dr. Stahl's scholarly interests include literacy history, postsecondary literacy, and research methods.

K. Bret Staudt Willet is a doctoral candidate in the Educational Psychology and Educational Technology Program at Michigan State University. His research focuses on networked learning at the intersection of information science and teacher education. Specifically, he has been exploring how social media platforms support induction and ongoing professional learning for K–20 educators.

John Z. Strong, PhD, is Assistant Professor in the Graduate School of Education at the University at Buffalo, State University of New York. His research interests include integrated reading and writing interventions in grades 4–12. His recent work has focused on measuring text structure awareness and investigating the effects of an informational text structure intervention on fourth- and fifth-grade students' reading comprehension and writing quality. Dr. Strong is coauthor of the books *Literacy Instruction with Disciplinary Texts: Strategies for Grades 6–12* and *Differentiated Literacy Instruction in Grades 4 and 5, Second Edition.*

Marinus H. van IJzendoorn, PhD, is Professor of Human Development at the Department of Psychology, Education and Child Studies, Erasmus University Rotterdam; Honorary Senior Visiting Fellow, Department of Public Health and Primary Care, School of Clinical Medicine, University of Cambridge; and Professor Emeritus of Leiden University. He studies the determinants of parenting and child development, with special emphasis on attachment, emotion regulation, differential susceptibility, and child maltreatment. The central question of his research is whether and how parents and other caregivers shape children's development in the current era of the genome and the brain.

Amy Vetter, PhD, is Professor in the School of Education at the University of North Carolina at Greensboro, where she teaches undergraduate courses in teaching practices and curriculum of English and literacy in the content areas, and graduate courses in youth literacies, teacher research, and qualitative research design. Her areas of research are literacy and identity, critical conversations, and the writing lives of teens.

Meaghan N. Vitale, MA, is a doctoral student in Economic Education at the University of Delaware. Her research interests include the measurement and evaluation of teaching and learning in economic classrooms with a focus on motivation and self-efficacy. She is currently exploring the relationships between teacher efficacy beliefs, professional development, and changes in curriculum.

Sharon Walpole, PhD, is Professor in the School of Education at University of Delaware and Director of its Professional Learning Center for Educators. Her research interests include the effects of curriculum, intervention, and professional learning on teaching and on student achievement. Dr. Walpole is the author of the open-access literacy curriculum Bookworms K–5 Reading and Writing and coauthor of several books, including *Differentiated Literacy Instruction in Grades 4 and 5, Second Edition.*

Rachelle D. Washington, PhD, is Executive Director of First Year Experience and Honors Programs at Allen University in Columbia, South Carolina, where she administers student-focused programming and teaches seminars with sociocultural emphases. Dr. Washington has published in the area of language and literacy and social justice.

Christina Weiland, EdD, is Associate Professor in the School of Education at the University of Michigan. Her research focuses on the effects of early childhood interventions and public policies on children's development, especially on children from low-income families.

Melissa B. Wilson, PhD, is an independent scholar. Her last position was as a senior lecturer at the Institute of Childhood and Education at Leeds Trinity University in the United Kingdom. Her work is focused on using international children's literature as a way to build bridges between (and among) cultures.

Foreword

Readers develop relationships with books. When reading novels, we are immersed in characters' lives for a sustained amount of time and experience joys, struggles, adventures, emotions, and more with them. When reading informational texts, we gain new knowledge and experience boundless opportunities—knowledge and experiences that expand our understanding and, indeed, our lives. We are often sad when we finish a book, not because it had a sad ending, but because our time in that book is over. Some books stay with us long after we finish them, and some books we return to time and time again to reenter that world and that experience.

Academics have relationships with texts as well. A rigorous study may cause us to rethink an investigation we are designing. An insightful book chapter might illuminate a construct or theory by discussing it in a new light. I remember a conversation at a group dinner at the Literacy Research Association conference one year, where we all shared the piece of scholarship that most substantially influenced our work. A nerdy dinner conversation, to be sure, but nonetheless all six or seven of us could name an impactful scholarly read—one that stayed with us, one that we returned to time and time again.

Literacy Research Methodologies is a book I have a relationship with. The first edition was a required text in a doctoral course I took with my mentor, Dr. Gerry Duffy, at the University of North Carolina at Greensboro in 2006. In the class, students selected five chapters from the book that we wanted to read, and we had to give a presentation on one of the selected chapters. I remember carefully poring over the table of contents, trying to choose the five I was going to read: "How can I choose with such a brilliant lineup?"

Years later, as a faculty member at George Mason University, I had the opportunity to teach the doctoral course "Research and Trends in Literacy." The text I assigned for that class—then and every time I have taught it since—was the second edition of *Literacy Research Methodologies*. Like Gerry, I ask doctoral students to choose one chapter that they will present to the class (along with an empirical study that exemplifies the use of the methodology). I watch as these early scholars study the table of contents, just as I did, considering their research interests, knowledge, plans, and curiosities as they examine the collection of chapters before them.

Literacy Research Methodologies has followed me, and I have followed it, from my doctoral program to the present. And it has influenced and guided my thinking all along the way. My copies of the previous editions are well worn, marked up, and dog-eared. I have read several of the chapters numerous times between my own research and teaching. Therefore, I was delighted when Marla and Nell invited me to write this foreword for the third edition.

For this edition, Mallette and Duke again bring together some of the best researchers and thinkers in the field of literacy to write chapters. Most chapters are updated, some chapters are new, and some chapters have new contributors. They have maintained the core of the book that has made it so helpful and so successful, and updated it to better reflect growing understanding and current developments in the field.

One of the reasons why previous editions of this text have been so successful is the centrality of the topic: research methodologies. Research is the best mechanism we have for developing an understanding of phenomena. That is the purpose of research: to build knowledge through rigorous investigation. Building knowledge requires a *body of research* that investigates phenomena repeatedly, in various contexts, using various methodologies. When results are taken together, and tested and scrutinized time and time again, this process leads to the development of a knowledge base. However, research results are only as insightful as the quality of the research methodologies employed. Methodologies are the fulcrum upon which the research enterprise rests.

Back in 2001, Duke and Mallette articulated the importance of deep and wide knowledge of diverse methodologies. They were concerned that new doctoral students were not gaining the breadth of methodological knowledge to engage in rigorous inquiry in "changing times" with diversification and advancement in methodologies. They also expressed concern about the fragmentation of the field of literacy on epistemological and methodological grounds. Unfortunately, I fear that this fragmentation still exists. My recent work investigating the theoretical and methodological landscape of literacy research revealed that literacy journals, which are typically associated with literacy organizations, tend to publish research from a particular paradigm (Parsons et al., 2016). For example, *Scientific Studies of Reading* publishes quantitative research almost exclusively, while *Research in the Teaching of English* publishes primarily qualitative research. There is nothing inherently wrong with these methodological leanings, but it does suggest some level of fragmentation in the field among researchers and organizations. It also makes it harder for literacy scholars to stay on top of current research that uses diverse methodologies. Therefore, I recommend that journal editors and association leaders reflect on their procedures and processes to ensure that they welcome and solicit rigorous research, regardless of epistemology or methodology.

I close, then, by reiterating Duke and Mallette's (2001) position that it is important for literacy scholars to have deep and wide knowledge of research methodologies and to apply methodologies rigorously. With increased knowledge, scholars are better positioned to appreciate research that uses diverse methodological approaches, and to recognize that such diversity enhances the nuance and depth of understanding about literacy phenomena. And therein lies the power of this book. It presents a diverse array of literacy research methodologies described by some of the best thinkers in the field. This new edition is an asset for literacy scholars and advances the field in the right direction. I know that my copy will become just as marked up and dog-eared as the previous editions as I use it in my research and teaching.

SETH A. PARSONS, PhD
George Mason University

REFERENCES

Duke, N. K., & Mallette, M. H. (2001). Critical issues: Preparation for new literacy researchers in multi-epistemological, multi-methodological times. *Journal of Literacy Research, 33*, 345–362.

Parsons, S. A., Gallagher, M. A., & the George Mason University Content Analysis Team. (2016). A content analysis of nine literacy journals, 2009–2014. *Journal of Literacy Research, 48*, 476–502.

Contents

CHAPTER 1

Introduction

Marla H. Mallette
Nell K. Duke

Methodology, as defined in *Webster's New World College Dictionary*, is "the science of method, or orderly arrangement; specifically, the branch of logic concerned with the application of the principles of reasoning to scientific and philosophical inquiry" (Anges, 1999, p. 906). *Method*, within that, is defined simply as "a way of doing anything" (Anges, 1999, p. 906). In the context of this volume, a method is a way of doing literacy research. And our emphasis in this volume is on the plural—methods or methodologies. That is, there are many ways of conducting literacy research.

We initially conceptualized this volume as including an exhaustive account of literacy research methodologies, but realized that it would be impossible to include every methodology and/or variation of methodology used. Thus we include here only a partial set of literacy research methodologies currently being used in the field. The process of determining which methodologies to include in the first edition began with brainstorming a list. The list was then reviewed by several colleagues, who were asked to add methodologies that were noticeably missing and to reduce redundancy in methodologies already included. For the second edition, we added chapters on long-standing methodologies we regretted not including in the first edition, as well as emerging methodologies coming into their own in literacy research.

In approaching this third edition, we began by returning to the core ideas that inspired us in our pursuit of this work:

1. Many different research methodologies—in fact, each research methodology discussed in this book and others—have valuable contributions to make to the study of literacy.
2. Different types of research are best suited for different types of

questions and claims. The match of research methodology to research questions and resulting claims is essential.

3. There are standards of quality for every type of research. There is better- and poorer-quality research of every methodology.
4. Synergy across research methodologies is possible, powerful, and advisable.
5. We must urgently and actively pursue synergy across research methodologies.

And it was with these ideas in mind that we have updated this volume. The chapter authors in this volume have stellar reputations for use of the methodology they write about, with numerous publications of rigorous research using that methodology. The chapters in this book strike a balance between maintaining each author's individual writing style/voice and achieving consistency across them. To achieve this consistency in core content, we maintained the same structure as in the previous editions, in which we asked the chapter authors to address the following questions:

1. What is this methodology (including a definition and description of the methodology, and, if possible, some key history of the methodology in literacy)?
2. What kinds of questions and claims is this methodology appropriate for?
3. What are standards for quality in this methodology?
4. What is one or more exemplar of this methodology (in literacy), and what makes it so good?

We suggest that readers approach each chapter with these four key questions in mind. We also strongly encourage readers to gather and read the exemplar or exemplars presented for each chapter. A listing of featured exemplars appears in two places: (1) in Appendix 1.1 at the end of this chapter, arranged by methodology, and (2) in the book's Appendix, arranged in alphabetical order.

Methodologies for conducting literacy research are growing in expansiveness and sophistication; yet, as Seth Parsons points out in the foreword, some publication outlets remain largely methodologically homogenous. Thus increasing our knowledge of a broad range of research methodologies can provide the foundation to enrich our understanding of literacy and inform our future research. This book, we hope, provides one tool for doing that.

REFERENCE

Anges, M. (Ed.). (1999). *Webster's new world college dictionary* (4th ed.). New York: Macmillan.

APPENDIX 1.1. Alphabetical Listing of the Exemplars, Arranged by Methodology

Ethnographies and Case Study

Dyson, A. H. (2013). *Rewriting the basics: Literacy learning in children's cultures.* New York: Teachers College Press.

Content Analysis

Beach, R., Enciso, P., Harste, J., Jenkins, C., Raina, S. A., Rogers, R., et al. (2009). Exploring the "critical" in critical content analysis of children's literature. In K. M. Leaner, D. W. Rowe, D. K. Dickinson, M. K. Hundley, R. T. Jamenez, & V. J. Risko (Eds.), *58th yearbook of the National Reading Conference* (pp. 129–143). Oak Creek, WI: National Reading Conference.

Dutro, E., & Haberl, E. (2018). Blurring material and rhetorical walls: Children writing the border/lands in a second-grade classroom. *Journal of Literacy Research, 50*(2), 167–189.

Hoffman, J. V., Sailors, M., Duffy, G. G., & Beretvas, N. (2004). The effective elementary classroom literacy environment: Examining the validity of the TEX-IN3 observation system. *Journal of Literacy Research, 36*, 303–334.

Kim, G. M. (2016). Transcultural digital literacies: Cross-border connections and self-representations in an online forum. *Reading Research Quarterly, 51*(2), 199–219.

Marshall, E. (2004). Stripping for the wolf: Rethinking representations of gender in children's literature. *Reading Research Quarterly, 39*(3), 256–270.

Moss, B. (2008). The information text gap: The mismatch between non-narrative text types in basal readers and 2009 NAEP recommended guidelines. *Journal of Literacy Research, 40*(2), 201–219.

Correlational Designs

Deacon, S. H., Kieffer, M. J., & Laroche, A. (2014). The relation between morphological awareness and reading comprehension: Evidence from mediation and longitudinal models. *Scientific Studies of Reading, 18*, 432–451. (**Longitudinal Autoregression**)

Kieffer, M. J., & Lesaux, N. K. (2008). The role of derivational morphological awareness in the reading comprehension of Spanish-speaking English language learners. *Reading and Writing: An Interdisciplinary Journal, 21*, 783–804. (**Correlation and Multiple Regression**)

Kieffer, M. J., & Lesaux, N. K. (2012). Development of morphological awareness and vocabulary knowledge for Spanish-speaking language minority learners: A parallel process latent growth model. *Applied Psycholinguistics, 33*, 23–54. (**Longitudinal Growth Modeling**)

Kieffer, M. J., Petscher, Y., Proctor, C. P., & Silverman, R. D. (2016). Is the whole more than the sum of its parts?: Modeling the contributions of language comprehension skills to reading comprehension in the upper elementary grades. *Scientific Studies of Reading, 20*, 436–454. (**Latent Variable Modeling**)

Levesque, K., Kieffer, M. J., & Deacon, S. H. (2017). Morphological awareness and reading comprehension: Examining mediating factors. *Journal of Experimental Child Psychology, 160,* 1–20. **(Mediation Analyses)**

Critical Race Methodologies

Kynard, C. (2010). From Candy Girls to cyber sista-cipher: Narrating Black females' color-consciousness and counterstories in and out of school. *Harvard Educational Review, 80*(1), 30–52.

Digital Contexts

Gillen, J. (2009). Literacy practices in Schome Park: A virtual literacy ethnography. *Journal of Research in Reading, 32*(1), 57–74.

Steinkuehler, C. (2006). Massively multiplayer online video gaming as participation in a discourse. *Mind, Culture and Activity, 13*(1), 38–52.

Steinkuehler, C. (2007). Massively multiplayer online gaming as a constellation of literacy practices. *E-Learning and Digital Media, 4*(3), 297–318.

Discourse Analysis

Albers, P. (2007). Visual discourse analysis: An introduction to the analysis of school-generated visual texts. In D. W. Rowe, R. T. Jiménez, D. L. Compton, D. K. Dickinson, Y. Kim, K. M. Leander, et al. (Eds.), *56th yearbook of the National Reading Conference* (pp. 81–95). Oak Creek, WI: National Reading Conference.

Wohlwend, K. (2012). The boys who would be princesses: Playing with gender identity intertexts in Disney Princess transmedia. *Gender and Education, 24*(6), 593–610.

Design-Based Research

Colwell, J., & Reinking, D. (2016). A formative experiment to align middle-school history instruction with literacy goals. *Teachers College Record, 118*(12), 1–42.

Causal Effects

Gamse, B. C., Jacob, R. T., Horst, M., Boulay, B., & Unlu, F. (2008). *Reading First Impact Study: Final report* (NCEE 2009-4038). Washington, DC: National Center for Education Evaluation and Regional Assistance, Institute of Education Sciences, U.S. Department of Education.

Justice, L. M., McGinty, A. S., Cabell, S. Q., Kilday, C. R., Knighton, K., & Huffman, G. (2010). Language and literacy curriculum supplement for preschoolers who are academically at risk: A feasibility study. *Language, Speech, and Hearing Services in Schools, 41,* 161–178.

Yoshikawa, H., Leyva, D., Snow, C. E., Treviño, E., Barata, M., Weiland, C., et al. (2015). Experimental impacts of a teacher professional development program in Chile on preschool classroom quality and child outcomes. *Developmental Psychology, 51,* 309–322.

Historical Research

Monaghan, E. J. (1991). Family literacy in early 18th-century Boston: Cotton Mather and his children. *Reading Research Quarterly, 26*(4), 342–370.

Instrument Development

Strong, J. Z. (2019). *Effects of a text structure intervention for reading and writing: A mixed methods experiment.* Unpublished doctoral dissertation, University of Delaware, Newark, DE.

Meta-Analysis

Bus, A. G., & van IJzendoorn, M. H. (1999). Phonological awareness and early reading: A meta-analysis of experimental training studies. *Journal of Educational Psychology, 91,* 403–414.

Mixed Research

Benge, C., Onwuegbuzie, A. J., Mallette, M. H., & Burgess, M. L. (2010). Doctoral students' perceptions of barriers to reading empirical literature: A mixed analysis. *International Journal of Doctoral Studies, 5,* 55–77.

Narrative Approaches

Gordon, E., McKibbin, K., Vasudevan, L., & Vinz, R. (2007). Writing out of the unexpected: Narrative inquiry and the weight of small moments. *English Education, 39*(4), 326–351.

Hankins, K. H. (2003). *Teaching through the storm: A journal of hope.* New York: Teachers College Press.

Neuroimaging

Nugiel, T., Roe, M. A., Taylor, W. P., Vaughn, S. R., Fletcher, J. M., Juranek, J., et al. (2019). Brain activity in struggling readers before intervention relates to future reading gains. *Cortex, 111,* 286–302.

Roe, M. A., Martinez, J. E., Mumford, J. A., Taylor, W. P., Cirino, P. T., Fletcher, J. M., et al. (2018). Control engagement during sentence and inhibition fMRI tasks in children with reading difficulties. *Cerebral Cortex, 28*(10), 3697–3710.

Single-Subject Experimental Design

Mudre, L. H., & McCormick, S. (1989). Effects of meaning-focused cues on underachieving readers' context use, self-corrections, and literal comprehension. *Reading Research Quarterly, 24,* 89–113.

Neuman, S. B., & Gallagher, P. (1994). Joining together in literacy learning: Teenage mothers and children. *Reading Research Quarterly, 29,* 382–401.

Survey Research

Baumann, J. F., Hoffman, J. V., Duffy-Hester, A. M., & Ro, J. M. (2000). *The first R* yesterday and today: U.S. elementary reading instruction practices reported by teachers and administrators. *Reading Research Quarterly, 35,* 338–377.

Mesmer, H. A. E. (2009). Beginning reading materials: A national survey of primary teachers' reported uses and beliefs. *Journal of Literacy Research, 38,* 389–425.

Verbal Protocols

Goldman, S. R., Braasch, J. L. G., Wiley, J., Graesser, A. C., & Brodowinska, K. (2012). Comprehending and learning from Internet sources: Processing patterns of better and poorer learners. *Reading Research Quarterly, 47*(4), 356–381.

Hartman, D. K. (1995). Eight readers reading: The intertextual links of proficient readers reading multiple passages. *Reading Research Quarterly, 30*(3), 520–561.

CHAPTER 2

Turtles, Tortoises, Ethnographies, and Case Study

NUANCES OF DIFFERENCE AND DESIGN

Catherine Compton-Lilly

Like turtles and tortoises, on the surface case studies and ethnographies look very much the same. Turtles and tortoises both have a protective shell, four short legs, pointed tails, and rounded heads, as well as the amazing capacity to fold their limbs inside their shells. However, when we look closely, turtles and tortoises are very different. Turtles spend most of their lives in the water, have webbed feet, and are agile swimmers. Tortoises live their lives on land and have powerful claws to negotiate rough terrain. While their bodies may appear the same, they are uniquely suited to different purposes. Case studies and ethnographies are the same; they look similar, share many characteristics, and attend to people within social spaces (White, Drew, & Hay, 2009). However, when we look closely, important and fundamental differences become apparent.

CASE STUDIES AND ETHNOGRAPHIES: STUNNING SIMILARITIES

In general, contemporary case studies and ethnographies use similar types of data, attend to details, use thick description, focus on people's experiences, entail subjectivities on the part of researchers, use similar analytic processes, and report their findings in similar ways. These characteristics can make case studies and ethnographies difficult to differentiate. Below, I describe the notable number of characteristics shared by many case studies and ethnographies.

- Perhaps the most obvious similarity between case studies and ethnographies involves the types of data collected. Both case studies and ethnographies can involve assemblages of observations, interviews, field notes,
documents, and artifacts.

- While the term *thick description* was coined by Geertz (1973), an
ethnographer, both case studies and ethnographies entail thick description
of phenomena. For case study researchers, this involves using multiple data
sources to thoroughly describe and understand a *case*. For ethnographers,
this entails careful observation to trace, track, and describe interactions
and meaning making within social spaces.

- Both case studies and ethnographies attend to "cultural practices"
(Dyson & Genishi, 2005; Heath & Street, 2008). As recurring events that
operate as social patterns, cultural practices are located within social and
institutional contexts and produce the meanings that accompany experience. Analysis of cultural practices, for both case study researchers and
ethnographers, reveals how everyday events implicate and involve people's
values, aesthetics, preferences, norms, and expectations.

- Both case studies and ethnographies focus on meaning construction. By attending to details of discourse, behavior, interaction, and context, researchers come to understand how people construct meaning and
make sense of themselves and their experiences. Case study researchers and
ethnographers construct "interpretations of other people's interpretations"
(Dyson & Genishi, 2005, p. 18) to reflect and describe people's worlds.

- Neither case study researchers nor ethnographers can claim to be
unbiased or neutral; all qualitative researchers play active roles in research,
and their backgrounds, beliefs, and experiences inevitably affect what they
observe, hear, feel, understand, and describe. Both case studies and ethnographies are inherently subjective and interpretative, and are never comprehensive.

- While both case study researchers and ethnographers generally enter
research spaces with general interests and questions, initial time spent in
research settings involves observations and noticings that help them to
transform general questions about phenomena into specific questions that
can be adequately addressed (Dyson & Genishi, 2005; Heath & Street,
2008; Stake, 1995).

- Both case studies and ethnographies situate ongoing activities and
experiences within larger contexts defined and affected by historical, institutional, political, cultural, and societal influences. Relevant context is identified during the research processes as researchers attend to contextualizing

factors that participants name and/or that define their experiences. Thus, the lines between micro and macro, and between contexts and phenomena, are always subjective and blurry. Case study researchers and ethnographers strive to recognize, consider, and explain relevant macro forces as they interpret phenomena.

- While case study researchers (Compton-Lilly, 2013; Creswell, 1998; Merriam, 1998; Smith, 1979; Stake, 1995; Yin, 2002) often argue that case studies can be characterized by the bounded nature of the phenomena under study, ethnographies also entail boundaries. As Heath and Street (2008) explain, ethnographers "set spatial and temporal boundaries when seeking the answer to questions" (p. 19). Thus, both case studies and ethnographies are bounded; however, their boundaries are drawn to encompass different types of entities.

- For both case study researchers and ethnographers, analysis of data is "inductive, grounded in particular pieces of data that are sorted and inter-related in order to understand the dimensions and dynamics of some phenomenon as it is enacted by intentional social actors in some time and place" (Dyson & Genishi, 2005, p. 82). This analysis can involve sorting and categorizing data, and developing the vocabulary needed to tell a story suggested by data. As Dyson and Genishi (2005) report, categories, patterns, lists, linked events, recurring practices, and shared perspectives voiced by participants lead to trails of "thematic threads, meaningful events, and powerful factors, that allow us [researchers] entry into the multiple realities and dynamic processes that constitute the everyday drama of language use in educational sites" (p. 111).

- Both case studies and ethnographies can occur in classrooms and schools (Erickson, 1984); case studies are likely to focus on particular issues or the experiences and perspectives of particular individuals, while ethnographies tend to focus on processes and practices within defined spaces—including the roles, activities, and meaning making that occur.

- Both case studies and ethnographies can be employed to explore the experiences of social groups that been historically underserved by schools. Thoughtful and sensitive research efforts can reveal and reflect on histories, ideological tensions, and power struggles that define people's lived experiences.

- The reporting of literacy case studies and ethnographies often assumes a form of "storytelling" (Dyson, 2013; Heath & Street, 2008; Stake, 1995). Vignettes, rich descriptions of places and people, and narrative-like storylines characterize the presentation of ethnographies and case study research.

• Both literacy case studies and ethnographies not only may attend to written representations of language, but may also reference multimodal literacies that include images, musical scores, computer languages, gestures, dramatic performances, charts, or signed languages for hearing-impaired people; thus, literacy is inherently connected to various communicative practices.

• Both case study and ethnography have been criticized as not being generalizable. Stake (1978) challenges this claim, arguing that case studies mimic the understandings that people gain "through direct and vicarious experience" (p. 5), and that researchers' words and illustrations emulate "natural experience acquired in ordinary personal involvement" (p. 5). Naturalistic generalizations invoke researchers' curiosity and assume personal, sensory, and narrative forms. Thus, naturalistic generalizations (Stake, 1995) result from the "full and thorough knowledge of the particular, recognizing it also in new and foreign contexts" (p. 6). As Dyson and Genishi (2005) explain, qualitative analyses have "contributed to and complicated generalizations about language and literacy teaching" (p. 113) weaving together ideas and creating "quilts" of understanding. They argue for the importance of naturalistic generalization as readers generalize "in private, personal ways, modifying, extending, or adding to their generalized understandings of how the world works" (p. 115). Understandings of a particular phenomenon or context allow researchers and educators to compare the particulars of various situated experiences to extend, complicate or modify existing knowledge.

When explicitly listed as they are above, the similarities between case studies and ethnographies are stunning; they explain the consternation that emergent scholars may feel as they attempt to distinguish these two methodologies (White et al., 2009).

Below, I explicitly name differences in foci and practices that distinguish case studies and ethnographies. Just as children learn to recognize turtles' and tortoises' bodies as suited to either living in water or on land, scholars are able to distinguish between case studies and ethnographies, once they are alerted to relevant differences. In what follows, I explore some of these critical differences. Some result from disparate histories, which have defined the emergence of these methodologies. Thus, I open each section with a discussion of the histories associated with each methodology.

WHAT MAKES A CASE STUDY A CASE STUDY?

Case studies and ethnographies have different historical roots. Case study research can be traced to the historical emergence of medicine, psychology, biology, and law, and has served as a primary method of learning for generations of physical, biological, and social scientists (Flyvbjerg, 2006). However, the cases described in these historical reports are very different from how qualitative case studies are currently conducted.

Biologists, doctors, and physicists learn through the careful observation of particular cases. For example, Anderson and Meier-Hedde (2001) describe how rich case reports of people who struggled with reading led to the development of various theories and interventions for people we now describe as having dyslexia. These cases often focused on individuals who had suffered some form of physical brain injury and involved close observation and tracking of individuals. As Flyvbjerg (2006) reports, observation and documentation of cases have always been critical to scientific endeavors; unfortunately, too often this *"force of example"* (p. 228, original emphasis) is underestimated and described as unscientific.

Across history, disciplines, and epistemological premises, varied methodological practices use the word *case* as they focus on particular entities, individuals, and phenomena; however, these methodologies can be very different from contemporary qualitative case studies as defined by Merriam (1998), Stake (1995), and Yin (2002). For example, Merseth (1991) provides an historical account of the early history of case-based instruction in the field of law. He locates its emergence at the Harvard Law School during the 1870s. The goal was for faculty to use the analysis and discussion of particular legal cases to apply legal precedents to new situations. Merseth discusses the implementation of similar instructional practices at the Harvard School of Business and advocates for case-based instruction as a viable educational practice for educators.

Certainly, there are examples of educators creating opportunities for case-based instruction. For example, Harry, Klingner, and Cramer (2007) present cases of minority students who have been placed in special education classrooms to engage preservice teachers and others in conversations about the disproportionality of special education placement for students from historically underserved communities. Jones, Clarke, and Enriquez (2010) present case studies of children in literacy classrooms to explore possibilities for instructional problem solving to address the particular challenges faced by young readers and writers. Similarly, Comber and Kamler (2005) present cases that reveal the resourceful and student-centered work of literacy teachers as they craft "turn-around pedagogies" (p. 1) that successfully serve children. The cases presented in these books share an epistemological commitment to using cases to support the learning of practicing and preservice teachers.

Another methodology that can be confused with case study is single-subject experimental design. Like many case studies, single-subject experiments focus on individuals; however, this method involves carefully delineated methods to examine the effects of an experimental treatment on participants: "In a single-subject experiment the investigator deliberately manipulates one or more independent variables. Single-subject experiments are designed to generate functional and causal statements, whereas case studies are designed to provide insight by describing phenomena" (Neuman, Chapter 16, this volume, p. 346) Single-subject experiments are explicitly designed to establish a causal relationship between interventions and outcomes. Thus, this method involves the manipulation of one or more variables and the tracking of change over time. While contemporary case studies, particularly longitudinal case studies, may also attend to change over time, their focus is on what happens across time in naturalistic settings. Yin (1981) defined the case study as a research strategy that is distinguished by its "attempts to examine (a) a contemporary phenomenon in its real-life context, especially when (b) the boundaries between phenomenon and context are not clearly evident" (p. 59).

Contemporary case studies are premised on the researcher's "interest in the local particulars of some abstract social phenomena" (Dyson & Genishi, 2005, pp. 2–3). They focus on a particular *social unit*—"a person, a group, a place or activity, or some combination of those units" (p. 3). This unit operates as an *example*—"case of something, of some phenomenon" (p. 3). As Stake (1995) explains, the goal is to capture the complexity of a specific case, perhaps the meaning making of an individual, the enactment of a particular practice, or activities that occur within a particular classroom. Dyson and Genishi (2005) argue that case studies are "constructed not found as researchers make decisions about how to angle their vision on places over-flowing with potential stories of human experience" (p. 2). Because any phenomenon of interest looks, sounds, and feels different depending on the social and cultural context in which it occurs, the case itself is not the phenomenon, but a contextualized instance of a phenomenon.

Contemporary case studies can also be very different from each other. For example, Merriam (1998), Stake (1995), and Yin (2002) present different visions of the nature of case studies (Yazan, 2015). Yin (2002) proposes a relatively positivistic view of case studies, referencing objectivity, validity, and traditional notions of generalizability. Merriam and Stake share a constructivist orientation that honors experiences constructed through social interactions; they strive to understand how people make sense and operate within their worlds. The generalizations I make about qualitative case study methodologies in this chapter are most closely aligned with the qualitative practices, analytic procedures, and epistemological stances described by Merriam and Stake.

Thus, case study research inevitably engages the "messy complexity of human experience" (p. 3) as phenomena are enacted, experienced, and encountered in multiple, complex, eternally emerging, and socially constructed contexts. The researcher's goal is to understand what a phenomenon of interest means as it is enacted within a particular social context (Dyson & Genishi, 2005).

Stake (1995) has identified three types of case studies. *Intrinsic case studies* and *instrumental case studies* are defined by the interests and intents of the case study researchers. An intrinsic case study is designed and implemented to allow a researcher to learn about a particular case—perhaps a person, a classroom, or a school. Generally, the researcher has identified a salient reason for choosing a particular case and believes that focusing on this case will lead to important insights and understandings. In contrast, instrumental case studies are designed and implemented in order to examine and explore a particular issue or situation. While instrumental case studies may involve particular people, classrooms, or schools, the researchers focus is on an identified phenomenon—perhaps the experiences of novice teachers, gifted children, or emerging bilingual students. Distinguishing between these two types of case studies is contingent on subtle differences in focus.

The third type of case study identified by Stake (1995) is the *collective case study.* Collective case studies can be either intrinsic or instrumental. An intrinsic collective case study looks across carefully chosen cases that describe and interpret the experiences of individual people, classrooms, and schools to contribute to findings that involve contrasts between these unique, individual experiences. An instrumental collective case study explores a particular issue as it plays out and affects people in various contexts. The goal is to contribute to a richer understanding of the issue and its affects.

Flyvbjerg (2006) distinguishes among *extreme/deviant cases, maximum variation cases, critical cases,* and *paradigmatic cases*:

- Extreme/deviant cases focus on unusual or problematic cases that complicate existing knowledge.
- Maximum variation cases attend to cases that have been carefully selected to account for high levels of variation. These cases may vary in accordance with student age, classroom organizational structure, or available resources.
- Critical cases seek information that supports or challenges existing knowledge. Critical case logic can either challenge or support existing understandings as they relate to a particular case.
- Paradigmatic cases establish a particular lens, metaphor, or understanding that can be applied to related cases.

These variations of case study research highlight the significance of case selection and the empirical rationale for choosing particular cases.

Flyvbjerg (2006) argues for significant learning from case studies. He notes that case studies produce "the type of content-dependent knowledge that research on learning shows to be necessary to allow people to develop from rule based beginners to virtuous experts" (p. 221). In other words, case studies can situate, nuance, and complicate the experiences of students and their teachers. Flyvbjerg argues that "experts operate on the basis of intimate knowledge of several thousand concrete cases in their areas of expertise. Context-dependent knowledge and experience are at the very heart of expert activity" (p. 222), and "case knowledge is central to human learning" (p. 222). He notes that case study learning is not about proving causality or establishing claims. Instead, careful case study research results in learning something about the phenomena of study, within a particular context, and as understood by a particular researcher.

Case study researchers can assume many roles; they can observe from a distance, operate as trusted allies, or serve as action researchers studying their own practice. Although acting as a participant observer is an option for case study researchers, the roles played by case study researchers tend to be more varied than the roles generally assumed by ethnographers, who often act as participant observers.

WHAT MAKES AN ETHNOGRAPHY AN ETHNOGRAPHY?

While case study researchers highlight phenomena or people, ethnographers focus on processes and practices within defined contexts. Case study researchers are more interested in understanding how a "phenomenon matters from the perspectives of participants" (p. 81). Modern ethnography has clear historical roots in anthropology (Atkinson & Hammersley, 1998). Around the beginning of the 20th century, anthropologists, particularly those working in South America and Asia, studied people's everyday social lives and practices.

Heath and Street (2008) identified two complementary and historical traditions, originating respectively in Britain and in North America, that inform modern ethnography. In Britain during World War I, Bronislaw Malinowski, a social anthropologist working in the Trobriand Islands, found himself breaking with traditional anthropological approaches (surveys, accounts from travelers) and conducting extended ethnographic fieldwork while locating his findings within larger economic, political, and social contexts. Malinowski's methods led to the preparation of new generations of social anthropologists and ethnographers committed to long-term projects in which they spent months and years embedded in local cultures, learning local languages, and documenting cultural practices.

During the early 20th century in the United States, North American scholars became aware of the pressing need to attend to the knowledge, languages, and cultural practices of indigenous communities (Heath & Street, 2008). Franz Boas at Columbia University was a leader among this group of anthropologists who "recognized that indigenous populations possessed critical knowledge of their regions as well as a historical understanding of human migration" (Heath & Street, 2008, p. 114). These interests expanded internationally as U.S. governmental agencies began to recognize the roles anthropologists and linguists could play in learning about the "range of social, ideological and cultural differences" (p. 115) in the world. While questions continue to emerge about whether and to what degree people can understand and describe other cultures, and what methodological and analytical practices might be ethical and helpful to local communities, these practices have served as the basis for contemporary ethnography, including ethnographies conducted in local communities and organizations.

Across the 20th century, ethnographers increasingly collected first-hand data and used those data to describe and explain social and cultural characteristics of communities and organizations. These practices were also applied to contemporary Western settings, including urban neighborhoods, religious and ethnic communities, and schools (Yon, 2003). Educational anthropology evolved from 1925 through 1955, leading to the publication of ethnographies that focused on classrooms and schools during the 1950s and 1960s (Yon, 2003). From anthropology, ethnographers have adopted and adapted a commitment to in-depth and often long-term study of social or cultural groups, a focus on everyday life and cultural practices, and the use of ethnographic tools (i.e., interviews, document analysis, observation, video/audio recording) (Green & Bloome, 1997). Participant observation in classrooms enabled researchers to observe children in naturalistic studies to document official and nonofficial goals of schools, hidden or unrecognized curricular effects, and the ways larger social changes affected schooling and participants' experiences of school.

Although not all educational ethnographies are classroom ethnographies, Heath and Street (2008) note that since the 1990s, classrooms have increasingly served as ethnographic sites. They remind us that classrooms are heavily influenced by forces beyond classroom walls, which typically determine the pace of instruction, instructional goals, schedules, and instructional methods and materials.

Atkinson and Hammersley (1998) note that there is no firm consensus on the definition of *ethnography,* but they do identify several substantial features, including an emphasis on the nature of social phenomena, the collection of "unstructured" data (p. 248), the investigation of a small number of cases, and the "explicit interpretation of the meanings and functions of human actions" (p. 248). Heath and Street (2008) define ethnography as "a theory building and theory dependent enterprise. Ethnographers construct, test, and amplify theoretical perspectives through systemic observing, recording, and analyzing of human behavior in specifiable spaces and interactions for the co-occurrence of language, literacy, and multimodalities for any situation or context selected as field site(s)" (p. 38). Heath and Street argue that culture should be recognized as "a verb rather than a noun" (p. 7). They describe culture as "unbounded, kaleidoscopic, and dynamic" (p. 7), referencing the eternally emergent and always multi-faceted nature of culture. Culture involves "ever-shifting active processes of meaning-making" (p. 7) and focuses on what happens in particular spaces, contexts, classrooms, communities, or affinity groups.

Heath and Street (2008) argue that ethnographers dive "head-first into *culture*" (p. 3, original emphasis). They attend to how people produce symbolic structures that accompany being, while honoring both the vast variability in the ways people "create, sustain, and adapt their modalities, including oral and written language" (p. 3). For example, ethnographers who study language and literacy may explore individual efforts to become experts in particular areas, identity making within groups, or meaning making within institutions of formal learning. For Heath and Street, ethnography entails tracking, describing, and enumerating the multimodal and semiotic processes within social spaces. These semiotic processes inevitably involve social interactions, social contexts, and cultural norms.

A tenet of ethnography is the construct of *thick description* (Geertz, 1973), mentioned earlier in this chapter. Thick description highlights the interpretation and pursuit of cultural meaning and understanding. Traditionally, and again drawing on anthropology, ethnographies entail spending sustained periods of time in a field (often several years). However, in recent years, some researchers have argued that ethnographic studies can be designed to compensate for shorter time frames (Heath & Street, 2008). These adaptations include the following:

- Briefer but more intensive data collection, paired with the careful identification of a singular and specific theme.
- Longer time frames and the selective identification of particular foci and events that enable the researcher to move in and out of the research space.
- Focusing on particular recurrent events or naturally occurring phases to monitor change over time.

Unlike case studies, which generally focus on individuals or issues, ethnography focuses on social networks (i.e., families, classrooms, schools). As Erickson (1984) has explained, an ethnography "not only treats a social unit of any size as a whole but . . . portrays events, at least in part, from the points of view of the actors involved in the events" (p. 52). Erickson notes that ethnographers combine their own firsthand experiences with the perspectives and insights of participants to produce informed descriptions of essential and partial aspects of a society. Such descriptions can lead to systematic definitions of the social whole that often challenge naïve explanations and deficit assumptions.

Drawing on Malinowski, Erickson (1984) describes educational ethnographies as focusing on schools as organizations that entail economies, myths, folk philosophies, and rituals. Thus, schools and classrooms can be treated as communities and analyzed in terms of the people involved—their statuses, roles, rights, and obligations. Economically, these communities entail contracts and exchanges; for instance, students defer to teachers in exchange for good treatment and access to knowledge. Myths, folk philosophies, and rituals determine what is taught, the cultural lens that is privileged, and the routines and rituals that guide successful participation. As Erickson notes, "ethnography, because of its holism and because of its cross-cultural perspective, provides an inquiry process by which we can ask open-ended questions that will result in new insights about schooling in American society" (p. 65).

A particularly salient dimension of ethnography is the role of the researcher. In many ethnographies and to various degrees, the researcher assumes the stance of a participant observer. This participant observer "intrudes into the situation to invite participants to record *their* observations" (Stenhouse, 1987, p. 34). Stenhouse contrasts this stance with that of researchers who rely only on interviews. He argues that the "interviewer is a collector of specimens for later examination" while the "participant observer cannot 'collect' his observations—he *makes them* in a much more thorough sense than the interviewer need, because he interprets in the field" (p. 35; emphasis added). At the same time, participant observers work to be both involved and engaged, while simultaneously remaining silent and communicating only in locally appropriate ways (see Dyson, 2013). As Atkinson and Hammersley (1998) argue, it is possible to claim that all social research involves participant observation, as all qualitative researchers participate to some degree in social spaces; however, ethnographers tend to claim a particularly active role in research contexts and with participants. In short, the ethnographer is the primary research instrument. Drawing on their anthropological roots, ethnographers aspire toward careful observation, attention to detail, and nuanced listening in order to make connections and see patterns within complex social spaces.

CASE STUDIES AND ETHNOGRAPHIES: A FEW REPRESENTATIVE EXAMPLES

While space limits prevent a comprehensive discussion of the many wonderful case studies and ethnographies that address literacy, on the following pages I describe a small set of research projects that begin to capture how case study and ethnography have been used to study literacy. Choosing these studies was a challenge. I sought studies that would be recognizable to readers and clearly represented case study and ethnography.

As readers might suspect, I revisited an earlier edition of this book to see what was previously written and which studies were cited. The second edition of *Literacy Research Methodologies* (Duke & Mallette, 2011) included separate chapters on case study and ethnography. Interestingly, when I examined those chapters, I noticed that some studies were discussed in both the case study chapter and the ethnography chapter. For example, *The Brothers and Sisters Learn to Write: Popular Literacies in Childhood and School Cultures* (Dyson, 2003), *Ways with Words: Language, Life and Work in Communities and Classrooms* (Heath, 1983), and *Other People's Words: The Cycle of Low Literacy* (Purcell-Gates, 1997) were discussed as examples of both case study and ethnography. This is not surprising, given their many shared characteristics discussed above. As described below in reference to another of Dyson's books, *Rewriting the Basics: Literacy Learning in Children's Cultures* (2013), researchers often draw on both case study and ethnography methodologies; these studies might best be described as *ethnographic case studies.*

A Few Case Studies

During the second half of the 20th century, a growing body of powerful literacy case studies appeared. These studies tracked the literacy development of individual children (Bissex, 1980; Butler, 1975; Calkins, 1983; White, 1956). For example, Bissex (1980) tracked her son's literacy development across several years to explore his emergent interactions with text and his increasing ability to connect oral language with print. These early case studies revealed the emergent nature of early literacy learning and have inspired generations of educators to attend to the literacy practices and abilities that children bring from home to formal literacy-learning experiences at school.

Whereas Bissex's primary emphasis was on an individual child, Taylor (1983) shifted her lens to examine what happened in families. Thus, rather than a targeted focus on children, Taylor attended to families and to the roles played by parents and their own literate histories. In a later coauthored study, Taylor and Dorsey-Gaines (1988) applied case study methods to examine literacy learning in low-income African American families whose children were successful in school. This study challenged assumptions about literacy practices in African American homes and revealed the resourcefulness and ingenuity of parents who often faced difficult situations with few resources.

My own work was heavily influenced by these case studies. As a graduate student in the 1990s, I read these texts. For my dissertation, I conducted a 1-year collective case study of 10 students from my first-grade classroom (Compton-Lilly, 2003). Although it was not my intention at the time, I ended up extending those case studies across a decade and following the children into grade 11 (Compton-Lilly, 2007, 2012, 2017). While the cases originally focused on literacy practices in children's homes, over time the stories told by families expanded to include the children's experiences of school, their literacy practices, and their identity construction. The families featured in these books, like those described by Taylor and Dorsey-Gaines (1988), challenged assumptions often made about poor African American families and revealed the knowledge, resources, and resilience of the families.

Each of these case studies provides a lens on literacy that helps educators to understand how literacy is learned, the roles it plays in people's lives, and the ways people experience literacy. These micro-level accounts, while contextualized by larger practices and policies, focus on people and their lived experiences or issues that have defined literacy learning and practices.

A Few Ethnographies

Although case studies can focus on larger social units (classrooms, schools, communities), a group focus often results in hybridity, as attention in social spaces is often drawn to interactions and social meanings in social spaces (Dyson, 2003; Heath, 1983; Purcell-Gates, 1997). Below, I explore three ethnographies that situate literacy learning and literacy practices in communities and classrooms.

Street (1984) used ethnography to examine literacy practices and learning in an Iranian village. He identified how literacies related to Koranic schooling influenced the emergence of commercial literacies. As he described these literacy flows, he made critical distinctions between autonomous and ideological models of literacy, challenging narrow and conventional views of literacy and literacy learning. Thus, Street's interest was in what happened within particular social spaces, the actors within those spaces, the roles they assumed, and the meanings that were made.

Focusing on perhaps a more familiar community, Barton and Hamilton (2012) explored the local literacies operating in Lancaster, England during the 1990s. They documented people's day-to-day literacy practices, with an emphasis on how focal individuals accessed and used local media. Less interested in the practices and perspectives of particular people, they highlighted the role of literacy in families and during leisure activities. Like Street, they were interested in what was happening with literacy in a particular community. What were the spaces within which literacy occurred, who were the actors within those spaces, what roles did they assume, and what meanings were made?

Finally, Lewis (2001) brought us into classrooms to explore classroom interactions and practices related to literacy. Specifically, Lewis spent a year in fifth- and sixth-grade classrooms observing children as they engaged in four literacy practices: read-aloud, peer-led discussions, teacher-led literature discussions, and independent reading. Her focus was on "how these practices were shaped by discourses and rituals within the classroom and by social codes and dominant cultural norms beyond the classroom" (p. 4). Thus, Lewis explicitly focused on what happened in classrooms and how meanings were made and shared.

Whereas the biology of turtles and tortoises prevents interbreeding, theories that espouse and support the social construction of knowledge suggest that hybridity is always possible and probably unavoidable. Thus, while discernible differences continue to define the two methodologies, many researchers have consciously and thoughtfully adopted and adapted methods and practices across this methodological divide. The result has been that in practice, differences between case study and ethnography must be conceptualized on a continuum rather than as distinct breaches (see Figure 2.1). Some case studies are notably ethnographic: Case study researchers might retain their attention to individual meaning making and experience, while adopting participant observer roles and attending to the social construction of meaning. Alternatively, ethnographers, through their

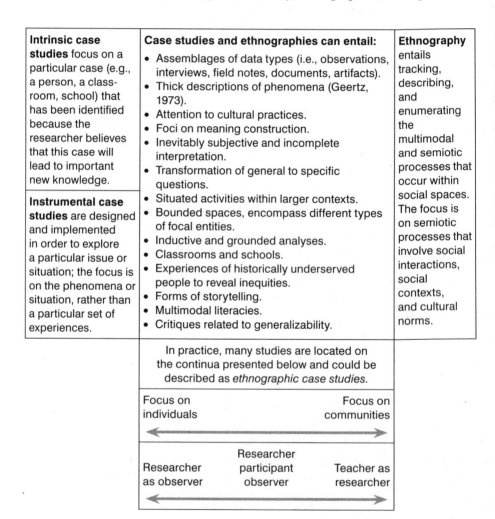

Intrinsic case studies focus on a particular case (e.g., a person, a class-room, school) that has been identified because the researcher believes that this case will lead to important new knowledge.	Case studies and ethnographies can entail:	Ethnography entails tracking, describing, and enumerating the multimodal and semiotic processes that occur within social spaces. The focus is on semiotic processes that involve social interactions, social contexts, and cultural norms.
Instrumental case studies are designed and implemented in order to explore a particular issue or situation; the focus is on the phenomena or situation, rather than a particular set of experiences.	• Assemblages of data types (i.e., observations, interviews, field notes, documents, artifacts). • Thick descriptions of phenomena (Geertz, 1973). • Attention to cultural practices. • Foci on meaning construction. • Inevitably subjective and incomplete interpretation. • Transformation of general to specific questions. • Situated activities within larger contexts. • Bounded spaces, encompass different types of focal entities. • Inductive and grounded analyses. • Classrooms and schools. • Experiences of historically underserved people to reveal inequities. • Forms of storytelling. • Multimodal literacies. • Critiques related to generalizability.	

In practice, many studies are located on the continua presented below and could be described as *ethnographic case studies*.

Focus on individuals		Focus on communities

Researcher as observer	Researcher participant observer	Teacher as researcher

FIGURE 2.1. A hybrid continuum: Case studies and ethnographies.

attention to focal participants, may embed case studies into their ethnographic accounts.

In this chapter, I differentiate between case studies and ethnographies—two methodological practices with many similarities. As readers who share a commitment to the social construction of knowledge and practice might expect, in practice the methods and epistemological frameworks that define modern case studies and ethnographies often merge. Case study researchers routinely read ethnographies, and ethnographers routinely read case studies. We attend the same conferences, write for the same journals, and cite each other's work. We share qualitative and often sociocultural and critical commitments, and are dedicated to understanding literacy practices and educational phenomena within naturalistic settings.

As a result of this cross-pollination, researchers have located themselves in various spaces on the case study–ethnography continuum. This hybrid result is often described as an *ethnographic case study*. Below, I describe what I believe is an exemplary ethnographic case study: *Rewriting the Basics* by Anne Haas Dyson (2013). Following my discussion of this study, I highlight criteria that defines quality for both case studies and ethnographies.

REWRITING THE BASICS (DYSON, 2013): AN EXEMPLARY ETHNOGRAPHIC CASE STUDY

Although there are many brilliant and compelling ethnographic case studies, when I think about literacy research, I am constantly drawn to the work of Anne Haas Dyson. As a first-grade teacher and graduate student who grappled with the readings assigned in my doctoral classes, I often found myself questioning the relevance of what we were required to read. I missed the voices of children; I also worried that the research I was reading was far removed from my work as a teacher, and that I might not rally the stamina needed to finish my doctorate. I vividly remember being assigned to read *Writing Superheroes* (Dyson, 1997) and finally thinking, "Wow, this makes sense! There is power in writing about children and their literacy learning." I remember being able to see myself as a qualitative researcher, writing about children and families, and telling their stories. I recognized the power in that approach. Thus, I return to the work of Dyson as an example of an exemplary ethnographic case study.

I focus on one of Dyson's more recent books, *Rewriting the Basics* (2013), as an excellent example of an ethnographic case study. Part of my selection process entailed confirming that this book qualifies as an ethnographic case study. In particular, I wondered how Dyson characterizes her own work. I knew that along with Celia Genishi, she had literally "written the book" on case studies (Dyson & Genishi, 2005). Thus, I consulted the book's index and searched for the terms *case study* and *ethnography*. I encountered two surprises. First, while the index includes no references to ethnography, the indexed references to *case study* brought me to a methodological appendix that opens with the words, "As an ethnographer . . ." (p. 180). This focus on ethnography is reiterated on pages 183 and 184, where Dyson describes her "ethnographic analysis/es." Intrigued, I perused the text and noted that Chapter 1 is titled "The 'Basics' and Society's Children: *Cases* of Classroom Writing" (p. 1; emphasis added).

These clues confirmed my thinking. First, yes, Dyson characterizes her work as drawing on both ethnography and case study methodologies. Second, these insights affirm the premise presented in this chapter: that hybrid models are possible and promising for exploring literacy learning and literacy practices. In short, Dyson focuses on what happens within social spaces—classrooms—alongside careful and thoughtful analyses of individual children, their experiences, and their literacy practices.

One of the strengths of this ethnographic case study is the clear articulation of the project's focus. In her methodological appendix (pp. 180–184), Dyson clearly articulates her focus and her interest in both social contexts and the children's sense making: "My overriding concern was to understand the ideological—indeed, the ethical—underpinnings of 'basics' in the official composing curricula, as materially given and interactionally enacted. Moreover, I aimed to understand how children, made sense of what was curricularly on offer in their own times and spaces" (p. 180).

Dyson provides a clear description of how this focus leads to the ideas presented in the book. After collecting official documents and curricula that defined learning in two classrooms, she identifies events and analyzes those events in terms of their focus, their place within larger routines, their thematic content, and the modalities involved. Dyson becomes particularly intrigued by the "fix-it events" (p. 183) in each classroom. She defines *fix-it events* as times when basic skills were invoked through correction by the teachers or students. Across the two classrooms, students fixed grammar; addressed content; adhered to writing conventions; and made choices about words, organization, and aesthetics. The fix-its defined what counted as "fair," "good," or "nice" (p. 183). Thus, Dyson thoroughly describes her methodological and analytic processes; she makes her process visible so that readers have a clear sense of what she did, and thus can discern the trustworthiness of her study.

Interestingly, toward the end of this appendix, Dyson provides a rare degree of transparency about her process. She identifies and lists possible themes that she does not discuss in this book: "descriptions of the kinds of play in which the children engaged," "new kinds of emerging play," and variation in the "focal children's use of semantic tools" (p. 184). She then describes starting with "thin tales" about writing, reading compelling theories, pouring over her data, and sketching out new types of analyses. Finally, the "plot thickened," the "characters emerged" (p. 184), and the book was written. This transparency about her process, and her honesty about the unplanned and unpredictable nature of her analysis, are reassuring to all of us who find ourselves with stacks of data and no clear path forward.

Across this ethnographic case study, Dyson demonstrates reflexivity, not only about her research process, but also about her role as a researcher. She admits that she intentionally selected classrooms where teachers demonstrated respect for children and would welcome her nontraditional presence. She acknowledges her "critical stance toward the highly regulated teaching situations" (p. 180). While attempting to be as innocuous as possible—listening, watching, audiotaping, copying children's work, and taking notes—she identifies how her presence probably affected the children and the teachers. Dyson makes no claims of objectivity and noninterference, but clearly describes the steps she took to minimize her influence on the children and their writing.

While Dyson's methodological descriptions and reflexive stance support the trustworthiness of the study, they do not capture the ultimate power of Dyson's work. Part of the contribution is her beautiful and compelling writing. Her thick descriptions of classrooms and apt articulations of children's voices transport readers into these classrooms, and specifically into buzzing writing workshops. We vicariously sit beside the children as they negotiate doing writing right, and we witness how they experience fix-it requests.

Each chapter opens with an anecdote that draws readers into a writing workshop. We accompany Dyson on her drive to the school, enter the classrooms with her, and are introduced to the teachers and children. We then encounter the official *basics* in kindergarten and first grade, including letters, their sounds, punctuation, spelling, grammar, and the spacing of words across a page. However, Dyson observes more than simple skill instruction. She complicates the basics by "examining the values and beliefs—the ideologies—they embody about proper language and proper children" (p. xi).

This interface among children, the basics, and accompanying fix-it strategies in writing workshops is not established by telling readers what happened. We are truly shown. We witness what Dyson witnessed through her careful observation and relentless recording of children's words, actions, and written texts. As we read the book and consider the children's experiences, Dyson creates a compelling case that reveals how attention to the basics has "drowned out talk of how children learn and, most relevant to this book, who they are, that is, their humanity" (p. 6). Significantly, Dyson does not dismiss the importance of official basics; instead, she argues for a "transformation [that] would stretch 'the basics,' because it would make relevant children's use of basic communicative actions" (p. 165). She insists on the humanity of children.

CLOSING AND CRITERIA

Although exemplary ethnographic case studies share many criteria, I highlight the following:

- A clear articulation of the project's ultimate focus.
- Attention to dimensions of education that matter for children.
- Rich and detailed descriptions of settings, participants, and methods.
- Thoughtful presentations of the voices and experiences of participants.
- Recognition of the complexity of social spaces and the people who occupy them.
- Acknowledgment of how power, in all its forms, affects children's lives and learning.
- Transparency and honesty in regard to the researcher's own practices and positionality.
- Excellent writing.
- Attention to the humanity of people as they live and learn in educational spaces.

Like turtles and tortoises, case studies and ethnographies can appear very similar (White et al., 2009). They use similar types of data, attend to details and entail thick description, focus on people's experiences, are subjective, use similar analytic processes, and report their findings in similar ways.

However, as Small (2009) notes, methods of scientific inquiry "are languages to the extent that they constitute systems of thought with terms and ways of framing problems that are specific to their systems" (p. 10). Thus, it is not the types of data, the level of detail, or the amount of subjectivity that distinguishes case studies from ethnographies. Instead, we recognize the systems of thought that accompany these methodologies and frame phenomena in ways that highlight either social processes or social mechanisms, perspectives or systems of meaning, individuals or networks, the particularistic or the interactive, individual experiences or lives within groups, and individual or cultural knowledge. Thus, the systems of thought that the researcher attends to are what make the difference. The good news is that, unlike turtles and tortoises, researchers can choose from both systems by locating themselves on a powerful continuum that offers a myriad of possibilities.

REFERENCES

Anderson, P. L., & Meier-Hedde, R. (2001). Early case reports of dyslexia in the United States and Europe. *Journal of Learning Disabilities, 34*(1), 9–21.

Atkinson, P., & Hammersley, M. (1998). Ethnography and participant observation. In N. K. Denzin & Y. S. Lincoln (Eds.), *Strategies of qualitative inquiry* (pp. 248–261). Thousand Oaks, CA: SAGE.

Barton, D., & Hamilton, M. (2012). *Local literacies: Reading and writing in one community*. New York: Routledge.

Bissex, G. L. (1980). *GNYS AT WRK: A child learns to write and read*. Cambridge, MA: Harvard University Press.

Butler, D. (1975). *Cushla and her books*. Boston: Horn Book.

Calkins, L. M. (1983). *Lessons from a child: On the teaching and learning of writing*. Portsmouth, NH: Heinemann.

Comber, B., & Kamler, B. (2005). *Turn-around pedagogies: Literacy interventions for at-risk students*. Newtown, New South Wales, Australia: Primary English Teaching Association.

Compton-Lilly, C. (2003). *Reading families: The literate lives of urban children*. New York: Teachers College Press.

Compton-Lilly, C. (2007). *Re-reading families: The literate lives of urban children, four years later*. New York: Teachers College Press.

Compton-Lilly, C. (2012). *Reading time: The literate lives of urban secondary students and their families*. New York: Teachers College Press.

Compton-Lilly, C. (2013). Case studies. In A. Trainor & E. Graue (Eds.), *Reviewing qualitative research in the social sciences* (pp. 54–65). New York: Routledge.

Compton-Lilly, C. (2017). *Reading students' lives: Literacy learning across time*. New York: Routledge.

Creswell, J. W. (1998). *Qualitative inquiry and research design: Choosing among five traditions*. Thousand Oaks, CA: SAGE.

Duke, N. K., & Mallette, M. H. (Eds.). (2011). *Literacy research methodologies* (2nd ed.). New York: Guilford Press.

Dyson, A. H. (1997). *Writing superheroes: Contemporary childhood, popular culture, and classroom literacy*. New York: Teachers College Press.

Dyson, A. H. (2003). *The brothers and sisters learn to write: Popular literacies in childhood and school cultures*. New York: Teachers College Press.

Dyson, A. H. (2013). *Rewriting the basics: Literacy learning in children's cultures*. New York: Teachers College Press.

Dyson, A. H., & Genishi, C. (2005). *On the case: Approaches to language and literacy research*. New York: Teachers College Press & NCRLL.

Erickson, F. (1984). What makes school ethnography ethnographic? *Anthropology and Education Quarterly, 15*(1), 51–66.

Flyvbjerg, B. (2006). Five misunderstandings about case-study research. *Qualitative Inquiry, 12*(2), 219–245.

Geertz, C. (1973). *The interpretations of cultures: Selected essays*. New York: Basic Books.

Green, J., & Bloome, D. (1997). A situated perspective on ethnography and ethnographers of and in education. In J. Flood, S. B. Heath, & D. Lapp (Eds.), *Handbook of research on teaching literacy through the communicative and visual arts* (pp. 181–202). New York: Routledge.

Harry, B., Klingner, J. K., & Cramer, E. P. (2007). *Case studies of minority student placement in special education*. New York: Teachers College Press.

Heath, S. B. (1983). *Ways with words: Language, life and work in communities and classrooms.* Cambridge, UK: Cambridge University Press.

Heath, S. B., & Street, B. V. (2008). *On ethnography: Approaches to language and literacy research.* New York: Teachers College Press & NCRLL.

Jones, S., Clarke, L. W., & Enriquez, G. (2010). *The reading turn-around: A five-part framework for differentiated instruction.* New York: Teachers College Press.

Lewis, C. (2001). *Literary practices as social acts: Power, status and cultural norms in the classroom.* Mahwah, NJ: Erlbaum.

Merriam, S. B. (1998). *Qualitative research and case study applications in education.* San Francisco: Jossey-Bass.

Merseth, K. K. (1991). The early history of case-based instruction: Insights for teacher education today. *Journal of Teacher Education, 42*(4), 243–249.

Purcell-Gates, V. (1997). *Other people's words: The cycle of low literacy.* Cambridge, MA: Harvard University Press.

Small, M. L. (2009). 'How many cases do I need?': On science and the logic of case selection in field-based research. *Ethnography, 10*(1), 5–38.

Smith, L. (1979). An evolving logic of participant observation, educational ethnography, and other case studies. In L. Shulman (Ed.), *Review of research in education* (pp. 316–377). Itasca, IL: Peacock.

Stake, R. E. (1978). The case study method in social inquiry. *Educational Researcher, 7*(2), 5–9.

Stake, R. E. (1995). *The art of case study research.* Thousand Oaks, CA: SAGE.

Stenhouse, L. (1987). Case study and case records: Towards a contemporary history of education. *British Educational Research Journal, 4*(2), 21–39.

Street, B. V. (1984). *Literacy in theory and practice.* Cambridge, MA: Cambridge University Press.

Taylor, D. (1983). *Family literacy: Young children learning to read and write.* Portsmouth, NH: Heinemann.

Taylor, D., & Dorsey-Gaines, C. (1988). *Growing up literate: Learning from inner-city families.* Portsmouth, NH: Heinemann.

White, D. (1956). *Books before 5.* New York: Oxford University Press.

White, J., Drew, S., & Hay, T. (2009). Ethnography versus case study: Positioning research and researchers. *Qualitative Research Journal, 9*(1), 18–27.

Yazan, B. (2015). Three approaches to case study methods in education: Yin, Merriam, and Stake. *The Qualitative Report, 20*(2), 134–152.

Yin, R. K. (1981). The case study crisis: Some answers. *Administrative Science Quarterly, 26*(1), 58–65.

Yin, R. (2002). *Case study research and applications: Design and methods.* Thousand Oaks, CA: SAGE.

Yon, D. A. (2003). Highlights and overview of the history of educational ethnography. *Annual Review of Anthropology, 32*(1), 411–429.

CHAPTER 3

Content Analysis

THE PAST, PRESENT, AND FUTURE

Samuel DeJulio
James V. Hoffman
Misty Sailors
Ramón A. Martínez
Melissa B. Wilson

Jg zpv dbo sfbe uijt, uibol b ufbdifs.
—BOPOZNPVT

In his popular children's book *The Riddle of the Rosetta Stone,* James Cross Giblin (1990) describes the path scholars followed to uncover the mysteries of hieroglyphics, using parallel texts in Greek and Egyptian. The essence of content analysis is to be found in this remarkable effort to reconstruct a written language that had been lost for centuries. On a much simpler scale, the quotation we offer at the start of this chapter can be seen as a similar kind of challenge. What does it say? Content analysis can lead readers to discover both the meaning behind, and the patterns used to obscure the meaning of, a text like this. More important in relation to the goals of this chapter, content analysis can reveal the subtle messages embedded in a text read by a child in a classroom or by a classroom teacher—for example, consulting a manual in preparation to teach a lesson.

Content analysis has found broad applications in the study of language and literacy, ranging from the analysis of book responses (audio-recorded and transcribed as in Sipe, 2000), to the analysis of students' writing (as in Aulls, 2003), to the analysis of the teacher's role in scaffolding of classroom discussion (as in Maloch, 2002), to the analysis of word choice, word repetition, and sentence complexity in beginning reading materials (as described by Hiebert & Martin, 2003), to the analysis of the content of textbooks (as in Beck, McKeown, & Gromoll, 1989), to the analysis of online interactions of youth in a Korean drama forum (as in Kim, 2016).

We begin this chapter with a general description of the focus and methods of content analysis, including attention to its historical roots, essential components, and standards for inquiry. We continue with a presentation of the kinds of questions that have been addressed in literacy-related research by investigators using this method. We include in this section the description of some exemplary studies that reflect the breadth of application of this method to literacy research. We believe that these reports could very well serve as mentor texts for those who hope to take up content analysis as a methodology for research. In the final section, we call attention to issues and trends for those who may be contemplating the use of content analysis in their own literacy research.

DEFINING CONTENT ANALYSIS

Content analysis is a flexible research method for analyzing texts and describing and interpreting the written artifacts of society (White & Marsh, 2006). Babbie (2007) defined content analysis as "the study of recorded human communications, such as books, websites, paintings and laws." Bernard Berelson (1952) defined content analysis as "a research technique for the objective, systematic and quantitative description of manifest content of communications" (p. 15). Neuendorf (2002) offered the following definition:

> Content analysis is an in-depth analysis using quantitative or qualitative techniques of messages using a scientific method (including attention to objectivity–intersubjectivity, a priori design, reliability, validity, generalizability, replicability, and hypothesis testing) and is not limited as to the types of variables that may be measured or the context in which the messages are created or presented.

Content analysis thus involves the inspection of patterns in written texts, often drawing on combinations of inductive, deductive, and abductive analytical techniques.

White and Marsh (2006) explained *abductive* analysis in terms of a researcher's using "rules of inference, to move from the text to the answers to the research questions" (p. 27). The rules of inference in this methodology are of this type: "Abductive inferences proceed across logically distinct domains, from particulars of one kind, to particulars of another kind" (Krippendorff, 2004, p. 36).

Content analysis has sometimes been challenged for being a positivist methodology; yet there are numerous examples of content analysis that rely on interpretive/qualitative principles (e.g., analysis of transcripts of classroom interactions). "Research using qualitative content analysis focuses on the characteristics of language as communication with attention to the content or contextual meaning of the text" (Hsieh & Shannon, 2005, p. 1278). The goal of this analysis is to provide "knowledge and understanding of the phenomenon under study" (p. 1278). In other words, content analysis is the method of making inferences from texts and making sense of these interpretations in a context surrounding the text.

HISTORICAL BACKGROUND ON CONTENT ANALYSIS

Content analysis has its beginnings in rhetorical analysis over 4,000 years ago. Aristotle, in his studies of rhetoric, was concerned with the content of argument when he "put the message content and form at the center of the argument—that we use communication to control our environment, including the actions of others" (Neuendorf, 2002, p. 31). Neuendorf (2002) traced the genesis of content analysis to another source, decryption. The Rosetta Stone discovery prompted Thomas Young to "translate between the three scripts through a process of quantifying occurrences of signs on the stone and other ancient sources" (p. 31).

Krippendorff (2004) began his search for the beginnings of content analysis at a somewhat later point: He traced this methodology's start to the 1600s, when theological scholars used content analysis in their dissertations. These scholars, at the Roman Catholic Church's behest, analyzed printed materials for heretical content. The next historical instances of content analysis developed in Sweden during the 18th century, when scholars systematically analyzed a new book of hymns for anti-Christian ideas (Hsieh & Shannon, 2005; Krippendorff, 2004).

Content analysis became more widely recognized and adopted in the early 20th century, when it was used in journalism schools to examine newspapers for "demoralizing, unwholesome, and trivial matters as opposed to worthwhile news items" (Krippendorff, 2004, p. 5). Both Krippendorff (2004) and Neuendorf (2002) note content analysis's major growth spurt in the United States and Western Europe in the 1930s and 1940s. Krippendorff described sociologists' extensive use of polling in the 1930s, and mass communications scholars' use of the methodology to analyze Nazi propaganda in the 1940s.

After World War II, "the use of content analysis spread to numerous disciplines" (Krippendorff, 2004). While it was used in the fields of psychology, anthropology, and history, it came to rest primarily in the field of communications, where it was used to analyze mass media. With the advent of better computers and software, much of the "analyzing" is now done on computers, "with text data coded into explicit categories and then described using statistics" (Hsieh & Shannon, 2005, p. 1278).

Although the tools for content analysis have expanded, particularly with the use of computers, the essential attention to patterns in text has remained the same. The applications of content analysis can be seen across many forms of human activity, ranging from national intelligence (e.g., the analysis of communications across the Internet that might signal terrorist activity), to business (e.g., analysis of newspaper advertisements that might signal buying and selling patterns), to psychology (e.g., patterns of behavior in problem solving), to sociology (e.g., sexist language patterns in public discourse).

ESSENTIAL FEATURES AND STANDARDS FOR CONTENT ANALYSIS IN LITERACY RESEARCH

Content analysis, as a tool in literacy research, typically focuses on the presence of certain words or concepts within a text or a set of texts. Researchers quantify and analyze the presence, meanings, and relationships of such words and concepts; they then make inferences about the messages within the text(s), the writer(s), the audience, and even the culture and time of which these are a part. *Texts* can be defined broadly as books, book chapters, essays, interviews, discussions, newspaper headlines and articles, historical documents, speeches, conversations, advertising, theater, informal conversation, or really any occurrence of communicative language.

Ole Holsti (1969) grouped the uses of content analysis into three basic categories: (1) making inferences about the antecedents of a communication (e.g., what messages, themes, belief systems can be inferred from this text?); (2) describing and making inferences about characteristics of a communication (e.g., what is the quality of the communication in this text measured against some standard?); and (3) making inferences about the effects of a communication (e.g., what impact does a particular text have on patterns of interaction?).

According to Krippendorff (2004), six questions must be addressed in every content analysis:

1. Which data are analyzed?
2. How are they defined?
3. What is the population from which they are drawn?
4. What is the context relative to which the data are analyzed?
5. What are the boundaries of the analysis?
6. What is the target of the inferences?

Neuendorf (2002) described a set of steps, or a progression, that is typical in any content analysis:

- *Theory/rationale.* The research must identify the focus for the analysis in terms of key variables and a theoretical framework. A hypothesized relationship or set of predictions may be posed. Alternatively, the research may rely on a set of questions to guide the study.
- *Conceptualizing decisions.* The researcher may limit the focus for

the content analysis to a particular purpose or set of variables. These decisions are described explicitly and with a rationale.

- *Operationalizing measures.* The researcher defines each variable or construct or process to be used to guide the analysis of the targeted text(s). These definitions must be described in relation to the theoretical framework, and explicit enough to guide possible replications.
- *Selecting/identifying a coding scheme.* The coding scheme may rely on computer-based or may rely on human analysis. The scheme may be drawn from previous research, adapted from previous research, or constructed for this study.
- *Sampling.* The researcher describes the sampling process used to gather the corpus of text to be analyzed.
- *Training and reliability.* Coders are trained in the process of analysis to levels of agreement. The checks focus on each of the critical variables.
- *Coding.* There must be at least two coders (with at least 10% overlap of material analyzed to check for levels of agreement). Even with computer analysis, there should be spot-checking on the reliability of coding.
- *Tabulation and reporting.* The research reports on the analysis procedures, including reliability, leading to the findings.

Of course, these procedures may be modified, depending on the content and focus for the study. However, these procedures set a clear standard for researchers who adopt content analysis as their primary method.

QUESTIONS ADDRESSED BY USING CONTENT METHODS IN LITERACY RESEARCH

Given that content analysis is focused on texts, there might be an expectation for broad application of this methodology in literacy research. But is this true? How often is content analysis used as the primary method of literacy research? What kinds of questions are addressed? Are there particular areas of focus that appear frequently in the literature? For our chapter published in the second edition of this book (2011), we undertook an examination of the research literature that has adopted this methodology. In the current chapter, we have updated our analysis to examine the ways content analysis is presently being used in the field of literacy research.

In the 2011 chapter, we excluded from our analysis studies that adapted applied methods of discourse analysis, historical analysis, and literature syntheses. We focused primarily on studies that examined curriculum materials used in instruction. We conducted this search with three goals in mind: to uncover the kinds of questions addressed in literacy research by investigators using this methodology; to examine the application of the methodology in recent research in terms of rigor and theoretical frameworks; and to identify a set of studies that might serve as mentor texts for inquiry within this methodology.

We set parameters on our examination of the research literature consistent with our questions. Specifically, we limited our inquiry to a particular time period and to a sample of research journals. We chose, as our starting point, Durkin's (1981) investigation of comprehension instruction in the basal teacher guides. There are certainly earlier examples of research in literacy that adopted a content analysis perspective (e.g., Chall's [1967] analysis of basal materials for code vs. meaning emphasis; Beck and McCaslin's [1978] study of commercial materials to determine how instruction is arranged with respect to decoding; and the many studies of readability from the 1940s through the 1970s). For us, the appeal of Durkin's study as a starting point was that this study was one of the first coming from the Center for the Study of Reading to use content analysis methods; it was published in the premier reading research journal (*Reading Research Quarterly*); and it was complemented by a replication study published in the same journal in 2009 (Dewitz, Jones, & Leahy, 2009). Following this rationale, we identified our time framework of 1981 to 2009. Second, we limited our examination to studies that had been published in four of the leading literacy research journals: *Reading Research Quarterly, Journal of Literacy Research* [formerly *Journal of Reading Behavior*], *Research in the Teaching of English,* and the *Yearbook of the National Reading Conference.* This was a limited sampling, and while it would not suffice in a comprehensive review, we were hopeful that this would be appropriate to examine our goal of determining the range of questions being asked through content analysis methods in literacy research.

In describing the findings from our initial investigation, we begin with Durkin's (1981) study and the follow-up study with a similar focus reported in 2009 by Dewitz and colleagues. Next, we offer a brief "content analysis" of research in literacy that has employed content analysis methods of curriculum materials, with a focus on the range of questions and topics addressed between the years 1981 and 2009. Next, we update our analysis with studies published between 2010 and 2019, to understand how content analysis is being applied in current literacy research. Finally, we offer a detailed description of the content analysis methods used in six studies that seem to represent the breadth of research in literacy.

COMPREHENSION INSTRUCTION

Durkin's (1981, 1990) research into comprehension instruction was conducted in her association with the Center for the Study of Reading at the University of Illinois, Champaign–Urbana, and was featured in two research reports. The first study, with some attention to content analysis, was an observational study investigating the amount and qualities of comprehension instruction in elementary schools. Durkin first developed an observational tool that was based on her analysis of the research literature on effective practices in the teaching of reading comprehension. She then used this tool to observe in classrooms from grades 3 through 6. Durkin's (1981) findings indicated that minimal comprehension instruction was offered in classrooms. She famously documented, instead, large doses of comprehension "mentioning," the frequent "interrogation" of students with comprehension questions, and the reliance on "worksheets" to practice comprehension. By the end of this study, Durkin puzzled over the causes for the near-absence of comprehension instruction in classrooms. She wondered whether this could be a result of the absence of guidance for such instruction in the curriculum guides provided for teachers.

Durkin followed this line of thinking into her second study of comprehension instruction, this time relying primarily on content analysis methods. Durkin used the same definition of comprehension instruction from her observational study in the analysis of the basal materials: "A manual suggests that a teacher do or say something that ought to help children acquire the ability to understand, or work out, the meaning of connected text" (p. 518). Durkin articulated specific guidelines for the analysis that included issues of what the coders of the materials would not consider—for example, "Headings for manual segments (e.g., Comprehension Instruction) will not be considered in classifying them" (p. 519). The guidelines also described what the coders would consider—for example, "Whenever a manual provides comprehension instruction about a topic that was covered earlier but adds something new that is judged to be significant for understanding connected text, it will be called 'elaboration' (not review) and will be counted as an additional instance of comprehension instruction" (p. 520). The features of the content analysis were indentified a priori and pilot-tested before they were incorporated in the research methods. Further classifications included definitions of terms such as *practice, application,* and *review.*

The procedures followed in the analysis provided for an initial reader's coding all of the materials and a second reader's analyzing all of the instances identified as comprehension instruction. All disagreements ("very few") were discussed and resolved between the reviewers. In addition, the second reviewer went back to the original materials to check on "missed" instances, and the few that were discovered were resolved through discussion. The first reviewer repeated the entire review process, once the initial round of reviewing was completed.

The findings were analyzed and reported by frequencies, and next broken down by grade level and then by categories (e.g., graphic signals, anaphora). These latter categories were not established a priori, but resulted from the content analysis itself. These categories were further divided by the support offered at "less" than the sentence level (20 categories) and "more" than the sentence level (14 categories). Further analysis focused on attention to the qualities of the "discourse" type (e.g., narrative, expository, poetry).

From this analysis, Durkin concluded that there was far more attention to application and practice to support instruction that there was guidance on explicit instruction. Overall, Durkin struggled with the extreme attention to questions and assessment rather than instruction. In terms of methodology, Durkin offered a good example of the use of a priori and constructed categories based on analysis. She offered substantial detail about coding, although there was far more attention to this in the technical report (Durkin, 1990) than in the journal article (Durkin, 1981). Although both Durkin's observational and basal analysis studies have been critiqued for the a priori definitions used, the studies have stood the test of time within the research community.

Dewitz and colleagues (2009) reported a curriculum analysis of comprehension instruction in basal reader guides (grades 3, 4, and 5). The study was framed by these questions:

- What skills and strategies are recommended to be taught?
- How are these skills and strategies recommended to be taught?
- What instructional designs do the programs employ?
- How do the spacing and timing of comprehension skill and strategy instruction in core programs compare with how these skills were taught in original research studies?

The researchers, for the most part, adopted Durkin's (1981) original definition for comprehension instruction. The researchers "read every lesson" of every program. They examined the scope and sequence for each program and looked for alignment between the two. They coded instructional "moves" in terms of what skill was in focus and what the teacher was directed to do. They adopted six a priori categories from Durkin (preparation, instruction, application, practice, review, and assessment) to create 10 codes. The need for the additional codes was recognized during the coding process, and the new categories were then created. Lessons that were coded as "direct explanation" were further analyzed according to Duffy and colleagues' (1986) criteria (e.g., identification of procedural knowledge, when strategy would be used). Dewitz and associates (2009), like Durkin, found little attention to comprehension instruction. They found few examples of instruction that met the criteria for explicitness set by Duffy and colleagues. Furthermore, they found little evidence in their analysis of timing that there was any attention to a "gradual release of responsibility" for the comprehension strategy from the teacher's control to the students.

In terms of method, the Dewitz and colleagues (2009) report offered remarkably little if any information on coding procedures or reliability checks on the coders, although the coding form was included in the appendix of the report. There was also no description of the process followed to construct the new categories in the coding system. In fact, there was less explicit attention to the method in the Dewitz and coauthors report than in the original by Durkin, and neither Durkin nor Dewitz and colleagues offered any explicit references to the methods used.

OUR 2011 SEARCH OF THE LITERATURE

To what degree were these two studies "typical" in terms of focus or methods? As noted earlier, to address the question for our 2011 chapter, we conducted a hand search of four literacy research journals (*Reading Research Quarterly, Research in the Teaching of English, Journal of Literacy Research* [formerly *Journal of Reading Behavior*], and the *Yearbook of the National Reading Conference*) from the years 1981 through 2009 for research reports that relied primarily on content analysis. We sought to identify studies that used content analysis of curriculum materials as the primary focus for the research questions and the primary methodology. We excluded studies that relied on discourse analysis, historical analysis, or literature syntheses. We conducted hand searches of each of the volumes from the target journals with these criteria.

In our initial analysis, we identified a total of 42 studies that met our criteria for inclusion. These studies were distributed across the four journals in the following manner: *Journal of Reading Behavior/Journal of Literacy Research* = 11; *Reading Research Quarterly* = 12; *Yearbook of the National Reading Conference* = 16; and *Research in the Teaching of English* = 3. We met and applied a constant-comparative method (Glaser & Strauss, 1967) to identify the major focus for the analysis in each of these reports. We identified five major categories:

1. *Leveled texts,* mostly basal readers (a focus on the features of the text materials read by students; N = 15 studies).
2. *Instruction* (a focus on the materials used by teachers to guide their teaching; N = 12).
3. *Literature* (a focus on the qualities of the literature; N = 9).
4. *Print environment* (a focus on the print qualities in the classroom environment; N = 4).
5. *Methods textbooks* (a focus on the texts used to prepare teachers; N = 1).

In some cases, the focus for a particular study spanned more than one area. However, for the initial presentation of this data, we classified each study by its major focus. Consistent with our purpose in conducting this review, we further examined each of the studies relative to the kinds of research questions addressed and the methodology.

Leveled Texts

The first category represented the largest group of studies in the pool identified. The vast majority of these studies focused on the analysis of basal readers or content area textbooks and related trends. These studies addressed questions related to the decoding demands and supportive features of the texts used in primary grades, and included studies of such traditional constructs as "readability." These were also studies that examined the distribution of different text "types" (e.g., the inclusion of informational texts) and the match between text types represented in the instructional materials as compared to the distribution in tests or in standards documents. None of the studies in this category described "content analysis" as their primary method; nor were there any citations to indicate the analytical framework being used.

Instructional Studies

The second category represented the second largest group of studies in the pool identified. The vast majority of these studies focused on the analysis of teacher guides in basal readers or content area textbooks. A large number of these reports focused on how, when, and if teachers were guided in the teaching of comprehension (e.g., were strategies taught explicitly?). As in the first category, none of the studies in the second category described "content analysis" as their primary method; nor were there any citations to indicate the analytical framework being used.

Literature Studies

Making up the third largest category, the literature studies tended to focus on questions related to the literary content of basal readers or children's literature or both. While there was almost no mention of content analysis as a method, many of the studies were explicit about the ways their analysis drew on sociological or literary theory.

Print Environment Studies

Although the fourth category comprised fewer studies, the number of studies in this category seemed to be increasing. The print environment studies we reviewed assumed a broader and more inclusive view of the qualities of texts and the functions served in the classroom environment. These studies ranged from examinations of the range of text types to examinations of particular kinds of texts (e.g., informational) or of a medium (e.g., electronic). Some of these studies included the examination of teachers and students as they engaged with texts in these print environments. There was little mention of content analysis as a method in these studies.

Methods Textbooks Studies

There were two studies represented in the fifth category. One study was focused on the attention to the particular needs of English language learners in literacy instruction. Interestingly, this study included an examination of journals on this same topic. There was no mention of content analysis as a primary method. The second study focused on references to "literacy" teachers in secondary methods textbooks. This study referenced content analysis in detail as part of the methods section.

UPDATED LITERATURE SCAN

For the current chapter, we revisited the literacy research literature, following two paths. In the first path, we revisited the four journals that we examined in our initial review (*Journal of Literacy Research, Reading Research Quarterly, Yearbook of the National Reading Conference,* and *Research in the Teaching of English*). We conducted a hand search of the journals from 2010 (where we had ended our last search) to 2019. As done previously, we excluded reviews of research or articles that were not research studies. We recorded each of the studies in a table (see Table 3.1), using the five categories described earlier. Our updated review of the journals led to the identification of 24 new studies. These studies were distributed across the four journals in the following manner: *Journal of Literacy Research* = 8; *Reading Research Quarterly* = 7; *Yearbook of the National Reading Conference* = 7; and *Research in the Teaching of English* = 2.

In the second path, we focused on studies that cited our 2011 chapter. This allowed us to see how researchers were using this chapter to apply content analysis to their work. Once again, we excluded publications that were not empirical studies. Using Google Scholar, we found 43 studies that cited this chapter for their research purposes and also met our criteria. We found four studies that were in both paths of our analysis (i.e., studies that were found in one of the four journals and that cited this chapter). Following the same process as we had in our review of the journals, we added articles to our table, continuing to revise the categories as needed. Table 3.2 shows articles identified in our review of studies that cited this chapter.

As we examined the studies, we began to add more categories to capture some of the ways content analysis was being done. We found that although the five initial categories still worked for studies focused on curricular materials (the principal focus of our earlier review), content analysis was being used in diverse ways, even within literacy research. We continued this process until we had completed both paths of our updated research. This led us to add five new categories.

TABLE 3.1. Studies from the Review of Journals (2010–2019)

	Categories used in our 2011 chapter					New categories added during this review					Named content analysis as primary method (Y/N)
	Leveled texts	Instructional studies	Literature studies	Print environment studies	Methods textbooks studies	Academic literature	Content standards	Preservice teachers	K–12 students, teachers, and administrators	Other	
Reading Research Quarterly											
Goldman, Braasch, Wiley, Graesser, & Brodowinska (2012)										X	N
Hutchison & Reinking (2011)									X		N
Hutchison, Woodward, & Colwell (2016)									X		N
Kim (2016)									X		Y
Reutzel & Mohr (2015)						X					N
Segal, Howe, Persram, Martin-Chang, & Ross (2018)									X		N
Silverman, Proctor, Harring, Doyle, Mitchell, & Meyer (2014)									X		N
Journal of Literacy Research											
Blackburn, Clark, & Nemeth (2015)			X								Y
Brooks & Cueto (2018)			X								Y
Certo (2015)									X		Y

Reference											Y/N
Dentith, Sailors, & Sethusha (2016)			X								N
Dutro & Haberl (2018)									X		N
Murphy, Andiliou, Firetto, Bowersox, Baker, & Ramsay (2016)									X		N
Parsons, Gallagher, & the George Mason University Content Analysis Team (2016)						X					Y
Sciurba (2017)			X								Y
Research in the Teaching of English											
Brooks, Sekayi, Savage, Waller, & Picot (2010)			X								N
Walters (2015)										X	N
Yearbook of the National Reading Conference											
Beckers, Saal, & Cheek (2014)									X		N
Dixon & Janks (2018)								X			Y
Everett (2016)									X		N
Hattan, Singer, Loughlin, & Alexander (2015)									X		N
Kerkhoff (2015)							X				Y
Taylor (2015)						X					Y
Patrick (2016)								X			Y
Total (24)	0	0	5	0	0	3	1	2	11	2	Y = 10/N = 14

Note. Full citations are available in the References.

TABLE 3.2. Studies That Cited Our 2011 Chapter

	Categories used in our 2011 chapter					New categories added during this review					Named content analysis as primary method (Y/N)
	Leveled texts	Instructional studies	Literature studies	Print environment studies	Methods textbook studies	Academic literature	Content standards	Preservice teachers	K-12 students, teachers, and administrators	Other	
Azano, Tackett, & Sigmon (2017)			X								Y
Biddle & Azano (2016)						X					Y
Dentith, Sailors, & Sethusha (2016)[a]			X								Y
Domke (2018)			X								Y
Gretter & Yadav (2018)								X			Y
Ikpeze (2018)								X			Y
Kerkhoff (2015)[a]							X				Y
Kumar (2014)					X						Y
Kumar (2016)								X			Y
Lochmiller & Mancinelli (in press)									X		Y
Marlatt (2018)								X			Y
Marlatt (2019)									X		Y
McIver (2018)			X								Y
Meixner, Peel, Hendrickson, Szczeck, & Bousum (2019)										X	N
Montero (2012)				X							Y
Morrison, Wilcox, Murdoch, & Bird (2018)	X										Y
Nguyen & Kebede (2017)						X					Y
Pantaleo (2012a)									X		Y
Pantaleo (2012b)									X		Y
Pantaleo (2013)									X		Y
Pantaleo (2014)									X		Y

40

											Y/N
Pantaleo (2015)										X		Y
Pantaleo (2016a)										X		Y
Pantaleo (2016b)										X		Y
Pantaleo (2016c)										X		Y
Pantaleo (2017)										X		Y
Pantaleo (2018)										X		Y
Pantaleo (2019)						X						Y
Parsons, Gallagher, & the George Mason University Content Analysis Team (2016)[a]						X						Y
Pelltari (2016)						X						Y
Ramanayake & Williams (2017)									X			Y
Roth (2017)					X							Y
Sailors, Orellana, Stortz, & Sellers (2019)				X								Y
Stagg Peterson, Parr, Lindgren, & Kaufman (2018)							X					Y
Stahl, Theriault, & Armstrong (2016)						X						Y
Taylor (2015)[a]						X						Y
West & Williams (2015)						X						Y
Williams & Lowrance-Faulhaber (2018)						X						Y
Wilson & Kumar (2017)									X			Y
Wright & Domke (2019)							X					Y
Wright & Peltier (2016)					X							Y
Yanoff, LaDuke, & Lindner (2014)			X									Y
Yeom (2018)										X		N
Total (43)	1	1	4	2	3	9	3	3	6	13	1	Y = 41/N = 2

Note. Full citations are available in the References.
[a]Study is also included in Table 3.1.

Academic Literature

The first new category consisted of studies that conducted content analysis using research journals or academic literature. This might include looking at current trends or changes in literacy research (Parsons et al., 2016), or at the construction of particular concepts in the research literature (Biddle & Azano, 2016). We found three studies that fit this category after our updated search of the four journals, and one study in our review of studies that cited this chapter.

Content Standards

Studies in the second new category focused on the analysis of educational standards. These studies, though few in number, might be focused on particular content area standards (e.g., writing) or might even look across contexts/borders to compare standards (Stagg Peterson, Parr, Lindgren, & Kaufman, 2018). Initially, there was only one study in this category, but three more were added after the second path of our work.

Preservice Teachers

Some of the studies were focused on content related to preservice teachers in higher education. These studies included content analyses of interviews, lesson plans created by preservice teachers, or written reflections. As with the content standards category, this category led us to only one study in our review of the four journals. However, in the second path, we identified six studies related to preservice teachers.

K–12 Students, Teachers, and Administrators

Of the five new categories we created, this was the one in which the greatest number of studies was included. Studies in this category included the analysis of student-created materials, interviews with students or teachers, surveys with administrators, or student responses to literature. In our analysis of the journals, we identified 11 studies in this category, and 13 in our review of chapter citations.

Other

We found a small number of studies that did not fit any of the old or new categories. We labeled these three studies as "other" from our review of the four journals, and one study that cited the 2011 chapter in this category. The focus of the studies in this category ranged from the analysis of interviews with undergraduates with disabilities (Walters, 2015) to an analysis of graphic novels, photographs, and podcasts (Meixner, Peel, Hendrickson, Szczeck, & Bousum, 2019).

The five categories from our 2011 chapter made up only a small portion of the studies we found in our updated search. Only 15 of the 63 new studies were coded in the original categories. We found only one study in which the primary focus was on leveled texts. This was a considerable shift, since this category was the largest of the four in our 2011 chapter. Even so, there were studies in which the authors attended to aspects of the readability as part of their analysis, even if it was secondary to the main purpose. We did not find any studies that focused on instructional texts. Again, this was somewhat surprising, considering the number of studies (N = 12) in the earlier review. There were nine studies in the literature studies category, the same number we identified in our initial analysis. We also found two studies in the print environment category, and three studies identified as methods textbooks studies. These numbers were relatively close to those in our earlier analysis, in which we found four studies and one study in these categories, respectively.

In our updated review of studies in the four journals, we found that nearly half (10/24) of the authors named content analysis as their primary method. In our initial review of these journals, none of the authors did so. In our review of studies that cited our 2011 chapter, nearly all of the authors (61/63) named content analysis as their primary method of analysis.

CONTENT ANALYSIS IN SIX REPRESENTATIVE STUDIES

Our findings represent the range of different questions that have adopted a content analysis perspective. Our next step was to identify examples of studies that reflected a breadth of questions, as well as studies that met the standards for procedures and reporting presented by Neuendorf (2002). We identified six studies. The first four studies were examples from our 2011 analysis; the last two studies were ones we identified in our current review. Below, we describe and highlight features of content analysis within each one.

Study 1: The Information Text Gap: The Mismatch between Non-Narrative Text Types in Basal Readers and 2009 NAEP Recommended Guidelines (Moss, 2008)

We chose Moss's (2008) study for several reasons. First, the study dealt with an area that has received a great deal of attention in literacy research (i.e., informational texts). Second, the study reflected one of the initial categories we identified as a prominent context for content analysis (i.e., basal reading programs). Third, we believe that the methods described in this study represented a good application of content analysis standards.

The Moss study was designed to compare the text genres represented in two recent California-adopted basal readers (grades 1–6). Moss documented the difficulty children had with comprehending expository passages. She argued that this difficulty might be attributed in part to the emphasis on the reading of narrative ("story") texts in the primary grades. Citing Duke (2000), Moss argued that few informational texts were available in classrooms, and that the engagement with these kinds of texts was limited for both teachers and students. Moss cited additional research suggesting that increased attention to informational texts might have benefits. Moss used the 2009 National Assessment of Educational Progress (NAEP) recommended guidelines (American Institutes for Research, 2005) as the primary referencing point for her investigation. The 2009 NAEP guidelines called for more informational texts in classrooms, recommending 50% informational texts at the grade 4 level, 55% at the grade 8 level, and 70% at the grade 12 level. Moss contextualized her research in terms of Reading First schools in California that were limited to the adoption of one of two core (basal) reading programs. She argued that for many children, this was the only exposure to texts they might receive in their classrooms. Thus, Moss set out to identify the kinds of text genres included in the student readers of these basal programs, as well as the "kinds" of nonfiction texts that were included.

Moss (2008) described the method of this study as a descriptive "content analysis" with two phases. For the first phase, Moss trained two graduate students to classify the selections included in the basal into four genres: narrative fiction, poetry, plays, or nonfiction. These categories were predetermined by Moss, using a modification of the classifications used in previous research by Flood and Lapp (1986). For the purposes of the Moss study, *nonfiction* was "defined as non-narrative texts that included information books, biographies, concept books, information storybooks, or books that combine narrative elements such as characters and plots with informational ones" (p. 208). There was an initial phase of training in which the same selections were classified and compared. Then each member of the research team independently classified each of the selections from all grade levels. The interrater reliability was calculated at .94. Discrepancies in coding were discussed and resolved. Pages and percentages of selections were then calculated for each genre.

In the second phase, each nonfiction selection was classified according to one of four categories specified in the 2009 NAEP guidelines: literary nonfiction or one of three types of informational texts (expository texts, argumentative and persuasive texts, or procedural texts and documents). The procedure for coding in this second phase was the same as in the first phase: one with an initial coding "together," independent coding (with calculation of reliability), and finally the negotiation of discrepancies. The independent coding agreement in this phase was calculated as .94.

The author reported the findings by using tables to compare pages and percentages of selections across the genres and then for the types of nonfiction texts. The findings suggested a high percentage of informational texts (i.e., about 40%). In one series, there was more of a progression toward larger percentages from the primary to the upper grades. In the other series, there was a more abrupt trend, with low levels of nonfiction in the primary grades and high levels in the upper grades. The author argued, using previous research reports, that these numbers represented a substantial increase in attention to informational texts. However, neither series met the guidelines put forward by NAEP. The author also argued, based on the findings, for the need to diversify the kinds of nonfiction texts. There was little in the way of persuasive and argumentative texts, or of procedural texts and documents.

While this study did not make any explicit reference to "content analysis" as a methodology, there was clear attention to each of the steps identified by Neuendorf (2002). The theory and rationale were clearly described with respect to the issues surrounding exposure to informational texts and previous research. The author was careful to identify decisions that were made in a focus on particular variables (e.g., informational texts) and materials (e.g., California basals). The author gave clear conceptual and operational definitions for each of the variables, most often linking them to previous research and to the coding scheme used. The sampling procedures and the training procedures were clearly described with attention to reliability of coding. Finally, the data were tabulated and reported in a format that directly reflected the movement from coding to analysis.

The author also addressed all six of the questions required by Krippendorff (2004) for content analysis with respect to the identification and definitions of the data to be analyzed, the population sampled (California basals), the context for the analysis (e.g., importance of informational texts, lack of attention to informational texts, and the policies shaping exposure such as No Child Left Behind). The boundaries were clearly identified (e.g., a focus on the texts read and not on the instructional support in teacher guides). And finally, the targets of the inferences—researchers and publishers in particular—were clearly identified.

Study 2: Exploring the "Critical" in Critical Content Analysis of Children's Literature (Beach et al., 2009)

We chose to focus on the Beach and colleagues (2009) study because of its focus on a version of content analysis that, at the time of our 2011 chapter, was relatively new in literacy research. This study adopted critical content analysis as its framework. These authors defined *critical content analysis* as a "close reading of small amounts of text that are interpreted by the analyst and then contextualized in new narratives; a definition that is a hermeneutic, reader response-oriented research stance that can be critical as well. What makes the study 'critical' is not the methodology, but the framework used to think within, through, and beyond the text" (Beach et al., 2009, pp. 130–131).

Content analysis is "critical" when the methodology is used to ferret out issues of overt or covert power found in texts. This kind of analysis requires a critical theoretical stance or framework to buttress an analyst's purpose for a study. Examples of critical theoretical stances include feminist studies, queer studies, and childhood studies.

Assumptions about the inherent qualities of texts must be transparent. In order to do a critical content analysis on texts, the features of texts must be discussed. Beach and colleagues adapted the following features from Krippendorff (2004, pp. 22–25):

1. Texts have no qualities without a reader. The meaning of the text is found in the reading event between the analyst and the text.
2. Texts contain multiple meanings. The meanings found are dependent on the reader's intentions and the context of the study.
3. Meanings found in texts do not need to be shared. It is legitimate if one scholar's reading and interpretation of the same text do not jibe with another scholar's reading and interpretation.
4. The meanings found in texts pertain to other contexts. The analyst uses the meanings from the text to make sense of something outside of the text. Again, the text itself is not the object of study. The object of reading the text is to inform another context.
5. Texts have meanings that speak to particular context. The purpose for the reading influences the meanings found.
6. Content analysts read to draw inferences from texts to be applied to the context of the study. The texts do not speak for themselves in this process, but rather speak to or for something else.

This report highlighted the reader response and hermaneutic nature of critical content analysis. Three scholars were asked to analyze the same picture book, *The Day of Ahmed's Secret*, written by Florence Parry Heide and Judith Heide Gilliland (1990) and illustrated by Ted Lewin. What made the analyses different were the different theoretical frameworks the three scholars used. The first analysis, by Vivian Yenika-Agbaw, employed postcolonial theory. She wrote that when she came upon a story set in a foreign culture, "I wonder why the author chose to set the story in a particular region of a country and how much the author knows about that culture" (Beach et al., 2009, p. 132). She used the lens of postcolonial theory because the story takes place in Cairo, Egypt—a place that is, in the Western mind, associated with the mythical "orient." Yenika-Agbaw saw through this lens "stereotypes of exoticism" (p. 4). To counterbalance this reading, she looked for a counter-discourse—in this case, the child protagonist's sense of agency. By looking at the child character, language use, and the plot, she created three analytical categories.

The first category was Ahmed's ownership of space; the second was his ownership of work; and the third was his ownership of personal and cultural identity. Within these categories, Yenika-Agbaw placed excerpts from the text that fit. In her discussion, she posited that despite the cultural stereotypes embedded in the text, her postcolonial reading (her counter-discourse), allowed her to understand the power dynamics that actually position Ahmed in a role of agency.

Christine Jenkins did a second analysis of the same text, using the Great Books Method. She focused on the "elusive interpretive questions" (Beach et al., 2009, p. 137) found in this method. She explained that she attended to parts of the book "where I paused" (p. 10). It was in this pause that Jenkins found anomalies to examine that took the form of questions. She argued that reading this way "is not simply the province of adult scholars, but can and should inform young people's reading experiences" (p. 12). Jenkins saw her focus of doing this critical content analysis as a jumping-off point for her to "provide readers with multiple opportunities to become critical readers on their own terms" (p. 12).

In the third critical content analysis of the Heide and Gilliland (1990) book, Rebecca Rogers used critical discourse theories. She decided on this frame because the child protagonist was not in school, but worked as a butane gas delivery boy. Rogers started her analysis by investigating the use of butane gas in Cairo at the time the book was published. She found that butane gas was a major fuel source in Egypt then, and that it was a dangerous job to lug it around crowded city streets. Rogers saw Ahmed as "literally situated in the economic market, a market that was experiencing severe restructuring" (Beach et al., 2009, p. 141). Rogers analyzed the story in terms of "the political–economic backdrop of Egypt during the early 1990s" (p. 13). Through this lens, she was concerned that the policies engineered by the International Monetary Fund (IMF) regarding butane gas hurt poor people like Ahmed. This positioning of the story in global economic terms led Rogers to ask how "Ahmed is positioned to both recognize and naturalize his rightful place in the world" (p. 14). Using textual and visual analyses, Rogers examined the "genre, discourse and style of the book" (p. 14) to look at what choices the writer and illustrator privileged and marginalized. "Unpacking dominant worldviews—in this book, neoliberalism—is an important task in making sure that reading global children's literature offers multi-perspectival learning spaces" (p. 18).

As seen in these three very different critical content analyses of the same book, the methodology was the same. Each analyst did a "close reading of small amounts of text" from a hermeneutic, reader-response-oriented research stance. Each scholar made abductive inferences; took the particulars from one domain, *The Day of Ahmed's Secret*; and applied them to another domain (in the three analyses, postcolonialism, reader response with children, and neoliberalism, respectively). Through these inferences, the researchers illustrated Krippendorff's (2004) qualitative content analysis text features: The same text was given different meanings through different reading events. The one text contained multiple meanings that were dependent upon the reader's individual intentions and the contexts of the study. The meanings found by the different scholars were all valid; it was all right that these three scholars found different meanings. The meanings found in *The Day of Ahmed's Secret* pertained to particular contexts. The object of reading the text was to inform the other contexts. These content analysts read to draw inferences from texts to be applied to the context of their particular studies. This all speaks to this method's being close to content analysis, as it seems to satisfy the requirements for qualitative content analysis.

These studies were also informed by critical discourse analysis. All three researchers had a social problem to solve through a text. In the case of Yenika-Agbaw, her concern rested with the social issue of the imbalance of power between the West and its colonized subjects. Jenkins's social problem was the limited opportunities students have to read critically and for themselves. Rogers's issues were with the IMF and the neoliberalization of the third world. The studies all addressed the ideologies surrounding and perpetuating various social problems by attending to power relationships and hierarchies. The three scholars all saw their job as excavating the covert discourses behind the story in order to disrupt the status quo.

Study 3: Stripping for the Wolf: Rethinking Representations of Gender in Children's Literature (Marshall, 2004)

We chose to include the Marshall (2004) article as an example of critical qualitative content analysis that reached outside this methodological approach's roots in traditional communications theory. Drawing on feminist poststructural literary theory, Marshall sought to move beyond liberal feminist analyses of children's literature that overemphasized sex-role theory. While she acknowledged the usefulness and importance of these more traditional feminist approaches to content analysis, she criticized the way in which they often framed gender as a neutral and static category. Over the previous three decades, Marshall noted, feminist critiques of children's literature had focused on the underrepresentation and stereotypical portrayal of girls and women, as well as on how these phenomena might serve to reinforce gender bias. Such a focus, Marshall argued, "sustains a male/female duality" and "relies primarily on white, Western, middle-class, heterosexual notions of femininity" (p. 260). What Marshall proposed instead was a poststructural theoretical framework for analyzing *how* gender is constructed and produced through the content of children's literature. She suggested that this framework would extend existing feminist perspectives by allowing for more dynamic theorizations of gender that would move beyond sex-role theory to situate the discursive construction of gender within particular cultural and historical contexts.

In order to illustrate the affordances of poststructural feminist theory, Marshall analyzed four different variants of the *Little Red Riding Hood* tale—an early oral version and three subsequent written versions. She selected (1) the earliest known oral variant of the tale, "The Story of Grandmother"; (2) Charles Perrault's 1697 iteration based on this oral version; (3) *Little Red Cap*, an 1819 adaptation by the Brothers Grimm; and (4) Trina Schart Hyman's (1983) picture book version, *Little Red Riding Hood*, which became a Caldecott Honor Book in 1984. Focusing on the construction of gender and sexuality in each of these versions, Marshall analyzed how the character Little Red Riding Hood was variously represented with respect to issues of femininity, morality, and sexual violation. Although Marshall did not explicitly refer to her approach as content analysis—indeed, she said almost nothing at all about her methods—her approach to analyzing the construction of gender was clearly informed by some of the key principles of qualitative content analysis. In particular, her insistence on situating each version of the *Little Red Riding Hood* tale within its respective historical and cultural context was consistent with Krippendorff's (2004) emphasis on identifying the context relative to which data are analyzed. Marshall explicitly connected each iteration of the tale with the construction of gender and sexuality in its respective historical period, interpreting each text in light of its particular context. Moreover, she explicitly discussed how multiple (and sometimes conflicting) interpretations could stem from each version of this story—an approach consistent with Krippendorff's discussion of how texts always contain multiple meanings.

Marshall's poststructural feminist analysis highlighted how competing discourses about gender, childhood, and sexuality intersect in children's literature, framing girls as both innocent and vulnerable on the one hand, and sexually enticing and in need of moral regulation on the other. As she noted, the four different versions of *Little Red Riding Hood* reflected different historical preoccupations with girls and their sexuality. The earliest oral version, for example, was intended for an audience of all ages and thus contained explicit references to violence, nudity, and sexual content. Marshall explained that Perrault's version, which was equally explicit, was intended as a cautionary tale and directed specifically toward young girls. She suggested that this adaptation essentially framed Little Red Riding Hood as responsible for her own violation. The Grimms' version, Marshall noted, featured the addition of a mother who warned her daughter not to stray from the path, converting this into a more transparent cautionary tale. Marshall argued that this version also differed from previous versions in that Little Red Riding Hood, although initially eaten by the wolf, emerged unharmed, representing the possibility of rehabilitation. With respect to Hyman's version, Marshall highlighted the author's addition of an interior monologue, which served to characterize Little Red Riding Hood as a rational subject. She further asserted that Hyman went out of her way to avoid addressing Little Red Riding Hood's sexuality, resulting in a sanitized version of the character that nonetheless reinscribed prescriptive notions of femininity. According to Marshall, despite their differences, all four versions of this tale converged in ultimately portraying the protagonist as responsible for policing herself and containing her latent sexuality by avoiding certain behaviors. She contended that while more recent iterations of the tale shed some of the explicit violence and sexual content of earlier versions and portrayed Little Red Riding Hood as more agentive, they reflected a "subtle, yet no less coercive, attempt to contain and regulate the feminine body" (Marshall, 2004, p. 262).

We considered this article an example of qualitative content analysis in the sense that it was consistent with some of the key principles guiding this methodological approach. Marshall foregrounded this question: What is the context relative to which the data are analyzed? She made inferences from four different texts and then made sense of these interpretations within the cultural and historical contexts surrounding each text. This article represented a *critical* approach to content analysis because the author challenged more traditional feminist approaches to content analysis that relied on binary definitions of gender. Marshall sought to unveil the ways in which dominant constructions of gender could be inscribed in children's literature, while also allowing for the possibility of multiple meanings and interpretations of the texts in question.

Study 4: The Effective Elementary Classroom Literacy Environment: Examining the Validity of the TEX-IN3 Observation System (Hoffman, Sailors, Duffy, & Beretvas, 2004)

We selected the Hoffman and colleagues (2004) study for two reasons. First, in our view, the methods in this study represent a good application of the standards for content analysis discussed thus far. Additionally, the study was an example of print environment studies—a category that was prominent in our 2011 analysis, but in which few studies have been published in recent years. This study offered an example of the diverse ways in which content analysis can be applied in literacy research.

The Hoffman and colleagues study was designed to validate an instrument that was grounded in a theoretical framework and connected to student achievement. This instrument focused on the assessment of the physical text environment of the classroom, the practices surrounding the use of the texts in the classroom environment, and the understanding and valuing of the texts in that same environment. Because it assessed the overall effectiveness of the classroom literacy environment, the instrument could be used to evaluate and support professional development efforts for teachers and can be used for classroom research.

In designing the instrument, Hoffman and his colleagues drew from the literature describing literacy as a social practice. Citing the New Literacy Studies Group (Barton, 1994, 2000; Barton & Hamilton, 2000; Barton, Hamilton, & Ivanic, 2000), the research team described literacy as "the way in which members of particular social groups use and value literacy" (Hoffman et al., 2004, p. 309). Furthermore, the intentions, uses, and values of the literacy practices by members of that society "are indicative of the role literacy plays in the lives of those members" (Hoffman et al., 2004, p. 310). In order to capture the social practices in elementary classrooms, the research team developed the instrument under study across a 2-year period and various phases. These development phases led to a fully developed instrument that contained three components. The first component, the text inventory, was an inventory scheme that included 17 different text types (with supporting rubrics quantifying the quality of those texts, based on a 5-point scale). The component yielded individual scores for each of the text types, a holistic score for the text environment, and a holistic rating of the local environment (those texts in the classroom that were written by teachers and students).

The second component, the "in-use" inventory, was designed to capture and record the engagement of the teachers and the children as they used the various texts found in the classroom. Each of the three observations focused on a particular subject area. The first of the two observations were intended to capture the use of text across an entire class; the second focused carefully on three students in the room ("on, below, and above-grade" level readers) and on how they were using texts. Data were collected across the observations, including data on the text type in which the students and teachers were engaged and the context of that engagement. These raw data eventually contributed to a Quality Time Engaged (QTE) score (a calculated score that weighted engagement with the quality of the text used during the engagement).

The third component of the instrument, the "text interviews," was designed to capture and record the understanding, interpretations, values, and beliefs about the texts located in the classroom environment. The teachers and the children who were the foci of the in-use observations were interviewed. Observers rated the responses of the students on a scale of 1 (low understanding) to 5 (high understanding). Observers rated the teachers on a similar scale; in addition, teachers were asked to rank the various text types located in their rooms from 1 (most valuable) to 17 (least valuable).

Hierarchical linear modeling was used to analyze the data, including the classroom environment data (TEX-IN3) and the student comprehension data collected with the Group Reading Assessment and Diagnostic

Evaluation (GRADE) (American Guidance Service, 2001). Findings from this analysis indicated that the holistic and the local text inventories were significant predictors of comprehension scores. The QTE scores that captured the teachers' engagement, and the measures averaged across the three representative students, were significantly related to adjusted posttest comprehension scores. Likewise, the average students' text understandings and those of the teachers were significant predictors when entered into the analysis equation.

The authors concluded their study by relating the findings to the importance of texts in classrooms; the use of the print with students; and the understanding, valuing, and interpretations of the texts as important in relationship to student comprehension growth.

Although this study did not make any explicit reference to content analysis as a methodology, there was clear attention to each of the steps identified by Neuendorf (2002). First, the theory and rationale were clearly described with respect to the role of print environments and literacy education. The authors were careful to attend to the sets of variables studied; the sets of rubrics clearly defined each set of operational measures in replicable ways. The coding scheme described in the study was drawn from previous research (time on task and follow-through studies), and the sampling for the corpus of texts to be studied was clearly described. The training and reliability of data collectors reached an appropriate level of agreement, and the tabulation and reporting were clear. Finally, the authors of this validation study also addressed all six questions posed by Krippendorff (2004) for content analysis.

Study 5: Transcultural Digital Literacies: Cross-Border Connections and Self-Representations in an Online Forum (Kim, 2016)

We chose the Kim (2016) study for three reasons. First of all, it pushed the boundaries of what might count as an educational setting. Kim's focus on the way multicultural learning could take place in online settings far removed from traditional school settings invited readers to rethink the whole concept of curricular content. The study also provided an example of the ways *texts* can be broadly defined within content analysis. The texts examined in Kim's study included interactions, images, and the content of online profiles. Finally, it was an example of the way literacy researchers sometimes combine qualitative content analysis with other methods of analysis in their research. Kim described her study as a "hybrid approach involving three genres of qualitative research: ethnography, case study, and content analysis" (p. 205).

Kim pointed out that although digital literacies and multicultural education have become increasingly important in school and society, the literature on the relationship between the two is still sparse. Addressing this need, Kim sought to understand the transcultural literacy practices of youth engaged in online spaces. She argued that online spaces can provide youth with opportunities to learn about other cultures and to negotiate identities in ways transcending traditional markers of identity, such as race or geographic location.

Kim used a transcultural digital literacies framework, which was informed by the literature on globalization, new literacies, and social networks. In accordance with her theoretical framework, Kim focused on particular content on the DramaCrazy website, a site dedicated to Asian television and film dramas. Within a Korean discussion forum on the site, she found eight discussion threads in which youth discussed topics other than dramas. She explained her rationale for focusing on this particular subset of content on the DramaCrazy website, saying that her purpose "was not [to examine] Korean dramas fandom" but rather to "understand literacy practices facilitated and supported within DramaCrazy's Korean dramas forum" (p. 206).

To begin, Kim analyzed the postings in each of the threads for content relating to issues of identity, community, and cultural information seeking and sharing. She moved from the content of the threads to the content of the participants' individual profiles. Analysis on the content of the participants' profiles allowed her to focus on identity development and contextualize the content of the discussion threads themselves.

In addition to finding that youth engaged in the threads wrote about a variety of topics outside of Korean dramas, Kim found four main constructs: "language learning, cross-border connections, cultural inquiry, and self-representations" (p. 208). Importantly, youth used the space to learn about other cultures and to construct identities. Within these online spaces, they were able to negotiate this multicultural learning and identify formation through the content of their online interactions, rather than through traditional markers such as race and nationality.

Unlike the authors of some other examples of content analysis examined in this chapter, Kim named content analysis as one part of her hybrid method. She also clearly addressed each of Krippendorff's (2004) six questions for content analysis. Even though she did not describe her coding scheme in detail or explain whether she used software to aid her in the analysis of the content, she thoroughly described the sampling process and rationale. The connections among her focus, her theoretical framework, her procedures, and her findings make this study a useful model for others interested in similar work. Just as Kim's study highlighted some of the ways in which the youth she studied pushed the boundaries between multicultural education and identity, it illustrated the ways in which content analysis can push the boundaries of what counts as text and curricular content.

Study 6: Blurring Material and Rhetorical Walls: Children Writing the Border/Lands in a Second-Grade Classroom (Dutro & Haberl, 2018)

We chose the Dutro and Haberl (2018) study for three reasons. First of all, it focused on a political and social context currently affecting classrooms across the United States. Second, the study focused on the work and identities of Latinx children in the elementary classroom. Finally, the authors focused their analysis on materials created by the students themselves.

In their article, Dutro and Haberl addressed each of Krippendorff's (2004) six questions. The authors began their article by addressing the political environment in the United States, particularly the election of Donald Trump and the anti-immigrant rhetoric that became a focal point of his campaign. They drew on Anzaldúa's (1987) concept of "border/lands," as well as on "feminist and critical poststructuralist theories" (Dutro & Haberl, 2018, p. 167). Through these lenses, the authors focused on how the binaries created by borders, political discourses, and schooling could be disrupted by children's writing, particularly through *testimonios* (Anzaldúa, 1987).

Dutro and Haberl focused on the writing of seven second-grade students from their 3-year study on "pedagogies of testimony and critical witness" (2018, p. 172). In the first phase of analysis, the authors conducted a content analysis of notebooks from across the larger study in which children kept the writing they did across the academic year. In addition to clearly outlining their rationale for their analysis, the authors described "creating tables with rows for each child and columns for noting genres, topics, connections to central research focus, and initial codes" (p. 174). The authors did not address coding agreement or specific details about the development of the codes used in their analysis. From this initial phase of analysis, the authors were able to identify focal stories on which to focus the next stage of their analysis. Dutro and Haberl explained, "This process allowed us to identify writing that indexed identities and relationships across national borders or impacts of systems of authority and enforcement" (p. 174).

In the next phase, Dutro and Haberl focused on the seven focal stories and engaged in what they described as a process of "close reading" (p. 174). The authors made a distinction between the way the term is sometimes used in schools and their approach, which "demand[ed] interpretive attention to affective and political dimensions of texts with the aim to illuminate and complicate meaning in ways that may open pathways to new understandings" (p. 174). Included in their analysis, the authors considered "imagery, symbolism, tropes, metaphor, temporality, and the linguistic, pictorial, and aesthetic echoes across children's writing and drawing" (p. 174). Dutro and Haberl reported themes of connections with family in children's stories that indicated both love and feelings of absence. The children's writing also included a second theme of threat and fear. The authors concluded that the children's writing functioned to "complicate geographic borders, as well as blur artificial borders of genre, space, time, and feeling" (p. 184).

Similar to the Kim (2016) study, this article might seem to stray away from what have traditionally been regarded as curricular materials. However, the children's experiences and identities within the border/lands became an essential part of the curriculum, and the context of violence and fear the children faced was made visible through the children's writing. Another similarity to Kim's approach was the combination of content analysis with other methods of analysis. The use of content analysis in the first phase of this study allowed the authors to focus on the seven focal students and conduct a deeper analysis through close reading. Importantly, the authors' use of content analysis was aligned with their theoretical approach and other methods of analysis, which were clearly outlined in the study.

SUMMARY

If you can read this, thank a teacher.
—ANONYMOUS

As astute readers of this chapter, applying content analysis methods, you may have already decoded the quotation used at the start of the chapter. Some of you may have even determined that we simply substituted the next letter in the alphabet to create the coded version—not a very sophisticated scheme, but one that can be used to illustrate the value of combining inductive and deductive processes in a content analysis to achieve goals. You may be using a similar process to infer, from the body of work cited in this chapter, the major points we would make regarding content analysis as a research method in literacy.

Our analysis of the recent literature suggests three important trends for content analysis. First, content is expanding beyond the traditional focus on studies of curriculum materials and into studies of teaching and teacher preparation. Content analysis can, it seems, be adapted to the times in terms of topics of interest. Second, content analysis is appearing more often now in combination with other research methods. This trend suggests that the traditional version of mixed methods (i.e., qualitative and quantitative) may need to be considered more broadly in the future. Third, content analysis is moving from the technical (and even tedious) studies of curriculum materials to the critical. We see this shift in the application of the method in the work of Kim (2016) and of Dutro and Haberl (2018). Again, this speaks to the flexibility and usefulness of content analysis as a method. We believe that these three trends bode well for the future of content analysis as a tool for literacy research in the coming decades.

REFERENCES

American Guidance Service. (2001). *GRADE: Group Reading Assessment and Diagnostic Evaluation* [Computer software]. Circle Pines, MN: Author.

American Institutes for Research. (2005). Reading framework for the 2009 National Assessment of Educational Progress pre-publication edition. Retrieved November 1, 2005, from *www.nagb.org/pubs/reading_fw_06_05_prepub_edition.doc.*

Anzaldúa, G. (1987). *Borderlands: Vol. 3. La frontera.* San Francisco: Aunt Lute.

Aulls, M. W. (2003). The influence of a reading and writing curriculum on transfer learning across subjects and grades. *Reading Pyschology, 24*(2), 177–215.

Azano, A. P., Tackett, M., & Sigmon, M. (2017). Understanding the puzzle behind the pictures: A content analysis of children's picture books about autism. *AERA Open, 3*(2).

Babbie, E. (2007). *The practice of social research* (10th ed.). Belmont, CA: Thomson/Wadsworth.

Barton, D. (1994). *Literacy: An introduction to the ecology of written language.* Oxford, UK: Blackwell.

Barton, D. (2000). Literacy practices. In D. Barton, M. Hamilton, & R. Ivanic (Eds.), *Situated literacies: Reading and writing in context* (pp. 7–15). London: Routledge.

Barton, D., & Hamilton, M. (2000). Literacy practices. In D. Barton, M. Hamilton, & R. Ivanic (Eds.), *Situated literacies: Reading and writing in context* (pp. 167–179). London: Routledge.

Barton, D., Hamilton, M., & Ivanic, R. (Eds.). (2000). *Situated literacies: Reading and writing in context.* London: Routledge.

Beach, R., Enciso, P., Harste, J., Jenkins, C., Raina, S. A., Rogers, R., et al. (2009). Exploring the "critical" in critical content analysis of children's literature. In K. M. Leaner, D. W. Rowe, D. K. Dickinson, M. K. Hundley, R. T. Jamenez, & V. J. Risko (Eds.), *58th yearbook of the National Reading Conference* (pp. 129–143). Oak Creek, WI: National Reading Conference.

Beck, I. L., & McCaslin, E. S. (1978, March). *An analysis of dimensions that affect the development of code-breaking ability in eight beginning reading programs.* Paper presented at the annual meeting of the American Educational Research Association, Toronto.

Beck, I. L., McKeown, M. G., & Gromoll, E. W. (1989). Learning from social studies texts. *Cognition and Instruction, 6*(2), 99–158.

Beckers, G., Saal, L. K., & Cheek, E. H. (2014). Interrupting and transforming mental models for social responsibility: Effects of an emancipatory interest curriculum for secondary disciplinary teachers. In P. J. Dunston, S. K. Fullerton, M. W. Cole, D. Herro, J. A. Malloy, P. M. Wilder, et al. (Eds.), *63rd yearbook of the Literacy Research Association* (pp. 326–339). Altamonte Springs, FL: Literacy Research Association.

Berelson, B. (1952). *Content analysis in communication research.* New York: Free Press.

Biddle, C., & Azano, A. P. (2016). Constructing and reconstructing the "rural school problem": A century of rural education research. *Review of Research in Education, 40*(1), 298–325.

Blackburn, M. V., Clark, C. T., & Nemeth, E. A. (2015). Examining queer elements and ideologies in LGBT-themed literature: What queer literature can offer young adult readers. *Journal of Literacy Research, 47*(1), 11–48.

Brooks, W., & Cueto, D. (2018). Contemplating and extending the scholarship on children's and young adult literature. *Journal of Literacy Research, 50*(1), 9–30.

Brooks, W., Sekayi, D., Savage, L., Waller, E., & Picot, I. (2010). Narrative significations of contemporary black girlhood. *Research in the Teaching of English, 45*(1), 7–35.

Certo, J. (2015). Poetic language, interdiscursivity and intertextuality in fifth graders' poetry: An interpretive study. *Journal of Literacy Research, 47*(1), 49–82.

Chall, J. (1967). *Learning to read: The great debate.* New York: McGraw Hill.

Dentith, A. M., Sailors, M., & Sethusha, M. (2016). What does it mean to be a girl?: Teachers' representations of gender in supplementary reading materials for South African schools. *Journal of Literacy Research, 48*(4), 394–422.

Dewitz, P., Jones, J., & Leahy, S. (2009). Comprehension strategy instruction in core reading programs. *Reading Research Quarterly, 44*(2), 102–126.

Dixon, K., & Janks, H. (2018). "My fish died and I flushed him down the toilet": Children disrupt preservice teachers' understandings of "appropriate" picture books for young children. *Literacy Research: Theory, Method, and Practice, 67*(1), 343–359.

Domke, L. M. (2018). Probing the promise of dual-language books. *Reading Horizons: A Journal of Literacy and Language Arts, 57*(3), 3.

Duffy, G. G., Roehler, L. R., Meloth, M. S., Vavrus, L. G., Book, C., Putnam, J., et al. (1986). The relationship between explicit verbal explanations during reading skill instruction and student awareness and achievement: A study of reading teacher effects. *Reading Research Quarterly, 21*(3), 237–252.

Duke, N. (2000). 3.6 minutes per day: The scarcity of informational texts in first grade. *Reading Research Quarterly, 35*, 202–224.

Durkin, D. (1981). Reading comprehension instruction in five basal reader series. *Reading Research Quarterly, 16*(4), 515–544.

Durkin, D. (1990). Comprehension instruction in current basal reader series (Center for the Study of Reading Technical Report No. 521). Champaign: University of Illinois at Urbana–Champaign.

Dutro, E., & Haberl, E. (2018). Blurring material and rhetorical walls: Children writing the border/lands in a second-grade classroom. *Journal of Literacy Research, 50*(2), 167–189.

Everett, S. (2016). "I just started writing": Toward addressing invisibility, silence, and mortality among academically high-achieving black male secondary students. *Literacy Research: Theory, Method, and Practice, 65*(1), 316–331.

Flood, J., & Lapp, D. (1986). Types of texts: The match between what students read in basals and what they encounter in tests. *Reading Research Quarterly, 21*(3), 284–297.

Giblin, J. C. (1990). *The riddle of the Rosetta Stone: Key to ancient Egypt.* New York: Crowell.

Glaser, B., & Strauss, A. (1967). *The discovery of grounded theory: Strategies for qualitative research.* New York: Aldine.

Goldman, S. R., Braasch, J. L., Wiley, J., Graesser, A. C., & Brodowinska, K.

(2012). Comprehending and learning from Internet sources: Processing patterns of better and poorer learners. *Reading Research Quarterly, 47*(4), 356–381.

Gretter, S., & Yadav, A. (2018). What do preservice teachers think about teaching media literacy?: An exploratory study using the theory of planned behavior. *Journal of Media Literacy Education, 10*(1), 104–123.

Hattan, C., Singer, L. M., Loughlin, S., & Alexander, P. A. (2015). Prior knowledge activation in design and in practice. *Literacy Research: Theory, Method, and Practice, 64*(1), 478–497.

Heide, F. P., & Gilliland, J. H. (1990). *The day of Ahmed's secret.* New York: Lothrop, Lee & Shepard.

Hiebert, E. H., & Martin, L. A. (2003). The texts of beginning reading instruction. In S. Neuman & D. Dickinson (Eds.), *Handbook of early literacy research* (Vol. 1, pp. 361–376). New York: Guilford Press.

Hoffman, J. V., Sailors, M., Duffy, G. G., & Beretvas, N. (2004). The effective elementary classroom literacy environment: Examining the validity of the TEX-IN3 observation system. *Journal of Literacy Research, 36*, 303–334.

Holsti, O. R. (1969). *Content analysis for the social sciences and humanities.* Reading, MA: Addison-Wesley.

Hsieh, H., & Shannon, S. E. (2005). Three approaches to qualitative content analysis. *Qualitative Health Research, 15*(9), 1277–1288.

Hutchison, A., & Reinking, D. (2011). Teachers' perceptions of integrating information and communication technologies into literacy instruction: A national survey in the United States. *Reading Research Quarterly, 46*(4), 312–333.

Hutchison, A. C., Woodward, L., & Colwell, J. (2016). What are preadolescent readers doing online?: An examination of upper elementary students' reading, writing, and communication in digital spaces. *Reading Research Quarterly, 51*(4), 435–454.

Hyman, T. S. (1983). *Little Red Riding Hood.* New York: Holiday House.

Ikpeze, C. H. (2018). Designing e-books: Enhancing prospective teachers' digital literacy skills. In *Best practices in teaching digital literacies* (pp. 29–42). Melbourne, Australia: Emerald.

Kerkhoff, S. N. (2015). Dialogism: Feminist revision of argumentative writing instruction. *Literacy Research: Theory, Method, and Practice, 64*(1), 443–460.

Kim, G. M. (2016). Transcultural digital literacies: Cross-border connections and self-representations in an online forum. *Reading Research Quarterly, 51*(2), 199–219.

Krippendorff, K. (2004). *Content analysis: An introduction to its methodology* (2nd ed.). Thousand Oaks, CA: SAGE.

Kumar, T. (2014). Where are "their" voices?: Examining power and privilege in a family literacy text. *School Community Journal, 24*(2), 127–146.

Kumar, T. (2016). "Something you can look back on": Teacher candidates, rap music, and P–12 social studies. *Urban Education.* [Epub ahead of print]

Lochmiller, C. R., & Mancinelli, J. L. (in press). Principals' instructional leadership under statewide teacher evaluation reform. *International Journal of Educational Management.*

Maloch, B. (2002). Scaffolding student talk: One teacher's role in literature discussion groups. *Reading Research Quarterly, 37*(1), 94–112.

Marlatt, R. (2018). This is what we do: Emphasizing discipline-specific literacy practices in teacher education. *Journal of Language and Literacy Education, 14*(2), 1–23.

Marlatt, R. (2019). "Ditch the study guide": Creating short films to analyze literature circle texts. *Journal of Adolescent and Adult Literacy, 63*(3), 311–321.

Marshall, E. (2004). Stripping for the wolf: Rethinking representations of gender in children's literature. *Reading Research Quarterly, 39*(3), 256–270.

McIver, P. (2018). A content analysis of multicultural children's books in the Republic of Korea and America. *Journal of Literature and Art Studies, 8*(1), 67–80.

Meixner, E., Peel, A., Hendrickson, R., Szczeck, L., & Bousum, K. (2019). Storied lives: Teaching memoir writing through multimodal mentor texts. *Journal of Adolescent and Adult Literacy, 62*(5), 495–508.

Montero, M. K. (2012). Literary artistic spaces engage middle grades teachers and students in critical-multicultural dialogue: Urban students write about their lives in one-word poems and on traveling scrawled walls. *Middle School Journal, 44*(2), 30–38.

Morrison, T. G., Wilcox, B., Murdoch, E., & Bird, L. (2018). Textual demands of passages in three English/language arts common core assessments and one core literacy program for intermediate elementary grades. *Reading Psychology, 39*(4), 362–383.

Moss, B. (2008). The information text gap: The mismatch between non-narrative text types in basal readers and 2009 NAEP recommended guidelines. *Journal of Literacy Research, 40*(2), 201–219.

Murphy, P. K., Andiliou, A., Firetto, C. M., Bowersox, C. M., Baker, M., & Ramsay, C. M. (2016). Intratextual persuasive messages as catalysts for higher-order thinking: An exploratory investigation. *Journal of Literacy Research, 48*(2), 134–163.

Neuendorf, K. A. (2002). *The content analysis guidebook*. Thousand Oaks, CA: SAGE.

Nguyen, C., & Kebede, M. (2017). Immigrant students in the Trump era: What we know and do not know. *Educational Policy, 31*(6), 716–742.

Pantaleo, S. (2012). Exploring grade 7 students' responses to Shaun Tan's *The Red Tree. Children's Literature in Education, 43*(1), 51–71.

Pantaleo, S. (2012). Exploring the intertextualities in a grade 7 student's graphic narrative. *L1 Educational Studies in Language and Literature, 12,* 23–55.

Pantaleo, S. (2013). Paneling "matters" in elementary students' graphic narratives. *Literacy Research and Instruction, 52*(2), 150–171.

Pantaleo, S. (2014). Exploring the artwork in picturebooks with middle years students. *Journal of Children's Literature, 40*(1), 15.

Pantaleo, S. (2015). Language, literacy and visual texts. *English in Education, 49*(2), 113–129.

Pantaleo, S. (2016). Primary students transgress story world boundaries in their multimodal compositions. *Journal of Research in Childhood Education, 30*(2), 237–251.

Pantaleo, S. (2016). Primary students' understanding and appreciation of the artwork in picturebooks. *Journal of Early Childhood Literacy, 16*(2), 228–255.

Pantaleo, S. (2016). Teacher expectations and student literacy engagement and achievement. *Literacy, 50*(2), 83–92.

Pantaleo, S. (2017). Critical thinking and young children's exploration of picture-book artwork. *Language and Education, 31*(2), 152–168.

Pantaleo, S. (2018). Elementary students' analytical responses about David Wiesner's *The Three Pigs. New Review of Children's Literature and Librarianship, 24*(2), 167–188.

Pantaleo, S. (2019). The semantic and syntactic qualities of paneling in students' graphic narratives. *Visual Communication, 18*(1), 55–81.

Parsons, S. A., Gallagher, M. A., & George Mason University Content Analysis Team. (2016). A content analysis of nine literacy journals, 2009–2014. *Journal of Literacy Research, 48*(4), 476–502.

Patrick, L. D. (2016). Found poetry: Creating space for imaginative arts-based literacy research writing. *Literacy Research: Theory, Method, and Practice, 65*(1), 384–403.

Pelttari, C. (2016). Imagination and literacy instruction: A content analysis of literature within literacy-related publications. *Language and Literacy, 18*(3), 106–122.

Ramanayake, S., & Williams, C. (2017). "I don't know why I'm learning this": Preservice English teachers' engagement in a language development course. *International Journal of Teaching and Learning in Higher Education, 29*(3), 447–457.

Reutzel, D. R., & Mohr, K. A. (2015). 50 years of *Reading Research Quarterly* (1965–2014): Looking back, moving forward. *Reading Research Quarterly, 50*(1), 13–35.

Roth, D. (2017). Morphemic analysis as imagined by developmental reading textbooks: A content analysis of a textbook corpus. *Journal of College Reading and Learning, 47*(1), 26–44.

Sailors, M., Orellana, P., Stortz, R., & Sellers, T. (2019). Exploring urban print environments: A comparative study across San Antonio and Santiago and implications for early childhood literacy practices. *Literacy, 53*(2), 102–111.

Sciurba, K. (2017). Journeys toward textual relevance: Male readers of color and the significance of Malcolm X and Harry Potter. *Journal of Literacy Research, 49*(3), 371–392.

Segal, A., Howe, N., Persram, R. J., Martin-Chang, S., & Ross, H. (2018). "I'll show you how to write my name": The contribution of naturalistic sibling teaching to the home literacy environment. *Reading Research Quarterly, 53*(4), 391–404.

Silverman, R. D., Proctor, C. P., Harring, J. R., Doyle, B., Mitchell, M. A., & Meyer, A. G. (2014). Teachers' instruction and students' vocabulary and comprehension: An exploratory study with English monolingual and Spanish–English bilingual students in grades 3–5. *Reading Research Quarterly, 49*(1), 31–60.

Sipe, L. R. (2000). The construction of literary understanding by first and second graders in oral response to picture storybook read-alouds. *Reading Research Quarterly, 35*(2), 252–275.

Stagg Peterson, S., Parr, J., Lindgren, E., & Kaufman, D. (2018). Conceptualizations of writing in early years curricula and standards documents: International perspectives. *The Curriculum Journal, 29*(4), 499–521.

Stahl, N. A., Theriault, J. C., & Armstrong, S. L. (2016). Four decades of JDE interviews: A historical content analysis. *Journal of Developmental Education, 40*(1), 4.

Taylor, L. A. (2015). From expressive reading to rapid reading: The rise in reading rate during the efficiency movement (1910–1925). *Literacy Research: Theory, Method, and Practice, 64*(1), 267–284.

Walters, S. (2015). Toward a critical ASD pedagogy of insight: Teaching, research-ing, and valuing the social literacies of neurodiverse students. *Research in the Teaching of English,* 340–360.

West, J. A., & Williams, C. (2015). Grounding our teaching in research: Implica-tions from research in the teaching of English, 2009–12. *English Journal, 104*(6), 17–24.

White, M. D., & Marsh, E. E. (2006). Content analysis: A flexible methodology. *Library Trends, 55*(1), 22–45.

Williams, C., & Lowrance-Faulhaber, E. (2018). Writing in young bilingual chil-dren: Review of research. *Journal of Second Language Writing, 42,* 58–69.

Wilson, M. B., & Kumar, T. (2017). Long ago and far away: Preservice teachers' (mis)conceptions surrounding racism. *International Journal of Multicultural Education, 19*(2), 182–198.

Wright, T. S., & Domke, L. M. (2019). The role of language and literacy in K–5 sci-ence and social studies standards. *Journal of Literacy Research, 51*(1), 5–29.

Wright, T. S., & Peltier, M. R. (2016). Supports for vocabulary instruction in early language and literacy methods textbooks. *Reading and Writing Quarterly, 32*(6), 527–549.

Yanoff, E., LaDuke, A., & Lindner, M. (2014). Common core standards, profes-sional texts, and diverse learners: A qualitative content analysis. *Language and Literacy Spectrum, 24,* 7–27.

Yeom, E. Y. (2018). How visual thinking strategies using picture book images can improve Korean secondary EFL students' L2 writing. *English Teaching, 73*(1).

CHAPTER 4

Correlational Designs and Analyses

Michael J. Kieffer

What is the association between children's phonological awareness and their decoding? How does vocabulary relate to reading comprehension for students with and without reading difficulties? Do particular teaching practices predict students' gains in reading? How do the reading growth trajectories of bilingual students compare to those of their monolingual peers? These are all *correlational* questions—questions about the relations between two or more variables. Such questions are ubiquitous in literacy research and answering them provides important insights to the field. This chapter introduces the designs and analyses that can best answer these types of correlational questions.

WHAT ARE CORRELATIONAL DESIGNS?
WHAT ARE THEIR STRENGTHS AND WEAKNESSES?

Correlational designs are observational in the sense that variables are not actively manipulated by researchers, but simply observed. This is in contrast to *experimental* designs (such as *randomized controlled trials*), in which variables are actively manipulated by researchers to determine the effects of those manipulations. For instance, an experiment may involve researchers' manipulating instruction by providing one type of instruction to one group and another type to a second group. Under correlational designs, research- ers instead collect data on naturally occurring phenomena and seek to extract patterns from those observations. For instance, researchers might observe students' levels of reading comprehension along with their levels of componential skills (e.g., decoding, listening comprehension; Hoover &

Gough, 1990). They do not intervene to improve componential skills (as they might in an experimental intervention study); rather, they leverage the natural variation in those skills to investigate how that variation relates to natural variation in reading comprehension. In another case, researchers might observe classroom practices as they naturally occur and vary, and explore how variation in those practices is associated with variation in students' gains in reading comprehension (e.g., Silverman et al., 2014).

It is worth noting that *correlational* has two common meanings in quantitative research. Under one meaning, it refers to a correlation (often Pearson's correlation coefficient), a specific statistic for the relation between two variables. In this chapter, however, *correlational designs* and *correlational research* are used more broadly to refer to nonexperimental, observational studies. The data from these studies can be analyzed in a wide variety of ways, including correlations but going far beyond them to include methods such as multiple regression, structural equation modeling, and individual growth modeling (see below). What correlational designs have in common is less their data-analytic approaches than the fact that variables are observed as they naturally vary, rather than being manipulated by researchers. That said, careful data analyses can mitigate some of the weaknesses of correlational designs, as described below.

What Are Third Variables?

A widely heard saying is that correlation does not equal causation. Just because variable *B* is at higher levels when variable *A* is at higher levels, this does not mean that *A* causes *B*. This is because of two problems inherent in correlational research (e.g., Cunningham, Stanovich, & Maul, 2011). The first problem is that of third variables. One is reminded of the positive correlation between ice cream sales and deaths by drowning. Clearly, ice cream consumption is not a cause of drowning but rather is an effect of hotter weather, which also leads to more swimming and thereby more frequent drowning. Hot weather is what we call a *third variable* or a *confounder*—an additional variable *C* that explains away the relation between variables *A* and *B*.

Third variables can be observed (i.e., captured by researchers' instruments) or unobserved. When observed in a study with a correlational design, third variables can be statistically controlled so that their confounding effect is taken into account. For instance, in the ice cream–drowning example, one could measure and statistically control for daily temperature, and this would likely make the spurious (untrue) relation between ice cream sales and deaths by drowning disappear. However, there are almost always some third variables that are unobserved in a study with a correlational design—either because they are difficult to observe, or because a researcher simply could not or did not think of them. In this case, they remain threats to the validity of causal inferences from the results; that is, they undermine the extent to which we can conclude that the predictor caused the outcome. Experimental studies, in which individuals or groups are randomly assigned to treatment conditions, can support causal claims because randomization eliminates the threat from all third variables, both observed and unobserved. When randomization is properly used, the treatment and control groups will be equivalent on all characteristics, on average in the population. Only the treatment will differ, so we can isolate its effect on the outcomes.

Careful researchers using correlational designs will use theory and evidence to identify and measure the third variables that represent the most logical counter-explanations to the relation of interest's being causal. They can never observe all third variables, so, unlike researchers conducting experiments, they can never be fully confident that A affects B rather than that some C affects both. Nonetheless, the quality of correlational research can be judged by the extent to which the most logical third variables were identified, measured, and appropriately controlled for in statistical models.

Why Worry about Directionality?

The second problem in correlational research is directionality. When an observational study collects data at one point in time (or analyzes cross-sectional relations in longitudinal data), it can be impossible to tell whether a relation between A and B means that A caused B or that B caused A. Consider, for instance, Kim's (2009) study of home literacy practices and early literacy in Korean children.[1] She found that parental teaching had a negative relation with early literacy skills (after she controlled for home language environments), such that parents who taught their children more frequently had children with lower literacy skills. A naïve interpretation of this relation—that assumes only a one-way path where teaching causes changes in skills—would be that the parents were hurting their children with their teaching. Kim's more thoughtful interpretation is that the children's literacy skills may in fact have been affecting the parents' teaching, such that parents were adjusting their teaching to their children's literacy acquisition, teaching them more often when their children were struggling. As a correlational study, Kim's work cannot by itself prove the direction of causality, though her thoughtful interpretation certainly goes a long way toward an understanding of these findings.

In addition to B's causing A, A and B can cause each other. In literacy, many skills are thought to be reciprocally related. For instance, vocabulary

---

[1]The Kim (2009) study was, in fact, a longitudinal study that examined relations between parental teach and students' growth and final status in emergent and conventional literacy skills. Thus, it had some potential to shed light on directionality. However, parent teaching predicted levels, but not rates, of growth in literacy, so the results do not provide direct evidence on directionality.

and reading comprehension likely demonstrate reciprocal causation; that is, knowing more words (and more about words) helps readers learn to comprehend text well, while successful comprehension also provides more opportunities to learn new word meanings (e.g., Cunningham & Stanovich, 1998; Stanovich, 1986). Experiments solve the directionality problem by manipulating one variable (the predictor or treatment causing effects) and evaluating its effects on another variable measured later (the outcome). Control over the manipulation eliminates the possibility that the outcome affects the level of the predictor. For instance, an experimental intervention study that teaches vocabulary and treats reading comprehension as an outcome can focus attention on the vocabulary → reading comprehension relation (e.g., Jones et al., 2019). In correlational research, a longitudinal design can often address the directionality problem. For instance, measuring vocabulary and reading comprehension over multiple time points and evaluating their longitudinal associations can help determine whether vocabulary predicts later reading comprehension, or vice versa, or both (e.g., Verhoeven & Van Leeuwe, 2008). However, observational longitudinal studies still suffer from the problem of third variables, so they cannot typically support strong inferences about cause and effect. For instance, the vocabulary–reading comprehension relationship could be driven (in part, at least) by other cognitive skills or educational experiences, rather than by direct causation.

So Why Conduct Correlational Studies?

If correlational designs suffer from these two problems, what are their benefits? First, correlational studies are possible to conduct in situations in which experimental studies are impractical, unethical, or too expensive to conduct. Consider the research that led to the conclusion that smoking causes cancer. This consensus conclusion from the medical community was not based on any randomized controlled field trials, because randomly assigning individuals to smoke was considered impractical and unethical. Second, correlational designs provide evidence that can accumulate over time and converge or diverge from theory in ways that support more definitive conclusions. In the smoking example, the broad causal consensus was based on a critical mass of correlational studies that tested several predictions following from the hypothesis that smoking causes cancer (Novella, 2009). For instance, they established that duration of smoking was associated with increased risk of causer, that stopping smoking was associated with reduced risk of cancer, that greater intensity of smoking was associated with increased risk, and that smoking unfiltered (vs. filtered) cigarettes was associated with higher risk. None of these individual findings established causality, but the weight of evidence from combining them informed a causal consensus. Third, correlational designs can provide the foundation for experimental studies by establishing that a relation of interest exists, to justify determining whether it is causal. Because well-conducted experiments are expensive and time-consuming, researchers are wise to have a foundation of correlational evidence before they pursue them. If a correlational relation does not exist, then a causal relation is unlikely, so an experiment is not warranted. In the area of literacy, researchers had well established the relations between phonological awareness and early reading (e.g., Share, Jorm, Maclean, & Matthews, 1984) and between vocabulary and reading comprehension (e.g., Anderson & Freebody, 1981) before conducting experiments to test whether these relations were causal.

WHAT ARE STANDARDS FOR QUALITY IN CORRELATIONAL RESEARCH?

There are many dimensions along which research with correlational designs can be judged. Many of these apply to all research or all quantitative research. For instance, there should be a close alignment between the research questions and the data sources, so that the questions posed can be answered with the data collected. The samples of participants need to be well chosen for the purposes of the research. The measures used need to be reliable and valid for the study's purposes. The procedures used need to be systematic and carefully documented. Standards of ethical treatment of human participants must be followed. Results need to be carefully interpreted in light of prior theory and evidence, and in relation to the limitations of the data.

Correlational research also has unique standards for quality. These follow directly from the problems of third variables and directionality discussed above. The first involves whether the statistical model and controls, if any, align with the underlying logic of the study. Every study has an underlying logic for the relations among the variables, and the quality of that logic—along with its empirical support in the results—determines the trustworthiness of conclusions. Specifically, correlational studies can be evaluated on whether and how they address counter-explanations contrary to their hypotheses. Strong correlational research can do this by identifying the most relevant third variables, measuring them, and statistically controlling for their confounding influence on the outcome of interest. This is an issue of design, not merely analysis, because the relevant third variables must be identified before the start of the study, so that they can be measured and later integrated into analyses.

For instance, consider my work (Kieffer, 2011) comparing the reading growth trajectories of language minority learners (i.e., students from homes in which English was not the primary language) with those of native English-speaking students across kindergarten through grade 8. In this study, socioeconomic status (SES) was a major confounder; language minority learners have substantially lower SES than native English speakers, and

SES also predicts reading achievement. So the logical counter-explanation would be that students' SES rather than their language background would predict their reading growth. In this paper, I found that controlling for this third variable indeed changed the description of students' growth trajectories substantially (see also Kieffer, 2008). Specifically, language minority learners with initially limited English proficiency had growth trajectories that remained substantially below national averages, but that converged with their peers from similar socioeconomic backgrounds during middle school.

Another, related standard for the quality of correlational research involves how well the authors address the directionality problem. If the study is longitudinal and appropriately models relations between earlier and later skills, then claims about the *temporal order* of the variables are warranted, but not necessarily causal claims (see the discussion of longitudinal analyses below). If the study is cross-sectional, the authors should carefully consider whether the relations of interest might operate in the opposite direction investigated or might be reciprocally related. These possibilities should be acknowledged, particularly if they have a basis in theory or past evidence, and the authors should be clear that their design does not eliminate those counter-interpretations.

A third standard for the quality of correlational research involves the careful use of language to report findings. Because correlational studies cannot support causal inferences, the language used to report findings needs to be careful not to suggest causality to readers. Terms such as *influence, affect,* and *consequence* are rarely warranted; these should be replaced with correlational language such as *associated with, relates to,* or *predicts.* Similarly, when studies are cross-sectional, terms connoting growth or gains over time, such as *improves, increases,* or *declines,* are usually not appropriate and should be replaced with language indicating *differences.*

EXEMPLAR: WHAT IS THE RELATION BETWEEN MORPHOLOGICAL AWARENESS AND READING COMPREHENSION?

For nearly 15 years, colleagues and I have been asking correlational questions about the relation between morphological awareness (MA) and reading comprehension. MA is defined as students' awareness of and ability to manipulate the smallest meaningful units in words (e.g., Carlisle, 1995; Kuo & Anderson, 2006). MA is thought to come into play as readers move past the primary grades and increasingly encounter morphologically complex words in text (e.g., Anglin, 1993; Nagy & Anderson, 1984). We hypothesize that readers who can decipher novel complex words by breaking them down into meaningful parts—to see the *complex* in *complexity,* or to recognize that *independence* is related to *independent* and is the opposite of *dependence*—are better equipped to navigate and comprehend challenging text.

Current models of reading comprehension (e.g., Perfetti, Landi, & Oakhill, 2005) support this notion by predicting two roles for morphology: first, as part of the lexicon supporting word recognition and second, as part of the linguistic system supporting comprehension. In the first role, MA may support word reading, given the challenges in recognizing morphological complex words (e.g., Deacon, Kieffer, & Laroche, 2014). In the latter role, MA may support comprehension directly by facilitating the extraction of meaning from morphologically complex words (e.g., Kieffer & Lesaux, 2008). Similarly, readers with developed MA may know more about the words they know (e.g., their morphological variants, syntactic roles), which leads to a connection between MA and depth of vocabulary knowledge (i.e., the richness of knowledge about the words that are known by an individual; Anderson & Freebody, 1981). In this vein, the *lexical quality hypothesis* (Perfetti & Hart, 2001) also supports a role for morphology in facilitating high-quality representations of words as tightly bonded phonological, orthographic, and semantic/syntactic features.

Within this theoretical framework, there are multiple third variables to consider (i.e., multiple reading-related skills that relate to MA as well as to reading comprehension and may confound the MA → reading comprehension relation). The first and most prominent is vocabulary knowledge. As noted above, morphological knowledge is sometimes considered a facet of vocabulary depth. Empirically, correlations between MA and vocabulary are typically moderate to strong, and studies have found reason to doubt the separability of these two constructs (e.g., Spencer et al., 2015). Given that and the strong relation between vocabulary knowledge and reading comprehension (e.g., Anderson & Freebody, 1981), there is a clear need to account for the counter-hypothesis that it is simply vocabulary and not MA that uniquely predicts reading comprehension.

Another third variable for the MA → reading comprehension relation is word reading. Theoretical models (e.g., Perfetti et al., 2005) and substantial evidence (e.g., Carlisle, 2000; Deacon & Kirby, 2004) implicate MA in word reading. Given the strong role of word reading in reading comprehension (e.g., National Reading Panel, 2000), it may also confound the relation between MA and reading comprehension. In addition, frequently used MA tasks may involve reading (often along with a researcher reading aloud) or spelling (e.g., writing the base word extracted from a morphologically complex word, such as *complex* from *complexity*). In this case, word-reading abilities (and related writing abilities) are introduced as third variables by the measurement paradigm and need to be taken into account.

On the other hand, vocabulary and word reading may be considered not as third variables, but rather as *mediating* variables. Mediation is the situation in which the relation from *A* to *B* is explained by an intervening variable, *M*. *A* predicts *M*, which in turn predicts *B*. In this case, MA may contribute to vocabulary (or word reading), which in turn contributes to reading comprehension. This would align with our hypothesis that MA promotes students' abilities to decipher new morphologically complex words, which in turn promotes their reading comprehension. Mediation can be expressed as indirect contributions, such as the indirect contribution of MA to reading comprehension via vocabulary. This is different from treating vocabulary as a confounder, because vocabulary is part of the underlying logic for the MA → reading comprehension relation, rather than a threat to that logic.

Beyond third variables and mediation, studying the relation between MA and reading comprehension involves a directionality problem. Although theory supports the idea that MA contributes to reading comprehension, it is also possible that reading comprehension supports the development of more advanced MA (Deacon et al., 2014; see below). For instance, successful reading experiences driven by good reading comprehension could provide students with more opportunities to decipher morphologically complex words and to generate abstract rules from examples.

Colleagues and I have investigated the relation between MA and reading comprehension—while working to address these third-variable and directionality concerns—in a series of correlational studies. Here, I briefly introduce the studies; in the next section, I describe their analytic approaches and findings. In the first study, Kieffer and Lesaux (2008), we followed a group of 87 Spanish-speaking English learners from fourth to fifth grade, assessing them annually on a battery of standardized and researcher-developed measures. Although the design was longitudinal, the primary aims involved cross-sectional analyses of concurrent relations. In Kieffer and Lesaux (2012a), we used data from this same cohort, now followed through seventh grade, with assessments each year, to conduct longitudinal analyses of the relation between MA and vocabulary. In Kieffer and Lesaux (2012b), we used a single wave of data with a broader sample of 952 students, including native English speakers and bilingual students from three different first-language backgrounds (Spanish, Filipino, and Vietnamese). In Deacon and colleagues (2014), we followed 100 native English speakers from third to fourth grade, assessed annually on standardized and researcher-created measures. In Kieffer, Petscher, Proctor, and Silverman (2016), we used data from two studies conducted with linguistically diverse samples (including both English learners and native English speakers), with 148 students in grade 6 (Study 1) and 311 students in grades 3–5 (Study 2). The studies used similar and overlapping, but not identical, batteries of measures, which allowed us to compare findings across approaches. In Levesque, Kieffer, and Deacon (2017), we assessed 221 native English speakers in grade 3, again on researcher-developed and standardized measures. All of these studies were observational and correlational; none involved experimental manipulation of variables. However, as we illustrate below, their designs and data-analytic approaches addressed third variables and directionality in several ways. Together, they provide compelling evidence for the important role of MA in reading comprehension across diverse language backgrounds.

WHAT ARE COMMON CORRELATIONAL DATA-ANALYTIC APPROACHES? WHAT ARE ILLUSTRATIONS OF EACH?

Colleagues and I have used a wide variety of correlational data-analytic approaches to explore the relation between MA and reading comprehension. In this section, I introduce some common approaches and illustrate them with my collaborative work on MA. It is worth noting that all of these data-analytic approaches can be used with data from experiments as well, but here I emphasize their affordances for addressing the problems inherent in correlational designs. Full descriptions of these methods are far beyond the scope of what is possible here, but I intend these brief introductions as invitations to the reader to learn more.

Correlations

The simplest approach for analyzing correlational data is the zero-order correlation (most commonly Pearson's correlation coefficient). *Zero-order* refers to the fact that the correlation is between two variables, *A* and *B*, and does not take into account any third variable, *C*. If there are any third variables at all, the correlation is biased; that is, it does not reflect the actual relation. Correlations run from 0 to 1, and their magnitudes or strength can be interpreted by using Cohen's (1992) standards, where .10 is small, .30 is medium, and .50 is large. In Kieffer and Lesaux (2008), we started by reporting the correlations between our researcher-developed measure of MA and Woodcock passage comprehension. These were .48 in fourth grade and .60 in fifth grade. Although these suggested large (strong) relations, the rest of the correlations suggested some bias threatening that conclusion. Both MA and reading comprehension were also positively related (with medium to large magnitudes) to the control variables of vocabulary, word reading, and phonological awareness. The correlations, then, are very likely to have been biased upward, suggesting that the relation is much stronger than it would be if we account for these third variables.

Multiple Regression

Multiple regression is perhaps the most common approach for analyzing correlational data. (For a more thorough explanation of multiple regression and correlational designs, see Cunningham et al., 2011. I relied heavily on their chapter in developing the current one.) In this approach, a primary question predictor is included in a regression model to predict an outcome, while also including control variables. The control variables are selected to account for third variables that represent counter-explanations to the hypothesis that the question predictor causes changes in the outcome. Controlling for these variables *partials out* variation associated with them in the outcome, so that we can determine whether the question predictor explains the remaining variation. Put another way, control variables are *held constant*, such that we compare outcomes for cases that have the same level of the control but different levels of the question predictor. (It is worth noting that analysis of covariance [ANCOVA] is a related method with the same underlying logic.)

In the Kieffer and Lesaux (2008) study, we used multiple regression to explore the relation between MA and reading comprehension, after controlling for the third variables of vocabulary, word reading, and phonological awareness. As noted above, we controlled for vocabulary because of its theoretical and empirical relation to both MA and reading comprehension. Likewise, we controlled for word reading because it might confound the relation between the constructs of interest, but also because our MA task involved reading along with the researcher and spelling (i.e., skills irrelevant to MA that we wanted to partial out). Phonological awareness has also been established as an important control in this work (e.g., Deacon & Kirby, 2004), because it relates to MA and is a strong predictor of reading skills. Controlling for or holding constant these variables meant that we were comparing students who had similar vocabulary, word reading, and phonological awareness, but differing MA, to see whether they would also have different levels of reading comprehension.

We found that the unique relation (i.e., the relation when we accounted for controls) between MA and reading comprehension was not statistically significant in fourth grade ($p = .093$), but was statistically significant in fifth grade ($p < .01$). *Statistical significance* here refers to the probability that the observed result (e.g., a unique relation different from 0) could have occurred if it is not the case in the population; a p-value less than .05 is the convention for calling a relation statistically significant. However, to determine if a relation has practical significance, we also have to interpret its magnitude. Using Cohen's (1992) rules of thumb for interpreting the magnitudes of relations, we found that the relation between MA and reading comprehension in fifth grade was moderate (standardized beta = .39). This relation was smaller than the correlation of .60 above, as we would expect, given the importance of the observed third variables. Considered differently, adding MA to the model explained an additional 8% of the variance in reading comprehension ($\Delta R^2 = .078$), above and beyond the variation explained by the control variables. These findings support the notion that MA contributes to reading comprehension to a meaningful extent, above and beyond at least some of the most relevant third variables. However, other third variables remain, such as nonverbal reasoning ability (given the reasoning involved in the MA task and in reading comprehension) and syntactic skills (given that there is a theoretical and empirical relation between MA and syntax [Kuo & Anderson, 2006] and between syntax and reading comprehension [Deacon & Kieffer, 2018]). In addition, because the main analyses were cross-sectional, the directionality of the relation could not be established, raising the need for further longitudinal research on this question.

Longitudinal Autoregression

To address the directionality problem, researchers can collect longitudinal data with the same participants observed at multiple points in time and predict skills from earlier to later waves. Among multiple approaches to analyzing these data, one common method is *autoregression*. Autoregression is a form of multiple regression in which a later outcome (Time 2 *B*) is predicted by an earlier question predictor (Time 1 *A*), even after a researcher controls for the autoregressor (Time 1 *B*)—that is, earlier levels of the outcome variable. The model typically also includes other controls for third variables measured at the earlier time point (Time 1 *C*'s). Controlling for the earlier level of the outcome variable is important in reading research, because skills tend to predict themselves over time, often strongly. If those earlier skills are also related to the question predictor, they become a third variable that needs to be taken into account. So, for instance, if we had Time 1 MA predicting Time 2 reading comprehension, but did not control for Time 1 reading comprehension, we would ignore the fact that readers who were good (or struggling) comprehenders at Time 1 tend to remain good (or struggling) comprehenders at Time 2. Because we already know that MA and reading comprehension are concurrently related at Time 1, ignoring the autoregressor would threaten the validity of results for the longitudinal relations of interest.

A single autoregression model can establish one direction for the temporal order of variables. To eliminate or establish the alternative direction, researchers can fit another model with the outcome–predictor relation reversed, again after controlling for earlier levels of the (new) outcome. For instance, if the main hypothesis is that *A* causes *B*, one autoregressive model (*A* causing *B*) would have Time 1 *A* predicting Time 2 *B*, controlling for the autoregressor Time 1 *B*, while the alternative model (*B* causing *A*) would have Time 1 *B* predicting Time 2 *A*, controlling for the autoregressor Time 1 *A*.

For instance, in the Deacon and colleagues (2014) study, we used autoregression to establish the temporal order of the relation between MA and reading comprehension. (For another example of autoregression on this topic, see Levesque, Kieffer, & Deacon, 2019.) Testing our main hypothesis—that MA predicts later reading comprehension—we investigated whether grade

3 MA would predict grade 4 reading comprehension, after we controlled for grade 3 reading comprehension (along with additional third variables measured in grade 3: vocabulary, word reading, phonological awareness, nonverbal reasoning, and age). In addition, we tested the other direction—that reading comprehension predicts later MA—by investigating whether grade 3 reading comprehension predicted grade 4 MA, after we controlled for grade 3 MA (along with the same additional third variables in grade 3).[2] We found evidence for both directions: Both MA and reading comprehension had small to moderate and statistically significant relations with later levels of the other, suggesting a reciprocal relation (from grade 3 MA to grade 4 reading comprehension: standardized regression path = .16, p = .0300; from grade 3 reading comprehension to grade 4 MA: standardized regression path = .25, p = .0119). The two paths were not significantly different from one another in magnitude, suggesting that both longitudinal relations are likely to be equally important. These findings support the MA → reading comprehension relation found in Kieffer and Lesaux (2008), among several others, but also suggest that the other direction (reading comprehension → MA) is important and worthy of study.

LONGITUDINAL GROWTH MODELING

Although widely used in reading research, autoregression models have been criticized for not capturing individual growth appropriately (e.g., Berry & Willoughby, 2017; Singer & Willett, 2003). While autoregressive models can assess the relation between early and later skills, they do not directly model intraindividual growth in those skills. *Growth models,* by contrast, use three or more waves of data to directly capture individual students' growth trajectories (Singer & Willett, 2003). Individual growth modeling uses longitudinal data to model individuals' status and rate of growth (as well as the correlation, if any, between status and rate of growth). *Status* is often specified as students' initial status (i.e., levels at the first time point), but can also be modeled as another meaningful point along students' trajectory (e.g., final status or midpoint status). Status can also be thought of as the elevation of students' trajectories, whereas *rate of change* refers to the slope of their trajectories. Having modeled these trajectories, researchers can evaluate whether independent variables predict students' status and/or rates of growth.

---

[2]In Deacon and colleagues (2014), we actually used path analysis, rather than multiple regression, to fit the two autoregression models simultaneously. This had the advantage of facilitating model comparisons and testing whether the two paths of interest had similar magnitudes. Nonetheless, the logic was the same as if we had fit two separate models by using multiple regression.

For instance, in the Kieffer and Lesaux (2012a) study, we used a variant of growth modeling called a *parallel process latent growth curve model* to investigate the relation between students' growth trajectories in MA and in vocabulary. Using four waves of data, we modeled students' initial (grade 4) status and rates of growth between grades 4 and 7 for both MA and vocabulary. Examining each variable individually, we found evidence for rapid growth in both MA and vocabulary during this period (i.e., more than half a standard deviation per year), consistent with prior research (e.g., Anglin, 1993). Despite this rapid growth, the sample of Spanish-speaking language minority learners remained far below national norms for vocabulary (i.e., more than 0.75 of a standard deviation in grade 7). We also found a strong relation between MA growth and vocabulary growth ($r = .67$), such that students with rapid growth in one also demonstrated rapid growth in the other. However, initial (grade 4) levels in neither skill predicted growth in the other, so there was less direct evidence for the directionality of this relation.

Latent Variable Modeling

As mentioned previously, correlational research must meet the standards for all quantitative research that measures should be reliable and valid. *Reliability* refers to the extent to which test scores are consistent (across repeated applications of the testing procedures), whereas *validity* refers to the strength of the evidence-based argument that a test score reflects what it claims to measure (e.g., American Educational Research Association [AERA], American Psychological Association, & National Council for Measurement in Education, 2014). In literacy research, many important constructs are challenging to measure and difficult to isolate from other constructs. Latent variable models—including confirmatory factor analysis, structural equation modeling, and item-response theory models—offer opportunities to maximize reliability and to assess and improve validity (e.g., Kline, 2016; Lord, 1980/2012), which are particularly valuable for modeling constructs like MA. (They also offer opportunities to estimate indirect effects in mediation models, as described in the section below.)

These opportunities come, in part, from the use of latent composites to capture the shared variance across multiple items or instruments. Specifically, when a reading-related skill is challenging to measure, we are well advised to measure it in multiple ways with different paradigms that tap different irrelevant skills. Then, by combining the overlapping information from the different tasks, we can capture the construct in more valid ways, with less influence from those irrelevant skills. For instance, one common measure for MA we have used is a decomposition task, in which students are read a word and sentence and have to decompose the word to give a written response completing the sentence (e.g., "*complexity. The problem is* _____"; Kieffer & Lesaux, 2008, based on Carlisle, 2000). A second common measure is a multiple-choice suffix choice task, in which students chose a nonsense word with an appropriate derivational suffix to complete a sentence (e.g., *"The man is a good _____. A) tranter B) tranting C) trantious D) trantiful"*; Kieffer & Lesaux, 2012b, based on Nagy, Berninger, & Abbott, 2006). The first task has the problem that it may tap students' spelling skills that are unrelated to their MA. The second task has the problem that its multiple-choice format might tap process-of-elimination strategies. However, because the two tasks have different problems, the overlapping information from the two tasks is less susceptible to those task-specific confounding skills. By creating a latent variable from the two tasks, we can isolate the shared variance (representing common skills) among them and partial out those task-specific irrelevant skills.[3]

For instance, in Kieffer and Lesaux (2012b), a study with sixth graders from diverse language backgrounds, we created a latent variable for MA by using scores from these two tasks. We simultaneously created a latent variable for reading comprehension by using the Gates–McGinitie reading comprehension test and a researcher-developed expository text comprehension task; this similarly combined information across two different paradigms for measuring reading comprehension, a construct that is notoriously difficult to measure (e.g., Keenan, Betjemann, & Olson, 2008). We found that latent MA strongly predicted latent reading comprehension, after we controlled (again) for the third variables of vocabulary and word reading (standardized regression coefficient = .480; $p < .0001$). We further found that this relation was not statistically significantly different for the different language groups (Spanish-speaking, Filipino-speaking, and Vietnamese-speaking language minority learners as well as native English speakers). This finding converged with the previous findings described above, while accounting better for measurement error and partialing out the irrelevant skills tapped by the individual MA tasks.

Using a different version of latent variable modeling, we (Kieffer et al., 2016) investigated whether MA would make a unique contribution to reading comprehension after we accounted for the skills common to MA, vocabulary, and syntax. This was another way to consider the third variables of vocabulary and syntax: Rather than statistically controlling for them, we used a bifactor model to capture what was shared and unique to each of the three aspects of language comprehension. Across two studies, we found that the bifactor model provided the best fit to the data, thus

---

[3]It is worth noting that latent variables with only two indicators (measured variables) are not identified and cannot be used to compare alternative measurement models (i.e., unidimensional vs. multidimensional models). In Kieffer and Lesaux (2012b), we overcame this problem by creating latent variables for both MA and reading comprehension, using a total of four indicators. I use the example of two measures because it is a clear illustration of the logic behind latent variables, not because it is recommended as best practice.

appropriately capturing the dimensionality of language comprehension, and that the general language comprehension factor (i.e., representing the common skills among the three aspects of language) was the most predictive. In Study 2, but not Study 1, we found that the unique MA factor also predicted reading comprehension above and beyond general language comprehension and word reading (standardized regression coefficient = .16; p = .001). Because Study 2 incorporated syntax, a third variable that was unobserved in many of the studies reviewed here, these findings further advance the case for a unique contribution of MA to reading comprehension.

Mediation Analyses

Often, literacy researchers' theories are more complicated than A causes B. Specifically, we frequently want to know about mediated relations (i.e., situations in which some variable A causes B via a hypothesized mechanism or mediator, M). Mediation analyses allow us to examine the "black box" that intervenes between two variables. By exploring the pathways by which variables relate to one another, we can test more sophisticated and likely more accurate theories about the phenomenon under study. More practically, unpacking mechanisms for relations can shed light on their inner workings, addressing not simply whether but how two variables relate. Among multiple approaches for mediation analyses, we have used two in our work: multivariate path analysis and structural equation modeling. Both approaches can model the direct and indirect relations hypothesized in a mediation model, but they treat measurement error differently. Structural equation modeling, as described above, uses the latent composites to capture the shared variance across multiple measures and partials out measurement error. Multivariate path analysis uses observed variables and does not account for measurement error, but is more appropriate when each construct of interest is measured by a single task.

As described above, MA likely contributes to reading comprehension via multiple mechanisms. The first is word reading. Students with better MA are likely to have a better organized lexicon, which supports word reading, which in turn supports reading comprehension (e.g., Perfetti et al., 2005). In the Deacon and colleagues (2014) study, we explored this hypothesis with data from third- and fourth-grade native English speakers. We used multivariate path analysis to test whether a mediation model—in which MA predicts word reading, which in turn predicts reading comprehension—fit the data better than models with no mediation. Again, we controlled for third variables (vocabulary, phonological awareness, nonverbal reasoning, and age). In both third and fourth grades, we found evidence for partial mediation; that is, the MA → word reading → reading comprehension pathway was uniquely significant, but so was the direct MA → reading comprehension pathway. The indirect effects were small to moderate and statistically significant (grade 3: standardized indirect effect

= .17, p < .05; grade 4: standardized indirect effect = .12, p < .05),[4] while the remaining direct effects from MA to reading comprehension were moderate and statistically significant (grade 3: standardized direct effect = .24, p < .05; grade 4: standardized direct effect = .30, p < .05). This partial mediation suggests that word reading is one, but not the only, mechanism to explain the relation between MA and reading comprehension.

In more recent work, we have explored other mechanism for the MA → reading comprehension relation. For instance, in the Levesque and colleagues (2017) study, we used structural equation modeling to explore four intervening variables through which MA may contribute indirectly to reading comprehension: word reading, vocabulary, morphological decoding (i.e., the ability to read morphologically complex words), and morphological analysis (i.e., the ability to analyze the meaning of morphologically complex words). We found two indirect pathways (after controlling for nonverbal ability and phonological awareness as well as the other pathway). In the first, MA predicted morphological decoding, which in turn predicted word reading and then reading comprehension (standardized indirect effect = .24; p < .05). In the second, MA predicted morphological analysis, which in turn predicted reading comprehension (standardized indirect effect = .20; p < .05). Like the results from Deacon and colleagues (2014), we found evidence for partial mediation, such that a direct MA → reading comprehension path remained statistically significant and moderate to large (.36; p < .01). This provides further support for the notion that we have identified some, but not all, of the mechanisms for the relation between MA and reading comprehension.

CONCLUSION

As these examples illustrate, correlational research has a great deal to offer literacy researchers. Although it can never support the strong causal inferences produced by experimental designs, the accumulation of evidence from multiple, well-designed correlational studies can move us closer to tentative conclusions about cause and effect. In the case of MA and reading comprehension, our line of work has addressed prominent counter-hypotheses by incorporating third variables as controls, including vocabulary, word reading, phonological awareness, syntactic skills, and nonverbal ability. Together, the evidence converges to indicate that MA makes a unique contribution to reading comprehension, above and beyond the contributions

---

[4]In Deacon and colleagues (2014) and Levesque and colleagues (2017), we evaluated indirect effects using bootstrapped 95% confidence intervals rather than traditional z statistics, because the latter are known to be biased for indirect effects (MacKinnon, Fairchild, & Fritz, 2007). For simplicity, we report p's here, but refer the reader to the original papers for the most complete reporting of mediation analyses.

of these related skills. The evidence also suggests that this relation may be bidirectional and mediated by multiple skills.

Researchers have many decisions to make when pursuing correlational research. First and foremost, they face design decisions that will determine whether they collect data that can be used to mitigate the limitations of correlational designs. They must identify the most logical counter-explanations represented as third variables, so that they can be measured and taken into account analytically. When doing so is feasible, they should collect longitudinal data to explore the directionality of relations and model individual growth. At the data-analytic stage, they also have many options, but should carefully consider how to control for relevant third variables, how to assess directionality through longitudinal analyses (when possible), how to maximize reliability and validity of measures (e.g., by using latent variable models), and how to consider mediated, indirect relations in their analyses. As our examples illustrate, no single correlational study is perfect or free from bias, but the cumulative process of correlational research can yield important insights about the nature of reading and writing.

REFERENCES

American Educational Research Association (AERA), American Psychological Association, & National Council on Measurement in Education. (2014). *Standards for educational and psychological testing.* Washington, DC: AERA.

Anderson, R. C., & Freebody, P. (1981). Vocabulary knowledge. In J. T. Guthrie (Ed.), *Comprehension and teaching: Research reviews* (pp. 77–117). Newark, DE: International Reading Association.

Anglin, J. M. (1993). Vocabulary development: A morphological analysis. *Monographs of the Society for Research in Child Development, 58*(Serial No. 238).

Berry, D., & Willoughby, M. T. (2017). On the practical interpretability of cross-lagged panel models: Rethinking a developmental workhorse. *Child Development, 88*(4), 1186–1206.

Carlisle, J. F. (1995). Morphological awareness and early reading achievement. In L. B. Feldman (Ed.), *Morphological aspects of language processing* (pp. 189–209). Hillsdale, NJ: Erlbaum.

Carlisle, J. F. (2000). Awareness of the structure and meaning of morphologically complex words: Impact on reading. *Reading and Writing, 12*(3), 169–190.

Cohen, J. (1992). A power primer. *Psychological Bulletin, 112*(1), 155.

Cunningham, A. E., & Stanovich, K. E. (1998). What reading does for the mind. *American Educator, 22,* 8–17.

Cunningham, A. E., Stanovich, K. E., & Maul, A. (2011). Of correlations and causes: The use of multiple regression modeling in literacy research. In N. K. Duke & M. H. Mallette (Eds.), *Literacy research methodologies* (2nd ed., pp. 50–69). New York: Guilford Press.

Deacon, S. H., & Kieffer, M. J. (2018). Understanding how syntactic awareness contributes to reading comprehension: Evidence from mediation and longitudinal models. *Journal of Educational Psychology, 111,* 72–86.

Deacon, S. H., Kieffer, M. J., & Laroche, A. (2014). The relation between morphological awareness and reading comprehension: Evidence from mediation and longitudinal models. *Scientific Studies of Reading, 18*, 432–451.

Deacon, S. H., & Kirby, J. R. (2004). Morphological awareness: Just "more phonological"? The roles of morphological and phonological awareness in reading development. *Applied Psycholinguistics, 25*(2), 223–238.

Hoover, W. A., & Gough, P. B. (1990). The simple view of reading. *Reading and Writing, 2*(2), 127–160.

Jones, S. M., LaRusso, M., Kim, J., Kim, H. Y., Selman, R., Uccelli, P., et al. (2019). Experimental effects of Word Generation on vocabulary, academic language, perspective taking, and reading comprehension in high-poverty schools. *Journal of Research on Educational Effectiveness, 12*(3), 448–483.

Keenan, J. M., Betjemann, R. S., & Olson, R. K. (2008). Reading comprehension tests vary in the skills they assess: Differential dependence on decoding and oral comprehension. *Scientific Studies of Reading, 12*(3), 281–300.

Kieffer, M. J. (2008). Catching up or falling behind?: Initial English proficiency, concentrated poverty, and the reading growth of language minority learners in the United States. *Journal of Educational Psychology, 100*, 851–868.

Kieffer, M. J. (2011). Converging trajectories: Reading growth in language minority learners and their classmates, kindergarten to grade eight. *American Educational Research Journal, 48*, 1157–1186.

Kieffer, M. J., & Lesaux, N. K. (2008). The role of derivational morphological awareness in the reading comprehension of Spanish-speaking English language learners. *Reading and Writing: An Interdisciplinary Journal, 21*, 783–804.

Kieffer, M. J., & Lesaux, N. K. (2012a). Development of morphological awareness and vocabulary knowledge for Spanish-speaking language minority learners: A parallel process latent growth model. *Applied Psycholinguistics, 33*, 23–54.

Kieffer, M. J., & Lesaux, N. K. (2012b). Direct and indirect roles of morphological awareness in the English reading comprehension of native Spanish, Filipino, Vietnamese, and English speakers. *Language Learning, 62*, 1170–1204.

Kieffer, M. J., Petscher, Y., Proctor, C. P., & Silverman, R. D. (2016). Is the whole more than the sum of its parts?: Modeling the contributions of language comprehension skills to reading comprehension in the upper elementary grades. *Scientific Studies of Reading, 20*, 436–454.

Kim, Y.-S. (2009). The relationship between home literacy practices and developmental trajectories of emergent literacy and conventional literacy skills for Korean children. *Reading and Writing: An Interdisciplinary Journal, 22*, 57–84.

Kline, R. B. (2016). *Principles and practice of structural equation modeling* (4th ed.). New York: Guilford Press.

Kuo, L. J., & Anderson, R. C. (2006). Morphological awareness and learning to read: A cross-language perspective. *Educational Psychologist, 41*(3), 161–180.

Levesque, K., Kieffer, M. J., & Deacon, S. H. (2017). Morphological awareness and reading comprehension: Examining mediating factors. *Journal of Experimental Child Psychology, 160*, 1–20.

Levesque, K. C., Kieffer, M. J., & Deacon, S. H. (2019). Inferring meaning from meaningful parts: The contributions of morphological skills to the development of children's reading comprehension. *Reading Research Quarterly, 54*, 63–80.

Lord, F. M. (2012). *Applications of item response theory to practical testing problems*. New York: Routledge. (Original work published 1980)

MacKinnon, D. P., Fairchild, A. J., & Fritz, M. S. (2007). Mediation analysis. *Annual Review of Psychology, 58*, 593–614.

Nagy, W. E., & Anderson, R. C. (1984). The number of words in printed school English. *Reading Research Quarterly, 19*, 304–330.

Nagy, W. E., Berninger, V. W., & Abbott, R. D. (2006). Contributions of morphology beyond phonology to literacy outcomes of upper elementary and middle-school students. *Journal of Educational Psychology, 98*, 134–147.

National Reading Panel. (2000). *Report of the National Reading Panel: Teaching children to read: An evidence-based assessment of the scientific research literature on reading and its implications for reading instruction. Reports of the subgroups* (NIH Publication No. 00-4754). Washington, DC: National Institute of Child Health and Human Development, National Institutes of Health.

Novella, S. (2009). Evidence in medicine: Correlation and causation. Retrieved September 4, 2019, from *https://sciencebasedmedicine.org/evidence-in-medicine-correlation-and-causation*.

Perfetti, C. A., & Hart, L. (2001). The lexical basis of comprehension skill. In D. S. Gorfein (Ed.), *On the consequences of meaning selection: Perspectives on resolving lexical ambiguity* (pp. 67–86). Washington, DC: American Psychological Association.

Perfetti, C. A., Landi, N., & Oakhill, J. (2005). The acquisition of reading comprehension skill. In M. J. Snowling & C. Hulme (Eds.), *The science of reading: A handbook* (pp. 227–247). Malden, MA: Blackwell.

Share, D. L., Jorm, A. F., Maclean, R., & Matthews, R. (1984). Sources of individual differences in reading acquisition. *Journal of Educational Psychology, 76*(6), 1309–1324.

Silverman, R. D., Proctor, C. P., Harring, J. R., Doyle, B., Mitchell, M. A., & Meyer, A. G. (2014). Teachers' instruction and students' vocabulary and comprehension: An exploratory study with English monolingual and Spanish–English bilingual students in grades 3–5. *Reading Research Quarterly, 49*(1), 31–60.

Singer, J. D., & Willett, J. B. (2003). *Applied longitudinal data analysis: Modeling change and event occurrence*. New York: Oxford University Press.

Spencer, M., Muse, A., Wagner, R. K., Foorman, B., Petscher, Y., Schatschneider, C., et al. (2015). Examining the underlying dimensions of morphological awareness and vocabulary knowledge. *Reading and Writing, 28*(7), 959–988.

Stanovich, K. E. (1986). Matthew effects in reading: Some consequences of individual differences in the acquisition of literacy. *Reading Research Quarterly, 21*(4), 360–407.

Verhoeven, L., & Van Leeuwe, J. (2008). Prediction of the development of reading comprehension: A longitudinal study. *Applied Cognitive Psychology, 22*(3), 407–423.

CHAPTER 5

Critical Race Methodologies

Alice Y. Lee
Amos J. Lee

Critical race methods and methodologies are analytic extensions of critical race theory (CRT), which offers an explanation of why race and racism are simultaneously insidious and common within the fabric of American life. CRT methodologies are both explanatory and problem-solving-oriented, and seek to "define, expose, and address educational problems" (Parker & Lynn, 2002, p. 7). CRT itself was conceived to expose, critique, and explain the central role of race within U.S. structures and institutions (e.g., government, judicial courts, schools, places of employment), and to demonstrate how white supremacy purposely marginalizes non-white[1] voices. In post-civil-rights America, particularly after the *Brown v. Board of Education* U.S. Supreme Court decision, critical race legal scholars (e.g., Derrick Bell, Kimberlé Crenshaw, Mari Matsuda, Richard Delgado) began to theorize about why racial discrimination persisted despite major judicial changes, and constructed a framework describing the all-encompassing nature of white supremacy. In an era in which many believed racial tensions and disparities had been ameliorated, critical race legal scholars debunked false notions of color-blindness and a postracial society, underscoring why racial reconciliation is infeasible without a dismantling of all forms of white dominance.

In the 1990s, CRT was shepherded into the field of education by Ladson-Billings and Tate (1995) in their seminal article, "Toward a Critical

---

[1] While the terms *Black*, *Brown*, and *Indigenous* as racial and/or ethnic identities are capitalized throughout this chapter, we have chosen not to capitalize the term *white*, to highlight a sociopolitical environment in which European American dominance is the norm throughout every economic, political, social, and religious sphere within the United States, and to highlight a power differential in which Black, Brown, and Indigenous communities continue to be left at the margins.

Race Theory of Education." In the 25 years since that article appeared, CRT educational researchers have developed methodologies, undergirded by CRT tenets, that focus on exposing and explaining the ways in which racism is endemic within U.S. schools. While the core tenets of CRT are widely known within the field (Crenshaw, Gotanda, Peller, & Thomas, 1996; Delgado & Stefancic, 2013, 2017; Ladson-Billings & Tate, 1995; Tate, 1997; Taylor, Gilborn, & Ladson-Billings, 2015), we provide a brief overview to familiarize readers with these tenets:

• *Centrality and interconnectedness of race and racism.* CRT rejects the notion of a postracial or color-blind society. CRT posits that race and racism are endemic within everyday life, have a permanency within U.S. society/institutions, and are so commonplace that only the most egregious forms of racism are acknowledged, thus deemphasizing all other forms of racism present in daily life.

• *Whiteness as property.* CRT also argues that U.S. society is based on property rights, and that people's whiteness is considered as their property. Under a system of white supremacy, whiteness incurs capital and material value, and racism is used to maintain a racial hierarchy in which white people dominate.

• *Interest convergence.* This notion posits that any progress made for people of color, particularly Black, Brown, and Indigenous communities, is achieved only when it "converges with the interests of whites" (Bell, 1980, p. 523). And, since racism is permanent, the progress established can be reversed on the basis of whether or not it continues to benefit white people.

• *Challenges to majoritarian views, meritocracy, neutrality, and ahistoricism.* Majoritarian views are narratives that substantiate ideologies rooted in ahistorical notions (e.g., slavery ended a long time ago and no longer affects us today). Ahistoricism rejects historical contexts (e.g., legal, social, political) and distorts our understandings of current forms of subordination. These notions often lead to myths of a meritocratic society, in which everyone has the same opportunities and chances to succeed; and to false beliefs that the law is neutral, objective, and fair to all people, regardless of race. While people of any racial background may hold these views and ideologies, they mostly serve the interests of white people, and thus support white supremacy.

• *Centering the experiential knowledge of people of color as sources of knowledge.* CRT purposefully centers the experiences, stories, and narratives of people of color as meaningful and instructive. People of color's voices are valuable and necessary, particularly to destabilize white hegemony.

• *Intersectionality and interdisciplinary.* While CRT promotes the centrality of race within analyses, it also acknowledges that race intersects with all other forms of subordination (classism, sexism, ableism, etc.), and thus must be interdisciplinary and intersectional in its interpretation and study of racial inequality (including such approaches as DisCrit, LatCrit, QueerCrit, TribCrit, etc.).

• *Commitment to justice and liberation.* CRT praxis moves CRT beyond intellectual endeavors, and underscores the need for a movement that directly influences and benefits communities of color as theory meets practice.

The CRT field has exponentially expanded, with a vast amount of research and intersecting subfields, and has laid a vital foundation in identifying and naming racism within U.S. schools. Critical race scholars are now mapping the next steps for the field to address tangible solutions to the racial ills that have been exposed (Dixson & Anderson, 2018; Lynn, 2019). They acknowledge, however, that a key difficulty in moving toward racial justice lies in the very architecture of American society. CRT is founded upon the understanding that the law is inherently grounded in white supremacy; thus, real solutions require the very nature of our society to change. Nevertheless, a core tenet of CRT is committed action to the justice of all people of color. In this vein, we provide a historical and methodological landscape for the ways CRT can enrich scholarly endeavors toward this end.

HISTORICAL PROGRESSION OF CRITICAL RACE METHODS

One avenue of dismantling white supremacy in research consists of expanding traditional methodologies and critically exploring *whose* voice and stories take center stage. Counter-storytelling and counter-narratives, which accentuate the voices of people of color, have been hallmark approaches to CRT methodologies. Shortly after the introduction of CRT into educational research, scholars such as Ladson-Billings and Tate (1995), Parker (1998), Solórzano and Yosso (2002), and DeCuir and Dixson (2004) spent the early years establishing the legitimacy of critical race methods as approaches to centering the experiential knowledge of people of color in a society that continues to marginalize their voices and perspectives. More specifically, articles in three special journal issues on qualitative inquiry (Dixson, Chapman, & Hill, 2005; Lynn, Yosso, Solórzano, & Parker, 2002; Parker, 2015), along with a few edited books (Hopson & Dixson, 2013; Lynn & Dixson, 2013; Parker, Deyhle, & Villenas, 1999), have sought to explain how a CRT epistemology can be infused into—and can change how we approach—research.

This literature was foundational for defining and explaining the analytic value of counter-storytelling (DeCuir & Dixson, 2004; Solórzano & Yosso, 2002), substantiating the approach's intersections with feminism (Alemán, Delgado Bernal, & Mendoza, 2013; Crenshaw, 1989; Delgado Bernal, Burciaga, & Flores Carmona, 2012), developing Indigenous methodologies (Brayboy, 2005, 2013), and employing Latinx critical theories in conjunction with CRT to explore Latinx educational experiences (Guadalupe Valles & Villalpando, 2013; Solórzano & Yosso, 2001). This work charted how the field currently conceptualizes CRT methods—from the use of counter-storytelling and counter-narratives to underscoring how the approach is inherently cross-disciplinary and intersectional. Undergirding CRT methodology is the notion that racial oppression does indeed intersect with multiple forms of subjugation in a racial caste system. Concurrently, CRT posits race as a central feature in U.S. oppression, which cannot be negated in conducting research. Within these core tenets, researchers continue to push the boundaries of critical race methodologies by mixing original forms of counter-storytelling with other intersecting approaches (e.g., ethnographies, mixed methods, quantitative analysis, geographic information systems, document or content analysis).

Most recently, and based on the continued evolution and growth of CRT within education, DeCuir-Gunby, Chapman, and Schutz (2019) have compiled emerging methodological approaches in *Understanding Critical Race Research Methods and Methodologies*. This edited volume newly features various critical race methodologies, including qualitative, quantitative, and mixed methods. It is significant to note the entrance of quantitative approaches, since CRT methods have been primarily qualitative in nature. Quantitative methods are often predicated on postpositivist ideologies, which assume an objective truth, and thus have been perceived as diametrically opposed to qualitative approaches rooted in postmodern and critical theories. New quantitative studies (Covarrubias, 2011; Covarrubias & Vélez, 2013; Crawford, Demack, Gillborn, & Warmington, 2019; Sablan, 2019), however, problematize such a bifurcated view, and offer quantitative methods that can align with CRT tenets. In the following sections, we discuss an original CRT method—counter-storytelling—as well as approaches that have emerged over the last decades. We also offer essential standards, questions, and claims for scholars pursuing CRT methodologies. We then examine how touchstone features of counter-storytelling are exemplified in a literacy study, and we conclude with thoughts about the significance of CRT methods in literacy research.

CRITICAL RACE METHODOLOGICAL APPROACHES

Counter-Storytelling

After CRT was introduced into the field of education, the initial methodological focus was on amplifying the voices and lived experiences of people of color—particularly through the use of *counter-storytelling*, which has been used interchangeably with the term *counter-narratives* by some scholars (e.g., Solórzano & Yosso, 2002). These methods functioned as explanatory tools in naming, explaining, and showing racial inequities that illuminated systems of whiteness and subordination of people of color.

Legal scholars were the first to employ storytelling and counter-storytelling as methods for broadly communicating CRT tenets. Derrick Bell (1987), a key founder of the CRT movement, utilized knowledge from history, politics, race studies, and the law to tell stories that allowed readers a more robust understanding of the actors and victims of racism. These stories functioned as more than anecdotes; their purposes were analytic in nature, interweaving interdisciplinary perspectives to question the status quo and majoritarian views that continue to subordinate people of color, particularly Black and Brown people. As Ladson-Billings (1998, 2000) further notes, composite counter-stories can involve fictitious characters based on the real-life experiences of those marginalized, and can be drawn from a multitude of people and many types of empirical data. Brayboy and Chin (2019) emphasize the power of composite counter-stories to disrupt the normalized reality of colonization, and to awaken white people through narratives that help them see the effects of colonization on Indigenous communities. Bell's (1992) seminal story, "The Space Traders," presents a window into the ways white people in power are willing to physically sacrifice Black lives for their own benefit. This composite story involves a fictional setting that parallels the treatment of Black people in this country. Historical evidence, therefore, is used to create the composite story, and it becomes an analytic tool to elucidate racial realism, which postulates the permanence of whiteness—as evidenced in the past, in the present, and certainly into the future.

Delgado and Stefancic (2017), also pioneering CRT legal scholars, discuss how stories can become avenues for white people to garner some understanding of the lived experiences of people of color, and to gain insight into a racial existence vastly different from their own. They contend that stories are often used by white people as a way of sustaining hegemonic views and a society structured by a racial hierarchy. A critical mass of counter-stories, therefore, can be a forceful way of unraveling oppressive and racist mindsets, especially since those in power are rarely cognizant of how their own actions oppress subordinate groups. Furthermore, the permanence of white supremacy is evident in the ways majoritarian narratives continue to be recycled and retold in iterative forms to convey the same messages. For this reason, counter-stories, too, must continue to be told as a way of disrupting and exposing ongoing majoritarian narratives. Only then can new paradigms be imagined for our society, showing the different possibilities available. As Delgado (1989) writes, "they [counter-stories] enrich imagination and teach that by combining elements from the story and current reality, we may construct a new world richer than either alone" (p. 2415). The purpose of counter-stories is to open up their readers' worldviews into realms that were uncritiqued and unobserved before.

Because people of color daily experience the injustices related to structural racism in their lives, they are the experts needed in order to counter
the stories told by the majority to retain their power, such as a narrative that
promotes a postracial, color-blind society. Therefore, counter-storytelling
centers people of color's lived expertise within the group of critical race
methodological approaches. Solórzano and Yosso (2002) define *critical
race methodology* in the following way:

> We define critical race methodology as a theoretically grounded approach
> to research that (a) foregrounds race and racism in all aspects of the
> research process. However, it also challenges the separate discourses on
> race, gender, and class by showing how these three elements intersect to
> affect the experiences of students of color; (b) challenges the traditional
> research paradigms, texts, and theories used to explain the experiences
> of students of color; (c) offers a liberatory or transformative solution to
> racial, gender, and class subordination; and (d) focuses on the racialized,
> gendered, and classed experiences of students of color. Furthermore, it
> views these experiences as sources of strength and (e) uses the interdis-
> ciplinary knowledge base of ethnic studies, women's studies, sociology,
> history, humanities, and the law to better understand the experiences of
> students of color. (p. 24)

They go on to divide the methodological approach of counter-
storytelling into three distinctive categories. The first category consists
of personal counter-stories or counter-narratives (used interchangeably).
These stories are primarily autobiographical and convey a person's encounters with varied forms of racism as it may intersect with other forms of
subordination (e.g., sexism, ableism). These personal narratives include the
tapestry of a person's lived experiences as it fits in with larger sociopolitical
frameworks that push back against a majoritarian perspective (Espinoza,
1990; Montoya, 1994; Williams, 1991). The second category is that of
other people's stories and/or narratives. These stories are told by a third
party, and constitute a way in which biographical data and the experiences of persons of color can illuminate experiences with race and racism
in their daily lives (DeCuir & Dixson, 2004; Dixson & Anderson, 2018;
Lynn & Dixson, 2013). The third category is that of composite narratives,
as described earlier in this section. The purposes of creating a composite
narrative are to expose and explain the ways in which subordination plays
out in everyday life; to push back against dominant views that continue to
privilege white people; and/or to be generative in providing an alternative,
more equal reality that currently does not exist under white supremacy
(Brayboy & Chin, 2019). Composite counter-stories are not mere fiction
in the traditional sense; rather, they incorporate multiple empirical data
sources within a sociopolitical and historical context (Bell, 1987; Ladson-
Billings, 1998; Solórzano & Yosso, 2002).

In the field of literacy, CRT has been increasingly used as a theoretical
framework for a variety of studies, particularly ones examining racial and

linguistic equity. Fewer studies have actually employed CRT methodologies, such as counter-storytelling (Willis, 2008). There has been work that features the voices of people of color (e.g., Haddix, McArthur, Muhammad, Price-Dennis, & Sealey-Ruiz, 2016), and further progress has been made through a special journal issue devoted to storytelling by early-career language and literacy scholars of color. This issue was published by the *Journal of Literacy Research* (Volume 49, Issue 4) to highlight the racialized experiences of the 2015–2017 STAR (Scholars of color Transitioning into Academic Research) cohort in the Literacy Research Association. The studies employed methodological approaches ranging from counter-storytelling to other forms of storytelling that push how we define racialized stories, and that draw on Black and African feminist traditions.

In particular, Gibbs Grey and Williams-Farrier (2017) "perform" counter-stories that invite readers into intimate dialogue regarding their experiences as Black female literacy scholars. Their stories highlighting white student resistance via end-of-semester evaluations and lack of participation function as analytic tools in understanding the challenges Black women scholars face when engaging in anti-racist pedagogy at historically white institutions. Jang (2017) also utilizes counter-stories to describe his racialized experiences as both an Asian and an international scholar. Through his stories, we gain access to personalized meanings of navigating deficit notions of foreignness, and we perceive how the "model minority" myth about Asian peoples pigeonholes them into narrow identities. Other literacy studies that have utilized counter-storytelling include the following: Han (2014) describes the linguistic racism and questioning of her professional expertise that she faced while teaching elementary literacy courses to white preservice teachers in a rural context; Johnson (2018) shares his journey in traveling to Ferguson, Missouri, shortly after the death of Trayvon Martin, and reflects on his experiences to theorize for a critical race English education (CREE) approach; and Lewis Ellison and Solomon (2019) tell the stories of a Black mother and two first-grade Black girls to problematize notions of a "digital divide" within Black communities, and to counter common deficit-based assumptions about Black students' digital literacies and access. Although this listing is only a sample, not a comprehensive summary of all literacy studies conducted utilizing counter-stories, the increasing usage of this methodology in the last decade in the field of literacy, with a special issue devoted to the stories of people of color in a major literacy research journal, shows promise for further usage of this approach in the future.

Intersectional Approaches

Intersectional approaches within critical race methodologies cross disciplines in order to fully examine the ways that race and racism are ingrained within U.S. society. Underpinning the interdisciplinary tenet of CRT is an acknowledgment of multiple forms of intersecting oppression.

Simultaneously, such interdisciplinary approaches must still draw on critical race legal scholarship, and underscore research paradigms that "explore the lives, successes, marginalization, and oppression of people of color both within and outside of the academy" (Tate, 1999, p. 268). The following intersectional CRT approaches accomplish these objectives. Please refer to additional citations for more reading on a specific approach.

• *Historical and archival analyses.* Such analyses emphasize the use of both historical knowledge and case law in analyzing historical events and presenting policy suggestions aimed at dismantling white supremacy within U.S. institutions (Donnor, 2013, 2019; Gillborn, 2013; Harris, 1995; Morris, 2001; Morris & Parker, 2019).

• *Tribal critical race theory (TribalCrit) and critical Indigenous research methodologies (CIRMs).* TribalCrit builds on CRT as it takes into account the history and pervasive effects of U.S. colonization on Indigenous communities and on their current experiences (Brayboy, 2005, 2013). CIRMs prioritize Indigenous knowledge, beliefs, and practices in the analysis process (Brayboy, Gough, Leonard, Roehl, & Solyom, 2012), and offer emancipatory possibilities for Indigenous groups (Brayboy & Chin, 2019).

• *Critical race ethnographies.* Critical race ethnographies are responses to critics who argue that counter-storytelling and the focus on marginalized voices are too subjective, and that they require readers to decide whether these stories are true or not true. Duncan (2017) proposes this CRT methodology as a specific extension of ethnographies in general; it draws on multi-ontological categories to study people in their own environments, and overlaps in epistemology and methods with counter-storytelling. (Duncan, 2002, 2005; Villenas & Deyhle, 1999).

• *CRT and participatory action research (PAR).* Dixson, James, and Frieson (2019) note that PAR draws from two major theoretical fields, as its name suggests: participatory research (Brydon-Miller & Maguire, 2009) and action research (Noffke, 1994). PAR seeks to disrupt the researcher/participant role by emphasizing the participation of people who have not been formally trained as researchers in the research process (Dixson et al., 2019; Noffke & Somekh, 2009). The intersection of CRT and PAR focuses on and values the experiential knowledge and voices of marginalized groups in naming racially oppressive structures within society.

• *Critical race feminist methodology.* This intersectional CRT methodology centers women of color in the analysis. Their experiences, stories, and *testimonios* take center stage within the methodology and analysis. Critical race feminist methodology represents the intersection of CRT and other bodies of feminist theoretical thought, such as Black feminism

(Crenshaw, 1989) and Chicana feminist theories (e.g., Alemán et al., 2013; Delgado Bernal, Pérez Huber, & Malagón, 2019; Delgado Bernal et al., 2012).

- *Critical race quantitative methodology (QuantCrit).* QuantCrit is a critical race methodology that focuses on how numbers can support equity, and that critiques/dismantles the ways in which numbers are used to defend and support oppression within a white supremacist society (Crawford et al., 2019). One key principle of QuantCrit is that numbers are neither objective or neutral; rather, data are shaped within the sociopolitical contexts in which they occur, and by researchers who are not neutral or objective in their search for data (Covarrubias & Vélez, 2013; Garcia, López, & Vélez, 2018). Numbers, therefore, cannot (as the common saying goes) "speak for themselves"; instead, they are shaped by the theoretical frames and bodies of knowledge that undergird the studies (Covarrubias, 2011). Hence, statistical research is not "value-free or politically neutral" (Crawford et al., 2019, p. 127). For a closer look into QuantCrit, see a special issue of *Race, Ethnicity and Education* (Volume 21, Issue 2).

- *Critical race mixed methodologies (CRMMs).* The usefulness of CRMMs is that as the field of CRT continues to grow, the methodologies for how we expose, explain, analyze, and propose solutions must grow with it. Although CRT has mainly taken qualitative approaches, QuantCrit as well as CRMM are now burgeoning areas. With the varied challenges related to race and racism in the United States, research methods that are responsive in solving the problems of inequity continue to be necessary (DeCuir-Gunby & Schutz, 2019). CRMMs provide frameworks for employing the most useful research methods, whether quantitative and/or qualitative, in addressing the structural issues of racism embedded in U.S. society and its institutions (DeCuir-Gunby & Schutz, 2019; DeCuir-Gunby & Walker-Devose, 2013).

- *Critical race spatial analysis.* This type of analysis uses maps in order to explore the intersection between race and space (Solórzano & Vélez, 2016). Using geographic information systems to create maps helps researchers toward a better understanding of the ways in which race and racism play central roles in the geohistorical/geopolitical realities of a community (Morrison, Ancy Annamma, & Jackson, 2017; Vélez & Solórzano, 2019).

ESSENTIAL FEATURES AND STANDARDS

CRT methodologies within literacy must center race and racism throughout the analysis process, and should seek to expose, explain, uncover, and undo the deeply embedded positions of racism and white supremacy within U.S. society and within the field of literacy studies (Parker & Lynn, 2002; Solórzano & Yosso, 2002). Moreover, discussions about racism must foreground its systemic nature, and focus on the structural changes needed at an institutional level (Parker & Lynn, 2002). This is significant, given the ways in which dominant, mainstream discourses have generally framed racism as individual rather than systemic—a framing that minimizes the role of structural racism (Omi & Winant, 1994). These dominant discourses, then, serve the interests of white supremacy, and propagate a reality in which the solution consists of changing individual persons' racist intentions instead of dismantling the systemic harm done to communities of color. Thus, literacy studies utilizing CRT methodologies should include the following: utilizing race and racism as these relate to CRT tenets in the analysis process; drawing on critical frameworks and intersectional epistemologies (e.g., feminism, Indigenous) to interpret data; illuminating how racism and white supremacy are inherently systemic; and discussing implications for institutional change. Winkle-Wagner, Sulé, and Maramba (2019) provide an example of incorporating CRT tenets in the analysis process through the selection of critical race-based themes or codes to analyze discourse in a qualitative policy study.

Equally important to the work of furthering CRT through intellectual and scholarly endeavors is the need for CRT methodologies to seek praxis (Gillborn, 2006; Roithmayr, 1999; Stovall, Lynn, Danley, & Martin, 2009). That is, the findings produced through studies should benefit the communities within which the research takes place, as well as include the communities in the research process itself. The purposes of CRT and its methodologies, after all, are to "define, expose, and address educational problems" (Parker & Lynn, 2002, p. 7), and to present radical solutions that will upend pervasive hierarchies and structures that continue to oppress people of color (Ladson-Billings & Tate, 1995). Lynn (2019) further exhorts scholars to push forward in the area of addressing educational problems by moving past "problem-posing," and to engage in "problem-solving" (p. x), which applies to both research and praxis.

Dixson and Anderson (2018) also address the issue of praxis in their article looking back on the 20+ years of CRT in the field of education since Ladson-Billings and Tate (1995) first introduced the theory. They note that while CRT has expanded beyond their imaginings, the question of how much impact the field has had on communities of color must be continually assessed. Dixson and Anderson agree with Gillborn (2006), Roithmayr (1999), Stovall (2013), and Yamamoto (1997) that CRT praxis is necessary—in other words, that researchers must move from the campus into the community in order to benefit communities of color. For example, Dixson and colleagues (2019) recount the ways in which they became "reluctant scholar activists" in their pursuit to "honor and serve" their participants and communities of color (p. 72). Derrick Bell himself contributed to CRT praxis by resigning from the University of Oregon when it chose not to hire an Asian American woman, and from Harvard University because it did not have any tenured faculty members who were Black women.

Finally, given the impetus behind the CRT tenets and the mandate for praxis, we propose that researcher positionality matters and is an essential feature and standard of critical race methodologies. This is especially true for white researchers conducting research among non-white people and communities. Kynard's (2010) counter-story casts light on the ways white researchers financially and socially benefit from conducting research in poor communities of color, yet fail to support the needs of students of color within their own departments. Willis (2008) contends that white researchers who do not deconstruct how their racial identity plays a role in their research are actually reifying whiteness as a normalized dominant status. Thus, white researchers telling the stories and counter-stories of communities of color have a particular obligation and responsibility to destabilize white supremacy, in contexts both inside and outside the academy.

QUESTIONS SUITABLE FOR CRITICAL RACE METHODOLOGIES

Critical race methodologies are focused on exposing, explaining, critiquing, and solving issues of inequities that stem from racism. Correspondingly, we now present a list of questions (though not an exhaustive one) suitable for this methodology in literacy research. The questions interrogate power structures related to race and racism, and focus on ways in which institutions and their actors are complicit with white-dominant norms. We also ask questions that provide space for members of marginalized communities who want to tell their own stories or have inside access. Finally, we pose questions that underscore the role of white supremacy—its intricate workings, the actors, and the researchers' positionality.

- In what ways and forms do white-dominant norms play out within literacy practices?
- What structural systems continue to promote a system that privileges white mainstream literacy and language practices over those of people of color?
- What can we learn from students of color (at all levels) and their experiential knowledge in regard to language and literacy practices?
- How do schools promote and privilege majoritarian literacy narratives that harm children of color?
- How can CRT tenets be used as analytic tools to examine, expose, and solve continued literacy-based inequities within public school systems?

- What roles do majoritarian views play in our understanding of language—its acquisition, processes, and learning—within and outside of school contexts?
- Who benefits from school literacy policies and practices, and who does not?
- What roles do teachers play in either dismantling or reinforcing white-dominant literacy norms in classroom spaces? And what tools and/or resources are used in accomplishing their work?
- What roles do literacy researchers and teacher educators in literacy play in dismantling or reinforcing white-dominant literacy norms in higher education? And what tools and/or resources are used in accomplishing their work?
- How does your research agenda benefit communities in which the research takes place?
- How does your positionality as a researcher shape your research methods and applications in the field?
- "Whose stories are privileged in educational contexts and whose stories are distorted and silenced?" (Solórzano & Yosso, 2002, p. 36)
- "What are the experiences and responses of those whose stories are often distorted and silenced?" (Solórzano & Yosso, 2002, p. 36)

EXEMPLAR OF COUNTER-STORYTELLING IN LITERACY RESEARCH

The exemplar we have selected for CRT methods is Carmen Kynard's *Harvard Educational Review* article, "From Candy Girls to Cyber Sista-Cipher: Narrating Black Females' Color-Consciousness and Counterstories in and out of School" (2010). Our selection of this piece is based on Solórzano and Yosso's (2002) definition and standards of critical race methods and counter-storytelling. We have specifically chosen a counter-storytelling exemplar, given its standing as a hallmark CRT method. Kynard's article focuses on the counter-stories of Black women in white-dominated higher educational spaces. Beyond meeting the criteria for counter-stories, her research utilizes these stories to give us a glimpse into the normalized racist experiences Black women face in white institutions, and also connects these stories to research documenting larger phenomena related to Black marginalization. In what follows, we divulge how her piece meets the criteria established by Solórzano and Yosso for counter-storytelling.

It should be noted that while Kynard methodologically locates this piece as a "narrative ethnography of sistahood," she does later in the article discuss her vignettes as "counterstories" that interrogate how systems of white supremacy punished the Black women in the "cyber hush harbor" (p. 45). More recently, when we asked her why she did not explicitly define counter-storytelling as the methodology she employed, she said that it was not considered a "real" method at that time, although it was her method of choice for the article (C. Kynard, personal communication, 2019). Kynard's piece was published in 2010, years after Solórzano and Yosso's (2002) original work on defining counter-stories—a fact that further illuminates the struggle for CRT methods to gain acceptance and legitimacy in traditional literacy research.

It Foregrounds Race/Racism in the Research Process and Offers Liberatory Solutions

Kynard opens her article with vignettes from her adolescence, when state-mandated school integration forced Kynard and other Black students to be bused into historically white schools. Survival in these newly diverse schools entailed forming social groups—hers was the Candy Girls (named after a popular New Edition song)—which mirrored her own racial, gender, and class experiences. Kynard draws on the Candy Girls' experiences and their intimate support network to teach us about contemporary forms of *hush harbors,* which were historically sites of resistance during African American enslavement. These spaces have been mainstays within the academic white spaces Kynard has traversed—in particular, the "cyber sista-cipher" group, which communicated virtually via an e-mail listserv. She shares these counter-stories to offer a new understanding of "schooling's processes of ethnic cleansing," and the ways Black women organize in resistance to them (p. 48). Race and racism, therefore, are foregrounded in her posing of this question: "What if school success is really—most of the time or even some of the time—about eradicating pan-African/black conscious identity and language or, at least, having to hide it and develop it somewhere else (which is still eradication)?" (p. 41). At the heart of her piece, Kynard sheds light on how racism and white supremacy govern the experiences of Black women in academic institutions.

Kynard uses her experiences at Champion State University (a pseudonym) to point to how racism pervades higher education in the research process. In particular, she calls out the researchers from her own department who were silent and inactive on matters related to the academic survival of students of color within their department, yet materially benefited from conducting research in poor communities of color. Instead, she offers an alternative ethical process tied to the governance of the institutional review board: Rather than merely checking for informed consent, an ethical process would involve checking in with the communities themselves and asking what has been done for them, as a form of accountability.

Other liberatory solutions she offers are tied to acknowledging the existence of hush harbor spaces. The world of hush harbors illuminate the spaces needed to support students of color, and to "teach working-class/working poor people alternate gendered and racialized roles in white institutions" (p. 33). Kynard argues that these spaces need to be part of historically white institutions, to function as a regular check on white-dominant norms, and to offer a liberatory space for people of color.

It Challenges Traditional Research Paradigms

Traditional paradigms regarding the culture and language of Black communities reflect deficit models (e.g., Bereiter & Engelmann, 1966). Linguists and sociolinguists have countered such models with a valuation of African American Language's (AAL's) linguistic legitimacy (Labov, 1972; Smitherman, 1977; Wolfram & Fasold, 1974) and rhetorical patterns (Smitherman, 1977). Despite decades of literature debunking deficit models, these models continue to thrive in society at large, based on their alignment with white supremacist notions of Black language and culture. Kynard draws on these theories to frame the discourse practices employed by the Candy Girls and the sista-cypher. She points out that research conducted by the American Institute for Research and the National Endowment for the Arts operationalized literacy as skills and behaviors for college students, producing a disconnect between the out-of-school literacies valued in K–12 literature and what should have been recognized as such for the sista-cypher. Kynard also draws on African American literacies (Richardson, 2003) to elucidate the unique worldview offered within AAL that the sista-cypher employed in responding to the daily microaggressions they experienced both inside and outside the university. The women in the sista-cypher further claimed their digital platform as a Black space by using AAL phonetics and spelling to identify themselves. For these reasons, Kynard points to the ways the members of the sista-cipher were "multiply silenced" (p. 35) for their race, class, and gender, as well as to the ways their discourse communities remained ignored and marginalized.

It Uses Interdisciplinary Knowledge to Understand Racialized, Classed, and Gendered Experiences as Strengths

While Kynard's article is written for an audience situated within the field of education, she draws on Black feminist theories to center and value the voices and collective experiences of Black females, as well as African American epistemologies to foreground the significance of hush harbors. The references to these sites in their contemporary forms draw on the historical knowledge of African American oppression in this country. Kynard also draws on historical and legal knowledge for the contextualization of the Candy Girls, as a group of Black female middle school students who were part of the aftereffects of state-sanctioned school integration. Kynard offers us localized understandings of the macro issues shaping the societal landscape at that time.

  Using such interdisciplinary knowledge, Kynard honors the racialized, classed, and gendered experiences of the Candy Girls and the sista-cypher as strengths. Kynard alludes to classed experiences the Candy Girls faced with "mothers [who] were single and worked long days and long nights" (p. 31), and to the sista-cypher's consisting of women who were all first-generation college students. She describes the Candy Girls as a "community of practice" whose members engaged in literary and artistic practices such as dance and rap, and who displayed leadership, loyalty, and creativity through the survival of a racially tense schooling environment. This was despite the white "bourgeois etiquette" norm that "actively disempowered" (p. 32) all the intersectional identities the Candy Girls held. Furthermore, Kynard credits their academic agency and excellence to their backgrounds with all-Black teachers throughout elementary school. This notion pushes back on dominant assumptions that school integration will offer better schooling for Black students.

CONCLUSION

Part and parcel of our lived realities are the narratives we tell ourselves to understand and interpret the world. CRT informs us that these narratives are not neutral and will be skewed toward mainstream ideologies that support white supremacy. In fact, research across methodologies often consists of analytic narratives that tell stories about the particularities of various people. For quite some time, communities of color have been central "subjects" of studies that distort their stories through a majoritarian lens, oftentimes unbeknownst to the people of color being studied. Yet what opportunity have people of color had to speak for themselves, as scholars of their own stories and experts in their own cultural contexts? Therein lies the power of CRT methodologies: to unleash data born out of the everyday lives of people of color through vantage points that have long been silenced. It is a travesty, therefore, that the stories (and studies) of people of color have only been believed in and considered "real" research when they have been narrated by white people, or in ways that reify hegemonic norms.

Solórzano and Yosso (2002) remind us, "If methodologies have been used to silence and marginalize people of color, then methodologies can also give voice and turn the margins into places of transformative resistance" (p. 37). The use and further development of CRT methodologies are thus active forms of resistance that offer a reimagination of our world, as it is currently known. This is particularly salient at the present historical juncture, when those running for the highest office in the United States broadcast majoritarian views of language. In 2015, during a Republican presidential primary debate, Donald Trump insisted on language "assimilation" when he stated, "This is a country where we speak English, not Spanish." In 2019 during a Democratic primary debate, Joe Biden announced that addressing the "word gap" was a key educational reform needed. These linguistically racist majoritarian views of language have long been debunked; yet society at large continues to privilege narratives that twist and marginalize the identities of people of color. The intricate workings of white supremacy never end, and continue to be recycled and repurposed to serve the interests of white people and their dominant language. The voices of people of color, then, must also speak their truths, and counter these dominant discourses that are oppressive. CRT methodologies, by centering people of color's voices and experiences, can foster new epistemologies that offer lifelines for both the tellers and hearers of these stories.

REFERENCES

Alemán, E., Delgado Bernal, D., & Mendoza, S. (2013). Critical race methodological tensions: Nepantla in our community-based praxis. In M. Lynn & A. Dixson (Eds.), *Handbook of critical race theory in education* (pp. 325–338). New York: Routledge.

Bell, D. (1980). Brown v. Board of Education and the interest-convergence dilemma. *Harvard Law Review, 93*(3), 518–533.

Bell, D. (1987). *And we are not saved: The elusive quest for racial justice.* New York: Basic Books.

Bell, D. (1992). *Faces at the bottom of the well: The permanence of racism.* New York: Basic Books.

Bereiter, C., & Engelmann, S. (1966). *Teaching disadvantaged children in the preschool.* Englewood Cliffs, NJ: Prentice-Hall.

Brayboy, B. M. J. (2005). Towards a tribal critical race theory in education. *The Urban Review, 37*(5), 425–446.

Brayboy, B. M. J. (2013). Tribal critical race theory: An origin story and future directions. In M. Lynn & A. D. Dixson (Eds.), *Handbook of critical race theory in education* (pp. 88–100). New York: Routledge.

Brayboy, B. M. J., & Chin, J. (2019). A match made in heaven: Tribal critical race theory and critical Indigenous research methodologies. In J. T. DeCuir-Gunby, T. K. Chapman, & P. A. Schutz (Eds.), *Understanding critical race research methods and methodologies* (pp. 51–63). New York: Routledge.

Brayboy, B. M. J., Gough, H. R., Leonard, R., Roehl, R. F., & Solyom, J. A. (2012). Reclaiming scholarship: Critical Indigenous research methodologies. In S. D. Lapan, M. T. Quartaroli, & F. J. Reimer (Eds.), *Qualitative research: An introduction to methods and design* (pp. 423–450). San Francisco: Jossey-Bass.

Brydon-Miller, M., & Maguire, P. (2009). Participatory action research: Psychology and social change. *Journal of Social Issues, 53*(4), 657–666.

Covarrubias, A. (2011). Quantitative intersectionality: A critical race analysis of the Chicana/o educational pipeline. *Journal of Latinos and Education, 10*(2), 86–105.

Covarrubias, A., & Vélez, V. (2013). Critical race quantitative intersectionality: An antiracist research paradigm that refuses to "let the numbers speak for themselves." In M. Lynn & A. D. Dixson (Eds.), *Handbook of critical race theory in education* (pp. 270–285). New York: Routledge.

Crawford, C. E., Demack, S., Gillborn, D., & Warmington, P. (2019). Quants and crits: Using numbers for social justice (or, how not to be lied to with statistics). In J. T. DeCuir-Gunby, T. K. Chapman, & P. A. Schutz (Eds.), *Understanding critical race research methods and methodologies* (pp. 125–137). New York: Routledge.

Crenshaw, K. W. (1989). Demarginalizing the intersection of race and sex: A Black feminist critique of antidiscrimination doctrine, feminist theory and antiracist politics. *University of Chicago Legal Forum, 1*(8), 139–167.

Crenshaw, K. W., Gotanda, N., Peller, G., & Thomas, K. (1996). *Critical race theory: The key writings that formed the movement.* New York: New Press.

DeCuir, J. T., & Dixson, A. D. (2004). So when it comes out, they aren't that surprised that it is there: Using critical race theory as a tool of analysis of race and racism in education. *Educational Researcher, 33*(5), 26–31.

DeCuir-Gunby, J. T., Chapman, T. K., & Schutz, P. A. (Eds.). (2019). *Understanding critical race research methods and methodologies.* New York: Routledge.

DeCuir-Gunby, J. T., & Schutz, P. A. (2019). Critical race mixed methodology: Designing a research study combining critical race theory and mixed methods research. In J. T. DeCuir-Gunby, T. K. Chapman, & P. A. Schutz (Eds.), *Understanding critical race research methods and methodologies* (pp. 166–179). New York: Routledge.

DeCuir-Gunby, J. T., & Walker-DeVose, D. C. (2013). Expanding the counterstory: The potential for critical race mixed methods studies in education. In M. Lynn & A. D. Dixson (Eds.), *Handbook of critical race theory in education* (pp. 248–259). New York: Routledge.

Delgado, R. (1989). Storytelling for oppositionists and others: A plea for narrative. *Michigan Law Review, 87*(8), 2411–2441.

Delgado, R., & Stefancic, J. (2013). *Critical race theory: The cutting edge.* Philadelphia: Temple University Press.

Delgado, R., & Stefancic, J. (2017). *Critical race theory: An introduction.* New York: New York University Press.

Delgado Bernal, D., Burciaga, R., & Flores Carmona, J. (2012). Chicana/Latina testimonio: Mapping the methodological, pedagogical, and political. *Equity and Excellence in Education, 45*(3), 363–372.

Delgado Bernal, D., Pérez Huber, L., & Malagón, M. C. (2019). Bridging theories to name and claim a critical race feminista methodology. In J. T. DeCuir-Gunby, T. K. Chapman, & P. A. Schutz (Eds.), *Understanding critical race research methods and methodologies* (pp. 13–23). New York: Routledge.

Dixson, A. D., & Anderson, C. R. (2018). Where are we?: Critical race theory in education 20 years later. *Peabody Journal of Education, 93*(1), 121–131.

Dixson, A. D., Chapman, T. K., & Hill, D. A. (2005). Extending the portraiture methodology. *Qualitative Inquiry, 11*(1), 16–26.

Dixson, A. D., James, A., & Frieson, B. L. (2019). Critical race theory, participatory research and social justice. In J. T. DeCuir-Gunby, T. K. Chapman, & P. A. Schutz (Eds.), *Understanding critical race research methods and methodologies* (pp. 64–75). New York: Routledge.

Donnor, J. K. (2013). Education as a property of whites: African Americans' continued quest for good schools. In M. Lynn & A. D. Dixson (Eds.), *Handbook of critical race theory in education* (pp. 195–203). New York: Routledge.

Donnor, J. K. (2019). Understanding the way of whiteness: Negrophobia, segregation, and legacy of white resistance to Black education in Mississippi. In J. T. DeCuir-Gunby, T. K. Chapman, & P. A. Schutz (Eds.), *Understanding critical race research methods and methodologies* (pp. 13–23). New York: Routledge.

Duncan, G. A. (2002). Critical race theory and method: Rendering race in ethnographic research. *Qualitative Inquiry, 8*(1), 83–102.

Duncan, G. A. (2005). Critical race ethnography in education: Narrative, inequality and the problem of epistemology. *Race, Ethnicity and Education, 8*(1), 93–114.

Duncan, G. A. (2017). Critical race ethnography in education: Narrative, inequality, and the problem of epistemology. In A. D. Dixson, C. K. Rousseau Anderson, & J. K. Donnor (Eds.), *Critical race theory in education: All God's children got a song* (pp. 65–86). New York: Routledge.

Espinoza, L. (1990). Masks and other disguises: Exposing legal academia. *Harvard Law Review, 103*, 1878–1886.

Garcia, N. M., López, N., & Vélez, V. N. (2018). QuantCrit: Rectifying quantitative methods through critical race theory. *Race, Ethnicity, and Education, 21*(2), 149–157.

Gibbs Grey, T., & Williams-Farrier, B. J. (2017). #Sippingtea: Two Black female literacy scholars sharing counter-stories to redefine our roles in the academy. *Journal of Literacy Research, 49*(4), 503–525.

Gillborn, D. (2006). Critical race theory and education: Racism and anti-racism in educational theory and praxis. *Discourse: Studies in the Cultural Politics of Education, 27*(1), 11–32.

Gillborn, D. (2013). The policy of inequity: Using CRT to unmask white supremacy in education policy. In M. Lynn & A. D. Dixson (Eds.), *Handbook of critical race theory in education* (pp. 129–139). New York: Routledge.

Guadalupe Valles, B., & Villalpando, O. (2013). A critical race policy analysis of the school-to-prison pipeline for Chicanos. In M. Lynn & A. D. Dixson (Eds.), *Handbook of critical race theory in education* (pp. 260–269). New York: Routledge.

Haddix, M., McArthur, S. A., Muhammad, G. E., Price-Dennis, D., & Sealey-Ruiz, Y. (2016). At the kitchen table: Black women English educators speaking our truths. *English Education, 48*(4), 380–395.

Han, K. T. (2014). Moving racial discussion forward: A counterstory of racialized dynamics between an Asian-woman faculty and white preservice teachers in traditional rural America. *Journal of Diversity in Higher Education, 7*(2), 126–146.

Harris, C. I. (1995). Whiteness as property. In K. Crenshaw, N. Gotanda, G. Peller, & K. Thomas (Eds.), *Critical race theory: The key writings that formed the movement* (pp. 292–302). New York: New Press.

Hopson, R. K., & Dixson, A. D. (Eds.). (2013). *Race, ethnography and education.* New York: Routledge.

Jang, B. G. (2017). Am I a qualified literacy researcher and educator?: A counter-story of a professional journey of one Asian male literacy scholar in the United States. *Journal of Literacy Research, 49*(4), 559–581.

Johnson, L. L. (2018). Where do we go from here?: Toward a critical race English education. *Research in the Teaching of English, 53*(2), 102–124.

Kynard, C. (2010). From Candy Girls to cyber sista-cipher: Narrating Black females' color-consciousness and counterstories in and out of school. *Harvard Educational Review, 80*(1), 30–52.

Labov, W. (1972). *Language in the inner city: Studies in the Black English vernacular.* Philadelphia: University of Philadelphia Press.

Ladson-Billings, G. (1998). Just what is critical race theory and what's it doing in a *nice* field like education? *International Journal of Qualitative Studies in Education, 1,* 7–24.

Ladson-Billings, G. (2000). Racialized discourses and ethnic epistemologies. In N. Denzin & Y. Lincoln (Eds.), *Handbook of qualitative research* (pp. 257–277). Thousand Oaks, CA: SAGE.

Ladson-Billings, G., & Tate, W. (1995). Toward a critical race theory of education. *Teachers College Record, 97*(1), 47–67.

Lewis Ellison, T., & Solomon, M. (2019). Counter-storytelling vs. deficit thinking around African American children and families, digital literacies, race, and the digital divide. *Research in the Teaching of English, 53*(3), 223–244.

Lynn, M. (2019). Moving critical race theory in education from a problem-posing mindset to a problem-solving orientation. In J. T. DeCuir-Gunby, T. K. Chapman, & P. A. Schutz (Eds.), *Understanding critical race research methods and methodologies* (pp. viii–xii). New York: Routledge.

Lynn, M., & Dixson, A. D. (Eds.). (2013). *Handbook of critical race theory in education.* New York: Routledge.

Lynn, M., Yosso, T. J., Solórzano, D. G., & Parker, L. (2002). Critical race theory and education: Qualitative research in the new millennium. *Qualitative Inquiry, 8*(1), 3–6.

Montoya, M. (1994). Mascaras, trenzas, y grenas: Un/masking the self while un/braiding Latina stories and legal discourse. *Chicano–Latino Law Review, 15,* 1–37.

Morris, J. E. (2001). Forgotten voices of African-American educators: Critical race perspectives on the implementation of a desegregation plan. *Educational Policy, 15*(4), 575–600.

Morris, J. E., & Parker, B. D. (2019). CRT in education: Historical/archival analyses. In J. T. DeCuir-Gunby, T. K. Chapman, & P. A. Schutz (Eds.), *Understanding critical race research methods and methodologies* (pp. 24–33). New York: Routledge.

Morrison, D., Ancy Annamma, S., & Jackson, D. D. (2017). *Critical race spatial analysis: Mapping to understand and address educational inequity.* Sterling, VA: Stylus.

Noffke, S. E. (1994). Action research: Towards the next generation. *Educational Action Research, 2*(1), 9–21.

Noffke, S. E., & Somekh, B. (Eds.). (2009). *The SAGE handbook of educational action research.* Thousand Oaks, CA: SAGE.

Omi, M., & Winant, H. (1994). *Racial formation in the U.S.: From the 1960s to the 1990s.* London: Routledge.

Parker, L. (1998). "Race is race ain't": An exploration of the utility of critical race theory in qualitative research in education. *International Journal of Qualitative Studies in Education, 11*(1), 43–55.

Parker, L. (2015). Critical race theory in education and qualitative inquiry: What each has to offer each other now? *Qualitative Inquiry, 21*(3), 199–205.

Parker, L., Deyhle, D., & Villenas, S. (Eds.). (1999). *Race is . . . race isn't: Critical race theory and qualitative studies in education.* Boulder, CO: Westview Press.

Parker, L., & Lynn, M. (2002). What's race got to do with it?: Critical race theory's conflicts with and connections to qualitative research methodology and epistemology. *Qualitative Inquiry 8*(1), 7–22.

Richardson, E. (2003). *African American literacies.* New York: Routledge.

Roithmayr, D. (1999). Introduction to critical race theory in educational research and praxis. In L. Parker, D. Deyhle, & S. Villenas (Eds.), *Race is . . . race isn't: Critical race theory and qualitative studies in education* (pp. 1–7). Boulder, CO: Westview Press.

Sablan, J. R. (2019). Can you really measure that?: Combining critical race theory and quantitative methods. *American Educational Research Journal, 56*(1), 178–203.

Smitherman, G. (1977). *Talkin' and testifyin': The language of Black America.* Boston: Houghton Mifflin.

Solórzano, D. G., & Vélez, V. (2016). Using critical spatial analysis to examine the Du Boisian color-line along the Alameda Corridor in Southern California. *Whittier Law Review, 27,* 423–437.

Solórzano, D. G., & Yosso, T. J. (2001). Critical race and LatCrit theory and method: Counter-storytelling. *Qualitative Studies in Education, 14*(4), 471–495.

Solórzano, D. G., & Yosso, T. J. (2002). Critical race methodology: Counter-storytelling as an analytical framework for education research. *Qualitative Inquiry, 8*(1), 23–44.

Stovall, D. (2013). "Fightin' the devil 24/7": Context, community, and critical race praxis in education. In M. Lynn & A. Dixson (Eds.), *Handbook of critical race theory in education* (pp. 289–301). New York: Routledge.

Stovall, D., Lynn, M., Danley, L., & Martin, D. (2009). Critical race praxis in education. *Race, Ethnicity and Education, 12*(2), 131–132.

Tate, W. F., IV. (1997). Critical race theory and education: History, theory, and implications. *Review of Research in Education, 22,* 195–247.

Tate, W. F., IV. (1999). Conclusion. In L. Parker, D. Deyhle, & S. Villenas (Eds.), *Race is . . . race isn't: Critical race theory and qualitative studies in education* (pp. 251–272). Boulder, CO: Westview Press.

Taylor, E., Gillborn, D., & Ladson-Billings, G. (2015). *Foundations of critical race theory in education.* New York: Routledge.

Vélez, V. N., & Solórzano, D. G. (2019). Critical race cartographies: Exploring map-making as anti-racist praxis. In J. T. DeCuir-Gunby, T. K. Chapman, & P. A. Schutz (Eds.), *Understanding critical race research methods and methodologies* (pp. 13–23). New York: Routledge.

Villenas, S., & Deyhle, D. (1999). Critical race theory and ethnographies challenging the stereotypes: Latino families, schooling, resilience and resistance. *Curriculum Inquiry, 29*(4), 413–445.

Williams, P. (1991). *The alchemy of race and rights: Diary of a law professor.* Cambridge, MA: Harvard University Press.

Willis, A. I. (2008). Critical race theory. In B. V. Street & N. H. Hornberger (Eds.), *Encyclopedia of language and education: Vol. 2. Literacy* (pp. 15–28). New York: Springer.

Winkle-Wagner, R., Sulé, V. T., & Maramba, D. C. (2019). Analyzing policy critically: Using critical race theory to analyze college admissions policy discourse. In R. Winkle-Wagner, J. Lee-Johnson, & A. N. Gaskew (Eds.), *Critical theory and qualitative data analysis in education* (pp. 193–203). New York: Routledge.

Wolfram, W., & Fasold, R. W. (1974). *The study of social dialects in American English*. Englewood Cliffs, NJ: Prentice-Hall.

Yamamoto, E. K. (1997). Critical race praxis: Race theory and political lawyering practice in the post-civil rights America. *Michigan Law Review, 95*(4), 821–900.

CHAPTER 6

Research Methods Unique to Digital Contexts

AN INTRODUCTION TO VIRTUAL ETHNOGRAPHY

Christine Greenhow
Sarah Galvin
K. Bret Staudt Willet

INTERNET TRENDS SHAPING LITERACIES, LITERACY RESEARCH METHODS, AND CONCEPTIONS OF SCHOLARSHIP

Ninety-five percent of American teens (ages 13–17) own a smartphone, and 45% report being online almost constantly. Another 44% are online multiple times per day. Nearly 90% of teens repeatedly find themselves in digital spaces on a daily basis.
—ANDERSON AND JIANG (2018)

We live in an age where online social networking is the dominant activity among young Americans during out-of-school leisure time (Anderson & Jiang, 2018). The proliferation of the Internet, and particularly of its emerging forms of social media, is shaping how people learn, work, play, communicate, share information, and spend their time and money. Human desires and changing practices, in turn, are shaping the cultural, social, and technological landscape. Indeed, the 21st century is witnessing a renaissance, in which young people especially are creating more, sharing more, advocating more, and communicating more in their online everyday lives (Rideout & Robb, 2018). They are pooling their time, effort, and knowledge into the publishing of potentially beneficial and revolutionary online resources (e.g., Wikipedia), with tremendous consequences for education and literacy education (Greenhow, 2008, 2010b; Greenhow, Galvin, Brandon & Askari, 2020; Greenhow & Gleason, 2012). Educational research today continues to question what should be valued as literacy, what should be valued as literacy in the classroom, and how literacies are evolving from and within virtual spaces (Ito et al., 2009; Lankshear & Knobel, 2006; Leu, Kinzer, Coiro, Castek, & Henry, 2017; Mills, 2010; Moje, 2016).

Not surprisingly, sectors outside education are considering how to harness this "cognitive surplus" (Shirky, 2008) to advantage on both a national and a global scale. Businesses are inquiring into how to tap their employees' "social connections, institutional memories and special skills—knowledge that large, geographically dispersed companies often have a difficult time obtaining" (Stone, 2008, p. C2)—by using social networking software to connect a company's employees into a single private Web forum (Gratton, 2007). News media are increasingly incorporating viewer participation in the form of online comments and testimonials, independently produced videos, and citizen journalist blog entries to enhance the truth and spread of centrally produced stories such as CNN's documentary *Black in America* (Nelson, 2008). Of course, evident in U.S. presidential election campaigns since 2008 has been a new style of "Netroots" politics: "open-sourced and inclusive, multi-racial and multicultural" (Sheehy, 2008, p. 79), in which potential voters don't just consume campaign propaganda, but help to write and disseminate it via online meet-ups, blogs, videos, and social networks.

The convergence of economic, social, and technological trends, as these examples suggest, warrants a reenvisioning of both the goals and means of production. In literacy education, this will require substantial inquiry and understanding of how new technological affordances and students' uses and needs reshape traditional literacy education agendas, pedagogies and the content that gets taught. This reimagining is already underway within organizations such as the National Council of Teachers of English (NCTE) and the International Literacy Association (ILA), formerly the International Reading Association (IRA). These organizations have observed that "new global employees engage with a technology-driven, diverse, and quickly changing 'flat world' " (NCTE, 2007, p. 14) to question traditional learning objectives and consider newly desired competencies (IRA, 2009; National Center on Education and the Economy, 2006). Students must now be able to navigate, read and compose in digital spaces to be successful in school and the workforce—practices that research highlights as different from, and uniquely complex compared to, traditional literacies (see, e.g., studies of hypertext and the Internet as an ill-structured domain; Coiro & Dobler, 2007; DeSchryver, 2014). See also Weinberger (2011) and Wolf (2018) for continued discussions of how technology is transforming our thinking and literacies. The NCTE (2018) is tackling these issues, posing questions that open up conceptualizations of *literacy* and possibilities for research, such as these: How has technology pluralized literacy, and what new skills do these new literacies require? How have the consumption and production of texts (including new media) changed with technology, and how can we best prepare students to become critical readers and composers?

As literacies evolve across a dynamic sociotechnical landscape, our scholarly practices and corresponding methods for literacy research also need to evolve in order to adequately capture, describe, and interpret these literacies (Greenhow, 2009; Greenhow, Robelia, & Hughes, 2009). What kinds of methods are needed? How are these unique to digital contexts? In this chapter, we highlight *virtual ethnography* as an evolving method uniquely suited to emerging and experienced scholars interested in researching and cultivating new literacies in digital contexts. The following sections first provide a survey of research methods for digital contexts; this is followed by a definition of virtual ethnography, locating it within prominent definitions of ethnography and the discourse surrounding the Internet's impact on identity, society, and culture that "bring into sharp relief assumed and invisible epistemologies and practices of inquiry" (Baym & Markham, 2009, p. vii). Next, we discuss questions and claims particularly suited to the application of virtual ethnographic methods in literacy research before turning to a discussion of methodological quality and rigor. The chapter concludes with examples of virtual ethnography for new and seasoned researchers seeking to adapt and apply this approach.

SURVEY OF METHODS FOR DIGITAL CONTEXTS

In the years since the second edition of this handbook was published, the number and scope of research methods for digital contexts have proliferated. Hewson (2017) has categorized these new approaches to Internet-mediated research as *obtrusive* (in which researchers interact with participants and data are largely self-reported) or *unobtrusive* (in which participants' data are collected through observation). Hewson has noted the potential of Internet-mediated research methods to expand the scope of unobtrusive approaches in particular because of the readily accessible *digital traces* left behind by numerous forms of online activity.

Hine (2017) notes several benefits of ethnographic research conducted in online settings, such as "demonstrating the complex social nature of Internet-based interactions and enabling us to explore the new cultural formations that emerge online" (p. 401). Researchers have studied ethnographic phenomena, including—but not limited to—the teaching of discourse patterns and community expectations in a video-game-related fan website supported by online discussion forums (Lammers, 2013); religious education teachers' professional identity development through engagement with Facebook groups and pages (Robson, 2018); the development of professional academic identity through scholars' participation on Twitter (Stewart, 2016); and young people's formal and informal learning in and through Twitter (Greenhow & Gleason, 2012).

Literacies are changing rapidly, as the technologies available are constantly changing. Within changing contexts, meanings are negotiated, shifting from space to space, person to person, moment to moment. The emphasis is on understanding the situated nature of literacy practices and the ways that membership in a particular social group is signaled (words, actions, values, and beliefs) (Gee, 1996). The writer of multimodal texts is in essence a designer "assembling according to one's designs" (Kress, 2003, p. 6), which allows meaning to be distributed across different modes. Assemblage composition— the remixing and repurposing of text pieces or media to create something new—in multimodal formats adds weight to texts' situated contexts: Meanings become layers of what text pieces *were* with what the new assembled text *is* (Yancey & McElroy, 2017). For example, various remixed media come together to create viral video clips that are humorous, but may also carry political or social significance to groups of viewers. Multimodal texts can also be interactive, as users can "write back"—further blurring the lines between/ among authorship, readership, production, and consumption, and requiring new skills, sensibilities, social practices, and roles for researchers.

What constitute literacy research methodologies in a world where data are continuously updated and can be collected around the clock, across the globe, without the costs (e.g., time, transcription errors) associated with more traditional methods of research? As literacy researchers, we need new competencies for conducting research in collaborative digital contexts; in developing these, we may find ourselves shifting not only our notions of *literacy* and *method,* but our fundamental ideas of scholarship and sense of our own identities. For instance, *social scholarship*—a practice being debated within library sciences, education, communications, and other disciplines (Cohen, 2007; Taraborelli, 2008)—applies Web 2.0 capabilities to change the ways in which academic writing is accomplished within social networks. It connects traditional, formal scholarship practices such as writing a research article with more informal, social Web-based practices such as posting unfinished writing in an online collaborative space and inviting readers to comment or even contribute (Greenhow & Gleason, 2014). Using social media tools such as Diigo and Pinterest, researchers can compile, annotate, recommend, and share resources (e.g., websites, journal articles, books, and contacts), and usher in new scholarly reading and writing practices (e.g., Dennen, Cates, & Bagdy, 2017; Gao, 2013). Another example of social scholarship is the Literacy, Equity + Remarkable Notes (LEARN) program, a "connected learning" effort (National Writing Project, 2018). LEARN uses a hashtag, #MarginalSyllabus, and a social annotation platform, Hypothes.is, to prompt and sustain conversations about literacy and equity issues. One benefit of such forms of social scholarship is that they "provide multiple ways to contribute to a collective learning experience (e.g., through textual response, personal experience, rhetorical response, intertextual connection, and more) and become the site for research on teaching" (Greenhow, Gleason, & Staudt Willet, 2019, p. 995).

AN INTRODUCTION TO VIRTUAL ETHNOGRAPHY

> Understanding the boringness and routineness of everyday Internet
> research is captivating and important work. One of the reasons for its
> importance is that research into digital literacies will, one hopes, yield
> richer understandings of non-digital literacies as well. One of our current
> limitations in achieving this kind of cross-fertilization of theory building
> is to confront . . . some of the haunting dichotomies: computer-mediated
> versus face-to-face, online versus offline, virtual versus real, and in the
> new literacy studies, in school versus out of school. How do we work
> toward building knowledge that might take Internet practice out of the
> exotic and assert their everydayness and their qualities of the *quotidian?*
> —LEANDER (2008, p. 33)

Early ethnographers, writing in the late 19th and early 20th centuries and
sprung from Western traditions, were drawn to exploring the "exotic other-
ness" of non-Western societies (Heath, 1983). By contrast, in the 21st century, studying the "boringness" of one's own culture, and oneself as part of
that culture—especially in the presence of rapid technological change—is
necessary, important, and (we hope) captivating work for literacy researchers (Patton, 2002, p. 84).

Virtual ethnography provides a particularly powerful tool in this
regard. To introduce it, we must first briefly review basic tenets of ethnography. Victoria Purcell-Gates's (2011) definition of *ethnography* is especially useful:

> Literacy researchers who operate out of a theoretical frame that views
> literacy as cultural practice are particularly drawn to ethnography as
> a methodological tool . . . ethnography is grounded in theories of cul-
> ture and allow researchers to view literacy development, instruction,
> learning and practices as it occurs naturally in sociocultural contexts
> . . . to explore and come to understand phenomena about which little is
> known . . . ethnographic consumers can use [these ethnographic find-
> ings] to enhance their own understandings of similar actors and con-
> texts. (p. 135)

Similarly, Patton (2002, p. 81) defines ethnography as the study of *culture,* or the collective set of patterns and beliefs that constitute standards
for decision-making and action. LeCompte and Schensul (1999) assert,
"Ethnography generates or builds theories of culture—or explanations of
how people think, believe, and behave—that are situated in local time and
space" (p. 8). Thus, appropriate questions for ethnographic research include
these (Anderson-Levitt, 2006; Patton, 2002; Purcell-Gates, 2004): What is
the culture of this group? What is happening, why, how, and what does it
look like? What does this mean to the different actors who make up the
situation? What are the layers of context surrounding this phenomenon?
How does my own experience of this culture connect with or offer insights?

Traditionally, ethnographers have used methods of *participant obser-vation,* which typically entails intensive *fieldwork,* in which the investigator is immersed in the culture under study (Patton, 2002, p. 81; see also Purcell-Gates, 2004, 2011). However, there is considerable variation in how these methods are interpreted and carried out in practice (Atkinson & Hammersley, 1994), and notions of *participation* and *field* have been problematized with the emergence of the Internet and digital contexts for research. For instance, how much the researcher is known by those studied (e.g., by all, only some, or no subjects in the case of a "lurking" researcher implementing unobtrusive methods), and how much the researcher participates and adopts the orientation of insider or outsider, will vary considerably.

Thus, arising from the ethnographic tradition, *virtual ethnography* or *digital ethnography* is an interpretive method for studying the dynamic culture of online communities or "virtual worlds" (Boellstorff, Nardi, Pearce, & Taylor, 2012; Hine, 2000, 2005). Its relevance for the field of literacy research can be traced to its roots in the 1990s, with the increasing mainstream adoption of the Internet. Researchers within computer-mediated communication, science, and technology circles and other fields sought to understand the Internet as a *tool*; as a *place* where one could shape relationships, identities, and so forth apart from the material world; and, eventually, as a *way of being* (Jones, 1995, 1997; Markham, 1998). Working from a variety of disciplinary traditions, virtual ethnographers have examined human relationships (Carter, 2005), social relations (Hine, 2000), and identity (Thomas, 2007; Turkle, 1995). For a more complete historical overview, see Christine Hine's *Virtual Ethnography* (2000), which discusses the schools of thought and issues that are foundational to the development of this method.

Moreover, virtual ethnography, like ethnography generally, relies on *mixed methods* approaches (see Onwuegbuzie & Mallette, 2011). It may combine more commonly known qualitative procedures for studying literacy, such as interviews, observations, think-alouds, focus groups, and document analysis, with qualitative and quantitative procedures appropriate to studying subjects within online contexts. For example, procedures important for documenting and capturing communication, online reading comprehension, and interactions within digital contexts include screenshot captures, monitoring of screen moves, eye tracking, recording of Internet usage statistics (e.g., Facebook or Google Analytics), online interviews, online focus groups, archived transcripts of online speech, and social network analysis. These have all been employed by literacy researchers applying virtual ethnography to explore, for example, World of Warcraft (Steinkuehler, 2006), Schome Park (Gillen, 2009), or Facebook (Greenhow & Robelia, 2009b) as both sites of literacy practices and new literacies in and of themselves.

That said, Leander's quotation at the opening of this section is cautionary; the "dichotomies" between computer-mediated and face-to-face,

real and virtual, online and offline, and in-school and out-of-school contexts are categorical conveniences at best, and harmful limitations to
research, at worst. The characteristics that distinguish ethnographies from
other methodologies—for example, ethnography is carried out in naturalistic settings rather than a laboratory; involves intimate face-to-face interactions with participants; presents an accurate reflection of participants'
perspectives and behaviors; and uses inductive, interactive, and recursive
data collection and analytic strategies to build local and cultural theories
(LeCompte & Schensul, 1999, p. 9)—must necessarily be renegotiated
in conducting virtual literacy ethnography (Gillen, 2009). For instance,
bounding the research context to the "online community" despatializes
notions of community, focusing on cultural processes rather than physical
space; however, this can also unduly minimize connections with offline life
when, in fact, our everyday literacies integrate online and offline contexts
seamlessly. Taking a *connective* approach to virtual ethnography (Hine,
2000; Leander, 2008) allows one to conceptualize the space for research as
"the space of flows" (flows of people, information, etc.), organized around
connection rather than location. This is important because it enables meaningful exploration of online–offline connections—for example, what does
the traversal of space (or not) mean to the participants, and what does
it accomplish?—rather than assuming the online–offline boundary. Similarly, applied to the study of literacy, the connective approach to virtual
ethnography is important because it "works the tension" between treating
digital literacy practices as fascinating, worthy of study, and unique, and,
on the other hand, "as flowing within and interconnected to streams of
other literacy practices, material culture, traditional media, movements of
people, identity practices, and social construction of technologies" (Leander, 2008, p. 34). Virtual ethnographic methods attend to the layers of
context and their interrelationships surrounding literacy practices (Purcell-
Gates, 2011).

QUESTIONS PARTICULARLY SUITED
TO VIRTUAL ETHNOGRAPHY

'Ethnographic' characterises a certain commonality of interest in
capturing the manifold dimensions of (new) literacy practices . . . for
those who practise virtual ethnography with particular attention to
literacy practices . . . there is an opening then to . . . applying diverse
interpretive methods and reflexive understandings to the meaning-
making practices of a virtual community, particularly attending to
the practices of authoring and reading written, multi-modal texts.
—GILLEN (2009, pp. 66–67)

Virtual ethnography is a methodology particularly well suited to researching literacy as tool, place, and way of being (Steinkuehler, Black, & Clinton,

2005). With the rapid pace of social, economic, and technological change, the concepts of *literacy* and of *being literate* are in a constant state of flux. Virtual ethnography offers a framework for systematic inquiry into literacy phenomena that are continuously changing or about which little is known. Although this list is by no means exhaustive, some questions appropriate for literacy research applying virtual ethnographic methods include the following:

- What literacy practices (e.g., forms and functions) are happening here, why, and how? And what are their essential characteristics?
- How do people understand or make sense of their digital experiences? What role or significance do these practices play in their lives?
- What roles do different languages, script systems, images, music, or other forms of communication play?
- How do language and modes of participation develop over time?
- How are digital literacy practices used to perform identity and social networks?
- Are online literacy practices experienced as different from ones that are offline, school-based, and so on? And, if so, how?
- How does my own experience of this connect with or offer insights?

ISSUES AND STANDARDS FOR QUALITY IN VIRTUAL ETHNOGRAPHY

> Virtual ethnography is a promising approach to studying (new) literacies in everyday life. It acknowledges and seeks to delineate complex literacy phenomena in digital contexts and beyond. Moreover, it can serve as a useful precursor to more focused inquiry and to other methodologies such as formative and design experiments.
> —Reinking and Bradley (2004)

Numerous scholars have debated the topic of quality in educational research. For instance, Freeman, deMarrais, Preissle, Roulston, and St. Pierre (2007), writing in *Educational Researcher,* argued for steps toward ensuring quality of evidence in qualitative research. They called for more thorough description of research designs and methods, including greater transparency in how researchers access and enter the research setting, and in how they select, collect, and analyze data. In writing up results, researchers should adequately demonstrate the relationship between claims and data and render a thoughtful consideration, or balancing, of the relative strengths and limitations of their methodological decisions and interpretations. Novice literacy scholars, especially, will benefit from reviewing these and similar guidelines for ensuring quality in the research process.

Beyond these general guidelines, Purcell-Gates (2004, 2011) has articulated well the competencies needed for conducting ethnographic research.

These include sharp observational skills, as well as the abilities to shape theory; to understand the perspectives of others; to write engagingly and vividly; to think generatively and analytically; and to adhere strictly to rules for rigorous data collection, data management, and data analysis.

Principles of Virtual Ethnography

Considering the conduct of virtual ethnography, Hine (2000, p. 63) lists six principles that are useful for conceptualizing this method and adapting it to one's research goals in reflexive and rigorous ways. These are paraphrased here for our purposes:

- Virtual ethnography is used to render the use of the Internet, and its new technologies, as *problematic*: The *status* of these technologies as literacy forms and functions, as ways of communicating, as sites of literacy practices, is accomplished (rather than predefined) in the ways in which they are used, interpreted, and reinterpreted.
- Interactive media such as the Internet can be understood as both cultures and cultural artifacts. Privileging one or the other perspective leads to an impoverished view.
- The concept of the field site is questioned. Concentration on flow and connectivity, rather than on location and boundary, serves as an organizing principle for inquiry.
- Boundaries are not assumed a priori, but interrogated through the course of study.
- Immersion in the setting is only partially achieved. Engagement with mediated contexts fits in with other interactions and activities of both the ethnographer and participants.
- Technology enables relationships, including researcher–participant relationships, to be intermittent or sustained across temporal and spatial divides. All forms of interaction are ethnographically valid, not just face-to-face interaction. Thus, the intimate, face-to-face interaction with participants often assumed in ethnographic research is problematized, and indeed often not possible, in virtual ethnography.

Applying virtual ethnography successfully is labor-intensive. To do it well requires inductive, interactive, and recursive data collection and analysis. Understanding of language and literacy *in situ* warrants the researcher's role as participant observer, but this can mean that the researcher is contributing to the construction of text and literacy practices "in the field." Performing rigorous virtual ethnography requires constant reflection and sensitivity to one's role in the culture under study and in the construction of cultural artifacts.

Methodological and Ethical Issues in Internet Research

We now turn to highlighting briefly some of the issues in conducting virtual ethnography, as a form of Internet research, that are worth considering at the outset. (For a more complete discussion, see Markham & Baym, 2009.) Indeed, the expansion of the Internet and the rise to mainstream prominence of social media (from 2003 to the present) have helped bring about four major transformations that affect the choice of research foci, engagement with research fields, and design and conduct of qualitative inquiry: (1) media convergence, (2) mediated identities, (3) redefinitions of social boundaries, and (4) transcendence of geographical boundaries (Baym & Markham, 2009, p. x). These trends make virtual ethnography an especially apt and important tool for the literacy researcher's toolkit, but also raise implementation issues.

First, media convergence, evident in the combination and collision of face-to-face conversation, telephones, radio, television, and film within single hand-held mobile devices, challenges the traditional distinctions between reading and writing, speaking and listening, and digital and nondigital communication that have partially ordered the foci and sites of literacy research.

Second, the mediation of identities, distributed and produced through multiple media, makes understanding one's participants, their perspectives, and their self-expressions an increasingly complex task. "When conceptualizing, defining, protecting, interviewing, or observing the subject of inquiry, tradition dictates that the research participants have demographically verifiable characteristics" (Baym & Markham, 2009, p. x); discerning the truth or reliability of participants is problematic in studying online–offline communities, where identity construction and playing with identity are central features.

Third, the shifting nature of public and private, highlighted by newer Web technologies and social media, challenges the researcher's ability to formulate clear boundaries for the research field, to define engagement in the field, and to obtain informed consent. For instance, in an online social network site it may be impossible to obtain informed consent from all the individuals who are writing, reading, chatting online, and invited into the site, with clear consequences for the dynamic content under study.

Fourth, people in today's digitally mediated world can communicate and interact presumably anytime, anywhere, without necessarily occupying the same geographic and/or temporal space. Researchers cannot always simply restrict a study to a physically grounded site or, in the case of literacy research, to face-to-face conversation or the printed page. Limiting the study of literacies to digital context and the study of place fails to represent adequately its cultural complexity (Hine, 2015, p. 10).

Just as the Internet can be understood as both ways of conducting social interactions (cultures) and products of those interactions (cultural artifacts) (Hine, 2000), so too virtual ethnography can be viewed as both a method and a product. When we are considering rigor in virtual ethnography, therefore, we need to consider how credible and transferable the researcher's presentation of the ethnography seems, as well as its apparent utility for an audience, such as the participants in the online community being researched, others interested in the phenomena, and other researchers adapting the methods (Hine, 2000). As mentioned above, we can judge the credibility of a virtual ethnographic work by looking at how well (or not well) the researcher has described the details of the ethnographic process, maintained a critical stance toward his or her own work, and returned to the field for feedback and analysis. For instance, has the researcher sufficiently described how access to and entry into the field of study were negotiated, including a critical examination of his or her roles as participant and observer both online and offline? Has the researcher demonstrated critical thinking in the formulation of boundaries for the research field and engagement in the field, resisting simple dichotomies and predefined limits? Were the field of study and the relevant background context (e.g., history, culture, technical architecture) sufficiently described that readers can situate themselves within it? This scene setting will often involve visual images of the online community and possibly hyperlinks, embedded videos, or other multimedia with which readers can interact if the ethnography is published online. We can judge how well the virtual ethnography transfers, or seems similar enough to other cases to illuminate them, by examining how clearly the methods of data collection, data management, and analyses were described and interrogated. For instance, did the researcher not only describe his or her data collection and analysis procedures, but also demonstrate a healthy skepticism toward methodological decisions, underlying assumptions, and interpretations? Was the digital context sufficiently and effectively mined for data, and where multiple forms of online data were available and continuously updating, how well did the researcher justify the choice of data sources? Did the researcher return results to the field of study, such as an online community, and describe how emerging ideas were tested and alternatives explored? Does the virtual ethnography appear to be an authentic account, and does it present insights that seem useful to those studied and to the world at large? These questions are by no means exhaustive, and not always applicable (e.g., returning results to an online community made up of young children would likely be inappropriate); they just indicate some of the marks of quality in virtual ethnography.

EXEMPLARS OF VIRTUAL ETHNOGRAPHY

Examples of virtual ethnography in literacy studies are gaining in popularity. A persistent theme in this chapter, however, is the need to resist oversimplified demarcations and superficial boundaries, and to move toward a more open and integrative approach. Literacy researchers who seek to employ ethnographic methods will gain from recognizing and collaborating with relevant research and theory occurring outside of language and literacy departments in the fields of communication (Holloway & Valentine, 2001), science and technology studies (Hine, 2000), cultural studies (Wilson, 2006), and information sciences (Ito et al., 2009), to name a few.

Next, we describe three ethnographic projects in language and literacy that apply virtual ethnographic methods. We chose two published studies to serve as exemplars because (1) the work was published recently in a well-regarded literacy journal; (2) the researchers demonstrated many of the elements of quality in virtual ethnographic research described above; and/or (3) the ethnographic findings have been recognized as significant to the field of literacy, digital media, and learning. Interestingly, a search in the contents of three prominent literacy journals—*Reading Research Quarterly, Journal of Adult and Adolescent Literacy,* and *Journal of Research in Reading*—revealed only a handful of articles from 2003 to 2019 (*N* = 13) employing virtual ethnography or some variation thereof (e.g., Black, 2005; Chandler-Olcott & Mahar, 2003; Gillen, 2009; Guzzetti & Foley, 2014; Jacobs, 2004; Leander, 2003; Luke, 2003; Moje et al., 2004; Wade & Fauske, 2004). Although virtual ethnography as a research method has been around for over a decade, its use in literacy studies is nascent and evolving (Lammers, 2016; Wargo, 2017). The two published studies we have selected are notable for their exploration of literacy practices and youth-initiated, emerging digital contexts (i.e., massively multiplayer online game worlds [Steinkuehler, 2006, 2007] and a three-dimensional virtual world [Gillen, 2009]). Furthermore, both studies embraced a connective approach, resisting simple dichotomies between online and offline or in-school and out-of-school practices in favor of the relationships and understandings across settings and media. Finally, we reflect upon our own work in studying the literacy practices of low-income, urban high school students and college students in naturally occurring online social network sites and a social networking application, respectively. For additional examples of virtual ethnography in literacy studies, see Lam's (2004) examination of digital literacy practices among immigrant youth in the United States, and Leander and McKim's (2003) tracing of adolescent practices across online and offline spaces.

Constance Steinkuehler (2006, 2007) applied virtual ethnographic techniques and Hutchins's (1995) notions of *cognitive* ethnography to studying a massively multiplayer online game called Lineage. She sought to understand the literacy practices that constituted young people's game play *within* the game (e.g., transcripts on online social interaction, in-game letters) and *beyond* the game (e.g., online game forums, created fan sites, and fan fiction). On the basis of her research, she argues against popular contempt for video games as replacing literacy activities. She suggests instead that a more accurate, evidence-based, and generative framing for educators and literacy researchers may be found in viewing game play as a "constellation" of literacy activities. She draws on Gee's (1996) notions of discourses to illuminate the complexities and manifold dimensions of gamers' literacy practices.

Julia Gillen (2009) also applied techniques of virtual ethnography to examine the multidimensional literacy practices of teenagers in Schome Park, an out-of-school project involving use of a (Teen) Second Life three-dimensional virtual world. As Steinkuehler did in her 2-year study, Gillen took a longitudinal approach (15 months) to analyzing the meaning-making practices of the virtual community. Specifically, she attended to the practices of authoring and reading written, multimodal texts, and analyzed data from various communicative channels: chat logs, wiki postings (including images captured "in-world" to record events), forum postings, in-world sensor measurements (of how many people were in-world and where, every minute), and field notes. Like Steinkuehler (2006, 2007), too, she argues for a more fruitful framing of adolescent literacy practices within and beyond popular-culture-inspired spaces, and against "overly dichotomised boundaries between new literacies and those more established" (Gillen, 2009, p. 67).

Both Gillen (2009) and Steinkuehler (2006, 2007) also demonstrated an adaptive approach to applying virtual ethnographic techniques. In both cases, the authors had to synthesize theory and methods to cultivate a research design that would work for their specific questions and purposes. As Hine (2000) and others have mentioned, there is no precise formula for virtual ethnographers to carry out—only detailed accounts of the journeys others have taken, the methodological decisions they have made, with what implementation issues and outcomes.

Finally, we conclude with a few reflections from our own work in taking a virtual ethnographic stance to understanding the literacy practices of different adolescent subgroups within and beyond online social networking sites (SNS) such as MySpace (Greenhow & Robelia, 2009a, 2009b; Greenhow, Walker, & Kim, 2009), and an open-source social networking application designed and implemented within Facebook for environmental education purposes (Greenhow, 2010a, 2010b). In both projects, the goals were to examine what was happening from the participants' perspectives. To do so required negotiating the boundaries of participant observation. For instance, to begin to identify students' perspectives, it was necessary to learn the sociotechnical features being used, and especially the ways to manipulate default settings and code (e.g., "pimp my profile") as the participants did. Gaining access to the dynamically updating network of SNS pages meant requesting "friend" status from our participants, and documenting complex series of decisions with respect to what we regarded as "public" versus "private" or "semiprivate" but usable under the informed consent process. In addition, strict adherence to rules for rigorous data collection, data management, and data analysis—as Purcell-Gates (2004) argues for in ethnographic research—became challenging in practice, as online comments, votes, chat transcripts, uploaded song lyrics, tagged images, and background layouts and graphics were seemingly transforming themselves minute by minute. Capturing, charting, and interpreting the nature and development of literacy practices as these were occurring forced us to come face to face with our own time and data management limitations and with life beyond the network. Such issues are the costs of doing virtual ethnography. The benefits are a more nuanced view of established literacy practices and those on the horizon, greater cross-fertilization with other fields, advancement of methods well suited to digital contexts, and a sense of ourselves as literacy scholars who are conversant in changing times.

REFERENCES

Anderson, M., & Jiang, J. (2018). Teens, social media and technology 2018 (Pew Research Center). Retrieved from *www.pewinternet.org/2018/05/31/teens-social-media-technology-2018*.

Anderson-Levitt, K. (2006). Ethnography. In J. Green, G. Camilli, & P. Elmore (Eds.), *Handbook of complementary methods in education research* (pp. 279–295). Mahwah, NJ: American Educational Research Association/Erlbaum.

Atkinson, P., & Hammersley, M. (1994). Ethnography and participant observation. In N. K. Denzin & Y. S. Lincoln (Eds.), *Handbook of qualitative research* (pp. 248–261). Thousand Oaks, CA: SAGE.

Baym, N. K., & Markham, A. N. (2009). Introduction: Making smart choices on shifting ground. In A. N. Markham & N. K. Baym (Eds.), *Internet inquiry: Conversations about method* (pp. i–xix). London: SAGE.

Black, R. (2005). Access and affiliation: The literacy and composition practices of English-language learners in an online fanfiction community. *Journal of Adolescent and Adult Literacy, 49*(2), 118–128.

Boellstorff, T., Nardi, B., Pearce, C., & Taylor, T. L. (2012). *Ethnography and virtual worlds: A handbook of methods.* Princeton, NJ: Princeton University Press.

Carter, D. (2005). Living in virtual communities: An ethnography of human relationships in cyberspace. *Information, Communication and Society, 8*(2), 148–167.

Chandler-Olcott, K., & Mahar, D. (2003). "Tech-savviness" meets multiliteracies: Exploring adolescent girls' technology-mediated literacy practices. *Reading Research Quarterly, 38*(3), 356–385.

Cohen, L. (2007, April 5). Social scholarship on the rise. Retrieved October 7, 2008, from *http://liblogs.albany.edu/library20/2007/04/social_scholarship_on_the_rise.html*

Coiro, J., & Dobler, E. (2007). Exploring the online reading comprehension strategies used by sixth-grade skilled readers to search for and locate information on the Internet. *Reading Research Quarterly, 42*, 214–257.

Dennen, V. P., Cates, M. L., & Bagdy, L. M. (2017). Using Diigo to engage learners in course readings: Learning design and formative evaluation. *International Journal for Educational Media and Technology, 11*(2), 3–15.

DeSchryver, M. (2014). Higher-order thinking in an online world: Toward a theory of web-mediated knowledge synthesis. *Teachers College Record, 116*, 1–44.

Freeman, M., deMarrais, K., Preissle, J., Roulston, K., & St. Pierre, E. A. (2007). Standards of evidence in qualitative research: An incitement to discourse. *Educational Researcher, 36*(1), 25–32.

Gao, F. (2013). A case study of using a social annotation tool to support collaboratively learning. *The Internet and Higher Education, 17*, 76–83.

Gee, J. P. (1996). *Social linguistics and literacies: Ideology in discourses* (2nd ed.). London: Taylor & Francis.

Gillen, J. (2009). Literacy practices in Schome Park: A virtual literacy ethnography. *Journal of Research in Reading, 32*(1), 57–74.

Gratton, L. (2007). *Hot spots: Why some teams, workplaces, and organizations buzz with energy—and others don't.* San Francisco: Berrett-Koehler.

Greenhow, C. (2008). Commentary: Connecting formal and informal learning in the age of participatory media: A response to Bull et al. *Contemporary Issues in Technology and Teacher Education, 8*(3).

Greenhow, C. (2009). Social scholarship: Applying social networking technologies to research practices. *Knowledge Quest, 37*(4), 43–47.

Greenhow, C. (2010a). *Literacies and community formation in social network sites: Understanding a complex ecology.* Paper presented at the annual meeting of the American Educational Research Association, Denver, CO.

Greenhow, C. (2010b). Youth as content producers in a niche social network site. *New Directions for Youth Development, 2010*(128), 55–63.

Greenhow, C., Galvin, S., Brandon, D., & Askari, E. (2020). A decade of research on K–12 teaching with social media: Insights on the state of the field. *Teachers College Record, 122*(6). Manuscript submitted for publication.

Greenhow, C., & Gleason, B. (2012). Twitteracy: Tweeting as a new literacy practice. *Educational Forum, 76*(4), 464–478.

Greenhow, C., & Gleason, B. (2014). Social scholarship: Reconsidering scholarly practices in the age of social media. *British Journal of Educational Technology, 45*, 392–402.

Greenhow, C. M., Gleason, B., & Staudt Willet, K. B. (2019). Social scholarship revisited: Changing scholarly practices in the age of social media. *British Journal of Educational Technology, 50*, 987–1004.

Greenhow, C., & Robelia, E. (2009a). Informal learning and identity formation in online social networks. *Learning, Media and Technology, 34*(2), 119–140.

Greenhow, C., & Robelia, E. (2009b). Old communication, new literacies: Social network sites as social learning resources. *Journal of Computer-Mediated Communication, 14*, 1130–1161.

Greenhow, C., Robelia, E., & Hughes, J. (2009). Web 2.0 and classroom research: What path should we take now? *Educational Researcher, 38*(4), 246–259.

Greenhow, C., Walker, J. D., & Kim, S. (2009). Millennial learners and net-savvy teens: Examining Internet use among low-income students. *Journal of Computing in Teacher Education, 26*(2), 63–69.

Guzzetti, B. J., & Foley, L. M. (2014). Literacy agents online. *Journal of Adolescent and Adult Literacy, 57*(6), 461–471.

Heath, S. B. (1983). *Ways with words*. Cambridge, UK: Cambridge University Press.

Hewson, C. (2017). Research design and tools for online research. In N. G. Fielding, R. M. Lee, & G. Blank (Eds.), *The SAGE handbook of online research methods* (2nd ed., pp. 57–75). Los Angeles: SAGE.

Hine, C. (2000). *Virtual ethnography*. London: SAGE.

Hine, C. (Ed.). (2005). *Virtual methods: Issues in social research on the Internet.* New York: Berg.

Hine, C. (2015). *Ethnography for the internet: Embedded, embodied and everyday.* London: Bloomsbury.

Hine, C. (2017). Ethnographies of online communities and social media: Modes, varieties, affordances. In N. G. Fielding, R. M. Lee, & G. Blank (Eds.), *The SAGE handbook of online research methods* (2nd ed., pp. 401–415). Los Angeles: SAGE.

Holloway, S. L., & Valentine, G. (2001). "It's only as stupid as you are": Children and adults' negotiation of ICT competence at home and at school. *Social and Cultural Geography, 22*, 25–42.

Hutchins, E. (1995). *Cognition in the wild*. Cambridge, MA: MIT Press.

International Reading Association (IRA). (2009). *New literacies and 21st century technologies: A position statement of the International Reading Association.* Newark, DE: Author. Retrieved May 13, 2019, from *www.literacyworldwide.org/docs/default-source/where-we-stand/new-literacies-21st-century-position-statement.pdf.*

Ito, M., Baumer, S., Bittanti, M., boyd, d., Cody, R., Herr-Stephenson, B., et al. (2009). *Hanging out, messing around, and geeking out: Kids living and learning with new media.* Chicago: MacArthur Foundation Series on Digital Media and Learning.

Jacobs, G. E. (2004). Complicating contexts: Issues of methodology in researching language and literacies of instant messaging. *Reading Research Quarterly, 39*(4), 394–406.

Jones, S. G. (1995). *Cybersociety: Computer-mediated communication and community.* Thousand Oaks, CA: SAGE.

Jones, S. G. (1997). *Virtual culture: Internet and communication in cybersociety.* London: SAGE.

Kress, G. (2003). *Literacy in the new media age*. New York: Routledge.

Lam, W. S. E. (2004). Second language socialization in a bilingual chat room. *Language Learning and Technology, 8*(3), 44–65.

Lammers, J. C. (2013). Fangirls as teachers: Examining pedagogic discourse in an online fan site. *Learning, Media and Technology, 38*, 368–386.

Lammers, J. C. (2016). "The hangout was serious business": Leveraging participation in an online space to design Sims fanfiction. *Research in the Teaching of English, 50*(3), 309–332.

Lankshear, C., & Knobel, M. (2006). *New literacies: Everyday practices and classroom learning* (2nd ed.). Maidenhead, UK: Open University Press.

Leander, K. M. (2003). Writing travelers' tales on new literacyscapes. *Reading Research Quarterly, 38*(3), 392–397.

Leander, K. M. (2008). Toward a connective ethnography of online/offline literacy networks. In J. Coiro, M. Knobel, C. Lankshear, & D. Leu (Eds.), *Handbook of research on new literacies* (pp. 33–65). New York: Erlbaum.

Leander, K. M., & McKim, K. K. (2003). Tracing the everyday "sitings" of adolescents on the Internet: A strategic adaptation of ethnography across online and offline spaces. *Education, Communication, and Information, 3*(2), 211–240.

LeCompte, M. D., & Schensul, J. J. (1999). *Designing and conducting ethnographic research.* Walnut Creek, CA: AltaMira Press.

Leu, D. J., Kinzer, C. K., Coiro, J., Castek, J., & Henry, L. A. (2017). New literacies: A dual-level theory of the changing nature of literacy, instruction, and assessment. *Journal of Education, 197*(2), 1–18.

Luke, A., (2003). Literacy and the other: A sociological approach to literacy research and policy in multilingual societies. *Reading Research Quarterly, 38*(1), 132–141.

Markham, A. (1998). *Life online: Researching real experience in virtual space.* Walnut Creek, CA: AltaMira Press.

Markham, A. N., & Baym, N. K. (Eds.). (2009). *Internet inquiry: Conversations about method.* London: SAGE.

Mills, K. A. (2010). A review of the "digital turn" in the new literacy studies. *Review of Educational Research, 80*(2), 246–271.

Moje, E. B. (2016). Youth literacy and cultural theories: A review of the science and implications for policy. *Policy Insights from the Behavioral and Brain Sciences, 3*(1), 70–76.

Moje, E. B., Ciechanowski, K. M., Kramer, K., Ellis, L., Carillo, R., & Tehani, C. (2004). Working toward Third Space in content area literacy: An examination of everyday funds of knowledge and discourse. *Reading Research Quarterly, 39*(1), 38–70.

National Center on Education and the Economy. (2006). *Tough choices or tough times: The report of the New Commission on the Skills of the American Workforce.* San Francisco: Jossey-Bass.

National Council of Teachers of English (NCTE). (2005). Multimodal literacies: A summary statement. Retrieved July 28, 2008, from *www.ncte.org/about/ over/positions/category/comp/123213.htm.*

National Council of Teachers of English (NCTE). (2007). 21st century literacies: A policy research brief. Retrieved May 2020, from *https://secure.ncte.org/ library/NCTEFiles/Resources/Positions/Chron1107ResearchBrief.pdf*

National Council of Teachers of English (NCTE). (2018). Beliefs for integrating technology into the English Language Arts classroom. Retrieved May 21, 2019, from *www2.ncte.org/statement/beliefs-technology-preparation-english-teachers.*

National Writing Project. (2018). Literacy, Equity + Remarkable Notes = LEARN: Marginal syllabus 2018–19. Retrieved from *https://educatorinnovator.org/campaigns/literacy-equity-remarkable-notes-learn-marginal-syllabus-2018-19.*

Nelson, M. (Executive Producer). (2008, July 23). *CNN presents: Black in America*

[Television broadcast]. New York: Turner Broadcasting Service. Retrieved March 23, 2010, from *www.cnn.com/SPECIALS/2008/black.in.america.*

Onwuegbuzie, A. J., & Mallette, M. H. (2011). Mixed research techniques. In N. K. Duke & M. H. Mallette (Eds.), *Literacy research methodologies* (2nd ed., pp. 301–330). New York: Guilford Press.

Patton, M. Q. (Ed.). (2002). *Qualitative research and evaluation methods* (3rd ed.). London: SAGE.

Purcell-Gates, V. (2004). Ethnographic research. In N. K. Duke & M. H. Mallette (Eds.), *Literacy research methodologies* (pp. 92–113). New York: Guilford Press.

Purcell-Gates, V. (2011). Ethnographic research. In N. K. Duke & M. H. Mallette (Eds.), *Literacy research methodologies* (2nd ed., pp. 135–154). New York: Guilford Press.

Reinking, D., & Bradley, B. A. (2004). Connecting research and practice using formative and design experiments. In N. K. Duke & M. H. Mallette (Eds.), *Literacy research methodologies* (pp. 149–169). New York: Guilford Press.

Rideout, V. J., & Robb, M. B. (2018). *Social media, social life: Teens reveal their experiences.* San Francisco: Common Sense Media.

Robson, J. (2018). Performance, structure and ideal identity: Reconceptualising teachers' engagement in online social spaces. *British Journal of Educational Technology, 49,* 439–450.

Sheehy, G. (2008, August). Campaign Hillary: Behind closed doors. *Vanity Fair,* pp. 79–86.

Shirky, C. (2008, April 23). *Massively multiplayer online video gaming as participation in a discourse.* Keynote for the Web 2.0 Expo, San Francisco, CA [Video file]. Retrieved May 13, 2019, from *https://youtu.be/oz1HZkaFz1w.*

Steinkuehler, C. (2006). *Mind, Culture and Activity, 13*(1), 38–52.

Steinkuehler, C. (2007). Massively multiplayer online gaming as a constellation of literacy practices. *E-Learning and Digital Media, 4*(3), 297–318.

Steinkuehler, C. A., Black, R., & Clinton, K. A. (2005). Researching literacy as tool, place, and way of being. *Reading Research Quarterly, 40*(1), 95–100.

Stewart, B. (2016). Collapsed publics: Orality, literacy, and vulnerability in academic Twitter. *Journal of Applied Social Theory, 1*(1), 61–86.

Stone, B. (2008, June 18). At social site only the businesslike need apply. *New York Times,* pp. C1–C2.

Taraborelli, D. (2008, May 20–23), Soft peer review. Social software and distributed scientific evaluation. *Proceedings of the 8th International Conference on the Design of Cooperative Systems* (COOP 08), Carry-Le-Rouet, France. Retrieved October 3, 2008, from *http://nitens.org/docs/spr_coop08.pdf.*

Thomas, A. (2007). *Youth online: Identity and literacy in the digital age.* New York: Peter Lang.

Turkle, S. (1995). *Life on the screen: Identity in the age of the Internet.* London: Weidenfeld & Nicolson.

Wade, S. E., & Fauske, J. R. (2004). Dialogue online: Prospective teachers discourse strategies in computer-mediated discussions. *Reading Research Quarterly, 39*(2), 134–160.

Wargo, J. (2017). "Every selfie tells a story . . . ": LGBTQ youth lifestreams and and new media narratives as connective identity texts. *New Media and Society, 19*(4), 560–578.

Weinberger, D. (2011) *Too big to know: Rethinking knowledge now that the facts aren't the facts, experts are everywhere, and the smartest person in the room is the room.* New York: Basic Books.

Wilson, B. (2006). *Fight, flight, or chill: Subcultures, youth, and rave into the 21st century.* Montreal: McGill–Queen's University Press.

Wolf, M. (2018). *Reader come home: The reading brain in a digital world.* New York: Harper-Collins.

Yancey, K. B., & McElroy, S. J. (2017). *Assembling composition.* Urbana, IL: Conference on College Composition and Communication/National Council of Teachers of English.

CHAPTER 7

Approaches to Discourse Analysis in Language and Literacy Research

Amy Vetter
Melissa Schieble

Originating from the field of linguistics, discourse analysis has become a vast field of study in multiple subject areas. Scholars across these areas, however, agree that discourse analysis is the "study of the ways sentences and spoken utterances [and other multimodal signs] are put together to make texts and interactions and how those texts and interactions fit into the social world" (Jones, 2019, p. 2). The many different approaches to discourse analysis include conversational analysis, ethnography of communication, and interactional sociolinguistics. For this chapter, we focus on specific approaches to discourse analysis that examine the relationship between interaction and literacy learning both in and out of school.

Language, including talk and texts, is at the center of classroom learning and instruction. Language, however, is not transparent and involves complex social, cultural, and political processes. Interactions between students and teachers, for example, involve issues of identity and power that can both hinder and foster learning. Researchers have been studying classroom talk for the past half-century both nationally and internationally to learn more about how students learn within specific contexts (e.g., Cazden, 1988; Mercer, 2000). Scholars have found discourse analysis to be a useful method for exploring these complex issues (e.g., Bloome, Carter, Christian, Otto, & Shuart-Faris, 2004; Thomas, 2015).

We used van Dijk's (2015) notion that discourse analysis is broad and interdisciplinary, and encompasses various analytic practices, to conceptualize the organization of this chapter. We aim to orient readers to the various analytical practices of discourse analysis as both a theory and a method. The approach to discourse analysis that a researcher invokes is that which is most relevant to the research question(s) and is coherent with the particularities of theory and design. However, some fundamental tenets are worth pointing out before we discuss the history of discourse analysis and branch out into the various approaches currently undertaken in language and literacy research.

THEORIZING DISCOURSE

At the heart of discourse analysis is a focus on the relationship between form and function of language, including other forms of nonverbal communication and digitization, and the social world (Gee, 2011). We define *discourse* as naturally occurring talk and nonverbal and/or multimodal communication in the context of any communicable event. Moje and Lewis (2007) refer to groups that share ways of using language as *discourse communities*.

To understand discourse analysis, it is important to understand what is meant by discourse. To define discourse, we propose a two-part definition that draws from Gee (2015), who uses capitalization of the letter D to distinguish between the moment-to-moment structures of language (*discourses*) and the ideologies or storylines we evoke about people, places, and events in the world through language and other sign systems (*Discourses*). Rogers and Wetzel (2014) note, "Discourses play many roles in the classroom. They sustain, build, resist, or transform existing narratives and ideologies" (p. 38). While Discourses are neither fixed nor stable, when evoked as familiar narratives by many actors and signs over time, they can take on a form of habitus in the social imagination (Bourdieu, 1977) and thus can also shape material conditions. For example, researchers have shown that teachers' deficit language (e.g., "My students lack basic skills . . .") about students of color in schools has contributed over time to low expectations for achievement (a Discourse about race and class as related to ability) and disproportionate referrals to special education (a material outcome) (Ahram, Fergus, & Noguera, 2011; Ladson-Billings, 2007; Valencia, 2012). Linguistic choices, and the Discourses to which literacy teachers subscribe, operate to privilege some students over others and play a major factor in students' opportunities for learning and material experiences in school and beyond.

Alternatively, discourse analysis may reveal that individuals position themselves in ways that are outside the group's accepted norms, and thus struggle to find acceptance. For example, a literacy teacher who identifies as a culturally responsive educator in a school that focuses on packaged literacy curriculum and test preparation would struggle for acceptance in this context; speaking back to powerful Discourses that promote testing and standardization (the Discourse of neoliberalism) is a frequent struggle for literacy educators. Discourse analysis in language and literacy research focuses on the ways these practices are enacted through everyday language use and communicative events within a situated context.

In the remainder of this chapter, we describe and explain some of the discourse analysis approaches that are used in literacy research. Approaches to discourse analysis can be undertaken after a language and literacy event, or as part of the ongoing and reflective work of teaching (see Rogers & Wetzel, 2014). We organize these approaches into two sections: discourse analysis (DA) and critical discourse analysis (CDA). We do so because our review of the scholarly literature suggests that the field is oriented to these two broader categories. While both DA and CDA researchers study discourse through analysis of textual and interactional data, CDA takes a more operative theoretical and methodological approach to studying the ways that discourse practices shape and are shaped by powerful discursive and structural exercises of privilege, oppression, liberation, and agency. While we agree with Gee (2017) that "all instances of language in use signal 'political meanings' and all discourse analysis does or ought to have a critical element" (p. 63), for the purpose of writing a chapter about discourse analysis, we see value to organizing the various approaches in the ways that are taken up in the field of literacy research.

DISCOURSE ANALYSIS

Modern DA originated in the 1960s with a focus on structural discourse analysis (e.g., Roland Barthes) that was mainly descriptive and focused on discourse genres, such as folktales. Burgeoning work in this time included Michael Halliday's systemic functional approach, which studied the relationship between language and its function in social settings. In addition, Dell Hymes (1964) published *Language in Culture and Society*—a collection of work from linguistic anthropology and sociolinguistics that drew attention to specific aspects of language (e.g., discourse and style), and to the ways in which social, cultural, and historical contexts shape interactions.

Building on this work, scholars in the 1970s developed a more systemic DA that was used in research across several disciplines. For example, scholars in sociolinguistics studied the connections between language and society, and the ways individuals use language in various contexts. Researchers in this area have examined, for example, how gender shapes communication (Tannen, 2001) and how language varies across contexts (Labov, 1972). Scholars also developed the concept of *speech acts*, in which verbal utterances such as apologizing or requestioning are also considered forms of social action (Austin, 1973; Searle, Kiefer, & Bierwisch, 1980). During this time, scholars began to focus on everyday social interaction (e.g., Goffman, 1981; Saks, Schlegoff, & Jefferson, 1974) by examining not only the rules of grammar, but also the rules of conversation, such as turn taking. Such work also led to the ethnography of communication, which analyzes communication within the social and cultural context of a particular speech community (Hymes, 1976). This approach examines which communication acts are important to a group of people and how they came to learn those conversational norms.

Scholars in literacy education have built on the history of this work. With the goal of improving teaching and learning in literacy education, studies in and out of classrooms demonstrate the importance of social interaction to learning, thus drawing on sociolinguistics and the ethnography of communication (Allington, 2002; Applebee, Langer, Nystrand, & Gamoran, 2003; Cazden, 1988; O'Connor, Michaels, Chapin, & Harbaugh, 2017). In this section, we focus on what Gee (2011) would call *descriptive discourse analysis*. The goal for this type of DA is to "describe how language works in order to understand it" (Gee, 2011, p. 9). The job of the analyst is to uncover how people use discourse to position themselves in strategic ways to belong to a particular group, and how this work distributes social and economic goods. For literacy researchers, this often means foregrounding the daily life of classrooms or other learning spaces. For example, Courtney Cazden's influential work, described in *Classroom Discourse: The Language of Teaching and Learning* (1988), has been used with educators to help them see how language is the primary medium of teaching and learning. She argued that in order to teach, teachers need tools to examine their own ways of using language with the students they teach. Shirley Brice Heath also contributed to this scholarship in *Ways with Words* (1983), which examined children learning to use language at home and school in two different communities within the Southeastern United States. In the book, Heath introduced the concept of *literacy events*, which involve uses of written language and talking about a text in a particular context. Heath argued that schools often privilege dominant literacy events and exclude the diverse linguistic practices that children bring with them from home. Such privileging hinders students' success in the classroom.

To find more equitable ways of teaching and learning, literacy research has also used DA to examine how all students can be successful in classrooms. Rex and colleagues (2010) engaged in an extensive literature review that examined such questions as "Whose literacies count?" In the review, the authors described researchers engaging in DA at three units of scale: *macro, micro,* and *meso*. At the macro level, studies focused on examining policy and curriculum. Studies focused on the micro scale investigate interactions and literacy practices in specific educational spaces, such as school. At the meso level, researchers explore genres of discourse types that are related to cultural, institutional, or social contexts such as churches, afterschool programs, district meetings, and/or PTO groups. Through this kind of DA, literacy researchers have been able to deconstruct traditional binaries (e.g., capable–incapable) and to problematize how equity and access have been defined. As a result, literacy instruction and learning are conceptualized as complex and dynamic processes that are shaped by the social, cultural, and political world.

Researchers have also used DA to unpack how students co-construct knowledge through dialogue, in a process known as *dialogic teaching* (Juzwik, Borsheim-Black, Caughlan, & Heintz, 2013; Mercer & Hodgkinson, 2008; Wells, 1999). Specifically, DA has illuminated how traditional instruction that utilizes a teacher initiation, student response, and teacher evaluation structure situates students as passive recipients of information (Nystrand, 1997; Rymes, 2016) through known-information questions (Mehan, 1979). Researchers have since examined how teachers can be effective at fostering talk as tools for collective learning by encouraging students to provide evidence for their views, providing mutual support during classroom discussions, and inviting students to take a student-led approach to discussion (Nassaji & Wells, 2000). By using specific talk patterns related to a dialogic stance, such as the utilization of uptake questions, narration, or speculation, teachers and students are more likely to learn through talk in a classroom (Juzwik et al., 2013).

More recently, researchers have focused on how using DA with teachers fosters critical reflection and improves literacy instruction and learning in the classroom (Juzwik & Ives, 2010). In *Using Discourse Analysis to Improve Classroom Interaction*, Rex and Schiller (2009) worked with teacher inquiry groups to analyze classroom interactions. They argued that encouraging teachers to study their own classroom discourse in a teacher research group contributed to their ability to be interactionally aware of their practices. For instance, one inservice teacher used discourse analysis to reframe situations from student behaviors to teacher actions. Such an approach shifted language from a "Kids can't . . ." to a "Let's try . . ." approach. Other research has found that preservice teachers who understand that identities are socially constructed have the opportunity to become more responsive to students' diverse learning identities because they recognize that learning is shaped by multiple factors (de Freitas, 2008). Another study used discourse analysis to help preservice English teachers in a student teaching seminar examine videos of their practice, to determine how their practice matched with their desired teaching identities (Vetter & Schieble, 2015). This study found that preservice teachers struggled with this alignment, and revealed that DA tools were generative in helping them reflect on and analyze their practice and develop strategies to match who they desired to be in the classroom with what they did in practice. Researchers have also found that the digital aspect helps teachers slow down the fast pace of classroom events and concentrate on close analysis of specific events (Sherin & van Es, 2009; van Es & Sherin, 2002). Teachers, then, are able to take "notice" of interactions and events that are not easily observed while teaching (Sherin & van Es, 2009) and to make connections between theory and practice (Brophy, 2004; Koc, Peker, & Osmanoglu, 2009).

Approaches to DA

Because there are many approaches to DA, it can be difficult to know which one to use in research. To provide some clarity, we highlight some of the approaches that have been most commonly used in, or that have great potential to contribute to, literacy research (Albers, Holbrook, & Flint, 2014). This list, however, is not exhaustive and is not intended to dictate what can and cannot be used to make sense of language in use in learning spaces. Before we describe those approaches, it is important to mention that scholars have developed similar elements of DA studies that are of high quality. For example, high-quality DA research provides clear documentation of the sources of information used, delimitation of data sources, and a description of the context of the study. High-quality studies also include clear explanations of the methods used to code and synthesize the data and how/why those methods helped to answer the stated research questions. Finally, in order to do high-quality DA, researchers should clearly describe how their own individual sociocultural positions may have influenced their interpretations.

Microethnographic DA

Microethnographic DA is an approach that "combines attention to how people use language and other systems of communication in constructing language and literacy events in classrooms with attention to social, cultural, and political processes" (Bloome et al., 2004, p. xv). This approach draws from social and cultural anthropology and sociology, including sociolinguistic ethnography (Gumperz & Hymes, 1972). Microethnographic approaches focus on the daily interactions of classrooms or other learning spaces. Specifically, research using this type of DA does so to examine how people make meaning through interactions with others. In relation to literacy research in this area (e.g., Cook-Gumperz, 1986; Gee, 2004; Heath, 2012), *literacy* is defined as a set of social and cultural events and practices. The term *literacy events* or *literacy practices* is used to describe spoken, written, and other modes of communication that are constructed during interactions. Literacies, then, are viewed as multiple and varied in context-dependent ways, and as reflecting ideologies of broader contexts and institutions.

Researchers using this approach do not come in with a priori notions of how literacy events and practices work within learning spaces. Instead, they observe and make sense of how literacy events occur within the moment, while recognizing the ways in which broad cultural, social, and political issues shape local interactions. Researchers taking this approach ask questions related to "how the ways people act and react to each other constitute literacy events and practices and the relationship of such social interactions to other social events and practices and to broader social contexts" (Bloome & Carter, 2014, p. 16). For example, researchers might ask: In what ways do social identities shape classroom language and literacy events? In what ways do power relations shape classroom language and literacy events? When following the approach of Bloom, Carter, Christian, Otto, and Shuart-Faris (2004), researchers would use six theoretical tools for analysis of classroom language and literacy events: (1) contextualization cues, (2) boundary making, (3) turn taking, (4) negotiating thematic coherence, (5) intertextuality, and (6) intercontextuality (juxtaposing contexts such as business and classroom contexts).

In Bloome and colleagues' book, *Discourse Analysis and the Study of Classroom Language and Literacy Events: A Microethnographic Perspective* (2004), the authors focus on key constructs for engaging in an ethnographic approach. By using data from classrooms, chapters in the book also highlight various uses of microethnographic DA, such as describing classroom literacy events as cultural action, examining the social construction of identities in literacy events, and exploring power relations in and through classroom literacy events. For example, in Chapter 3 the authors describe how one student (Andrew) was consistently positioned as a nonreader by his teacher and classmates. Although Andrew resisted this positioning in many ways, the teacher and students did not recognize this resistance, leaving the researchers to wonder what else Andrew could do to become a member of that classroom. This kind of analysis illuminates how literacy identities are related to both local and broader social, cultural, and political issues. Thus, this work has contributed to more in-depth understanding about the dynamics of social identities and the ways these identities shape classroom language and literacy events. Overall, Bloome and colleagues exemplify a microethnographic approach by first describing the literacy events and context of the classrooms and then providing detailed analyses of the classroom interactions.

Temporal DA

Temporal DA is "an analysis of discourses across time, and highlights time as a constitutive dimension of experience that people use to conceptualize their experiences with literacy, schooling, and identity" (Compton-Lilly, 2013, p. 46). This approach is used to illuminate how individuals make sense of their experiences across and within time. Specifically, researchers might ask questions about how individuals construct meaning about literacy across time, and how those constructions relate to how individuals engage in literacy learning and construct literate identities. Researchers can use this approach to examine time over extended periods (10 years) or over short classroom periods (50 minutes), for example. During analysis, researchers can identify temporal language of participants ("When I was 12 . . ." or "When I'm older . . ."), and they can also search for language that situates individuals in historical accounts ("When schools were segregated, I . . ."). Researchers can also look for repeated, revised, and revisited stories or discourses that occur across time.

Compton-Lilly's (2007) work in this area is an example of high-quality DA research because of her longitudinal and systematic analysis of students' literacy experiences and identities over time. To engage in that analysis, Compton-Lilly identified five types of temporal discourse: (1) the language people use to situate themselves in time; (2) references to the pace of schooling and the timelines that operate in schools; (3) comments and practices that reflect long social histories; (4) repeated discourses over time; and (5) repeated stories that present changing or consistent meanings. She used these when analyzing data in a longitudinal study (11 years) that followed seven African American individuals (originally from her first-grade class) and their families. For example, Compton-Lilly illustrated how Marvin's family used temporal discourses (e.g., "Every Saturday . . . ," "Every single day . . .") to describe how they engaged in literacy practices, such as going to the library and reciting the ABCs. These temporal discourses were also repeated across time and extended across generations. As a result, readers can understand the storylines and behaviors this family followed in order to situate their child as a reader year after year. Such work can provide insight into the roles that agency and social/cultural/political contexts play in shaping children's literacy identities over time.

Multimodal Interaction Analysis

Multimodal interaction analysis (Norris, 2004) is an approach that emphasizes human actions, such as talk or gestures, as mediated actions. Researchers using this approach, then, study individuals interacting with others, the environment, and technology (Norris, 2014). Thus, multimodal interaction analysis focuses on examining the multiple activities individuals are involved in when interacting (Jones, 2019). This approach draws from mediated DA (Scollon & de Saint-Georges, 2012), interactional sociolinguistics (Goffman, 1974; Gumperz, 1982; Tannen, 1984), and social semiotics (Kress & van Leeuwen, 2001, 2006). Researchers in a classroom can analyze video and other multimodal data at micro, meso, and macro levels to better understand how learning is occurring. Analysts typically examine language, gestures, furniture, posture, proxemics, and music in a theoretically founded way by taking the mediated action as the unit of analysis (Scollon & de Saint-Georges, 2012; Wertsch, 1998). This approach focuses on the social actors, what these actors do (actions performed), and how actions are performed (the mediated means/cultural tools used to perform actions).

According to Norris (2014), researchers using this approach might ask questions such as "What makes reading possible?" or "How can a distinction between various levels of action allow us to better understand the process of reading?" (p. 72). Researchers using this approach focus on a social action being performed, such as a child reading a book. Every action is made up of a social actor and a mediational means or cultural tool. The unit of analysis is the mediated action (in this case, the child reading the book). Analysts look at levels of actions within that unit, such as lower-level actions (e.g., a gesture unit or postural shift) and higher-level actions (e.g., the coming together of multiple chains of lower-level actions). For example, a researcher might be interested in the role that posture plays in turn taking during a classroom dialogue. As a result, the researcher would look for patterns in the ordering of posture (Jones, 2019). Transcription is image based with transcribed dialogue or sound to illustrate the interactions taking place.

Norris (2011) engaged in an ethnographic longitudinal study and used multimodal interaction analysis to illustrate the practices of identity production in the lives of two German women. Through this high-quality analysis, Norris developed a well-articulated set of theoretical constructs for discourse analysts interested in the various features of identity production in interaction. Specifically, she expands notions of identity construction and illustrates how this approach can demonstrate how social actors shift identities in and out of focus; explain how social actors change identities; and/or present how social actors sustain identities across time, place, and activities.

Such work has implications for learning more about literacy learning. For example, Andrea, one of the participants in Norris's research, had recently become nearsighted. As a result, the simple task of seeing a small number on a paintbrush became a difficult task that caused frustration for Andrea. As Norris (2014) described, "A simple lower-level action of reading even just one number for Andrea, who is fully literate, turns into a complex higher-level action that needs to be focused upon" (p. 74). With this example, Norris suggests that literacy studies would benefit from using micro-level analysis of readers to better understand their actions. Such analysis could offer insight into how young readers develop over time. This information can also help scholars learn more about the history of actions related to reading, for example, to derive new knowledge about the macro societal levels of literacy.

Visual DA

Visual DA (VDA) is an approach to analyzing visual language within naturally occurring environments like a classroom. This approach is grounded in semiotics (Hodge & Kress, 1988), a theory that examines the study of signs and symbols and their use or interpretation. VDA is also informed by DA in general (Gee, 2004) and by the grammar of visual design (Kress & van Leeuwen, 2006). This approach defines a visual text as a "structure of messages within which are embedded social conventions and/or perceptions, and which also present the discourse communities to which the visual textmaker identifies" (Albers et al., 2014, p. 86).

According to Albers (2014), four principles of VDA foster high-quality analysis. First, VDA is reflexive, which means that visual language creates and reflects the context people are in. Visual language allows for situated meanings, which means that images or texts that are made on the spot are informed by learners and their interaction with other texts/conversations. Visual languages are also composed of many different social languages, meaning that students expressing their thoughts visually will sound different from artists speaking. Finally, cueing systems (e.g., tactile, semantic, structural) help understand how, why, and what students draw upon as they construct meaning (Albers, 2007). This kind of analysis allows educators to understand how students communicate about literacy, which is not always oral or written and can offer insights into the students' beliefs, thoughts, and practices. Questions that guide VDA include the following: "How is language used to communicate (use of technique, design, color, and so on)?" or "What is revealed about the textmaker through the image (attention to discourses and systems of meaning that underpin the visual text)?" (Albers et al., 2014, p. 86).

One exemplar of VDA is an interpretive study done by Albers, Frederick, and Cowan (2009), in which they use those four principles with 38 fifth-grade students. The study examined how elementary students sent messages about the experiences and interests of boys and girls through their visual texts in their English/language arts class. Data included students' drawings from two classes that were created during a unit focused on stereotypes. One key finding in the study showed that visual conversations about gender occurred between and across texts, and that some students drew things in similar ways, indicating a "unified expression of a social collective" (Albers et al., 2014, p. 91). Second, they found clear discourses of gender in the visual texts. When asked to draw what boys like, girls typically drew video games and cars, for example, while boys typically drew romance or beauty for girls. Thus, students took up available discourses of their own and the other gender, and visually represented their beliefs about the other. Students, then, were able to explore those beliefs through art, which opened opportunities for play and performance. VDA is one way, then, to study how students make meaning of and interact with visual texts in classrooms, which can also tell us how they make meaning of their social, cultural, and political worlds.

CRITICAL DISCOURSE ANALYSIS

CDA is a set of theories and methods that researchers invoke to study questions in the social sciences grounded in critical social theory perspectives. That is, critical approaches to DA are concerned with an investigation of the ways power is enacted through discourse that both shapes and is shaped by institutions and social structures in particular contexts and over time. The theories and methods associated with work by Norman Fairclough, Ruth Wodak, Teun van Dijk, and Theo van Leeuwen are considered foundational within CDA. Approaches to CDA associated with

Norman Fairclough, James Gee, and Guenther Kress are representative of CDA studies in education (Rogers, 2011). Although there are elemental differences among these approaches as defined by the scholars associated with them, there is hybridity in both theory and method within and across approaches. Rogers (2011) emphasizes the importance of noting the methodological tools and limits of each approach, but also notes how each analytic practice (or new ones) may be invoked in innovative ways, depending on the social events and practices under study.

In contrast, the term *critical discourse studies* is an umbrella term for an interdisciplinary set of approaches that, as van Dijk (2015) explains, connotes an integrated focus on theory and method. Gee (2004) distinguishes *Critical Discourse Analysis* as Fairclough's (1995) approach, and uses the lowercase term *critical discourse analysis* to refer to other approaches, which today include mediated DA, positive DA, public consultative DA, nexus analysis, and narrative analysis, among additional approaches. What makes any approach to DA critical is a *critical perspective* (van Dijk, 2015); any of the approaches foregrounded in the earlier section on DA can be framed as a CDA approach if the researcher invokes one or more critical perspectives. For readability, we use the abbreviation CDA as a reference to encompass this large body of work. All approaches within CDA share a concern with studying the form and function of text and talk in relation to social and institutional structures that are either oppressive or liberating. What binds CDA approaches is a critical perspective that is epistemologically and ontologically oriented to the ways that talk and text operate in relationship to power, with a goal of fostering positive social change.

Background of CDA

Some of the earliest principles of CDA were present in the Frankfurt School of critical theory and in British Cultural Studies (van Dijk, 2015; Rogers, 2011). Critical social theory perspectives focus on both critique of and resistance to domination in tension with the potential for human agency and liberation. Critical linguistics, which emerged primarily in the United Kingdom and Australia toward the end of the 1970s, oriented a critical perspective to the study of language and discourse. CDA also emerged alongside a critical turn in the social sciences, sociolinguistics, and psychology, among other fields, as early as the 1970s and may have been a critical response to the decontextualized and ahistorical paradigms in linguistics and conversation analysis that were dominant in prior decades (van Dijk, 2015).

Foundational tenets of CDA include attempts to describe and explain social problems within a situated social and political context. Specifically, CDA focuses on interaction and institutional structures, and on the ways discourses are construed within relations of dominance–liberation (Gee, 2004; Lewis, 2006; Rogers, 2013; van Dijk, 2015). Notably, Fairclough and Wodak (1997) posit that CDA shares a view of discourse as ideological, historical, and a form of social action. Thus, CDA approaches seek to uncover the workings of text and talk as powerful and mutually constitutive of society, culture, and the distribution of wealth and social goods.

Because CDA approaches are so varied, no single or unifying theoretical framework undergirds all of these approaches. Most approaches, however, share a focus on asking questions about the role of text and talk in social dominance and/or liberation. The social context of text and talk may include classroom interactions, written documents, news and other mass media, video-recorded interactions in and/or out of school, and visual forms such as image and film. Like DA in general, CDA approaches emphasize how everyday language in use and other semiotic modes (micro-level) are linked with macro-level ideas about power and inequality at the institutional level through the enactment and enforcement of laws and policies, or narratives that shape dominant cultural norms, values, and social practices. The critical discourse analyst moves back and forth recursively between the micro (and/or meso) layers of text and talk and a broader macro context to deconstruct and reconstruct the social world. The boundaries of context within CDA have been the subject of much discussion (Rogers, 2011), and it is the job of the analyst to delineate these constructs. To analyze the links between and among micro–macro structures, analysts look to how individual social acts are constitutive of normalized social group values and behaviors, and/or are related to state or national legislation or organizational policies.

CDA has been taken up in language and literacy research to study how discourses related to race, class, gender, sexuality, ability, and religion shape and are shaped by talk and text. In particular, CDA has been used to highlight how everyday language and literacy practices in and out of schools are value-laden and distribute social and cultural capital—such as who is deemed a "good student" and/or a "good reader" (Brown, Souto-Manning, & Tropp Laman, 2010) by literacy teachers and leaders (e.g., instructional coaches or literacy professional developers), and by other stakeholders such as policy makers. CDA offers language and literacy researchers theories and methods to investigate the forms and functions of talk and text at the micro level, and to connect these instantiations of language use to macro-level ideological constructs such as race, whiteness, and White supremacy. For example, CDA has been used to study racial literacy among second graders when whiteness is both enacted and disrupted in the context of guided reading and whole-class discussion (Rogers & Mosley, 2006); whiteness frameworks have also been invoked to study how race intersects with class and gender in the construction of characters' identities in adolescent literature (Schieble, 2012). CDA is invoked in literacy and language research to show how minoritized students' language and literacy practices are devalued and constructed as deficiencies in classrooms and schools (Alford, 2014); this research also illustrates ways in which literacy teachers and students challenge dominant language expectations of school and literacies as a decontextualized set of skills devoid of social practice.

How is quality characterized in CDA studies? Rogers and Schaenen (2013) conducted a large-scale literature review of studies in education published from 2004 until 2012 that explicitly invoked a CDA approach. In doing so, they arrived at the following touchstones for quality within a CDA tradition:

- *Reflexivity:* The ways in which a researcher's identity is implicated in the analytic process, from methodological choices to interpretation.
- *Context:* Social, cultural, political, and additional meaning frames that shape and arc shaped by discourse practices.
- *Deconstruction–reconstruction:* Analytic practices that address both pillars of domination and means of agency/liberation.
- *Social action:* Analytic procedures and implications that lead to an interruption of the commonplace and reimagine positive social change.

Additionally, Rogers (2013) outlines markers of quality in CDA studies, from the construction of a transcript to transparency in analysis. It is beyond the scope of this chapter to attend to all issues pertaining to quality outlined by these sources, and we encourage readers to refer to them for further discussion. However, we describe and explain how these characteristics are exemplified in the following three studies that took different approaches to CDA.

Approaches to CDA

Mediated DA

Mediated DA places a focus on sociocultural activity as a unit of analysis and is considered a more action-oriented approach to CDA. Wohlwend (2012) drew on the work of Scollon (2001) and Scollon and Scollon (2004) to bring mediated DA to literacy research. In her study, she examined children's play with Disney Princess dolls as transmedia artifacts to understand "collaborative understandings of play texts and contexts" (Wohlwend, 2012, p. 599) in an early childhood classroom. Wohlwend analyzed the ways in which an interplay of artifacts and contexts mediated how the children enacted gendered figured worlds and identities. She located the moment-to-moment interactions of their play within multiple contextual sites, including the narratives about gender constructed through Disney Princess dolls as global marketing ploys, a shared peer culture, and the teaching and learning context. Wohlwend's study demonstrated quality through the ways she analyzed children's play practices by attending to the interactions of micro-level play with macro-level rich layers of context that indexed how globally circulated narratives about gender roles and hyper-femininity also mediated the children's play activity. While Wohlwend's analysis was deconstructive with respect to gender discourses, she also noted moments when the children asserted agency and improvised gender trouble (Butler, 1990) in ways that challenged discourses of the "boy problem," in which boys enact identities typically reserved for girls in peer culture (Martino, 2004). Her study exemplifies the ways in which moment-to-moment language and literacy events can be studied by using a CDA approach that foregrounds interaction mediated by artifacts and context.

Positive DA

Positive DA represents a change in analytic focus from how discourses are dominating to ways in which everyday instances of talk and text create spaces for agency and liberation. This approach addresses a critique of DA studies, in that for too long they have focused the discursive reproduction of oppression (Luke, 2004). Rogers and Wetzel (2013) used positive DA to study how one teacher in a Midwestern city demonstrated agency through her transformational understanding of culturally relevant pedagogy and her efforts to educate colleagues in this approach through a workshop presentation at a local conference. By creating a multimodal transcript (Norris, 2004) and using the tools of Fairclough's (2011) orders of discourse, the researchers noted ways in which the teacher positioned her identities as educator (including teacher educator) and change agent. For example, the teacher consistently used third-person, collective pronouns to demonstrate solidarity with workshop attendees, as well as counter-narratives to challenge dominant conceptualizations of pedagogy (Rogers & Wetzel, 2013). A turn toward the positive represents a shift in analytic focus, and there is a need for more studies that invoke this analytic practice to highlight openings in language and literacy practices that enact social change and agency.

CDA and Critical Race Theory

Brown and colleagues (2010) used critical race theory to analyze three ethnographic case studies of representations of racism in three early childhood classrooms in the United States. Their research sought to highlight the ways in which seemingly normalized practices in schools (e.g., a PTA fundraiser) and literacy programs (e.g., an accelerated reading program) are instantiations of race and class systems of oppression that position White middle-class students in ways in which they are perceived as "good students" in the schools. By creating narrative vignettes of three racialized classroom events, and the ways each author was implicated in and reflective of the changes needed to create more equitable spaces in school for students of color and/or students living in poverty, their analyses demonstrated quality: They were both deconstructive and reconstructive, and the authors were highly reflexive of their own positionings and how they potentially shaped events and how they might reconstruct those events in more equitable ways. Their analysis of the three case studies more broadly analyzed the ways that race and class Discourses were normalized in school practices, rather than a fine-grained analysis of specific moments of classroom talk. For example, Souto-Manning analyzed the implementation of a mandated reading program (Accelerated Reader) at one elementary school in one of the poorest counties in the United States. Her analysis showed how Accelerated Reader's packaged curricula, promoted by the No Child Left Behind Act and "scientifically valid" research, contributed to racial segregation at the school and maintained whiteness. Dominant discourses about race were upheld through the required books' inauthentic representations of characters of color as acting in "White ways" (p. 520), and through the promotion of European American cultural practices such as competitiveness (e.g., the only rewards for students' reading were the points they received on an Accelerated Reader test). The authors show how a critical race theory framework can be intersected with the tools of CDA to reveal the ways in which well-intentioned school literacy practices contribute to race and class segregation.

These three approaches represent some of the many high-quality studies that employ CDA in language and literacy research. For further discussion of exemplary studies that employ CDA, see Rogers's (2014) analysis of Dutro (2010) and Haddix (2010).

CONCLUSION

As this chapter highlights, discourse analysis is a varied set of theoretical and methodological approaches. It is the analyst's job to make clear how approaches are reflective of a particular tradition or brought together (or created anew) in innovative ways to build new knowledge about the relationship between language and literacy practices and the social world. Our review of DA and CDA studies has noted a few important areas of need for students and scholars who wish to contribute to this vast and interdisciplinary work. First, research is emerging that uses DA to study communicative events mediated by digital technologies (Lewis Ellison & Solomon, 2019). Also of note is the need for more examples of positive DA: studies that show how the forms and functions of talk and text interact with the social world in ways that lead to community solidarity and transformational change (see Rogers, 2018), including how youth engage in activism through literate practices in and out of school spaces.

In what ways might DA and CDA contribute to literacy research in the current moment? In other words, what might literacy researchers need from this methodology? One possibility DA and CDA approaches may lend to the field is a better understanding of the ways in which literacy education has avoided race, for example, when Discourses about race are so entrenched in literacy classrooms. It is clear from reviewing the history of DA and the novel approaches that are appearing on the language and literacy research landscape that there is much promise and potential for DA and CDA to be leveraged in ways that open more meaningful and just literacy learning opportunities in and out of school.

ACKNOWLEDGMENT

We thank Melissa Wetzel at the University of Texas at Austin for feedback on an earlier draft of this chapter.

REFERENCES

Ahram, R., Fergus, E., & Noguera, P. (2011). Addressing racial/ethnic disproportionality in special education: Case studies of suburban school districts. *Teachers College Record, 113*(10), 2233–2266.

Albers, P. (2007). Visual discourse analysis: An introduction to the analysis of school-generated visual texts. In D. W. Rowe, R. T. Jiménez, D. L. Compton, D. K. Dickinson, Y. Kim, K. M. Leander, et al. (Eds.), *56th yearbook of the National Reading Conference* (pp. 81–95). Oak Creek, WI: National Reading Conference.

Albers, P. (2014). Visual discourse analysis. In P. Albers, T. Holbrook, & A. S. Flint (Eds.), *New methods of literacy research* (pp. 85–98). New York: Routledge.

Albers, P., Frederick, T., & Cowan, K. (2009). Features of gender: A study of the visual texts of third grade students. *Journal of Early Childhood Literacy, 9*(2), 243–269.

Albers, P., Holbrook, T., & Flint, A. S. (Eds.). (2014). *New methods of literacy research.* New York: Routledge.

Alford, J. H. (2014). "Well, hang on, they're actually much better than that!": Disrupting dominant discourses of deficit about English language learners in senior high school English. *English Teaching: Practice and Critique, 13*(3), 71–78.

Allington, R. L. (2002). What I've learned about effective reading instruction: From a decade of studying exemplary elementary classroom teachers. *Phi Delta Kappan, 83*(10), 740–747.

Applebee, A. N., Langer, J. A., Nystrand, M., & Gamoran, A. (2003). Discussion-based approaches to developing understanding: Classroom instruction and student performance in middle and high school English. *American Educational Research Journal, 40*(3), 685–730.

Austin, J. L. (1973). Speech acts. *Edinburgh Course in Applied Linguistics, 1,* 37–53.

Bloome, D., & Carter, S. P. (2014). Microethnographic discourse analysis. In P. Albers, T. Holbrook, & A. S. Flint (Eds.), *New methods of literacy research* (pp. 3–18). New York: Routledge.

Bloome, D., Carter, S. P., Christian, B. M., Otto, S., & Shuart-Faris, N. (2004). *Discourse analysis and the study of classroom language and literacy events: A microethnographic perspective.* New York: Routledge.

Bourdieu, P. (1977). *Reproduction in education, society and culture.* London: SAGE.

Brophy, J. (2004). Discussion. In J. Brophy (Ed.), *Using video in teacher education: Advances in research on teaching* (Vol. 10, pp. 287–304). Amsterdam: Elsevier.

Brown, S., Souto-Manning, M., & Tropp Laman, T. (2010). Seeing the strange in the unfamiliar: Unpacking racialized practices in early childhood settings. *Race Ethnicity and Education, 13*(4), 513–532.

Butler, J. (1990). *Gender trouble: Feminism and the subversion of identity.* New York: Routledge.

Cazden, C. B. (1988). *Classroom discourse: The language of teaching and learning.* Portsmouth, NH: Heinemann.

Compton-Lilly, C. (2007). *Re-reading families: The literate lives of urban children, four years later.* New York: Teachers College Press.

Compton-Lilly, C. (2014). Temporal discourse analysis. In P. Albers, T. Holbrook, & A. S. Flint (Eds.), *New methods of literacy research* (pp. 40–55). New York: Routledge.

Cook-Gumperz, J. (1986). Caught in a web of words: Some considerations on language socialization and language acquisition. In J. Cook-Gumperz, W. A. Cosaro, & J. Streeck (Eds.), *Children's worlds and children's language* (pp. 37–68). New York: New Babylon.

de Freitas, E. (2008). Troubling teacher identity: Preparing mathematics teachers to teach for diversity. *Teaching Education, 19*(1), 43–55.

Dutro, E. (2010). What "hard times" mean: Mandated curricula, class-privileged assumptions, and the lives of poor children. *Research in the Teaching of English, 44*(3), 255–291.

Fairclough, N. (1995). *Critical discourse analysis: The critical study of language.* London: Longman.

Fairclough, N. (2011). Semiotic aspects of social transformation and learning. In R. Rogers (Ed.), *An introduction to critical discourse analysis in education* (2nd ed., pp. 119–126). New York: Routledge.

Fairclough, N., & Wodak, R. (1997). Critical discourse analysis. In T. van Dijk (Ed.), *Discourse as social interaction* (pp. 258–284). London: SAGE.

Gee, J. P. (2004). *Situated language and learning: A critique of traditional schooling.* London: Routledge.

Gee, J. P. (2011). *An introduction to discourse analysis: Theory and method* (3rd ed.). New York: Routledge.

Gee, J. P. (2015). Discourse, small d, big D. In K. Tracy (Ed.), *The international encyclopedia of language and social interaction* (Vol. 1, pp. 418–422). Malden, MA: Wiley-Blackwell.

Gee, J. P. (2017). Discourse analysis. In E. Weigand (Ed.), *The Routledge handbook of language and dialogue* (pp. 62–77). New York: Routledge.

Goffman, E. (1974). *Frame analysis.* New York: Harper & Row.

Goffman, E. (1981). *Forms of talk.* Philadelphia: University of Pennsylvania Press.

Gumperz, J. (1982). *Discourse strategies.* Cambridge, UK: Cambridge University Press.

Gumperz, J., & Hymes, D. (Eds.). (1972). *Directions in sociolinguistics: The ethnography of communication*. New York: Holt, Rinehart & Winston.

Haddix, M. (2010). No longer on the margins: Researching the hybrid literate identities of Black and Latina preservice teachers. *Research in the Teaching of English, 45*(2), 97–123.

Heath, S. B. (1983). *Ways with words: Language, life and work in communities and classrooms*. Cambridge, UK: Cambridge University Press.

Heath, S. B. (2012). *Words at work and play: Three decades in family and community life*. Cambridge, UK: Cambridge University Press.

Hodge, R., & Kress, G. (1988). *Social semiotics*. Cambridge, UK: Polity Press.

Hymes, D. (Ed.). (1964). *Language in culture and society: A reader in linguistics and anthropology*. New York: Harper & Row.

Hymes, D. (1976). *Foundations in sociolinguistics: An ethnographic approach* (8th ed.). Philadelphia: University of Pennsylvania Press.

Jones, R. H. (2019). *Discourse analysis: A resource book for students* (2nd ed.). New York: Routledge.

Juzwik, M. M., Borsheim-Black, C., Caughlan, S., & Heintz, A. (2013). *Inspiring dialogue: Talking to learn in the English classroom*. New York: Teachers College Press.

Juzwik, M., & Ives, D. (2010). Small stories as resources for performing teacher identity: Identity-in-interaction in an urban language arts classroom. *Narrative Inquiry, 20*(1), 37–61.

Koc, Y., Peker, D., & Osmanoglu, A. (2009). Supporting teacher professional development through online video case study discussions: An assemblage of preservice and inservice teachers and the case teacher. *Teaching and Teacher Education, 8*, 1158–1168.

Kress, G., & van Leeuwen, T. (2001). *Multimodal discourse: The modes and media of contemporary communication*. London: Edward Arnold.

Kress, G., & van Leeuwen, T. (2006). *Reading images: The grammar of visual design* (2nd ed.). New York: Routledge.

Labov, W. (1972). *Language in the inner city: Studies in the Black English vernacular*. Philadelphia: University of Pennsylvania Press.

Ladson-Billings, G. (2007). Pushing past the achievement gap: An essay on the language of deficit. *Journal of Negro Education, 76*(3), 316–323.

Lewis, C. (2006). At last: "What's discourse got to do with it?": A meditation on critical discourse analysis in literacy research. *Research in the Teaching of English, 40*(3), 373–379.

Lewis Ellison, T., & Solomon, M. (2019). Counter-storytelling vs. deficit thinking methods around African American children and families, digital literacies, race, and the digital divide. *Research in the Teaching of English, 53*(3), 223–244.

Luke, A. (2004). Notes on the future of critical discourse studies. *Critical Discourse Studies, 1*(1), 149–152.

Martino, W. (2004). The boy problem: Boys, schooling, and masculinity. In R. P. Transit (Ed.), *Disciplining the child via the discourse of the professions* (pp. 19–33). Springfield, IL: Charles C Thomas.

Mehan, H. (1979). *Learning lessons: Social organization in the classroom*. Cambridge, MA: Harvard University Press.

Mercer, N. (2000). *Words and minds: How we use language to think together*. New York: Routledge.

Mercer, N., & Hodgkinson, S. (Eds.) (2008). *Exploring talk in school: Inspired by the work of Douglas Barnes*. London: SAGE.

Moje, E. B., & Lewis, C. (2007). Examining opportunities to learn literacy: The role of critical sociocultural literacy research. In C. Lewis, P. Enciso, & E. B. Moje (Eds.), *Reframing sociocultural research on literacy: Identity, agency, and power* (pp. 15–48). Mahwah, NJ: Erlbaum.

Nassaji, H., & Wells, G. (2000). What's the use of "triadic dialogue"?: An investigation of teacher–student interaction. *Applied Linguistics, 21,* 376–406.

Norris, S. (2004). *Analyzing multimodal interaction: A methodological framework*. London: Routledge.

Norris, S. (2011). *Identity in (inter)action: Introducing multimodal (inter)action analysis* (Vol. 4). Berlin: de Gruyter.

Norris, S. (2014). Multimodal (inter)action analysis. In P. Albers, T. Holbrook, & A. S. Flint (Eds.), *New methods of literacy research* (pp. 70–84). New York: Routledge.

Nystrand, M. (1997). *Opening dialogue: Understanding the dynamics of language and learning in the English classroom*. New York: Teachers College Press.

O'Connor, C., Michaels, S., Chapin, S., & Harbaugh, A. G. (2017). The silent and the vocal: Participation and learning in whole-class discussion. *Learning and Instruction, 48,* 5–13.

Rex, L. A., Bunn, M., Davila, B. A., Dickinson, H. A., Ford, F. C., Gerben, C., et al. (2010). A review of discourse analysis in literacy research: Equitable access. *Reading Research Quarterly, 45*(1), 94–115.

Rex, L. A., & Schiller, L. (2009). *Using discourse analysis to improve classroom interaction*. New York: Routledge.

Rogers, R. (2011). *An introduction to critical discourse analysis in education*. New York: Routledge.

Rogers, R. (2013). Critical discourse analysis. In A. A. Trainor & E. Graue (Eds.), *Reviewing qualitative research in the social sciences* (pp. 66–81). New York: Routledge.

Rogers, R. (2014). Critical discourse analysis in literacy research. In P. Albers, T. Holbrook, & A. S. Flint (Eds.), *New methods of literacy research* (pp. 19–39). New York: Routledge.

Rogers, R. (2018). *Reclaiming powerful literacies: New horizons for critical discourse analysis*. New York: Routledge.

Rogers, R., & Mosley, M. (2006). Racial literacy in a second grade classroom: Critical race theory, whiteness studies, and literacy research. *Reading Research Quarterly, 41*(4), 462–495.

Rogers, R., & Schaenen, I. (2013). Critical discourse analysis in literacy education: A review of the literature. *Reading Research Quarterly, 49*(1), 121–143.

Rogers, R., & Wetzel, M. M. (2013). Studying agency in teacher education: A layered approach to positive discourse analysis. *Critical Inquiry into Language Studies, 10*(1), 62–92.

Rogers, R., & Wetzel, M. M. (2014). *Designing critical literacy education through critical discourse analysis: Pedagogical and research tools for teacher-researchers*. New York: Routledge.

Rymes, B. (2016). *Classroom discourse analysis: A tool for critical reflection* (2nd ed.). New York: Routledge.

Saks, H., Schegloff, E. A., & Jefferson, G. (1974). The simplest systematics for the organization of turntaking for conversations. *Language, 50*(4), 696–735.

Schieble, M. (2012). Critical conversations on whiteness with young adult literature. *Journal of Adolescent and Adult Literacy, 56*(3), 212–221.

Scollon, R. (2001). *Mediated discourse: The nexus of practice.* London: Routledge.

Scollon, R., & Scollon, S. W. (2004). *Nexus analysis: Discourse and the emerging Internet.* New York: Routledge.

Scollon, S. W., & de Saint-Georges, I. (2012). Mediated discourse analysis. In J. P. Gee & M. Handford (Eds.), *The Routledge handbook of discourse analysis* (pp. 66–78). New York: Routledge.

Searle, J. R., Kiefer, F., & Bierwisch, M. (Eds.). (1980). *Speech act theory and pragmatics* (Vol. 10). Dordrecht, the Netherlands: Reidel.

Sherin, M., & van Es, E. A. (2009). Effects of video club participation on teachers' professional vision. *Journal of Teacher Education, 60*(1), 20–37.

Tannen, D. (1984). *Conversational style: Analyzing talk among friends.* Norwood, NJ: Ablex.

Tannen, D. (2001). The relativity of linguistic strategies: Rethinking power and solidarity in gender and dominance. In M. Wetherell, S. Taylor, & S. J. Yates (Eds.), *Discourse theory and practice: A reader* (pp. 150–166). London: SAGE.

Thomas, E. E. (2015). "We always talk about race": Navigating race talk dilemmas in the teaching of literature. *Research in the Teaching of English, 50*(2), 154–175.

Valencia, R. R. (2012). *The evolution of deficit thinking: Educational thought and practice.* New York: Routledge.

van Dijk, T. A. (2015). Critical discourse analysis. In D. Tannen, H. E. Hamilton, & D. Schiffrin (Eds.), *The handbook of discourse analysis* (pp. 466–485). Hoboken, NJ: Wiley.

van Es, E., & Sherin, M. G. (2002). Learning to notice: Scaffolding new teachers interpretations of classroom interactions. *Journal of Technology and Teacher Education, 10*(4), 571–596.

Vetter, A., & Schieble, M. (2015). *Observing teacher identities through video analysis: Practice and implications.* New York: Routledge.

Wells, G. (1999). *Dialogic inquiry: Toward a sociocultural practice and theory of education.* Cambridge, UK: Cambridge University Press.

Wertsch, J. V. (1998). *Voices of the mind: A sociocultural approach to mediated action.* Cambridge, MA: Harvard University Press.

Wohlwend, K. (2012). The boys who would be princesses: Playing with gender identity intertexts in Disney Princess transmedia. *Gender and Education, 24*(6), 593–610.

CHAPTER 8

Design-Based Research in Literacy

Gay Ivey

The past decade has brought numerous calls for building bidirectional, inextricable links between research and practice in education. At the 2014 Wallace Foundation Distinguished Lecture at the annual meeting of the American Educational Research Association (AERA), Catherine Snow (2015) referred to "a remarkable shift . . . in the rhetoric relating educational research to practice," which "moved beyond the mottos of the 20th century—from research to practice, doing translation science—to a new model that emphasizes the interconnections between research and practice rather than the gap between them" (p. 460). At that same conference, Anthony Bryk (2015), in the AERA Distinguished Lecture, argued for practice-based evidence that addresses the variability of complex educational settings, and thus the variable effectiveness of interventions. Others (e.g., Malouf & Taymans, 2016; Pogrow, 2017) have offered cautionary messages regarding the practical value of randomized controlled experimental designs, and the danger of relying on existing evidence bases most frequently invoked in educational reform initiatives, such as the What Works Clearinghouse.

Growing interest in the general notion that research ought to be more directly shaping of and shaped by practice is also apparent within the literacy research community. In his presidential address to the Literacy Research Association, David Reinking (2012) argued that our existing metaphors for research—laboratory or lens—have rendered our efforts to produce changes in literacy learning and teaching relatively inconsequential. He argued for a new set of metaphors—chefs (rather than cooks), evolution, engineering—that emphasize the care, time, and complexity of research that might make a difference, and the need to refocus our attention on multiperspective, goal-oriented actions, rather than simply asking questions about "what works" and what is.

Reinking (2012) suggested design-based research as having strong potential to transform the consequences of research on outcomes for children and adult literacy learners. He and Barbara Bradley wrote chapters on design-based research for previous editions of this handbook. Since the second edition appeared in 2011, literacy researchers have published design-based studies on a range of topics, including preservice teacher learning (Chandler-Olcott et al., 2018; Paratore, O'Brien, Jiménez, Salinas, & Ly, 2016), vocabulary development (Neuman & Dwyer, 2011; Parsons & Bryant, 2016; Wang, Christ, & Chiu, 2014), writing/composing (Howell, Butler, & Reinking, 2017; Philippakos, MacArthur, & Munsell, 2018; Tracy & Headley, 2013), digital literacies (Colwell, Hunt-Barron, & Reinking, 2013; Rowe & Miller, 2016), disciplinary literacies (Colwell & Reinking, 2016; Doerr & Temple, 2016), and classroom talk (Caughlan, Juzwik, Borsheim-Black, Kelly, & Fine, 2013; Hall, 2016), among others. A handbook on educational design research (Plomp & Nieveen, 2013) included a range of examples written by literacy researchers. At this writing, there were 121 subscribers to a listserv sponsored by the Literacy Research Association's Formative Experiments and Design-Based Research Innovative Community Group. Thus, the status of design-based research in literacy has continued to grow in recent years, undoubtedly in no small part because of David Reinking's efforts to bring it to the forefront of methodological conversations.

The appeal of design-based research in the literacy community is likely linked in part to decades of frustration over a string of failed educational policies. These policies have privileged programs that promised improvement, but that were based on conventional experimental research that failed to take into account the complex ecologies of classrooms, the multidimensionalities of children's and teachers' lives, the range of literate practices in which people engage, and the broader forms of development made possible by and through literacy. For instance, two defining features of Reading First, a multibillion-dollar initiative funded by the U.S. government, were its emphasis on "scientifically based research" (i.e., randomized controlled experiments) and its arguably narrow focus on phonemic awareness, phonics, fluency, vocabulary, and comprehension—the constructs promoted as most essential by the National Reading Panel (2000) and perpetuated by the 2001 No Child Left Behind Act. Yet the Reading First Impact Study (Gamse, Jacob, Horst, Boulay, & Unlu, 2008) reported that despite the vast financial and human resources devoted to this undertaking, improvement in student reading achievement was limited. Specifically, results indicated that Reading First "produced a positive and statistically significant impact on amount of instructional time spent on the five essential components of reading instruction promoted by the program (phonemic awareness, phonics, vocabulary, fluency, and comprehension) in grades one and two," but "did not produce a statistically significant impact on student reading comprehension test scores in grades one, two or three" (Gamse et al., 2008, p. xv). An analysis of the outcomes of response to intervention, an approach to early intervention to prevent reading difficulties that was generated through the 2004 reauthorization of the Individuals with Disabilities Education Act, revealed similar problems, but with the added problem of negative impacts (Balu et al., 2015).

There is also increasing movement in the literacy research community toward intentionally mitigating inequities through design-oriented studies. Gutiérrez (2018), for instance, has argued for literacy research focused squarely on "designing educational practices that contribute to the social good, as well as have transformative and enduring consequences for people in vulnerable communities" (p. 103).

In this chapter, I offer my understandings of design-based research as it is currently taken up, including some types of questions that can be addressed through this methodology, along with some considerations regarding methodological standards. I include an extended example of a study in literacy that employed principles of design-based research. Finally, I consider some possible future directions and expansions of design-based research in literacy.

WHAT IS DESIGN-BASED RESEARCH?

At the risk of oversimplifying, we might think of design-based research as setting a particular educational goal; designing or employing an intervention that stands the best chance of leading participants to that goal; and then tweaking it, via systematic examinations of how well it is working, until all participants have achieved what we hoped they might. Design-based research in education has been primarily situated in the learning sciences, and its origins are routinely traced back to Brown (1992) and Collins (1992), who called for "design experiments" in which interventions and tools might be tested and refined in actual classroom settings. The basic premise of design experiments was that intervention research should directly improve classroom practice. Ann Brown's reflection on the evolution of her research makes clear that for experimental and developmental psychologists of the time, this call would require a substantial shift not only in what research should accomplish, but also in what researchers should do:

> As a design scientist in my field, I attempt to engineer innovative educational environments and simultaneously conduct experimental studies of those innovations. This involves orchestrating all aspects of a period of daily life in classrooms, a research activity for which I was not trained. My training was that of a classic learning theorist prepared to work with "subjects" (rats, children, sophomores), in strictly controlled laboratory

settings. The methods I have employed in my previous life are not readily transported to the research activities I oversee currently. (p. 141)

This new set of activities would include looking beyond singular variables, she reported, to simultaneously studying multiple parts of a system (e.g., students, teachers, curriculum) and how changes in one area potentially generate changes in the whole. Clear from the beginnings of this approach to educational research was the dual goal of generating both theoretical and practical implications. In other words, particular classrooms that served as settings and objects of research were the targets of improvement, but there was an expectation that the research would contribute to theories about learning that could be applied to other classrooms.

Over the next several decades, the fundamental principles of early design experiments began to appear in various disciplines in educational research—beyond experimental psychology and the learning sciences— and under varied labels, including *design-based research* (Design-Based Research Collective, 2003), *formative experiments* (Reinking & Bradley, 2008), *formative interventions* (Engeström, 2011), *lesson study* (Lewis, Perry, & Murata, 2006), *design-based implementation research* (Penuel, Fishman, Cheng, & Sabelli, 2011), *social design experiments* (Gutiérrez & Vossoughi, 2010), *researcher–practitioner partnerships* (Coburn, Penuel, & Geil, 2013), and *participatory design research* (Bang & Vossoughi, 2016). The most recent iterations in this group represent an expansion of the goals of design-oriented research. Researchers are using this approach not only to influence classroom learning in a conventional sense, but also to intentionally aim for larger social change. Most of the more recent iterations also focus not just on changing the roles of researchers, in line with Brown's (1992) early reflections, but on paying attention to the roles of teachers and other collaborators (Engeström, 2011; Penuel, Coburn & Gallagher, 2013).

Characteristics of Design-Based Studies

Although there are variations in how design-based research is conceived, particularly in newer iterations and expansions, researchers generally agree that at its core, design-based research is defined by the multifaceted, iterative relationship between theory and practice. It can be distinguished from action research in that although it aims to create possibilities and solutions at the local level, it also aspires to promote theoretical understandings that can be taken up across contexts.

The principles of design-based research across these variations mentioned previously are too nuanced to detail specifically here, but the most common characteristics are still likely those suggested by Cobb, Confrey, diSessa, Lehrer, and Schauble (2003). They submit that design-based research (1) generates theories about learning and about instruction; (2) capitalizes on intervention; (3) places existing learning theories at risk;

(4) employs iterative design featuring cycles of intervention, inquiry, and revision; and (5) generates new theories that have an instrumental impact on practice.

Drawing on the work of Cobb and colleagues (2003), but expanding these characteristics on the basis of their own experiences in conducting formative experiments, Reinking and Bradley (2008, pp. 17–22) offered these principles, which I detail here because they have been invoked most frequently in design-oriented research in literacy:

- *Intervention-focused within an authentic context.* The research needs to focus on an intervention or instructional practice, which must be studied within a real instructional setting. The intervention under study may be an existing intervention, and the focus on the research may be on the interplay between the intervention and the particular context in which it is being used. The intervention can also be new and innovative, but informed by existing research.

- *Theoretical.* Design-based research is driven by theories not only about how to create conditions to make an intervention work toward a specified goal, but also by theories explaining why an intervention did or did not work. Thus, preliminary theories are placed at risk and potentially tweaked, depending on modifications that proved necessary to make interventions effective for all participants.

- *Goal-oriented.* Studies are driven by explicitly stated goals—in other words, what the intervention or instructional practice under consideration is intended to affect in positive ways. These goals must be justified by existing research, theory, and practice, and researchers need to argue why a particular goal is warranted. This goal serves as a touchstone throughout the research to determine whether an intervention is having the intended result.

- *Adaptive and iterative.* Whereas traditional experiments are concerned with fidelity and aim to report the effects of an intervention *on average,* the point of design-based research is to modify the intervention to the point that it is producing positive outcomes for *all* participants. Steeped in authentic contexts, these studies more closely match the processes effective teachers use and the goals of actual schools and other educational settings.

- *Transformative.* Beyond addressing the goal explicitly stated by a study, design-based research opens the possibility for larger transformations of teaching, learning, and the learning environment. The documentation of unintended consequences of the intervention is essential for understanding not only potential negative side effects of an intervention (Zhao, 2017), but also the possibility of unanticipated, expanded learning that leads to new theoretical understandings and practices (e.g., Ivey & Johnston, 2015a).

- *Methodologically inclusive and flexible.* Design-based studies are not bound to any particular methods of collecting or analyzing data. Studies may employ quantitative, qualitative, or mixed methods approaches. The most important determining factor for selection of methods is that they sufficiently capture whether or not an intervention is working, in addition to the factors that are supporting or hindering effectiveness.

Design-Based Research for Social Change

A diverging group of studies related to design-based traditions aims explicitly to affect social change, as mentioned earlier. Stemming primarily from Engeström's (2011) notion of *formative intervention,* much of this work is rooted in cultural–historical activity theory. The core of this work is located not so much in changing an intervention to make it work as in designing it to expand the agency of participants so that they can transform their own circumstances and social institutions (Gutiérrez & Jurow, 2016; Penuel, 2014). In particular, this approach takes up intentionally the tensions between existing educational ecologies and the lives and experiences of nondominant students and their communities. Key properties are the shifting roles of researchers and participant collaborators, far beyond those that were proposed in the earliest iterations of design-based research. Sannino, Engeström, and Lemos (2016) explain that the participants themselves are the primary designers: "Whereas [Ann] Brown innovatively advocated the collaborative role of participants in design experiments, we seek to take a step further, seeing ourselves as intervening in design processes of which we cannot possibly be the engineers in control" (p. 600). They explain that the researcher's role, rather than to design interventions, is to "intervene by provoking and supporting the process led and owned by the learners" (p. 600). As other researchers outside the area of learning sciences take up the general notion of design, but employ different theoretical orientations and include participants of very different communities, it is likely that what it means to be "design-based" will continue to evolve and expand.

WHAT KINDS OF QUESTIONS CAN BE ADDRESSED WITH DESIGN-BASED STUDIES?

In general, design-based research is appropriate for studies that ask overarching questions about *how,* rather than *what is, what is the relationship,* or *what is better.* As an example, Howell and colleagues (2017) asked, "How can using digital tools within a process orientation to writing be integrated into conventional instruction to help students construct effective multimodal and conventional arguments?" (p. 186). The point of the question was to make the change happen. This might be contrasted with an ethnographic study that asks, hypothetically, "What is the nature of students' multimodal and conventional written arguments when digital tools within a process orientation to writing are integrated into conventional instruction?" As another contrast, a conventional experimental study might test the effects of digital tool use versus conventional instruction on students' argumentative writing. In these two examples, although the results might be used to drive a change in policy or instruction, the research itself is not intended to catalyze change in the context in which it is conducted. This important distinction is one of the defining features of questions most suited for design-based studies.

In order to fully understand the complexity of a learning environment and the conditions under which an intervention or practice is most or least effective, though, researchers use additional questions beyond the starting point to help drive the process. Reinking and Bradley (2008) suggest guiding questions such as these: (1) What are the factors that enhance or inhibit an intervention's effectiveness in moving toward the stated pedagogical goal? (2) How do modifications based on these factors help improve the effectiveness of the intervention? (3) What are the unanticipated outcomes of the intervention? Questions such as these help to maintain the dual purposes of design-based studies—that is, to inform practical knowledge and to leverage theoretical developments.

WHAT ARE THE STANDARDS OF QUALITY FOR DESIGN-BASED STUDIES IN LITERACY?

Design-based research has been described as "a meta-methodology that integrates other methods into a process" (Easterday, Rees Lewis, & Gerber, 2018, p. 136). Furthermore,

> DR [design research] does not commit researchers to a specific theoretical perspective, type of data collection, or analytical approach, but rather, the researcher must deploy these methods in a way that is appropriate to the iterative, empirical development of the theoretical and empirical products of design research. This explains the shape-shifting nature of DR—DR looks like other forms of research because it employs these methodologies to do its work. (Easterday et al., 2018, p. 148)

How Standards of Quality for Design-Based Studies Intersect with Conventional Standards

Because design-based studies employ multiple methods, many of the acceptable standards of rigor that apply to more conventional methods still apply to those methods when they are used within the process of design-based studies. A colleague and I (Ivey & Johnston, 2011), however, have described how some methods are used in slightly different ways. For example, testing claims of causality may be appropriate in design-based studies, but in contrast to more familiar experimental approaches, this happens within the process of the study rather than at the end. In addition, efforts at change in design research are theoretically motivated and need to be tested not only at the group level, but also at the individual level;, thus it is necessary to use the negative case analysis of ethnographic work to test the theoretical frame. A major difference, though, is that this analysis will have to be accomplished somewhat on the run because it will be essential to identify why an intervention is not working as efficiently and promptly as possible in order to make necessary adjustments, and thus to ameliorate the differences in student outcomes. An outlier, in this sense, is not viewed as a nuisance, as it might be in controlled experiments, but as an invaluable source of information: It can be used to drive improvement, and also simultaneously to help researchers retheorize the study based on these changes.

Ethnography and design-based research also share the burden of documenting in painstaking detail the context of a study, particularly the social context. A key divergence when it comes to design-based research is that a single statement of context is insufficient. Because the idea is that the context will change as a result of the intervention and as an outcome of the intervention, documentation of the context is ongoing, and identifying the sources and consequences of these shifts is key to developing theories.

Distinctive Standards for Design-Based Research

Here I want to highlight three areas that seem to have growing importance in the evolution of design-based research and its emergence as a valued, rigorous approach to educational research: (1) the importance of developing and demonstrating a chain of logic that both produces and explains the process and the instrumental and theoretical outcomes; (2) arranging for the agency of participants; and (3) dealing with intervention side effects.

Establishing a Chain of Logic

Because design-based research is both multiphased and iterative, researchers must clearly document not just the overall design and methods—which in many cases cannot be codified at the beginning of a study—but also the reasoning or goals behind a set of methods nested within the larger research process (Easterday et al., 2018). To offer a perhaps overly simplistic example, a study designed to increase children's time spent reading might begin with a survey to establish a baseline for students' reading habits at both the group and individual levels, followed by the introduction of an intervention that both the existing professional literature and practical knowledge suggest has the best chance for producing the desired outcome. A next phase might include observations of students during a scheduled time for self-selected reading, along with students' logging the number of pages they read each day for a particular period of time. The analysis of this data might lead the researcher to identify students who are reading more than what their initial surveys suggested, and students whose reading habits did not seem to be changing. Interviews with these selected students might be designed to determine what at this point was enhancing or inhibiting students' reading experiences, and corresponding modifications might be made to the intervention, following by another round of surveys or observations, and so on. The rounds of data collection and analysis, regardless of methods, are driven by the goal of the intervention.

In design-based studies specific to literacy, it appears that presently there is great variability in the extent to which a chain of logic is included, with a few studies providing painstaking detail, and others providing only intervention outcomes derived at the conclusion of a study. A persistent challenge of the need to explain the logic driving an entire study (much more complex than the example I have offered, of course) is how to have it published in outlets that expect a relatively straightforward, formulaic description of methods.

Arranging for Agency of Participants

Many failed reform efforts in recent years have constrained teachers' efforts to contribute their own expertise (Snow, 2015), much less to develop new ways of thinking about learning and teaching. There continues to be some ambiguity and inconsistency in the role of practitioners and in the role of practical knowledge in the development of design-based interventions (Ormel, Pareja Roblin, McKenney, Voogt, & Pieters, 2012). But research aimed at directly shaping classroom practice must not simply enlist teachers and students as collaborators; it must centralize their involvement. In order for the outcomes of design-based research to be taken up and sustained, studies must intentionally account for how participants (e.g., teachers and students) might assume ownership of the tools and practices developed through the intervention.

In some cases, the possibilities for teacher agency can be increased explicitly by making it the precise object of the intervention (Severance, Penuel, Sumner, & Leary, 2016). In other cases, though, special care should be taken to ensure that participants not only maintain the intervention, but even expand it on the basis of new learning. In my own work in this area, I have recognized the need to make adjustments. In one formative experiment designed to increase literacy engagement among adolescent English learners (Ivey & Broaddus, 2007), an unanticipated outcome of the intervention was that the researchers had assumed far too many of the teaching opportunities, particularly when it came to the students most difficult to engage, rendering the teacher in that study considerably less autonomous and the intervention more difficult to sustain. In contrast, eighth-grade teachers in a subsequent formative experiment designed to increase reading engagement (Ivey, 2013) were enlisted from the beginning as codesigners of the intervention. The long-term result was an expansion of the original goals of the intervention (Ivey & Johnston, 2013), but also transformations in the teaching activity and relationships between the teachers, as well as increases in student agency (Ivey & Johnston, 2015a).

Dealing with Side Effects

In their guiding principles for formative experiments, Reinking and Bradley (2008) recommend the deliberate identification of both positive and negative outcomes of the interventions that were not originally intended by the researchers. Hypothetically, researchers developing an intervention to increase kindergarteners' writing engagement might learn, for instance, that this process inadvertently resulted in children's expanding their vocabularies—an outcome most people would welcome. A key aspect of data collection and analysis would be to try to understand, from both a practical and a theory-expanding standpoint, how those developments were coming about.

On the other hand, interventions created even with the best of intentions may also have damaging effects. Zhao (2017) has argued that if medical research is going to be held up as the gold standard for educational research, as it has been in contemporary educational policies, then randomized controlled experiments in education such as those favored in the What Works Clearinghouse need to be held to the same standard as the U.S. Food and Drug Administration requires for drugs before they are introduced into the marketplace. That is, they need to be tested for any unwanted damaging effects. In other words, "when studying and reporting the benefits or effectiveness, one must also study and report the risks" (Zhao, 2017, p. 2). Zhao goes on to offer the hypothetical example of an intervention that is shown to raise reading test scores, but also to make children hate reading. This would give potential users and consumers all sides of the issue.

The iterative nature of design-based studies gives them the potential not only to detect (quickly) any potential negative impacts of the intervention, but also to mitigate them as part of the design process. One might imagine, for instance, an intervention designed to increase third-grade students' fluency instruction that had the unwanted effect of privileging reading speed at the cost of comprehension. In a high-quality design-based study, it would be necessary not only to detect the problem, but also to modify or perhaps redesign the study so that fluency and comprehension would be developed simultaneously, with perhaps other benefits sought in the process. Likewise, that study would produce practical knowledge about what inhibits or enhances the synchronous development of fluent, meaning-oriented reading.

It is important to note that there may be a significant burden on ethical rigor for researchers engaging in design-based research. Although the idea of designing research that deliberately and explicitly aims for impact appears to be a prosocial enterprise, there are potential downsides and unforeseen negative consequences. Individuals in the research actively transform the learning environment and take up the constructs that are generated, for better or for worse. Students and teachers are fully involved and take risks as part of the change process. Researchers have to make many decisions in the moment, and these may create many gray areas that cannot be preapproved by institutional review boards; yet not addressing them would be equally unethical. At the same time, because change is not simply decided by researchers, the participants have ownership of consequences, both good and bad—so there is to some extent a higher level of personal risk on the participants' part.

AN EXEMPLAR STUDY

Colwell and Reinking (2016) conducted a study characterized as a formative experiment (Reinking & Bradley, 2008) that exemplifies many of the principles of high-quality design-based research described in this chapter. The primary purpose of their study was to "investigate how middle school history instruction could be transformed to align with the literacy goals addressed in new curricular standards and to better understand within a typical instructional context the pedagogical influences and outcomes associated with such a transformation" (p. 1). They collaborated with an eighth-grade teacher in her history classroom as she learned to align history instruction with literacy instruction, and they sought to understand how this change might occur.

As expected from design-oriented studies, the purpose of the study was responsive to both practical and theoretical conundrums. From the practical side, there were new curricular imperatives that required instruction linking history and language arts. On the research side, they drew from existing theories suggesting that this challenge might be appropriately addressed through a focus on disciplinary literacy, but also from a lack of evidence on how the process of teaching could be transformed to align history and literacy. Their initial intervention was drawn from three elements supported by the literature, and thus was intended to represent strategies with the best chance of catalyzing change toward the desired goal: (1) reading primary and secondary sources; (2) explicit instruction on critical reading and analyzing historical texts; and (3) responding to the reading of historical texts through blogging. To promote autonomy, the researchers provided some suggestions, but they asked the teacher to choose the precise materials and strategies to be used.

The intervention took place over a period of 10 consecutive weeks, following a time of planning and of the researchers' collecting data to understand the instructional context—the larger context of the district, as well as that of the classroom. During the implementation of the intervention, the researchers conducted an embedded case study (Yin, 2009). Data included classroom observations, participant observations, video recordings of lessons, informal interviews and debriefings with the teacher, semistructured interviews with the teacher, focused group discussions with the students, and students' blog posts.

The intervention consisted of five instructional units, and each of these units served not only to demarcate an embedded case, but also to define cycles of data collection and analysis. As Colwell and Reinking (2016) described it, "data collection and analysis within each topical unit informed modifications to the next unit, iterative across the five units" (p. 11). Whereas ongoing analysis prompted practical changes to the intervention, a retrospective analysis (Gravemeijer & Cobb, 2006), in which the researchers analyzed data from across the whole intervention, produced theoretical outcomes.

In reporting their results—often a challenging process in writing up design-based studies—Colwell and Reinking (2016) shared several pedagogical assertions (generated through retrospective analysis), each followed by key events that led to modifications in the intervention, a description of the modification, and the outcomes of the change. For example, the first assertion was "A teacher's beliefs are foundational to aligning history instruction and literacy goals, but instantiating those beliefs in instruction is mediated by previous, imagined, and enacted practice" (p. 13). In explaining key events that led to the modification linked to this assertion, the researchers described the teacher's resistance to using graphic organizers as a way to support students' critical reading of history (a strategy encouraged by the researchers at the outset of the intervention). Their analysis of interview data revealed three possible reasons for this apprehension: (1) the teacher's concern that students would not be successful in using this strategy; (2) her hesitance to abandon familiar instructional routines; and (3) a commitment to instruction, such as teaching for rote learning of facts, that would help students with standardized tests. The subsequent modification was the introduction of a model blog activity in which the teacher could share an example of how someone might respond critically to a text. This particular activity was chosen because the teacher had been observed using model examples elsewhere in her teaching. The outcome shared by the researchers was that both the teacher and her students were enthusiastic about the blog activity. Their analysis indicated that the teacher's enthusiasm was likely due to observing her own students' engagement, seeing their success with the activity, and seeing them think critically as they read the historical texts. The researchers noted that this was an important first turn in the transformation of her teaching.

Unanticipated outcomes catalyzed by the intervention included the teacher's unprompted decision later in the intervention to use instructional tools (such as the graphic organizer) that she had originally rejected, and also to use online activities that involved critical reading. Colwell and Reinking (2016) also observed a change in her perspective toward lower-achieving students. As they described it, "[the teacher] was moving away from a deficit stance, acquiring more confidence that all of her students, with the right support could engage successfully with the intervention and with texts in a manner more consistent with her conceptions of disciplinary literacy" (p. 25). They noted that during the final two units, the teacher was more enthusiastic about working with these students. Overall during the final two units, the researchers were collecting substantial evidence that instruction was being transformed.

This particular study provides an incredibly useful model for the complex, inseparable relationship between practical activity and theoretical development in design-based research. It also serves as a good example of how to write up research with processes and results that do not resemble conventional structures.

FUTURE CONSIDERATIONS

While developing this chapter, I was in the midst of some challenging work with a laboratory school—a public charter school—that emerged from a state mandate to partner universities with low-performing schools in an effort to improve and expand student outcomes and experiences through research and professional development. The project was given 5 years because it was believed that real transformation would require that much time. At the beginning of the second year of my involvement, I have certainly come to share that belief.

Likewise, when it comes to design-based research, we would be wise not to think in terms of "quick fixes" or to place too much emphasis on isolated, one-time studies, even those reflecting the highest methodological standards. Erickson (2014) had an interesting perspective on how we might think about the role of design-based research within the research–policy–practice dynamic. He proposed a "Lake Wobegon" approach that shifts away from "best practices" toward "pretty good practices," and from "high-fidelity implementation" toward "low-fidelity implementation," for interventions that can and should be modified for local contexts. He argued that instead of scaling *up* so-called "replicable findings" from research, we consider scaling *down*. The reduced expectation, he suggested, is not for the magnitude of the work, but instead for the pace at which this work is accomplished, particularly given the recent history of school reform efforts:

> Recognize that real school improvement will take years upon years . . . because good teaching is labor-intensive, and there is no end run about that. Two generations of teachers have been de-skilled by highly scripted teaching materials in an attempt at installing "teacher-proof" curriculum. Instead, what is needed is serious investment in long term continuing education—support for the clinical judgment of teachers rather than vain attempts to replace the complexity of that judgment with simple compliance to administrative fiat. (p. 3)

In a similar vein, Goatley and Johnston (2013) have described important innovations in literacy teaching that came about through small-scale "tinkering" rather than through grand, large-scale design. Drawing on Johnson's (2010) work on the history of innovation, they propose that these innovations evolved through small advancements in practice that led to the "adjacent possible," or as they put it, "a small succession of realizations—a continuous process of local transformation and knowledge building over time," rather than through a "big vision" (Goatley & Johnston, 2013, p. 95).

Over the past decade, I have been fortunate to catch a glimpse of how innovation and theoretical breakthroughs can occur through such small successions of realizations, all prompted by a design-based study. In all, I spent approximately 6 years studying reading engagement in the classrooms of the same group of eighth-grade teachers in one school. The original goal of the intervention was to tweak instruction so that all students in these classrooms became engaged as readers over the course of the year, backed by the evidence-based rationale that the amount of voluntary, purposeful reading would be linked to higher reading achievement (Ivey, 2013).

The teachers and I started with a theoretically defensible intervention— offering students high-interest books, permission to choose what they read, regular times to read in school, and freedom from assignments attached to their reading. With relatively few modifications needed over one school year, most students became enthusiastic, engaged readers. But becoming engaged readers opened up new possibilities for students. The students began to express how, through engagement, they became personally involved with characters; they then began to turn to each other, family members, and their teachers to talk about interesting and unsettling dilemmas they were encountering through characters' lives. They claimed that they were not merely reading more or changing as readers, as the initial intervention intended; they were changing as people.

On an informed hunch that there was more to this, I stayed longer than I intended, returning to these same teachers' classrooms the next year and enlisting help. Peter Johnston and I (Ivey & Johnston, 2013) studied a new set of students in these classrooms where teachers' practices were now evolving. For instance, in addition to abandoning whole-class reading for student choices, they loosened their requirement for "silent" reading time—not only allowing but encouraging students to talk to each other as they read, and rearranging desks to make that more possible. Our interviews and observations revealed that, indeed, students were experiencing a range of consequences they attributed to engagement and to their teachers' decisions about instruction. They reported not only reading more (and better); they suggested a range of personal, social, relational, academic, and intellectual development. Their reports of their experiences suggested that engaged reading—previously theorized as a motivated, strategic, but primarily cognitive enterprise supported by the social context (e.g., Guthrie, Wigfield, & You, 2012)—was substantially social and inseparably cognitive and social, particularly when reading fiction.

A subsequent study involved a cultural–historical analysis of the evolution of teaching and classroom practices and interactions over a 4-year period (Ivey & Johnston, 2015a), which illuminated how the innovation had occurred. Students and teachers, we learned, had transformed not only the literacy practices in these classrooms, but also the cultures in these classrooms, relationships and roles (as teaching became distributed across teachers and students), and ultimately the goals of reading instruction. In short, just getting readers engaged for the purpose of higher achievement was no longer a sufficient goal. Students and their teachers deliberately set out to use reading and conversations about books to grow as people, to expand their relationships, and to think about their futures. It would have been naïve to believe that the story ended there, though. Several years later, we revisited student participants from two of the study cohorts, then 2 or 3 years removed from eighth grade (Ivey & Johnston, 2015b). Without the supportive contexts of their eighth-grade classrooms, the persistence of engaged reading was limited—although, surprisingly, students maintained detailed memories and strong feelings from their experiences with eighth-grade reading and relationships. These findings have opened the door to more questions.

Among the many things I have learned in this process, particularly in reflecting on research I conducted prior to that period, is that we know very little from "one-and-done" studies, regardless of methodology. If we imagine that design-based research in literacy could help to substantially change the experiences of literacy learners and teachers, we need to consider the possibilities offered by prolonged, multilayered studies in the same contexts. In particular, if teacher and student agency is to be privileged in studies, then steps should be taken to understand and support where that agency might lead. Indeed, it is the infinite potential afforded by human agency, with tools and expertise made available by knowledgeable researchers, that will help design-based research in literacy deliver on its promise of transformation.

REFERENCES

Balu, R., Zhu, P., Doolittle, F., Schiller, E., Jenkins, J., & Gersten, R. (2015). *Evaluation of response to intervention practices for elementary school reading* (NCEE 2016-4000). Washington, DC: National Center for Education Evaluation and Regional Assistance, Institute of Education Sciences, U.S. Department of Education.

Bang, M., & Vossoughi, S. (2016). Participatory design research and educational justice: Studying learning and relations within social change making. *Cognition and Instruction, 34*(3), 173–193.

Brown, A. L. (1992). Design experiments: Theoretical and methodological challenges in creating complex interventions in classroom settings. *Journal of the Learning Sciences, 2,* 141–178.

Bryk, A. S. (2015). 2014 AERA Distinguished Lecture: Accelerating how we learn to improve. *Educational Researcher, 44*(9), 467–477.

Caughlan, S., Juzwik, M. M., Borsheim-Black, C., Kelly, S., & Fine, J. G. (2013). English teacher candidates developing dialogically organized instructional practices. *Research in the Teaching of English, 47*(3), 212–246.

Chandler-Olcott, K., Dotger, S., Waymouth, H., Crosby, M., Lahr, M., Hinchman, K., et al. (2018). Teacher candidates learn to enact curriculum in a partnership-sponsored literacy enrichment program for youth. *The New Educator, 14*(3), 192–211.

Cobb, P., Confrey, J., diSessa, A., Lehrer, R., & Schauble, L. (2003). Design experiments in educational research. *Educational Researcher, 32*(1), 9–13.

Coburn, C. E., Penuel, W. R., & Geil, K. E. (2013). *Research–practice partnerships: A strategy for leveraging research for educational improvement in school districts.* New York: William T. Grant Foundation.

Collins, F. (1992). Toward a design science of education. In E. Scanlon & T. O'Shea (Eds.), *New directions in educational technology* (pp. 83–103). New York: Springer-Verlag.

Colwell, J., Hunt-Barron, S., & Reinking, D. (2013). Obstacles to developing digital literacy on the Internet in middle school science instruction. *Journal of Literacy Research, 45*(3), 295–324.

Colwell, J., & Reinking, D. (2016). A formative experiment to align middle-school history instruction with literacy goals. *Teachers College Record, 118*(12), 1–42.

Design-Based Research Collective. (2003). Design-based research: An emerging paradigm for educational inquiry. *Educational Researcher, 32*(1), 5–8.

Doerr, H. M., & Temple, C. (2016). "It's a different kind of reading": Two middle grader teachers' evolving perspectives on reading in mathematics. *Journal of Literacy Research, 48*(1), 5–38.

Easterday, M. W., Rees Lewis, D. G., & Gerber, E. M. (2018). The logic of design research. *Learning: Research and Practice, 4*(2), 131–160.

Engeström, Y. (2011). From design experiments to formative interventions. *Theory and Psychology, 21*(5), 598–628.

Erickson, F. (2014). Scaling down: A modest proposal for practice-based policy research in teaching. *Education Policy Analysis Archives, 22*(9), 1–7.

Gamse, B. C., Jacob, R. T., Horst, M., Boulay, B., & Unlu, F. (2008). *Reading First Impact Study: Final report* (NCEE 2009-4038). Washington, DC: National

Center for Education Evaluation and Regional Assistance, Institute of Education Sciences, U.S. Department of Education.

Goatley, V. J., & Johnston, P. (2013). Innovations, research, and policy: Evolutions in classroom teaching. *Language Arts, 91*(2), 94–104.

Gravemeijer, K., & Cobb, P. (2006). Design research from a learning design perspective. In J. van den Akker, K. Gravemeijer, S. McKenney, & N. Nieveen (Eds.), *Educational design research* (pp. 17–51). New York: Routledge.

Guthrie, J. T., Wigfield, A., & You, W. (2012). Instructional contexts for engagement and achievement in reading. In S. Christenson, C. Wylie, & A. Reschly (Eds.), *Handbook of research on student engagement* (pp. 601–634). New York: Springer.

Gutiérrez, K. D. (2018). Social design-based experiments: A proleptic approach to literacy. *Literacy Research: Theory, Method, and Practice, 67*(1), 86–108.

Gutiérrez, K. D., & Jurow, A. S. (2016). Social design experiments: Toward equity by design. *Journal of the Learning Sciences, 25*(4), 565–598.

Gutiérrez, K. D., & Vossoughi, S. (2010). Lifting off the ground to return anew: Mediated praxis, transformative learning, and social design experiments. *Journal of Teacher Education, 61*(1), 100–117.

Hall, L. A. (2016). "I don't really have anything good to say": Examining how one teacher worked to shape middle school students' talk about texts. *Research in the Teaching of English, 51*(1), 60–83.

Howell, E., Butler, T., & Reinking, R. (2017). Integrating multimodal arguments into high school writing instruction. *Journal of Literacy Research, 49*(2), 181–209.

Ivey, G. (2013). Developing an intervention to increase engaged reading among adolescents. In T. Plomp & N. Nieveen (Eds.), *Educational design research—Part B: Illustrative cases* (pp. 235–251). Enschede, the Netherlands: SLO.

Ivey, G., & Broaddus, K. (2007). A formative experiment investigating literacy engagement among adolescent Latina/o students just beginning to read, write, and speak English. *Reading Research Quarterly, 42,* 512–545.

Ivey, G., & Johnston, P. H. (2011, December). *Using young adult fiction to increase engagement in reading.* Paper presented at the annual conference of the Literacy Research Association, Jacksonville, FL.

Ivey, G., & Johnston, P. H. (2013). Engagement with young adult literature: Outcomes and processes. *Reading Research Quarterly, 48*(3), 255–275.

Ivey, G., & Johnston, P. (2015a). Engaged reading as a collaborative transformative practice. *Journal of Literacy Research, 47*(3), 297–327.

Ivey, G., & Johnston, P. (2015b). *The persistence of the experience of engaged reading.* Paper presented at the annual conference of the Literacy Research Association, Carlsbad, CA.

Johnson, S. (2010). *Where good ideas come from: The natural history of innovation.* New York: Riverhead Books.

Lewis, C., Perry, R., & Murata, A. (2006). How should research contribute to instructional improvement?: The case of lesson study. *Educational Researcher, 35*(3), 3–14.

Malouf, D. B., & Taymans, J. M. (2016). Anatomy of an evidence base. *Educational Researcher, 45*(8), 454–459.

National Reading Panel. (2000). *Report of the National Reading Panel: Teaching children to read: An evidence-based assessment of the scientific research literature on reading and its implications for reading instruction: Reports of the subgroups* (NIH Pub. No. 00-4754). Washington, DC: National Institute of Child Health and Human Development, National Institutes of Health.

Neuman, S. B., & Dwyer, J. (2011). Developing vocabulary and conceptual knowledge for low-income preschoolers: A design experiment. *Journal of Literacy Research, 43*(2), 103–129.

Ormel, B. J. B., Pareja Roblin, N. N., McKenney, S. E., Vogt, J. M., & Pieters, J. M. (2012). Research-practice interactions as reported in recent design studies: Still promising, still hazy. *Educational Technology Research and Development, 60*(6), 967–986.

Paratore, J. R., O'Brien, L. M., Jiménez, L., Salinas, A., & Ly, C. (2016). Engaging preservice teachers in integrated study and use of educational media and technology in teaching reading. *Teaching and Teacher Education, 59,* 247–260.

Parsons, A. W., & Bryant, C. L. (2016). Deepening kindergarteners' science vocabulary: A design study. *Journal of Educational Research, 109*(4), 375–390.

Penuel, W. R. (2014). Emerging forms of formative intervention research in education. *Mind, Culture, and Activity, 21*(2), 97–117.

Penuel, W. R., Coburn, C. E., & Gallagher, D. J. (2013). Negotiating problems of practice in research-practice design partnerships. *National Society for the Study of Education, 112*(2), 237–255.

Penuel, W. R., Fishman, B. J., Cheng, B. H., & Sabelli, N. (2011). Organizing research and development at the intersection of learning, implementation, and design. *Educational Researcher, 40*(7), 331–337.

Philippakos, Z. A. T., MacArthur, C. A., & Munsell, S. (2018). Collaborative reasoning with strategy instruction for opinion writing in primary grades: Two cycles of design research. *Reading and Writing Quarterly, 34*(6), 485–504.

Plomp, T., & Nieveen, N. (Eds.). (2013). *Educational design research—Part B: Illustrative cases.* Enschede, the Netherlands: SLO.

Pogrow, S. (2017). The failure of the U.S. education research establishment to identify effective practices: Beware effective practices policies. *Education Policy Analysis Archives, 25*(5), 1–19.

Reinking, D. (2012). Beyond the laboratory and lens: New metaphors for literacy research. In P. L. Dunston, L. B. Gambrell, S. K. Fullerton, P. M. Stecker, V. R. Gillis, & C. C. Bates (Eds.), *60th yearbook of the Literacy Research Association* (pp. 1–17). Oak Creek, WI: Literacy Research Association.

Reinking, D., & Bradley, B. A. (2008). *Formative and design experiments: Approaches to language and literacy research.* New York: Teachers College Press.

Rowe, D. W., & Miller, M. E. (2016). Designing for diverse classrooms: Using iPads and digital cameras to compose eBooks with emergent bilingual/biliterate four-year-olds. *Journal of Early Childhood Literacy, 16,* 425–472.

Sannino, A., Engeström, Y., & Lemos, M. (2016). Formative interventions for expansive learning and transformative agency. *Journal of the Learning Sciences, 25*(4), 599–633.

Severance, S., Penuel, W. R., Sumner, T., & Leary, H. (2016). Organizing for teacher agency in curricular co-design. *Journal of the Learning Sciences, 25,* 531–564.

Snow, C. E. (2015). Rigor and realism: Doing educational science in the real world. *Educational Researcher, 44*(9), 460–466.

Tracy, K. N., & Headley, K. N. (2013). I never liked to read or write: A formative experiment on the use of a nonfiction-focused writing workshop in a fourth-grade classroom. *Literacy Research and Instruction, 52*(3), 173–191.

Wang, X. C., Christ, T., & Chiu, M. M. (2014). Exploring a comprehensive model for early childhood vocabulary instruction: A design experiment. *Early Child Development and Care, 184*(7), 1075–1106.

Yin, R. (2009). *Case study research: Design and methods* (4th ed.). Thousand Oaks, CA: SAGE.

Zhao, Y. (2017). What works may hurt: Side effects in education. *Journal of Educational Change, 18*(1), 1–19.

CHAPTER 9

Identifying Causal Effects in Literacy Research

RANDOMIZED TRIALS AND REGRESSION DISCONTINUITY DESIGNS

Christina Weiland
Anna Shapiro
Julia Lindsey

Literacy researchers, practitioners, and schools are often charged with making decisions that require answers to *causal* questions. For example, what approach to teaching early literacy leads to higher achievement in kindergarten? What form of teacher training results in the greatest likelihood of high-quality literacy instruction? What is the most effective intervention for a student who is falling behind his or her peers in literacy development? Making evidence-based decisions to questions like these requires studies that can determine that a given approach or curriculum—and not any other factor—leads to improved teacher instruction and/or students' gains in literacy. In other words, answering these important questions requires research designs that can identify *cause-and-effect* relationships.

Fortunately, a great deal of progress has been made over the last 20 years in designing and conducting studies that can identify causal effects. There are now highly readable texts on designing such studies (Angrist & Pischke, 2009; Banerjee & Duflo, 2017; Bloom, 2005; Murnane & Willett, 2010), as well as guidance from the U.S. Department of Education's *What Works Clearinghouse Standards Handbook* on what constitutes a high-quality causal study in education (National Center for Education Evaluation and Regional Assistance [NCEE], 2017). The research arm of the U.S. Department of Education, the Institute of Education Sciences, has since 2002 encouraged research that can identify causal effects across the PreK–12 spectrum and across content areas (Murnane & Willett, 2010). As a result of these advances, literacy studies that can identify causal effects have proliferated. There are now strong examples of large- and small-scale causal studies in literacy policy and practice, including studies of the federal Reading First program (Gamse, Jacob, Horst, Boulay, & Unlu, 2008); a large-scale state literacy-focused coaching program for teachers in Ohio (Piasta et al., 2017); literacy-focused professional development for preschool teachers in Chile (Yoshikawa et al., 2015); eight different preschool literacy curricula (Jenkins et al., 2018); reading intervention in first grade (Baker, Smolkowski, Chaparro, Smith, & Fien, 2015; Case et al., 2014); adolescent reading curricula and interventions (Cantrell, Almasi, Carter, Rintamaa, & Madden, 2010; Kim et al., 2016); and parent-targeted literacy interventions (Cabell, Zucker, DeCoster, Copp, & Landry, 2019; Mayer, Kalil, Oreopoulos, & Gallegos, 2019; York, Loeb, & Doss, 2018).

In this chapter, we discuss several common methodologies for estimating causal effects in literacy research studies. We focus on randomized trials and regression discontinuity designs—two types of designs that can identify causality and are in wide use in literacy research. We also cover pre–post designs, a method that cannot identify causality but is often useful when more rigorous approaches are not possible. First, however, we cover three concepts important to design (and to research broadly): sampling, external validity, and internal validity. We then delve into the specifics of these three types of designs, providing a concrete example of each from a real-world literacy study.

We have written this chapter for *consumers* of literacy research, although we encourage you, our readers, to pursue resources such as those cited in this chapter's second paragraph to learn to produce research that enables causal inference. Whether or not you conduct research that enables causal inference, it is important to understand this type of research, particularly for those who are or will be in positions to use research to inform critical decisions about literacy policies and practices. We hope this chapter proves useful as a primer in how to identify stronger versus weaker causal studies, as well as in understanding to whom results of a given study apply. Improving literacy instruction and important student outcomes requires connecting research to practice. Researchers must understand practice, and practitioners must understand research.

THREE CRITICAL CONCEPTS: SAMPLING, EXTERNAL VALIDITY, AND INTERNAL VALIDITY

Three concepts are critical to understanding the specific designs that follow this section. The first is *sampling*. In designing a study, a researcher has to choose participants to include in the study. This decision depends both on the research question and on practicalities. Is the researcher interested in the effects of a reading program on all students, students of certain ages or at certain grade levels, or students at certain levels of reading achievement? The researcher may also be interested less in student subgroups and more interested in school types. For example, does a particular reading policy have positive effects when implemented in charter schools? On the practical side, *who* is willing to participate in a given study also matters, as not all students, teachers, and schools are equally willing to participate in research. Defining the broader population of interest and then sampling from it constitute one of the first and most important steps in research studies.

Determining the broader population and then sampling from it is related to our second concept: *external validity*. After a research study is complete, external validity describes to whom the study's results apply. Most strictly, if the researcher has sampled students from only elementary schools in one district, the subsequent study's results apply technically only to elementary school students in that district. They do not apply to middle school students in that same district, or to elementary school students in another district. To be sure, a well-conducted study of the effects of a reading program on a given sample can be suggestive of the *likely* effects for a different sample. But students in the original study district may differ from students in other districts in ways that make an intervention, program, or policy affect students in that district differently from students elsewhere. If the researcher has used a nationally representative sample, only then can we interpret the results of a given study as relevant to all students of the included grades nationally. Determining to whom the researcher would like to generalize is a critical step in making sampling decisions. For consumers, being mindful of external validity is critical in identifying which studies are more versus less relevant to their district, school, or classroom.

Our third critical concept is *internal validity*. This term refers to whether we are sure that we got the right answer for the population of interest. To have strong internal validity, we must be able to rule out that the results of the study were due to anything other than the intervention, program, or policy of interest. If we are evaluating a classroom phonics program for kindergarten students, for example, we want to know if any learning gains we observe at the end of kindergarten are due to the program and not to student characteristics (early reading skills, gender, race/ethnicity, etc.), or to attending better-funded schools or living in more resource-rich neighborhoods. What we are trying to avoid is *selection bias*, or findings that are due to which participants sorted themselves into a given intervention and not to the actual intervention received.

As we walk through our three designs, we touch on each of these three concepts. As you become a critical consumer of research, you should also keep the three critical concepts in mind as you read any language and literacy research studies. They are highly useful across many types of research studies, beyond the three designs we describe here.

PRE–POST DESIGNS

Basics

A very common approach in educational research is measuring students' targeted skills before and after an intervention or policy is put in place, for a sample of a defined population. Then the researcher compares the differences in students' pre- and post-intervention scores, often statistically controlling for (or removing the influence of) any important factors about the students that might also affect their growth, such as family socioeconomic status (SES) or gender. Especially if the researcher can compare the students' means to national norms, this can provide a hint as to whether the intervention or policy might have led to stronger or weaker gains than expected among other similar students. However, as mentioned earlier and explained in more detail below, this design cannot identify causal effects of a given program.

A simple illustration of this design appears in Figure 9.1. Imagine that an elementary school reading specialist is interested in whether the Lindamood Phoneme Sequencing (LiPS) program, which is rated by the What Works Clearinghouse (NCEE, 2015) as having potentially positive effects on children's comprehension and alphabetic skills in early elementary school, is working for students who need intervention supports. The specialist tests their reading fluency on a nationally normed assessment where 100 is the national average and finds that at pretest, students on average score an 85, or about one standard deviation below the national norm for their age. At the end of the intervention period, she measures

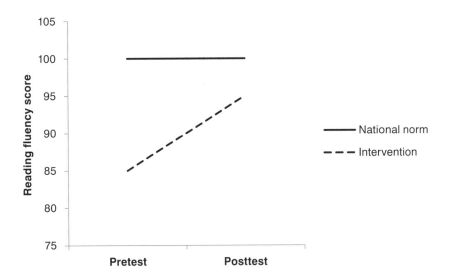

FIGURE 9.1. Pre–post design example.

them again and finds that they now score 95, a marked improvement over their baseline scores.

Is this definitive evidence that the LiPS approach *caused* students' improvements? It isn't. Something else—improvements to the school's library program, increased reading at home, improvements in classroom instruction—might have led to the gains shown in Figure 9.1, even in the absence of LiPS. If researchers know and have measures of every other such factor, then they can control for (or remove the effect of) these factors in their models and rule out these other explanations. The trouble is that without a source of randomization, there are always additional potential confounders or alternative explanations that researchers cannot rule out. In other words, to return to our three critical concepts, there are serious threats to the *internal validity* of the findings of pre–post designs. Designs that can identify causal effects—like the two designs we discuss in the rest of this chapter—are necessary to rule out these other explanations. But we include this approach in our chapter, even though it does not provide causal estimates, both because it is commonly used and because the kinds of designs we discuss in the rest of the chapter are often difficult to do. In our view, pre–post designs can provide some valuable evidence about students' progress, even if that evidence is not definitive.

Pre–Post Designs in Action

Researchers can and do use pre–post designs, particularly when they are developing and initially testing a given policy, curriculum, or intervention. For example, Justice and colleagues (2010) used such a design to investigate a language and literacy curriculum in preschool classrooms. This study hoped to address a major problem facing literacy researchers, educators, and policy makers: How do we ensure high-quality preschool literacy instruction for the unprecedented number of young children in the United States attending public preschools? To begin to answer this question, Justice and colleagues asked 11 preschool teachers to implement a research-based, scripted literacy and language curriculum for a year. These classrooms were intervention classrooms (i.e., the children in these classrooms were supposed to receive a literacy intervention). The children in these classrooms were assessed on measures of child language and measures of emergent literacy skills in the fall and in the spring. By comparing these children's scores at the beginning and end of the year, the researchers estimated the growth in language and literacy skills shown by children in the intervention classrooms. Over the year, children did make progress in language and literacy. For example, children's scores on vocabulary in the intervention classrooms increased an average of 7.6 points.

So could Justice and colleagues say, "This curriculum improves children's language and literacy, so everyone should use it"? Not quite (and don't worry; these researchers did not say that!). There are too many other possible explanations for why these children's scores improved. Children's scores often improve with age, regardless of the intervention. Perhaps these students' scores would have improved with any type of preschool language literacy curriculum, not just with this specific one. Or perhaps the children's scores improved because their parents increased their home language and literacy supports. In pre–post designs, it is not possible to say that an intervention *caused* an outcome because we simply do not have enough information to rule out other possible explanations for any observed changes.

In pre–post designs, however, researchers can bolster the rigor of their studies. As discussed above, researchers might compare students to national norms. Alternatively, they might select other students or classrooms not implementing the intervention to include in their study as points of comparison. Justice and colleagues (2010), for example, also assessed children in nine other preschool classrooms that were not implementing the intervention curriculum. They tried to pick a group of comparison preschool classrooms that were similar (in demographics and teacher characteristics) to the intervention classrooms. Comparing students in intervention and comparison classrooms provided a suggestive benchmark—though not a definitive one—for gauging the success of the intervention. In addition, future research ideally would include a sample from a clearly defined population, so that we can determine more rigorously not only what the impact of this program is but for whom (i.e., strong external validity). Despite these limitations, findings from the study suggested that the curriculum was worthy of more rigorous research, using designs that could rule out other explanations; we discuss two such designs next.

RANDOMIZED CONTROLLED TRIALS

Basics

Randomized controlled trials (RCTs) are the "gold standard" of causal inference. When executed correctly, this powerful experimental technique allows researchers to conclude that an intervention, policy, or curriculum *worked* (or did not work). The key is the random assignment of a given sample drawn from a defined population (e.g., students, teachers, schools, districts) to treatment and control conditions. The intervention is then implemented in the treatment group and not the control group. At the end of intervention, a simple comparison of the treatment and control groups' average outcomes provides a causal answer to whether the intervention worked. Importantly, randomization can occur at different levels. Researchers might randomize districts, schools, teachers, or children, for example, depending on the question they hope to answer and the context.

As illustrated in Figure 9.2, in a simple example of this design, a researcher randomly assigns a group of second-grade students to two smaller groups: one using a new type of small-group reading activity (i.e.,

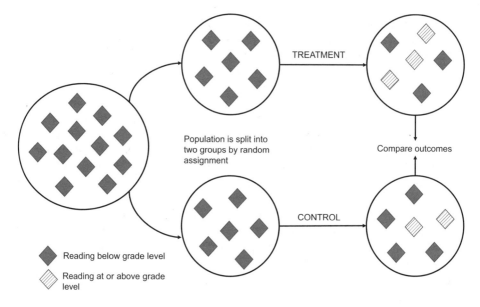

FIGURE 9.2. Simple RCT example.

the treatment group) and one using typical small-group reading activities (i.e., the control group). After the small-group intervention has been implemented with treatment group children, the researcher then collects postintervention reading assessment data from all the children in the study. A simple comparison of the average score in the treatment group with the average score in the control group is the *causal impact* of the new small-group reading activities. The researcher would use a simple technique known as a *Student's t-test* to examine whether any difference in outcomes by treatment status is *statistically significantly different* from zero (in other words, whether the difference is unlikely to be due to chance and likely to be due to the intervention).

Why does such a simple design lead to a causal answer? There are two reasons. First, if done correctly, random assignment should produce groups that are *equivalent at baseline* in their characteristics. In randomly assigning students, for example, there should be an approximately equal number of boys versus girls, higher- versus lower-achieving students, and higher- versus lower-SES students in the treatment and control groups. Assuming that data on such sample characteristics are collected by or available to researchers, the researchers directly check after random assignment that the treatment and control groups are indeed balanced in terms of these *observable* participant characteristics. Beyond these direct checks, the power of this approach is that randomization allows us to assume that there are no differences on unobservable baseline variables (anything the researchers do not or are not able to measure) across the two groups. Thus, when groups are similar before the study begins, then any differences at the end of the study can be attributed to the intervention and to the intervention only. Second, this design leads to a causal answer because the control group's average outcome provides a counterfactual for the treatment group's outcome. In other words, the control group's outcome captures what would have happened to the treatment group in the absence of the treatment.

As you read RCT studies, you will likely notice that the design is not quite so simple in practice. Specifically, you will likely notice that researchers almost always include other variables in calculating the treatment effect. They might, for example, include baseline test scores, child gender, and child free/reduced lunch status. Why do they do so? Technically, if random assignment is successful, the treatment and control groups should be balanced at baseline on these and all other characteristics, and including such variables is not necessary for calculating the causal effect. But including such characteristics (called *covariates*) explains some of the variation in the outcome that is due to factors other than the treatment. And for statistical reasons, explaining some of this variation with covariates means that a researcher can include fewer participants in a study. This both saves money and limits burden on participants—a win–win.

Common Problems in RCTs

RCTs are popular in part because the researcher's job—comparing means on outcomes for the treatment and control groups and then testing whether the difference is statistically significant (i.e., unlikely to be due to chance)— is simple and results in estimates of intervention impact that have strong internal validity. However, the internal validity of the estimates from an RCT can easily be undermined in practice. There are several "look-fors" that you should attend to when reading RCT studies, to separate stronger RCT studies from weaker ones.

The biggest potential threat to an RCT's internal validity is *nonrandom biasing attrition*. Attrition is the loss of participants from a study. Some attrition is expected in studies, particularly in ones that follow participants over many years. But attrition becomes an issue when the treatment and control groups are no longer balanced. For example, if more males drop out of a study in the treatment group than in the control group, we no longer have assurance that the treatment and control groups are equivalent in their observed and unobserved background characteristics. As you read RCTs, you should always look for a description of how much attrition there was overall, whether the attrition rate was different for the treatment versus control groups, and whether those participants who remained in the study were still balanced across groups in their background characteristics. The What Works Clearinghouse (NCEE, 2017) offers guidelines for researchers and readers to assess the impact of different levels of overall attrition and attrition from each group. When the balance between overall attrition and attrition from each group is at a potentially problematic level, it can bias the causal estimate. In other words, if there are attrition problems, we can no longer be sure that the difference in treatment and control outcomes we detect is due only to the treatment and not to other factors. Selection bias can creep in, and strong internal validity is no longer assured.

Another common issue or "look-for" in RCTs is that study participants do not always comply with their assigned treatment or control status. A participant assigned to the treatment group may not take up an offered treatment. A participant assigned to the control group may find a way into a given intervention, even if he or she was assigned to a business-as-usual condition. In the first nationally representative RCT of Head Start, for instance, about 87% of families assigned to an offer of a year of preschool in a Head Start center took up the offer and enrolled their children in Head Start. About 17% of control families were also able to enroll their children in a Head Start center in that same year (Bloom & Weiland, 2015). A standard comparison of treatment and control groups outcomes at the end of preschool would still identify the causal impact of being offered a seat in Head Start for 1 year. But it would not, however, identify the causal effect of *enrolling* in Head Start because not all participants complied with their random assignment status. To estimate the effect of enrolling in Head Start, we can perform a simple calculation in which we attribute any benefits of treatment only to those who stuck to their treatment assignment status. We divide the causal impact of being offered a place in Head Start by the proportion of those who complied with their treatment assignment. In this example, let's say that the causal impact of being offered a seat in Head Start on vocabulary was 2 points. We calculate the effect of enrolling in Head Start as 2 divided by 0.6 (i.e., $0.87 - 0.17 = 0.70$), or 3.3 points.

Both the effect of being offered a treatment and the effect of taking it up are important. But they are important for different reasons. Often, in policy, we may be able to *offer* a treatment, but not to force constituents to take it up. An example is public preschool. Several states such as Georgia, Oklahoma, and West Virginia offer a free year of public preschool to all 4-year-olds, but do not require families to take it up. Knowing the effect of *offering* public preschool on important student outcomes, regardless of take-up rates, informs policy decisions about the potential benefits of adopting a universal preschool program. But stakeholders are generally also interested in the effects for those who actually enroll in public preschool, since these are the children who have directly experienced the program. Generally, if some treatment group members did not take up an offered treatment and some control members did so, RCT studies include estimates of both the effect of being offered a treatment and the effect of taking it up. The Head Start study discussed above, for example, included both types of estimates (Puma, Bell, Cook, & Heid, 2010). Look for both types as you read descriptions of RCTs, and consider which type of estimate is most relevant to the decision you may be trying to make for your state, district, school, or students.

Still another "look-for" as you read descriptions of RCTs is fidelity of implementation. In real educational contexts, interventions are rarely implemented perfectly across all participants. Teachers may modify a curriculum in ways they think will benefit their students, for example, but that depart from the intervention model. High-quality educational interventions studied today accordingly often include measures of the degree to which an intervention was implemented as intended (Hulleman, Rimm-Kaufman, & Abry, 2013). A study with low fidelity of implementation may indicate (1) that the intervention is very hard to implement in real-world conditions or (2) that training supports in the RCT were poor, and that as such, this particular RCT may not have been a fair trial of the intervention. Discerning between (1) and (2) is critical in making sense of the results of a given study and deciding whether the results apply to your context.

A final "look-for" is the specifics of what the control group received, versus what the treatment group received (called *the treatment–control contrast*; Weiss, Bloom, & Brock, 2014). This is important because some educational practices are widespread and may already be present in classrooms, even in the absence of intervention. For example, an intervention that encourages more frequent small reading groups may not have positive impacts on treatment group students if the control group uses frequent small reading groups as well. One recent study found that Head Start had positive impacts on treatment group students' vocabulary scores at kindergarten entry only when these students were compared to control group children who did not attend preschool. When the Head Start students were compared to control group children who attended other preschool programs, Head Start had no such impacts (Feller, Grindal, Miratix, & Page, 2016; Morris et al., 2018). The treatment–control contrast was too modest for children attending other preschool programs. Particularly when a study finds no impacts of a given intervention or policy, identifying what the control group received is critical for understanding the "why" behind the findings.

Example of an RCT in Action

An example of an RCT in action in literacy research comes from a preschool and kindergarten teacher professional development program in Santiago, Chile, called Un Buen Comienzo (UBC; Yoshikawa et al., 2015). UBC was created using research-based principles for enriching preschool language and literacy environments (Snow, Burns, & Griffin, 1998). It was of interest to Chilean stakeholders because previous research had shown that early education settings in Chile focused very little on vocabulary, reading, or alphabet-focused activities (Pontificia Universidad Católica de

Chile, 2011; Strasser & Lissi, 2009). The UBC program consisted of 12 modules delivered across 2 years (6-month-long modules per year). The modules combined language- and literacy-content-focused strategies for teachers and coaching components, along with a library of roughly 100 books per classroom. Each module consisted of four weekly activities, beginning with a 4-hour workshop to introduce a particular topic and the corresponding instructional strategies (e.g., supporting children's predictions in read-alouds). Following the workshops, each teacher received two classroom visits from a trained coach—first to model the strategies introduced at the workshop, and then to provide feedback on the teacher's implementation of the strategy in the classroom. Every 2 months, teachers took part in a group reflection session at their school to discuss the successes and challenges of the module's topic and strategies.

To choose a sample for the UBC RCT, the research team first defined a set of criteria for municipalities (i.e., neighborhoods) in Santiago that spanned student characteristics (at least 20% of primary-school-age children had to be considered at risk), the total number of schools in each municipality, and responsiveness of neighborhood leadership. Ultimately, six municipalities were selected for the study, and schools were randomized to treatment versus control status within each municipality. The research team examined the external validity of this sample by comparing the fourth-grade test scores and household SES of selected municipalities to eligible but not selected municipalities, finding no statistically significant differences. This bolstered the external validity of their sample to some degree, though ultimately impact estimates applied only to schools in the six municipalities that participated in the study, due to how municipalities were selected for the study.

In all, a total of 64 schools, 90 classrooms, 119 teachers, 94 aides, and 1,876 children (age 4) participated in the study (32 schools, 51 classrooms, 66 teachers, 54 aides, and 1,033 children in the treatment condition; 32 schools, 39 classrooms, 53 teachers, 40 aides, and 843 children in the control condition). The team demonstrated that the sample was balanced by treatment status on 11 different child, teacher, and classroom baseline characteristics. Attrition in the trial was also very minimal and did not differ in rate, or in who was left in the study, by treatment status. The baseline balance checks and attrition analysis together showed that the estimates from the trial had good internal validity; they represented the causal impact of the UBC intervention on participants.

The research team collected data on classroom-level instructional quality by observing both treatment and control classrooms directly. Trained assessors tested children on their targeted language and literacy outcomes at the end of Year 1 and Year 2 of the 2-year intervention. The research team used these data to estimate the impacts of UBC. They found that the program had moderate to large impacts on measures of teaching quality in preschool; small impacts on measures of teaching quality in kindergarten;

and no impacts on child vocabulary, early reading, or early writing in either preschool or kindergarten. A subsequent study that used data on fidelity of implementation (Mendive, Weiland, Yoshikawa, & Snow, 2016) suggested why there were no impacts on children: By the end of preschool and kindergarten, treatment teachers increased their use of targeted language and literacy strategies to about 12 minutes, just about 5 minutes more than the control group—a very modest treatment–control contrast.

RCTs are informative for the field when they do not find effects, as well as when they do. Ultimately, the research team and stakeholders determined from these results that coaching alone was not enough in this context. Teachers needed more support and direction. Curriculum materials and more structured, data-driven guidance for teachers were subsequently introduced and tested, with evidence of promising effects on important student language and literacy outcomes so far (Arbour et al., 2015).

REGRESSION DISCONTINUITY DESIGNS

Although RCTs are considered the "gold standard" for estimating causal relationships, conducting an RCT to evaluate an education program is not always feasible. Districts, for example, may not be willing to randomize which of their schools receives a given intervention. RCTs also can require considerable foresight. Perhaps you are interested in evaluating a program or policy that was put in place in the past. You cannot go back and retroactively conduct an experiment to evaluate its effectiveness. However, social scientists have found many instances in which experimental conditions occurred naturally as education policies and programs were enacted or discontinued over time. These "natural experiments" can be used to estimate causal relationships between education programs and student outcomes. In this section, we discuss what is often considered (if implemented appropriately) the most rigorous type of these "natural experiments": regression discontinuity designs (RDDs).

Basics

Decision makers often impose rules to allocate resources and influence behaviors. Under the right conditions, the rules that govern what we do and when we can do it can create a valuable natural experiment (Angrist & Pischke, 2014). Think, for example, of kindergarten entrance age laws. In most states, children are eligible to attend kindergarten when they turn 5 years old. However, children turn 5 every day of the year, including in the middle of the school year. Therefore, states set rules that determine by what date in a calendar year students must be 5 years old in order to start kindergarten in September with their peers or else wait until the next school year. This administrative cut point date creates a sharp distinction between otherwise similar children and in turn creates the ideal conditions to conduct a natural experiment.

An RDD is one method social scientists use to generate causal evidence from a natural experiment of this type. There are two key components of an RDD. The first is the presence of a measure that sorts people along a continuum of values. This measure is called the *assignment variable,* the *forcing variable,* or the *running variable,* interchangeably. In this discussion, we refer to it as the running variable. The second key component of an RDD is that along the running variable, there is a cut point that determines whether an individual is eligible for an intervention, program, or policy. Just above the cut point, participants are offered a given treatment and form the treatment group. Just below the cut point, participants are not offered the treatment and form the control group.

Figure 9.3 demonstrates how an RDD works. The solid line represents the relationship between the running variable (x axis) and the outcome of interest (y axis), and the vertical dashed line represents the cut point along the running variable. As you can see, those with values of x to the right of the cut point (the treatment group) have higher outcome values (y) than those to the left of the cut point (the control group). In other words, at the cut point, the value of the outcome jumps *discontinuously.* In the RDD, the

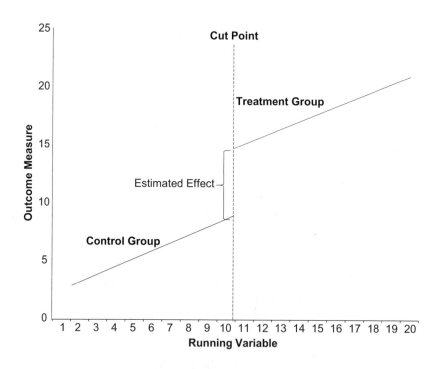

FIGURE 9.3. Hypothetical RDD analysis.

researcher estimates the magnitude of this discontinuity and considers it as the causal effect of the intervention, program, or policy.

Importantly, an RDD generates a causal estimate of a program for participants just around the cut point, not for all participants in the study. This is because an RDD is akin to an RCT near the cut point only; we have assurance that those just on either side of the cut point are similar to each other in their background characteristics. But those farther away from the cut point are likely to be quite different from each other. RCTs, in contrast, estimate an average treatment effect for all program participants. This facet of the external validity of an RDD is important to remember when you are interpreting the estimates of an evaluation using this method. Results of an RDD study generally have weaker external validity than those of an RCT.

RDD Specifics

Trusting results from an RDD as identifying the causal effect of an intervention requires several key pieces of evidence. These "look-fors" as you read descriptions of RDD studies are as follows.

First, the key assumption underlying the internal validity of an RDD is that those immediately on each side of the cut point are "equal in expectation" in all ways, except for which side of the cutoff they fall on. Because the cutoff determines which group is assigned to the treatment group and which to the control condition, this is akin to those on one side being randomly assigned to treatment and the those on the other, to control (Murnane & Willett, 2010). If this assumption holds, then the RDD identifies the causal impact of the program, policy, or intervention. For this to be the case, the cut point must be *exogenously* determined. What does that mean? Much as in an RCT, where treatment assignment is determined independently from study participants, participants should not be able to manipulate precisely on which side of the cut point they fall. This would be akin to participants' determining for themselves whether they are in the treatment or control group, which would open the door to selection bias. How would a researcher know whether manipulation occurred? A simple way is to look for "bunching" of participants around the cut point. If there are many more observations just above the cut point than just below, this is a sign of manipulation. If this occurs, participants appear to have found a way to influence whether they fell on their desired side of the cut point. Another way is to check that the characteristics of participants are not different on either side of the cut point. If one side of the cut point has all boys, while girls are represented equally on either side, this is evidence that something fishy has occurred. Parents of boys may have thought that their sons would benefit from a treatment and found a way to be eligible for it (i.e., they were not randomly assigned to the program).

As a second "look-for," we have to be sure that the cut point is not used for assignment to other programs that may affect the outcomes of study participants (NCEE, 2017). For example, if the same cut point used to determine children's kindergarten starting year was also used to determine which students were eligible for a community health program, the estimated effect of starting kindergarten early could be confounded with a potential effect of greater health care access. Drawing causal conclusions from an RDD study requires that the researcher understand the context of the rule (i.e., how it was determined and to what it applies).

In addition, for an RDD to provide a trustworthy estimate of the treatment effect, the researcher has to model the relationship between the running variable and the outcome of interest correctly. If age is the running variable and vocabulary is the outcome, does a straight line best describe their relationship? Or perhaps a curve? To calculate the effect of the treatment at the cut point correctly, this relationship must be modeled appropriately. When you read descriptions of RDD studies, look for attention to the shape of this relationship.

Finally, the researcher should also demonstrate that their estimate of the treatment effect is not sensitive to whether participants farther away from the cut point are included or excluded. In an RDD, a researcher would ideally include only those participants *immediately* on either side of the cut point. But generally there are not enough such participants, so the researcher "borrows strength" from those farther away. If the answer is highly sensitive to how far away from the cut point the researcher goes, that is a sign that we should place less confidence in the answer regarding whether a treatment worked or did not work.

Research using the RDD approach is extremely active, with new studies and guidance released frequently. For additional state-of-the-art tests of RDD assumptions and modeling approaches, see Angrist and Pischke (2014), Cattaneo, Idrobo, and Titiunik (2018), and Murnane and Willett (2010).

Example of an RDD in Action

To illustrate the RDD design in practice, we turn to an evaluation of the Reading First initiative. Reading First was a federally funded program established by the No Child Left Behind Act of 2001; it was designed to help all children in the United States read at or above grade level by third grade. More specifically, the initiative allocated $1 billion per year to states and school districts to implement a set of research-based reading instruction practices in early elementary school. Within the federal guidelines of the initiative, the states and school districts that received grants decided how to allocate the money to individual schools and what specific approaches, materials, and curricula to use (Gamse, Bloom, Kemple, & Jacob, 2008).

Within the group of states and school districts that received Reading First grants, local decision makers were left to decide which schools would participate in the program, due to limited funding. In some cases, the grant recipient (either a state or a school district) chose to assign the program to schools by using a systematically ordered ranking system, creating the necessary conditions for an RDD. More specifically, these districts ordered their schools by the previous year's third-grade reading test scores and then set a cut point to determine program participation, based on the amount of available funding. For example, if School District *A* had 30 elementary schools but only enough funding to implement the program in 10 schools, the district would rank all 30 elementary schools by the prior year's third-grade reading scores and implement the program in the 10 lowest-scoring schools. Thus, the previous year's third-grade reading scores served as the running variable, and an RDD was used to estimate the effect of the program for schools that had just made the cut (i.e., the 10th lowest-scoring school in each district) compared to those who had just missed it (i.e., the 11th lowest-scoring school). Importantly, the treatment schools in this study were those with lower prior reading scores, and the control schools in the study were those with slightly higher prior reading scores.

As previously mentioned, the Reading First initiative was a federal grant program that set guidelines for research-based reading instruction. Grant recipients could only use the funds for reading curricula and materials that focused on phonemic awareness, phonics, vocabulary, fluency, and comprehension; professional development and coaching for how to use research-based reading practices and how to teach struggle readers; and student screening, intervention for struggling readers, and monitoring of student progress to diagnosis and prevent reading difficulties. Within these guidelines, however, localities had flexibility to decide which materials to use within each category and how exactly resources would be allocated across the three categories. Therefore, while the specific implementation of the Reading First program varied by recipient, the overall approach and goals were the same across localities. Overall, the Reading First evaluation included a sample of 248 schools from 18 grant recipient sites and over 36,000 students in those schools, with 125 schools in the Reading First program and 123 control group schools.

To measure the effect of the Reading First initiative, the authors used the RDD described above to estimate the effects of participating in Reading First on overall reading comprehension in first, second, and third grades (as assessed with the Stanford Achievement Test 10) and on reading fluency in first grade (as assessed with the Test of Silent Word Reading Fluency). The authors also estimated the effects of participating in the program on classroom reading instruction practices in first and second grades, as assessed by the following measures created for the research: Instructional Practice in Reading Inventory, Student Time-on-Task and Engagement with Print, and Global Appraisal of Teaching Strategies. Finally, the authors measured the professional development component of the program via teacher, principal, and reading coach surveys and district staff interviews in the first and third years of the program.

The authors conducted a number of tests (i.e., our RDD "look-fors") to assess the internal validity of their estimates. First, they tested for baseline differences between the schools that did and did not receive the Reading First program on measures like the characteristics of the student body, the size and location of the schools, and their prior third-grade reading scores. They found no statistically significant differences between the treatment and control schools on these measures, providing evidence that the schools around the cut point were "equal in expectation" before the program began. Second, the authors tested the sensitivity of their estimates to modeling the relationship between the running variable and the outcome in different ways. In addition to estimating program effects by using the preferred linear model specification, the authors also reestimated the program effects after dropping observations with outlying values of the running variable, allowing the relationship between the outcome and the running variable to be different on each side of the cutoff; and by using a quadratic, or curvilinear, model. Their answers to whether the program worked were not different across these checks (Gamse, Jacob, et al., 2008), increasing their confidence in their results.

Overall, the researchers found that the program modestly increased the amount of time devoted to instruction in five components of reading in grades 1 and 2, and had a small positive impact on decoding in grade 1 in one of the 3 years studied, though there were no effects on student reading comprehension at grades 1, 2, or 3 in any of the 3 years studied (Gamse, Bloom, et al., 2008). The research team posited that these results may ultimately have been due to the fact that the type of reading instruction promoted by Reading First was already in wide use, due to several influential reports encouraging these practices and to funding from the Reading Excellence Act of 1998 (Herlihy, Kemple, Bloom, Zhu, & Berlin, 2009). Essentially, although the program increased the use of what the authors called "scientifically based reading instruction practices" in the treatment group, control group teachers spent the majority of their reading instructional block on the same Reading First core components (i.e., there was only a modest treatment–control contrast). There also were intriguing findings that Reading First did improve students' reading comprehension in sites that received larger grants, sites that served lower-achieving students, and sites in which control group counterparts spent less time on the Reading First core components. Ultimately, this use of an RDD enabled policy makers to draw conclusions about the impacts of a specific policy initiative without employing an RCT.

CONCLUSION

National tests show that only 36% of U.S. fourth graders are proficient in reading, with evidence of large opportunity gaps for children by income and race (National Center for Education Statistics, 2018). Improving reading and other literacy outcomes for students requires understanding what works for whom, under what conditions. Rigorous research like the designs we present here, when implemented well, can help to point the way to more efficient, effective, and engaging instruction for all students. But research only has the potential to improve outcomes for students when it is used to inform policy and practice decisions. Researchers, district leaders, principals, and teachers trained in how to read and apply research are an important part of bridging the current research-to-practice gap. We hope that our chapter makes a contribution to your training as a literacy leader, poised to use research to inform critical decisions to improve the life chances of all students.

ACKNOWLEDGMENTS

We would to like thank Robin Jacob and Catherine Snow for sharing their insights with us on the Reading First evaluation. Anna Shapiro's work on this chapter was supported by the Institute of Education Sciences Predoctoral Fellowship at the University of Michigan (No. R305B150012).

REFERENCES

Angrist, J. D., & Pischke, J.-S. (2009). *Mostly harmless econometrics: An empiricist's companion*. Princeton, NJ: Princeton University Press.

Angrist, J., & Pischke, J.-S. (2014). *Mastering 'metrics: The path from cause to effect*. Princeton, NJ: Princeton University Press.

Arbour, M. C., Yoshikawa, H., Atwood, S., Duran, F. R., Godoy, F., Trevino, E., et al. (2015). Quasi-experimental study of a learning collaborative to improve public preschool quality and children's language outcomes in Chile. *BMJ Quality and Safety, 24*(11).

Baker, S. K., Smolkowski, K., Chaparro, E. A., Smith, J. L., & Fien, H. (2015). Using regression discontinuity to test the impact of a Tier 2 reading intervention in first grade. *Journal of Research on Educational Effectiveness, 8*, 218–244.

Banerjee, A. V., & Duflo, E., (Eds.). (2017). *Handbook of field experiments* (Vol. 1). Amsterdam: North-Holland.

Bloom, H. S. (Ed.). (2005). *Learning more from social experiments: Evolving analytic approaches*. New York: Russell Sage Foundation.

Bloom, H. S., & Weiland, C. (2015). *Quantifying variation in Head Start effects on young children's cognitive and socio-emotional skills using data from the National Head Start Impact Study* (MRDC Working Paper) New York: MDRC.

Cabell, S. Q., Zucker, T. A., DeCoster, J., Copp, S. B., & Landry, S. (2019). Impact of a parent text messaging program on pre-kindergarteners' literacy development. *AERA Open, 5*.

Cantrell, S. C., Almasi, J. F., Carter, J. C., Rintamaa, M., & Madden, A. (2010).

The impact of a strategy-based intervention on the comprehension and strategy use of struggling adolescent readers. *Journal of Educational Psychology, 102,* 257–280.

Case, L., Speece, D., Silverman, R., Schatschneider, C., Montanaro, E., & Ritchey, K. (2014). Immediate and long-term effects of Tier 2 reading instruction for first-grade students with a high probability of reading failure. *Journal of Research on Educational Effectiveness, 7,* 28–53.

Cattaneo, M. D., Idrobo, N., & Titiunik, R. (2018). A practical introduction to regression discontinuity designs: Vol. I. *Cambridge Elements: Quantitative and Computational Methods for Social Science, 1,* 113.

Feller, A., Grindal, T., Miratrix, L., & Page, L. C. (2016). Compared to what?: Variation in the impacts of early childhood education by alternative care type. *Annals of Applied Statistics, 10,* 1245–1285.

Gamse, B. C., Bloom, H. S., Kemple, J. J ., & Jacob, R. T. (2008). *Reading First Impact Study: Interim report* (NCEE 2008-4016). Washington, DC: National Center for Education Evaluation and Regional Assistance, Institute of Education Sciences, U.S. Department of Education.

Gamse, B. C., Jacob, R. T., Horst, M., Boulay, B., & Unlu, F. (2008). *Reading First Impact Study: Final report* (NCEE 2009-4038). Washington, DC: National Center for Education Evaluation and Regional Assistance, Institute of Education Sciences, U.S. Department of Education.

Herlihy, C., Kemple, J., Bloom, H., Zhu, P., & Berlin, G. (2009). Understanding Reading First: What we know, what we don't, and what's next (MRDC Policy Brief). New York: MDRC. Retrieved June 6, 2019, from *www.mdrc.org/sites/default/files/understanding_reading_first.pdf.*

Hulleman, C. S., Rimm-Kaufman, & Abry, T. (2013). Innovative methodologies to explore implementation: Whole–part–whole—construct validity, measurement, and analytical issues for intervention fidelity assessment in education research. In T. Halle, A. Metz, & I. Martinez Beck (Eds.), *Applying implementation science in early childhood programs and Systems* (pp. 65–93). Baltimore: Brookes.

Jenkins, J. M., Duncan, G. J., Auger, A., Bitler, M., Domina, T., & Burchinal, M. (2018). Boosting school readiness: Should preschool teachers target skills or the whole child? *Economics of Education Review, 65,* 107–125.

Justice, L. M., McGinty, A. S., Cabell, S. Q., Kilday, C. R., Knighton, K., & Huffman, G. (2010). Language and literacy curriculum supplement for preschoolers who are academically at risk: A feasibility study. *Language, Speech, and Hearing Services in Schools, 41,* 161–178.

Mayer, S. E., Kalil, A., Oreopoulos, P., & Gallegos, S. (2019). Using behavioral insights to increase parental engagement: The Parents and Children Together intervention. *Journal of Human Resources, 54*(4), 900–925.

Mendive, S., Weiland, C., Yoshikawa, H., & Snow, C. (2016). Opening the black box: Intervention fidelity in a randomized trial of a preschool teacher professional development program. *Journal of Educational Psychology, 108,* 130–145.

Morris, P. A., Connors, M., Friedman-Krauss, A., McCoy, D. C., Weiland, C., Feller, A., et al. (2018). New findings on impact variation from the Head Start Impact Study: Informing the scale-up of early childhood programs. *AERA Open, 4.*

Murnane, R., & Willett, J. (2010). *Methods matter: Improving causal inference in educational and social science research.* New York: Oxford University Press.

National Center for Education Evaluation and Regional Assistance (NCEE), Institute of Education Sciences. (2015). *Intervention report: Lindamood Phoneme Sequencing (LiPS).* Washington, DC: Author.

National Center for Education Evaluation and Regional Assistance (NCEE), Institute of Education Sciences. (2017). *What Works Clearinghouse Standards Handbook Version 4.0.* Washington, DC: Author. Retrieved from *https://ies.ed.gov/ncee/wwc/Docs/referenceresources/wwc_standards_handbook_v4.pdf.*

National Center for Education Statistics, Institute of Education Sciences. (2018). *NAEP reading report card.* Washington, DC: Author. Retrieved from *https://nces.ed.gov/nationsreportcard/reading.*

No Child Left Behind Act of 2001, Pub. L. No. 107-110, 20 U.S.C. § 6319 (2002).

Piasta, S. B., Justice, L. M., O'Connell, A. A., Mauck, S. A., Weber-Mayrer, M., Schachter, R. E., et al. (2017). Effectiveness of large-scale, state-sponsored language and literacy professional development on early childhood educator outcomes. *Journal of Research on Educational Effectiveness, 10,* 354–378.

Pontificia Universidad Católica de Chile, Facultad de Educación. (2011). *Informe final. Alfabetización en establecimientos Chilenos subvencionados.* Retrieved from *www.educacion2.udp.cl/seminarios/201109/ppt/Alfabetizacion-Informe-final.pdf.*

Puma, M., Bell, S. H., Cook, R., & Heid, C. (2010). *Head Start Impact Study: Final report.* Washington, DC: U.S. Department of Health and Human Services, Administration for Children and Families.

Snow, C. E., Burns, M. S., & Griffin, P. (Eds.). (1998). *Preventing reading difficulties in young children.* Washington, DC: National Academy Press.

Strasser, K., & Lissi, M. R. (2009). Home and instruction effects on emergent literacy in a sample of Chilean kindergarten children. *Scientific Studies of Reading, 13,* 175–204.

Weiss, M. J., Bloom, H. S., & Brock, T. (2014). A conceptual framework for studying the sources of variation in program effects. *Journal of Policy Analysis and Management, 33,* 778–808.

York, B. N., Loeb, S., & Doss, C. (2019). One step at a time: The effects of an early literacy text -messaging program for parents of preschoolers. *Journal of Human Resources, 54*(3), 537–566.

Yoshikawa, H., Leyva, D., Snow, C. E., Treviño, E., Barata, M., Weiland, C., et al. (2015). Experimental impacts of a teacher professional development program in Chile on preschool classroom quality and child outcomes. *Developmental Psychology, 51,* 309–322.

CHAPTER 10

Doing Historical Research on Literacy

Norman A. Stahl
Douglas K. Hartman

Everything has a history. Every textbook, chapbook, trade book, picture book, notebook, workbook, blue book, hornbook, scrapbook, copybook, yearbook, audiobook, and e-book reveals its past in some way. "The house of the present is filled with windows into the past," as Benjamin (2018, p. 2) has explained. The purpose of this chapter is to strengthen the ways in which literacy scholars gaze through these windows.

Take, for example, the anthologies currently used for formal reading instruction in elementary classrooms across the United States and Canada. These comprehensive programs of leveled stories, skills, activities, worksheets, videos, apps, and websites are the prevailing instruments for teaching reading throughout North America—and have been for many decades. To the keen eye of a literacy historian, the design and content of these anthologies include features that are traceable to reading materials published in previous centuries, most notably to the "Dick and Jane" readers of the mid-20th century, the *McGuffey's Eclectic Readers* of the latter 19th century, Webster's "Blueback Spellers" of the 18th century, and the *New England Primer* of the 17th century. To rephrase Benjamin (2018), the reading anthologies of today are filled with windows onto the reading materials of yesteryear.

Recognizing the features that appear, coappear, disappear, and reappear across time in these reading materials is like being an archeologist or geologist. But instead of digging into the earth to excavate the past, the literacy historian traverses the material landscape of reading to map the elemental, organizational, or topical terrain of a moment, period, era, epoch, or age. The features, design, and content of the current anthologies merely form the uppermost layer of history. Deeper, more discerning inferences about authorial and ideological continuity and change in the curriculum, schools, and society for a given time period or across centuries can be worked out from subaltern-focused analyses.

To compare McGuffey's rural farm ditties with Dick and Jane's suburban neighborhood happenings to today's anthologized tales from urban and global communities is to realize a number of cultural, political, demographic, technological, and economic movements that shaped successive editions of reading materials and spans of reading instruction. The more we understand the continuities and changes in these materials—when they were made, who made them, and why—the better equipped we will be to see into the kind of future where we as literacy professionals may be heading. The corollary to Benjamin's (2018) metaphor is that the house of the present is also filled with windows that open onto the future.

Looking through windows into the past requires literacy scholars to look *at* the windows too. Why? The trim or frame or glass may skew the scholars' view of the artifact in a way that distorts or decontextualizes. To study oneself looking through a window requires a kind of "double-double" vision, in which a scholar looks not only at the historical artifact (such as a textbook), but also at him- or herself analyzing the artifact, as well as the academic field, which is likely grappling with making sense of many related artifacts. This expanding view of historical scholarship suggests a model composed of three concentric circles: the literacy artifact(s) in the inner circle, literacy scholars in the middle circle, and the literacy profession in the outer one. To understand the workings of such a model, this chapter begins by focusing on the outer circle, the profession. The questions and conversations that occupy the profession have a history of their own. In our minds' eyes, this outer circle is the logical starting place for learning to look through windows into literacy's past. The fundamental questions for anyone embarking on historical work in any area are *What is history?* and *Why should we do it?*

WHAT IS HISTORY?

There is no single, once-and-for-all answer to the first question, *What is history?* But there are answers that mark the terrain better than others. Gray (1991) suggests that three features are essential to any response: history as a happening, as the record, and as a field of study.

History Is a Happening

First and foremost, *history is a happening.* Every aspect of a happening (a person, object, identity, event, action, symbol, thought, etc.), from the beginning of time until this moment, is history. If a student learned to read with a "Dick and Jane," that is a historical happening. If a company designed and marketed an SRA kit to teach reading skills, that happening is history too. The current moment is but fleeting because it quickly becomes a contribution, meaningful or not, to history. It is only the future that is infinite and beyond the scope of history until it too becomes history—something that is assured to happen.

History Is the Record

Second, *history is the record* of things in the present that become the past. This is the record we studied as part of a 5th-grade social studies unit on the Civil War with Miss Jameson or in our foray into 10th-grade world history at Abraham Lincoln High School. The locations of these happenings for each of us are different, as were the times, but the experience was likely to have been much the same. We studied the record of important events and the thoughts and actions of those of great minds (i.e., the elite), as selected for us by the elders of our society. Yet for most of us, history as a record of world literacy or reading instruction never received more than passing attention in our undergraduate or graduate training, either.

Unlike history as a happening, history as a record has quite finite parameters. About 5,000 years ago, with the growing complexity of economic and political activity throughout ancient Mesopotamia and Egypt, writing was invented—and the record of history began (Clayton, 2013; Clodd, 1907; Diringer, 1962; Fischer, 2001). The great preponderance of the Western historical record is focused on the period since then. With the development of printing in the West, the documentary record was more likely to survive. Furthermore, with each new technology for capturing the present, there is less and less that cannot be preserved for the historical record if there is an archive, whether physical or digital, to preserve the documentary evidence.

In the field of literacy, we may propose three areas of history as record: the history of reading instruction (e.g., Lamport, 1935; Mathews, 1966; Reeder, 1900; Shannon, 1989; Smith, 2002), the history of literacy (e.g., Cavallo & Chartier, 2003; Fischer, 2019; Lyons, 2010; Manguel, 1996), and the history of the book or print culture (e.g., Darnton, 1990; Diringer, 1982; Johns, 2000; Suarez & Woudhuyen, 2013). While these examples often cross boundaries, each area provides opportunity to learn of aspects of literacy history. We suggest that any literacy historian or doctoral student take the time to sample works in each of these classifications. Still, we must be careful not to confuse the study of history with the conduct of the historical method (Leedy & Ormrod, 2019).

History Is a Field of Study

Finally, *history is a field of study* where historical methods—known as *historiography*—are undertaken by institutionally trained academics or self-studied citizen historians. Thousands of years ago, though, history was written by scribes in the form of chronicles that praised a monarch or glorified a city or state (referred to as *hagiographies*). With the coming of Herodotus and Thucydides in the 5th century B.C., the writing of history began to seek the "truth" and examine relationships between cause and effect. During the Middle Ages and the decline of classical civilization in the West, the truth-seeking methods of historians also slipped into the dark ages. Not until rationalist philosophy evolved during the Enlightenment of the 18th century did the idea of rigorously studying history once again emerge. It was in Germany, at the University of Berlin in the 1820s, that Leopold von Ranke advocated the systematic approach to evaluating primary source documents and the practice of presenting the past "as it actually happened" (*wie es eigentlich gewesen ist*). As *historicism* spread throughout the European academic community, the fundamental tenets for history as an academic discipline based on examination and evaluation of primary sources were set in place for the modern era. Over the next two centuries, new approaches and concepts for the conduct of historical research developed, such as positivist, progressive, Marxist, *Annales*, cliometric, Freudian, and postmodern approaches, to name a few (Brundage, 2018; Gilderhus, 2009).

These different approaches provide complementary and incompatible ways of analyzing, knowing, and representing the past. A single interpretation of events has become untenable. As a result, history has grown into a more diverse field of study, likely to continue developing in new directions (Gilderhus, 2009; Gunn & Faire, 2016; Tosh, 2015).

A WORKING DEFINITION OF HISTORY

With Gray's (1991) three features in mind—history as happening, record, and field of study—we propose a working definition of *history,* akin to that of Borg, Gall, and Gall (1993): History is the *interpretive reconstruction of the known past.* This definition highlights three elements of historical analysis:

1. History is an *interpretation* of the past. It involves the careful weighing and sorting of evidence into patterns, arguments, and narratives based on judgment. It is more than marshaling a chronology of facts. History is the production of meanings for an audience relative to a purpose.
2. History is a *reconstruction* of the past. It is a refabricating of something that once was. It is not the same thing as the actual event or episode. History is a "making again" of a happening, account, or explanation that re-presents what already happened.
3. History is about the *known* past. There is much in the past that

existed and happened, but we can only know pieces and parts of it because of the evidence that remains. That which can be known, then, is that which has been saved or survived into the present for interpretation and reconstruction.

We think that, as a whole, this working definition offers considerable flexibility. The focus can be on an individual, a group, a movement, an institution, a place, or an era (Best & Kahn, 1989; Skager & Weinberg, 1971). In the literacy field, this flexible focus could animate historical investigations on the impact of educational policies, legislation, and laws (e.g., Right to Read, Goals 2000, No Child Left Behind, Race to the Top, Common Core); curriculum models and movements (e.g., basal systems, whole-language philosophy, Initial Teaching Alphabet, direct instruction, guided reading, disciplinary literacy); instructional methods and materials (e.g., KWL, phonics workbooks, Dolch word materials); and assessment practices (e.g., informal reading inventories, miscue analysis, standardized testing) across time or within defined eras. The focus could also be on the lives and contributions of distinguished literacy pioneers, such as Edmund Burke Huey, William S. Gray, Noah Webster, or Arthur I. Gates; or on the literative lives of current literacy heroes or everyday educators, be they teachers, administrators, or former students (e.g., Ayres, 1988; Taylor, 2016).

The historical process could be used to study the development and influence of specific educational institutions either in higher education (e.g., the Center for the Study of Reading and the college reading programs in Georgia throughout the 1980s) or in the PreK–12 environment (e.g., the Benchmark School, the Calhoun Colored School, and the University of Chicago Laboratory School). Finally, the literacy historian could delve into the roots of current literacy practices, techniques, or strategies to understand whether they were developed to meet instructional parameters that no longer exist today, or to learn whether they have fallen victim to the "confusions of time" to such an extent that application and delivery no longer resemble the original constructs (Skager & Weinberg, 1971). Conversely, the literacy historian could identify instructional activities or movements that were lost to the times (Stahl, King, & Eilers, 1996) but could have practical relevance for the current educational scene.

In history as an interpretive and reconstructive process, historical topics are not considered in isolation. Each one builds on, borrows from, and gives to the philosophies, constructs, and movements of institutions within a particular era or an identified setting. In addition, the researcher must be cognizant of the historical events beyond the literacy field that may have influenced the issue or event. For instance, the growth of postsecondary reading programs in the early 1950s, as well as the birth of professional associations like the Southwest Reading Conference (which became the National Reading Conference and is now the Literacy Research

Association, or LRA) and the College Reading Association (now the Association of Literacy Educators and Researchers, or ALER) occurred soon after Congress passed the Serviceman's Readjustment Act of 1944 (i.e., the GI Bill of Rights), which enrolled tens of thousands of returning service personnel in postsecondary education and in college reading courses. Knowing the larger social and cultural context can help us understand more specific issues or events.

A working definition of history, such as the one we have proposed, is rooted in two long-standing approaches to historical research. One is *document/artifact analysis*, which moves the researcher to interpret existing documents/artifacts from the past, such as birth records, census data, photographs, correspondence (written and digital), contracts, commission reports, textbooks, trade books, workbooks, newspapers, periodicals, manuscripts, diaries/journals, video recordings, and speech transcripts (McDowell, 2002). The other broad category of historical research is *oral history analysis*,[1] where individuals who lived through a happening, event, or era—or knew individuals of importance to an area of study—are interviewed by a historian. The interview thus produces the evidence, which is preserved through the process of transcription, and then interpreted by the historian (Baum, 1995; Caunce, 1994; Kyvig & Marty, 2019; Perks & Thomson, 2016; Sitton, Mehaffy, & Davis, 1983; Thompson & Bornat, 2017). Recent methodological innovations have expanded the range of approaches available to historians. The digital humanities, in particular, have been a hotbed for creating digital tools like text-mining software, computer-aided design, geographic information systems, and statistical analysis software.

WHY DO HISTORICAL RESEARCH?

The second question fundamental to those embarking on historical research in literacy is *Why do it?* Not surprisingly, there are a number of related responses to this question (Cohen, Manion, & Morrison, 2018; Good, 1966; Stahl, 2002). One is that historical research in literacy forms the reading field into a professional community with a history that is known, valued, and disseminated to the current and future generations of literacy specialists. History provides us with a sense of honor as a profession, all the while focusing us on the unique responsibilities we bear as reading educators and researchers.

The research also yields insights into pedagogical problems that cannot be achieved by other means. It informs us about how our current curricular systems came into being and to how to build a sound basis for

---

[1] Oral history analysis is also referred to as *oral biography, oral chronicles,* and *life history* in the professional literature.

future directions. It permits us to use past practices to evaluate emerging and current practices. It allows us to identify and evaluate recurrent trends in literacy education. It assists us in understanding the relationships between politics and literacy education, school and society, local and central governments, and teachers and students. It provides a greater understanding about the dynamics of change in education. And finally, historical research in literacy informs us that variations of even the most protracted problems of our day have been tackled in one manner or another by previous generations of literacy specialists.

THE RESEARCH PROCESSES FOR THE HISTORICAL ANALYSIS OF LITERATE PRACTICE

We now turn from the larger questions about historical methodology to the specific skills, strategies, and procedures that mark the path through historical inquiry in literacy. As with any research endeavor, there is a process that outlines the general flow of historical research, allowing for false starts, recursions, digressions, and revisions. The outline that follows suggests the general flow of historical inquiry, but also acknowledges the vagaries inherent to the flow. We begin with the all-important first step, choosing a topic.

Choosing the Topic

When we as historical researchers are selecting a topic, Gray (1991) recommends considering the topic's (1) value, (2) originality, (3) practicality, and (4) unity of theme. Nailing down the topic enables us to focus on those things that will help us tell our story. Conversely, it helps us set aside things that are not useful to our storytelling. Experience shows us that the beginning researcher of literacy's history often proposes a topic that is too broad in nature. A topic's focus may be delimited chronologically, spatially, thematically, or by a combination of these three parameters. Hence we may need to focus—and refocus—the investigation through a continuous narrowing process. Often this action includes the formulation of at least a tentative working hypothesis or a set of guiding questions. Yet a working hypothesis may be revised through new questions, new foci, or new goals after the collection, evaluation, and initial analysis of appropriate data.

Collecting Evidence

Unlike other types of researchers, a historian does not create evidence. Rather, the historian uses that which is available. In collecting evidence, the researcher is likely to examine both primary sources and secondary sources. *Primary sources* are original documents, artifacts, remains, or relics associated with the topic under investigation. Documents and artifacts are records of eyewitnesses or direct outcomes of incidents. These items are intentionally or unintentionally left in order to provide a firsthand record of the event. As Ary, Jacobs, and Razavich (2002) note, "Only the mind of the observer intrudes between the original event and the investigator" (p. 450).

Examples of primary sources for literacy education would include those works of (1) a personal nature (e.g., manuscripts, personal journals, memoirs, diaries, marginal notes, blogs, autobiographies, private and public letters, memos, and emails); (2) a public nature (e.g., written transcriptions and oral testimonies from participants and observers, photographs, films, and audio, video, or digital recordings); (3) a professional nature (e.g., community and school newspapers, magazines, journals, school bulletins, curriculum guides, courses of study/units, textbooks/workbooks, children's books, software, student work, portfolios, report cards, record books, and examinations); and (4) an official nature (e.g., official records, minutes, and reports of legislatures, school boards, state and county offices of education, specific schools, postsecondary institutions, or special task forces; certificates, licenses, and credentials; evaluation and research data/ reports to local, state, and federal agencies; and census reports, immigration records, and laws) (see Butchart, 1986).

Remains or relics associated with a particular person, group, institution, or periods in time were not meant to transmit information across time as part of the record, but nonetheless they can shed light on a research question. In literacy education, these may include school buildings and specific rooms (e.g., reading clinics and resource rooms), classroom furniture (e.g., language centers), period technology (e.g., tachistoscopes, controlled readers, and language masters), tools (e.g., handwriting implements), teaching materials (e.g., basals and software), student work samples (e.g., completed handwriting manuals, spelling books, and portfolios), and so on.

Secondary sources do not have a direct relationship to the case under study. An individual writing or talking about an event was not present as the incident unfolded; rather, this narrator obtained the description of the event or era from another source, which may or may not have been a primary source (e.g., Wyatt, 1992). Examples of secondary sources covering literacy history include textbooks (Anderson & Dearborn, 1952), history books (Balmuth, 2009), articles in an encyclopedia (Monaghan, Hartman, & Monaghan, 2002; Rose, 2002), reviews of research (Stahl & Henk, 1986), reprints or reproductions of materials (Gorn, 1998; Robinson, 2002), or prints of originals (Nolin, Swan, & West, 1991). The literacy historian may find that a valuable source would be the annotated bibliography *Historical Sources in U.S. Reading Education 1900–1970* (Robinson, 2000), as well as Graff's (1981) extensive interdisciplinary research bibliography.

Secondary source materials will be of interest as they present particular vantage points on primary sources and the topic itself. Secondary sources may also review previously unread bibliographic information that should be read on the topic of interest. Furthermore, the review of secondary sources will assist the researcher in focusing on or narrowing down a topic of interest, and hence assist with the development of research questions.

Nevertheless, secondary sources are always imbued with points of view or subject to erroneous information as interpretations of primary sources reconveyed from person to person or from text to text. In addition, such works inevitably include the prejudices and the assumptions of the authors. The final point to be made is that each secondary source should be used with great care, with accurate citation, and with appropriate critique of the perspectives and biases found within the work. The reality is that most historical work in literacy will use a combination of primary and secondary sources.

With most historical investigations, the primary sources are available in the rare book rooms of public and academic libraries or in archives associated with learned societies, religious groups, museums, and other archival sites around the globe; to a greatly expanding degree, they are also available on the Internet (e.g., Internet Archives, Google Scholar, the European Library/Europeana, and Project Gutenberg). Archives that include artifacts needed for research in the history of literacy can be difficult to locate.

More recently, the field of historiography has been able to draw the growing number of sources that can be classified as reproductions of primary and secondary sources (e.g., *New England Primer Enlarged,* 1800/1975; Stickney, 1885/1985; Webster, 1866/n.d.), many of which are out of copyright protection and reproduced by services outside the United States (e.g., Gray, 1917; Judd, 1918). Monaghan and Hartman (2000) note that printed copies reproduced with "scrupulous care" can be acceptable substitutes for actual primary sources if the reproduction of the material fits the purpose of the research.

As we move more fully into the digital age, many primary and secondary sources are being preserved via digital technologies in Internet archives (e.g., Internet Archive, Google Scholar). Such practices make the use of primary sources accessible to all historians, but these technologies require that the literacy historian become knowledgeable about and competent with online catalogs, online networks, and search engines from the perspective of "big historical data" (see Benjamin, 2018; Galgano, Arndt, & Hyser, 2012; Graham, Milligan, & Weingart, 2016; Greenstein, 1994; Nicholson, 2016; Reiff, 1991).

With the coming of Internet archives, archival work is more than simply reading a recently found source, as archival endeavors now permit the mining of data within a text and across sources. Indeed, a whole new world of historiography has opened up to the literacy researcher, but new and sophisticated skills are now required in regard to the data, the metadata, and the interface with the site (Nicholson, 2016). When such materials are used in the research process, it is imperative that citations note the actual sources of the evidence.

While printed reproductions or digitalized sources from archives may be used in the comfort of one's home or office (often for free or for nominal costs) rather than through traveling at great cost to a distant archive, the review of a document or an image over the Internet will never replace the materiality associated with the source (i.e., size, weight, texture), the sensual experience, or the experience of being at one with the author through holding and perusing the primary source or examining a relic at first hand. Furthermore, as digitally oriented generations continue to enter the professoriate, there is a clear danger that digital sources will be privileged—and since not all sources are being digitalized, historically important primary and secondary sources will be overlooked. The problem is exacerbated as libraries purge holdings, so that important works become difficult to access or must be procured through the used-book market.

Regardless of the use of primary sources versus secondary sources, or of originals versus reproductions, historians must understand from the onset of their research that they can only investigate those topics (whether about events or people) for which either public or private documents and artifacts were preserved by official action or by happenstance for posterity, or those events or people for which there are available and cognizant witnesses willing to discuss them for the record. As such, historians should strive to review conscientiously the available data, and then within their reports discuss the depth and the breadth of the existing pool of documents (and, as possible, the degree to which historical traces have been lost over the years). Unfortunately, many historical narratives published in the education journals fail to provide information about the location, selection, and evaluation of both primary and secondary sources. Willis (2002), in her work on the Calhoun Colored School, presents such information in the text of the article.

Evaluating Evidence

While there is a degree of thrill in the hunt for materials, the responsibility of the historian does not end there. Indeed, potential problems may arise with the documents that have survived for the historian's review. In his seminal work on educational historiography, Kaestle (1988) poses four evaluative questions that literacy historians should use when interpreting artifacts:

1. How conscientiously were the data reported in the first place?
2. What individuals and institutional biases may have affected the results?
3. What are the contradictions between different sources that claim to measure the same variables in the same population?
4. Since the artifact of interest is removed in time (and likely in space) from the present, could its fundamental purpose or definition have been interpreted differently in the previous era than it is today?

These concerns call for us to evaluate critically the information under review. Historical criticism is the underlying foundation of historiography. Every time a historian accepts a piece of evidence or rejects another source and then interprets data in a research report, the act of historical criticism either external or internal is taking place (Isaac & Michael, 1995). Careful and ordered evaluation of evidence in historical research leads the process to be more demanding than experimental methods. The analysis is not a one-time procedure that is run to "crunch" data, but an ongoing vigilance to the questioning of data across the life of the project and at times well beyond that point. Kaestle's (1988) four questions serve as a kind of analytic mantra to be repeated and answered for all data gathered in historical research.

When we say that evidence is evaluated critically, we mean that it is evaluated through a two-step process of external and internal criticism. The act of *external criticism* (sometimes referred to as *lower criticism*) asks this question: Is the evidence under consideration authentic and genuine? There is a focus on the textual integrity of the document or source rather than the message it carries. In other words, the historian asks four further questions: Who wrote the work? Where was the work authored? When was the document developed? Under what conditions was the work authored?

All the while, the historian is looking for frauds, distortions, or ghost-written works. For documents, this process may include several steps: (1) the authentication of authorship through signatures, script, handwriting, and spelling style by comparison to known signatures, script, handwriting, and spelling from a particular person and historical period; (2) the verification through physical and chemical tests that the document's paper, parchment, cloth content, or inks were available in the period the document was purportedly written; and (3) the matching of writing style and the point of view as evidenced in the document with texts previously verified as written by the individual. For relics, external criticism might include chemical analysis of paints and inks, or even carbon dating of relics and remains.

The act of *internal criticism* (sometimes referred to as *higher criticism*) asks this question: What is the accuracy and worth of the evidence that has been unearthed? This is the case for both document analysis and oral history interviews. The historian seeks to establish the credibility of each informant by asking whether the individual was a credible or reliable observer/recorder of the event, as well as whether any motives might have induced the informant to overstate, misconstrue, or overlook information. Indeed, the historian looks for bias that is both sympathetically and antagonistically constituted within the data. For instance, the literacy historian would ask what the bias or subjectivity of information is, based on the social, cultural, economic, or educational values and backgrounds of the individual(s) who authored the documents or provided the testimonies of the events of interest. The historian must query whether the informant's participation in the event influenced the reporting of the event and whether there is agreement in the report with other descriptions and reports of the event. And, if there are quantitative data, the historian must question whether it seems to be reasonable.

Internal criticism also requires that the historian turn inward to assess the extent and position of an implicit or explicit personal perspective demonstrated through the selection of either documents/artifacts or quantitative data to support the hypothesis and thus shape the interpretation of the evidence in the report. With oral history, the researcher must ask about the bias or subjectivity that emerges from the interaction between interviewee and interviewer. Authors of literacy-oriented histories do not tend to describe explicitly how they undertook either external or internal criticism. Still, such information is often hinted at within the footnotes for each article or chapter of a book.

Some scholars (e.g., Gray, 1991) think that the distinction between external and internal criticism is somewhat artificial. Instead, Gray suggests a set of heuristic questions that deal with opportunity, objectivity, transmission, and meaning. Whether historians engage in formal criticism or follow Gray's (1991) informal approach, their historical research should report the processes of criticism used, as well as their evaluation of the adequacy of the data used to support the hypothesis.

Working with Evidence

The activity of taking notes when reviewing a document is as individualistic as is each historian, and in some cases, it depends on the era in which the individual was trained. A time-honored tradition is the development of a manual note card system for both bibliographic notes and content notes— whether paper or digital cards are used.

Bibliographic cards contain standard reference information, including the name of the library or archive; specific cataloguing information for the document; and information about the source, the author, or the site. It is important to include complete documentation because reference styles for different scholarly journals and book publishers require different degrees of completeness for a referenced source.

Content cards contain the working material or facts that are extracted from the particular piece of evidence. In taking notes, one should be generous in the use of cards, as this action will promote ease with the organization of the research report. The page number for the information's bibliographic source should be written down; verbatim quotes must be so noted but used sparingly on cards and in the report; and summarization of ideas and data should be used, rather than simple copying of words (this prevents plagiarism). Personal inferences or ideas about the documents must be recorded, so that they will not be confused with facts from the document when both are reviewed at a later date. While photocopying or scanning of documents might be desirable, many archives will not permit such activities, as the process damages the primary sources.

There are, however, traditions and inventions other than note cards for recordkeeping. We have colleagues who prefer to take notes in a composition book or journal and then reorganize the notes at a later date on note cards or in a digital data file. Others have recommended the use of an audio recorder with which they dictate notes for future transcriptions and organization. Still others choose to use a laptop computer or netbook, so that digital note cards are taken at the time the source is reviewed, and then each saved digital note card is organized in a file corresponding to each source in a database. Through the use of a find feature, recurring words and phrases permit the location of text that can be moved into appropriate files. Still others use digital cameras or speech-to-text translation software (e.g., Dragon Speech Recognition).

Regardless of the process or medium used, it is always imperative to match the information recorded to the source and the actual placement of the information in the source. This is particularly important when the archive is not immediately or readily available, so that reviewing the primary sources for a second time is not possible.

Analyzing and Interpreting Evidence

In analyzing data, the first task is to make sure it is dependable and relevant to the topic. Then the evidence is synthesized into a pattern that tests the hypothesis or answers questions guiding the work. This synthesis first requires that one employ a systematic plan for the organization, storage, and retrieval of the data collected. When Leedy (1958) undertook his expansive history of postsecondary reading, he organized data by cross-filing the bibliographic and factual data (cards or files) in triplicate by three general categories: (1) chronological order, (2) author or informant, and (3) subject of theme. Through such a scheme he was able to cross-reference, or link, common subject data separated by the intervention of other events and the passage of time. More recently, he advocated (Leedy & Ormrod, 2019) the use of a fourth classification, geography of event. The preparation and then use of multiple files are facilitated through the use of index cards color-coded to the classification category.

The process of constructing history is shaped by three factors: the philosophical stance held by the writer, the evidence that was examined in the available primary and secondary sources, and the researcher's interpretation of the data. The facts that are gathered by the historian say little in and of themselves. The interpretation of those facts is what leads to understanding the hypothesis that was posed and the answering of the questions driving the study. The process of inductively interpreting the facts individually or in sets depends on having both mastery of the data and an understanding of the significance of that material.

Best and Kahn (1989) point out that a work can fall short because of oversimplification and illogical analysis when there are multiple and complex causes of events. On the other hand, the presentation of overgeneralizations based on insufficient evidence, or of false analogies when there are only superficial similarities, is an equally serious problem. Kaestle (1988) follows the same track as he cautions that one must be careful not to confuse correlation with causality. Just because two events occurred successively, this does not mean that one event caused the other.

While it is expected that one will build an interpretive stance based on one's philosophy, politics, or even pedagogy of literacy, as well as prior knowledge of the historical era and practice of historiography, the interpretation must be the result of acceptable and ethical scholarship. Making a case based on the selection of facts that agree with the hypothesis, while ignoring data that are not in accordance with a preferred outcome, is not acceptable. The context of quoted ideas and passages must be honored, people and ideas must be treated in a just and scholarly manner, and both criticism and admiration will be tempered through professional ethics. Best and Kahn (1989) offer sage advice when they state that impartiality and not neutrality is the aim of systematic research presentation in history.

Kaestle (1988) suggests that, as historians, we consider two potentially overlooked issues when interpreting the evidence. First, we must distinguish between the evidence of ideas about how people should behave and the evidence about how people actually behaved during an era. Most of us are quite familiar with the oft-quoted statement that regardless of the policies and curriculum adopted by a school district, when a teacher closes the classroom door, literacy instruction becomes that with which there is the greatest comfort. Simply put, people may be told that they need to act in a particular way, but the actual behavior may be different, either explicitly or covertly.

Second, it is necessary to distinguish between intent and consequence because the consequences of an event or a movement do not provide evidence of the participants' intent in undertaking the action under study. Intent must be based on specific evidence, not inferred from the consequences of the event. A historian has a great advantage in having the power of hindsight (Fendler, 2008). However, the participant in an event in history did not have clairvoyant powers to predict the future.

Writing the Article or Book

Finally, the research article, thesis, dissertation, or book should be written to present the analysis in an understandable and interesting manner. Authors should be careful not to be overly sentimental, didactic, or persuasive. Generally, the work is presented in a form of a narrative, with an underlying chronological discourse pattern. Yet, as presented earlier in this chapter, discourse patterns associated with the theoretical perspectives of historiography have evolved in many directions; thus, there are no hard and fast structures for reporting a study. Still, several recommendations for writing a report have been put forward by literacy historians over the years.

First, the argument that drives the hypothesis should be stated explicitly in the initial stages of the work. Then, as each concept underlying the argument is put forth, it should be followed by examples for support and explication. Equally important is the provision for general historical context in the report, as literacy events and personalities are intertwined with the greater cultural and societal events of the times. For instance, the impact of the Elementary and Secondary Education Act of 1965 on the nation's literacy instruction during the presidency of Lyndon Johnson cannot be examined without attention to the administration's War on Poverty or the civil rights movement.

Second, the meaning of key terms should be clear. Kaestle (1988) describes two potential problems with the use of key terms in a research report. There is *vagueness,* or the use of umbrella/overarching terms that do not carry the necessary degree of specificity when precision of language is essential. Many terms, such as *literacy* itself, have lost the precision and focus that were once associated with these terms. Furthermore, there is *presentism,* or the act of applying current-era terms that did not exist in the past or that have since evolved etymologically to carry different denotations or connotations to past events, movements, and so on. For instance, we would need to consider carefully our era-appropriate use of terms such as *work-type skills, work–study skills, study skills, study strategies,* and *learning strategies* as the underlying concept evolved across the 20th century.

Third, the unresolved issues of our research findings should not be glossed over or hidden. Points in our work that are still open to conjecture or yet to be validated should be treated openly. Footnotes or endnotes should explicate the issue and evenhandedly present the logic and evidence supporting each one.

Fourth, both the audience and the disciplinary medium that is best suited to our work should guide where the manuscript is disseminated in the field of literacy. Historical works in literacy are welcomed in the literacy journals sponsored by the International Literacy Association, the LRA, the ALER, and the College Reading and Learning Association, among others. Such works may also find homes in other education journals or history journals or may become books or monographs published by university and scholarly presses. We suggest that any author new to the field review Monaghan and Hartman (2000) before selecting a potential vehicle for publication. Finally, let us not forget that the field has welcomed dissertations focusing on our history since the early 1900s (e.g., Lamport, 1935; Reeder, 1900; Smith, 1934).

Now we wish to make a point that comes from our shared experiences in reviewing historical research reports for journals, book publishers, and yearbooks over several decades. A manuscript that has problems with the presentation of the findings can often be revised to find an academic home and contribute to the scholarship of the profession. But a historical manuscript that rests on insufficient, flawed, or shoddy analysis of the data will be doomed from the start if the investigator did not employ appropriate and rigorous historical research methods. In other words, there is truth in the old adage that an ounce of prevention is worth a pound of cure.

ORAL HISTORY

In 1989, Norman Denzin authored his seminal text *Interpretive Biography,* in which he made a coherent case for oral history, life history, biography, autobiography, memorials, and case histories to be integrated in an all-encompassing classification of biography. To cover such a broad subject would require another chapter in this text. Hence we concentrate on oral history and its close cousin, life history, as focused on the literacy profession. Having noted this delimitation, we do suggest that readers interested in biography and autobiographies as related to life history and oral history should review Cowman (2016), Hitchcock and Hughes (1995), Kridel (1998), Tosh (2015), and Zimmer (2007) for discussions of methodology, and Ayres (1988), Havinghurst (1971), Israel and Monaghan (2007), Rose (1989), and Taylor (1937) for examples of the craft as associated with individuals within reading pedagogy.

The oral history project uses the most fragile and irreplaceable form of historical trace, human memory, to reconstruct the known past. Indeed, the fleeting nature of memory is best expressed in the old African adage acknowledging that whenever an elder member of a community dies, an entire library is lost (Zimmerman, 1982). By extending this acknowledgment, Stahl and King (2000) argue that the legacy of the literacy community must be preserved through gathering transcriptions of personal and professional recollections and life stories of our senior colleagues. Stahl, King, Dillon, and Walker (1994) suggest that the oral history projects of the ALER (Linek et al., 2010a, 2010b), the LRA, and the learning assistance program at National Louis University (Casazza & Bauer, 2006) have allowed us to (1) learn about the impact of both educational events and individuals through the saving of participants' and observers' recollections, which are unlikely to be saved in documents or the public record; (2) gain a more holistic perspective on our entire reading community by studying the observations of PreK–16 literacy teachers; and (3) know the lineage of each succeeding academic generation, to understand the impact our professional ancestors have had on each of us.

We believe that oral historians of literacy pedagogy can take the same step that Brandt (2001) did when she interviewed community members about the their literacy experiences across their school years and lifespans (also see Lyons & Taska, 1992). Hence the primary responsibility of these historians is to save the records of individuals' contributions to the profession, as well as individuals' views on pedagogical movements or literacy experiences encountered across the professional lifespan. Furthermore, oral historians have the opportunity to identify and record the underlining reasons, motivations, policies, and experiences behind individuals' life actions and scholarly endeavors.

The groundwork for undertaking an oral history interview involves immersion in the era or context in which the interviewee observed or participated. Interviewers in any project should consult era-appropriate primary sources and a range of secondary sources before conducting any interviews, and then again in seeking clarification of points raised during an interview. These works may include those that influenced the interviewee or were authored by the individual. If the oral history project focuses on a non-elite member of a professional group, interviewers should consider visiting a state or local historical society's archive for regional data, a school district's or state educational agency's repository for district records and curriculum materials, or a postsecondary institution (such as the University of Pittsburgh or Northern Illinois University) that has a textbook collection. Review of such documents should help in the development of a purpose statement and the preparation of the questions to appear in the interview guide. In addition, gaining local color is possible through initial interviews of community members or family members.

The first step in undertaking an oral history project is the selection of individuals to be interviewed. Interviewees in the ALER and LRA projects were from the category of individuals who have left a legacy through presentations at reading conferences; publication of professional articles, chapters, and books; or service activities for organizations. Numerous individuals participating in the National Louis University project were not as likely to leave a written legacy of their careers or experiences. It may be even more important to capture the perspectives of the non-elite on the role literacy played within their personal or professional lives. Brandt (2001) demonstrates with her exemplary study of literacy in the lives of typical Americans the importance of selecting participants from varied economic, geographic, and cultural communities.

Once a potential interviewee has agreed to be interviewed, that person must be informed of the project's focus and the nature of questions to be asked. The greater the rapport between the interviewer and the interviewee, the more likely it is that cooperation will be achieved and the interview process will be completed, particularly if there is a need for multiple interviews. The interviewee must be comfortable with the interview process and the recording of recollections through either audio or video technology.

Three cautionary notes need to be considered at this point in our discussion. First, it is essential that any participant possess the physical and mental capabilities to participate in the oral history interview. Second, unlike in other historical investigations that do not focus on the personal element, obtaining the interviewee's consent to participate in the study and to permit archiving and future research use of the transcription is standard procedure. (Policies pertaining to institutional review of research involving human subjects are not quite as clear for oral history work as for most other forms of human subjects research. Hence all literacy historians should read Shopes's [n.d.] treatise on the topic and then check with the office of research compliance at their own institutions to learn of local requirements.) Finally, it is imperative that the researcher be competent with the technology to be used during the interview.

An interview guide composed of open-ended questions should be used to informally direct the interview process. Although not every oral historian uses such a guide, these are helpful for the less experienced interviewer, and guides assist an interviewer with the obtaining of data for cross-case analysis. Participants in the first LRA project were given an 11-stage lifespan guide with multiple subcategories for interviewing members of the literacy profession (Stahl & King, 2000). Brandt (2001) includes an excellent guide that should be consulted in designing a protocol for interviewing individuals from the general public. As important as an interview guide might be, Stahl and King (2000) note that an interviewer should not be a slave to the guide, but instead should use it as a starting point for the interview process.

The heart of the oral history process is the interview. To ensure an optimal interview, we recommend taking several preparatory steps before the interview begins. First, in laying the groundwork, the interviewer must visit the interview site to learn about possible distractions or background noises that could interfere with the interview. The interviewer must be sure that both interviewer and interviewee will be seated comfortably, and that the recorder will not be in direct view of the interviewee. The interviewer should keep the initial dialogue conversational to break the ice, all the while making sure the technology is functioning properly. The opening recorded statements should identify the participant's name, the date, the time, the location, and the subject matter. Finally, the interviewer should share four or five statements about the topic of the interview with the respondent, to activate prior knowledge. Throughout the interview, the questions in the guide provide a basic street map of the process. We are influenced by the seminal work of Baum (1995) for interview guidelines and suggest that the reader review this source for a comprehensive set of recommendations for undertaking the actual interview.

Once each interview is complete, the same identifying information as noted previously (e.g., interviewee's name, date, time) should be read into the recording. Shortly after the session is over, an initial review of the recording should be undertaken, so that any problems with the recording can be identified and self-notes can be taken while information is still fresh in the interviewer's mind. A copy of the recording should be produced and stored in an alternative setting for safekeeping, according to an institution's institutional review board policies.

The transcription process should be undertaken shortly after the interview session. Transcriptions are developed directly from the recording in a verbatim manner. The transcript must be an accurate accounting of the verbal dialogue between the interviewee and the interviewer. (See Yow, 2015, for additional information on transcribing issues and procedures.) At a later date, the interviewer should ask the respondent to review the transcript for accuracy, as well as for personal comfort with the information provided.

The dissemination stage of a project is composed of two parts: immediate dissemination, and long-term archival and dissemination functions. Immediate dissemination often takes the form of giving a presentation at an annual conference, publishing a report of an individual oral history (e.g., Dillon, 1985), or publishing a report of thematically categorized oral histories (e.g., Clegg, 2003; King, 1991; Lyons & Taksa, 1992). Long-term archival requires that the researcher find a depository for the transcripts and the recordings/digital files, so that future generations of researchers can review these materials in the years ahead. In some cases, local or state historical societies or university libraries will undertake the archival responsibilities for a project, or an organization's historian or archivist will maintain the project's data.

OPPORTUNITIES FOR HISTORICAL RESEARCH

The opportunities for individuals to raise and then answer questions through the historical method are numerous, going back to Huey's (1908/1968) seminal text, and are certainly needed at the cross-national, national, regional, and local levels. Topics that have been studied in the past are also always open for revisionist interpretations, based on new and overlooked evidence as well as different philosophical perspectives. Hence, rather than offering specific topics for potential research, we refer the reader to the broadly defined avenues for historical research as put forward by Stahl and Hartman (2004) for literacy education, Stahl and King (2018) for postsecondary reading, and Skager and Weinberg (1971) for the general field of education.

The selection of a research topic is a very personal activity, based on interest, prior knowledge, questions, and personal commitment. The researcher's selection of a method—whether document analysis, oral history, or a mixed method—will rest on the questions driving the research. Certainly, an individual should have the degree of interest in the topic and the competence with the method(s) that will drive the research endeavors forward through a multitude of tasks and across what is often a lengthy period of time. Any research undertaking should also be guided by an understanding of the standards and the parameters described throughout this chapter.

An evolving mastery of the historical method should not stop an individual from undertaking historical research or from becoming a literacy historiographer. As Butchart (1986) counsels, "There is no need to be intimidated. You need not know all the methods or even most of them. The work of the historian has more in common with old craft traditions than with modern professions. Native intelligence, careful work, and a willingness to learn are the only prerequisites" (p. 9). Still, our experience suggests that a new literacy historian will find value in reading texts on historiography (Tosh, 2015), pedagogical historiography (Butchart, 1986; Goodson & Sikes, 2001; McCulloch & Richardson, 2000), and literacy historiography (Gilstad, 1981; Monaghan & Hartman, 2000; Moore, Monaghan, & Hartman, 1997).

Furthermore, the first steps of becoming a literacy historian need not be taken in monastic solitude. The new historiographer will find support through membership in the History of Literacy Innovative Community Group of the LRA, or in Division F (History and Historiography) of the American Educational Research Association (*www.aera.net/Division-F/History-Historiography-F*).

EXEMPLAR

We selected an exemplar study of historical research on literacy research by drafting a list of texts that demonstrated the essential criteria for good historiography outlined earlier in this chapter. While the list of texts was not as long as might be developed for some empirical methodologies, there were numerous works, both recent and older, that could serve the purpose of exemplifying well-researched and well-written historical research on literacy. Through several conversations in trying to narrow down the options, we kept coming back to E. Jennifer Monaghan's body of work. Indeed, we came to understand that there are really two definitions of the word *exemplar*. First, the word can refer to an individual who has been a torchbearer, a mentor, and a legacy for the profession. Second, it can refer to a particular professional work that serves as a model work for future researchers. For us, E. Jennifer Monaghan and her work are the prime examples of the first and second definitions, respectively. (For a similar type of analysis, see Kaestle, 1988.)

Author

Monaghan, who has authored such seminal works as *A Common Heritage: Noah Webster's Blue-Back Speller* (1983) and *Learning to Read and Write in Colonial America* (2005), is one of the most important literacy researchers to publish in the field across the past four decades. From her exemplary body of research on literacy history and historiography, we have selected Monaghan's (1991) article "Family Literacy in Early 18th-Century Boston: Cotton Mather and His Children," which appeared in *Reading Research Quarterly*, as an exemplar of historical research in literacy.

Introductory Matter

Monaghan begins the exemplar with a brief discussion of what was in 1991 the literacy field's evolving understanding of family literacy, emergent literacy, and out-of-school literacy practices. In a sense, this introductory section provides an advance organizer that assists with activating the reader's prior knowledge of topics in the article that are removed in time (if not space). While such might not be important in a scholarly venue for historians with a specialization in colonial America, it serves an important purpose for the typical readership of *Reading Research Quarterly*.

Following the same line of reasoning, Monaghan then discusses the shift in the research in educational history from in-school practices to influences external to the schoolhouse, such as the community, church, and home. Yet Monaghan points out, "Despite these similar changes of heart within the two separate disciplines of reading research and the history of education, scholars have yet to take a fresh look at a history of American reading instruction that has been informed by these insights" (1991, p. 344). The published work on literacy education in colonial America as found in 1991 focused on textbooks or English spelling. Research also existed on the colonial family, as historians had been studying quantitative data from demographic sources to learn about family structure and governance, as well as qualitative data found in diaries, letters, and religious materials/records to learn about the psychological aspects of family life. Yet the study of literacy within the family circle presented a pristine topic, and diaries and letters could serve as a window into the literacy life of the colonial family. A set of diaries authored by Cotton Mather, serving as primary sources, provided just such a window.

Cotton Mather and His Works

Cotton Mather (1663–1728) was an iconic figure in early New England as one of the ministers in Boston's North Church and as the author of numerous religious texts and tracts, including *Wonders of the Invisible World, Magnalia Christi Americana, Bonifacius*, and *Ratio Disciplinae*. Throughout his life Mather kept a diary, starting a new journal each year on his birthday. While not all of his diaries survive, 16 diaries can be found in the Massachusetts Historical Society archives, 9 diaries are in the archives of the American Antiquarian Society, 1 diary is housed with the Congregational Library Society, and 1 can be found at the University of Virginia.

More importantly for the scope of this research, these works have been edited and published in three volumes, which served as the primary sources for Monaghan's work. As noted earlier, when based on proper historical criticism of the primary sources (as had been done with the diaries), such reproductions and collections can serve as de facto primary sources (while protecting fragile works). Still, one must understand that since the research is limited to the diaries that have been located and preserved, there are gaps in the corpus that could suggest alternative theories if the missing diaries were available. In order to gain a fuller picture of Mather's life and beliefs, Monaghan consulted his other works, including *Paterna*, his autobiography, and *The Life of the Very Reverend and Learned Cotton Mather, D.D., & F.R.S.*, the biography authored by his son Samuel Mather (1729).

Purpose for Research

As with any research endeavor, the researcher must formulate a guiding purpose for any historical study. Monaghan wished to learn about early colonial New England family literacy practices as evidenced within the entries found in the extant Mather diaries. More specifically, she was interested in determining how the Mather children surviving beyond infancy developed literacy, how these literate behaviors were employed at home, how the parents and other adults influenced their literacy activities, and what literacy experiences were engaged in by the household. Monaghan directed specific attention to variables of gender, class, and race. Yet she provided a caveat from the onset that, given Mather's highly literate background and his elite status in the community, the findings from the research should not be considered either typical or representative of the entire New England population.

Mather: The Man

In the first formal section of the article after the frontmatter, Monaghan provides the readership with fundamental knowledge of the man, the time, and the place. Initially, she covers the scholarship on Cotton Mather. Monaghan drew heavily on the work of respected scholars who focused on the colonial era. Through these secondary sources, we learn that Mather was at the very least a complex individual, with interests in theology, medicine, science, community charity, and even the evils of witchcraft. His *Magnalia Christi Americana* is considered one of the early classics of American literature. Monaghan notes that while his three biographers have examined his family life, other scholars have paid less attention to the topic. As for other scholars drawing upon the diaries to examine the family, there had been but a small degree of their use before this article was authored. In her background coverage of Mather, Monaghan employs secondary sources. This is a rather typical way in which scholars develop initial knowledge of an individual or an event before narrowing a research topic and then proceeding to delve into primary sources. Monaghan gives credit to Kenneth Silverman's (1984) biography, *The Life and Times of Cotton Mather,* for providing her with numerous references that assisted her in undertaking this work.

Monaghan next describes the literacy environment in Boston during the first 20 years of the 18th century. Without such background information, the reader would have difficulty in understanding the primary source examples drawn from the diaries that follow later in the article. Again, the author uses respected secondary sources to demonstrate that Boston had grown into an urbanized center of commerce, social sophistication, and greater secularization. The educational environment included three writing (penmanship/bookkeeping) schools and two Latin schools preparing boys for college and the ministry. She also shows that Boston had a flourishing trade in both imported and indigenously prepared books, a growing printing capacity, and two newspapers. Literacy instruction in New England is portrayed by examining accounts in secondary sources, as well as the author's extensive research on colonial literacy. After noting that our knowledge of teaching literacy in this environment contains holes, she discusses what is known about the period: The teaching of reading was followed by writing instruction, which was followed by mathematics instruction; initial instruction was provided by females, and later instruction was delivered by males; and reading and writing in the colony served both important religious purposes and necessary secular purposes.

Monaghan then turns to examine Mather's literacy background. She contends that the education of Mather's children can only be understood in the context of his own education. Hence, she first details the literate lives of his grandfather, Richard Mather, and then his father, Increase Mather, and his mother, Maria Mather—all important figures in the development of the Massachusetts Bay Colony. As the narrative continues, the author draws from both Mather's autobiography as well as respected secondary sources to paint a picture of a young man gifted in communicative arts who taught himself to write before attending school; who read voraciously, exhibiting skill with skimming, summarizing, and paraphrasing; who mastered Latin by age 11; who graduated from Harvard at age 15; and who was ordained at 22 years of age. Throughout his life he valued reading and writing (composition) to such a degree that he attempted regularly to impart such values to others. By the time he passed on, he had authored at least 444 books or pamphlets, including a reading instructional text for youngsters entitled *Good Lessons for Children.*

The Diaries

As the author transfers attention to the diaries, she first informs the reader that Mather sought to use his diaries as a vehicle for spiritual improvement.

While he does mention important personal events, he does not dwell on external events. He had no desire for the audience of the journals to be the greater public. Quite the contrary, he hoped that they would provide guidance to his children, as well as explanation for his fatherly actions. In addition, the diaries became sources as he worked on *Paterna*, his autobiography. Monaghan points out that such purposes must be kept in mind as one judges the value of the works as evidence.

Besides considering the purpose of the diaries, Monaghan felt that Mather's process of composing these works was also worthy of consideration. Throughout each of his "natal years" from February 1681 to February 1711, Mather kept regular notes on the events of his life. Then, at the end of each natal year, he transferred the most important transcriptions into a diary. Each year he also developed a list of "Contrivances to do good," which were also integrated into the annual diary. Monaghan points out that these diaries were thus retrospective in nature, as opposed to regular records. Furthermore, we do not know what information Mather chose not to integrate into the annual diary, or why certain notes might have been cast aside.

Then in 1711 through 1724, the content of Mather's diaries shifted from recollections of past actions to a focus on his plans for improvement, entitled "Good Devised." These entries took the form of questions pertaining to different groups in his life including his family. A most positive happenstance for this study was that the "Good Devised" for Mondays was "What is to be done in my family," within which included Mather's literacy plans for his children. The diaries from this era tended to be longer, and the entries were often more explicit in detailing his planned activities with his children, although we do not know the degree to which these plans were implemented. Still, Monaghan assumes that Cotton was a man who did carry out his plans, and she points out that intent provides valuable insight into a person's value system.

Finally, Monaghan considers the diaries' "veracity as a source," as a form of criticism. In other words, might Mather have distorted the entries for any reason? When one reads the entries pertaining to his troubled marriage to his third wife, some distortions or extreme prejudices might be inferred. Yet Monaghan believes that his entries pertaining to his children's literacy provided fair treatment, showing both desired outcomes and less than desired outcomes equally. Therefore, she felt that there was no reason to disbelieve the evidence that surfaced.

Diary Evidence

The heart and soul of this article for both the educational historian and the literacy professional is the second major section, which focuses on the primary source diary evidence. Monaghan parses the diary evidence in such a way that the segments correspond roughly to each of his three marriages: to

Abigail Philips from 1686 to 1702, with four of nine children living beyond infancy (Katharin, 1689; Abigail, 1694; Hannah, 1697; and Increase Jr., 1699); to the widow Elizabeth Clark Hubbard from 1703 to 1714, with two of six children living beyond infancy (Elizabeth, 1704, and Samuel, 1706); and to Lydia George (1715–1728)—a union that produced no children, but in time produced a fair degree of turmoil and stress for Mather.

Hence, as would be expected, Monaghan's narrative is presented in a chronological discourse pattern. Throughout the analysis of the diaries, Monaghan follows a macrostructure in which she integrates a life event with a family-literacy-oriented theme, which she then explicates by presenting specific events and quotations from the respective diary. Across the years (diaries) and the many entries, themes appear, evolve, and reappear. The examples of family literacy practices woven throughout the diary entries included oral reading in various family settings; personal and educative writing activities; sharing of religious and other texts; summarization and interpretation of texts; reading and writing as 1700s versions of bibliotherapy; and formal and informal education practiced in the greater family circle, as influenced by the pious and often stark realities of urban life in early colonial New England.

Integration of the Findings

In the final (discussion) section of the article, Monaghan pulls together the various data points that she has mined from Mather's many diary entries across the years of his maturity. It is here that her work comes full circle back to the very purposes and questions that guided the initial work. Superordinate themes have emerged from the study of the diaries and the associated primary sources. First, Monaghan draws conclusions about general literacy instruction of the period, in that she confirms the earlier research findings on the sequence of literacy instruction; the importance of religion, but with the growing secular nature of education; the gender of teachers at the various levels; and the content of instruction. Second, she addresses the role of gender, class, and race. The Mather home was patriarchal, and the males were the favored gender, with greater attention directed to their formal and informal educations. Yet, given the class distinctions in the New England early colonial society, the Mather daughters, as members of the middle class, were expected to master the pen. Furthermore, Mather was interested in the literacy development of his slaves, at least in the sense of having them learn to read for the sake of their conversion. In fact, he opened a school for African Americans and Native Americans in 1717.

Another theme is presented through Monaghan's discussion of literacy in the family setting. She proposes that literacy through "bed-book" reading, peer and intergenerational instruction, and Mather's literacy assignments for the children had an important but not overreaching role in promoting family interactions. Literacy was a communal family activity, particularly through oral reading of the scriptures and Mather's Bible stories. Mather promoted family literacy in that he modeled literate behaviors; directed his children to complete specific reading and writing assignments; taught them how to comprehend text through both examples and explanation; and demonstrated how "life, language, and literacy" are interrelated.

The last theme is in a sense an assessment of Mather's success as a literacy promoter and provider. Monaghan points out that none of the children rose to his level as an author; given his prodigious production of texts, however, such a goal would have been unreachable to all but a limited number of gifted individuals. Still, she suggests that the members of the family upon reaching adulthood held the same views of the importance of literate behaviors as did the family patriarch.

What, then, does this study demonstrate to the potential literacy historian? Clearly, it answers questions about how one family from early colonial New England used both reading and writing as part of and in promotion of a literate environment. And while the Mather family can hardly be called typical of colonial America or even colonial Boston, the work served as one of the cornerstones for what was to become Monaghan's defining tome on literacy in colonial America from north to south, *Learning to Read and Write in Colonial America* (Monaghan, 2005).

But Monaghan's study does more than provide a historicized piece to the family literacy puzzle. As an exemplary study, it illustrates the two core strategies for doing sound methodological work with data from literacy's past: *questioning* and *connecting*. She questioned and connected at several levels in her study. At the data level, Monaghan *questioned* the data by interrogating the motives and purposes of the sources (and their authors), asking why some data were available but not others, and framing queries that guided her ongoing handling of the data. She *connected* the data by linking primary and secondary sources, sequencing them temporally and thematically, and comparing differences and similarities. At the interpretive level, Monaghan *questioned* her interpretations of the data by cross-examining the durability of the connections she'd made between data to warrant her claims. She *connected* her interpretations of the data to her other interpretations, sorting and sifting interpretive themes into more encompassing themes. And at the discourse level, Monaghan questioned her interpretations of the data by pitting them against the interpretations of other scholars, asking how they would challenge the robustness of her themes. She connected her interpretations of the data by associating them with the interpretations of other scholars, acknowledging points where her interpretations imbricate, valvate, and separate from those of others.

We close this chapter where we began. Everything has a history—including literacy. Everything that exists in the present—textbooks, articles, correspondence, tests, methods, theories, diaries, software, this chapter, and the other chapters in this volume—comes out of literacy's past. There are rigorous methods for interpreting these artifacts from the past.

The twin strategies for doing rigorous interpretive work on literacy's history are *questioning* and *connecting*. Through interrogation and linking, an interpretive reconstruction of our knowable past is made. Regrettably, relatively little is known about literacy's past compared to other fields and professions. Fortunately, ample data and new interpretive tools are available for making that past known. There has never been a better time, or a greater need, for such research to be conducted.

REFERENCES

Anderson, I. H., & Dearborn, W. F. (1952). *The psychology of teaching reading.* New York: Roland Press.

Ary, D., Jacobs, L. C., & Razavich, A. (2002). *Introduction to research in education* (6th ed.). Belmont, CA: Wadsworth/Thomson Learning.

Ayres, D. (1988). *Let my people learn: The biography of Dr. Wil Lou Gray.* Greenwood, SC: Attic Press.

Balmuth, M. (2009). *The roots of phonics* (rev. ed.). Baltimore: Brookes.

Baum, W. K. (1995). *Oral history for the local historical society* (3rd ed.). Nashville, TN: American Association for State and Local History.

Benjamin, J. R. (2018). *A student's guide to history* (14th ed.). New York: Bedford/St. Martin's.

Best, J. W., & Kahn, J. V. (1989). *Research in education* (6th ed.). Englewood Cliffs, NJ: Prentice-Hall.

Borg, W. R., Gall, J. P., & Gall, M. D. (1993). *Applying educational research: A practical guide* (3rd ed.). New York: Longman.

Brandt, D. (2001). *Literacy in American lives.* Cambridge, UK: Cambridge University Press.

Brundage, A. (2018). *Going to the sources: A guide to historical research and writing* (6th ed.). Hoboken, NJ: Wiley.

Butchart, R. E. (1986). *Local schools: Exploring their history.* Nashville, TN: American Association for State and Local History.

Casazza, M. E., & Bauer, L. (2006). *Access, opportunity, and success: Keeping the promise of higher education.* Westport, CT: Greenwood Press.

Caunce, S. (1994). *Oral history and the local historian.* London: Longman.

Cavallo, G., & Chartier, R. (2003). *A history of reading in the West.* Amherst: University of Massachusetts Press.

Clayton, E. (2013). *The golden thread: The story of writing.* Berkeley, CA: Counterpoint.

Clegg, L. B. (2003). *The empty schoolhouse: Memories of one-room Texas schools.* College Station: Texas A&M University Press.

Clodd, E. (1907). *The story of the alphabet.* New York: Appleton.

Cohen, L., Manion, L., & Morrison, K. (2018). *Research methods in education* (8th ed.). London: Routledge.

Cowman, K. (2016). Collective biography. In S. Gunn & L. Faire (Eds.), *Research methods for history* (2nd ed., pp. 85–103). Edinburgh, UK: University of Edinburgh Press.

Darnton, R. (1990). What is the history of the books? In R. Darnton (Ed.), *The kiss of Lamourette: Reflections in cultural history* (pp. 107–135). New York: Norton.

Denzin, N. K. (1989). *Interpretive biography.* Newbury Park, CA: SAGE.

Dillon, D. (1985). Ira E. Aaron: A qualitative case study of a career history. *Georgia Journal of Reading, 11*(1), 18–25.

Diringer, D. (1962). *Writing.* New York: Praeger.

Diringer, D. (1982). *The book before printing: Ancient, medieval and oriental.* New York: Dover.

Fendler, L. (2008). The upside of presentism. *Paedagogica Historica, 44*(6), 667–690.

Fischer, S. R. (2001). *A history of writing.* London: Reaktion Books.

Fischer, S. R. (2019). *A history of reading* (rev. ed.). London: Reaktion Books.

Galgano, M. J., Arndt, J. C., & Hyser, R. M. (2012). *Doing history: Research and writing in a digital age.* Belmont, CA: Wadsworth Cengage Learning.

Gilderhus, M. T. (2009). *History and historians: A historiographical introduction* (7th ed.). Englewood Cliffs, NJ: Prentice-Hall.

Gilstad, J. R. (1981). Methodology of historical research of reading instruction: Principles and criteria. *Reading World, 20,* 185–196.

Good, C. V. (1966). *Essentials of educational research.* New York: Meredith.

Goodson, I., & Sikes, P. (2001). *Life history research in educational settings.* Buckingham, UK: Open University Press.

Gorn, E. J. (Ed.). (1998). *The McGuffey readers: Selections from the 1879 edition.* Boston: Bedford/St. Martin's.

Graff, H. J. (1981). *Literacy in history: An interdisciplinary research bibliography.* New York: Garland Press.

Graham, S., Milligan, I., & Weingart, S. (2016). *Exploring big historical data: The historian's macroscope.* London: Imperial College Press.

Gray, C. T. (1917). *Types of reading ability as exhibited through tests and laboratory experiments.* Chicago: University of Chicago Press. (Reprinted on demand, 2018, Facsimile Publisher, Delhi, India)

Gray, W. (1991). *Historian's handbook: A key to the study and writing of history* (2nd ed.). Prospect Heights, IL: Waveland Press.

Greenstein, D. I. (1994). *A historian's guide to computing.* New York: Oxford University Press.

Gunn, S., & Faire, L. (Eds.). (2016). *Research methods for history* (2nd ed.). Edinburgh, UK: University of Edinburgh Press.

Havinghurst, R. J. (Ed.). (1971). *Leaders in American education: Seventieth yearbook of the National Society for the Study of Education, Part II.* Chicago: University of Chicago Press.

Hitchcock, G., & Hughes, D. (1995). *Research and the teacher.* London: Routledge.

Huey, E. B. (1968). *The psychology and pedagogy of reading.* Cambridge, MA: MIT Press. (Original work published 1908)

Isaac, S., & Michael, W. B. (1995). *Handbook in research and evaluation* (3rd ed.). San Diego, CA: EdITS.

Israel, S. E., & Monaghan, E. J. (Eds.). (2007). *Shaping the reading field: The impact of early reading pioneers, scientific research, and progressive ideas.* Newark, DE: International Reading Association.

Johns, A. (2000). *The nature of the book: Print and knowledge in the making.* Chicago: University of Chicago Press.

Judd, C. H. (1918). *Reading: Its nature and development*. Chicago: University of Chicago Press. (Reprinted on demand, 2018, Facsimile Publisher, Delhi, India)

Kaestle, C. F. (1988). Recent methodological developments in the history of American education. In R. M. Jaeger (Ed.), *Complementary methods for research in education* (pp. 61–71). Washington, DC: American Educational Research Association.

King, J. R. (1991). Collaborative life history narratives: Heroes in reading teachers' tales. *Qualitative Studies in Education, 4*(1), 45–60.

Kridel, C. (Ed.). (1998). *Writing educational biography*. New York: Garland Press.

Kyvig, D. E., & Marty, M. A. (2019). *Nearby history* (4th ed.). Lanham, MD: Rowman & Littlefield.

Lamport, H. B. (1935). *A history of the teaching of beginning reading* (Doctoral dissertation). Available from ProQuest Dissertations and Theses database. (UMI No. T-09249)

Leedy, P. D. (1958). *A history of the origin and development of instruction in reading improvement at the college level*. Unpublished doctoral dissertation, New York University. (University Microfilms No. 59-01016)

Leedy, P. D., & Ormrod, J. E. (2019). *Practical research: Planning and design* (12th ed.). Boston: Pearson.

Linek, W. M., Massey, D. D., Sturtevant, E. G., Cochran, L., McClanahan, B., & Sampson, M. B. (2010a). *The College Reading Association legacy: A celebration of fifty years of literacy leadership* (Vol. 1). St. Cloud, MN: Association of Literacy Educators & Researchers.

Linek, W. M., Massey, D. D., Sturtevant, E. G., Cochran, L., McClanahan, B., & Sampson, M. B. (2010b). *The College Reading Association legacy: A celebration of fifty years of literacy leadership* (Vol. 2). St. Cloud, MN: Association of Literacy Educators & Researchers.

Lyons, M. (2010). *A history of reading and writing*. London: Palgrave.

Lyons, M., & Taksa, L. (1992). *Australian readers remember: An oral history of reading 1890–1930*. Melbourne, Australia: Oxford University Press.

Manguel, A. (1996). *A history of reading*. New York: Viking Penguin.

Mathews, M. (1966). *Teaching to read: Historically considered*. Chicago: University of Chicago Press.

McCulloch, G., & Richardson, W. (2000). *Historical research in educational settings*. Buckingham, UK: Open University Press.

McDowell, W. H. (2002). *Historical research: A guide for writers of dissertations, theses, articles and books*. New York: Longman.

Monaghan, E. J. (1983). *A common heritage: Noah Webster's blue-back speller*. Hamden, CT: Archon Books.

Monaghan, E. J. (1991). Family literacy in early 18th-century Boston: Cotton Mather and his children. *Reading Research Quarterly, 26*(4), 342–370.

Monaghan, E. J. (2005). *Learning to read and write in colonial America*. Amherst: University of Massachusetts Press.

Monaghan, E. J., & Hartman, D. K. (2000). Undertaking historical research in literacy. In M. Kamil, P. Mosenthal, P. D. Pearson, & R. Barr (Eds.), *Handbook of reading research* (Vol. 3, pp. 109–121). Mahwah, NJ: Erlbaum.

Monaghan, E. J., Hartman, D. K., & Monaghan, C. (2002). History of reading instruction. In B. J. Guzzetti (Ed.), *Literacy in America: An encyclopedia of history, theory, and practice* (Vol. 1, pp. 224–231). Santa Barbara, CA: ABC/CLIO.

Moore, D. W., Monaghan, E. J., & Hartman, D. K. (1997). Values of literacy history. *Reading Research Quarterly, 32*(1), 90–102.

New England Primer Enlarged. (1975). Highland Park, NJ: Drier Educational Systems. (Original work published 1800)

Nicholson, B. (2016). Digital research. In S. Gunn & L. Faire (Eds.), *Research methods for history* (2nd ed., pp. 170–190). Edinburgh, UK: University of Edinburgh Press.

Nolin, L., Swan, H. A., & West, P. C. (1991). *Historical images of education: Prints from the Blackwell history of education research collection.* DeKalb: Northern Illinois University.

Perks, R., & Thomson, A. (Eds.). (2016). *The oral history reader* (3rd ed.) Abingdon, UK: Routledge.

Reeder, R. (1900). *Historical development of school readers and methods in teaching reading.* New York: Macmillan.

Reiff, J. L. (1991). *Structuring the past: The use of computers in history.* Washington, DC: American Historical Association.

Robinson, R. D. (2000). *Historical sources in U.S. reading education 1900–1970: An annotated bibliography.* Newark, DE: International Reading Association.

Robinson, R. D. (2002). *Classics in literacy education: Historical perspectives for today's teacher.* Newark, DE: International Reading Association.

Rose, J. (2002). History of the book. In B. J. Guzzetti (Ed.), *Literacy in America: An encyclopedia of history, theory, and practice* (Vol. 1, pp. 231–233). Santa Barbara, CA: ABC/CLIO.

Rose, M. (1989). *Lives on the boundary.* New York: Penguin.

Shannon, P. (1989). *Broken promises: Reading instruction in twentieth-century America.* Granby, MA: Bergin & Garvey.

Shopes, L. (n.d.). Oral history, human subjects, and institutional review boards. Retrieved September 15, 2019, from *www.oralhistory.org/about/do-oral-history/oral-history-and-irb-review.*

Silverman, K. (1984). *The life and times of Cotton Mather.* New York: Harper & Row.

Sitton, T., Mehaffy, G. L., & Davis, O. L. (1983). *Oral history: A guide for teachers (and others).* Austin: University of Texas Press.

Skager, R. W., & Weinberg, C. (1971). *Fundamentals of educational research: An introductory approach.* Glenview, IL: Scott, Foresman.

Smith, N. B. (1934). *A historical analysis of American reading instruction.* New York: Silver Burdett.

Smith, N. B. (2002). *American reading instruction* (special ed.). Newark, DE: International Reading Association.

Stahl, N. A. (2002). Epilogue. In N. B. Smith, *American reading instruction* (special ed., pp. 413–418). Newark, DE: International Reading Association.

Stahl, N. A., & Hartman, D. K. (2004). Doing historical research on literacy. In N. K. Duke & M. H. Mallette (Eds.), *Literacy research methodologies* (pp. 170–196). New York: Guilford Press.

Stahl, N. A., & Henk, W. A. (1986). Tracing the roots of textbook-study systems: An extended historical perspective. In J. A. Niles & R. V. Lalik (Eds.), *Solving problems in literacy: Learners, teachers, and researchers: 35th yearbook of the National Reading Conference* (pp. 366–374). Rochester, NY: National Reading Conference.

Stahl, N. A., & King, J. R. (2000). Preserving the heritage of a profession through California Reading Association oral history projects. *The California Reader, 34*(1), 14–19.

Stahl, N. A., & King, J. R. (2018). History. In R. F. Flippo & D. C. Caverly (Eds.), *Handbook of college reading and study strategy research* (3rd ed., pp. 3–26). New York: Routledge.

Stahl, N. A., King, J. R., Dillon, D., & Walker, J. (1994). The roots of reading: Preserving the heritage of a profession through oral history projects. In E. G. Sturtevant & W. Linek (Eds.), *Pathways for literacy: 16th yearbook of the College Reading Association*. Commerce: East Texas State University.

Stahl, N. A., King, J. R., & Eilers, V. (1996). Postsecondary reading strategies: Rediscovered. *Journal of Adolescent and Adult Literacy, 39*(5), 368–379.

Stickney, J. (1985). *Classics for children: A primer*. Boston: Ginn. (Original work published 1885)

Suarez, M. F., & Woudhuysen, H. R. (Eds.). (2013). *The book: A global history*. Oxford, UK: Oxford University Press.

Taylor, D. (Ed.). (2016). *Great women scholars*. New York: Garn Press.

Taylor, E. A. (1937). *Controlled reading*. Chicago: University of Chicago Press.

Thompson, P., & Bornat, J. (2017). *The voice of the past: Oral history* (4th ed.). Oxford, UK: Oxford University Press.

Tosh, J. (2015). *The pursuit of history* (6th ed.). New York: Routledge.

Webster, N. (n.d.). *The elementary spelling book, being an improvement on the American spelling book*. New York: American Book. (Original work published 1866)

Willis, A. I. (2002). Literacy at Calhoun Colored School 1892–1945. *Reading Research Quarterly, 37*(1), 8–44.

Wyatt, M. (1992). The past, present, and future need for college reading courses in the U.S. *Journal of Reading, 36*(1), 10–20.

Yow, V. R. (2015). *Recording oral history: A guide for the humanities and social sciences* (3rd ed.). Lanham, MD: Rowman & Littlefield.

Zimmer, J. E. (2007). Hints on gathering biographical data. In S. E. Israel & E. J. Monaghan (Eds.), *Shaping the reading field: The impact of early reading pioneers, scientific research, and progressive ideas* (pp. 417–420). Newark, DE: International Reading Association.

Zimmerman, W. Z. (1982). *Instant oral biographies*. New York: Guarionex.

CHAPTER 11

Instrument Development

Sharon Walpole
John Z. Strong
Meaghan N. Vitale

Many inspiring meetings between advisees and their mentors, or among team members preparing grant proposals, do not yield action plans. Invariably, someone says, "Yes, but how would we measure it?" If no one has ever measured it, that can be the end of the discussion. But it need not be. We can commit to generating the possibility that this conversation ends instead with someone saying, "I know a measure that we could use."

As we begin this chapter, we want to make the case that wide engagement in the instrument development process will advance the literacy research field. Perhaps the counter-argument is most convincing: If we do not engage widely in instrument development, we are all constrained by the set of instruments currently available. We cannot pursue new areas of interest; we cannot conduct research with new populations. In short, we cannot keep up. Even our funding agencies acknowledge that instrument development is an important part of the research process. In the request for applications for 2020 research grants from the Institute of Education Sciences (IES), for example, instrument development projects are specifically detailed as one of four IES project types; valid and reliable outcome measures are also required for each of the other project types (IES, 2019).

Why not rely solely on subtests from large assessment batteries? Think about the many studies yielding positive results on a set of researcher-designed measures, but no transfer to such large-scale measures. The sensitivity and specificity of standardized measures of reading have been challenged (e.g., Kame'enui et al., 2006; Kent, Wanzek, & Yun, 2019), and we expect that the same criticisms are valid for standardized measures of writing. A sensitive instrument consistently identifies a high number of true positives (e.g., students actually benefiting from an instructional program) and a low number of false negatives; specific instruments consistently identify true negatives (e.g., students not benefiting) and fewer false positives (Compton, Fuchs, Fuchs, & Bryant, 2006). Perhaps, because standardized measures of reading comprehension are limited in their accuracy, they should be avoided altogether in favor of curriculum-sensitive measures developed for more precise purposes (Catts & Kamhi, 2017; Kamhi & Catts, 2017).

But there is a more positive argument to advance as well. Developing an instrument requires a deep dive into the literature. It helps an investigator to locate and consider previous work, to refine his or her language, and to test and retest definitions of constructs. It builds methodological proficiencies. It presents an opportunity for managing the data collection process from start to finish. If done well, it provides a publication opportunity and then connections to other researchers interested in similar ideas. Each of us has engaged in instrument development, and we are convinced that it has advanced and deepened our scholarship.

RELIABILITY AND VALIDITY

If we are to engage in instrument development that advances our work and the work of others, we must keep our eye squarely on quality. Instrument quality is dependent on *reliability* and *validity*, including the theoretical soundness of the constructs being measured. Instruments themselves, however, are not reliable or unreliable, nor are they valid or invalid. Establishment of quality requires nuanced decisions that interact with the instrument's purpose. That is easier to understand if you accept that instruments are neither valid nor reliable at their face; the data they produce and the decisions they influence are what must be subjected to careful scrutiny. But what does it mean for those data to be reliable and valid, and for those decisions to be warranted? You will see that instrument development requires both the skills developed in social science methods classes and the theoretical understandings that come from deep understanding of the literacy literature.

Reliability describes the consistency and precision of data. It can refer to individual scores remaining consistent across testing periods and raters, assuming there is no reason for the scores to change. Reliability can also refer to the consistent measurement of a construct across the instrument (Huck, 2008). In other words, reliability is the reduction of measurement error. Depending on the instrument and its purpose, reliability can be established in numerous ways.

Frequently cited measures of reliability in instrument development studies are equivalence (alternate forms), stability (test–retest), internal consistency, and interrater reliability. Selection of a particular strategy for determining reliability depends on the instrument. Equivalence is established through correlational analyses on alternate or parallel versions of an instrument using the same sample. Stability is established through test–retest procedures with the same sample. Internal consistency is typically established through split-half testing, calculation of coefficient alpha, or use of the Kuder–Richardson Formula 20 (KR-20). Split-half testing divides a test into equal parts (odd vs. even, first half vs. second half, etc.), requires administration to separate groups of test takers, and then requires correlational analyses. Coefficient alpha measures the correlation between items of a test. KR-20 is used for dichotomous choices. Lastly, interrater reliability is established by comparing the scores from two or more raters observing the same event. We select from a set of statistics to establish interrater reliability, including percentage of agreement, Pearson's correlation (product–moment), Kendall's coefficient of concordance, Cohen's kappa, or the intraclass correlation coefficient (Huck, 2008). Each of these analyses has a different purpose and may privilege different aspects of the data. Establishing reliability adequately, with the appropriate statistics, is one step toward determining quality.

We also must establish validity. Validity estimates the "legitimacy of the scores as a measure of the intended attribute" and is the "most fundamental consideration in developing tests and evaluating tests" (American Educational Research Association [AERA], American Psychological Association, & National Council on Measurement in Education, 2014, p. 11). Different sources of evidence support different claims of validity: *content validity, construct validity,* and *criterion validity.* Although there are claims that "no single aspect of validation [is] sufficient on its own" (Abell, Springer, & Kamata, 2008, p. 99), the type (and amount) of evidence needed depends on how the data will be interpreted and used (AERA et al., 2014). Content validity is established by experts and is important in designing instruments intended to assess cognition. It is the degree to which an instrument is representative of a topic and contains relevant items (Colton & Covert, 2007). Construct validity is the degree to which an instrument measures a given construct. It can be established through judgments of test content, factor analysis of the instrument's internal structure, analysis of response processes, convergent or discriminant associations with other variables, or consequences of use (AERA et al., 2014; Furr, 2018; Huck, 2008). Criterion validity is the degree to which the instrument can accurately estimate the results of another measure collected concurrently or at different time points (predictive validity). It is established through correlational analyses (Colton & Covert, 2007).

Evidence of both reliability and validity is vital to the development of an instrument. Moreover, because reliability and validity are characteristics of the data and not of the instrument itself, Huck (2008) suggests not only citing the reliability of an instrument from its original publication, but also revalidating and reestablishing reliability when using or modifying an existing instrument. As part of Standard 2.0, AERA and colleagues (2014) advise that "appropriate evidence of reliability/precision should be provided for the interpretation for each intended score use" (p. 42). Uses that have significant consequences necessitate a higher degree of reliability compared to those with lower stakes; however, there is no singular cutoff score for reliability. Though reliability and validity are different, when scores lack consistency or contain a high degree of measurement error, their principled use is limited; this fact affects their validity (AERA et al., 2014, p. 35). As you develop instruments, you have important decisions to make, and you must be prepared to defend them. Next, we contextualize the establishment of quality within the overall sequential actions and decisions generally required in the development of a new instrument, and with examples of the development of instruments useful in literacy research.

STEPS FOR DEVELOPING A RESEARCH INSTRUMENT

Developing a valid and reliable research instrument is, without a doubt, a lengthy process. McCoach, Gable, and Madura (2013) proposed a 16-step process for developing an instrument, and we have condensed their steps into 10 "blocks," summarized and presented in Table 11.1.

To illustrate this process, we describe the steps we took to develop two literacy instruments. The first, the Text Structure Identification Test (TSIT), is an assessment of fourth- and fifth-grade students' awareness of informational text structures (e.g., sequence, compare–contrast, cause–effect, problem–solution) that Strong (2019) developed to measure the effects of an informational text structure intervention for his dissertation. The other is a survey designed to measure the self-efficacy and collective efficacy beliefs of teachers that Vitale, Strong, and Walpole are currently developing. Both examples illustrate the actual steps researchers take in the instrument development process, following the blocks in Table 11.1.

Determine the Purpose

The first block of steps in developing a research instrument is guided by its intended use. It must be contextualized in a specific future study. What do we actually need to measure? In instructional research, for example, we need to measure whether the instruction actually influenced the aspects of achievement for which it was designed, so the instrument must be clearly aligned with the instructional goals (O'Reilly, Weeks, Sabatini, Halderman, & Steinberg, 2014). Once the goals are clear, researchers must search the literature to see whether an existing instrument meets them (McCoach et al., 2013). If so, the researcher should use that instrument, especially if it has convincing evidence of reliability and validity.

When developing the TSIT, Strong searched the existing literature for measures of text structure awareness. Since one purpose of his dissertation was to measure the effects of an intervention delivered at the classroom level on students' text structure awareness, it was important that the instrument be administered in a group. He found evidence that other researchers called for design of classroom-based instruments that could be more easily scored than the time-consuming analyses of oral or written summaries used in previous research (e.g., Ray & Meyer, 2011). He also found measures of text structure awareness using paragraph identification tasks that had been used recently, but none were publicly available. Strong had a mandate to design a new instrument.

TABLE 11.1. Steps in the Instrument Development Process

Block	Description
1	Determine the purpose of the proposed instrument to be used in a study, and identify whether there is an existing instrument available that serves the same purpose.
2	Conduct a comprehensive literature review on the topic, in order to develop conceptual definitions of the construct(s) and dimensions measured by the proposed instrument.
3	Develop items that adequately and proportionally measure each dimension of the construct(s), and select a measurement scale or scaling method for the instrument.
4	Collect evidence of content validity by asking content experts to provide qualitative feedback and quantitative ratings of items; analyze the readability of test items.
5	Prepare a version of the instrument to be piloted, including directions for administering and/or responding to the items, as well as clear formatting.
6	Gather feedback on the instrument with a small sample from the population to be studied, in order to make necessary revisions to the instrument.
7	Pilot the instrument with a larger, representative sample from the population to be studied, in order to investigate its internal structure and internal consistency reliability.
8	Analyze the pilot data by conducting exploratory factor analysis and internal consistency reliability procedures; revise the instrument based on these analyses.
9	Administer the instrument and analyze the data by conducting confirmatory factor analysis and reliability analyses, as well as gathering additional evidence of validity.
10	Prepare a test manual and/or a manuscript of the instrument validation study to publish.

Note. Based on McCoach, Gable, and Madura (2013).

Vitale, Strong, and Walpole also needed to create a new instrument because those that were available did not suit their purpose. They wanted to measure teacher efficacy beliefs under conditions of curricular change and after professional learning opportunities. They found instruments measuring self-efficacy beliefs and collective efficacy beliefs—for example, the Teachers' Sense of Efficacy Scale (Tschannen-Moran & Woolfolk Hoy, 2001) and the Collective Teacher Efficacy Scale (Goddard, Hoy, & Woolfolk Hoy, 2000). These measures, however, involve domain-general beliefs about teaching rather than teachers' beliefs surrounding change. Therefore, designing a new instrument was necessary to suit their purpose.

Review Existing Literature

The next block of steps encompasses an iterative process that should be part of any study—a comprehensive review of the existing literature. Researchers must understand theoretical perspectives on the construct(s) they seek to measure (McCoach et al., 2013). Searching databases such as Education Source for all of the published research on a topic must be part of the research process in designing an instrument (Suter, 2012). This search must produce conceptual definitions of a construct and its underlying dimensions to ensure that the instrument is consistent with, or advances, the construct as it has been defined by the field over time.

When Strong reviewed the research on informational text structures, he was aided by recently published meta-analyses (e.g., Hebert, Bohaty, Nelson, & Brown, 2016; Pyle et al., 2017) and systematic reviews (e.g., Meyer & Ray, 2011), but he went back to all of the original studies. This allowed for a theoretical understanding that text structure awareness depends on reader (e.g., age and reading ability) and text (e.g., type of structure) characteristics. Specifically, older and more skilled readers possess greater awareness of informational text structures, and more organized structures (e.g., compare–contrast) lead to greater recall than do less organized structures (e.g., description; Ray & Meyer, 2011). Strong learned that a theoretically sound measure should reveal greater text structure awareness in patterns that are consistent with the reader and text characteristics found in previous research.

Vitale, Strong, and Walpole needed to understand how the constructs of self-efficacy and collective efficacy were defined in the literature if they intended to create their own instrument. They discovered that definitions of teacher self-efficacy have evolved considerably. The literature currently uses Bandura's definition of self-efficacy. It takes an agent–means approach and involves beliefs about capabilities. However, the first definitions of teacher self-efficacy were grounded in Rotter's locus of control theory, which took a means–end approach and focused on beliefs about outcomes (Wyatt, 2016).

Develop Items

Once the not-small undertaking of reviewing the literature is complete, researchers begin developing a bank of items. Multiple items are necessary to adequately measure a construct generally, and each of its specific dimensions proportionally (McCoach et al., 2013). Item development also prompts selection of a measurement scale. Measurement in psychological domains involves assigning a quantitative value to an observable behavior or unobservable attribute along one of four measurement scales: nominal (group membership), ordinal (ordered ranking), interval (additive values with arbitrary zero), or ratio (additive values with absolute zero; see Furr, 2018).

Most hypothesis tests based on frequentist statistics, such as *t*-tests and *F*-tests, require data at the interval or ratio level of measurement (Field, 2018). For measurement of affective constructs, Likert scales, which span a continuum of agreement or disagreement with an item, are commonly employed (Henk, McKenna, & Conradi, 2011; McCoach et al., 2013). However, there are disagreements about whether tests that employ Likert scales should be treated as interval-level data (Furr, 2018). While a complete discussion of scaling and measurement is beyond the scope of this chapter, it is important for researchers to start with a broad picture of the statistical analyses and interpretations that will be possible. As a general rule, longer instruments are more reliable (Furr, 2018), but we must maximize data collection efficiency. Instrument development requires a large item pool to start (O'Reilly et al., 2014).

For the initial version of the TSIT, Strong developed 20 items to measure students' awareness of four informational text structures (sequence, compare–contrast, cause–effect, and problem–solution), due to their inclusion in the Common Core State Standards (National Governors Association Center for Best Practices & Council of Chief State School Officers, 2010). On the TSIT, each item consists of a well-structured paragraph using one of the four organizational structures for which awareness is measured. Students read each item and select the structure from multiple choices. Strong developed the same number of items for each structure, as an unequal weight favoring a potentially more familiar structure such as compare–contrast might skew the overall score. In addition, he needed to start with a greater number of items because several might be deleted later. He developed 5 items of each type. As for scaling, the instrument produced a raw score between 0 and 20 that would allow for statistical analyses appropriate only for data on the interval or ratio level of measurement (Furr, 2018).

To develop items for the instrument measuring self- and collective efficacy, Vitale, Strong, and Walpole consulted the results of factor analyses for the existing instruments. They identified 10 factors of interest: instruction, curriculum, assessment, academic pressure, school environment, teacher perception of student engagement/motivation, communication, group dynamics, professional development, and task analysis. They used these factors to write their own items. In other words, they created items that they believed would represent categories already identified in the literature. In total, they wrote 114 items to pilot-test. While this was a large number of items, not all of them would survive the instrument development process. As with previous measures, they decided on a Likert-type scale with seven categories.

Collect Validity Evidence

Establishing initial validity requires a series of actions. Instrument developers first check test content with experts to establish at the most basic level that the items seem to measure what they are intended to measure. Content experts can provide quantitative ratings and/or qualitative feedback regarding how adequately and clearly the instrument covers relevant content, including the wording of items and appropriateness of the measurement scale (Furr, 2018; McCoach et al., 2013). Beyond this check, researchers typically collect a variety of validity evidence to convey confidence that the interpretation of data obtained from the instrument will represent a construct both theoretically and empirically (Furr, 2018). In addition to test content, construct validity can be established with four types of evidence: internal structure, response processes, associations with other variables, and consequences of use (AERA et al., 2014; Furr, 2018). In addition, researchers should always analyze the readability of the test items to ensure that the word- and sentence-level text complexity is appropriate for the participants who will be asked to complete the instrument (McCoach et al., 2013).

Since the TSIT aimed to measure a single construct (awareness of informational text structures), evidence of content validity was limited to obtaining experts' ratings of whether each item accurately represented the intended structure. Strong asked several graduate students in education to read each item and select the structure, providing initial evidence that each item represented a distinct text structure. He also calculated the readability of the items to ensure consistency. If the items varied in terms of text complexity, some items might be more difficult than others due to differences in readability rather than differences in the underlying text structure construct. Strong computed the text complexity of each item by using the Lexile Analyzer (MetaMetrics, 2018), which produces the word count, mean log word frequency, mean sentence length, and Lexile measure for pieces of texts. He then ran statistical tests to determine that the items were not statistically significantly different on any of these measures. These simple steps provided evidence that the items were consistently written at an appropriate reading level for students in fourth and fifth grade (the intended participants for data collection).

For the self- and collective efficacy instrument, this process was more time-consuming. Vitale solicited feedback from current teachers and instructional coaches with varying content area and grade-level expertise. Vitale asked them to think aloud as they answered the items to see whether participants interpreted the items in similar ways. At several places, she prompted the participants to restate the question in their own words, to see whether questions were interpreted as intended. These validity explorations led to item revisions. The final pool comprised items derived from constructs in the literature and then reviewed by two different groups of experts.

Prepare Pilot Instrument

The next steps are fairly straightforward. A researcher must format the instrument and write directions (McCoach et al., 2013). Respondents (e.g., students, teachers) and individuals who may administer the instrument (e.g., graduate students, teachers) both need clear sets of directions. In addition, the pilot instrument should look professional and be easy for respondents to complete (McCoach et al., 2013). In the case of surveys, for example, researchers may wish to use web-based software, such as Survey-Monkey or Qualtrics, to aid in formatting and facilitate data collection.

While this step may seem unnecessary to describe, the pilot instrument must be usable. In the case of the TSIT, the 20-item pilot instrument required simple directions for students to read each paragraph and select the multiple-choice response that indicated the text structure the author used. Strong arranged four items on each page for a total of five pages. He took care that no item continued across a page break because that might have made an item more difficult. Strong also wrote directions for classroom teachers to use to administer the TSIT to their students. The directions included reminders for a teacher to hand out the test, ask students to write their names on the test, tell students how to complete the test items, collect the test when students were finished, and check to ensure that students responded to all items. This level of detail is important to ensure that the data collection process goes smoothly. Teachers in Strong's (2019) study reported that they appreciated this level of detail.

It was more complex to prepare the self- and collective efficacy instrument for piloting. Vitale, Strong, and Walpole used Qualtrics so that they could pilot-test the instrument anonymously with a large sample. With a large number of items to test, they were concerned about skipped items. Missing responses can complicate data analysis and trigger recruitment of additional participants. Therefore, it was important to determine the best formatting of the questions to minimize missing responses, and to ensure (to the extent possible) that if questions were accidentally skipped, they would be missing at random. The team selected a multiple-choice format rather than a matrix design and limited the number of items per page to five. They also randomized the questions so that the items at the end of instrument would always be different.

Gather Feedback on Instrument

The best intentions can still yield errors that will scuttle the instrument development process. Experts caution that a "final review" of an instrument is worth the effort (McCoach et al., 2013, p. 280). It may take various forms, including asking two or three colleagues to read the directions, ensure the readability of the items, and even complete the instrument to provide feedback on the process. Alternatively, researchers can administer the pilot instrument to a small number of participants (e.g., 5–10 people) from the same population that will be included in the piloting. The researchers can observe participants as they complete the form and gather an additional round of feedback about the clarity of the directions and items (McCoach et al., 2013). Interviewing respondents to check whether the psychological processes they actually use while completing the instrument match the processes the author intended can provide an additional type of validity evidence—response process validity (Furr, 2018).

The final check on the TSIT was fairly brief, as it is a relatively simple instrument. Unable to gather feedback about fourth- and fifth-grade students' perceptions of the test prior to collecting pilot data, Strong instead asked a small group of undergraduate students in teacher education to complete the instrument. He was able to observe the amount of time it took for them to complete the instrument and estimate how much longer it might take for upper elementary students. In addition, he was able to gather feedback from his students about each item after they finished. This step promoted confidence that the instrument was potentially clear and usable for intended participants.

Current teachers and instructional coaches were not the only groups to provide feedback for the efficacy survey. Vitale also asked graduate students who had been teachers to evaluate the format of the survey on Qualtrics, as well as answer the questions to provide an estimate of the time requirement. They were prompted to provide suggestions about question phrasing and overall design critiques. Together, these sources provided enough assurance that the instrument was ready to be piloted.

Collect Pilot Data

Pilot data are key for establishing an instrument's validity and reliability. Researchers will have to obtain approval from their institutional review board (IRB) to collect these data. The sample must include a large number of participants representative of the population to which the research aims to generalize (Furr, 2018). The number of participants required for a pilot study should equal 10–15 times the number of items on the instrument (Field, 2018; McCoach et al., 2013). For example, researchers should expect to recruit 200–300 participants in a pilot study for a 20-item instrument. Novice researchers may be shocked that such a large number of participants is necessary. While a full discussion of statistical theory is beyond the scope of this chapter, suffice it to say that the statistical tests used for analyzing reliability and validity are problematic if they are attempted with small sample sizes (Field, 2018; McCoach et al., 2013). In general, researchers should aim for at least 300 participants, regardless of the length of the instrument, in order to conduct a factor analysis (Comrey & Lee, 1992; Tabachnik & Fidell, 2007). That said, there may be times when researchers must use a smaller sample for convenience, but this is only especially problematic when the sample is not representative of the population (McCoach et al., 2013). The goal of collecting pilot data is to obtain variance in responses that will allow for successful analyses of the internal structure and internal consistency reliability of the instrument.

The pilot study of the TSIT was smaller than the ideal sample size, due to the use of a fixed convenience sample. While it would have been preferable to recruit at least 200 students to complete the 20-item instrument, Strong conducted the pilot study with all fourth- and fifth-grade students in one elementary school (approximately 150 students). This reference sample was a diverse group of students with racial and socioeconomic proportions very similar to the distribution among elementary students statewide. Conducting the pilot study with all students in this elementary school was an important decision to ensure variance in the data collected from the instrument.

Obtaining a larger sample for the efficacy survey was expedited by the use of a purposive, volunteer sample. Participants were recruited through the Qualtrics targeted sample service. Elementary school teachers who volunteered to complete the survey were recruited to join a panel by Qualtrics and received compensation. Vitale, Strong, and Walpole pilot-tested the survey with 606 teachers who taught at least one grade between kindergarten and fifth grade and who reported teaching English language arts. Conducting the pilot study with a larger sample, though not necessarily representative of the population, was necessary due to the large number of items on the survey.

Analyze Pilot Data and Revise Instrument

Analysis of the data collected with the pilot instrument is the longest, and possibly most important, step in the development process. Researchers will have to conduct two analyses: exploratory factor analysis (EFA) and internal consistency reliability analysis. Each of these analyses will reveal revisions that need to be made to the instrument, including adding, deleting, or revising items to improve reliability and validity (McCoach et al., 2013). Methodological references (e.g., Field, 2018; Furr, 2018) provide full descriptions of the statistical analyses required in this step, but each is briefly described below.

Exploratory Factor Analysis

Recall from our initial discussion of validity that there are several types of validity evidence. Test content validity is established through expert reviews. The purpose of conducting an EFA is to establish another type of validity evidence—the internal structure (or dimensionality) of the instrument. Essentially, factor-analytic evidence is an empirical test of whether the actual internal structure of the instrument is consistent with the theoretical structure of the construct that the researchers used to develop items (Furr, 2018; McCoach et al., 2013). Many instruments are developed to measure multiple dimensions, or factors, associated with a construct. Items intended to measure the same factor should, conceptually, be highly correlated with one another and less correlated with items intended to measure a different factor (Furr, 2018). Factor analysis allows researchers to use empirical evidence to retain a certain number of factors, and specific items measuring those factors, based on the associations among items in the data. It can also prompt redefinition of constructs as item associations reveal new relationships.

There are three important considerations in conducting an EFA to investigate an instrument's internal structure: determining the number of factors to retain, examining the correlations between factors, and identifying which items load on which factors (Furr, 2018). After conducting the EFA with statistics software such as SPSS, researchers examine the output for Bartlett's test of sphericity (Bartlett, 1954) and the Kaiser–Meyer–Olkin (KMO) measure of sampling adequacy (Kaiser, 1974) to ensure that the data are appropriate for a factor analysis. A statistically significant (less than .05) Bartlett's test and a KMO statistic greater than .50 generally indicate that the data are appropriate (Field, 2018).

The process of factor extraction, or determining the number of factors to retain, requires researchers to make a subjective judgment based on several guidelines (Furr, 2018). Two of the most common methods are Kaiser's (1960) criterion and Cattell's (1966) scree test. Kaiser's (1960) criterion involves examining the EFA output and retaining factors with eigenvalues greater than 1.0. While this is the most common guideline used by researchers, it tends to be less accurate than other methods (Field, 2018; Furr, 2018). Statistics software such as SPSS also produces a scree plot. Cattell's (1966) scree test involves examining the plotted eigenvalues and retaining the number of factors above the point of inflection where the plot begins to flatten or level off (Field, 2018; Furr, 2018). Once the number of factors to extract has been determined, researchers should run the EFA again with a fixed number of factors and an appropriate method of factor rotation, either oblique or orthogonal (see Field, 2018). After conducting the EFA a second time, researchers should examine the factor correlation matrix in the output to determine whether the factors are associated with each other in a way that is consistent with theoretical expectations (Furr, 2018). Finally, the pattern (or factor) matrix in the output displays the factor loadings, or item–factor associations, for each item. Factor loadings above .30 should be considered reasonably strong correlations, while loadings above .70 should be considered very strong (Comrey & Lee, 1992; Furr, 2018; Tabachnik & Fidell, 2007). The last step in interpreting the EFA results requires researchers to examine these item–factor associations and name each factor based on the items that show strong loadings on that factor. It may also be necessary to delete items that don't load on any factor and conduct the EFA again without those items (Furr, 2018).

Conducting an EFA requires some level of subjectivity. To illustrate, we provide a brief description of the EFA conducted with the TSIT pilot data. First, Strong conducted a principal-components analysis (PCA)—an analysis that precedes an EFA (see Field, 2018)—to determine the appropriateness of the data for EFA and the number of factors to retain. Because Bartlett's (1954) test was statistically significant and the KMO statistic was above .60, EFA was appropriate for the pilot data. Although Kaiser's (1960) criterion indicated that eight factors (those with eigenvalues greater than 1.0) should be retained, Cattell's (1966) scree test suggested that one factor should be retained. The scree plot from the TSIT data is displayed in Figure 11.1, which shows a clear leveling off of the plot after the first eigenvalue. As a result, the EFA was rerun with the number of factors fixed to one. An examination of the factor matrix showed that 13 of the 20 items had factor loadings above .30 on the single factor that was extracted. The 7 items with factor loadings below .30 were deleted from the TSIT. Among the

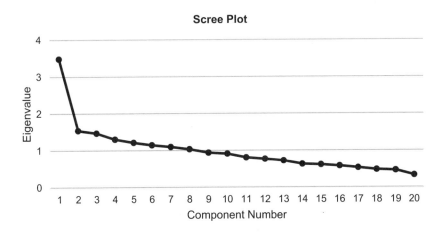

FIGURE 11.1. Scree plot for the TSIT pilot data.

13 remaining items, 4 measured awareness of compare–contrast structure, and 3 items measured each of the other three text structures (cause–effect, problem–solution, and sequence). Thus, the EFA provided evidence that the internal structure of the instrument was valid for measuring a single factor or construct, which Strong named *informational text structure awareness*.

Most instruments, however, will measure more than one construct, but the procedure is the same. Vitale, Strong, and Walpole first conducted a PCA and then an EFA with the efficacy survey pilot data. There was a large discrepancy between Kaiser's (1960) criterion, which suggested that 20 factors should be retained, and Cattell's (1966) scree test suggesting five factors. As a result, the team conducted a third test: Glorfeld's (1995) extension of parallel analysis (PA; Horn, 1965). PA involves comparing the eigenvalues from the actual data with eigenvalues from randomly generated data, retaining all of the factors for which the actual eigenvalues are larger. Confirming the results of Cattell's scree test, PA showed that five factors should be retained. Next, the team conducted an EFA with five factors extracted using principal axis factoring. Due to the number of items, the team decided to use Comrey and Lee's (1992) stricter guidelines for examining the factor loadings, with .55 being considered the cutoff for good loadings. An examination of the rotated pattern matrix showed that 14 items had good loadings on the first factor, 14 items had good loadings on the second factor, and 17 items had good loadings on the third factor. No items showed good loadings on the fourth or fifth factor, and the 56 items that did not show good loadings on any factor were deleted. After examining the items that loaded on each factor, the team found that the first factor measured self-efficacy, the second measured collective efficacy, and the third measured negative self-efficacy. Thus, the EFA provided evidence that the survey was valid for measuring these three constructs.

Internal Consistency Reliability

For the instrument being developed to be useful, it has to be reliable. In general, as noted earlier, reliability means that data obtained from the instrument are consistent both over time and across individuals (Field, 2018). In practice, researchers can estimate three types of reliability: alternate forms reliability, test–retest reliability, and internal consistency reliability (Furr, 2018). At this point in the instrument development process, the researcher has collected data on one form of an instrument (the pilot instrument) at one point in time. Therefore, calculating alternate forms reliability, which requires two parallel forms of the instrument, and test–retest reliability, which requires two administrations of the instrument with the same participants, is not yet possible. Estimating the reliability of the initial form of the pilot instrument can be done through internal consistency reliability (Furr, 2018; McCoach et al., 2013). Internal consistency reliability tests whether the items are correlated with each other and with the instrument as a whole, and both are influenced by instrument length (Furr, 2018). This is why it is desirable to develop more test items than necessary. There are three main ways of estimating internal consistency: split-half reliability, which randomly splits the items into two halves of the instrument; "raw" coefficient alpha, or Cronbach's alpha (or KR-20 for dichotomous items); and "standardized" coefficient alpha. Estimating reliability using split-half reliability is less common than calculating Cronbach's alpha (Field, 2018; Furr, 2018). In general, values for Cronbach's alpha above .70 or .80 are considered acceptable (Field, 2018).

Internal consistency reliability analyses can be conducted with statistics software such as SPSS (see Field, 2018). For the purpose of developing and refining an instrument, the analysis is conducted separately for each set of items that load on each factor or dimension (Field, 2018; Furr, 2018). This requires several steps. The first step is checking Cronbach's alpha for the overall reliability to determine whether it is acceptable. The next step is examining the item–total statistics, including the corrected item–total correlations. Researchers may decide to delete or revise items with item–total correlations below .30 (Field, 2018). In addition, the output displays the value for Cronbach's alpha for each item if it is deleted. It may also be wise to delete or revise items that would improve the overall reliability of the instrument. Finally, researchers will run the reliability analyses again to check the final results after deleting any items (Field, 2018). Of course, it may also be necessary to collect new pilot data with revised items in a revised instrument.

To return to the example of the TSIT's development, the next step after establishing validity of internal structure was to estimate its internal consistency reliability. Cronbach's alpha for the 13 remaining items on the TSIT was calculated as .74, which is above the acceptable level of .70 (Field, 2018; Furr, 2018). The item–total statistics identified 2 items with item–total correlations below .29, indicating that responses to those items were less consistent with the total score. Furthermore, the output suggested that Cronbach's alpha would be similar if these items were deleted. After the deletions, Cronbach's alpha for the remaining 11 items on the TSIT was still above the acceptable level at .73. Thus, the reliability analysis provided evidence that the revised instrument produced internally consistent data.

The same procedure was used to estimate the internal consistency reliability of the efficacy survey. Cronbach's alpha for the 45-item survey was calculated as .87, indicating that the items have relatively high internal consistency. Together, the validity and reliability evidence indicated that the items could be finalized and the shortened instrument used.

Administer Final Instrument and Analyze Data

Depending on the extensiveness of revisions to the pilot instrument, researchers may decide to collect additional pilot data and repeat the analyses in the previous step, or to administer the final version of the instrument and conduct a new set of analyses (McCoach et al., 2013). For this second study, researchers will want a sample size large enough (at least 200 participants) to run a confirmatory factor analysis (CFA), a type of structural equation modeling used to test an a priori model of the instrument's internal structure (McCoach et al., 2013). The procedures for conducting a CFA are more complex than those for an EFA. Researchers should consult references for conducting CFA with software such as Amos (e.g., Byrne, 2016) or Mplus (e.g., Byrne, 2013). Researchers may also wish to conduct a Rasch analysis (see Bond & Fox, 2015) with the newly collected data to interpret the difficulty of individual items (McCoach et al., 2013).

In the second study, researchers will want to collect additional data to provide evidence of different types of reliability and validity. In addition to analyzing internal consistency reliability, researchers should administer the instrument to the same participants on more than one occasion to analyze test–retest reliability, which provides evidence that data obtained from the instrument are consistent at different time points (Furr, 2018; McCoach et al., 2013). This is an important step in the validation process as well because an instrument must be able to be used reliably in order for it to produce valid results (Field, 2018). The second study should also be designed to collect an additional type of validity evidence—associations with other variables (McCoach et al., 2013). Researchers will want to administer previously validated measures of construct(s) that should be related to the construct(s) measured by the instrument of interest, in order to calculate correlations between the two sets of scores (Furr, 2018). This is also known as *convergent evidence,* but it may be just as important to look for *discriminant evidence,* showing that scores obtained from the instrument are not correlated with measures of unrelated constructs (Furr, 2018). When multiple measures are administered, it is also important to consider whether to provide *concurrent evidence* (associations with other variables measured at the same time) or *predictive evidence* (associations with other variables measured at a later point in time; Furr, 2018). At this point, it should be clear that researchers can make a variety of decisions with the second study, some of which may require extensive data collection or longitudinal designs. What is important is obtaining evidence to justify the instrument's reliability and validity.

To conclude the example of the development of the TSIT, Strong (2019) collected additional reliability and validity evidence within the context of an experimental study with an alternating treatments pretest–posttest design (see Shadish, Cook, & Campbell, 2002). Because the TSIT was not substantially revised following the pilot study, no additional factor-analytic procedures were conducted. However, 1 item that had been deleted was revised, in order to retain 3 items measuring each structure on the final version. Internal consistency reliability of the 12-item test was calculated, and Cronbach's alpha remained above the acceptable level of .70 (Field, 2018; Furr, 2018). Test–retest reliability was calculated using the pretest and posttest data (collected 10 weeks apart) for the group of approximately 200 fourth- and fifth-grade students in the comparison group (who were expected not to change in their level of text structure awareness between testing occasions), showing statistically significant ($p < .05$), moderate ($r > .50$) correlations. Strong was also able to calculate associations with other variables, including the Gray Silent Reading Test (GSRT; Wiederholt & Blalock, 2000), a validated measure of reading comprehension. This analysis also showed statistically significant ($p < .05$), moderate ($r > .50$) correlations, providing some evidence of association between text structure awareness measured with the TSIT and reading comprehension measured with the GSRT. We hope that this illustration of the development of the TSIT shows that instrument development is a worthwhile process that can be undertaken in different ways. After multiple phases of data collection and analyses, the final step in the development of the TSIT, as for other instruments, is to share the results.

Prepare Test Manual or Manuscript for Publication

After the final study has been conducted and results have been analyzed, researchers should share the instrument with people who may be able to use it (McCoach et al., 2013). Many well-known instruments in the field of literacy are published and sold by commercial vendors; however, anyone who has used these will attest to the cost they add to research studies. Others are reported in articles in peer-reviewed journals such as *Assessment for Effective Intervention*. In such an article, researchers may choose to report the theoretical framework underlying the instrument, the instrument development process, administration and scoring procedures, reliability and validity evidence, and recommendations for interpretations based on the results (McCoach et al., 2013). Readers may have noticed that we have not discussed collecting and reporting one of the five types of validity evidence—consequences of testing. This type of validity requires evidence of the intended effects, unintended differential effects on particular groups, and unintended systemic effects for individuals who complete the instrument, such as students in schools (Furr, 2018). In order for researchers to collect evidence of the consequences of testing, an instrument has to be used widely and over time. That makes this final step in the instrument development process of publishing and sharing researcher-developed instruments with other individuals who may be able to use them all the more important.

TAKING STOCK OF EXISTING INSTRUMENTS

It is always easier to read about instruments developed to test areas about which we are well versed. Table 11.2 provides a sample of published studies that attend to instrument development. We have identified the constructs

TABLE 11.2. Reliability and Validity Evidence for Instruments Measuring Literacy Constructs

Construct	Instrument	Dimensions	Reliability evidence	Validity evidence
Phonological awareness	Web-based phonological awareness (PA) assessment (Carson, 2017)	Rhyme oddity, initial phoneme identity, final phoneme identity, letter knowledge tasks	Interrater, internal consistency, and test–retest	Associations with other variables
Phonics	Informal Decoding Inventory (IDI; McKenna, Walpole, & Jang, 2017)	Short vowels, blends and digraphs, r-controlled vowels, vowel–consonant-e, vowel teams	Internal consistency	Internal structure, criterion, and associations with other variables
Fluency	Multicomponent measure of prosodic sensitivity (Holliman et al., 2014)	Stress, intonation, and timing at the word, phrase, and sentence levels	Internal consistency, test–retest	Internal structure, associations with other variables
Vocabulary	Multidimensional word knowledge assessment (Cervetti et al., 2012)	Recognition, definition, example, context, application, and relatedness	Internal consistency	Internal structure
Language comprehension	Assessment of Story Comprehension (ASC; Spencer et al., 2017)	Literal and inferential questions, story grammar, and vocabulary	Interrater, internal consistency, alternate forms	Associations with other variables, internal structure
Reading comprehension	Global Integrated Scenario-Based Assessment (GISA; O'Reilly et al., 2014)	Scenario-based tasks for reading U.S. history, literature, and biology	Internal consistency, alternate forms	Internal structure
Language expression	Narrative Assessment Protocol (NAP; Justice et al., 2010)	Oral narrative using a wordless book	Interrater, internal consistency	Internal structure, criterion, associations with other variables

(continued)

TABLE 11.1. *(continued)*

Construct	Instrument	Dimensions	Reliability evidence	Validity evidence
Written expression	Sentence Writing (Coker & Ritchey, 2010); Story Starter and Picture Story (Ritchey & Coker, 2013)	Total words written, correctly spelled words, correct word sequences, and quality ratings	Interrater, alternate forms, internal consistency	Associations with other variables, criterion
Written argumentation	Scenario-based assessments (SBA; Deane et al., 2019)	Summary and argument writing tasks	Internal consistency, alternate forms, interrater	Internal structure
Motivation.	Reading attitudes survey (McKenna et al., 2012)	Recreational and academic reading in print and digital settings	Internal consistency	Internal structure
Literacy instruction	Individualizing Student Instruction (ISI) observation system (Connor et al., 2009)	Time in teacher-managed, teacher- and child-managed, and child-managed instruction	Interrater	Associations with other variables
Shared reading instruction	Systematic Assessment of Book Reading (SABR; Pentimonti et al., 2012)	Language development, abstract thinking, print/ phonological skills, climate	Internal consistency, alternate forms, interrater	Internal structure, criterion, associations with other variables
Literacy environment	TEX-IN3 (Hoffman et al., 2004)	Text inventory, text in-use observations, teacher and student reports	Interrater	Content, association with other variables

and dimensions, as well as the reliability and validity evidence that the designers collected. As in many areas of literacy research, finding a set of mentor papers to aid in study design and reporting can be a powerful strategy. We invite you to read these papers with an eye toward instrument design, tracking the decisions researchers made. As we have said at the start of the chapter, we need a constantly growing set of reliable and valid instruments. We need instruments to measure development in reading, writing, and knowledge across ages and stages, as well as across disciplines. We need instruments to measure student motivation and teacher efficacy. We need measures of literacy instruction, literacy environments, and literacy leadership. We need measures of outside-of-school literacies. Better measures of evolving constructs can help all of us understand our core work more deeply.

REFERENCES

Abell, N., Springer, D. W., & Kamata, A. (2008). *Developing and validating rapid assessment instruments*. New York: Oxford University Press.

American Educational Research Association (AERA), American Psychological Association, & National Council on Measurement in Education. (2014). *Standards for educational and psychological testing*. Washington, DC: AERA.

Bartlett, M. S. (1954). A further note on the multiplying factors for various chi square approximations in factor analysis. *Journal of the Royal Statistical Society, 16*, 296–298.

Bond, T. G., & Fox, C. M. (2015). *Applying the Rasch model: Fundamental measurement in the human sciences* (3rd ed.). New York: Routledge.

Byrne, B. M. (2013). *Structural equation modeling with Mplus: Basic concepts, applications, and programming*. New York: Routledge.

Byrne, B. M. (2016). *Structural equation modeling with Amos: Basic concepts, applications, and programming*. New York: Routledge.

Carson, K. L. (2017). Reliability and predictive validity of preschool web-based phonological awareness assessment for identifying school-aged reading difficulty. *Communication Disorders Quarterly, 39*(1), 259–269.

Cattell, R. B. (1966). The scree test for the number of factors. *Multivariate Behavioral Research, 1*, 245–276.

Catts, H. W., & Kamhi, A. G. (2017). Prologue: Reading comprehension is not a single ability. *Language, Speech and Hearing Services in Schools, 48*(2), 73–76.

Cervetti, G. N., Tilson, J. L., Castek, J., Bravo, M. A., & Trainin, G. (2012). Examining multiple dimensions of word knowledge for content vocabulary understanding. *Journal of Education, 192*(2/3), 49–61.

Coker, D. L., Jr., & Ritchey, K. D. (2010). Curriculum-based measurement of writing in kindergarten and first grade: An investigation of production and qualitative scores. *Exceptional Children, 76*(2), 175–193.

Colton, D., & Covert, R. (2007). *Designing and constructing instruments for social research and evaluation*. San Francisco: Jossey-Bass.

Compton, D. L., Fuchs, D., Fuchs, L. S., & Bryant, J. D. (2006). Selecting at-risk readers in first grade for early intervention: A two-year longitudinal study of decision rules and procedures. *Journal of Educational Psychology, 98*(2), 394–409.

Comrey, A. L., & Lee, H. B. (1992). *A first course in factor analysis* (2nd ed.). Hillsdale, NJ: Erlbaum.

Connor, C. M., Morrison, F. J., Fishman, B. J., Ponitz, C. C., Glasney, S., Underwood, P. S., et al. (2009). The ISI classroom observation system: Examining the literacy instruction provided to individual students. *Educational Researcher, 38*(2), 85–99.

Deane, P., Song, Y., van Rijn, P., O'Reilly, T., Fowles, M., Bennett, R., et al. (2019). The case for scenario-based assessment of written argumentation. *Reading and Writing, 32*(6), 1575–1606.

Field, A. (2018). *Discovering statistics using IBM SPSS statistics* (5th ed.). Thousand Oaks, CA: SAGE.

Furr, R. M. (2018). *Psychometrics: An introduction* (3rd ed.). Thousand Oaks, CA: SAGE.

Glorfeld, L. W. (1995). An improvement on Horn's parallel analysis methodology for selecting the correct number of factors to retain. *Educational and Psychological Measurement, 55,* 377–393.

Goddard, R., Hoy, W., & Woolfolk Hoy, A. (2000). Collective teacher efficacy: Its meaning, measure, and impact on student achievement. *American Educational Research Journal, 37*(2), 479–507.

Hebert, M., Bohaty, J. J., Nelson, J. R., & Brown, J. (2016). The effects of text structure instruction on expository reading comprehension: A meta-analysis. *Journal of Educational Psychology, 108*(5), 609–629.

Henk, W. A., McKenna, M. C., & Conradi, K. (2011). Developing affective instrumentation. In N. K. Duke & M. H. Mallette (Eds.), *Literacy research methodologies* (2nd ed., pp. 242–269). New York: Guilford Press.

Hoffman, J. V., Sailors, M., Duffy, G. R., & Beretvas, S. N. (2004). The effective elementary classroom literacy environment: Examining the validity of the TEX-IN3 observation system. *Journal of Literacy Research, 36*(3), 303–334.

Holliman, A. J., Williams, G. J., Mundy, I. R., Wood, C., Hart, L., & Waldron, S. (2014). Beginning to disentangle the prosody–literacy relationship: A multicomponent measure of prosodic sensitivity. *Reading and Writing, 27*(2), 255–266.

Horn, J. (1965). A rationale and test for the number of factors in factor analysis. *Psychometrika, 30,* 179–185.

Huck, S. (2008). *Reading statistics and research* (5th ed.). Boston: Pearson/Allyn & Bacon.

Institute of Education Sciences (IES). (2019). *Request for applications: Education research grants (FY 2020).* Washington, DC: U.S. Department of Education.

Justice, L. M., Bowles, R., Pence, K., & Gosse, C. (2010). A scalable tool for assessing children's language abilities within a narrative context: The NAP (Narrative Assessment Protocol). *Early Childhood Research Quarterly, 25*(2), 218–234.

Kaiser, H. F. (1960). The application of electronic computers to factor analysis. *Educational and Psychological Measurement, 20,* 141–151.

Kaiser, H. F. (1974). An index of factorial simplicity. *Psychometrika, 39,* 31–36.

Kame'enui, E. J., Fuchs, L., Francis, D. J., Good, R., O'Connor, R. E., Simmons,

D. C., et al. (2006). The adequacy of tools for assessing reading competence: A framework and review. *Educational Researcher, 35*(6), 3–11.

Kamhi, A. G., & Catts, H. W. (2017). Epilogue: Reading comprehension is not a single ability—implications for assessment and instruction. *Language, Speech and Hearing Services in Schools, 48*(2), 104–107.

Kent, S. C., Wanzek, J., & Yun, J. (2019). Screening in the upper elementary grades: Identifying fourth-grade students at-risk for failing the state reading assessment. *Assessment for Effective Intervention, 44*(3), 160–172.

McCoach, D. B., Gable, R. K., & Madura, J. P. (2013). *Instrument development in the affective domain: School and corporate applications.* New York: Springer.

McKenna, M. C., Conradi, K., Lawrence, C., Jang, B. G., & Meyer, J. P. (2012). Reading attitudes of middle school students: Results of a U.S. survey. *Reading Research Quarterly, 47*(3), 283–306.

McKenna, M. C., Walpole, S., & Jang, B. G. (2017). Validation of the Informal Decoding Inventory. *Assessment for Effective Intervention, 42*(2), 110–118.

MetaMetrics. (2018). The Lexile Analyzer. Retrieved from *https://lexile.com/educators/tools-to-support-reading-at-school/tools-to-determine-a-books-complexity/the-lexile-analyzer.*

Meyer, B. J. F., & Ray, M. N. (2011). Structure strategy interventions: Increasing reading comprehension of expository text. *International Electronic Journal of Elementary Education, 4*(1), 127–152.

National Governors Association Center for Best Practices & Council of Chief State School Officers. (2010). *Common Core Standards for English language arts and literacy in history/social studies, science, and technical subjects.* Washington, DC: Authors.

O'Reilly, T., Weeks, J., Sabatini, J., Halderman, L., & Steinberg, J. (2014). Designing reading comprehension assessments for reading interventions: How a theoretically motivated assessment can serve as an outcome measure. *Educational Psychology Review, 26*(3), 403–424.

Pentimonti, J. M., Zucker, T. A., Justice, L. M., Petscher, Y., Piasta, S. B., & Kaderavek, J. N. (2012). A standardized tool for assessing the quality of classroom-based shared reading: Systematic Assessment of Book Reading (SABR). *Early Childhood Research Quarterly, 27*(3), 512–528.

Pyle, N., Vasquez, A. C., Lignugaris/Kraft, B., Gillam, S. L., Reutzel, D. R., Olszewski, A., et al. (2017). Effects of expository text structure interventions on comprehension: A meta-analysis. *Reading Research Quarterly, 52*(4), 469–501.

Ray, M. N., & Meyer, B. F. (2011). Individual differences in children's knowledge of expository text structures: A review of literature. *International Electronic Journal of Elementary Education, 4*(1), 67–82.

Ritchey, K. D., & Coker, D. L. (2013). An investigation of the validity and utility of two curriculum-based measurement writing tasks. *Reading and Writing Quarterly, 29*(1), 89–119.

Shadish, W. R., Cook, T. D., & Campbell, D. T. (2002). *Experimental and quasi-experimental designs for generalized causal inference.* Belmont, CA: Wadsworth Cengage Learning.

Spencer, T. D., Goldstein, H., Kelley, E. S., Sherman, A., & McCune, L. (2017). A curriculum-based measure of language comprehension for preschoolers:

Reliability and validity of the assessment of story comprehension. *Assessment for Effective Intervention, 42*(4), 209–223.

Strong, J. Z. (2019). *Effects of a text structure intervention for reading and writing: A mixed methods experiment.* Unpublished doctoral dissertation, University of Delaware, Newark, DE.

Suter, W. N. (2012). *Introduction to educational research: A critical thinking approach* (2nd ed.). Thousand Oaks, CA: SAGE.

Tabachnick, B. G., & Fidell, L. S. (2007). *Using multivariate statistics* (5th ed.). Boston: Allyn & Bacon/Pearson Education.

Tschannen-Moran, M., & Woolfolk Hoy, A. (2001). Teacher efficacy: Capturing an elusive construct. *Teaching and Teacher Education, 17*(7), 783–805.

Wiederholt, J. L., & Blalock, G. (2000). *Gray Silent Reading Tests.* Austin, TX: PRO-ED.

Wyatt, M. (2016). "Are they becoming more reflective and/or efficacious?": A conceptual model mapping how teachers' self-efficacy beliefs might grow. *Educational Review, 68*(1), 114–137.

CHAPTER 12

Meta-Analysis

Adriana G. Bus
Marinus H. van IJzendoorn
Suzanne E. Mol

WHAT IS META-ANALYSIS?

Meta-analysis is the empirical analysis of empirical studies—that is, the quantitative analysis and synthesis of a set of related empirical studies in a well-defined domain. Similar to narrative reviews of extant literature on a specific hypothesis or theory, meta-analysis tests hypotheses and aims at uncovering trends and gaps in a field of inquiry. Different from narrative reviews, meta-analysis uses rigid, replicable analytic procedures. A common and defining characteristic of all meta-analytic approaches is the use of a specific set of statistical methods compared with the methods used in primary research. The reason is simple: In primary research the unit of analysis is the individual participant (or class or other group), whereas the unit of meta-analysis is the study result. Study results are usually based on different numbers of participants, and they are, therefore, point estimates with different precision and confidence boundaries (Mullen, 1989). It would be incorrect to give a significant correlation of .30 in a sample of 50 participants (confidence interval: [.02, .53]) the same weight as a correlation of .30 in a sample of 500 participants (confidence interval: [.22, .38]). Basically, however, meta-analytic research follows the same steps and standards as empirical research.

Meta-Analysis as a Step in a Research Program

Meta-analysis can be applied most fruitfully within research programs in which studies with similar designs or measures accumulate over the years. In the spiral of research efforts, primary studies, secondary analyses, replications, and meta-analyses each play their crucial roles in promoting our understanding (see van IJzendoorn, 1994, for further details). In primary studies, data are collected to test a hypothesis derived from a well-articulated theory; the hypothesis often will be stated in the form: Variable X is associated with variable Y, or X is causally related to Y. In correlational or experimental designs, measures prototypical to assess X and Y are being used, and the results are, therefore, comparable across studies. If the results of the first empirical study on the association between X and Y are remarkable because of their effect size or direction, the next step in the spiral of research may be the secondary analysis of this first study. The secondary analysis uses the data as collected in the primary study, and through recoding with a different coding system and reanalyzing these data with different statistical methods, the original outcome is scrutinized.

The reanalysis may lead to falsification of the original outcome, as in Kamin's (1974) reanalysis of some of Burt's data on the heredity of intelligence in twins. In some cases, it may be difficult, however, to make the original data available for further study (Wolins, 1962). In any case, replication studies should then be performed to test the same hypothesis with new data that are collected in a different sample and with different designs or measures. If the number of replications increases, and if characteristics of replication studies vary, the meta-analytic approach is feasible to synthesize the literature and to test the effects of variations in study characteristics on the outcome of the studies. Because meta-analyses are based on numerous decisions about collecting, coding, and analyzing the pertinent studies, meta-analytic results, in their turn, need to be replicated as well (Lytton, 1994). Even if replications of meta-analyses yield the same results, they will never constitute the final argument in the spiral of scientific research. On the contrary, the most fruitful meta-analyses will lead to new hypotheses for further primary study (Eagly & Wood, 1994).

Meta-analyses have not been positioned in a more crucial role than any other systematic form of inquiry. Meta-analyses are part of a series of connected steps in the description and explanation of human behavior that never reaches a final point (van IJzendoorn, 1994).

A BRIEF HISTORY OF META-ANALYSIS

Karl Pearson (1904) reported on one of the first meta-analytic combinations of the outcomes of a set of medical studies, and the approach became extremely popular in the so-called evidence-based medical science. It was the educational researcher Glass (1976) who coined the concept *meta-analysis* and introduced it into the educational and behavioral science. He provided one of the most controversial examples of its application on psychotherapy studies, arguing that, in general, psychotherapy had considerable effect but that no specific treatment modality stood out (Smith & Glass, 1977).

To our knowledge, one of the first meta-analyses in reading was conducted by Kavale on correlates of reading: visual perceptual skills, auditory perceptual skills, and auditory–visual integration. He simply provided average correlations across studies between these predictors and success or failure in reading (Kavale, 1980, 1981, 1982; Kavale & Forness, 2000). Meta-analysis has become widely used and hotly disputed in educational science. In fact, it seems that it has been applied on a much wider scale in education than in any other social or behavioral science. The reason may be that educational policy decisions (like medical decisions) are supposed to be based on a firm foundation of empirical data (Slavin, 2002). Every decade the number of scientific papers is doubling (Garfield, 1979), and it becomes impossible even for the specialists—let alone the policymakers and practitioners—to keep track of the literature in their own field. The What Works Clearinghouse (WWC; see *ies.ed.gov/ncee/wwc*) is set up to support educators and the U.S. Department of Education in making evidence-based recommendations about the effectiveness of programs, policies, and practices in a wide range of areas. More importantly, meta-analyses are increasingly being used to monitor new developments in any area of the social and behavioral sciences (Sutton & Higgins, 2008). In reading research an abundance of meta-analyses have been conducted, in particular on interventions to enhance the development of reading abilities in children (see Table 12.1).

In the past, narrative reviews were considered the royal road to the synthesis of literature, and some narrative reviews indeed were very powerful in shaping the future of a field of inquiry (e.g., Adams, 1990). In a narrative review of high standards, the author tries to make sense of the literature in a systematic and, at the same time, creative way. In formulating a hypothesis for review in a precise manner, and in collecting systematically the pertinent papers to address the issue, the narrative reviewer does not act much differently from the meta-analyst. It is in the stage of data analysis that the narrative and meta-analytic reviewer go separate ways. Narrative reviewers may have the focus of telling readers what the field has and has not investigated more than what has been found. Insofar as they focus on conceptual analysis of studies, these might not include numerical results at all—as in a review of ethnographies of home literacy practices in different communities. The meta-analysts, on the contrary, proceed in a statistically rigorous way, analyzing studies that include numerical results. Effect sizes, quantitative indexes of relations among variables, are used to compare and communicate the strength of the summarized research findings (Hedges, 2008).

Cooper and Rosenthal (1980) showed experimentally that narrative reviewers are more inclined to commit type II errors (i.e., they tend to not reject the null hypothesis although it should be rejected on statistical grounds). Cooper and Rosenthal asked 41 graduate students and senior researchers to review a set of seven studies on the association between sex

TABLE 12.1. Focal Questions in Meta-Analyses in the Domain of Reading Carried Out between 1980 and 2010

Book reading

- Is there a relation between parent–preschooler book reading and emergent and conventional reading? (Bus et al., 1995)
- Does book reading in schools affect oral language and reading skills? (Blok, 1999)
- Does dialogic reading intensify the effects of parent–child picture storybook sharing? (Mol, Bus, De Jong, & Smeets, 2008)
- Does trained interactive teacher behavior as a part of book reading improve young children's language and print-related skills? (Mol, Bus, & De Jong, 2009)
- Do shared-reading interventions impact young children's early literacy skills? (NELP, 2008, Chap. 4)

Phonemic awareness instruction

- Does phonemic awareness training affect learning-to-read processes in a positive and substantial way, and are programs combining phonemic awareness training with letters and words more effective? (Bus & van IJzendoorn, 1999)
- Is phonemic awareness instruction effective in helping children learn to read? If so, under what circumstances and for what children? (Ehri, Nunes, Willows, et al., 2001)

Preschool intervention

- Do preschool intervention programs cause a positive effect on reading achievement? (Goldring & Presbrey, 1986; NELP, 2008, Chap. 6)
- What are the effects of preschool programs on children's intellectual, socio-emotional, and language abilities? (Leseman, Otter, Blok, & Dekkers, 1998, 1999)

Beginning reading methods

- Are whole-language or language experience approaches more effective than basal readers? (Stahl & Miller, 1989)
- Is whole-language instruction effective compared with basal instruction for kindergarten to third-grade students with low socioeconomic status? (Jeynes & Littell, 2000)
- Does systematic phonics instruction help children learn to read more effectively than nonsystematic phonics instruction or instruction teaching no phonics (i.e., language activities)? (Camilli, Vargas, & Yurecko, 2003; Camilli, Wolfe, & Smith, 2006; Ehri, Nunes, Stahl, & Willows, 2001; Hammill & Swanson, 2006; Stuebing, Barth, Cirino, Francis, & Fletcher, 2008)

Reading comprehension instruction

- Does vocabulary instruction affect reading comprehension? (Stahl & Fairbanks, 1986)
- Does sentence-combining promote reading comprehension? (Fusaro, 1992)
- Does instruction in question asking affect reading comprehension? (Rosenshine, Meister, & Chapman, 1996)
- Which forms of comprehension instruction improve reading comprehension? (National Reading Panel, 2000)
- How effective is repeated reading on comprehension, and what are essential instructional components? (Therrien, 2004)
- Does enhancing students' reading engagement increase reading comprehension? (Guthrie, McRae, & Klauda, 2007)
- What is the role of classroom discussion on students' text comprehension? (Murphy, Wilkinson, Soter, Hennessey, & Alexander, 2009)

(continued)

TABLE 12.1. *(continued)*

Acquiring vocabulary through reading

- Does instruction in deriving meaning from context improve skills to derive meaning from context? (Fukkink & De Glopper, 1998)
- Do children incidentally derive new words from texts? (Swanborn & De Glopper, 1999)

Effects of multimedia

- Does the Lightspan program (computer games to improve school-based achievement) improve reading comprehension, reading vocabulary, sounds/letters, and word reading? (Blanchard & Stock, 1999)
- How effective are computer-assisted instruction programs in the phase of beginning reading? (Blok, Oostdam, Otter, & Overmaat, 2002)
- What is the effectiveness of information and communication technology on the teaching of spelling? (Torgerson & Elbourne, 2002)
- How effective is the use of technology (e.g., electronic books) in language education and language learning? (Zhao, 2003; Zucker, Moody, & McKenna, 2009)
- What is the effect of using glosses (e.g., level of instruction, text type) in multimedia learning environments for enhancing L2 reading comprehension? (Abraham, 2008; Taylor, 2006)
- What is the impact of digital tools on the reading performance of middle school students? (Moran, Ferdig, Pearson, Wardrop, & Blomeyer, 2008)

Other aspects of reading instruction

- Does some form of guided oral reading stimulate reading achievement? (National Reading Panel, 2000)
- What is the impact of summer school programs (i.e., remedial, acceleration) on students' reading skills? (Cooper, Charlton, Valentine, & Muhlenbruck, 2000)
- Do cognitive paradigms targeting domain-specific learning activities improve effectiveness of reading instruction? (Seidel & Shavelson, 2007)

Bilingual education

- Does learning to read in the native language promote reading achievement in the second language? (Greene, 1997; Rolstad, Mahoney, & Glass, 2005; Slavin & Cheung, 2005; Willig, 1985)

Instruction of children with reading disabilities

- What is the overall effectiveness of sight word teaching for individuals with moderate and severe disabilities? (Browder & Xin, 1998)
- Does direct instruction yield higher effect sizes than strategy instruction in groups with learning disabilities? (Swanson, 1999; Swanson & Hoskyn, 1998)
- Do studies using strategy instruction or direct instruction yield higher effect size estimates than studies using competing models? (Swanson & Sachse-Lee, 2000)
- Do instructional components predict positive outcomes for adolescents with learning disabilities on measures of higher order processing? (Swanson, 2001)
- How effective is the Reading Recovery program for low-performing first-grade students? (D'Agostino & Murphy, 2004)
- Does treatment to improve expressive or receptive phonology, syntax, or vocabulary affect children with primary developmental speech and language disorders? (Law, Garrett, & Nye, 2004)
- What is the supplemental effect of out-of-school programs on reading achievement of at-risk students from kindergarten to high school? (Lauer et al., 2006)

(continued)

TABLE 12.1. *(continued)*

- Do metacognitive strategies improve the reading comprehension levels of students with learning disabilities? (Sencibaugh, 2007)
- How do interventions targeting decoding, fluency, vocabulary, and comprehension influence comprehension outcomes for secondary students with reading difficulties? (Edmonds et al., 2009)

Effects of grouping and tutoring

- Does one-to-one tutoring on reading promote reading skills? (Elbaum, Vaughn, Hughes, & Moody, 2000)
- Is effect size of reading instruction related to grouping format (e.g., pairing, small groups)? (Elbaum et al., 1999; Elbaum, Vaughn, Hughes, Moody, et al., 2000)
- Is parental involvement related to children's academic achievement (i.e., reading)? (Fan & Chen, 2001; Jeynes, 2002, 2005; NELP, 2008, Chap. 5; Sénéchal & Young, 2009)
- Do volunteer tutoring programs in elementary and middle school improve reading skills? (Ritter, Barnett, Denny, & Albin, 2009; Torgerson, King, & Sowden, 2002)

Effects of school organization

- Do second graders who have received 2 years of instruction in smaller classes score significantly higher in reading than second graders in larger classes? (McGiverin, Gilman, & Tillitski, 1989)
- Does reading achievement decline over summer holiday? (Cooper, Nye, Charlton, & Lindsay, 1996)
- Does homework improve academic achievement (i.e., reading)? (Cooper, Robinson, & Patall, 2006)

Processes explaining reading (dis)abilities

- Are auditory perception skills related to reading? (Kavale, 1980, 1981)
- Is visual perception an important correlate of reading achievement? (Kavale, 1982)
- Which of six variables (language, sensory skills, behavioral-emotional, soft neurological, IQ, and teacher ratings) provide the best early prediction of later reading difficulties? (Horn & Packard, 1985)
- Do dyslexic readers and normal readers differ in terms of phonological skill despite equivalent word-recognition abilities? (Herrmann, Matyas, & Pratt, 2006; van IJzendoorn & Bus, 1994)
- Do measures that tax the processing as well as the storage resources of working memory predict reading comprehension better than measures that tax only the storage resources? (Daneman & Merikle, 1996)
- Is a regularity effect also present in a group with learning disabilities? (Metsala, Stanovich, & Brown, 1998)
- Do children with learning disabilities differ from normal-achieving children in immediate memory performance, and does this difference continue? (O'Shaughnessy & Swanson, 1998)
- Do underachieving students with and without a learning disabilities label differ in reading performance? (Fuchs, Fuchs, Mathes, & Lipsey, 2000)
- Do children with reading disabilities and low achievers share a common deficit in phonological processing, memory, and visual-spatial reasoning? (Hoskyn & Swanson, 2000)
- What is the relative importance of auditory and visual perception in predicting reading achievement? (Kavale & Forness, 2000)
- Is it valid to use IQ discrepancy for the classification of reading disabilities? (Steubing et al., 2002)

(continued)

TABLE 12.1. *(continued)*

- Which brain areas are consistently activated during aloud single word-reading tasks? (Turkeltaub, Eden, Jones, & Zeffiro, 2002)
- Are rapid naming and phonological awareness as strong predictors of word reading as related reading abilities? (Swanson, Trainin, Necoechea, & Hammill, 2003)
- What is the influence of school mobility in the United States on reading achievement in the elementary grades? (Mehana & Reynolds, 2004)
- Can the relative variability of psychophysical performance in dyslexic readers compared with normal readers be attributed to general nonsensory difficulties? (Roach, Edwards, & Hogben, 2004)
- Does sampling affect studies linking genes to complex phenotypes such as reading ability/disability and related componential processes? (Grigorenko, 2005)
- What are the patterns of convergence in neuroanatomical circuits underlying phonological processing in reading alphabetic words and logographic characters? (Tan, Laird, Li, & Fox, 2005)
- Are gender differences present in reading achievement, and do these change with age? (Lietz, 2006; Lynn & Mikk, 2009)
- What is the magnitude and consistency of balance difficulties in the dyslexia population, and which sampling or stimulus characteristics modulate this effect? (Rochelle & Talcott, 2006)
- Do children with and without specific language impairments show performance differences in nonword repetition? (Graf Estes, Evans, & Else-Quest, 2007)
- What are the links between school entry skills/school readiness and later school reading achievement? (Duncan et al., 2007; La Paro & Pianta, 2000)
- What is the role of working memory measures (e.g., task modality, the attentional control involved) in distinguishing between performance of poor and good reading comprehenders? (Carretti, Borella, Cornoldi, & De Beni, 2009)

and persistence in performing rather dull tasks. Half of the reviewers were randomly assigned to a course on meta-analysis. Seventy-three percent of the untrained narrative reviewers found no association; only 32% of the meta-analysts came to this conclusion. The correct outcome was that female participants are significantly more persistent in performing boring tasks than males. In particular, in cases in which studies show insignificant trends, the accumulated effect size across these studies tends to be underestimated. Besides, narrative reviews are also more vulnerable to psychological factors. Bushman and Wells (2001) had 280 undergraduate students review 20 fictional studies, of which the salience of the title and serial order were manipulated. Interestingly, salient titles for the positive results led to overestimates of the actual relation, whereas salient titles for the negative results led to an underestimation of the effect magnitude (Bushman & Wells, 2001). It should be noted that despite this potential bias, narrative reviews remain indispensable, in particular in those areas in which a restricted number of empirical studies have been conducted or in the absence of strong research programs that unify the empirical approaches and make them comparable for meta-analytic purposes. Researchers sometimes persist in conducting a meta-analysis even when the exhaustive literature search results in the inclusion of only two or three studies (e.g.,

Sénéchal & Young, 2008; Torgerson, Porthouse, & Brooks, 2003; Zucker, Moody, & McKenna, 2009).

STAGES AND QUALITY STANDARDS IN META-ANALYSIS

Meta-analysis and primary studies are structured in similar ways. In fact, meta-analysts should proceed through the same stages as the primary researchers (Cooper, 1982). The meta-analysis should start with the formulation of a specific, theoretically relevant conceptual framework. Its domain should be clearly defined, and the central meta-analytic question should be theoretically derived and meaningful ("precise and relevant hypothesis"). When a meta-analyst is not sensitive to such substantive issues, a meta-analysis can become a pointless, merely statistical exercise (Littell, Corcoran, & Pillai, 2008). For example, when synthesizing the effects of interventions on struggling readers' reading comprehension, the validity and/or practical use of the summary effects can be questioned when interventions with a focus on fluency, decoding, comprehension, and multiple components are heaped together (see Edmonds et al., 2009). That is, even though the dependent measure is comparable and the target groups are similar, it is difficult to disentangle the kind of intervention that might support the comprehension skills of children with reading disabilities, especially when the number of studies per subtype is less than four.

In the next stage, the meta-analyst should systematically collect the relevant published as well as unpublished literature from at least three different sources. The "snowball" method (using references lists from key papers in the field), the "invisible college" approach (using key figures in the field to collect recent or unpublished materials), and computer searches of subject indexes such as ERIC, PsycINFO, MEDLINE, ProQuest UMI Dissertations, and Google Scholar or citation indexes such as SSCI or SCI may be used in a multimethod combination.

In some meta-analytic approaches, selection of studies is based on the idea that only randomized experimental designs produce valid findings to be taken seriously. The WWC (2008), for example, uses eligibility screens in which randomization, level of attrition, and equivalence of treatment and control groups are taken into account to select studies that meet the evidence standards fully or with reservations. The National Reading Panel (NRP) also objects to inclusion of all studies regardless of design features. Restrictions of the type of papers to be included, however, may imply an untenable reduction of the available evidence. For instance, the NRP discards the many correlational investigations in the area of reading research (NRP, 2000; Williams, 2001), which means a loss of potentially important information. It should also be noted that in this respect the meta-analytic method is basically indifferent: The central hypothesis should decide about the feasibility of selection criteria, and when this hypothesis is not stated in strictly causal terms there is no reason to leave correlational studies aside. Furthermore, the impact of the quality of research on effect sizes can be examined by testing whether the overall effect is influenced by the presence of studies with other designs than randomized controlled trials (Rosenthal, 1995). In this respect, the exhaustive search for pertinent literature is preferred compared with the best evidence approach (Slavin, 1986), in which only the qualitatively sound studies would be allowed to enter a meta-analysis. Because of their emphasis on explanation of variability in effect sizes, in recent meta-analytic approaches it is preferred to test whether quality of research (which always is a matter of degree and a matter of different strengths and weaknesses) explains variation in study results in order to make the process of study selection and evaluation transparent and to maximize the power of the analyses. Mol, Bus, and De Jong (2009), for instance, created a scale to score whether the researchers checked the use of trained techniques in the experimental group, the quality of reading sessions within the control group, and the actual frequency of book reading in the experimental and the control groups. Experimental designs outperformed quasi-experiments on the scale, but intervention outcomes were not affected by the experiment fidelity score; nor did quasi-experiments reveal higher effect sizes than true experiments for children's language and literacy measures.

The basic problem to be faced in this stage of the meta-analysis is the "file drawer" problem (Rosenthal, 1991). Primary researchers know that it is easier to get papers published in which they report significant results than to guide papers into print with null results regardless of the quality of the study (Begg, 1994). This publication bias may even lead to the unfortunate situation that the majority of papers remain in the file drawers of disappointed researchers, whereas only a minority of papers with significant results are published (Cohen, 1990). Average or combined effect sizes of published papers may, therefore, present an inflated picture of the real state of the art in a specific field. The number of unpublished papers with null findings that are needed to make the meta-analytic outcome insignificant can be estimated (the "fail-safe number"; Rosenthal, 1991). A publication bias can be visually inspected by a funnel plot, which is a scatter plot of the effect size against sample size that will be skewed and show asymmetry (i.e., due to a lack of small effect sizes) when a publication bias is present (Lipsey & Wilson, 2001). The file drawer problem may suggest that a priori selection of only published papers is not always warranted. Although published studies have been subjected to more or less thorough reviewing procedures and, therefore, seem to carry more quality weight than unpublished studies, the reasons for remaining unpublished may be unrelated to quality. In many cases, it is, therefore, better to collect all studies regardless of origin or status and to analyze post hoc whether publication status makes a difference in combining effect sizes ("unbiased and exhaustive set of papers"). To assess the likely impact of a publication bias, the "trim and fill" method can be used to estimate the unbiased effect size, by estimating the number of missing studies from an asymmetrical funnel plot and calculating an adjusted point estimate and variance (Duval & Tweedie, 2000a, 2000b).

Studies may report effects on several dependent measures for similar outcome measures. To avoid a situation in which studies with more results have a greater impact, the effect sizes should be aggregated within studies and domains. For example, when a study reports outcomes for one receptive and two expressive vocabulary measures, the expressive outcomes are aggregated in a first step (domain) and combined with the effect size of the single receptive measure in a second step in order to calculate a vocabulary composite per study. Separate meta-analyses can be conducted to examine differential treatment effects per outcome measure (e.g., Does dialogic reading affect expressive vocabulary more strongly than receptive vocabulary skills?; see Mol, Bus, De Jong, & Smeets, 2008) as long as each study contributes one effect size to each analysis. Creating a rather broad composite such as "academic achievement," in which a variety of reading, mathematical, and/or grade-related measures are aggregated, might limit the interpretation of specific treatment effects. Another complicating factor may be that experiments include two or more interventions but only one control group. Effect sizes are dependent if the same control group is used to calculate the effect sizes for each treatment (e.g., Ehri, Nunes, Willows, et al., 2001). Gleser and Olkin (1994) state that in multiple-treatment studies "the treatments may all be regarded as instances or aspects of a common treatment construct." Furthermore, they state that "there is strong reason a priori to believe that a composite effect size of treatment obtained by combining the end point effect sizes would adequately summarize the effect of treatment" (p. 351). Another, more pragmatic solution of the multiple-interventions problem is to divide the sample size of the control group in the same number of subgroups as there are interventions in order to avoid the situation in which control subjects count for more than one unit of analysis.

Studies may use a variety of outcome measures to test effects, which makes outcomes difficult to interpret. For instance, Stahl, McKenna, and Pagnucco (1994) noted that whole-language researchers increasingly preferred to use attitude toward reading rather than direct measures of performance assessment. Whole-language advocates assert that the key to learning language well rests in enjoying the learning process. They state that because whole language constitutes a more natural way of learning language, students will enjoy learning more and hence learn more. For instance, the study by Jeynes and Littell (2000) includes various attitude measures, and it is unclear what nonattitudinal effects are measured. The lower effect sizes for reading achievement measures indicates that measures such as attitude toward reading produce larger effect sizes than direct measures of performance.

The retrieved papers, dissertations, and unpublished documents are considered to be the raw data to which a coding system is applied to produce the variables to be used in the analysis. The application of the coding system should be tested for intercoder reliability. The coding system contains potential moderator variables that can be used to explain the variability of the effect sizes in the specific set of studies. The variables in the coding system should, therefore, be theoretically relevant and constitute pertinent moderator hypotheses. In view of the relatively small number of studies included in most meta-analyses, the coding system should not be too extended. If potential moderators exceed the number of studies, inflated meta-analytic outcomes may be the nonreplicable result ("reliable and concise coding system"). On the other hand, if the number of studies per moderator is too small, the power will be too low to detect meaningful differences in effects across subgroups (Hedges & Pigott, 2004). We suggest that a minimum of four (Bakermans-Kranenburg, van IJzendoorn, & Juffer, 2003; Mol et al., 2008, 2009) or five (Seidel & Shavelson, 2007) studies per subgroup is needed to reliably interpret any contrast.

Data analysis often consists of three steps (Mullen, 1989). First, the central tendency of the study results is computed (i.e., the combined effect size). Because p values heavily depend on the number of observations, recent meta-analyses focus on the combined standardized differences between the means of the experimental and the control groups. The statistic used to assess the effectiveness of a treatment or other variable is the effect size (ES), d, which measures how much the mean of the treatment group exceeds the mean of the control group in standard deviation units. ES expresses how many standard deviation units treatment groups differ from control groups without treatment. An ES of 1.0 indicates that the treatment group mean is 1 standard deviation higher than the control group mean, whereas an ES of 0 indicates that treatment and control groups mean are identical. A mean effect, of which the precision is addressed by the 95% confidence interval (CI), is considered significant if the CI does not include zero. Differences between estimates can be interpreted as significant when the CIs do not overlap. According to Cohen (1988), an ES of $d = 0.20$ is considered small, an ES of $d = 0.50$ moderate, and an ES of $d = 0.80$ or above large ($r = .10$ is small, $r = .30$ is moderate, $r = .50$ is large). Translated into percentiles, $d = 0.20$ indicates that the treatment has moved the average child from the 50th to the 58th percentile; $d = 0.50$ indicates that the treatment has moved the child, on average, to the 69th percentile; $d = 0.80$ indicates that the treatment has moved the child, on average, to the 79th percentile. In addition, and more importantly, authors should examine prior relevant research to provide some indication of the magnitude obtained in previous studies on different types of outcomes. As an alternative, Rosenthal and Rubin (1982) suggested the binominal ES display (BESD), which indicates the change in predictive accuracy attributable to the relationship in question and is computed from the formula $.50 \pm (r/2)$. The BESD shows the extent to which prediction is enhanced (i.e., the percentage increase in prediction) with the use of intervention X to predict reading skill Y (for details, see later discussion).

A weighted ES is mostly used to adjust for the bias resulting from small sample sizes (i.e., the tendency of studies with small samples to overestimate effects). Unweighted *d*s are sometimes presented to provide information about the direction of biases related to sample size. The ES can be computed on the basis of the standard deviations of the control group (Glass, 1976), the pooled standard deviations (Rosenthal, 1991), or the pooled variance (Hedges & Olkin, 1985). Cohen's *d*, for instance, is calculated as the difference between control and experimental treatment posttest mean scores (partialed for the influence of pretest scores if information is available) divided by the pooled standard deviation. Alternatively, the test statistics (F, t, χ^2) can be transformed into an ES (Rosenthal, 1991). In practice, different strategies do not seem to make a substantial difference (Johnson, Mullen, & Salas, 1995).

Second, the variability of the results around this central tendency is assessed, and outliers as well as homogeneous subsets of studies are identified. To determine whether a set of *d*s shares a common ES, a homogeneity statistic—Q, which approximates chi-square distribution with k − 1 degrees of freedom, where k is the number of ESs—can be computed. Homogeneity analysis compares the amount of variance exhibited by a set of ESs with the amount of variance expected if only sampling error is operating. *I*-squared (I^2), another indicator of homogeneity, describes the impact of heterogeneity on a meta-analysis by measuring the degree of inconsistency between studies. Values that exceed 70% should invite caution about the homogeneity of the mean effect (Petticrew & Roberts, 2006). If sets of study results remain heterogeneous, combined ES computed on the basis of the fixed model may be biased estimates; that is, it cannot be concluded that they are a sample from the same population, and a random model should be preferred (Hedges, 1994). In the random-effects model, studies are also weighted by the inverse of its variance, but, in addition, it accounts for within-study error as well as between-study variation in true effects (Borenstein, Hedges, Higgins, & Rothstein, 2009). If a distribution of study results is extremely skewed and shows several outlying values, the average ES does not adequately represent the central tendency.

Third, through a moderator analysis, the meta-analysts try to explain the variability on the basis of study characteristics. A significant chi-square indicates that the study features significantly moderate the magnitude of ESs. For example, intervention studies with randomized designs may, on average, yield smaller effects than those without randomization. Mostly the analyses do not include tests of interactions between moderator variables because the number of comparisons is insufficient in many cases. It should be noted that in meta-analytic as well as in primary studies every subject or sample should be counted independently from each other and only once. That is, if a study presents more than one ES for the same hypothesis, these ESs should be combined within the study before it is included in the overall meta-analysis ("independent and homogeneous ESs").

The interpretation of the size of the combined effects is a matter of much debate (McCartney & Rosenthal, 2000). In a meta-analysis, van IJzendoorn and Bus (1994) showed that a powerful explanation of dyslexia, the phonological deficit hypothesis, explains only 6% of the variance in dyslexia ($d = 0.48$), which is about a 0.5 standard deviation difference between the experimental and the control groups. Bus, van IJzendoorn, and Pellegrini (1995) showed that the association between preschool storybook sharing and later literacy was even stronger ($d = 0.59$), explaining about 8% of the variance in children's literacy skills. A correlation of .28 between book sharing and reading may seem a rather modest outcome. However, in terms of the BESD (Rosenthal, 1991), this effect is sizable. The BESD is defined as the change in success ratio because of an intervention. The BESD shows the extent to which prediction is enhanced (i.e., the percentage increase in prediction) with the use of intervention X to predict reading skill Y. If we equal the combined ES $d = 0.59$ with an $r = .28$, the success ratio in the experimental group would be .50 + (.28/2) = .64; the success ratio in the control group would be .50 − (.28/2) = .36. It should be noted, therefore, that it certainly can make a tremendous difference in the lives of young children whether or not they are read to by their parents. The difference between the experimental and the control groups would amount to a substantial difference if we translate this outcome to the millions of children who may profit from book reading (Rosenthal, 1991). Taking into account that experimental studies revealed outcomes similar to correlational/longitudinal/retrospective studies, this meta-analysis provides a clear and affirmative answer to the question of whether or not storybook reading is one of the most important activities for developing the knowledge required for eventual success in reading. Therefore, parental storybook reading should be recommended because in terms of BESD it makes a difference for many thousands of preschoolers ("BESD interpretation of ES"). In the same vein, phonological deficit is correctly considered as a main cause of dyslexia.

The basic stages and quality standards of a meta-analysis may be summarized as follows:

1. Hypothesis formulation
   - *Precise and relevant hypothesis*
2. Retrieval and coding of studies
   - *Unbiased and exhaustive set of papers*
   - *Reliable and concise coding system*
3. Analysis of study results and characteristics
   a. Central tendency
   b. Variability
   c. Moderators
   - *Independent and homogeneous ESs*
4. Interpretation of meta-analytic outcomes
   - *BESD interpretation of ES*

WHAT KINDS OF QUESTIONS ARE APPROPRIATE FOR META-ANALYSIS?

Review of Meta-Analyses in Reading Research

In his comprehensive book *Progress in Understanding Reading*, Keith Stanovich (2000) states that we make progress by accumulating evidence from a host of interlocking studies, each of which may be of fairly low diagnosticity but that, taken together, present a coherent picture and warrant firm conclusions. He concludes: "We are a science that is custom-made for meta-analysis" (p. 3). To find out to what extent the advice of one of the most influential reading researchers was followed, we listed the meta-analyses in the various domains of reading carried out between 1980 and 2010 in Table 12.1 on pages 238–240. We used a computer search of PsycINFO and ISI, with the key words *literacy and meta-analysis* and *reading and meta-analysis* to trace the relevant meta-analyses. In 2003, when the first version of this chapter was written, about 40 studies were detected since 1982. Even after excluding book chapters and dissertations, an additional set of about 60 meta-analyses on reading resulted from a new search in 2009 (see Table 12.1 for a summary of the reviews we could trace). Assuming that since 1966 approximately 130,000 research studies on reading have been conducted, with perhaps another 15,000 appearing before that time (NRP, 2000), only a small part of all available studies is meta-analyzed. The 90 meta-analyses cover at most 5% of all available studies on reading.

Meta-analysis appears a useful tool to test theories of reading problems, as Metsala, Stanovich, and Brown (1998) showed. Their synthesis of research counters a prediction based on classic dual-route models of word recognition that children with reading disabilities show an absent or reduced regularity effect even though separate studies support this hypothesis. The regularity effect in reading has been defined as the observation of superior performance in recognition of regular versus exception words. It is assumed that if the phonological route is less available as a result of impairment, the advantage for regular words should be eliminated or reduced. Children with learning disabilities should prefer a direct visual route without phonological mediation above an indirect route through phonological processing that involves stored spelling–sound correspondences in order to circumvent phonological coding. The synthesis of a series of small-scale studies is not in line with the dual-route model. It shows that both individuals with reading disabilities and normally achieving readers show a regularity effect and that ESs indicating higher scores on regularly spelled words were not related to reading level. Regardless of the reading level, regularly spelled words are easier to read than irregularly spelled words. Metsala and colleagues reported heterogeneity in ESs that cannot be explained as an effect of reading level. Carrying out secondary analyses on this data set with Comprehensive Meta-Analysis (Statistical Solutions Limited), the ESs appear to be homogeneous within the groups of normally developing and children with learning disabilities.

Even though not all individual studies report a regularity effect for children with reading problems, the results combined across the studies revealed a regularity effect. This finding is similar to results from the van IJzendoorn and Bus (1994) and Herrmann, Matyas, and Pratt (2006) meta-analyses on the pseudoword deficit of individuals with reading problems. That is, even when individual studies did not report a significant pseudoword reading deficit for participants with reading disabilities relative to reading level–matched participants, overall the studies did show this pattern when the results were combined across studies. The synthesis of studies on the regularity effect does not harmonize with the available theoretical models, and thus new models and further research are required to understand reading problems. The finding that both groups are susceptible to the regularity effect is inconsistent with the dual-route models of word reading but consistent with emerging connectionist models and their empirical findings on reading disability.

Most meta-analyses on reading synthesize the results of intervention studies. In an attempt to settle an ongoing debate on the best method to teach beginning reading skills, studies contrast whole language with basals (Jeynes & Littell, 2000; Stahl & Miller, 1989), systematic phonics instruction with no or incidental instruction in phonics (Ehri, Nunes, Stahl, & Willows, 2001), or reading instruction in the first or second language for bilingual children (Greene, 1997; Rolstad, Mahoney, & Glass, 2005; Slavin & Cheung, 2005). Other studies synthesize effects of special measures: programs to instruct phonemic awareness (Bus & van IJzendoorn, 1999; Ehri, Nunes, Willows, et al., 2001), guided oral reading (NRP, 2000), book reading in groups (Blok, 1999; Mol et al., 2009), question generation (NRP, 2000), repeated reading (Therrien, 2004), reading engagement (Guthrie, McRae, & Klauda, 2007), classroom discussion (Murphy, Wilkinson, Soter, Hennessey, & Alexander, 2009), or learning to derive word meaning from context (Fukkink & De Glopper, 1998). Furthermore, it is evaluated how direct and strategy instructions support groups with learning disabilities (Edmonds et al., 2009; Sencibaugh, 2007; Swanson & Sachse-Lee, 2000) and whether one-to-one tutoring in reading (D'Agostino & Murphy, 2004; Elbaum, Vaughn, Hughes, & Moody, 2000; Ritter, Barnett, Denny, & Albin, 2009; Torgerson, King, & Sowden, 2002) or instruction in small groups especially stimulates these children's reading development (Elbaum, Vaughn, Hughes, & Moody, 1999; Elbaum, Vaughn, Hughes, Moody, & Schumm, 2000). Few studies test effects of school organization on reading achievement: class size (McGiverin, Gilman, & Tillitski, 1989) or summer holiday (Cooper, Nye, Charlton, & Lindsay, 1996). The effectiveness of children's learning experiences outside the classroom is examined by evaluating studies on parent involvement (National Early Literacy Panel [NELP], 2008; Sénéchal & Young, 2008) and out-of-school programs (Cooper, Charlton, Valentine, & Muhlenbruck, 2000; Lauer et al., 2006). Only a few studies focus on interventions in the preschool ages and test effects of book reading in the family (Bus et al., 1995; Mol et al., 2008; NELP, 2008) or preschool intervention programs (Goldring & Presbrey, 1986; Leseman, Otter, Blok, & Dekkers, 1998, 1999; NELP, 2008). The increasing number of single studies that explore the opportunities of the computer for language instruction culminated in a new set of meta-analyses since the beginning of this century (Blok, Oostdam, Otter, & Overmaat, 2002; Moran, Ferdig, Pearson, Wardrop, & Blomeyer, 2008; Torgerson & Elbourne, 2002; Zucker et al., 2009).

Not all research domains are ready for meta-analysis despite numerous studies. The NRP did not succeed in finding sufficient studies to meta-analyze effects of all formal efforts to increase the amounts of independent or recreational reading that children engage in, including sustained silent reading programs, because of a lack of studies that meet NRP standards such as experimental or quasi-experimental designs, including a control group (NRP, 2000). They concluded that it would be difficult to interpret the small collection of studies that remained as representing clear evidence that encouraging students to read more actually improves reading achievement. Only three of the remaining studies reported any clear reading gains from encouraging students to read. However, one may wonder to what extent the selection criteria were responsible for this (counterintuitive) result. The selection of studies did not include a screening of studies in order to ensure that the participants needed what the treatment was designed to influence. The NRP routinely selected and analyzed studies that experimentally tested the efficacy of encouraging students to read more without ensuring that the participants in the selected studies indeed did not have the ability and opportunity outside of school to read independently (cf. Cunningham, 2001). Interestingly, the number of studies that correlated leisure-time reading activities to students' reading abilities is largely sufficient to synthesize quantitatively. Mol and Bus (2011) included 40 studies targeting children attending grades 1–12 and 30 studies targeting undergraduate and graduate students. Their meta-analysis showed that the correlation between leisure-time reading and students' reading comprehension and technical reading and spelling skills became stronger with age, which is in line with a model of reciprocal causation. More proficient readers are more likely to choose to read more frequently, which, in turn, will improve their reading abilities and their eagerness to read (Stanovich, 1986).

Meta-Analyses about Meta-Analyses

The set of meta-analyses reports effects of instruction on reading comprehension ($N = 19$) and on word recognition ($N = 11$). In 2003 we carried out a similar meta-analysis of meta-analyses. A striking result is that since then the number of meta-analyses targeting word recognition hardly increased ($N = 1$), whereas there was a substantial growth in number for reading comprehension ($N = 6$). From the stem-and-leaf display (Figure 12.1), it appears that both word recognition and reading comprehension are susceptible to specific forms of instruction. Insofar as several dependent measures were available, we selected tests with established (by the experimenter or someone else) construct validity and reliability (using multiple measures of reliability) above experimenter tests.

When a series of word-recognition outcomes were reported, we left out outcomes for selected words (e.g., pseudo- or only regularly spelled words). For both word recognition and reading comprehension, outcomes are homogeneous according to an analysis on this data set with Comprehensive Meta-Analysis, even though the interventions cover a variety of instructions varying in form (group vs. one-to-one tutoring) and ranging from phonemic awareness to deriving meaning from context. Only a meta-analysis on the effects of reading comprehension interventions revealed

Word Recognition		Reading Comprehension
	1.2	3
	1.1	8
	1.0	
	.9	15
2	.8	
5	.7	2
	.6	7
7554	.5	
10	.4	133
2	.3	01245666
70	.2	58
	.1	
	0	

FIGURE 12.1. Stem-and-leaf display of d indexes for effects of interventions on achievement test scores in word recognition and reading comprehension. Combine the stem (.1, .2, .3, etc.) with the leaves to the left and to the right to find d values. Stem combined with leaves to the right represents reading comprehension and stem combined with leaves to the left word recognition. For instance, in the range .2 to .3 one intervention caused an effect size (ES) of 0.28 on reading comprehension and another caused an ES of 0.27 on word recognition. Note that many ds for reading comprehension concentrate between 0.3 and 0.4 and ds for word recognition between 0.5 and 0.6.

outlying results (d = 1.23; Edmonds et al., 2009). As outlined previously, a rather diverse mix of intervention types might result in summary effects that are hard to interpret theoretically.

Another notable result is that ESs for word-recognition skills exceed those for reading comprehension. With word recognition as a dependent variable, the median ES of interventions is about 0.5 standard deviation. With reading comprehension as the dependent measure, it is about 0.33 standard deviation. These outcomes are similar whatever the focus of the study: improving word recognition, practicing comprehension skills, or one-to-one tutoring. In other words, word recognition is more susceptible to instruction than text comprehension. Reading comprehension is more strategic and based on higher level skills and may, therefore, be less trainable than decoding that is based on low-level skills. Interventions that include strategic and other higher level processes promise progress in comprehension (Pressley & Harris, 1994), but not to the same extent as a training of lower-level skills warrants progress in word recognition. Because the interventions varied so much, we were unable to test characteristics of instruction. For instance, assuming that instruction on comprehension supports skills beyond those stimulated by word recognition, one may expect that the effect of comprehension instruction on comprehension is quite a bit higher than the effect of word-recognition instruction on comprehension, particularly after the early grades.

Quality of Meta-Analyses in Reading

Most syntheses of research satisfy the criterion that ESs across comparisons are independent (68%). Intercoder reliability for coding the set of studies on these methodological characteristics and hereafter discussed measures was satisfactory. Reliabilities of moderator variables are not always reported (36%), and neither do meta-analysts always make an estimate of a publishing bias (21%). To prevent independence of ESs various strategies may be used. Some adjust the sample size for significance tests so that a single subject's data did not count more than once. In other studies a combined effect is estimated, and subsequent contrasts between two or more kinds of interventions are not tested (Bus & van IJzendoorn, 1999). Some studies ignore the problem and use the same control group more than once (e.g., Ehri, Nunes, Willows, et al., 2001).

In most cases, Q statistics are reported (70%), but a majority of studies applied a fixed model even though the populations did not involve a common ES estimate, as indicated by the tests of homogeneity (e.g., Bus et al., 1995; Elbaum, Vaughn, Hughes, & Moody, 2000), or did not report which model was used at all (e.g., Sencibaugh, 2007; Therrien, 2004). Sometimes authors may draw strong conclusions and bold implications for practice from a combined ES even though the point estimate is not representative of the central tendency in the total set of studies. In that case, conclusions are at least premature. Large variation in ESs requires a random-effects model, which may imply a broader confidence interval and a higher chance that the ES is not significantly different from zero. This scenario, however, does not always hold, as can be illustrated for the book-reading study. We reanalyzed the data of the book-reading meta-analysis with a random-effects model because the overall point estimate of ES was not based on a homogeneous set of studies (Bus et al., 1995). Reanalyzing the combined effects for book-reading outcomes with a random-effects model, we found outcomes that were very similar to those resulting from a fixed model. A point estimate of $r = .27$ for the overall effect of book reading on emergent literacy, reading achievement in school age, and language skills remains significant, as indicated by a 95% CI ranging from .21 to .32. A meta-analytic update of parent–child book reading, covering studies between 1994 and 2008, showed almost identical random effect sizes: $r = .34$ (95% CI = [.26, .40]) for oral language and $r = .28$ (95% CI = [.22, .36]) for emergent literacy (Mol & Bus, 2011).

META-ANALYTIC EXEMPLAR

Numerous studies relate phonemic awareness and reading achievement, but various questions remain unresolved because characteristics of replication studies vary. As the number of studies replicating the relationship between reading and phonemic awareness increases, quantitative synthesis of the research is warranted to test the effects of variations in study characteristics on the outcome of the studies (Bus & van IJzendoorn, 1999).

Precise and Relevant Hypotheses

First, we wondered whether phonemic awareness indeed is the single strongest predictor of reading development, as is often suggested (e.g., Elbro, 1996), and whether effects of alternative experiences as book reading are minor compared with a training of phonemic awareness. Another aim of this meta-analysis was to test whether children learn about the phonemic structure of words more easily when they learn to interpret spellings as maps for pronunciations. Therefore, we tested effects of characteristics of training programs, making a distinction between purely phonetic training, phonetic training embedded in letter practice, and phonetic training embedded in reading and writing practice.

A Homogeneous Set of Studies

Several meta-analyses have been subjected to thorough and sometimes harsh criticism because of the heterogeneity of independent variables across intervention studies and the heterogeneity of the interventions themselves

(Dunst & Snyder, 1986; but see Casto & Mastropieri, 1986). Dunst and Snyder (1986), for example, conclude that the Casto and Mastropieri (1986) findings cannot be the basis for policy: It would be both dangerous and unwarranted to develop policy about early intervention based on their flawed meta-analyses. We circumvented this problem by carefully selecting studies that test effects of training phonological awareness. We put considerable effort into excluding reading instruction programs that focus on the instruction of reading skills.

Reliable and Concise Coding System

As we have shown earlier, the heterogeneity of the studies can be productively used to explain variation between study outcomes. The meta-analysts should pay systematic attention to the discrimination of relevant subsets of more homogeneous studies, using quantitative approaches based on expert ratings. In the synthesis of phonemic awareness research, we therefore coded characteristics of the training program (purely phonetic, embedded in a letter training, or embedded in reading and writing practice), setting (training with a group or individual), number of training sessions, and the person who implemented the training (teacher vs. examiner). Quality of study designs is never an easy all-or-nothing decision; in the meta-analysis of training phonological awareness, quality dimensions were tested by coding design characteristics (randomized, matched, or not) and kind of control group (no treatment, dummy treatment, or some related training). Two coders coded all relevant studies separately and succeeded in reaching agreement on these characteristics of the phonemic awareness interventions.

The synthesis of phonemic awareness training studies revealed that a purely phonemic training such as the thoroughly replicated Lundberg program is less effective than a program such as Sound Foundations that includes letter training in addition to phonological awareness. This meta-analytic finding is in line with Ehri's (1979) assumption that letters appear to function as an intermediary because they may facilitate the discrimination of phonemes. The results support a theory with important practical implications; that is, letters draw the child's attention to the sounds in spoken words, and a distinct visual symbol for each phoneme may anchor the phonemes perceptually (Adams, Treiman, & Pressley, 1998).

Independent and Homogeneous ESs

An important criticism concerns the dependence of ESs within a study, thus violating crucial assumptions of independence of observations. To prevent studies with more than one training group and only one control group from inflating the number of participants, we combined the ESs of the interventions within the study. This practice is now recommended in standard introductions to meta-analysis (Cooper & Hedges, 1994), and it would be important to replicate the contaminated meta-analyses following this guideline.

Diffuse comparisons of ESs within phonemic awareness training studies showed considerable heterogeneity of results, which led to a search for a more homogeneous subset of studies. The training experiments with randomized or matched groups of participants from the United States met this criterion, and we computed a point estimate of the ES for this subset of studies separately. In this homogeneous set of experimental studies with more than 700 children, experimentally manipulated phonological awareness explains about 12% of the variance in word-identification skills. The combined effect with controlled designs is $d = 0.70$, $r = .33$ ($p < .001$) for reading.

New Insights and New Hypotheses to Be Tested

From a meta-analysis of 36 studies, we concluded that experimentally manipulated phonological awareness is a substantial predictor of reading but not the single strongest predictor. Compared with the outcome for phonemic awareness, early storybook reading leading to emergent literacy skills predicts reading skills somewhat less strongly than experimentally manipulated phonological awareness, but the difference is only marginal (Bus et al., 1995). Interestingly, Mol and colleagues (2009) showed that knowledge about reading skills in kindergartners gained about 7% ($d = 0.53$) from reading storybooks interactively, while adults in the experimental groups were not instructed to refer to letters or sounds in words. In other words, it is not only direct training of phonemic awareness that supports emergent literacy and thus later literacy. Emergent literacy supported by phonological awareness training as well as book reading appears to be important in shaping the early reading process. Thus, these meta-analyses may mark a new stage in the systematic study of reading development with emphasis on both "outside-in" as well as "inside-out" factors that stimulate emergent literacy (cf. Whitehurst & Lonigan, 1998). Future research should test the specific additive or interactive effects of formal and informal experiences with aspects of written language and how they promote reading development.

CONCLUSION

Meta-analysis not only provides a summary of research but also produces new insights and facts. Through meta-analysis we use the combined power of the primary studies to address issues that otherwise would require hundreds of participants and many different interventions within the same study. Only a meta-analysis could show that the teacher expectancy effect works better when the teachers do not know their pupils for more than a few weeks (Raudenbush, 1984).

Combining the results of several meta-analyses, researchers are able to construct models of associations between theoretically important variables that are not yet combined in any separate empirical study and to show at what point the model still is incomplete. For instance, we combined meta-analyses on the associations between book reading and literacy and phonemic training and reading to show that not just formal training but informal experiences are relevant to becoming literate. New meta-analytic approaches for creating and testing causal and multilevel models have been proposed (Cook et al., 1992; van den Noortgate & Onghena, 2003) and will continue to develop in decades to come.

REFERENCES

Abraham, L. B. (2008). Computer-mediated glosses in second language reading comprehension and vocabulary learning: A meta-analysis. *Computer Assisted Language Learning, 21*, 199–226.

Adams, M. J. (1990). *Beginning to read. Thinking and learning about print.* Cambridge, MA: MIT Press.

Adams, M. J., Treiman, R., & Pressley, M. (1998). Reading, writing, and literacy. In I. E. Sigel & K. A. Renninger (Eds.), *Handbook of child psychology: Child psychology in practice* (Vol. 4, pp. 275–355). New York: Wiley.

Bakermans-Kranenburg, M. J., van IJzendoorn, M. H., & Juffer, F. (2003). Less is more: Meta-analyses of sensitivity and attachment interventions in early childhood. *Psychological Bulletin, 129*, 195–215.

Begg, C. B. (1994). Publication bias. In H. Cooper & L. V. Hedges (Eds.), *The handbook of research synthesis* (pp. 399–409). New York: Russell Sage Foundation.

Blanchard, J., & Stock, W. (1999). Meta-analysis of research on a multimedia elementary school curriculum using personal and video-game computers. *Perceptual and Motor Skills, 88*, 329–336.

Blok, H. (1999). Reading to young children in educational settings: A meta-analysis of recent research. *Language Learning, 49*, 343–371.

Blok, H., Oostdam, R., Otter, M. E., & Overmaat, M. (2002). Computer-assisted instruction in support of beginning reading instruction: A review. *Review of Educational Research, 72*, 101–130.

Borenstein, M., Hedges, L. V., Higgins, J. P. T., & Rothstein, H. R. (2009). *Introduction to meta-analysis.* Chichester, UK: Wiley.

Browder, D. M., & Xin, Y. P. (1998). A meta-analysis and review of sight word research and its implications for teaching functional reading to individuals with moderate and severe disabilities. *Journal of Special Education, 32*, 130–153.

Bus, A. G., & van IJzendoorn, M. H. (1999). Phonological awareness and early reading: A meta-analysis of experimental training studies. *Journal of Educational Psychology, 91*, 403–414.

Bus, A. G., van IJzendoorn, M. H., & Pellegrini, A. D. (1995). Joint book reading makes for success in learning to read: A meta-analysis on intergenerational transmission of literacy. *Review of Educational Research, 65,* 1–21.

Bushman, B. J., & Wells, G. L. (2001). Narrative impressions of literature: The availability bias and the corrective properties of meta-analytic approaches. *Personality and Social Psychology Bulletin, 27,* 1123–1130.

Camilli, G., Vargas, S., & Yurecko, M. (2003). Teaching children to read: The fragile link between science & federal education policy. *Education Policy Analysis Archives, 11.* Retrieved November 11, 2009, from *epaa.asu.edu/ epaa/v11n15/.*

Camilli, G., Wolfe, P. M., & Smith, M. L. (2006). Meta-analysis and reading policy: Perspectives on teaching children to read. *Elementary School Journal, 107,* 27–36.

Carretti, B., Borella, E., Cornoldi, C., & De Beni, R. (2009). Role of working memory in explaining the performance of individuals with specific reading comprehension difficulties: A meta-analysis. *Learning and Individual Differences, 19,* 246–251.

Casto, G., & Mastropieri, M. A. (1986). The efficacy of early intervention programs: A meta-analysis. *Exceptional Children, 52,* 417–424.

Cohen, J. (1988). *Statistical power analysis for the behavioral sciences.* Hillsdale, NJ: Erlbaum.

Cohen, J. (1990). Things I have learned (so far). *American Psychologist, 45,* 1304–1312.

Cook, T. D., Cooper, H., Cordray, D. F., Hartman, H., Hedges, L. V., Light, R., et al. (1992). *Meta-analysis for explanation: A casebook.* New York: Russell Sage.

Cooper, H., Charlton, K., Valentine, J. C., & Muhlenbruck, L. (2000). Making the most of summer school: A meta-analytic and narrative review. *Monographs of the Society for Research in Child Development, 65,* 1–127.

Cooper, H., & Hedges, L. V. (Eds.). (1994). *The handbook of research synthesis.* New York: Russell Sage.

Cooper, H., Nye, B., Charlton, K., & Lindsay, J. (1996). The effects of summer vacation on achievement test scores: A narrative and meta-analytic review. *Review of Educational Research, 66,* 227–268.

Cooper, H., Robinson, J. C., & Patall, E. A. (2006). Does homework improve academic achievement?: A synthesis of research, 1987–2003. *Review of Educational Research, 76,* 1–62.

Cooper, H. M. (1982). Scientific guidelines for conducting integrative research reviews. *Review of Educational Research, 52,* 291–302.

Cooper, H. M., & Rosenthal, R. (1980). Statistical versus traditional procedures for summarizing research findings. *Psychological Bulletin, 87,* 442–449.

Cunningham, J. W. (2001). The National Reading Panel report. *Reading Research Quarterly, 36,* 326–335.

D'Agostino, J. V., & Murphy, J. A. (2004). A meta-analysis of reading recovery in United States schools. *Educational Evaluation and Policy Analysis, 26,* 23–38.

Daneman, M., & Merikle, P. M. (1996). Working memory and language comprehension: A meta-analysis. *Psychonomic Bulletin and Review, 3,* 422–433.

Duncan, G. J., Claessens, A., Huston, A. C., Pagani, L. S., Engel, M., Sexton, H., et al. (2007). School readiness and later achievement. *Developmental Psychology, 43,* 1428–1446.

Dunst, C. J., & Snyder, S. W. (1986). A critique of the Utah State University early intervention meta-analysis research. *Exceptional Children, 53*, 269–276.

Duval, S., & Tweedie, R. (2000a). A nonparametric "trim and fill" method for accounting for publication bias in meta-analysis. *Journal of the American Statistical Association, 95*, 89–98.

Duval, S., & Tweedie, R. (2000b). Trim and fill: A simple funnel-plot-based method of testing and adjusting for publication bias in meta-analysis. *Biometrics, 56*, 455–463.

Eagly, A. H., & Wood, W. (1994). Tying research synthesis to substantive issues. In H. Cooper & L. V. Hedges (Eds.), *The handbook of research synthesis* (pp. 485–502). New York: Russell Sage.

Edmonds, M. S., Vaughn, S., Wexler, J., Reutebuch, C., Cable, A., Tackett, K. K., et al. (2009). A synthesis of reading interventions and effects on reading comprehension outcomes for older struggling readers. *Review of Educational Research, 79*, 262–300.

Ehri, L. C. (1979). Linguistic insight: Threshold of reading acquisition. In G. Waller & G. MacKinnon (Eds.), *Reading research: Advances in theory and practice* (Vol. 1, pp. 63–111). New York: Academic Press.

Ehri, L. C., Nunes, S. R., Stahl, S. A., & Willows, D. M. (2001). Systematic phonics instruction helps students learn to read: Evidence from the National Reading Panel's meta-analysis. *Review of Educational Research, 71*, 393–447.

Ehri, L. C., Nunes, S. R., Willows, D. M., Schuster, B. V., Yaghoub-Zadeh, Z., & Shanahan, T. (2001). Phonemic awareness instruction helps children learn to read: Evidence from the National Reading Panel's meta-analysis. *Reading Research Quarterly, 36*, 250–287.

Elbaum, B., Vaughn, S., Hughes, M. T., & Moody, S. W. (1999). Grouping practices and reading outcomes for students with disabilities. *Exceptional Children, 65*, 399–415.

Elbaum, B., Vaughn, S., Hughes, M. T., & Moody, S. W. (2000). How effective are one-to-one tutoring programs in reading for elementary students at risk for reading failure? A meta-analysis of the intervention research. *Journal of Educational Psychology, 92*, 605–619.

Elbaum, B., Vaughn, S., Hughes, M. T., Moody, S. W., & Schumm, J. S. (2000). How reading outcomes of students with disabilities are related to instructional grouping formats: A meta-analytic review. In R. M. Gersten & E. P. Schiller (Eds.), *Contemporary special education research: Syntheses of the knowledge base on critical instructional issues. The LEA series on special education and disability* (pp. 105–135). Mahwah, NJ: Erlbaum.

Elbro, C. (1996). Early linguistic abilities and reading development: A review and a hypothesis. *Reading and Writing, 8*, 453–485.

Fan, X., & Chen, M. (2001). Parental involvement and students' academic achievement: A meta-analysis. *Educational Psychology Review, 13*, 1–22.

Fuchs, D., Fuchs, L. S., Mathes, P. G., & Lipsey, M. W. (2000). Reading differences between low-achieving students with and without learning disabilities: A meta-analysis. In R. M. Gersten & E. P. Schiller (Eds.), *Contemporary special education research: Syntheses of the knowledge base on critical instructional issues* (pp. 81–104). Mahwah, NJ: Erlbaum.

Fukkink, R. G., & De Glopper, K. (1998). Effects of instruction in deriving word meaning from context: A meta-analysis. *Review of Educational Research, 68,* 450–469.

Fusaro, J. A. (1992). Meta-analysis of the effect of sentence-combining on reading comprehension when the criterion measure is the test of reading comprehension. *Perceptual and Motor Skills, 74,* 331–333.

Garfield, E. (1979). *Citation indexing. Its theory and application in science, technology, and humanities.* New York: Wiley.

Glass, G. V. (1976). Primary, secondary and meta-analysis of research. *Educational Research, 5,* 3–8.

Gleser, L. J., & Olkin, I. (1994). Stochastically dependent effect sizes. In H. Cooper & L. V. Hedges (Eds.), *The handbook of research synthesis* (pp. 339–355). New York: Russell Sage.

Goldring, E. B., & Presbrey, L. S. (1986). Evaluating preschool programs: A meta-analytic approach. *Educational Evaluation and Policy Analysis, 8,* 179–188.

Graf Estes, K., Evans, J. L., & Else-Quest, N. M. (2007). Differences in the non-word repetition performance of children with and without specific language impairment: A meta-analysis. *Journal of Speech, Language, and Hearing Research, 50,* 177–195.

Greene, J. P. (1997). A meta-analysis of the Rossell and Baker review of bilingual education research. *Bilingual Research Journal, 21,* 103–122.

Grigorenko, E. L. (2005). A conservative meta-analysis of linkage and linkage-association studies of developmental dyslexia. *Scientific Studies of Reading, 9,* 285–316.

Guthrie, J. T., McRae, A., & Klauda, S. L. (2007). Contributions of concept-oriented reading instruction to knowledge about interventions for motivations in reading. *Educational Psychologist, 42,* 237–250.

Hammill, D. D., & Swanson, H. L. (2006). The National Reading Panel's meta-analysis of phonics instruction: Another point of view. *Elementary School Journal, 107,* 17–26.

Hedges, L. V. (1994). Statistical considerations. In H. Cooper & L. V. Hedges (Eds.), *The handbook of research synthesis* (pp. 29–38). New York: Russell Sage.

Hedges, L. V. (2008). What are effect sizes and why do we need them? *Child Development Perspectives, 2,* 167–171.

Hedges, L. V., & Olkin, I. (1985). *Statistical methods for meta-analysis.* New York: Academic Press.

Hedges, L. V., & Pigott, T. D. (2004). The power of statistical tests for moderators in meta-analysis. *Psychological Methods, 9,* 426–445.

Herrmann, J. A., Matyas, T., & Pratt, C. (2006). Meta-analysis of the nonword reading deficit in specific reading disorder. *Dyslexia, 12,* 195–221.

Horn, W. F., & Packard, T. (1985). Early identification of learning problems: A meta-analysis. *Journal of Educational Psychology, 77,* 597–607.

Hoskyn, M., & Swanson, H. L. (2000). Cognitive processing of low achievers and children with reading disabilities: A selective meta-analytic review of the published literature. *School Psychology Review, 29,* 102–119.

Jeynes, W. H. (2002). A meta-analysis: The effects of parental involvement on minority children's academic achievement. *Education and Urban Society, 35,* 202–218.

Jeynes, W. H. (2005). A meta-analysis of the relation of parental involvement to urban elementary school student academic achievement. *Urban Education, 40,* 237–269.

Jeynes, W. H., & Littell, S. W. (2000). A meta-analysis of studies examining the effect of whole language instruction on the literacy of low-SES students. *Elementary School Journal, 101,* 21–33.

Johnson, B. T., Mullen, B., & Salas, E. (1995). Comparison of three meta-analytic approaches. *Journal of Applied Psychology, 80,* 94–106.

Kamin, L. J. (1974). *The science and politics of I.Q.* New York: Wiley.

Kavale, K. A. (1980). Auditory-visual integration and its relationship to reading achievement: A meta-analysis. *Perceptual and Motor Skills, 51,* 947–955.

Kavale, K. A. (1981). The relationship between auditory perceptual skills and reading ability: A meta-analysis. *Journal of Learning Disabilities, 14,* 539–546.

Kavale, K. A. (1982). Meta-analysis of the relationship between visual perceptual skills and reading achievement. *Journal of Learning Disabilities, 15,* 42–51.

Kavale, K. A., & Forness, S. R. (2000). Auditory and visual perception processes and reading ability: A quantitative reanalysis and historical reinterpretation. *Learning Disability Quarterly, 23,* 253–270.

La Paro, K. M., & Pianta, R. C. (2000). Predicting children's competence in the early school years: A meta-analytic review. *Review of Educational Research, 70,* 443–484.

Lauer, P. A., Akiba, M., Wilkerson, S. B., Apthorp, H. S., Snow, D., & Martin-Glenn, M. L. (2006). Out-of-school-time programs: A meta-analysis of effects for at-risk students. *Review of Educational Research, 76,* 275–313.

Law, J., Garrett, Z., & Nye, C. (2004). The efficacy of treatment for children with developmental speech and language delay/disorder: A meta-analysis. *Journal of Speech, Language, and Hearing Research, 47,* 924–943.

Leseman, P. P. M., Otter, M. E., Blok, H., & Dekkers, P. (1998). Effecten van voor- en vroegschoolse educatieve centrumprogramma's. Een meta-analyse van studies gepubliceerd tussen 1985 en 1996 [Effects of preschool intervention programs. A meta-analysis of studies published between 1985 and 1996]. *Nederlands Tijdschrift voor Opvoeding, Vorming en Onderwijs, 14,* 134–154.

Leseman, P. P. M., Otter, M. E., Blok, H., & Dekkers, P. (1999). Effecten van voorschoolse educatieve centrumprogramma's. Een aanvullende meta-analyse van studies gepubliceerd tussen 1985 en 1996 [Effects of preschool intervention programs. An additional meta-analysis of studies published between 1985 and 1996]. *Nederlands Tijdschrift voor Opvoeding, Vorming en Onderwijs, 15,* 28–37.

Lietz, P. (2006). A meta-analysis of gender differences in reading achievement at the secondary school level. *Studies in Educational Evaluation, 32,* 317–344.

Lipsey, M. W., & Wilson, D. B. (2001). *Practical meta-analysis.* Thousand Oaks, CA: Sage.

Littell, J. H., Corcoran, J., & Pillai, V. K. (2008). *Systematic reviews and meta-analysis.* New York: Oxford University Press.

Lynn, R., & Mikk, J. (2009). Sex differences in reading achievement. *TRAMES, 13,* 3–13.

Lytton, H. (1994). Replication and meta-analysis: The story of a meta-analysis of parents' socialization practices. In R. van der Veer, M. H. van IJzendoorn, & J. Valsiner (Eds.), *Reconstructing the mind: Replicability in research on human development* (pp. 117–150). Norwood, NJ: Ablex.

McCartney, K., & Rosenthal, R. (2000). Effect Size, practical importance, and social policy for children. *Child Development, 71,* 173–180.

McGiverin, J., Gilman, D., & Tillitski, C. (1989). A meta-analysis of the relation between class size and achievement. *Elementary School Journal, 90,* 47–56.

Mehana, M., & Reynolds, A. J. (2004). School mobility and achievement: A meta-analysis. *Children and Youth Services Review, 26,* 93–119.

Metsala, J. L., Stanovich, K. E., & Brown, G. D. A. (1998). Regularity effects and the phonological deficit model of reading disabilities: A meta-analytic review. *Journal of Educational Psychology, 90,* 279–293.

Mol, S. E., & Bus, A. G. (2011). To read or not to read: A meta-analysis of print exposure from infancy to early adulthood. *Psychological Bulletin, 137,* 267–276.

Mol, S. E., Bus, A. G., & De Jong, M. T. (2009). Interactive book reading in early education: A tool to stimulate print knowledge as well as oral language. *Review of Educational Research, 79,* 979–1007.

Mol, S. E., Bus, A. G., De Jong, M. T., & Smeets, D. J. H. (2008). Added value of dialogic parent–child book readings: A meta-analysis. *Early Education and Development, 19,* 7–26.

Moran, J., Ferdig, R. E., Pearson, P. D., Wardrop, J., & Blomeyer, R. L. (2008). Technology and reading performance in the middle-school grades: A meta-analysis with recommendations for policy and practice. *Journal of Literacy Research, 40,* 6–58.

Mullen, B. (1989). *Advanced basic meta-analysis.* Hillsdale, NJ: Erlbaum.

Murphy, P. K., Wilkinson, I. A. G., Soter, A. O., Hennessey, M. N., & Alexander, J. F. (2009). Examining the effects of classroom discussion on students' comprehension of text: A meta-analysis. *Journal of Educational Psychology, 101,* 740–764.

National Early Literacy Panel (NELP). (2008). *Developing early literacy: Report of the National Early Literacy Panel.* Washington, DC: National Institute for Literacy.

National Reading Panel (NRP). (2000). *Report of the National Reading Panel: Teaching children to read: An evidence-based assessment of the scientific research literature on reading and its implications for reading instruction: Reports of the subgroups.* Washington, DC: National Institute of Child Health and Human Development.

O'Shaughnessy, T. E., & Swanson, H. L. (1998). Do immediate memory deficits in students with learning disabilities in reading reflect a developmental lag or deficit?: A selective meta-analysis of the literature. *Learning Disability Quarterly, 21,* 123–148.

Pearson, K. (1904). Report on certain enteric fever inoculation statistics. *British Medical Journal, 3,* 1243–1246.

Petticrew, M., & Roberts, H. (2006). *Systematic reviews in the social sciences; A practical guide.* Oxford, UK: Blackwell.

Pressley, M., & Harris, K. R. (1994). Increasing the quality of educational intervention research. *Educational Psychology Review, 6,* 191–208.

Raudenbush, S. W. (1984). Magnitude of teacher expectancy effects on pupil IQ as a function of the credibility of expectancy induction: A synthesis of findings from 18 experiments. *Journal of Educational Psychology, 76,* 85–97.

Ritter, G. W., Barnett, J. H., Denny, G. S., & Albin, G. R. (2009). The effectiveness of volunteer tutoring programs for elementary and middle school students: A meta-analysis. *Review of Educational Research, 79,* 3–38.

Roach, N. W., Edwards, V. T., & Hogben, J. H. (2004). The tale is in the tail: An alternative hypothesis for psychophysical performance variability in dyslexia. *Perception, 33,* 817–830.

Rochelle, K. S. H., & Talcott, J. B. (2006). Impaired balance in developmental dyslexia?: A meta-analysis of the contending evidence. *Journal of Child Psychology and Psychiatry, 47,* 1159–1166.

Rolstad, K., Mahoney, K., & Glass, G. V. (2005). The big picture: A meta-analysis of program effectiveness research on English language learners. *Educational Policy, 19,* 572–594.

Rosenshine, B., Meister, C., & Chapman, S. (1996). Teaching students to generate questions: A review of the intervention studies. *Review of Educational Research, 66,* 181–221.

Rosenthal, R. (1991). *Meta-analytic procedures for social research* (rev. ed.). Newbury Park, CA: Sage.

Rosenthal, R. (1995). Writing meta-analytic reviews. *Psychological Bulletin, 118,* 183–192.

Rosenthal, R., & Rubin, D. B. (1982). Further meta-analytic procedures for assessing cognitive gender differences. *Journal of Educational Psychology, 74,* 708–712.

Seidel, T., & Shavelson, R. J. (2007). Teaching effectiveness research in the past decade: The role of theory and research design in disentangling meta-analysis results. *Review of Educational Research, 77,* 454–499.

Sencibaugh, J. M. (2007). Meta-analysis of reading comprehension interventions for students with learning disabilities: Strategies and implications. *Reading Improvement, 44,* 6–22.

Sénéchal, M., & Young, L. (2008). The effect of family literacy interventions on children's acquisition of reading from kindergarten to grade 3: A meta-analytic review. *Review of Educational Research, 78,* 880–907.

Slavin, R. E. (1986). Best-evidence synthesis: An alternative to meta-analytic and traditional reviews. *Educational Researcher, 15,* 5–11.

Slavin, R. E. (2002). Evidence-based education policies: Transforming educational practice and research. *Educational Researcher, 31,* 15–21.

Slavin, R. E., & Cheung, A. (2005). A synthesis of research on language of reading instruction for English language learners. *Review of Educational Research, 75,* 247–284.

Smith, M. L., & Glass, G. V. (1977). Meta-analysis of psychotherapy outcome studies. *American Psychologist, 32,* 752–760.

Stahl, S. A., & Fairbanks, M. M. (1986). The effects of vocabulary instruction: A model-based meta-analysis. *Review of Educational Research, 56,* 72–110.

Stahl, S. A., McKenna, M. C., & Pagnucco, J. R. (1994). The effects of whole-language instruction: An update and a reappraisal. *Educational Psychologist, 29,* 175–185.

Stahl, S. A., & Miller, P. D. (1989). Whole language and language experience approaches for beginning reading: A quantitative research synthesis. *Review of Educational Research, 59,* 87–116.

Stanovich, K. E. (1986). Matthew effects in reading: Some consequences of individual differences in the acquisition of literacy. *Reading Research Quarterly, 21,* 360–407.

Stanovich, K. E. (2000). *Progress in understanding reading; Scientific foundations and new frontiers.* New York: Guilford Press.

Stuebing, K. K., Barth, A. E., Cirino, P. T., Francis, D. J., & Fletcher, J. M. (2008). A response to recent reanalyses of the National Reading Report: Effects of systematic phonics instruction are practically significant. *Journal of Educational Psychology, 100,* 123–134.

Stuebing, K. K., Fletcher, J. M., Ledoux, J. M., Lyon, G. R., Shaywitz, S. E., & Shaywitz, B. A. (2002). Validity of IQ-discrepancy classifications of reading disabilities: A meta-analysis. *American Educational Research Journal, 39,* 469–518.

Sutton, A. J., & Higgins, J. P. T. (2008). Recent developments in meta-analysis. *Statistics in Medicine, 27,* 625–650.

Swanborn, M. S. L., & De Glopper, K. (1999). Incidental word learning while reading: A meta-analysis. *Review of Educational Research, 69,* 261–285.

Swanson, H. L. (1999). Reading research for students with LD: A meta-analysis in intervention outcomes. *Journal of Learning Disabilities, 32,* 504–532.

Swanson, H. L. (2001). Research on interventions for adolescents with learning disabilities: A meta-analysis of outcomes related to higher-order processing. *Elementary School Journal, 101,* 331–348.

Swanson, H. L., & Hoskyn, M. (1998). Experimental intervention research on students with learning disabilities: A meta-analysis of treatment outcomes. *Review of Educational Research, 68,* 277–321.

Swanson, H. L., & Sachse-Lee, C. (2000). A meta-analysis of single-subject-design intervention research for students with LD. *Journal of Learning Disabilities, 33,* 114–136.

Swanson, H. L., Trainin, G., Necoechea, D. M., & Hammill, D. D. (2003). Rapid naming, phonological awareness, and reading: A meta-analysis of the correlation evidence. *Review of Educational Research, 73,* 407–440.

Tan, L. H., Laird, A. R., Li, K., & Fox, P. T. (2005). Neuroanatomical correlates of phonological processing of Chinese characters and alphabetic words: A meta-analysis. *Human Brain Mapping, 25,* 83–91.

Taylor, A. (2006). The effects of CALL versus traditional L1 glosses on L2 reading comprehension. *CALICO Journal, 23,* 309–318.

Therrien, W. J. (2004). Fluency and comprehension gains as a result of repeated reading: A meta-analysis. *Remedial and Special Education, 25,* 252–261.

Torgerson, C. J., & Elbourne, D. (2002). A systematic review and meta-analysis of the effectiveness of information and communication technology (ICT) on the teaching of spelling. *Journal of Research in Reading, 25,* 129–143.

Torgerson, C. J., King, S. E., & Sowden, A. J. (2002). Do volunteers in schools help children learn to read?: A systematic review of randomised controlled trials. *Educational Studies, 28,* 433–444.

Torgerson, C. J., Porthouse, J., & Brooks, G. (2003). A systematic review and meta-analysis of randomised controlled trials evaluating interventions in adult literacy and numeracy. *Journal of Research in Reading, 26,* 234–255.

Turkeltaub, P. E., Eden, G. F., Jones, K. M., & Zeffiro, T. A. (2002). Meta-analysis of the functional neuroanatomy of single-word reading: Method and validation. *NeuroImage, 16,* 765–780.

van den Noortgate, W., & Onghena, P. (2003). Multilevel meta-analysis: A comparison with traditional meta-analytical procedures. *Educational and Psychological Measurement, 63,* 765–790.

van IJzendoorn, M. H. (1994). Process model of replication studies: On the relations between different types of replication. In R. van der Veer, M. H. van IJzendoorn, & J. Valsiner (Eds.), *Reconstructing the mind: Replicability in research on human development* (pp. 57–70). Norwood, NJ: Ablex.

van IJzendoorn, M. H. (2002). Methodologie: Kennis door veranderen, de empirische benadering in de pedagogiek. In M. H. van IJzendoorn & H. de Frankrijker (Eds.), *Pedagogiek in beeld* [Education in pictures] (pp. 2–35). Houten, The Netherlands: Bohn Stafleu Van Loghum.

van IJzendoorn, M. H., & Bus, A. G. (1994). Meta-analytic confirmation of the nonword reading deficit in developmental dyslexia. *Reading Research Quarterly, 29,* 266–275.

What Works Clearinghouse. (2008, December). Procedures and standards handbook (version 2.0). Retrieved November 28, 2009, from *ies.ed.gov/ncee/wwc/pdf/wwc_procedures_v2_standards_handbook.pdf.*

Whitehurst, G. J., & Lonigan, C. J. (1998). Child development and emergent literacy. *Child Development, 69,* 848–872.

Williams, J. (2001). Commentary: Four meta-analyses and some general observations. *Elementary School Journal, 101,* 349–354.

Willig, A. C. (1985). A meta-analysis of selected studies on the effectiveness of bilingual education. *Review of Educational Research, 55,* 269–317.

Wolins, L. (1962). Responsibility for raw data. *American Psychologist, 17,* 657–658.

Zhao, Y. (2003). Recent developments in technology and language learning: A literature review and meta-analysis. *CALICO Journal, 21,* 7–27.

Zucker, T. A., Moody, A. K., & McKenna, M. C. (2009). The effects of electronic books on pre-kindergarten-to-grade-5 students' literacy and language outcomes: A research synthesis. *Journal of Educational Computing Research, 40,* 47–87.

CHAPTER 13

Mixed Research Approaches in Literacy Research

Anthony J. Onwuegbuzie
Marla H. Mallette

In the concluding chapter of this volume, Duke and Mallette present five messages that they hope readers will consider regarding literacy research methodologies. Message 4 ("Synergy across research methodologies is possible, powerful, and advisable") and Message 5 ("We must urgently and actively pursue synergy across research methodologies") apply not only across the contents of this volume, but also within this single chapter on mixed research in literacy. Although we agree that synergy can be achieved by looking across studies that use a single methodology (i.e., monomethodology), we contend that synergy can be achieved within a well-designed mixed research study as well.

WHY MIXED RESEARCH?

As can be seen from some of the other excellent chapters in this book, quantitative research represents a very useful set of techniques for addressing research questions in the field of literacy that necessitate the collection, analysis, and interpretation of numeric data. In particular, quantitative research is extremely useful for describing, explaining, and predicting human phenomena. Quantitative researchers often attempt to study phenomena under controlled conditions via experiments as a means of identifying cause-and-effect relationships. Under optimal conditions (e.g., large and random samples), findings from quantitative research studies can be generalized from the sample to the population from which the sample was drawn. When designed in an optimal way, in which rigor (e.g., reliability and validity of findings) is maximized, quantitative research can inform the field of literacy.

In contrast, qualitative research represents a very useful set of techniques for addressing research questions in the field of literacy that necessitate the collection, analysis, and interpretation of non-numeric data (e.g., words, observations, drawings, pictures, images). Qualitative research is extremely useful for exploring, discovering, describing, and constructing human phenomena. More specifically, it is generally used to obtain insights into experiences and the meaning(s) attached to these experiences of selected individuals (e.g., biography, autobiography, case study, life history, oral history, autoethnography) and groups (e.g., ethnography, grounded theory, phenomenology, critical theory), which, under optimal conditions (e.g., theoretical saturation, data saturation, informational redundancy, trustworthiness), can achieve *verstehen,* or understanding. Qualitative research can inform theory and model development if it is conducted in a way that yields insights into psychological, social, and/or cultural processes and practices that exist within a specific setting, location, context, event, activity, incident, time, and/or experience.

Unfortunately, although both quantitative and qualitative research represent powerful approaches for addressing an array of research questions in the field of literacy, each type has important weaknesses. In particular, quantitative research studies typically yield data that do not explain the reasons underlying prevalence rates, relationships, or differences that have been observed by literacy researchers. Simply put, quantitative research is not adequate for addressing "why" and "how" questions. Rather, it is better suited to "answering questions of who, where, how many, how much, and what is the relationship between specific variables" (Adler, 1996, p. 5). In contrast, as noted by Onwuegbuzie and Johnson (2008), "Qualitative research is typically based on small, nonrandom samples which means that qualitative research findings are often not very generalizable beyond the local research participants" (p. 441). Instead, the strength of qualitative research lies in its ability to understand the *emic,* or insider's, perspective; to capture the essence of an experience lived by one or more individuals; to identify the structure of a lived experience; to understand the meaning of psychological phenomena; to understand the role that culture (e.g., ethnicity, gender, age) plays in the context of phenomena; and to understand psychological processes that are reflected in language, thoughts, and behaviors from the perspectives of the participants themselves.

Because of the strengths and weaknesses inherent in monomethodological research, researchers from various fields and disciplines have been advocating that research studies include *both* quantitative and qualitative research within the same inquiry, commonly termed *mixed methods research*—or what we and several other researchers (e.g., Johnson & Onwuegbuzie, 2004) prefer to call *mixed research,* to reflect the fact that this research paradigm involves much more than the mixing of methods.

According to Johnson, Onwuegbuzie, and Turner (2007), mixed methods research or mixed research, broadly speaking, is

> an intellectual and practical synthesis based on qualitative and quantitative research; it is the third methodological or research paradigm (along with qualitative and quantitative research). It recognizes the importance of traditional quantitative and qualitative research but also offers a powerful third paradigm choice that often will provide the most informative, complete, balanced, and useful research results. Mixed methods research is the research paradigm that (a) partners with the philosophy of pragmatism in one of its forms (left, right, middle); (b) follows the logic of mixed methods research (including the logic of the fundamental principle and any other useful logics imported from qualitative or quantitative research that are helpful for producing defensible and usable research findings); (c) relies on qualitative and quantitative viewpoints, data collection, analysis, and inference techniques combined according to the logic of mixed methods research to address one's research question(s); and (d) is cognizant, appreciative, and inclusive of local and broader sociopolitcal realities, resources, and needs. Furthermore, the mixed methods research paradigm offers an important approach for *generating* important research questions *and* providing warranted answers to those questions. This type of research should be used when the nexus of contingencies in a situation, in relation to one's research question(s), suggests that mixed methods research is likely to provide superior research findings and outcomes. (p. 129)

The institutionalization of mixed methods as a distinct methodological orientation marked the beginning of conversations between quantitative and qualitative researchers; the publication of seminal works promoting mixed research as a separate research movement; the widespread publication of mixed research studies throughout the human sciences; and the conceptualization that "much if not most research is inherently mixed" (Teddlie & Johnson, 2009, p. 79).

Mixed research is not new. In fact, as Tashakkori and Teddlie (2003) contend, "Some of the most famous and influential research of the 20th century could be accurately referred to as mixed methods" (p. 697). However, despite researchers' inherent tendency to mix methods, early mixed studies were not systematically designed as mixed research; they did not involve the use of mixed research in any formal manner; and the researchers did not refer to their studies as representing mixed research.

Mixed Research in the Literacy Field

Researchers in the field of literacy also have informally been mixing methods for decades, although these studies were not classified as mixed research. Thus, the emergence of (formal) mixed research as an explicit design in particular and as a research methodology is still in its early stages (see, e.g., Calfee & Sperling, 2010).

In tracing the history of mixed research in literacy, we characterize its evolution in four phases. In the first phase, from the 1970s through the 1980s, mixed research studies, although limited in number, typically were quantitative, with qualitative data added to support the quantitative findings. One of the earliest examples of mixed research that we located was a study by Fareed (1971). Fareed investigated how skilled middle school students comprehended both historical and biological texts. As a Phase 1 study, this research was written with a predominantly quantitative focus. However, representative of this phase, qualitative data were included in the discussion under the heading of "Ancillary Findings" (p. 522). Perhaps even more interesting, considering the time of this study, was the qualitative language the author used in characterizing these data as *emerging* findings. A second example, by Garner (1980), followed a similar structure. Garner investigated comprehension monitoring of good and poor middle school readers. Similar to that of Fareed, Garner's study was a quantitative research report with qualitative findings added to the discussion to support the statistical results.

In contrast to the Phase 1 studies, Phase 2 research—which began in the late 1980s and continued through the early 2000s—was characterized by studies that included both quantitative and qualitative methods, and in which both types were described in the "Methods" section and reported in the "Results" section. Typically, these studies could be best characterized as having separate quantitative and qualitative sections; yet the authors tended to weave the findings together in the discussion. O'Brien and Martin's (1988) study on the nature of figurative language in comprehension represents an early example of mixed research. Their research comprised three types of analyses: (1) correlations, (2) regression analyses, and (3) logical analyses. As was characteristic of this phase of mixed research, O'Brien and Martin reported the results from each of the analyses separately and then integrated the findings in the discussion section.

A second common feature of mixed research during this time was the selection of a subsample from the larger sample for the qualitative phase. For example, Purcell-Gates and Dahl (1991) chose 12 "focal children" (p. 4) from their larger sample of 35 children in their study investigating how children of low socioeconomic status experienced a skills-based curriculum. Freppon (1991) chose 24 informants, six children from four classrooms, for the qualitative dimension in her study comparing skills-based classrooms with literature-based classrooms. Interestingly (and perhaps caught in the midst of the qualitative and quantitative paradigm wars), in both of these studies the subsamples were randomly as opposed to purposefully selected, with the latter being more typical of qualitative research.

Toward the end of this period, with qualitative research being embraced and legitimized in the field of literacy, researchers began providing stronger and more compelling rationales for the qualitative component of their mixed research. For example, Gaskins (1996) explored the effects of emotional involvement with text on reading comprehension. Although the primary analysis in this study involved a comparison of differences in responses between two experimental groups and a control group, Gaskins also interviewed the participants. What set this study apart were the inclusion of qualitative data and the rationale that Gaskins provided for its inclusion:

> *Data pertaining to the research questions.* In addition to providing support for key assumptions underlying the study, the subjects' comments provided a means for gaining further insights into the effect of issue-related emotional involvement on a subject's interpretation of a text pertaining to that issue. The subjects' comments are particularly important because they provide a vital manifestation of the effects the quantitative data support without voice. The quantitative data analyses provided statistically significant support for the hypothesis that subjects' degree of emotional involvement with one of the teams in the passage would have an effect on the way in which the subjects interpreted that passage, but the subjects' comments elaborated on that finding and gave the data a more personal voice. (pp. 395–396)

Bloodgood (1999) examined the importance of name writing among young children. In her abstract, she identified the design as representing both quantitative and qualitative research. She stated: "Sixty-seven 3-, 4-, and 5-year-olds, their teachers, instructional aides, and six case-study parents participated in a yearlong qualitative and quantitative study" (p. 343). In the "Methods" section, Bloodgood further elaborated on the importance of mixing both qualitative and quantitative methodologies:

> Experimental and naturalistic strategies were used in this study to explore name's role in literacy acquisition. Quantitative measures provided a database that was analyzed for evidence of growth across the year and relationships among literacy tasks. Qualitative information from observations and interviews supplied the why and how behind the data through prolonged engagement, thick description, and analysis of emerging . . . (1999, p. 348)

Through her use of mixed methods techniques, Bloodgood provided compelling evidence for the importance on name writing in early literacy learning. Although the quantitative data clearly demonstrated the importance of name writing as an indicator of early literacy knowledge, the qualitative data provided a more nuanced understanding of the various patterns that occur in how that knowledge develops.

The third phase, consisting of research published from the early 2000s to the present, includes studies in which authors explicitly state that their design represents mixed research, and as such the methodology is more integrative. In addition (and in contrast to the previous phase), rather than providing rationales for quantitative and qualitative methods, researchers tend to provide a theoretical rationale for the use of mixed research. One of the first examples of research in this time period that we located was Bauman et al.'s (2002) study on the effectiveness of teaching morphemic analysis and context clues on reading vocabulary and comprehension. They described the design as follows:

> The overall design involved a mixed method of quantitative and descriptive design. Specifically, one of Tashakkori and Teddlie's (1998) "dominant-less dominant mixed method designs" was employed, "in which one paradigm and its methods are dominant, while a small component of the overall study is drawn from an alternative design" (p. 44). The dominant design was quantitative and involved a between-subjects, pretest-posttest, control-group, quasi-experiment . . . , with the student as the unit of analysis. The independent variable was group membership, which had four levels: morphemic-only instruction (MO), context-only instruction (CO), combined morphemic-context instruction (MC), and instructed control (IC). The less-dominant design involved descriptive data on students' vocabulary learning gathered through individual interviews with students selected from each treatment group. (p. 156)

They provided similar support in their explanation of data analysis: "Data from the dominant–less-dominant design were analyzed according to a sequential quantitative–qualitative data analysis process (Tashakkori & Teddlie, 1998, p. 127)" (p. 161). In the "Results" section, they separated the quantitative and qualitative findings; yet, the discussion centered on the findings as a mixed research study, thereby providing a more complex understanding of their findings.

At present, we are entering a fourth phase, which is characterized by growing sophistication in conceptualizing mixed research. Johnson (2017) details a theoretical foundation for understanding the complexity of mixed research through a *metaparadigm* that requires "empathetically and thoughtfully work with more than one paradigm (or perspective or theory) to produce a new, more complex 'whole'" (p. 159). Specifically, he contends that dialectical pluralism "allows and thrives on conflicting positions and offers a strategy for dynamically 'merging' or combining ideas into new broader/thicker viewpoints" (p. 159), and offers a *metavoice* to research through the combination of divergent ideas.

Indubitably, one of the biggest advances in the field of mixed research has been the promotion of integration. In the field of literacy research and beyond, mixed research has been defined via what has been termed the "1 + 1 = 3 integration formula," which translates to "qualitative + quantitative

= more than the individual components" (Fetters & Freshwater, 2015, p. 116). However, as noted by Onwuegbuzie and Hitchcock (2019), this 1 + 1 = 3 methodological formula represents the low end of the integration continuum. And because this formula "reifies a quantitative–qualitative dichotomy that can undermine a fuller and more seamless kind of integration" (Onwuegbuzie, Hitchcock, Natesan, & Newman, 2018, p. 666), Onwuegbuzie and Hitchcock propose what they refer to as the "1 + 1 = 1 integration approach" (p. 100), which represents the full integration of qualitative and quantitative elements at the data collection, data analysis, and data interpretation phases. This 1 + 1 = 1 integration formula also advances the use of what Onwuegbuzie and Combs (2010) refer to as *cross-over mixed analyses,* wherein one or more analysis types associated with one tradition (e.g., qualitative analysis) are used to analyze data associated with a different tradition (e.g., quantitative data). An example of a 1 + 1 = 1 integration approach is the use of Bayesian techniques to conduct what Onwuegbuzie et al. (2018) refer to as *fully integrated Bayesian thinking meta-analyses,* which involves the integration of *both* qualitative and quantitative findings—either sequentially or simultaneously—as opposed to classical meta-analyses (Glass, 1976), wherein only the quantitative findings are integrated via the use of effect sizes.

Hitchcock and Onwuegbuzie (2020) advance the framework by suggesting crossover mixed analyses that can be used in "the mixing or combining of paradigmatic assumptions and stances with each tradition" (p. 72). Cronenberg (2020) proposes the *paradigm parley,* involving four aspects to achieve integration: (1) dialogue among differing paradigms, (2) dialogue voice priority and equality, (3) data integrity, and (4) exploring convergence and divergence. In addition, as emphasized by Sanscartier (2020), achieving holistic integration in mixed research requires researchers to be flexible, to embrace nonlinearity, and (perhaps most importantly) to embrace and explore divergence. Furthermore, until recently, *qualitizing* has been defined as the process of converting quantitative data into data that can be analyzed qualitatively (Tashakkori & Teddlie, 1998). However, Onwuegbuzie and Leech (2019) have expanded the concept of qualitizing as follows:

> The technique of qualitizing involves transforming data into qualitative form. The data that are qualitized can either stem directly from quantitative data, or from qualitative data that are converted to numeric form (i.e., quantitized), or both. The qualitizing process can involve one or more qualitative analysis and/or one or more quantitative analysis (e.g., descriptive analyses, exploratory analyses, inferential analyses) that represent either a single analysis (i.e., single qualitizing) or multiple analyses (i.e., multi-qualitizing), which, optimally, involves the full integration of qualitative and quantitative research approaches (i.e., 1 + 1 = 1 integration formula) that yield fully integrated analysis. Some form of qualitizing can be undertaken by quantitative researchers, qualitative

researchers, and mixed researchers that represent a variety of ontological, epistemological, and methodological assumptions and stances. The qualitizing process can yield numerous representations that include codes, categories, sub-themes, themes, figures of speech, meta-themes, and narratives (i.e., prose or poetry). (p. 122)

Prevalence of Mixed Research Studies in Literacy Research

Although, as noted previously, mixed research studies in the area of literacy have been published for several decades, and despite an increased prevalence of mixed research in mathematics education (Onwuegbuzie & Corrigan, 2014) and online research journals (Bangi, 2018)—literacy research has been dominated by monomethodological research approaches. Parsons et al. (2016) conducted an extensive examination of content, methodology, and theoretical perspectives of articles published in nine literacy journals between 2009 and 2014. Through qualitative content analysis, they found that the number of mixed research studies still remained low (i.e., 7%). Additionally, after *Reading and Writing Quarterly* (the one journal that accounted for 30% of all articles analyzed) was removed to provide a more balanced perspective across journals, the number of mixed research studies was 9%, with 67% of the published articles being quantitative and 24% being qualitative. Interestingly, in the *Scientific Studies of Reading*, where approximately 90% of the published articles were quantitative, and in *Research in the Teaching of English*, where approximately 70% of the published articles were qualitative, each journal published only one mixed research study during the 5-year period under analysis. These findings demonstrate the consistency in the limited number of mixed research publications in literacy research (cf. Mallette, Moffit, Onwuegbuzie, & Wheeler, 2008; Wilkinson & Staley, 2019).

In seeking to provide evidence into the dearth of published mixed research studies, Wilkinson and Staley (2019) examined the reviewers' comments from the mixed research studies submitted to *Reading Research Quarterly* between 2006 and 2010. Of the 698 manuscripts received during that time period, 37 (i.e., 5%) were mixed research. Of these 37 manuscripts, 22 were sent out for review, with 17 of them rejected and five accepted. However, it is important to note that upon revision, only three were published as mixed research studies, whereas two were revised and published as monomethodological studies. Wilkinson and Staley analyzed the 79 reviews for the 22 manuscripts. Through their content analysis of these reviews, they were able to identify the following six common problems in the mixed research submitted: (1) underdeveloped qualitative data, analysis, and sampling; (2) underdeveloped quantitative data, analysis, and design; (3) flawed logic of inquiry; (4) lack of focus; (5) weak articulation; and (6) what they called "methodological handwringing."

STAGES OF THE MIXED RESEARCH PROCESS

Our goal in the remainder of this chapter is to facilitate readers' understanding of conducting high-quality, methodologically sound, and rigorous mixed research in the field of literacy research through deepening their understanding of mixed research and suggesting ways of improving methodological rigor. Through thoughtful conceptualization, careful planning, and systematic implementation, mixed research can reach its potential to address complex issues in the field of literacy, which are detailed by Collins, Onwuegbuzie, and Sutton (2006) in their three-stage, 13-step framework. These 13 steps are both interactive and recursive. What most clearly distinguishes the mixed research process from the monomethodology research processes is that the former necessitates decisions not only about the individual quantitative research and qualitative research components, but also about how these components relate to each other (e.g., 1 + 1 = 3 vs. 1 + 1 = 1).

Research Conceptualization Stage

Determining the goal (Step 1) involves making a decision about the overall long-term aim of the mixed research study. Here, researchers can use Newman, Ridenour, Newman, and DeMarco's (2003) framework as a guide. These authors have identified nine goals: The researcher can aim to predict; add to the knowledge base; have a personal, social, institutional, and/or organizational impact; understand complex phenomena; measure change; test new ideas; generate new ideas; inform constituencies; or examine the past.

The research goal leads directly to the research objective (Step 2). In this step, the researcher should determine which of the following six major standard research objectives are pertinent for both the quantitative and qualitative phases of the study: *exploration* (i.e., using primarily inductive techniques to explore a concept, phenomenon, or context in order to make tentative inferences; *description* (i.e., identifying and describing the antecedents and nature of phenomena); *understanding* (i.e., attempting to understand the subjective viewpoints and/or experiences of the underlying participant[s] and/or group[s]); *explanation* (i.e., developing or expanding theory in an attempt to clarify the relationships among concepts, constructs, or phenomena and identify reasons for occurrences of events); *prediction* (i.e., using prior knowledge or extant theory to predict what will occur at a later point); and *influence* (i.e., manipulating one or more variables or conditions in an attempt to produce an expected or desired result) (Johnson & Christensen, 2020).

The third step of the mixed research process is to determine the research/mixing rationale. This step involves not only determining the rationale of the study (i.e., why the study is needed), but also identifying the rationale for mixing quantitative and qualitative approaches. Collins et al. (2006) identified the following four major rationales for mixing quantitative and qualitative approaches (i.e., reasons why mixing is needed): *participant enrichment* (i.e., mixing quantitative and qualitative techniques for the rationale of optimizing the sample—e.g., increasing the number of participants); *instrument fidelity* (i.e., maximizing the appropriateness and/or utility of all quantitative and qualitative instruments used in the study—e.g., via a pilot study); *treatment integrity* (i.e., mixing quantitative and qualitative procedures in order to assess the fidelity of interventions, treatments, or programs); and *significance enhancement* (i.e., mixing quantitative and qualitative techniques in order to optimize data interpretations).

Alongside identifying the research/mixing rationale, researchers should determine the research/mixing purpose (Step 4). Collins et al. (2006) identified 65 purposes for mixing quantitative and qualitative approaches (i.e., how the mixing will occur), categorized under one of the four major rationales (i.e., participant enrichment, instrument fidelity, treatment integrity, significance enhancement). Also, in determining the purpose of mixing, we recommend Greene, Caracelli, and Graham's (1989) framework, in which they identified five broad purposes of mixed research studies: *triangulation* (i.e., seeking convergence and corroboration of findings from different methods that examine the same phenomenon); *complementarity* (i.e., seeking elaboration, enhancement, illustration, and clarification of the findings from one method with results from the other method); *initiation* (i.e., identifying paradoxes and contradictions that lead to the reframing of the research questions); *development* (i.e., using the findings from one method to help inform the other method); and *expansion* (i.e., seeking to expand the breadth and depth of the study by using different methods for different research components).

Identifying the research purpose helps the researcher develop appropriate research questions (Step 5). For example, if the purpose of the research is triangulation, then both the quantitative and qualitative sets of research questions should most likely lead to an investigation of the same outcome or phenomenon. Conversely, if the purpose of the research is initiation or development, then the quantitative research question should be conditional on the qualitative research question or vice versa (cf. Onwuegbuzie & Leech, 2006).

Determining the research question(s), the fifth and final step of the research conceptualization stage, is central in the mixed research process. However, the development of research questions does not occur only at this step of the mixed research process; these questions are reevaluated during data collection (Step 8), data analysis (Step 9), data legitimation (Step 10), and/or data interpretation (Step 11), and might be reframed at any of these phases. Furthermore, these research questions are reevaluated after the study has been completed, leading to modified and/or additional research questions (Step 13).

Onwuegbuzie and Leech (2006) introduced the concept of *mixed research questions,* defining them as

> questions that embed both a quantitative research question and a qualitative research question within the same question. That is, mixed methods research questions combine or mix both the quantitative and qualitative research questions. Moreover, a mixed methods research question necessitates that both quantitative data and qualitative data be collected and analyzed either concurrently, sequentially, or iteratively before the question is addressed. (p. 483)

During the research conceptualization stage, the review of the literature is vital, and the role of the literature review should be made explicit. As recommended by Onwuegbuzie and Frels (2016), literacy researchers should treat the information from articles extracted for their literature review as data that provide both qualitative and quantitative information, and that therefore can be analyzed using qualitative and quantitative approaches—what Sandelowski, Voils, and Barroso (2006) call *mixed research syntheses*—including creating *metainferences* (i.e., inferences from qualitative and quantitative information integrated into a whole). Studies involving meta-analyses (Glass, 1976), metasyntheses (Sandelowski & Barroso, 2006), and metasummaries (Sandelowski & Barroso, 2003)—which involve analysis of a set of quantitative or qualitative studies on a given topic—play a vital role in mixed research syntheses whenever they are available. Furthermore, all literature should be examined and assessed for trustworthiness, credibility, dependability, legitimation, validity, plausibility, applicability, consistency, neutrality, reliability, objectivity, confirmability, and/or transferability (cf. Leech, Dellinger, Brannagan, & Tanaka, 2010).

Research Planning Stage

In Collins et al.'s (2006) mixed research process framework, the research planning stage involves selecting the mixed sampling design (Step 6) and the mixed research design (Step 7). These steps are both interactive and iterative because choice of sampling design affects the selection of research design and vice versa. With regard to the sampling design, Onwuegbuzie and Collins (2007) provided a typology for classifying mixed sampling designs according to the time orientation of the components or phases and the relationship of the qualitative and quantitative samples, as follows: *identical* (i.e., exactly the same participants are involved in both the qualitative and quantitative phases of the study); *parallel* (i.e., the samples for the qualitative and quantitative components of the research are different but are drawn from the same population of interest); *nested* (i.e., the participants selected for one phase of the study represent a subset of those sample members selected for the other component of the research); or *multilevel* (i.e., two or more sets of samples are extracted from different levels of the population of interest—e.g., elementary school children vs. language arts teachers). The two criteria—time orientation (two levels) and sample relationship (four levels)—yield eight different types of major sampling designs that mixed researchers have at their disposal. Another useful typology of sampling schemes is that developed by Teddlie and Yu (2007), who subdivided sampling schemes into the following four types: probability sampling, purposive sampling, convenience sampling, and mixed methods sampling.

For the research design step (Step 7), numerous useful typologies and frameworks have emerged. A particularly useful typology is that developed by Teddlie and Tashakkori (2006). These authors conceptualized what they termed the *methods–strands matrix* by crossing the number of methods used with the number of research components, or strands. The multistrand–mixed methods cell in the matrix contains five families of mixed research designs: *parallel* (i.e., the quantitative and qualitative phases of the study occur in a parallel manner, either at approximately the same time or with a time lag); *sequential* (i.e., the quantitative and qualitative phases of the study occur in chronological order); *conversion* (i.e., the mixing of quantitative and qualitative approaches occurs when one type of data [quantitative or qualitative] is transformed and then analyzed both quantitatively and qualitatively); *multilevel* (i.e., the quantitative data are collected at one level of analysis [e.g., child], and the qualitative data are collected at another level [e.g., parent], either concurrently or sequentially); and *fully integrated* (i.e., the mixing of quantitative and qualitative approaches occurs in an interactive [e.g., interdependent, iterative] manner at all stages of the study).

Teddlie and Tashakkori (2009) outlined seven criteria that authors use to create their mixed research design typologies: number of methodological approaches used, number of strands or phases, type of implementation process, stage of integration of approaches, priority of methodological approach, functions of the research study, and theoretical or ideological perspective. These authors also separate mixed research designs into mixed methods *monostrand* designs (i.e., comprising monostrand conversion designs, which "are used in single-strand studies in which research questions are answered through an analysis of transformed [quantitized and qualitized] data" [p. 149]) and mixed methods *multistrand* designs (i.e., containing at least two research strands that comprise the following five families: parallel mixed designs, sequential mixed designs, conversion mixed designs, multilevel mixed designs, and fully integrated mixed designs).

Leech and Onwuegbuzie (2009) presented a three-dimensional typology, in which mixed designs can be represented as a function of three dimensions: *level of mixing* (i.e., fully mixed [mixing of quantitative and qualitative approaches within or across the data collection, analysis, and interpretation stages] vs. partially mixed [mixing only at the data interpretation stage]), *time orientation* (i.e., concurrent [quantitative and qualitative phases occur at approximately the same point in time] vs. sequential [phases occur one after the other]), and *emphasis of approaches* (i.e., equal status [quantitative and qualitative components have approximately equal emphasis] vs. dominant status [one component has higher priority than the other]). Leech and Onwuegbuzie's typology thus can be characterized as a 2 (fully mixed vs. partially mixed) × 2 (concurrent vs. sequential) × 3 (equal status vs. dominant status quantitative vs. dominant status qualitative) matrix, which yields 12 types of mixed research designs.

Johnson et al. (2007) provided a useful way of framing mixed research studies. Specifically, they conceptualized mixed research as being either quantitative dominant, qualitative dominant, or equal status. According to Johnson and coauthors, "Qualitative dominant mixed methods research is the type of mixed research in which one relies on a qualitative, constructivist-poststructuralist-critical view of the research process, while concurrently recognizing that the addition of quantitative data and approaches are likely to benefit most research projects" (p. 124). In contrast, "Quantitative dominant mixed methods research is the type of mixed research in which one relies on a quantitative, postpositivist view of the research process, while concurrently recognizing that the addition of qualitative data and approaches are likely to benefit most research projects" (p. 124). Finally, equal status designs involve the approximately equal use of quantitative and qualitative epistemologies, techniques, methods, approaches, concepts, or language within the same mixed research study.

The utility of this tripartite conceptualization of mixed research designs is that it allows mixed research to be conducted within both quantitative and qualitative research studies without the researchers having to be mixed researchers. In other words, researchers with a quantitative orientation can conduct mixed research and yet maintain quantitative assumptions and stances (e.g., postpositivism). Similarly, researchers with a qualitative orientation can conduct mixed research and yet maintain qualitative assumptions and stances (e.g., constructivism, critical theory). Thus, this tripartite conceptualization makes mixed research accessible not only for mixed researchers, but also for both quantitative and qualitative researchers.

Research Implementation Stage

The research implementation stage comprises the following four interactive and cyclical steps: data collection (Step 8), data analysis (Step 9), data legitimation (Step 10), and data interpretation (Step 11). With respect to data collection, Johnson and Turner's (2003) typology contains six specific data collection strategies in mixed research: mixture of open- and closed-ended items on one or more questionnaires; mixture of depth and breadth interviewing; mixture of a priori and emergent/flowing focus group strategies; mixture of standardized open- and closed-ended predesigned tests; mixture of standardized/confirmatory and less structured/exploratory observation, alternating between participatory and nonparticipatory researcher roles; and mixture of non-numeric and numeric documents, consisting of archived data based on open- and closed-ended items. More recently, Teddlie and Tashakkori (2009) presented 30 between-strategies mixed data collection combinations (e.g., quantitative observations with qualitative-based focus groups) and six within-strategies mixed methods data collection combinations (e.g., quantitative interview and qualitative interview).

Data collection is followed by data analysis (Step 9). Onwuegbuzie and Combs (2010) conducted a comprehensive review of the literature, identifying virtually every known methodological work (e.g., article, editorial, book chapter, conference paper) in the area of mixed analyses at the time of writing, and identified 13 criteria that authors had used to create their mixed analysis typologies. This led them to develop the following comprehensive and inclusive definition or summary of what is called mixed analysis:

> Mixed analysis involves the use of both quantitative and qualitative analytical techniques within the same framework, which is guided either a priori, a posteriori, or iteratively (representing analytical decisions that occur both prior to the study and during the study). It might be based on one of the existing mixed methods research paradigms (e.g., pragmatism, transformative–emancipatory) such that it meets one or more of the following rationales/purposes: triangulation, complementarity, development, initiation, and expansion. Mixed analyses involve the analyses of one or both data types (i.e., quantitative data *or* qualitative data; or quantitative data *and* qualitative data) which occur either concurrently (i.e., in no chronological order), or sequentially in two phases (in which the qualitative analysis phase precedes the quantitative analysis phase or vice versa, and findings from the initial analysis phase informs the subsequent phase) or more than two phases (i.e., iteratively). The analysis strands might not interact until the data interpretation stage, yielding a basic parallel mixed analysis, although more complex forms of parallel mixed analysis can be used, in which interaction takes place in a limited way before the data interpretation phase. The mixed analysis can be design-based, wherein it is directly linked to the mixed methods design (e.g., sequential mixed analysis techniques used for sequential mixed methods designs). Alternatively, the mixed analysis can be phase-based, in which the mixed analysis takes place in one or more phases (e.g., data transformation). In mixed analyses, either the qualitative or quantitative analysis strands might be given priority or approximately equal priority as a result of a priori decisions (i.e., determined at the research conceptualization phase) or decisions that emerge during the course of the study

(i.e., a posteriori or iterative decisions). The mixed analysis could represent case-oriented, variable-oriented, and/or process/experience-oriented analyses. The mixed analysis is guided by an attempt to analyze data in a way that yields at least one of five types of generalizations (i.e., external statistical generalizations, internal statistical generalizations, analytical generalizations, case-to-case transfer, naturalistic generalization). At its most integrated form, the mixed analysis might involve some form of cross-over analysis, wherein one or more analysis types associated with one tradition (e.g., qualitative analysis) are used to analyze data associated with a different tradition (e.g., quantitative data). (Onwuegbuzie & Combs, 2010, pp. 425–426)

In Step 10, the legitimation of both the quantitative and the qualitative data is assessed. For the quantitative phase, literacy researchers should assess threats to internal validity and external validity (e.g., Campbell, 1957; Onwuegbuzie, 2003), as well as to measurement validity (Messick, 1995; Onwuegbuzie, Daniel, & Collins, 2009). With regard to the qualitative phase, literacy researchers should assess threats to trustworthiness, credibility, dependability, authenticity, verification, plausibility, applicability, confirmability, and/or transferability of data (e.g., Creswell & Poth, 2018; Guba & Lincoln, 1989; Lather, 1993; Lincoln, 1995; Maxwell, 1992; Miles & Huberman, 1994; Onwuegbuzie & Leech, 2007).

Onwuegbuzie and Johnson (2006) developed a typology for legitimation issues that are pertinent to the overall mixed research study. Specifically, this typology consists of nine legitimation types pertaining to the overall mixed research process: *sample integration* (i.e., extent to which the relationship between the quantitative and qualitative sampling designs yields high-quality metainferences); *inside–outside* (i.e., extent to which the researcher accurately presents and appropriately utilizes the insider's [emic] view and the observer's [etic] view for purposes such as description and explanation); *weakness minimization* (i.e., extent to which the weakness from one approach is compensated for by the strengths from the other approach); *sequential* (i.e., extent to which the researcher has minimized the potential problem wherein the metainferences could be affected by reversing the sequence of the quantitative and qualitative phases); *conversion* (i.e., extent to which the quantitizing or qualitizing yields high-quality metainferences); *paradigmatic mixing* (i.e., extent to which the researcher's epistemological, ontological, axiological, methodological, and rhetorical assumptions and stances that underlie the quantitative and qualitative approaches are successfully combined or blended into a usable package); *commensurability* (i.e., extent to which the metainferences made reflect a mixed worldview based on the cognitive process of gestalt switching and integration); *multiple validities* (i.e., extent to which addressing legitimation of the quantitative and qualitative components of the mixed research study results from the use of quantitative, qualitative, *and* mixed validity types, yielding high-quality metainferences); and *political* (i.e., extent to which the consumers of mixed research value the metainferences stemming from both the quantitative and the qualitative components of a study).

Once validated/legitimated, these data then are interpreted (Step 11). Leech and Onwuegbuzie (2004) identified four types of significance in social science research, which very much apply to literacy research: *statistical significance* (i.e., the probability that observed results from the sample could have occurred if the null hypothesis is true), *practical significance* (i.e., the educational value of the results—e.g., effect size, which represents a family of indices that measure the size of a relationship or difference), *clinical significance* (i.e., the extent that an intervention or treatment makes a real difference to the quality of life of the participants or to those with whom they interact or encounter), and *economic significance* (i.e., economic value of the finding—e.g., effect of the intervention).

With respect to the overall mixed research study, Teddlie and Tashakkori (2009) developed an interpretive framework for inference quality. This framework comprises the following 10 aspects of quality: *design suitability* (i.e., "Are the methods of study appropriate for answering the research questions?"; "Does the design match the research questions?"; "Does the mixed methods design match the stated purpose for conducting an integrated study?"; "Do the strands of the mixed methods study address the same research questions [or closely related aspects of the research question]?"); *design fidelity* (i.e., "Are the qualitative, quantitative, and mixed methods procedures or design components capturing the meanings, effects, or relationships?"); *within-design consistency* (i.e., "Do the components of the design fit together in a seamless manner?"; "Do the strands of the mixed methods study follow each other [or are they linked] in a logical and seamless manner?"); *analytic adequacy* (i.e., "Are the data analysis procedures/strategies appropriate and adequate to provide possible answers to research questions?"; "Are the mixed methods strategies implemented effectively?"); *interpretive consistency* (i.e., "Do the inferences closely follow the relevant findings in terms of type, scope, and intensity?"; "Are multiple inferences made on the basis of the same findings consistent with each other?"); *theoretical consistency* (i.e., "Are the inferences consistent with theory and state of knowledge in the field?"); *interpretive agreement* (i.e., "Are other scholars likely to reach the same conclusions on the basis of the same results?"; "Do the inferences match participants' constructions?"); *interpretive distinctiveness* (i.e., "Is each inference distinctively more credible/plausible than other possible conclusions that might be made on the basis of the same results?"); *integrative efficacy* (i.e., "Do the metainferences adequately incorporate the inferences that are made in each strand of the study?"; "If there are credible inconsistencies between inferences made within/across strands, are the theoretical explanations for these inconsistencies explored and possible explanations offered?"); and *interpretive correspondence* (i.e., "Do the inferences correspond to the stated purpose/

questions of the study?"; "Do the inferences made in each strand address the purposes of the study in that strand?"; "Do the metainferences meet the stated need for using a mixed methods design?").

Writing the research report (Step 12) is the penultimate step in the mixed research process. Several authors have provided guidelines for writing mixed research reports (e.g., Creswell & Plano Clark, 2017; Johnson & Onwuegbuzie, 2008; Leech, Onwuegbuzie, & Combs, 2011; Tashakkori & Creswell, 2007a).

Once the research report has been written, the researcher conceptualizes the research questions (Step 13); this, in turn, might lead to a reconceptualization of the research goal (Step 1), research objective (Step 2), research/mixing rationale (Step 3), and/or research/mixing purpose (Step 4) in subsequent studies. Alternatively, the research goal, research objective, and research purpose may not be changed; instead, the reconceptualization of the research question leads directly to a reconceptualization of the mixed sampling design (Step 6) and research design (Step 7). Thus, in subsequent studies, Steps 6–11 are repeated until all research goals, objectives, purposes, and questions are adequately addressed and *verstehen* is reached.

APPROPRIATE RESEARCH QUESTIONS FOR MIXED RESEARCH

As noted earlier, research questions play a central role in mixed research. In the words of Johnson and Onwuegbuzie (2004), "What is most fundamental is the research question—research methods should *follow* research questions in a way that offers the best chance to obtain useful answers" (pp. 17–18). Tashakkori and Creswell (2007b) have conceptualized an excellent typology for classifying mixed research questions, which outlines three ways that such questions are constructed. The first technique for constructing research questions in mixed research involves writing separate quantitative and qualitative questions followed by an explicit mixed research question. The second method involves writing an overarching mixed or integrated research question, subsequently broken down into separate quantitative and qualitative subquestions to address in each phase or component of the investigation. Tashakkori and Creswell contend that this type of research question is more common in parallel studies (i.e., the findings of both the quantitative and the qualitative phases are interpreted and written up separately) and concurrent studies (i.e., the findings stemming from one phase [e.g., quantitative phase] do not inform the other phase [e.g., qualitative phase]) than in sequential studies (i.e., either the quantitative or qualitative phase is conducted first, which then informs the subsequent phase). Although this overarching question may be implicitly present, it may not be explicitly stated. In the third method, research questions for each phase are written as the study evolves. If the first phase is quantitative in nature, the question is framed as a quantitative research question. If the second phase is qualitative, the question is framed accordingly. As such, this method of constructing research questions is more relevant to sequential studies than to concurrent or parallel studies. Consistent with Onwuegbuzie and Leech (2006), Tashakkori and Creswell recommended the development of a single mixed research question that addresses the nature of mixing and integration, or a single mixed research question that transcends any subsequent quantitative and qualitative subquestions.

CLAIMS FOR MIXED RESEARCH

Mixed researchers make several common claims about mixed research. The ultimate common claim is that mixed research represents a distinctive methodology—that it is a methodology distinct from both quantitative and qualitative methodologies (cf. Greene, 2006, 2008). Stemming from this claim are many others about mixed research. In particular, a major premise of mixed research is that "many research questions and combinations of questions are best and most fully answered through mixed research solutions" (Johnson & Onwuegbuzie, 2004, p. 18). However, some of the claims differ as a function of the philosophical assumptions and stance of the mixed researchers. The following are possible stances in mixed research: pragmatism-of-the-middle philosophy (Johnson & Onwuegbuzie, 2004), pragmatism-of-the-right philosophy (Putnam, 2002; Rescher, 2000), pragmatism-of-the-left philosophy (Maxcy, 2003; Rorty, 1991), anticonflationist philosophy (Bryman, 1992; Hammersley, 1992; Roberts, 2002), critical realist orientation (Christ, 2010; Houston, 2001; McEvoy & Richards, 2006), dialectical (Greene, 2008; Maxwell & Loomis, 2003), complementary strengths (Brewer & Hunter, 1989; Morse, 2003), transformative–emancipatory (Mertens, 2003), aparadigmatic (Patton, 2002; Reichardt & Cook, 1979), substantive theory (Chen, 2006), and communities of practice (Denscombe, 2008). The most recently suggested stance is dialectical pluralism (Johnson, 2017), which involves the use of "back-and-forth disputation and examination and can include the dynamic logic of thesis, antithesis, and synthesis" (p. 157).

STANDARDS OF QUALITY FOR MIXED METHODOLOGY RESEARCH

O'Cathain (2010) developed a comprehensive framework for assessing quality in mixed research across eight domains. Table 13.1 provides an overview of the standards of quality within each domain. In addition to standards of quality, Onwuegbuzie and Corrigan (2014) detail evidence-based guidelines for conducting and reporting mixed research. These guidelines are grounded in two essential aspects of the standards for reporting research established by the American Educational Research Association (AERA, 2006): the importance of research studies being warranted and transparent. Furthermore, Onwuegbuzie and Corrigan contend that, taken together, warranted and transparent research studies embody rigor. They describe the following five elements as necessary in achieving rigor in mixed research:

1. *Comprehensive:* All steps of the research process are followed.
2. *Systematic:* A sound and logical sequence of steps is followed.
3. *Evaluative:* Each step of the research process is evaluated.
4. *Defensible:* A rationale supporting design and inquiry decisions is provided.
5. *Transparent:* The logic of the inquiry is clearly documented.

Although rigor in conducting and reporting mixed research is an important mechanism in evaluating standards of quality, Onwuegbuzie and Corrigan view the attention to rigor as reflecting much more of an ethical issue. That is, because quantitative, qualitative, and mixed researchers are essentially united by a goal to achieve meaning making, a question that researchers should ask in every empirical research study is this: "To what extent have I/ we minimized threats to verification/trustworthiness/legitimation/authenticity/credibility/transferability/dependability/confirmability?" (p. 278).

AN EXEMPLAR OF MIXED RESEARCH

We selected "Doctoral Students' Perceptions of Barriers to Reading Empirical Literature: A Mixed Analysis" (Benge, Onwuegbuzie, Mallette, & Burgess, 2010) as our exemplar study because it adheres to all of the standards of quality in mixed research (O'Cathain, 2010) and the elements of rigor in such research (Onwuegbuzie & Corrigan, 2014) discussed previously. Also, this study is consistent with the 1 + 1 = 1 integration approach because, for example, multivariate analyses (e.g., canonical correlation analyses) were used simultaneously to analyze (i.e., correlate) qualitative data (i.e., emergent themes) and quantitative data (e.g., reading ability variables).

The planning quality domain is evident in the section describing the study. In providing a rationale, the authors not only make a claim for the importance of the study, but also provide a compelling rationale for using a mixed design. The design quality domain suggests the importance of the research questions matching the design. In high-quality mixed studies, there can be qualitative questions and quantitative questions; yet, most importantly, there ought to be mixed research questions. In the Benge et al. (2010) study, there is a good balance of qualitative and quantitative questions, and the overarching questions are mixed.

TABLE 13.1. Assessing Quality in Mixed Research across Eight Domains

Planning quality

- *Foundational element:* The extent to which the literature review situates the study and drives the study design.
- *Rationale transparency:* The extent to which a justification is provided for using mixed research approaches.
- *Planning transparency:* The extent to which elements of the mixed study are described in sufficient detail.
- *Feasibility:* The extent to which the design can be undertaken, given the available resources.

Design quality

- *Design transparency:* The extent to which there is adequate description of the mixed research design.
- *Design suitability:* The extent to which the design is appropriate for addressing the overall research question, consistent with the rationale for combining approaches, and is appropriate for the stated paradigm.
- *Design strength:* The extent to which the strengths and weaknesses of the methods are considered, in order to minimize bias and to optimize the breadth and depth of the mixed research study.
- *Design rigor:* The extent to which methods are implemented consistently with the mixed research design.

Data quality

- *Data transparency:* The extent to which each method is described in sufficient detail.
- *Data rigor/design fidelity:* The extent to which each method is implemented with rigor.
- *Sampling adequacy:* The extent to which the sampling for each method is adequate for the underlying design.
- *Analytic adequacy:* The extent to which data analysis techniques are appropriate and adequately undertaken.
- *Analytic integration rigor:* The extent to which integration at the analysis stage is robust.

Interpretive rigor

- *Interpretive transparency:* The extent to which it is clear which findings emerged from which methods.
- *Interpretive consistency:* The extent to which inferences are consistent with findings on which they are based.
- *Theoretical consistency:* The extent to which inferences are consistent with current knowledge or theory.
- *Interpretive agreement:* The extent to which other researchers are likely to arrive at the same interpretations.
- *Interpretive distinctiveness:* The extent to which conclusions drawn are credible.
- *Interpretive efficacy:* The extent to which the metainferences from the whole study adequately reflect inferences that stem from both the qualitative and the quantitative findings and inferences.
- *Interpretive bias reduction:* The extent to which explanations are given for inconsistencies that emerge between the findings and inferences.
- *Interpretive correspondence:* The extent to which the inferences correspond to the purpose of the study.

(continued)

TABLE 13.1. *(continued)*

Inference transferability

- *Ecological transferability:* The extent to which metainferences/conclusions can be transferred to other contexts.
- *Population transferability:* The extent to which metainferences/conclusions can be transferred to other populations.
- *Temporal transferability:* The extent to which metainferences/conclusions can be transferred to the future.
- *Theoretical transferability:* The extent to which metainferences/conclusions can be transferred to other methods.

Reporting quality

- *Report availability:* The extent to which the study is successfully completed within allocated resources.
- *Reporting transparency:* The extent to which the key aspects of the study are reported.
- *Yield:* The extent to which the whole is greater than the sum of its parts.

Synthesizability[a]

- *Mixed research components:* Justification of the mixed methods design, combination of qualitative and quantitative data collection analysis techniques or procedures, and integration of qualitative and quantitative data or results.

Utility

- *Utility quality:* The extent to which the findings are used by consumers and policy makers.

Note. Based on O'Cathain (2010).
[a]O'Cathain (2010) recommends the use of Pluye, Gagnon, Griffiths, and Johnson-Lafleur's (2009) scoring system for appraising mixed research.

The next several domains—data quality, interpretive rigor, and transferability—are necessary in all rigorous research. However, in mixed studies, it is imperative that the standards of quality be met for qualitative, quantitative, and mixed research. Benge et al. (2010) met these standards by beginning with a large sample size ($N = 205$), using multiple data sources (i.e., the Nelson–Denny Reading Test and the Reading Interest Survey), and sophisticated data analysis techniques. The analytic scheme was a sequential mixed analysis (SMA; Onwuegbuzie & Teddlie, 2003; Tashakkori & Teddlie, 1998), which

> involved the use of both qualitative and quantitative data analysis procedures in a sequential manner—specifically, an iterative manner—commencing with quantitative analyses, followed by qualitative analyses that built upon the quantitative analyses, followed by quantitative analyses of the qualitative data. This sequence of analysis involved abductive reasoning that oscillated between inductive reasoning and deductive reasoning . . . (p. 6)

Furthermore, the goal of the SMA was typology development (Greene et al., 1989).

The SMA included six analytic stages utilizing descriptive statistics, thematic analysis, principal components analysis, correlations, canonical correlation analysis, and confirmatory analysis.

Perhaps, though, it is the reporting quality domain that truly makes this an exemplar study. That is, the written report of this study follows the format suggested in this chapter by detailing the 13 methodological steps. In fact, these steps are used as section headings, which aids in understanding the importance of each step in the research process. This study exemplifies the standards of quality in mixed research, and in doing so not only reports the findings, but also builds the case for the importance of mixed research in literacy.

CONCLUSIONS

Approximately 40 years have passed since the publication of the first mixed research article in a first-tier journal representing the field of literacy. Although this time period has witnessed rapid growth in the number of mixed research studies published that represent other fields, the field of literacy has not kept pace. Yet, as observed in the exemplar study discussed in this chapter, combining quantitative and qualitative research approaches has conceptual and methodological appeal, enabling literacy researchers "to be more flexible, integrative, and holistic in their investigative techniques, as they strive to address a range of complex research questions that arise" (Powell, Mihalas, Onwuegbuzie, Suldo, & Daley, 2008, p. 306).

REFERENCES

Adler, L. (1996). Qualitative research of legal issues. In D. Schimmel (Ed.), *Research that makes a difference: Complementary methods for examining legal issues in education* (NOLPE Monograph Series No. 56, pp. 3–31). Topeka, KS: National Organization on Legal Problems of Education.

American Education Research Association. (2006). Standards for reporting on empirical social science research in AERA publications. *Educational Researcher, 35*(6), 33–40.

Bangi, Y. I. (2018). Prevalence of mixed methods research in education journals. *International Journal of Academic Research in Business and Social Sciences, 8,* 109–122.

Bauman, J. F., Edwards, E. C., Font, G., Tereshinki, C. A., Kame'enui, E. J., & Olejnik, S. (2002). Teaching morphemic and contextual analysis to fifth-grade students. *Reading Research Quarterly, 37,* 150–176.

Benge, C., Onwuegbuzie, A. J., Mallette, M. H., & Burgess, M. L. (2010). Doctoral students' perceptions of barriers to reading empirical literature: A mixed analysis. *International Journal of Doctoral Studies, 5*, 55–77.

Bloodgood, J. W. (1999). What's in a name?: Children's name writing and literacy acquisition. *Reading Research Quarterly, 34,* 342–367.

Brewer, J., & Hunter, A. (1989). *Multimethod research.* Thousand Oaks, CA: SAGE.

Bryman, A. (1992). Quantitative and qualitative research: Further reflections on their integration. In J. Brannen (Ed.), *Mixing methods: Qualitative and quantitative research* (pp. 89–111). Aldershot, UK: Avebury Press.

Calfee, R., & Sperling, M. (2010). *On mixed methods: Approaches to language and literacy research.* New York: Teachers College Press.

Campbell, D. T. (1957). Factors relevant to the validity of experiments in social settings. *Psychological Bulletin, 54,* 297–312.

Chen, H. T. (2006). A theory-driven evaluation perspective on mixed methods research. *Research in the Schools, 13*(1), 75–83.

Christ, T. W. (2010, April). *Critical realism and pragmatism as a lens for mixed methods research.* Paper presented at the annual meeting of the American Educational Research Association, Denver, CO.

Collins, K. M. T., Onwuegbuzie, A. J., & Sutton, I. L. (2006). A model incorporating the rationale and purpose for conducting mixed methods research in special education and beyond. *Learning Disabilities: A Contemporary Journal, 4,* 67–100.

Creswell, J. W., & Plano Clark, V. L. (2017). *Designing and conducting mixed methods research* (3rd ed.). Thousand Oaks, CA: SAGE.

Creswell, J. W., & Poth, C. N. (2018). *Qualitative inquiry and research design: Choosing among five approaches* (4th ed.). Thousand Oaks, CA: SAGE.

Cronenberg, S. (2020). Paradigm parley: A framework for the dialectic stance. *Journal of Mixed Methods Research, 14*(1), 26–46.

Denscombe, M. (2008). Communities of practice: A research paradigm for the mixed methods approach. *Journal of Mixed Methods Research, 2,* 270–283.

Fareed, A. H. (1971). Interpretive responses in reading history and biology: An exploratory study. *Reading Research Quarterly, 6,* 493–532.

Fetters, M. D., & Freshwater, D. (2015). The 1 + 1 = 3 integration challenge. *Journal of Mixed Methods Research, 9,* 115–117.

Freppon, P. A. (1991). Children's concepts of the nature and purpose of reading in different instructional settings. *Journal of Reading Behavior, 23,* 139–163.

Garner, R. (1980). Monitoring of understanding: An investigation of good and poor readers' awareness of induced miscomprehension of text. *Journal of Reading Behavior, 12,* 55–63.

Gaskins, R. W. (1996). "That's just how it was": The effect of issue-related emotional involvement on reading comprehension. *Reading Research Quarterly, 31,* 386–405.

Glass, G. V. (1976). Primary, secondary, and meta-analysis of research. *Educational Researcher, 5*(10), 3–8.

Greene, J. C. (2006). Toward a methodology of mixed methods social inquiry. *Research in the Schools, 13*(1), 93–98.

Greene, J. C. (2008). Is mixed methods social inquiry a distinctive methodology? *Journal of Mixed Methods Research, 2,* 7–22.

Greene, J. C., Caracelli, V. J., & Graham, W. F. (1989). Toward a conceptual framework for mixed-method evaluation designs. *Educational Evaluation and Policy Analysis, 11*, 255–274.

Guba, E. G., & Lincoln, Y. S. (1989). *Fourth generation evaluation*. Newbury Park, CA: SAGE.

Hammersley, M. (1992). Deconstructing the qualitative–quantitative divide. In J. Brannen (Ed.), *Mixing methods: Qualitative and quantitative research* (pp. 39–55). Aldershot, UK: Avebury Press.

Hitchcock, J. H., & Onwuegbuzie, A. J. (2020). Developing mixed methods crossover analysis approaches. *Journal of Mixed Methods Research, 14*(1), 63–83.

Houston, S. (2001). Beyond social constructionism: Critical realism and social work. *British Journal of Social Work, 31*, 845–861.

Johnson, R. B. (2017). Dialectical pluralism: A metaparadigm whose time has come. *Journal of Mixed Methods Research, 11*, 156–173.

Johnson, R. B., & Christensen, L. (2020). *Educational research quantitative, qualitative, and mixed approaches* (7th ed.). Thousand Oaks, CA: SAGE.

Johnson, R. B., & Onwuegbuzie, A. J. (2004). Mixed methods research: A research paradigm whose time has come. *Educational Researcher, 33*(7), 14–26.

Johnson, R. B., Onwuegbuzie, A. J., & Turner, L. A. (2007). Toward a definition of mixed methods research. *Journal of Mixed Methods Research, 1*, 112–133.

Johnson, R. B., & Turner, L. A. (2003). Data collection strategies in mixed methods research. In A. Tashakkori & C. Teddlie (Eds.), *Handbook of mixed methods in social and behavioral research* (pp. 297–319). Thousand Oaks, CA: SAGE.

Lather, P. (1993). Fertile obsession: Validity after poststructuralism. *Sociological Quarterly, 34*, 673–693.

Leech, N. L., Dellinger, A., Brannagan, K. B., & Tanaka, H. (2010). Evaluating mixed research studies: A mixed methods approach. *Journal of Mixed Methods Research, 4*, 17–31.

Leech, N. L., & Onwuegbuzie, A. J. (2004). A proposed fourth measure of significance: The role of economic significance in educational research. *Evaluation and Research in Education, 18*, 179–198.

Leech, N. L., & Onwuegbuzie, A. J. (2009). A typology of mixed methods research designs. *Quality and Quantity: International Journal of Methodology, 43*, 265–275.

Leech, N. L., Onwuegbuzie, A. J., & Combs, J. C. (2011). Writing publishable mixed research articles: Guidelines for emerging scholars in the health sciences and beyond. *International Journal of Multiple Research Approaches, 5*(1), 7–24.

Lincoln, Y. S. (1995). Emerging criteria for quality in qualitative and interpretive research. *Qualitative Inquiry, 1*, 275–289.

Mallette, M. H., Moffit, C., Onwuegbuzie, A. J., & Wheeler, K. (2008, December). *Early literacy research: Exploring trends and political influences.* Paper presented at the annual meeting of the National Reading Conference, Orlando, FL.

Maxcy, S. J. (2003). Pragmatic threads in mixed methods research in the social sciences: The search for multiple modes of inquiry and the end of the philosophy of formalism. In A. Tashakkori & C. Teddlie (Eds.), *Handbook of mixed methods in social and behavioral research* (pp. 51–89). Thousand Oaks, CA: SAGE.

Maxwell, J. A. (1992). Understanding and validity in qualitative research. *Harvard Educational Review, 62*, 279–299.

Maxwell, J. A., & Loomis, D. M. (2003). Mixed methods design: An alternative approach. In A. Tashakkori & C. Teddlie (Eds.), *Handbook of mixed methods in social and behavioral research* (pp. 241–272). Thousand Oaks, CA: SAGE.

McEvoy, P., & Richards, D. (2006). A critical realist rationale for using a combination of quantitative and qualitative methods. *Journal of Research in Nursing, 11*, 66–78.

Mertens, D. (2003). Mixed methods and the politics of human research: The transformative-emancipatory perspective. In A. Tashakkori & C. Teddlie (Eds.), *Handbook of mixed methods in social and behavioral research* (pp. 135–164). Thousand Oaks, CA: SAGE.

Messick, S. (1995). Validity of psychological assessment: Validation of inferences from persons' responses and performances as scientific inquiry into score meaning. *American Psychologist, 50*, 741–749.

Miles, M., & Huberman, A. M. (1994). *Qualitative data analysis: An expanded sourcebook* (2nd ed.). Thousand Oaks, CA: SAGE.

Morse, J. M. (2003). Principles of mixed methods and multimethod research design. In A. Tashakkori & C. Teddlie (Eds.), *Handbook of mixed methods in social and behavioral research* (pp. 189–208). Thousand Oaks, CA: SAGE.

Newman, I., Ridenour, C. S., Newman, C., & DeMarco, G. M. P. (2003). A typology of research purposes and its relationship to mixed methods. In A. Tashakkori & C. Teddlie (Eds.), *Handbook of mixed methods in social and behavioral research* (pp. 167–188). Thousand Oaks, CA: SAGE.

O'Brien, D. G., & Martin, M. A. (1988). Does figurative language present a unique comprehension problem? *Journal of Reading Behavior, 20*, 63–87.

O'Cathain, A. (2010). Assessing the quality of mixed methods research: Towards a comprehensive framework. In A. Tashakkori & C. Teddlie (Eds.), *Handbook of mixed methods in social and behavioral research* (2nd ed., pp. 531–558). Thousand Oaks, CA: SAGE.

Onwuegbuzie, A. J. (2003). Expanding the framework of internal and external validity in quantitative research. *Research in the Schools, 10*(1), 71–90.

Onwuegbuzie, A. J., & Collins, K. M. T. (2007). A typology of mixed methods sampling designs in social science research. *The Qualitative Report, 12*, 281–316. Retrieved from *www.nova.edu/ssss/QR/QR12-2/onwuegbuzie2.pdf*.

Onwuegbuzie, A. J., & Combs, J. P. (2010). Emergent data analysis techniques in mixed methods research: A synthesis. In A. Tashakkori & C. Teddlie (Eds.), *Handbook of mixed methods in social and behavioral research* (2nd ed., pp. 397–430). Thousand Oaks, CA: SAGE.

Onwuegbuzie, A. J., & Corrigan, J. A. (2014). Improving the quality of mixed research reports in the field of human resource development and beyond: A call for rigor as an ethical practice. *Human Resource Development Quarterly, 25*(3), 273–299.

Onwuegbuzie, A. J., Daniel, L. G., & Collins, K. M. T. (2009). A meta-validation model for assessing the score-validity of student teacher evaluations. *Quality and Quantity: International Journal of Methodology, 43*, 197–209.

Onwuegbuzie, A. J., & Frels, R. K. (2016). *Seven steps to a comprehensive literature review: A multimodal and cultural approach.* London: SAGE.

Onwuegbuzie, A. J., & Hitchcock, J. H. (2019). Toward a fully integrated approach to mixed methods research via the 1 + 1 =1 integration approach: Mixed research 2.0. *International Journal of Multiple Research Approaches, 11*(1), 7–28.

Onwuegbuzie, A. J., Hitchcock, J. H., Natesan, P., & Newman, I. (2018). Using fully integrated Bayesian thinking to address the 1 + 1 = 1 integration challenge. *International Journal of Multiple Research Approaches, 10*(1), 666–678.

Onwuegbuzie, A. J., & Johnson, R. B. (2006). The validity issue in mixed research. *Research in the Schools, 13*(1), 48–63.

Onwuegbuzie, A. J., & Johnson, R. B. (2008). Mixed research. In R. B. Johnson & L. B. Christensen (Eds.), *Educational research: Quantitative, qualitative, and mixed approaches* (3rd ed., pp. 439–459). Thousand Oaks, CA: SAGE.

Onwuegbuzie, A. J., & Leech, N. L. (2006). Linking research questions to mixed methods data analysis procedures. *The Qualitative Report, 11,* 474–498. Retrieved from *www.nova.edu/ssss/QR/QR11-3/onwuegbuzie.pdf.*

Onwuegbuzie, A. J., & Leech, N. L. (2007). Validity and qualitative research: An oxymoron? *Quality and Quantity: International Journal of Methodology, 41,* 233–249.

Onwuegbuzie, A. J., & Leech, N. L. (2019). On qualitizing. *International Journal of Multiple Research Approaches, 11,* 98–131.

Onwuegbuzie, A. J., & Teddlie, C. (2003). A framework for analyzing data in mixed methods research. In A. Tashakkori & C. Teddlie (Eds.), *Handbook of mixed methods in social and behavioral research* (pp. 351–383). Thousand Oaks, CA: SAGE.

Parsons, S. A., Gallagher, M. A., & the George Mason University Content Analysis Team. (2016). A content analysis of nine literacy journals, 2009–2014. *Journal of Literacy Research, 48,* 476–502.

Patton, M. Q. (2002). *Qualitative research and evaluation methods.* Thousand Oaks, CA: SAGE.

Pluye, P., Gagnon, M., Griffiths, F., & Johnson-Lafleur, J. (2009). A scoring system for appraising mixed methods research, and concomitantly appraising qualitative, quantitative and mixed methods primary studies in mixed studies reviews. *International Journal of Nursing Studies, 46,* 529–546.

Powell, H., Mihalas, S., Onwuegbuzie, A. J., Suldo, S., & Daley, C. E. (2008). Mixed methods research in school psychology: A mixed methods investigation of trends in the literature. *Psychology in the Schools, 45,* 291–309.

Purcell-Gates, V., & Dahl, K. L. (1991). Low-SES children's success and failure at early literacy learning skills-based classroom. *Journal of Reading Behavior, 23,* 1–34.

Putnam, H. (2002). *The collapse of the fact/value dichotomy and other essays.* Cambridge, MA: Harvard University Press.

Rescher, N. (2000). *Realistic pragmatism: An introduction to pragmatic philosophy.* Albany: State University of New York Press.

Roberts, A. (2002). A principled complementarity of method: In defense of methodological eclecticism and the qualitative–qualitative debate. *The Qualitative Report, 7*(3), 1–18. Retrieved from *www.nova.edu/ssss/QR/QR7-3/roberts.html.*

Rorty, R. (1991). *Objectivity, relativism, and truth: Philosophical papers* (Vol. 1). Cambridge, UK: Cambridge University Press.

Sandelowski, M., & Barroso, J. (2003). Creating metasummaries of qualitative findings. *Nursing Research, 52,* 226–233.

Sandelowski, M., & Barroso, J. (2006). *Handbook for synthesizing qualitative research.* New York: Springer.

Sandelowski, M., Voils, C. I., & Barroso, J. (2006). Defining and designing mixed research synthesis studies. *Research in the Schools, 13*(1), 29–40.

Sanscartier, M. D. (2020). The craft attitude: Navigating mess in mixed methods research. *Journal of Mixed Methods Research, 14*(1), 47–62.

Tashakkori, A., & Creswell, J. W. (2007a). Developing publishable mixed methods manuscripts [Editorial]. *Journal of Mixed Methods Research, 1,* 107–111.

Tashakkori, A., & Creswell, J. W. (2007b). Exploring the nature of research questions in mixed methods research [Editorial]. *Journal of Mixed Methods Research, 1,* 207–211.

Tashakkori, A., & Teddlie, C. (1998). *Mixed methodology: Combining qualitative and quantitative approaches* (Applied Social Research Methods Series, Vol. 46). Thousand Oaks, CA: SAGE.

Tashakkori, A., & Teddlie, C. (2003). The past and future of mixed methods research: From data triangulation to mixed model designs. In A. Tashakkori & C. Teddlie (Eds.), *Handbook of mixed methods in social and behavioral research* (pp. 671–701). Thousand Oaks, CA: SAGE.

Teddlie, C., & Johnson, R. B. (2009). Methodological thought since the 20th century. In C. Teddlie & A. Tashakkori (Eds.), *Foundations of mixed methods research: Integrating quantitative and qualitative techniques in the social and behavioral sciences* (pp. 62–82). Thousand Oaks, CA: SAGE.

Teddlie, C., & Tashakkori, A. (2006). A general typology of research designs featuring mixed methods. *Research in the Schools, 13*(1), 12–28.

Teddlie, C., & Tashakkori, A. (2009). *Foundations of mixed methods research: Integrating quantitative and qualitative approaches in the social and behavioral sciences.* Thousand Oaks, CA: SAGE.

Teddlie, C., & Yu, F. (2007). Mixed methods sampling: A typology with examples. *Journal of Mixed Methods Research, 1,* 77–100.

Wilkinson, I. A. G., & Staley, B. (2019). On the pitfalls and promises of using mixed methods in literacy research: Perceptions of reviewers. *Research Papers in Education, 34*(1), 61–83.

CHAPTER 14

Narrative Approaches

EXPLORING THE PHENOMENON AND/OR METHOD

M. Kristiina Montero
Rachelle D. Washington

I believe one of the principal ways in which we acquire,
hold, and digest information is via narratives.
—Toni Morrison (1993)

Fundamental to understanding narrative as a research method and/or phenomenon to be studied is that people live out their lives narratively. People relate their lived experiences as stories—actual, fictional, or hypothetical. Some write them down while others engage in their oral tellings or retellings. Lived experiences can be narrated in linguistic (e.g., prose, poetry, oral storytelling) or nonlinguistic (e.g., painting, photography, collage, music, film, dance, sculpture) ways or some combination of the two (Barone & Eisner, 2006; Eisner, 1997).

Narrative research is about understanding experience as lived and told stories that capture unquantifiable personal and human dimensions of life (Clandinin & Connelly, 2000). It is the systematic study of plots, "the narrative structure through which people understand and describe the relationship among the events and choices of their lives" (Polkinghorne, 1995, p. 7), as well as a form of inquiry in which the researcher studies the lives of individuals and asks one or more individuals to provide stories about their lives through living, telling, retelling, and/or reliving (Connelly & Clandinin, 2006). Narrative research, a collaborative effort between researcher and participants, is an effective way to see the world through the eyes of others by using the lived, told, retold, and/or relived experiences as theory, data, and method. The narratives become subjects of interpretation

291

to be guided by the various epistemological stances that guide individual and collective research agendas.

Through narratives, researchers and writers use multiple lenses to access richly textured human experiences (Coles, 1989; Morrison, 1993; Polkinghorne, 1988). These experiences can be captured in audio and video recordings and in transcriptions, field notes, journals, cultural artifacts, and other types of texts and have traditionally been analyzed and represented as autobiography, biography, and memoir, autoethnography, personal narrative, life and oral history, and forms of literary journalism (Alvermann, 2000). The globalized and far more socially conscious world in which we live facilitates communication across sociocultural, geopolitical, and socioeconomic boundaries. With this comes the need for a multifaceted understanding of narrative.

Autobiography, biography, and memoir, for example, have evolved as more a Western narrative construction and may not exist as genres in non-Western cultures or may exist differently from temporally structured Western narratives (Pavlenko, 2002). Because the organizational plot of any given story is not universal in nature, but bound by myriad sociocultural rules of form and purpose, and narrative research involves the study of human experiences as expressed in narrative, researchers need to carefully consider their research subjectivities and knowledge of narrative structure when reading and/or conducting cross-cultural narrative research. For example, in Africanist traditions, oral storytelling is cyclical in nature, and storytelling structures have been expressed through ring circles, which, in addition to linguistic communication, offer dance as communicative, spiritual, and sacred. Dau (2007), a member of the Dinka tribe in Sudan, explained how storytelling took on an important educational role to his people:

> I never had formal schooling in Duk County. The only schools were Muslim ones for the Arabs in the north, or Christian ones in the biggest villages of the south. But I did have an informal education based on stories and riddles. Father and mother told them at home, and the children shared them as well. The youngest boys and girls took their goats and sat under a tree to swap stories. I sat with them often. (p. 30)

Narrated experiences are open to interpretation (Bakhtin, 1935/1981), and in narrative inquiry narrated experiences must be interpreted. A narrative researcher accommodates the story, the teller, the context, and the listener by melding data collected from various sources into a collective narrative (Creswell, 2007; Patton, 2002). As a result, narratives are the stories that are lived, reserved, stored, storied, told, collected, written, researched, and validated. When dealing with narrative research that crosses sociocultural boundaries, the crises of legitimation and representation (Alvermann, 2000) are further compounded.

KEY HISTORY OF NARRATIVE INQUIRY
IN LITERACY RESEARCH

Narrative inquiry has its intellectual roots in *narratology*. Some researchers' initial foray into narratives began by "drawing on narratology and the practices of writers" (Coulter & Smith, 2009, p. 608). The theory and study of narrative structure and its effects on the way individuals perceive the world around them is rhizomatic. The study of narrative occurs across myriad disciplines: literary theory, history, anthropology, drama, art, film, theology, philosophy, psychology, linguistics, and education in general (Connelly & Clandinin, 1990, p. 2). Relatively speaking, narrative inquiry is a growing methodology in education and the social sciences (Connelly & Clandinin, 2006), but in literacy education it is only in its embryonic stages.

Connelly and Clandinin (2006), leading authorities in narrative inquiry research in educational contexts, noted that narrative inquiry was only included in the last iteration of the American Education Research Association's *Handbook of Complementary Methods for Research in Education* (Green, Camilli, & Elmore, 2006); it did not appear in its preceding edition (Jaeger, 1988). Similarly, narrative inquiry was not included among the literacy research methodologies highlighted in the first edition of this book (Duke & Mallette, 2004). This omission was not a negligent act; rather, we believe it was narrative inquiry's lack of presence among influential literacy-related research. Simply put, narrative approaches to literacy research were not on the radar screen of most literacy researchers.

A landmark exploration of narrative approaches in literacy research appeared in the *Handbook of Reading Research*, Volume 3 (Kamil, Mosenthal, Pearson, & Barr, 2000). In Chapter 9 of the handbook, Alvermann (2000) presented literacy researchers with issues that define narrative inquiry as a way of knowing and writing and the implications of these issues for research and practice in literacy. She also provided three examples of how literacy researchers used narrative approaches to understand their own literate lives and the lives of those whom they study. However, because of the nascent nature of narrative inquiry in literacy research, the examples did not explicitly explore narrative inquiry, either as a method or as a phenomenon; rather, the examples were based on Alvermann's accurate interpretation of narrative approaches (autobiography and genres of narrative representation: performance texts and confessionals) as used in literacy-related research. A rich tradition of narrative inquiry has developed in the field of teacher education over the past two decades; however, narrative inquiry and inquiry into narrative as explicitly stated research methods have emerged in literacy researchers' gold standard publishing outlets (*Journal of Literacy Research* and *Reading Research Quarterly*) since approximately 2004.

In the field of literacy research, narrative research seems to be attractive to those who define literacy broadly. Such a definition considers the

294   LITERACY RESEARCH METHODOLOGIES

social, cultural, historical, and political dimensions of literacy: for example, a multiliteracies definition of literacy, which focuses on broader modes of representation—linguistic, visual, audio, spatial, and gestural (Cope & Kalantzis, 2000)—or a definition of literacy as a social process (Barton, 1994; Street, 1995). It is also interesting to scholars who approach their work from a critical theory and social justice perspective because narrative inquiry has the potential to address grassroots issues such as learning about the impact of authentic writing experiences for incarcerated youth (Gordon, McKibbin, Vasudevan, & Vinz, 2007) or gaining insight into early language and literacy development rooted in family, cultural, school, and community experiences and contexts (Lapadat, 2004).

NARRATIVE INQUIRY AS SOCIALLY JUST RESEARCH

Narrative inquiry has the potential to use forms of expression relevant to the examination and celebration of lives, like grandmothers or community members called *lanterns* (Edelman, 1999), Holocaust survivors, students of limited formal education, busing and/or segregation victims to name a few. Narrative researchers can offer contextually, temporally, and socially rich understandings about research topics, such as the cultural contexts of literacy, literacy practices and processes, and literacy learning and teaching.

Narrative inquiry explores questions that lead to the understanding of storied human experiences and their impact on past, present, and future experiences of participants and researchers. It is a mode of inquiry that lends itself nicely to exploring questions about the relationship between thought and action (Hankins, 2003). For example, Montero's doctoral student, Joanne O'Toole, studied the contribution of prior language-learning experiences to the personal practical knowledge general education teachers draw on when teaching English language learners (ELLs) by exploring teachers' language-learning experiences, how they made sense of these experiences, and how these experiences impacted their attitudes toward ELLs and their teaching practices (O'Toole, 2010). Clandinin's doctoral students examined the lives of children, teachers, parents, and administrators as composed and lived out on school knowledge landscapes. Specifically, they examined what it meant to teach children in ethnically responsive and responsible ways and how parents were positioned in relation to the landscape of schools (Clandinin, Pushor, & Orr, 2007).

Narrative inquiry affords researchers a space to get up close and personal with their research participants. A valued characteristic in narrative inquiry design is that researchers need to deliberately imagine themselves as integral participants of the inquiry without necessarily being autobiographically involved. (The personal nature of narrative research is also viewed as an area of contention for individuals who believe that proximity to research distances oneself from objectivity of that which is being studied.) As narrative researchers, we aimed to decrease the distance between researcher and participant and opened ourselves to a form that was more congruent for the telling of stories. For example, in Washington, Bauer, Edwards, and McMillon-Thompson (2008), stories recollected from the authors' past lives and through dialoguing about both the process and product provided rich and diverse narratives of ways Black communities "do" language and literacy development. For example, consider the following:

> Every Sunday evening we attended Baptist Training Union where we learned about church etiquette, how to present ourselves properly in public, how to sit, walk, and curtsy. Everyone was taught how to speak clearly, using great inflection. Oral language development was a major part of our training. In fact, we practiced repeatedly until everything was second nature. (pp. 222–223)

According to Washington and her colleagues (2008), topics such as uncovering new literacies in and out of classrooms, acknowledging the role of family as a key to academic and social successes, using literacy to teach for social justice, and heightening awareness of ELLs' needs are brought into their classrooms via stories. Stories can provide insight into and significance of the larger society, protect children from the pain the authors felt, and promote the learning of the whole child. The authors' specific stories acknowledged the power of narratives and the opportunity to write new pages to a history that has silenced and marginalized their presence and insistence to "hear our [their] own hearts and voices" (Omolade, 1994, p. 9).

Within Africanist communities, church is among the many spaces that contribute to literacy development. Consider the insights made by Hankins (2003) about Randel, the first-grade preacher in her narrative inquiry. When studying Martin Luther King, Jr.'s birthday, a student announced to Hankins that he, too, knew how to preach. Hankins ignored the student at first. She admitted in her notes, her data, that she was tired and frustrated that morning and wanted to get through the day. The student's incessant hand waving and wriggling in his seat led Hankins to let him go to the front of the room.

> "Well Randel, if you were going to preach today, what would you say?" I fully expected him to shrug his shoulders or give me a one-sentence answer. Instead, he slowly rose to his feet, then stood behind his chair, looking down at his hands for a moment as they gripped the back of it.
>
> Then he squared his shoulders and raised his voice, hands and eyes in tandem saying, "Does anyone have a problem they'd like to *lift up* today?"
>
> The children came to attention, as I did, and he repeated the question, "I say! Does anyone have a problem they'd like to lift up today?"

He had the intonation of every Black preacher I'd ever heard. Then he began to move, to walk rhythmically a little to the right and a little to the left, issuing the call. We were all responding to it at varying levels. (pp. 35–36)

What unfurled was spectacular. Randel proceeded to engage his classmates and teacher in the prosody and performance demonstrated by Black preachers. Randel's call and response was well received by many of his peers, who were familiar with this cultural practice. Hankins's (2003) use of narrative as theory, data, and method revealed experiences that articulate common mis/understandings. Students' agency and literacy development through performance found its place inside her classroom *and* alongside other acceptable literacy practices by incorporating culturally congruent practices, such as performance, into her teaching practice. Through Randel, we learn how students' cultural contexts allow us to hear the voice of the unheard.

As we look at those who arrived at their voice, largely represented in published autobiographies, biographies, and memoirs, there exist unheard voices that are equally relevant to understanding human experiences. Narrative research creates a space to listen to the voices of the unheard and to learn from them in a representation of their voice. In oral history and life history research, for example, one of its purposes is "to offer a voice to the unheard and unseen" (Howarth, 1998, p. v). Examples of such purpose can be seen in the work of Clegg (1997), who recorded the experiences of students who attended one-room schoolhouses in Texas; of Santoli (1988), who traveled across the United States and recorded the experiences of immigrants to the United States; and of Terkel (1972/1990), who recorded the experiences of the blue-collar worker in his book *Working: People Talk About What They Do All Day and How They Feel About What They Do*. In each of these oral history exemplars, the oral historians worked with everyday people. Terkel poignantly stated that he purposefully left out the voices of the dentists, doctors, and clergy people of the world because they had other forums in which to express themselves.

Conversely, narratives that reconnoiter the disruption of *common misunderstandings* (Barone, 2009; Coulter & Smith, 2009; Riessman, 1993) of those who reside on the periphery of society can benefit from the integration of narrative works in general and in literacy research specifically. To that end, there has to be a place to celebrate participants' performance (Hankins, 2003); unparallel storytelling (Pavlenko, 2002); cultural habits and language practices (Delpit, 1995; Heath, 1983); or definition of story (Coulter & Smith, 2009; Morrison, 1993). The richness of voice, of embodied presence available in modes (e.g., auditory, gestural, visual) tend to lie flat in traditional modes. However, narratives with its supportive strategies and techniques (e.g., poetic inquiry, arts-based inquiry, performance) possess a potent power for the otherwise powerless to effect change beyond the old modes of support, which have served the underrepresented or oppressed in limited ways.

Analyzing narratives can be seen as a "flexible and responsive methodology" that allows the voices of the participants to shine (Johnson-Bailey, 2002, p. 235); therefore, when using identifiers to draw attention to details in stories and to answer questions (Alexander, 1988; Etter-Lewis, 1993), the use of indicators of salience, such as frequency, omission, uniqueness, primacy, hesitation, negation, error, incompletion, and isolation (Alexander, 1988) could be identified as necessary elements in examining inquiry into narrative. As such, readers of research relying on the stories of human experience as primary sources of data "hope for a description and analysis of its complexity that identify concepts not previously seen or fully appreciated" (Glesne, 2005, p. 153).

Other researchers have found that—from self-study (Bullough & Pinnegar, 2001), study at the margins to center (hooks, 1996), study of the marginalized (Hankins, 2003; Johnson-Bailey, 2002, 2003), and study honoring the marginalized (Etter-Lewis, 1993)—documenting the lives of historically oppressed people can be transformative and celebratory. Riessman (1993) argued that narrative researchers must attend to what is said, the relationship between speakers, and how points are connected as key points in recognizing *story* as the object of investigation.

INQUIRY INTO NARRATIVE AND NARRATIVE INQUIRY: WHAT'S THE DIFFERENCE?

Narrative inquiry can be considered a subfield of qualitative research, which has the potential to address limitless questions concerning the qualities of human experience. It is used to describe research that relies on human stories as data, narrative in data analysis, and/or narrative as data representation. The distinctions and tensions are described in the literature under inquiry into narrative and/or analysis of narrative and narrative inquiry and/or narrative analysis. Note that the latter terms are the most confusing because they seem to connote a method; however, as is described later in this chapter, narrative inquiry or narrative analysis is both method and data or, for some, theory (Hankins, 2003). Narrative analysis, as described herewith, does not imply a method to analyze the various sources of narrative data as the term is used by Riessman (2008), Labov (1997) and Labov and Waletzky (1967/1997) or in methods of cultural (Tillman, 2002) and poetic (Prendergast, Leggo, & Sameshima, 2009) analyses, methods of data analysis that may offer unique vantage points of the stories of human experience. This said, such methods are useful when working with narrated stories as found in oral history or life history interview data, for example.

In this chapter, we try to clarify the confusion many novice researchers have between *inquiry into narrative* and *narrative inquiry*, but because inquiry into narrative receives greater attention in literacy research, we focus a large part of our attention on narrative inquiry. Both types of narrative research rely on many of the same data collection tools (e.g., interviews, journals/diaries, collection of artifacts, observation, field notes, data memos) as conventional qualitative research traditions. These tools help to elicit and capture the narrative construction through which people make sense of their lives and the lives of others. As with other forms of qualitative research, narrative approaches, generally, are small in scope and time-consuming. It is nearly impossible for one narrative researcher to work with many participants and still remain true to the process. The sociocultural contexts of participants, however, can be large (e.g., students' experiences in a school setting, children's experiences in an after-school reading program). For example, in recent work with students of interrupted formal education, Montero worked with a team of five doctoral students to understand the storied lives of 16 students from Burundi, Liberia, Somalia, Sudan, and Nepal (Montero et al., 2009).

Narrative can be used as a way of making sense of the data as well, and this is what primarily sets *inquiry into narrative* apart from *narrative inquiry*. As such, narrative inquiry has a "rough sense of narrative as both phenomena under study and method of study" (Clandinin & Connelly, 2000, p. 4). The narratives gathered through interview, for example, are the phenomenon of which narrative inquirers try to make sense, and narrative is also the method of analysis and representation. Some narrative researchers argue that interview data generate stories, and the narratives are ways of "recounting, constituting, representing and constructing the story" (Gordon, McKibbin, Vasudevan, & Vinz, 2007, p. 327). Qualitative researchers can and do produce powerful narratives; however, not all qualitative researchers are narrative researchers. Narrative inquiry moves beyond just telling stories; it retells and relives stories through analysis (Clandinin & Connelly, 1998, 2000). As such, narrative inquiry will rarely be presented uniquely as a narrative: Through the analysis, researchers make sense of the narratives under study (Bell, 2002).

Hankins (2003) creatively described narrative inquiry in the following manner: "Narrative data hold the confusions. Narrative methodology dissects it" (p. 15). Dissecting the confusion involves placing the narrative in a meaningful context that encompasses narrative inquiry's three elements: (1) temporality (understanding an event, person, or object in light of the past, present, and future); (2) sociality (understanding the personal conditions [e.g., feeling, hopes, desires] and the social conditions [e.g., environment, surrounding factors, forces]); and (3) place (understanding the geophysical space in which the inquiry takes place) (Connelly & Clandinin, 2006). To dissect the confusions in the data, we narrate, in linguistic and/or nonlinguistic ways, in research diaries, field texts, data memos, audio recordings, and drawings and doodles, for example, thereby making narrative the method as well as the data.

Narrating provides a space to think through, analyze, and process the confusions in the data. This also affords a space to incorporate data that are not part of the observable research (e.g., interview transcripts, field notes, examined archival documents, photographs) such as the narratives that take place during events, interpretive narratives about events, and/or the narrative that drove the selection of the event to analyze (Hankins, 2003). St. Pierre (1997) also offers us different types of nontraditional data—emotional, dream, sensual, and response—to interrupt the linear nature of narrative knowledge production in traditional qualitative research practices.

What serves as narrative data in narrative inquiry? Narratives are not found—they are co-constructed texts between researcher and participant (Riessman, 2008). Connelly and Clandinin (2006) describe two ways of conducting narrative inquiry: telling and living. *Telling* narrative inquiry focuses on the stories of life as lived and told in the past, such as those found in autobiographical, biographical, memoirs, and oral and life histories. These stories are best captured through interviews that are audio recorded and transcribed. It is the stories in the transcribed text that telling narrative inquirers must tease out and then make sense of through thematic, structural, dialogic/performance, and visual methods of analysis (Riessman, 2008), for example.

We relate Clandinin and Connelly's telling narrative inquiry to Polkinghorne's (1995) analysis of narrative or what Clandinin and Connelly (1994) termed *inquiry into narrative*, which moves from stories to common elements by using told stories as the data to be analyzed with paradigmatic processes such as methods consistent with grounded theory (Glaser & Strauss, 1967; Strauss & Corbin, 1998). In inquiry into narrative, researchers' interests are on the stories told or the interpretations and meaning generated (Connelly & Clandinin, 2006) in an effort to answer how and why a particular outcome came about or to understand how an individual acted in the concrete social world (Polkinghorne, 1995). Over a decade later, Polkinghorne (Clandinin & Murphy, 2007) went on record saying that analysis of narrative is a more general form of qualitative research and is not true to narrative inquiry, "which understands lives as unfolding temporally, as particular events within a particular individual's life" (Clandinin & Murphy, 2007, p. 636). Because this distinction has been made, researchers must be careful not to equate the analysis of interview data with narrative inquiry simply because "stories" were analyzed or a narrative text has been generated as part of the research findings. Key to narrative inquiry, whether telling or living, are the common elements of narrative inquiry discussed earlier in the chapter. It might be useful to think of narrative inquiry as an ecological, grassroots, and comprehensive approach to studying human experiences.

At this point in the history of literacy research, it is *inquiry into narrative* that one will find in most peer-reviewed academic journals. We believe that inquiry into narrative offers the literacy research community insights that perhaps would not easily be made without analyzing the lived experiences of others. For example, Chandler-Olcott and Kluth's (2008) examination of parents' roles in supporting the literacy development of students with autism analyzed narrative using book-length autobiographies authored directly by individuals with autism. According to the norms of inductive data analysis, these researchers developed a set of criteria by which to choose the texts and then began to analyze them inductively by first developing a coding scheme and then reading the identified texts and analyzing them according to the rules they devised. On the basis of their inquiry into narrative, Chandler-Olcott and Kluth provided the literacy research community with insights into the various roles parents played in supporting literacy development for their children with autism-spectrum labels and advance preliminary knowledge about literacy development for students with autism researched from the perspective of individuals living with the disorder. Certainly, this is an advantage of narrative research: insight into an issue of interest from the perspective of those directly impacted. In this example, narrative research offers voice to the traditionally unheard and, therefore, could be considered, as we suggest, a socially just research methodology.

Living narrative inquiry is what distinguishes narrative inquiry most drastically from other modes of qualitative research. We relate Clandinin and Connelly's (2007) *living* narrative inquiry to Polkinghorne's (1995) narrative analysis, which moves from elements to stories and where the focus is on the local and the individual in relation to larger social, cultural, historical, and political contexts. Narrative analysis is a collection of described events that are synthesized or configured by a plot into a story or into a multitude of stories (Polkinghorne, 1995).

The path to narrative inquiry is not direct; rather, it is full of twists and turns (Clandinin & Connelly, 2000; Pinnegar & Daynes, 2007). Researchers often turn from positivistic research conceptions to narrative inquiry when they question the use of numbers as the exclusive way of representing data about human experience and/or question the adequacy of quantifiable data (survey questions, test scores) to account for the experiences they represent (Pinnegar & Daynes, 2007). The path to narrative inquiry is quick for some authors, and slow—perhaps spiraling or retreating—for others. We argue that the research traditions of any specific field of study frames how different approaches to research are communicated in the early stages of entrée into the field.

Considering the positivistic research traditions in literacy research (e.g., one of the gold standard journals for the field, *Journal of Literacy Research*, was called *Journal of Reading Behavior* until 1995), it is not surprising that in 1999, when Fitzgerald and Noblit published their study of first-grade ELLs' emergent reading, narrative inquiry was not identified as a methodological framework. Rather, they seemed to have written up their research framed according to the norms of the paradigmatic cognition (Polkinghorne, 1995) but having pushed the boundaries to be "more narrative than envisioned by Glaser and Strauss" (p. 174). Consider Fitzgerald's (1999) reflections on analyzing the data in her study, with Noblit, on first-grade ELLs' emergent reading. Their work echoes the characteristics of *living* narrative inquiry, the study of life as it unfolds:

> During my year with the children, my appraisal of the children's development happened daily. I was not just immersed in it; I was part of it, and it was part of me. . . . I had been listening to some of the children's oral reading tapes, and the children's voices on the tapes had quite suddenly made me feel closer to them . . . we talked about how we wanted the writing to convey some feeling about the scenes and the children and their families—because these were all central to the children's reading growth. . . . The interpretation of the data would be conveyed in part not just by what we said, but also by how we said it. "As we do the analyses and writing," George said, "think scene. Think "how can I show this, not tell it." (pp. 174–175)

Following suit to their narrative goals, the authors thought "scene" and were guided by the narrative research mantra: "How can I show this, not tell it?" (p. 175). Although Fitzgerald and Noblit (1999) did not explicitly state that they had engaged in a *living* narrative inquiry, their methodological description of data collection, analysis, and representation take into consideration many of the eight key elements of designing, conducting, and representing narrative inquiries (Clandinin et al., 2007), as described in the next section.

NARRATING STANDARDS: FIXED AND FLUID

The field of narrative inquiry is currently in a state of "fluid inquiry" (according to Schwab, as cited in Connelly & Clandinin, 2006)—a time "when longstanding assumptions and norms of a field are reexamined" (p. 478). As such, the criteria to define exemplary work in narrative inquiry are shifting as narrative researchers continue to define and redefine the method and phenomenon of their own work. Although guidelines for what constitutes quality narrative inquiry exist, the field of literacy research will eventually need to define its own criteria in recognition that "issues of quality and credibility intersect with audience and intended research purpose" (Patton, 2002, p. 1189) and explore in what ways narrative inquiry will best serve the field. For now, we can borrow and learn from researchers who engage in narrative inquiry across a variety disciplines.

What makes for good narrative research? The answer to this question largely depends on whether one considers *inquiry into narrative* or *narrative inquiry* (Connelly & Clandinin, 1990, p. 2). Standards for inquiry into narrative are more readily found in the literature because, as noted earlier, inquiry into narrative aligns more closely with well-established qualitative research (e.g., ethnography, case study, grounded theory). These methods have been widely used across time and disciplines, rich discussions have occurred over what is considered to be standards for quality research, and such standards have been more or less defined around the issues of trustworthiness and methodological rigor (see, e.g., Charmaz, 2005; Creswell, 2007; Lincoln & Guba, 1985; Miles & Huberman, 1994; Patton, 2002). Although the standards can be viewed as fixed in inductive types of research, they become more fluid in narrative inquiry research because the evaluation criteria are still under development (Connelly & Clandinin, 2006). Before beginning to delineate what defines "good" and "bad" narrative inquiry research, we would like to echo Smith and Hodkinson's (2005) thoughts that any list of criteria used to distinguish the "good" research from the "bad" can (and should) be challenged, changed, and/or modified according to the specific needs of the research under production.

When trying to explicitly lay out the standards of quality narrative inquiry, we found ourselves in a difficult position because those who engage in narrative inquiry generally believe that researchers should not get lost in policing the rigor of a field under development at the expense of developing the method (Mishler, 1999), that the criteria that will define quality narrative inquiry should develop naturally as narrative inquirers conduct and publish their research and generate a critical mass of studies from which more specific standards of quality can be amassed and put to the test of time. In the same way, exemplars will also be more readily identified; for example, in ethnography, Heath's (1983) *Ways with Words*, which continues to be cited as an exemplar, has stood the test of time. However, this rationale is not particularly useful, especially for the novice narrative inquirer, who may need a zoomed-in roadmap.

Connelly and Clandinin (2006) and Clandinin and colleagues (2007) stated that "good" narrative inquiry must address the commonplaces of narrative inquiry that frame the dimensions of the inquiry space (temporality, sociality, and place, as discussed earlier) and should be guided by eight key design elements. Next is a skeletal outline of the elements that should be considered when designing, conducting, and representing narrative inquiry research (for more detailed information on the key elements, we recommend you consult the previously cited texts):

1. Explicit details of the personal, practical, and social reasons to justify the research.
2. Explicit explanation of the phenomenon being studied through a narrative lens.
3. Explicit description of research methods used to study the phenomenon to figure out the kinds of field texts needed to research the phenomenon while being attentive to the three commonplaces.

4. Explicit description of the analysis and interpretation process while considering the importance of the contextual and relational.

5. Clear explanation of how the phenomenon under study is situated in relation to the existing literature both within and outside the epistemological and ontological assumptions of the research being undertaken.

6. Explicit explanation of how the distinctive lenses are used to inquire into the respective phenomena.

7. Explicit understanding that the ethical responsibilities of narrative inquiry go far beyond the ethical requirements of a university's ethics review board.

8. The research process, from beginning to end, must be narrative.

Clandinin, Connelly, and colleagues offer a detailed roadmap for evaluating narrative inquiry research; however, although their voices are prominent, they are not the only ones in the conversation. Next, we present what some of the conversations about quality narrative inquiry sound like.

Narrative inquiry distinguishes itself from traditional research methods in matters of purpose. It does not strive to discover and verify knowledge about the real state of the world; rather, it strives to portray experience, to question common understandings, and to offer a degree of interpretive space (Coulter & Smith, 2009, p. 577). Narrative inquiry is about questioning rather than hypothesizing, listening rather than categorizing, and presenting ambiguities rather than certainties (Gordon et al., 2007). Because narrative inquiry differs from paradigmatic research methods, Connelly and Clandinin (1990) caution that researchers cannot force traditional quantitatively oriented language, such as validity, reliability, and generalizability, to evaluate narrative research. Qualitative researchers like Denzin and Lincoln (2003), Lincoln and Guba (1985), and Peshkin (1988) have been making this point for decades, and narrative inquirers insist to join the same conversation.

Researchers conducting narrative inquiry have begun to acknowledge certain characteristics of quality pieces of narrative inquiry. Clandinin and Connelly argue that Van Maanen's (1988) criteria have been put forth as a starting point: *apparency* (easy to see and understand), *verisimilitude* (the quality of appearing to be true or real), and *transferability* (makes connections between elements of the study and readers' own experiences). Blumenfeld-Jones (1995) suggested that "fidelity" be a criterion for practicing and evaluating narrative research. Key to understanding fidelity is contrasting it with truth. He noted that in narrative inquiry it is not important to confirm or disconfirm the told story of experience (as historiographers try to do); rather, what is valued is that the researcher be able to accurately represent what the experience meant to the teller of the tale. Hence, fidelity according to Blumenfeld-Jones is "an obligation to preserve the bonds between the teller and receivers by honoring the self-report of the teller and the obligation of the original teller to be as honest as possible in the telling" (p. 28).

Our aim is to list criteria that are more specific to narrative inquiry. A good starting point to understanding what is valued in narrative inquiry research is eliminating that which is unvaluable, in other words, identifying characteristics of a "bad" narrative inquiry. Connelly and Clandinin (1990) noted that good pieces of narrative inquiry avoid the following errors: writing up the narrative of inquiry with "the illusion of causality" (p. 7) and writing numerous "I's" (researcher participant, teacher) with an uncomfortable fraternal intimacy. Narrative inquiry aims to explain the whole: Narratives should not be driven toward a model of cause and effect; rather, a narrative helps explain the big picture in such a way that the reader is always connected to the whole without getting lost in the minutiae.

A good narrative influences the thinking, inquiry, and writing of other researchers. Peshkin (cited in Connelly & Clandinin, 1990, p. 8) suggested that a test to this end is to have others read the narrative inquiry research text and respond to a question such as "What do you make of it for your situation?" The transferability of the narrated experience is personal in nature, and one can only confirm the effect of the research text's transferability by receiving feedback from those who have read it. For example, evidence that there was transferability of Hankins's work was demonstrated in Dwayne Wright's thoughts, as quoted by Allen (2003), after having read her book.

> Dr. Hankins' book affected me as a teacher, researcher, activist, and human being. . . . Although [much] educational research focuses on those who are on the periphery of society, their actual voices are not present in the research. Hankins' narratives provide the vehicle for the historic voiceless to take part in the construction of the classroom. (p. x)

Additionally, when writing across the different voices represented in narrative inquiry, the writer (researcher) must be careful to respect the role of researcher subjectivities (Peshkin, 1988). Should these subjectivities get muddled, the generated narratives become chaotic in nature and, therefore, have more inherent limitations than application.

Researchers need to confront candidly issues of quality in research and particularly to thwart challenges associated with qualitative designs (Patton, 2002). To that end, researchers' tasks involve consideration of power and positionality coupled with deliberate jottings and note takings related to the same (Hankins, 2003; Wolcott, 2009). For example, Hankins noted how eye-opening these practices could be as she struggled with her subjectivities, power, and position. In one narrative account of children, she wrote:

> There are common teacher gripes about children which I abhor, argue against, am sickened by. There are statements such as "He started

behind." " . . . I know what to do; I just need better clients." I fight those words but accept too easily the confirmation I see everywhere that education is not the promise for poor children of color that it is for "us" [White, middle-class teachers]. It is monstrous that I moved all kinds of boundaries in my thinking when Eric [White student] couldn't read and added extra support to the fences of acceptance that Tommy [Black student] couldn't read. (p. 90)

Reflexivity aids researchers and practitioners in the telling of their work. Hankins's willingness to open up her teaching and learning journals, to "bear the burden," allows readers to witness the power of reflexive practice.

Narrative inquiry may be challenging to grasp for some readers because the "answers" may not be explicitly provided in a "findings" section of a research report; rather, they are found in contextualized text obtained through interpreted narratives of lived experience. To evaluate narrative inquiry, one must be of a narrative mindset when asking questions such as: Is the narrative inquiry easy to understand? Does the narrative appear to be real or true? Does the text transact with the reader in meaningful ways? What does the reader make of the text? Note that some of these questions cannot be answered unless multiple readers engage in the evaluation process.

EXEMPLARS OF NARRATIVE INQUIRY

To date, the use of narrative inquiry in literacy research has been limited both in quantity and in types of experience examined. Literacy researchers have primarily examined autobiographical (oral or written) accounts of experiences (e.g., Bell, 1995; Chandler-Olcott & Kluth, 2008; Lapadat, 2004; Lazar, 2007; McKinney & Giorgis, 2009; Perry, 2007, 2008; Rogers, Marshall, & Tyson, 2006; Syed, 2008) conducted in the framework of *inquiry into narrative*. Because narrative inquiry research is text-heavy, many article-length reports discuss the methodological issues, for the most part, and narrative inquiry research is more completely written up as monographs. In educational studies, most of the exemplars we found were in the field of teacher education (see, e.g., Clandinin & Huber, 2005; Craig, 2009; Johnson & Golombek, 2002), perhaps because narrative inquiry is a methodology that appeals to teachers and teacher educators (Clandinin et al., 2007). Finding exemplars of narrative inquiry that explicitly examined issues related to literacy proved challenging. Herewith, we discuss two scholarly pieces: "Writing Out of the Unexpected: Narrative Inquiry and the Weight of Small Moments" (Gordon et al., 2007) and *Teaching through the Storm: A Journal of Hope* (Hankins, 2003).

Hankins's (2003) book-length narrative inquiry offers an example of a *living* narrative inquiry that uses narrative as data and method, whereas

Gordon and colleagues' (2007) article-length narrative inquiry addresses "one of the unexpected moments of the project" (p. 329) as a way to learn how to conduct narrative inquiry and to add to the knowledge base of how narrative inquiry can inform language and literacy education. The two examples are different but will, it is hoped, serve to illustrate the multiple layers of narrative inquiry.

Although it is outside the scope of this chapter to discuss all of the points that one could evaluate in a piece of narrative inquiry, we deemed it important to discuss briefly how the three commonplaces of narratives inquiry are simultaneously explored in narrative inquiry—the defining characteristics that set narrative inquiry apart from other forms of qualitative research that explores narrative structures. Therefore, a beginning place to identify "good" narrative research is to find work that addresses the commonplaces—temporality, sociality, and place—simultaneously.

What make makes these exemplars "good" narrative inquiry? Both exemplars, from the beginning, draw the reader into the work, much like an award-winning author seduces the nighttime reader to keep reading into the wee hours of the morning. The narratives are multidimensional, and in the analyses the authors explicitly identified how their work was constantly being reshaped as a result of new information and the reading and rereading of created narratives used as data and in analysis. As Hankins (2003) noted, "Narrative method requires me to contextualize each narrative within the history of the classroom, within my own knowledge of the participant's past, within narrative theory, and within pedagogical considerations" (p. 15).

Hankins demonstrated deep understandings of time, personal conditions, and place in which the inquiry takes place. Consider the following excerpt, in which Hankins places the reader within her research context and helps the reader understand all of the complexities of teaching literacy skills to first graders in a school that caters to children from families living at or near the poverty line:

> I remember that I reached out to touch her arm. "I promise I will not neglect him. I promise I will protect him and teach him where he is and take him as far as he can go with me. I also promise you that I will not refer him for any testing or special service. He is *your* child. Help me know what you want me to do; we will work together."
>
> I told her about my sister and the pain that I recognized as belonging also to my own life. She listened as I talked about Kathy's struggles as a child with brain damage from birth, the multiple learning problems and the accompanying emotional distress it caused for her and for our entire family. I talked briefly about the pain of the unfixable. I saw her silent acknowledgment of my mother's pain as the briefest hint of softness passed her face. She nodded and stood up.
>
> As we walked to the door together, I gave her my home number. She took it but did not put it in her purse, which she clutched less tightly now. She turned and said "OK, then . . . I'll call you next week." Her voice

seemed tired but there was no mistake in her message of watchfulness as she left. (pp. 3–4)

In this short excerpt, we gain a better understanding of a child's mother, who is angry toward the institution of school and is hypervigilant of her son's progress in the hands of the "system." Earlier in the narrative, Hankins provides the reader with information about the mother's past that influences her reactions in the present and how she will act in the future. Through the narrative, we are also privy to the personal conditions of both the mother's and the teacher's feelings—fears in particular. We are also privy to rich description about the physical environment in which the scene takes place. The narrative presents an ecology of the situation that is easy to understand, appears true, and has the potential to make connections between elements of the study and the reader's own experiences.

Gordon and colleagues (2007) worked as a research team to understand how authentic writing experiences could be used as a tool to engage incarcerated students in writing. The article they wrote was a way to work through the challenges of narrative inquiry, so in a sense they engaged in a narrative inquiry of their personal experience of putting thought to action. As they worked, they "constantly reviewed our fieldnotes, transcripts of our ongoing discussion, and the questions that interested each of us" (p. 328). They each decided to write about a particular situation that occurred during the project and shared these writings with each other, which methodologically is an interesting way to approach narrative inquiry done as a group project.

Learning about data representation and use of co-constructed stories occurred after one of the researchers wrote the following text and presented it to her research group:

A couple of weeks later, Elaine stopped me in the hallway to tell me what great success she was having with the oral histories. The students were reading and having animated discussions, and she was just about to assign the first writing assignment. I jumped at the chance when she invited me to listen as the kids read and discussed pieces from *Killing the Sky*. What I wasn't prepared for was how it felt to watch these student-readers, strangers to the Rikers Island student-writers I had come to know, interpret the lives and "characters" of the writers. It occurred to me that here was the—or at least one—audience that Jermaine and the others had been writing for, the nameless, faceless readers to whom they told their stories and had the power to "read" them as they wished. While on Rikers Island with Jermaine we could only imagine our readers, here was a very real classroom whose reading of the student-inmates cast new light on issues of representation. (Gordon et al., 2007, p. 344)

Resulting from the contextualized understanding of issues of representation in their work was an understanding that "collective narrative inquiry was less about the pursuit of consistency and more about the fuller understanding we can achieve through multiple perspectives" (Gordon et al., 2007, p. 348). What made this work interesting to us was that the article represented both the process and the product of their inquiry as highly contextualized. Narrative inquiry forges a space to show the process as part of the product.

CONCLUDING THOUGHTS

Realistically, we acknowledge that there will never be a paradigm shift to narrative inquiry in the field of literacy research (nor are we arguing that there should be); however, we believe there should be a place for researchers to examine the living, telling, retelling, and reliving of human experiences that flesh out the three commonplaces of human experience: temporality, sociality, and place (Connelly & Clandinin, 2006). By including more narrative inquiry in the literacy research repertoire, readers may become more intimately connected to others' experiences and may look at their own research and life experiences in different ways in order to exact change. The appropriateness of narrative research to study the storied human experiences is reiterated by Hankins (2003):

> Recognizing and piecing together what we understand of our own narratives and then connecting them, with some understanding, to the lives of others is somewhat like finding small pieces of a jigsaw puzzle that fit together, however gradually, to create a more complete picture. (p. 109)

Whether narratives help us make sense of our world as researchers or practitioners, we can use the diversity of narrative research to frame, invite, or expose issues relative to social justice, equity, classroom hierarchy, language habits and practices, curriculum and instruction, and literacy development inside and outside of schools.

REFERENCES

Alexander, I. E. (1988). Personality, psychological assessment, and psychobiography. In D. P. Adams & R. L. Ochberg (Eds.), *Psychobiography and life narratives* (pp. 265–294). Durham, NC: Duke University Press.

Allen, J. (2003). Foreword. In K. H. Hankins (Ed.), *Teaching through the storm: A journal of hope* (pp. ix–x). New York: Teachers College Press.

Alvermann, D. E. (2000). Narrative approaches. In M. J. Kamil, P. B. Mosenthal, P. D. Pearson, & R. Barr (Eds.), *Handbook of reading research: Volume III* (pp. 123–140). Mahwah, NJ: Erlbaum.

Bakhtin, M. M. (1981). Discourse in the novel (C. Emerson & M. Holquist, Trans.). In M. Holquist (Ed.), *The dialogic imagination* (pp. 259–422). Austin: University of Texas Press. (Original work published 1935)

Barone, D. (2009). Comments on Coulter and Smith: Narrative researchers as witnesses of injustice and agents of social change? *Educational Researcher, 38*(8), 591–597.

Barone, T., & Eisner, E. W. (2006). Arts-based educational research. In J. L. Green, G. Camilli, & P. B. Elmore (Eds.), *Handbook of complementary methods in education research* (pp. 95–110). Mahwah, NJ: Erlbaum.

Barton, D. (1994). *Literacy: An introduction to the ecology of written language.* Cambridge, MA: Blackwell.

Bell, J. S. (1995). The relationship between L1 and L2 literacy: Some complicating factors. *TESOL Quarterly, 29*(4), 687–704.

Bell, J. S. (2002). Narrative inquiry: More than just telling stories. *TESOL Quarterly, 36*(2), 207–213.

Blumenfeld-Jones, D. (1995). Fidelity as a criterion for practicing and evaluating narrative inquiry. *International Journal of Qualitative Studies in Education, 8*(1), 25–35.

Bullough, R., & Pinnegar, S. (2001). Guidelines for quality in autobiographical forms of self-study research. *Educational Researcher, 30*(3), 13–21.

Chandler-Olcott, K., & Kluth, P. M. (2008). "Mother's voice was the main source of learning": Parents' role in supporting the literacy development of students with autism. *Journal of Literacy Research, 40*(4), 461–492.

Charmaz, K. (2005). Grounded theory in the 21st century: Application in social justice. In N. K. Denzin & Y. S. Lincoln (Eds.), *Handbook of qualitative research* (3rd ed., pp. 507–535). Thousand Oaks, CA: Sage.

Clandinin, D. J., & Connelly, F. M. (1994). Personal experience methods. In N. K. Denzin & Y. S. Lincoln (Eds.), *Handbook of qualitative research* (pp. 413–427). Thousand Oaks, CA: Sage.

Clandinin, D. J., & Connelly, F. M. (1998). Asking questions about telling stories. In C. Kridel (Ed.), *Writing educational biography: Explorations in qualitative research* (pp. 245–254). New York: Garland.

Clandinin, D. J., & Connelly, F. M. (2000). *Narrative inquiry: Experience and story in qualitative research.* San Francisco: Jossey-Bass.

Clandinin, D. J., & Connelly, F. M. (Eds.). (2007). *Handbook of narrative inquiry: Mapping a methodology.* Thousand Oaks, CA: Sage.

Clandinin, D. J., & Huber, M. (2005). Shifting stories to live by: Interweaving the personal and professional in teachers' lives. In D. Beijaard, P. C. Meijer, G. Morine-Dershimer, & H. Tillema (Eds.), *Teacher professional development in changing conditions* (pp. 43–59). Dordrecht, The Netherlands: Springer.

Clandinin, D. J., & Murphy, M. S. (2007). Looking ahead: Conversations with Elliot Mishler, Don Polkinghorne, and Amia Lieblich. In D. J. Clandinin (Ed.), *Handbook of narrative inquiry: Mapping a methodology* (pp. 632–650). Thousand Oaks, CA: Sage.

Clandinin, D. J., Pushor, D., & Orr, A. M. (2007). Navigating sites for narrative inquiry. *Journal of Teacher Education, 58*, 21–35.

Clegg, L. B. (1997). *The empty schoolhouse: Memories of one-room Texas schools.* College Station: Texas A&M University Press.

Coles, R. (1989). *The call of stories: Teaching and the moral imagination.* Boston: Houghton Mifflin.

Connelly, F. M., & Clandinin, D. J. (1990). Stories of experience and narrative inquiry. *Educational Researcher, 19*(5), 2–14.

Connelly, F. M., & Clandinin, D. J. (2006). Narrative inquiry. In J. L. Green, G. Camilli, & P. B. Elmore (Eds.), *Handbook of complementary methods in education research* (pp. 477–487). Mahwah, NJ: Erlbaum.

Cope, B., & Kalantzis, M. (Eds.). (2000). *Multiliteracies: Literacy learning and the design of social futures.* New York: Routledge.

Coulter, C. A., & Smith, M. L. (2009). The construction zone: Literary elements in narrative research. *Educational Researcher, 38*(8), 577–590.

Craig, C. J. (2009). Research in the midst of organized school reform: Versions of teacher community in tension. *American Educational Research Journal, 46*(2), 598–619.

Creswell, J. W. (2007). *Qualitative inquiry and research design: Choosing among five approaches* (2nd ed.). Thousand Oaks, CA: Sage.

Dau, J. B. (2007). *God grew tired of us: A memoir.* Washington, DC: National Geographic.

Delpit, L. (1995). *Other people's children: Cultural conflict in the classroom.* New York: New Press.

Denzin, N. K., & Lincoln, Y. S. (Eds.). (2003). *Handbook of qualitative research* (3rd ed.). Thousand Oaks, CA: Sage.

Duke, N. K., & Mallette, M. H. (Eds.). (2004). *Literacy research methodologies.* New York: Guilford Press.

Edelman, M. W. (1999). *Lanterns: A memoir of mentors.* Boston: Beacon Press.

Eisner, E. W. (1997). The promise and perils of alternative forms of data representation. *Educational Researcher, 26*(6), 4–10.

Etter-Lewis, G. (1993). *My soul is my own: Oral narratives of African American women in the professions.* New York: Routledge.

Fitzgerald, J., & Noblit, G. W. (1999). About hopes, aspirations, and uncertainty: First-grade English-language learners' emergent reading. *Journal of Literacy Research, 31*(2), 133–182.

Glaser, B. G., & Strauss, A. L. (1967). *The discovery of grounded theory: Strategies for qualitative research.* New York: Aldine de Gruyter.

Glesne, C. (2005). *Becoming qualitative researchers.* New York: Allyn & Bacon.

Gordon, E., McKibbin, K., Vasudevan, L., & Vinz, R. (2007). Writing out of the unexpected: Narrative inquiry and the weight of small moments. *English Education, 39*(4), 326–351.

Green, J. L., Camilli, G., & Elmore, P. B. (Eds.). (2006). *Handbook of complementary methods in education research.* Mahwah, NJ: Erlbaum.

Hankins, K. H. (2003). *Teaching through the storm: A journal of hope.* New York: Teachers College Press.

Heath, S. B. (1983). *Ways with words.* Cambridge, UK: Cambridge University Press.

hooks, b. (1996). *Bone black: Memories of girlhood.* New York: Holt.

Howarth, K. (1998). *Oral history: A handbook.* Phoenix Mill, UK: Sutton.

Jaeger, R. M. (Ed.). (1988). *Complementary methods for research in education.* Washington, DC: American Educational Research Association.

Johnson, K. E., & Golombek, P. R. (Eds.). (2002). *Teachers' narrative inquiry as professional development.* Cambridge, UK: Cambridge University Press.

Johnson-Bailey, J. (2002). Cathy, the wrong side of the tank. In S. Merriam (Ed.), *Qualitative research in practice: Examples for discussion and analysis* (pp. 314–326). San Francisco: Jossey-Bass.

Johnson-Bailey, J. (2003). Enjoining positionality and power in narrative work: Balancing contentious issues and modulating forces. In K. deMarrais & S. D. Lapin (Eds.), *Perspectives and approaches for research in education and the social sciences* (pp. 123–138). Mahwah, NJ: Erlbaum.

Kamil, M., Mosenthal, P., Pearson, P. D., & Barr, R. (Eds.). (2000). *Handbook of reading research: Volume III*. Mahwah, NJ: Erlbaum.

Labov, W. (1997). Some further steps in narrative analysis. *Journal of Narrative and Life History, 7*(1–4), 395–415.

Labov, W., & Waletzky, J. (1997). Narrative analysis: Oral versions of personal experience. *Journal of Narrative and Life History, 7*, 3–38. (Original work published 1967)

Lapadat, J. C. (2004). Autobiographical memories of early language and literacy development. *Narrative Inquiry, 14*(1), 113–140.

Lazar, A. M. (2007). It's not just about teaching kids to read: Helping preservice teachers acquire a mindset for teaching children in urban communities. *Journal of Literacy Research, 39*(4), 411–443.

Lincoln, Y. S., & Guba, E. G. (1985). *Naturalistic inquiry*. Newbury Park, CA: Sage.

McKinney, M., & Giorgis, C. (2009). Narrating and performing identity: Literacy specialists' writing identities. *Journal of Literacy Research, 41*(1), 104–149.

Miles, M. B., & Huberman, A. M. (1994). *Qualitative data analysis* (2nd ed.). Thousand Oaks, CA: Sage.

Mishler, E. G. (1999). *Storylines: Craftartists narratives of identity*. Cambridge, MA: Harvard University Press.

Montero, M. K., Crandall, B., Mwambari, D., O'Toole, J., Stahl, N. A., Stevens, E., et al. (2009, December). *Local literacies, global visions: Documenting SIFEs' learning histories using oral history methodology*. Paper presented at the 58th National Reading Conference, Albuquerque, NM.

Morrison, T. (1993). Nobel lecture. In S. Allén (Ed.), *Nobel Lectures, Literature 1991–1995* (pp. 47–56). Singapore: World Scientific Publishing.

Omolade, B. (1994). *The rising song of African American women*. New York: Routledge.

O'Toole, J. (2010). *Language-learning experiences as a source of personal practical knowledge for general classroom teachers of English language learners*. Unpublished doctoral dissertation, Syracuse University.

Patton, M. Q. (2002). *Qualitative research and evaluation methods* (3rd ed.). Thousand Oaks, CA: Sage.

Pavlenko, A. (2002). Narrative study: Whose story is it, anyway? *TESOL Quarterly, 36*(2), 213–218.

Perry, K. H. (2007). Sharing stories, linking lives: Literacy practices among Sudanese refugees. In V. Purcell-Gates (Ed.), *Cultural practices of literacy: Case studies of language, literacy, social practice, and power* (pp. 57–84). Mahwah, NJ: Erlbaum.

Perry, K. H. (2008). From storytelling to writing: Transforming literacy practices among Sudanese refugees. *Journal of Literacy Research, 40*(2), 317–358.

Peshkin, A. (1988). In search of subjectivity—one's own. *Educational Researcher, 17*(7), 17–21.

Pinnegar, S., & Daynes, J. G. (2007). Locating narrative inquiry historically. In D. J. Clandinin (Ed.), *Handbook of narrative inquiry: Mapping a methodology* (pp. 3–34). Thousand Oaks, CA: Sage.

Polkinghorne, D. E. (1988). *Narrative knowing and human sciences*. Albany: State University of New York Press.

Polkinghorne, D. E. (1995). Narrative configuration in qualitative analysis. *International Journal of Qualitative Studies in Education, 8*(1), 5–23.

Prendergast, M., Leggo, C., & Sameshima, P. (Eds.). (2009). *Poetic inquiry: Vibrant voices in the social sciences*. Boston: Sense.

Riessman, C. K. (1993). *Narrative analysis* (Vol. 30). Thousand Oaks, CA: Sage.

Riessman, C. K. (2008). *Narrative methods for the human sciences*. Thousand Oaks, CA: Sage.

Rogers, T., Marshall, E., & Tyson, C. A. (2006). Dialogic narratives of literacy, teaching, and schooling: Preparing literacy teachers for diverse settings. *Reading Research Quarterly, 41*, 202–224.

Santoli, A. (1988). *New Americans: An oral history*. New York: Ballantine Books.

Smith, J. K., & Hodkinson, P. (2005). Relativism, criteria, and politics. In N. K. Denzin & Y. S. Lincoln (Eds.), *Handbook of qualitative research* (3rd ed., pp. 915–932). Thousand Oaks, CA: Sage.

St. Pierre, E. A. (1997). Methodology in the fold and the irruption of transgressive data. *International Journal of Qualitative Studies in Education, 10*(2), 175–189.

Strauss, A., & Corbin, J. (1998). *Basics of qualitative research: Techniques and procedures for developing grounded theory*. Thousand Oaks, CA: Sage.

Street, B. (1995). *Social literacies*. New York: Longman.

Syed, K. T. (2008). Voicing teachers' perspectives on professional development in literacy education. *Alberta Journal of Educational Research, 54*(3), 383–392.

Terkel, S. (1990). *Working: People talk about what they do all day and how they feel about what they do*. New York: Ballantine Books. (Original work published 1972)

Tillman, L. (2002). Culturally sensitive research approaches: An African-American perspective. *Educational Researcher, 31*(9), 3–12.

Van Maanen, J. (1988). *Tales of the field: On writing ethnography*. Chicago: University of Chicago Press.

Vasudevan, L., & Vinz, R. (2007). Writing out of the unexpected: Narrative inquiry and the weight of small moments. *English Education, 39*(4), 326–351.

Washington, R. D., Bauer, E., Edwards, P., & McMillon-Thompson, G. (2008). *Self-portraits of Black women scholars' literacy and identity*. In Y. Kim, V. V. Risko, D. Compton, D. Dickinson, M. Hundley, R. Jiménez, et al. (Eds.), *57th Yearbook of the National Reading Conference* (pp. 221–236). Chicago: National Reading Conference.

Wolcott, H. F. (2009). *Writing up qualitative research* (3rd ed.). Thousand Oaks, CA: Sage.

CHAPTER 15

Neuroimaging

Jessica A. Church
Jack M. Fletcher

The development of neuroimaging technologies permits an unprecedented look at human brain structure and function. Neuroimaging studies of the reading process attract attention in scientific circles, from educators, and from the mass media. Although many of these studies involve children and adults identified with reading difficulties, studies using neuroimaging tools also examine children in the process of learning to read. Excitingly, with the ongoing development of neuroimaging technology and child-friendly techniques, labs are collecting data from ever-younger children. Using a variety of structural and functional imaging modalities, these studies address fundamental questions about the neural mechanisms supporting reading development.

In this chapter, we examine the application of neuroimaging technologies to the study of reading. We begin with a brief explanation of different methods for structural and functional neuroimaging, focusing especially on functional magnetic resonance imaging (fMRI) studies because this method is seeing widespread application. We then examine a few recent results of studies applying these technologies to a variety of questions involving the neural correlates of reading, with a specific focus on evaluating changes in brain activation patterns over time during reading intervention. These studies are especially important because they demonstrate the malleability of the brain in response to learning to read, which is an acquired skill.

THE HUMAN BRAIN: A VERY BRIEF OVERVIEW

The human brain consists of neural cells (*neurons*); their connections (*dendrites* and *axons*); supportive cells (*glial cells*), which consist of many different types and their connections; and spaces (*ventricles*) filled with cerebrospinal fluid. Interestingly, while direct blood contact is toxic to the brain's cells, blood carries the critical fuel from the body to satisfy the brain's large energy demand (up to 20% of the body's total) relative to its size (about 2–3% of body weight). The brain is divided into anatomical lobes, all with left and right sides: The *cerebrum* consists of the frontal, parietal, temporal, and occipital lobes, while the *cerebellum* is a relatively separate structure that resides below the occipital lobes (see Figure 15.1). Neuronal cell bodies make up the *gray matter* of the brain and live near the surface of the brain, making up the *cortex*. Clumps of cell bodies deeper in the brain form the *subcortical nuclei* (e.g., the thalamus), which are critical relay stations for all sorts of different sensory, motor, and cognitive functions. Communication between neurons via their *axons* make up the *white matter* of the brain, so called because of the white, fatty insulation (*myelin*) around these connections, like coatings on electrical wires. The *corpus*

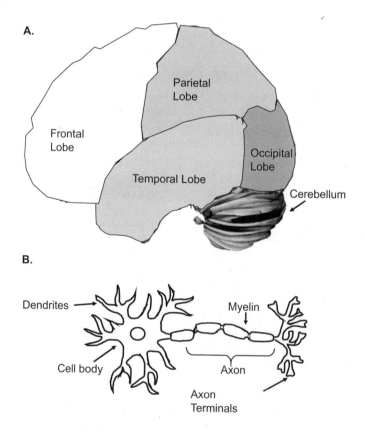

FIGURE 15.1. (A) The primary lobes of the cortex and the cerebellum. (B) Key parts of a neuron, the primary cell type of the brain.

callosum is an information superhighway of axons (neuronal connections) that transmits information between the two halves of the brain (between the left and right hemispheres). With different noninvasive neuroimaging techniques, we can study the structure of the brain in great detail; we can measure energy use related to the neuronal activity; and we can even estimate the motion of water molecules along different axon paths. We have come a long way in neuroimaging technologies over a relatively short time.

THE GOALS OF NONINVASIVE STUDY OF THE BRAIN

Neuroimaging research approaches aim to measure the structure and/or function of the human brain in a noninvasive manner. Structural neuroimaging captures high-resolution images of anatomy, allowing comparison of brain structures across different samples of people, or in the same individuals over time. Functional neuroimaging measures changes in brain activity over moments in time, or during a cognitive task, such as when a person is reading or listening to voices speak in familiar or unfamiliar languages. Functional neuroimaging depends on structural neuroimaging in order for researchers to know which areas of the brain participate when completing a particular task (e.g., deciding if two words rhyme).

One of the initial goals of functional neuroimaging was the localization of function to specific areas of the brain. Recently, however, functional neuroimaging researchers are also becoming interested in the brain as a series of interconnected networks that cooperate to perform cognitive functions. As illustrated in this chapter, it is an oversimplification to view neuroimaging as merely using medical tools to address social and behavioral research; however, much work remains before researchers can fully integrate neuroimaging findings with and translate them into educational practice. As with any method or technology, the research questions that drive the use of the method are the critical aspect. The use of theory and rationale behind the application of a particular neuroimaging tool, and the integration of results *across different methodologies* on a topic, such as reading, are how the field ultimately moves forward.

NEUROIMAGING ORIGINS

Both structural and functional neuroimaging have their origins in the need for noninvasive methods to examine clinical populations characterized by some form of brain injury, disease, or disorder. Prior to the advent of computed tomography (CT) scanning and magnetic resonance imaging (MRI) in the 1970s, methods for identifying brain abnormalities in clinical populations were often surgically invasive, based on attempts to follow radioactive tracers through the vascular system of the brain (angiography) or the injection of air into the ventricular system (pneumoencephalography). The resolution of these methods is poor.

For patients undergoing neurosurgery, it is always ideal not to injure the patient further by removing an area of the brain critical for language or motor function. Mapping studies to identify areas of the brain that are lesioned or responsible for seizures are critical to surgery and other treatment decisions. Reorganization of brain function can take place with aggressive tumors or early brain damage, further necessitating mapping approaches. Early functional mapping methods were also invasive, involving selective anesthesia of one of the cerebral hemispheres to broadly lateralize language or memory, known as the Wada technique (Wada & Rasmussen, 1960)—a technique still used as part of neurosurgical mapping today, especially for epilepsy, despite a growing number of less invasive approaches. For similar purposes, direct electrical stimulation of the cortex to map function in patients undergoing surgical removal of brain tissue for control of epilepsy dates back to the seminal studies of Penfield and Roberts (1959). A related approach, electrocorticography (ECoG)—begun by Penfield and Jasper, and elaborated for research (Miller et al., 2007)—places electrodes on the surface of the brain itself and monitors patients over time, sometimes days, in order to capture seizure activity as it happens.

LESION STUDIES

Studies of patient populations with brain injury, such as epilepsy or stroke, have long been used to advance hypotheses about the relations of brain and behavior. However, there are well-known limits of inferences from injury or disease. Damage to a particular area of the brain does not necessarily indicate that this area would mediate function in a non-brain-injured person and does not indicate how the behavior was acquired by the brain over time (Benton, 1962; Fletcher & Taylor, 1984). Moreover, brain lesions (e.g., from stroke) may damage passing axons under the cell bodies, disrupting communication between critical brain regions not at the site of injury. Thus, researchers interested in questions concerning how the brain mediates and acquires behavior have long desired methods for the noninvasive study of the brain, both in clinical populations and in typically developing individuals.

RADIOACTIVE MEASUREMENTS

With the development of CT scanning in the 1970s, modern neuroimaging began to take advantage of the growing availability of computer technologies. In a CT scan, X-ray technology is used to take successive pictures (slices) of the brain, and then this image series is reconstructed by computer technologies, thus revealing brain anatomy with much greater resolution. However, while CT scanning is a significant advance over older methods, the skull is a significant source of CT artifacts; the images have relatively poor resolution; and CT's use of radiation means that it is of limited utility for research purposes.

Radioactive isotopes have been and continue to be highly informative about the brain's metabolism of different chemicals. Briefly, positron emission tomography (PET) and its cousin, single-positron emission computed tomography (SPECT) detect radionucleotides. A biologically active molecule, like glucose, is paired with a radioactive tracer, which is injected into a vein or inhaled. PET or SPECT can detect the emissions of the radioactive tracer inside the brain and determine the location(s) where the glucose is being used. These types of imaging are particularly helpful for tracing molecules related to disease, like beta-amyloid in Alzheimer's disease. However, these tools, like CT, are rarely used in children or other nonclinical populations because of the small dose of radioactivity.

CURRENT NONINVASIVE METHODS

Electroencephalography

One of the earliest noninvasive neuroimaging approaches, electroencephalography (EEG), was invented in 1924 by Hans Berger (1940; see also Millett, 2001). EEG traces neuronal electrical activity through the skull via electrodes placed against the scalp. Because the skull scatters the electrical signals coming from the brain, EEG is not good with localization of function, and is highly sensitive to other sources of electrical noise. However, while it lacks good localization of function, EEG and a related approach, event-related potentials (ERPs), have excellent time sensitivity (tens of milliseconds); as such, their use can shed light on the timing of brain activity related to desired (e.g., reading) and undesired (e.g., seizure) events in a nonsurgical manner (Papanicolaou, 2017).

Structural MRI

The development of different aspects of MRI in the mid- to late 20th century was a revelation for human diagnostics and research (e.g., Lauterbur, 1973). For human research, MRI quickly rose to favor because it is noninvasive and represents minimal risk to participants at standard magnetic strengths: no radiation is used, and even pregnant women and very young infants are usually able to participate in a study. The primary limitation of MRI is that because it takes a series of images over time that are later reconstructed with computer programs, it is very sensitive to participant motion during scanning; participants have to be able to understand this requirement and cooperate. Also, because MRI research involves lying down in a tube, and because most types of MRI scans can be quite noisy, some participants can find the environment challenging.

MRI scanning is an application of physics (Krasuski, Horowitz, & Rumsey, 1996). A simplified explanation revolves around the spinning of protons and neutrons in atoms of the human body. The spin results in the generation of magnetic energy. In an MRI machine, this magnetic spin is greatly magnified by applying a strong magnetic field, so that small differences in the magnetic energy can be detected. By manipulating magnetic pulse sequences, the MRI scanner is able to assess the magnetic energy generated by atoms in different brain tissues. Structural MRI scans can therefore reveal the brain's gray matter, white matter, cerebrospinal fluid, and peripheral components (e.g., the skull). With the use of special software packages, the origin of these magnetic signals can be calculated precisely, so that an actual image of the brain can be constructed in high resolution over three dimensions (height, width, and depth) (see Figure 15.2). The results of an MRI scan are a set of digital images, and software can be used to measure the volume of selected brain regions. In addition, the image can be resliced in different planes, depending on the question of interest (Krasuski et al., 1996; Papanicolaou, 2017).

Structural imaging studies are usually based on some type of size measurement of gray or white matter, or total brain volume, in particular brain regions. Programs for this type of analysis have been rapidly advancing and now can automatically calculate different brain volumes when provided a set of high-resolution ($1 \times 1 \times 1$ mm) images of the entire brain. The recent ability to take pictures at very high resolution allows more accurate differentiation between gray matter and white matter, and more precise volume estimates, than in earlier studies.

Structural MRI	Functional (task) MRI	Diffusion Tensor Imaging
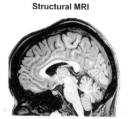	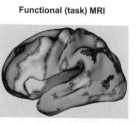	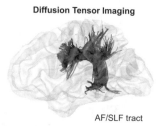
	Reading sentences	AF/SLF tract

FIGURE 15.2. MRI tools allow the study of brain structure, function, and connectivity. The middle image is based on data from Roe et al. (2018). The image at right is used with permission from Jenifer Juranek.

Diffusion-Weighted MRI

As a droplet of rain falling in a puddle makes a circular ripple, unrestricted water will spread out (diffuse) equally in all directions. When restricted by different brain anatomy, water molecules will move faster in some directions than others over time; this creates *anisotropy,* or uneven diffusion. At about the same time as the advent of fMRI methods (see below), a type of structural MRI sequence was invented that was sensitive to the movement of water molecules: diffusion-weighted imaging (DWI) approaches (DWI, also widely known as diffusion tensor imaging, or DTI) (Basser, Mattiello, & LeBihan, 1994; Mori & Zhang, 2006). Like other MRI sequences, DTI involves no contrast or radioactivity. When a water molecule is moving along a neuron's axon, the insulation of that axon is going to make traveling along the axon faster than trying to cross it. By rapidly tracking the motion of water molecules in different directions, researchers can use computers to model the major axon bundles, or white matter, of the brain (see Figure 15.2). These algorithms can create dramatic rainbow fiber pictures of the brain's information superhighways. The diffusion of water molecules along fiber pathways is reported as measures of fractional anisotropy (FA). DTI modeling can allow measurement of the size/density of white matter fiber bundles for comparison across individuals, with the hypothesis that some individuals (e.g., struggling readers) may have more or fewer structural connections between neuronal areas known to be important for a cognitive task (e.g. reading). As with all MRI studies, structural or functional, image quality can be harmed through various sources of noise that generate artifacts in the signal, such as those from participant motion; data quality has to be carefully assessed. A further limitation is that DTI is a model-based analysis, and there are debates as to which algorithms best deal with multiple axon bundles crossing in the same space.

Functional MRI

The development of methods for rapid acquisition of MRI slices in the 1990s generated better temporal resolution (on the order of a few seconds or less between sets of whole-brain pictures), which allowed the possibility for study of brain function. These methods essentially use conventional MRI scanners with software that permits fast image acquisition to detect alterations in blood flow and volume. Functional MRI (fMRI) scans take advantage of a very neat property of blood: Fresh, oxygenated blood has a different magnetic signal from that of used, deoxygenated blood because oxygen shields the (magnetic) iron molecules on blood cells. In the 1990s, it was discovered that MRI could be tuned to be sensitive to the difference between oxygenated and deoxygenated blood across the brain. The logic behind fMRI is this: Brain cells cannot store energy, so when they are active, they immediately need fresh energy from the body, via blood. When a region of the brain is active, therefore, fresh blood flows to that part of the brain, changing the ratio of used and fresh blood in the region. Thus, the fMRI signal is not capturing brain activity per se, but the blood-oxygenation-level-dependent (BOLD) signal related to the brain's energy use. While the measurement of brain activity via BOLD signal is indirect and provides a slow time course (~12–15 seconds for the BOLD signal to locally increase and then go back down), fMRI has excellent spatial localization, allowing unprecedented noninvasive windows on brain function.

For traditional fMRI studies that study brain activity related to a particular task, the distribution of BOLD signal is measured in a participant at rest over several seconds and then in response to task engagement. Any changes in BOLD at different points in the brain are depicted as color-coded maps overlaid upon the MRI images (Krasuski et al., 1996) (see Figure 15.2). The changes in BOLD are measured before, during, and after the person's engagement in a cognitive task. Inferences are then made about the cognitive processes engaged in the task, based on the brain regions that are active. BOLD changes between different tasks can be compared within an individual or group, and researchers can note BOLD changes specific to a particular task (e.g., reading) versus changes in regions common across multiple tasks (e.g., regions engaged in goal achievement, or aspects of executive function).

Recently a non-task-dependent version of fMRI analysis, termed *resting-state functional connectivity* MRI, has exploded in popularity. This type of BOLD imaging asks a participant simply to lie in the scanner, either with eyes open or eyes closed (though not sleeping). By looking at a very low-frequency part of the BOLD signal over several minutes of time, scientists have found that parts of the brain that work together to perform tasks (e.g., the motor system), also show a strong correlation together in this type of signal at rest (Biswal, Van Kylen, & Hyde, 1997; Power, Schlaggar, & Peterson, 2014). Thus, it is possible to extract a passive individual's functional brain networks, or groups of distant brain regions that correlate together at rest, through 10–20 minutes of scanning. This is a highly active area of neuroimaging research, potentially providing great insights about patient groups that are hard to study with task-based analyses, because they are unable to respond to task stimuli due to cognitive or physical limitations. Data of the brain at rest also illuminate a more fundamental organization of functional brain architecture across humans. A drawback of resting-state fMRI analysis is that because it is not constrained by a task, it is *especially* susceptible to motion and other sources of noise on the BOLD signal. Participants have to hold much more still than they do in task fMRI analyses to find reliable signals that are not colored by these artifacts.

Functional Near-Infrared Spectroscopy

More mobile than MRI machines (the instrumentation can be attached to the head via a cap), functional near-infrared spectroscopy (fNIRS) uses light to measure differences in oxygenated and deoxygenated blood in brain tissue (Ferrari & Quaresima, 2012). Light from the near-infrared part of the light spectrum passes pretty easily through skin and skull, while deoxygenated blood cells are strongly absorbent. Using a series of emitters and collectors against the scalp, light can be sent from an emitter, bounced off the brain, and refracted to the light collectors. Difference in absorbance rates between different collector locations on the head can reveal where the BOLD signal is changing due to brain activity. Although fNIRS is more portable and cheaper than fMRI while using similar techniques, it cannot measure brain activity very deeply below the skull surface, and is limited in localization based on the physical spacing of the collectors and emitters around the head. Furthermore, certain hair types and skull thickness changes over age can change signal clarity. fNIRS has had strong success in neonatal intensive care units for studying the youngest infants when their skulls are quite thin, and in going "out in the field" to locations (e.g., bedsides, schools) where MRIs cannot go (e.g., Arimitsu et al., 2018).

Magnetoencephalography

Along with fNIRS, magnetoencephalography (MEG), also known as magnetic source imaging (MSI), is a fairly recent invention. MEG uses magnetic fields similar to those of MRI, but can study signals more similar to those measured by EEG. MEG signals detect the magnetic field generated from electric currents in the dendrites of neurons. Local, transient changes in magnetic flux are recorded by superconducting loops of wire (magnetometers) that are contained in a helmet-like device covering the head. Based on the recorded changes in the surface distribution of electromagnetic energy, researchers obtain precise location estimates for active neurons, using simple statistical modeling techniques (Papanicolaou, 2017). MEG has the advantage of better temporal resolution than MRI, but has surface and modeling limitations similar to those of fNIRS: It cannot study deeper brain locations, and the source of signals is based on the type of localization model used (Papanicolaou, 2017).

NEUROIMAGING STUDY DESIGN CONSIDERATIONS

In evaluating an imaging study, the consumer must understand these issues and the strengths and weaknesses of different modalities. Consider, for example, the spatial resolution and temporal sensitivity of three neuroimaging modalities. The metabolic activity recorded by PET and fMRI takes place after the actual processing has occurred, so the temporal resolution of these methods is weak. The spatial resolution of PET is poor, so the maps are aligned with a structural MRI scan to allow precise localization of brain activity associated with performance of a particular task. MEG, on the other hand, affords measurement of neurophysiological activity in real time (down to the millisecond) and provides information on the actual time course of neuronal events. MEG scans, however, do not convey structural information for the brain being imaged, so MEG activation maps are also superimposed onto a structural MRI scan. fMRI partially overcomes the temporal limitations of MRI by rapidly collecting serial images in order to measure the changes in blood flow associated with cognitive activity over time (Papanicolaou, 2017). Thus, spatial resolution with fMRI is excellent, despite weak temporal resolution. These strengths and weaknesses help the consumer evaluate the contribution of different imaging studies.

In addition to selecting the appropriate technology to address a research question, investigators must balance several other aspects of the experimental design. First, nearly all of the approaches need multiple repetitions of a type of stimuli to produce a reliable signal (e.g., multiple trials of sentences where participants decide if they make sense or not, in a task designed to evaluate reading comprehension), so the task stimuli need to be carefully selected for difficulty, emotional tone, and so forth. Second, tasks need to be limited to button press responses or other small movements that will not generate much motion artifact in the measurements. Unfortunately, reading aloud or speaking in neuroimaging studies typically generates too much motion noise in the signal. Third, the tasks need to be interesting enough to keep participants engaged and motivated to complete the study, while being as simple and specific to the cognitive task of interest as possible. Many studies are now moving toward "naturalistic" stimuli like movie clips or virtual reality tasks, but these complex stimuli can make isolating the ability of interest challenging. Fourth, the researchers need to consider any biological differences between populations of interest (e.g., children and adults). Many studies have worked to demonstrate that the BOLD signal is similar between adults and children, and that head size differences do not alter results (this is true from the elderly down to children 6 or 7 years of age, but then different steps need to be taken with very young children's heads) (Church, Petersen, & Schlaggar, 2010). Finally, there are the considerations needed for any type of research experiment (e.g., participant diversity vs. homogeneity, statistical power to detect effects, cost).

THE NEUROSCIENCE OF READING

It is worth noting up front that human brains did not evolve to read. The need for reading arose with the invention of writing, which is only about

5,000 years old, and some cultures still have no need for reading at all. The process of reading demands that the brain engage language and visual mechanisms together in a fairly unique and precise way. Therefore, it may not be surprising that a proportion (5–15%) of the human population struggles to read in a literate society; this number is larger if illiteracy is considered, representing people who may never have the exposure and instruction needed to develop literacy (Wolf, 2007). Without exposure to print, reading does not develop; it is not an evolutionary skill, and thus the brain must reorganize to allow fluent reading, which it does by scaffolding on areas evolved for language and visual attention (Dehaene, 2009; Vogel, Petersen, & Schlaggar, 2014). There is thus much to learn about how the brain learns (or struggles to learn) a task like reading, and this understanding has broad implications for our understanding of education, remediation, and brain plasticity.

There has been great historical interest in brain structure and function in children and adults with unexpected reading difficulties. The earliest observations of unexpected reading failure led to hypotheses about the neural underpinnings of these severe disabilities (Hinschelwood, 1902). These early observations were fueled by studies of clinical populations who lost some aspect of reading and subsequently underwent postmortem examination. By identifying the areas of the brain that had been damaged, and linking findings across patients, researchers began to develop theories of language and reading that were ultimately extended to children with reading difficulties and no brain injury (Benton, 1975). These theories led to the conviction that these reading difficulties were intrinsic to a child and not due to environmental causes (Critchley, 1970; Orton, 1927). However, despite the tenacity of these convictions, the hypotheses were not really testable until the advent of modern neuroimaging, which has moved research from simple questions such as "Is the brain related to reading disability?" or "What areas of the brain 'cause' reading disability?" to much more complex questions involving the interplay of experience, instruction, age, and the brain in learning to read.

LIMITATIONS OF POSTMORTEM AND LESION STUDIES

Early clinicians could not assess brain–behavior relationships until after their patients died and postmortem studies were conducted. In early postmortem brain analyses, two different types of language disruptions (aphasias) were related to strokes in the brain in particular locations: Broca's area in the left frontal lobe, and Wernicke's area in the posterior temporal lobe, so named after the clinicians who described patients' symptoms after strokes in those areas (Fiez, Tranel, Seager-Frerichs, & Damasio, 2006). Later clinicians observed that reading was often impaired in strokes that impacted the left inferior parietal lobe, bottom part of the left occipital lobe, or cerebellum (Desmond & Fiez, 1998; Finch, Nicolson, & Fawcett, 2002). However, because literacy was not a cultural expectation until relatively recently, and because strokes do not generally happen in young people, the study of patients after strokes has substantial limitations in understanding reading and reading difficulties (Fletcher & Taylor, 1984).

The postmortem studies of people with a history of reading difficulties have not been without controversy (Fletcher, Lyons, Fuchs, & Barnes, 2019; Galaburda, 1993). People do not usually die from reading-related problems, so it is a small, unusual sample of brains. In addition to concerns about the nature and definition of reading difficulties after the fact, it is not possible to relate the findings of a postmortem study to actual reading performance. Thus, when noninvasive tools became available, they were almost immediately used to study brain structure and function in children and adults with reading difficulties.

INFLUENTIAL BRAIN MODELS OF READING

These early lesion and surgery results, along with many studies in vision and language more generally, led to some clear consistencies in findings regarding areas of the brain for vision and language. First, for the majority of people, language ability is often left-lateralized, meaning that the left hemisphere of the brain plays a bigger role in language than the right does. Similarly, while reading-related brain engagement appears to be happening in both hemispheres, it is also stronger in the left hemisphere. Visual information proceeds from the eyes, to the thalamus, to the back of the brain (the occipital lobe). From there, visual information spreads in two primary pathways: a "where" pathway that travels up through the parietal lobe, and a "what" pathway that travels along the ventral surface of the cortex toward the temporal lobe. Many models have been proposed to explain how the visual and language systems work together in the brain to read. A few have been particularly influential: the dual-route model (Coltheart, Rastle, Perry, Langdon, & Ziegler, 2001; Pugh et al., 2001) and the triangle model (Seidenberg, 2005).

The dual-route model proposes that words are read through two simultaneous visual pathways similar to other types of visual information. The proposed ventral pathway is the "orthographic" route, where information proceeds from letter, to morpheme, to word level recognition areas. The proposed dorsal "phonological" pathway involves language areas in inferior parietal and superior temporal cortex. Both pathways then involve left frontal cortex and motor cortex for articulatory processes related to verbal expression or task response (see Figure 15.3).

The triangle model proposes a set of semantic processors in addition to the phonological and orthographic processing. Semantic processing may involve the angular gyrus and midtemporal cortex, among other regions,

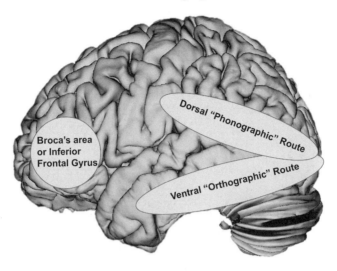

FIGURE 15.3. Key reading-related brain areas in the left hemisphere, including the left inferior frontal gyrus and temporal, parietal, and occipital cortex. To use the dual-route model as an example, visual information travels from the back of the brain (the occipital lobe) forward via a dorsal "phonological/sublexical" pathway and a ventral "lexical/visual recognition" pathway.

but has also recently been shown to be widely distributed across the brain (Huth, de Heer, Griffiths, Theunissen, & Gallant, 2016; Seidenberg, 2017). Given what we know about visual and language processing by the brain, reading-related analyses have often focused on the left hemisphere, and on regions related to the pathways just described. These regions and their interactions vary with proficiency, showing different patterns of activation in poor readers versus more skilled readers.

In summary, the areas most consistently involved in reading include the ventral temporo-occipital region in the base of the brain; the more dorsal temporoparietal cortex (including the posterior portion of the superior temporal gyrus, the angular and supramarginal gyri); and inferior frontal regions, predominantly in the left hemisphere (Church, Coalson, Lugar, Petersen, & Schlaggar, 2008; Dehaene, 2009; Fletcher et al., 2019) (see Figure 15.3).

STRUCTURAL NEUROIMAGING STUDIES OF READING DISABILITY

Comparisons of Regional Brain Volumes

Many morphometry studies of brain anatomy—comparisons of brain volumes in "regions of interest"—have now been completed with children and adults who experience reading difficulties. These studies implicate several structures and regions of the brain (Fletcher et al., 2019). The age and reading fluency of the participants may greatly affect the results, and thus careful characterization is necessary. Most consistent across studies are findings of thinner cortex in various language- and reading-related regions in children who struggle to read, or who are at risk due to family history of reading difficulties (e.g., Altarelli et al., 2013; Black et al., 2012; Hosseini et al., 2013; Hugdahl et al., 2003; Qi et al., 2016; Richlan, Kronbichler, & Wimmer, 2013).

Large research collaborations, such as the Pediatrics Imaging Neurocognition Genetics (PING) study and the Texas Center for Learning Disabilities (TCLD) research, have recently been able to amass large data collections for structural analysis to improve on previous smaller studies. Using precision measurements of the cortical surface, such as the local gyrification index, a study from the TCLD has found that cortex is thinner in poor readers in reading-related regions of the bilateral occipital, temporal, and parietal cortex (Williams, Juranek, Cirino, & Fletcher, 2018). The PING study has recently found that genetic markers of dyslexia were associated with cortical thickness in temporal cortex (Eicher et al., 2016).

Diffusion Tensor Imaging

Several studies have compared white matter structure, or the structural brain connectivity, in good and poor readers by using DTI techniques. Many DTI studies have associated poor reading with poor white matter integrity in tracts important for the dorsal (phonological) and ventral (orthographic) reading areas (e.g., Arrington, Kulesz, Juranek, Cirino, & Fletcher, 2017; Carter et al., 2009; Horowitz-Kraus, Wang, Plante, & Holland, 2014; Vandermosten et al., 2012). A few specific major white matter bundles are typically tested to relate to reading performance. The major tracts thought to be important for phonological processing are the arcuate fasciculus (AF) and the superior longitudinal fasciculus (SLF), especially in the left hemisphere. The SLF has been shown to correlate with the rate of reading development in children over time (Yeatman, Dougherty, Ben-Shachar, & Wandell, 2012). The major tracts investigated related to orthography and fluency are the inferior fronto-occipital fasciculus (IFOF), the inferior longitudinal fasciculus (ILF), and the uncinate fasciculus (UF) (Schlaggar & McCandliss, 2007). Examinations of the FA of these tracts have correlated with different reading measures across studies. Because some tracts overlap and cross in the brain, some newer studies are pushing methodological approaches for reducing overlap (e.g., Arrington et al., 2017). The Arrington and colleagues (2017) study found that the left ILF was related to reading comprehension abilities in poor readers, while reading fluency was related more to the left IFOF and right UF.

As DTI measures do not require task performance in the scanner, many studies of young children are being done with this approach (e.g., kindergarteners: Ozernov-Palchik et al., 2019; Vanderauwera, Wouters, Vandermosten, & Ghesquiere, 2017; preschoolers: Wang et al., 2017; infants: Langer et al., 2017). For example, the Langer and colleagues (2017) study assessed infants ages 6–18 months whose parents had reading difficulties, and who were thus at risk for reading difficulties themselves. Those infants with a family history of reading difficulties showed altered FA in the left AF, and a measure of infant expressive language positively correlated with FA in the AF across the whole dataset. Thus, many studies of reading using DTI are finding alterations in FA in white matter tracts that are believed to connect neurons in different parts of the reading network to each other.

Structural Neuroimaging Considerations

Many of the differences across structural neuroimaging studies reflect variations in participant characteristics and imaging methods. This is technically complicated and time-consuming research. Although acquiring the images is relatively simple, the machines vary in technical characteristics and resolution. Methods for acquiring and analyzing images vary and evolve over time with improved technology. Determining brain volume or gray/white matter thickness is a tedious and time-consuming process, despite recent automatization. Someone must digitize the scans, and often a team must manually outline the regions of interest, though automatized segmenting tools are being developed to address this aspect. Thus, samples tend to be small and variable. Participant motion is difficult to quantify and control for in structural scans. Factors such as age, gender, and handedness influence the anatomical organization of the brain, and these effects are magnified in small samples (Schultz et al., 1994). Thus, there is a strong push for larger samples and longitudinal measures in participants over time, with rich characterization of participant behaviors and abilities. Collaborations across multiple imaging sites are increasing to address this need.

FUNCTIONAL NEUROIMAGING STUDIES OF READING DISABILITY

As discussed earlier, functional neuroimaging studies assess changes in brain metabolism or neuronal signaling, often in response to some type of specific task. Thus, for example, children might be asked to read words or sentences. As they read words, changes in the rate of communication among brain cells in different regions take place, resulting in increased regional brain metabolism, and a local increase in blood flow, reflected by change in the local BOLD signal. In contrast somewhat to studies of brain structure, the results of research on brain function tend to converge fairly well across methods and laboratories in depicting brain differences between good and poor readers (Fletcher et al., 2019; Price & McCrory, 2005; Seidenberg, 2017), although there are ongoing debates and nuances with respect to the roles of particular brain regions (Poeppel, 1996; Price & McCrory, 2005; Vogel et al., 2013).

In this section of the chapter, we review neuroimaging studies involving reading, focusing on fMRI as the most frequently applied and least invasive paradigm. However, across modalities, the findings converge in suggesting that tasks involving different aspects of reading are associated with the brain regions described earlier (see Figure 15.3). It is apparent that a network of brain areas is commonly engaged across neuroimaging methods, and that these areas are engaged to different degrees, depending on the presentation modality, neuroimaging approach, and type of reading task.

Functional studies of reading have typically used word recognition tasks. Word recognition tasks can be manipulated to address a variety of component processes that are common to both aural language function and reading, such as phonological and semantic analysis, and others that are specific to understanding of print (visual and orthographic processing). It is also possible to image other, more complex aspects of reading, such as fluency and passage or sentence comprehension. This goal is far more difficult to achieve because fluency and comprehension involve several component processes, the contributions of which yield a larger and more complex pattern of brain activity. However, as neuroimaging moves toward more naturalistic stimuli, this type of research is happening more often (Huth et al., 2016; Roe et al., 2018).

fMRI Studies of Reading Disability

fMRI studies have proliferated to a point where meta-analytic syntheses have been performed that permit estimation of results across studies (e.g., Houdé, Rossi, Lubin, & Joliot, 2010; Maisog, Einbinder, Flowers, Turkeltaub, & Eden, 2008; Martin, Schurz, Kronbichler, & Richlan, 2015; Paulesu, Danelli, & Berlingeri, 2014; Richlan, Kronbicher, & Wimmer, 2009). Paulesu and colleagues (2014) completed a meta-analysis of fMRI and PET studies of children and adults with dyslexia and of control participants with typical reading. Across studies, they found reduced activation in struggling readers in left-hemisphere regions involving ventral visual (occipitotemporal) cortex, temporoparietal cortex (inferior parietal cortex, superior temporal gyrus), thalamus, and inferior frontal gyrus (see Figure 15.4, scatterplot in left inferior parietal cortex). Differences linked to reading ability have been largely consistent across studies of children and adults. This reduced activation has also been seen in children at risk for becoming

Correct Sentence Comprehension Trials vs. Rest
All readers (*N* = 92)

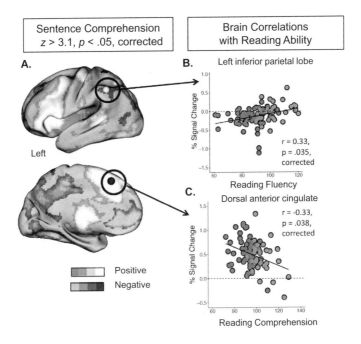

FIGURE 15.4. A sample of readers in grades 4–5 with a wide range of reading ability. (A) Left-hemisphere fMRI brain activity during a sentence comprehension task. Two regions of interest from the literature are shown as colored spheres overlaid on the brain activity. (B) A region in the left inferior parietal lobe was underactive in readers with poorer fluency. (C) An executive control region in dorsal anterior cingulate cortex was recruited more strongly by readers with poorer comprehension scores. Adapted from Roe et al. (2018). Copyright © 2018 Oxford University Press. Adapted by permission.

struggling readers due to family history (Raschle, Zuk, & Gaab, 2012). More mixed results across studies were found in the right hemisphere: Some studies found stronger right-hemisphere activity in struggling readers, while others found decreased activity (akin to the decreases observed in the left hemisphere).

Another meta-analysis (Richlan et al., 2009) involved 17 fMRI or PET studies of reading or phonological processing in samples described simply as "dyslexic" versus "controls." No age restrictions were introduced. Reduced activation in the dyslexic groups was apparent in left-hemisphere regions involving the temporoparietal (inferior parietal, superior, middle and inferior temporal) and occipitotemporal regions. Underactivation of the inferior frontal gyrus and hyperactivity of the primary motor cortex and anterior insula were found.

Both these meta-analyses concurred in identifying areas outlined in Figure 15.3 as dysfunctional in poor readers. One of the most consistent results across studies is underactivation in struggling readers of an occipitotemporal region that is often referred to as a visual "word form" region along the ventral visual pathway. This region is thought to be involved in the rapid processing of letter strings and orthographic patterns that is linked to higher-order representations of words (Price & McCrory, 2005). In addition, there is underactivation of the dorsal temporoparietal system involved in assembling phonological representations of words in oral language processing and in reading (Richlan et al., 2009). There is evidence for underactivation of an inferior frontal region that may mediate articulation in struggling readers, and yet also conflicting evidence for increased activity of mouth motor regions. The motor activity is often interpreted as a potential compensatory mechanism in struggling readers, involving efforts to articulate either overtly (out loud) or implicitly (internally recruiting motor strategies) while reading.

Resting-State Functional Connectivity Studies of Reading Disability

When reading is analyzed by using resting-state data (in the absence of an overt task), an interesting aspect of the functional reading network emerges: The activity of the reading-related brain regions is not strongly correlated. Rather, reading-related regions belong to multiple resting networks, including vision, hearing, and domain-general control networks (Bailey, Aboud, Nguyen, & Cutting, 2018; Vogel et al., 2013, 2014). The idea that reading-related brain regions connect broadly to other brain regions, and may even be hubs for information transfer, underscores the remarkable brain engagement that the reading process requires. Connectivity analysis approaches have also been applied during reading tasks (Aboud, Bailey, Petrill, & Cutting, 2016; Finn et al., 2014). They support the presence of altered reading network connectivity in poor readers during reading, providing a different look at dysfunction during reading tasks from that afforded by traditional task activation analyses.

MEG Studies of Reading Disability

In a series of MEG studies of adults and children varying in reading proficiency, good and poor readers did not differ in activation patterns when they *listened* to words, showing patterns predominantly in the left hemisphere that would be expected for such a task (Simos et al., 2007a, 2007b, 2011). However, on tasks involving recognition of *printed* words, striking differences in the activation patterns of good and poor readers occurred.

In the children who were good readers, there was a characteristic pattern in which the occipital areas of the brain that support primary visual processing were initially activated. Then the ventral visual association cortices in both hemispheres were activated, followed by simultaneous activation of three areas in the *left* temporoparietal region (essentially the angular, supramarginal, and superior temporal gyri, which relate to the dorsal reading pathway). In the children with reading problems, the same pattern and time course were apparent, but the temporoparietal areas of the *right* hemisphere were activated.

Recent MEG studies have also been testing struggling readers with non-reading-related stimuli (e.g. Simos, Rezaie, Fletcher, & Papanicolaou, 2013). Two recent studies have found that correlations among resting MEG signal fluctuations were reduced in the left temporoparietal regions in struggling readers, even in the absence of any task (Dimitriadis et al., 2013; Dimitriadis, Simos, Fletcher, & Papanicolaou, 2018). The connectivity results suggest that alterations in reading-related regions' brain activity may be affecting information transfer between those regions and across the brain. In addition to studying the brain mapping to word stimuli, a recent MEG study of 4- to 8-year-olds found some evidence that general object recognition signaling might also strengthen with reading acquisition (Caffarra et al., 2017).

Conclusions of Functional Studies of Reading Disability

Altogether, these functional neuroimaging studies suggest that in children with reading difficulties, the functional connections among brain areas are what account for differences in brain activation, as opposed to specific or general dysfunction of any single brain area. A critical question is whether at least some of the patterns seen in the poor readers are compensatory, and the greater activity sometimes found in the right hemisphere is often interpreted in that manner. The decreased activity observed in struggling readers is generally interpreted to reflect the failure of the brain to co-opt vision and language mechanisms through typical levels of reading instruction. Perhaps most importantly, studies generally show reduced activity in struggling readers within the same neural network identified in children and adults who are developmentally proficient in reading. At this point, there are not separate theories of good and poor reading in the brain; they are opposite sides of the same coin.

The field is actively pursuing research into what changes in the brain during reading intervention in struggling readers, what happens as very young children undergo the reading process, and what happens in the brains of adults learning to read for the first time (or anew after injury). These studies provide windows onto how the brain and environment interact in forming the neural networks supporting an acquired ability like reading. This neuroscience research is especially pertinent in demonstrating that reading is not a natural ability, and that for many, mere exposure is not sufficient to support the brain reorganization required for proficient reading.

CHANGES IN BRAIN ACTIVATION IN RELATION TO INTERVENTION

The relation of neuronal activation changes and response to intervention (RTI) has been evaluated in a growing number of studies using MRI and MEG. The growth in intervention research parallels a growing interest in the intersection of education and neuroscience (e.g., Eden et al., 2004; Meyler, Keller, Cherkassky, Gabrieli, & Just, 2008; Rezaie et al., 2011a, 2011b; Richards & Berninger, 2008; Shaywitz et al., 2004; Simos et al., 2002, 2007a, 2007b). Enough studies have begun to investigate reading intervention with neuroimaging that a recent meta-analysis was possible (Barquero, Davis, & Cutting, 2014).

As we have been discussing, studies of struggling readers consistently find underactivations in reading-related regions identified in studies of proficient readers. After intervention, many studies find increased (improved) activation within the same set of regions. To illustrate, Meyler and colleagues (2008) used fMRI to study children in U.S. grade 5 after a year-long intervention. A sentence comprehension task was used to assess brain activity. The primary finding was that the temporoparietal areas were underactivated bilaterally in poor readers at prior to intervention, but normalized with successful intervention. Some studies have also found compensatory activity in improved readers, particularly in the right inferior frontal gyrus (e.g., Eden et al., 2004; Meyler et al., 2008; Shaywitz et al., 2004), but also find improvement related to left inferior frontal gyrus as well (Hoeft et al., 2011).

In one of the earliest studies, Simos and colleagues (2002) employed MEG before and after children with severe reading disability participated in an intense phonologically based intervention. These children ranged in age from 7 to 17 years and had severe word recognition difficulties. Six of eight children read at the 3rd percentile or below, with the other two children reading at the 13th and 18th percentiles. The children received intervention for 2 hours a day, 5 days a week, over an 8-week period (i.e., about 80 hours of intensive phonologically based instruction per child). Before intervention, the eight children with dyslexia uniformly displayed an aberrant pattern of activation in the right hemisphere. After intervention, the children's word-reading accuracy scores improved into the average range. In addition, in each case, there was significant activation of neural circuits in the left hemisphere commonly associated with proficient word-reading ability. There was also a tendency for reduction in right-hemisphere activity.

More recent studies have begun to examine individuals whose RTI is inadequate. Odegard, Ring, Smith, Biggan, and Black (2008) conducted a postintervention comparison of adequate and inadequate responders, and found differences predominantly in the left inferior parietal region. These results are consistent with temporoparietal regions' changing in activation between pre- and postintervention comparisons of neural activity. It is likely that future studies will begin to focus more on children and adults who do not respond adequately to instruction (e.g., Nugiel et al., 2019).

These studies clearly show that the neural systems of poor readers are malleable and respond to instruction. In addition, while some compensatory changes are apparent, most changes reflect changes over intervention in the known reading-related areas seen in typically developing children.

TWO REPRESENTATIVE NEUROIMAGING STUDIES OF READING DIFFICULTIES

For the purpose of illustrating the use of functional neuroimaging in the study of reading, we highlight a pair of fMRI studies we and our colleagues recently completed (Nugiel et al., 2019; Roe et al., 2018). These studies involved a group of children identified as struggling readers in U.S. grades 4 and 5, and a comparison group of children in the same classrooms who were typical readers. The struggling readers received different reading interventions during the school year. As part of this study, a subset of the struggling and nonstruggling readers received MRI scanning in the fall of the school year, prior to the bulk of the reading intervention; at the end of the school year, struggling readers were scanned postintervention.

The research goal for both studies was based on the observation that in addition to decreased activity in struggling readers in the reading network, studies also often find altered activity in brain regions important for executive functioning. *Executive functioning* refers to the large set of cognitive processes needed to control one's own behavior and to accomplish desired goals. Studies are finding differences in brain regions important for executive functioning, but largely have only tested reading-related tasks. Our critical questions in these studies were these: (1) Would any executive function differences seen during a reading task in struggling readers also be seen in a nonreading but demanding executive function task? (2) Would children who improved from a reading intervention also show change in non-reading-related brain regions, or during a nonreading task?

Procedures: MRI Study of Struggling Readers and Intervention

The educational reading intervention study (Vaughn, Solis, Miciak, Taylor, & Fletcher, 2016) took place in multiple school districts in two large urban areas in central and eastern Texas. Half of the struggling readers were assigned a pull-out, small-group reading intervention, while the other half remained in the classroom and received whatever intervention (if any) that their schools would normally pursue. The experimental interventions took place in small groups, each with a trained tutor supervised by the researchers. The instruction took place for about 40 minutes each day for 16 weeks. A substantial focus of the intervention and the neuroimaging measures was on reading comprehension, and on the potential contribution of executive functioning to comprehension abilities. Families from all three groups (typical, struggling + intervention, and struggling + business-as-usual) were recruited to volunteer for the MRI study. Each MRI visit lasted about 2 hours, including informed consent, metal safety screening, and structural MRI/fMRI scans. Children watched a movie during structural MRI scans, and then performed two different behavioral tasks during the fMRI scans: a sentence comprehension (SC) task and a nonlexical executive function inhibition task.

The SC task required participants to read a short sentence presented on the screen and press a button to indicate whether the sentence "made sense" (e.g. "The key opened the carrot" vs. "The cat sat on the chair"). Words were high-frequency, and sentence length and verb tense were carefully controlled across stimuli. The SC stimuli were modeled after those used by Meyler and colleagues (2007).

The nonlexical executive functioning task was a visual version of a classic stop-signal task (SST). This task presented arrows at the center of the screen, and the participant indicated via button press which direction the arrow was pointing, unless a red X suddenly appeared over the arrow, in which case participants were supposed to try to refrain from button pressing. The red X appeared randomly, and would come faster or slower in a trial depending on whether the participant was successful at inhibiting the previous X button press or not (staircasing). The SST design was modeled after that used by Aron and Poldrack (2006).

Results: Struggling Readers versus Nonstruggling Readers

An MRI analysis of 60 struggling readers in grades 4–5 and 32 nonstruggling same-age readers found differences between the groups on the SC task. In brief, struggling readers had lower activity in the left posterior temporal cortex than nonstruggling readers did when making sentence judgments. This result was consistent with the lower reading-related regional activity seen in struggling readers by many other groups. Engagement during the SC task in bilateral temporal and parietal regions also correlated with word reading ability across the whole sample (Figure 15.4, A and B). Comprehension ability across the whole sample correlated with activity in a key executive function region, the anterior cingulate cortex (Figure 15.4, C). Thus, struggling readers were showing executive function differences during a reading-related task.

Critically, no group differences, or significant correlations with reading ability across the whole sample, were found during the nonlexical SST.

Thus, from this first analysis (Roe et al., 2018), we gained evidence that any general control or executive function difficulties experienced by struggling readers may be tied to the reading process. However, it is important to note that this experiment only looked at one reading task and one nonreading executive function task; it is quite possible that struggling readers could have deficits on other nonreading tasks that were not assessed.

Results: Improved Struggling Readers versus Nonimprovers

To follow up on that baseline MRI analysis between struggling and non-struggling groups, we took a closer look at the struggling readers themselves. We looked at the outcomes of the struggling readers at the end of the school year, after either business-as-usual or an experimental reading intervention. Children were categorized as "improved" if they gained more than expected for their age on a subset of the pre- and postachievement assessments; otherwise, they were categorized as "nonimproved." The MRI data collected prior to intervention were then sorted by those later outcome labels, resulting in 19 "future improvers" and 27 "future nonimprovers." We then tested whether there were any differences between the improver and nonimprover groups on either the SC or SST task. For the SC task, struggling readers who went on to improve had stronger activity in the right ventral visual pathway than future nonimprovers did (see Figure 15.5). Right fusiform activity was also correlated with reading gain when the participants were scanned after intervention. This right-hemisphere region has been seen in other intervention studies, and has been suggested to serve a compensatory function in readers who improve.

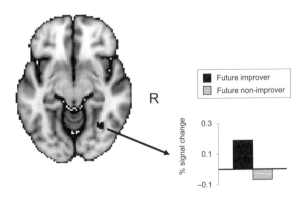

FIGURE 15.5. A right-hemisphere ventral visual region was more engaged by struggling readers *before intervention* who later improved in their reading. Adapted from Nugiel et al. (2019). Copyright © 2019 Elsevier. Adapted by permission.

Again, there were no group differences during the nonlexical SST. These results were interpreted as again suggesting that struggling readers' brain differences may be specific to the reading process, rather than more general, and in supporting the findings in the literature that stronger right-hemisphere brain activity in reading can serve as a potential marker for reading improvement.

RELEVANCE OF NEUROIMAGING TECHNOLOGIES TO READING RESEARCH

Educators commonly ask why neuroimaging studies are relevant to reading research. It might be better to reverse the question: Why is reading research relevant to neuroimaging? Reading is a wonderful exemplar of a skill that is not innate or evolutionary; reading must be taught. Thus, reading provides neuroscientists with a unique window on skill learning and brain plasticity. Studies of adults learning to read, or learning to read novel languages, inform our understanding of later-life brain plasticity; studies of reading and reading problems in children provide unique opportunities to study the impact of education and intervention on the developing brain. In many of the studies that have been described, the key has been theory-driven application of the technology to different research questions (e.g., comparing phonological vs. orthographic stimuli in struggling readers). The application of the imaging modality and the interpretation of the results have been heavily dependent on theory and research in the cognitive sciences (e.g., the assessment test results between struggling and typical readers on orthographic and phonological tasks). The appropriate use of previous behavioral research has helped focus the lens of the technology so that appropriate questions are asked, and so that appropriate tasks are designed.

The neuroimaging studies help explain why early intervention is more effective than later remediation. Words have no significance to the untrained brain. A young child or illiterate adult may be able to match the letters as visual stimuli, but the only way to access a word itself begins at the sublexical level and is tied to speech. Thus, in learning to read, a young child or illiterate adult must be able to link the visual stimulus with oral language, which involves what we have referred to as the dorsal sublexical or phonological route in a dual-route model. As soon as the brain begins to link speech and print, the ventral lexical route becomes activated. As a general visual expertise area, these regions begin to process increasingly large chunks of words so that the brain is able, with training, to recognize whole words quickly. These regions, especially in the left hemisphere, show remarkable reorganization for the processing of print with no loss of other abilities (Dehaene, 2009). Programming these ventral regions requires repeated exposures to words and word patterns in order to specialize for rapid, automatic, and effortless processing. If individuals have no print exposure or are delayed because they struggle to relate print and speech, the ventral systems do not develop the level of specialization needed for proficient reading. It is not surprising, then, that recent educational studies comparing the effects of instruction and intervention with struggling readers show much more efficacy in grades 1 and 2 than in grade 3 and beyond (Connor et al., 2013; Lovett et al., 2017). Delay in accessing print means that an older child would have to read a great deal to catch up in experience and develop a level of automaticity (Torgesen et al., 2001).

There are growing attempts to link the education and neuroscience fields more strongly, in the hope that better understanding of how the brain learns can lead to better educational practices. There is hope for a growing symbiosis between education and neuroscience. Educators understand the practical constraints on instruction and learning, and can help research study designs to be more applicable to the "real world." Questions of interest to reading educators have been asked in neuroimaging because educators have collaborated with neuroimaging studies, and because schools and families have participated in the research process. Thus, the early focus of the imaging studies on the results of intervention studies has been critical for the development and enhancement of neuroimaging technologies. By the same token, using neuroimaging in reading research, particularly in the intervention studies, has helped advance understanding of how children learn to read and why some struggle. In this regard, the results can be integrated into the larger body of knowledge regarding the critical role of phonological processing and word recognition in learning to read. We can now understand where brain differences are occurring for many children who do not develop adequate word recognition strategies.

The fact that neural systems can be shown to develop through interactions with the environment implies that they are not hard-wired at birth, and that certain types of experiences are critical in developing these systems. Moreover, when children who are struggling to learn to read are examined, it becomes apparent that neural systems are malleable. The greatest relevance of neuroimaging studies is the clear indication that effective instructional approaches (across ages, types, and abilities) can modify aspects of brain functioning that are known to be critical for the cognitive operations targeted by instruction. Ultimately, it is the teacher who provides instruction and experiences that affect the organization of the brain to generate reading ability.

In this chapter, we have attempted to show that the application of neuroimaging methods to the study of reading is a significant research accomplishment. These applications are dependent on other areas of reading research that both define the purpose of the imaging studies, and are critical for the interpretation of results. Together, the accumulating evidence across neuroimaging and non-neuroimaging studies suggests modifications of theories of reading development. Neuroimaging studies cut across multiple research domains, including reading development, processing, and RTI for various age groups and levels of proficiency. This type of knowledge must be integrated into the broader knowledge of research on reading. At the most basic level, neuroimaging research shows that teaching affects the brain in positive, long-term ways that are essential for a reader's development.

ACKNOWLEDGMENTS

Work reported in this chapter was supported in part by a grant from the Eunice Kennedy Shriver National Institute of Child Health and Human Development (No. P50 HD052117, Texas Center for Learning Disabilities). We greatly thank the other authors of the previous editions of this chapter: David L. Molfese, Panagiotis G. Simos, Andrew C. Papanicolaou, and Carolyn Denton. We also thank Alexis Boucher, Mary Abbe Roe, and Tehila Nugiel for reading over drafts of this chapter. The content is solely our responsibility and does not necessarily represent the official views of the Eunice Kennedy Shriver National Institute of Child Health and Human Development, or the National Institutes of Health.

REFERENCES

Aboud, K. S., Bailey, S. K., Petrill, S. A., & Cutting, L. E. (2016). Comprehending text versus reading words in young readers with varying reading ability: Distinct patterns of functional connectivity from common processing hubs. *Developmental Science, 19*(4), 632–656.

Altarelli, I., Monzalvo, K., Iannuzzi, S., Fluss, J., Billard, C., Ramus, F., et al. (2013). A functionally guided approach to the morphometry of occipitotemporal regions in developmental dyslexia: Evidence for differential effects in boys and girls. *Journal of Neuroscience, 33*(27), 11296–11301.

Arimitsu, T., Minagawa, Y., Yagihashi, T. O., Uchida, M., Matsuzaki, A., Ikeda, K., et al. (2018). The cerebral hemodynamic response to phonetic changes of speech in preterm and term infants: The impact of postmenstrual age. *NeuroImage: Clinical, 19*, 599–606.

Aron, A. R., & Poldrack, R. A. (2006). Cortical and subcortical contributions to stop signal response inhibition: Role of the subthalamic nucleus. *Journal of Neuroscience, 26*(9), 2424–2433.

Arrington, N. C., Kulesz, P. A., Juranek, J., Cirino, P. T., & Fletcher, J. M. (2017). White matter microstructure integrity in relation to reading proficiency. *Brain and Language, 174*, 103–111.

Bailey, S. K., Aboud, K. S., Nguyen, T. Q., & Cutting, L. E. (2018). Applying a network framework to the neurobiology of reading and dyslexia. *Journal of Neurodevelopmental Disorders, 10*(1), 37.

Barquero, L. A., Davis, N., & Cutting, L. E. (2014). Neuroimaging of reading intervention: A systematic review and activation likelihood estimate meta-analysis. *PLOS ONE, 9*(1), e83668.

Basser, P. J., Mattiello, J., & LeBihan, D. (1994). MR diffusion tensor spectroscopy and imaging. *Biophysical Journal, 66,* 259–267.

Benton, A. L. (1962). Behavioral indices of brain injury in school children. *Child Development, 33,* 199–208.

Benton, A. L. (1975). Developmental dyslexia: Neurological aspects. *Advances in Neurology, 7,* 1–47.

Berger, H. (1940). *Psyche.* Jena, Germany: Gustav Fischer.

Biswal, B. B., Van Kylen, J., & Hyde, J. S. (1997). Simultaneous assessment of flow and BOLD signals in resting-state functional connectivity maps. *NMR in Biomedicine, 10*(4–5), 165–170.

Black, J. M., Tanaka, H., Stanley, L., Nagamine, M., Zakerani, N., Thurston, A., et al. (2012). Maternal history of reading difficulty is associated with reduced language-related gray matter in beginning readers. *NeuroImage, 59*(3), 3021–3032.

Caffarra, S., Martin, C. D., Liazrazu, M., Lallier, M., Zarraga, A., Molinaro, N., et al. (2017). Word and object recognition during reading acquisition: MEG evidence. *Developmental Cognitive Neuroscience, 24,* 21–32.

Carter, J. C., Lanham, D. C., Cutting, L. E., Clements-Stephens, A. M., Chen, X., Hadzipasic, M., et al. (2009) A dual DTI approach to analyzing white matter in children with dyslexia. *Psychiatry Research: Neuroimaging, 172,* 215–219.

Church, J. A., Coalson, R. S., Lugar, H. M., Petersen, S. E., & Schlaggar, B. L. (2008). A developmental fMRI study of reading and repetition reveals changes in phonological and visual mechanisms over age. *Cerebral Cortex, 18*(9), 2054–2065.

Church, J. A., Petersen, S. E., & Schlaggar, B. L. (2010). The "Task B" problem and other considerations in developmental functional neuroimaging. *Human Brain Mapping, 31*(6), 852–862.

Coltheart, M., Rastle, K., Perry, C., Langdon, R., & Ziegler, J. (2001). DRC: A dual route cascaded model of visual word recognition and reading aloud. *Psychological Review, 108*(1), 204–256.

Connor, C. M., Morrison, F. J., Fishman, B., Crowe, E. C., Al Otaiba, S., & Schatschneider, C. (2013). A longitudinal cluster-randomized controlled study on the accumulating effects of individualized literacy instruction on students' reading from first through third grade. *Psychological Science, 24*(8), 1408–1419.

Critchley, M. (1970). *The dyslexic child.* Springfield, IL: Charles C Thomas.

Dehaene, S. (2009). *Reading in the brain: The new science of how we read.* London: Penguin.

Desmond, J. E., & Fiez, J. A. (1998). Neuroimaging studies of the cerebellum: Language, learning and memory. *Trends in Cognitive Sciences, 2*(9), 355–362.

Dimitriadis, S. I., Laskaris, N. A., Simos, P. G., Micheloyannis, S., Fletcher, J. M., Rezaie, R., et al. (2013). Altered temporal correlations in resting-state connectivity fluctuations in children with reading difficulties detected via MEG. *NeuroImage, 83,* 307–317.

Dimitriadis, S. I., Simos, P. G., Fletcher, J. M., & Papanicolaou, A. C. (2018). Aberrant resting-state functional brain networks in dyslexia: Symbolic mutual information analysis of neuromagnetic signals. *International Journal of Psychophysiology, 126,* 20–29.

Eden, G. F., Jones, K. M., Cappell, K., Gareau, L., Wood, F. B., Zeffiro, T. A., et al. (2004). Neural changes following remediation in adult developmental dyslexia. *Neuron, 44,* 411–422.

Eicher, J. D., Montgomery, A. M., Akshoomoff, N., Amaral, D. G., Bloss, C. S., Libiger, O., et al. (2016). Dyslexia and language impairment associated genetic markers influence cortical thickness and white matter in typically developing children. *Brain Imaging and Behavior, 10*(1), 272–282.

Ferrari, M., & Quaresima, V. (2012). A brief review on the history of human near-infrared spectroscopy (fNIRS) development and fields of application. *Neuro-Image, 63*(2), 921–935.

Fiez, J. A., Tranel, D., Seager-Frerichs, D., & Damasio, H. (2006). Specific reading and phonological processing deficits are associated with damage to the left frontal operculum. *Cortex, 42*(4), 624–643.

Finch, A. J., Nicolson, R. I., & Fawcett, A. J. (2002). Evidence for a neuroanatomical difference within the olivo-cerebellar pathway of adults with dyslexia. *Cortex, 38,* 529–539.

Finn, E. S., Shen, X., Holahan, J. M., Scheinost, D., Lacadie, C., Papademetris, X., et al. (2014). Disruption of functional networks in dyslexia: A whole-brain, data-driven analysis of connectivity. *Biological Psychiatry, 76*(5), 397–404.

Fletcher, J. M., Lyon, G. R., Fuchs, L. S., & Barnes, M. A. (2019). *Learning disabilities: From identification to intervention* (2nd ed.). New York: Guilford Press.

Fletcher, J. M., & Taylor, H. G. (1984). Neuropsychological approaches to children: Towards a developmental neuropsychology. *Journal of Clinical Neuropsychology, 6,* 39–56.

Galaburda, A. M. (1993). The planum temporale. *Archives of Neurology, 50,* 457.

Hinschelwood, J. (1902). Congenital word blindness, with reports of 10 cases. *Opthalmology Review, 21,* 91–99.

Hoeft, F., McCandliss, B. D., Black, J. M., Gantman, A., Zakerani, N., Hulme, C., et al. (2011). Neural systems predicting long-term outcome in dyslexia. *Proceedings of the National Academy of Sciences of the USA, 108*(1), 361–366.

Horowitz-Kraus, T., Wang, Y., Plante, E., & Holland, S. K. (2014). Involvement of the right hemisphere in reading comprehension: A DTI study. *Brain Research, 1582,* 34–44.

Hosseini, S. M., Black, J. M., Soriano, T., Bugescu, N., Martinez, R., Raman, M. M., et al. (2013). Topological properties of large-scale structural brain networks in children with familial risk for reading difficulties. *NeuroImage, 71,* 260–274.

Houdé, O., Rossi, S., Lubin, A., & Joliot, M. (2010). Mapping numerical processing, reading, and executive functions in the developing brain: An fMRI meta-analysis of 52 studies including 842 children. *Developmental Science, 13*(6), 876–885.

Hugdahl, K., Heiervang, E., Ersland, L., Lundervold, A., Steinmetz, H., & Smievoll, A. I. (2003). Significant relation between MR measures of planum temporal area and dichotic processing of syllables in dyslexic children. *Neuropsychologia, 41,* 666–675.

Huth, A. G., de Heer, W. A., Griffiths, T. L., Theunissen, F. E., & Gallant, J. L. (2016). Natural speech reveals the semantic maps that tile human cerebral cortex. *Nature, 532,* 453–458.

Krasuski, J., Horowitz, B., & Rumsey, J. M. (1996). A survey of functional and anatomical neuroimaging techniques. In G. R. Lyon & J. M. Rumsey (Eds.), *Neuroimaging: A window to neurological foundations of learning and behavior in children* (pp. 25–55). Baltimore: Brookes.

Langer, N., Peysakhovich, B., Zuk, J., Drottar, M., Silva, D. D., Smith, S., et al. (2017). White matter alterations in infants at risk for developmental dyslexia. *Cerebral Cortex, 27*(2), 1027–1036.

Lauterbur, P. C. (1973). Image formation by induced local interactions: Examples of employing nuclear magnetic resonance. *Nature, 242,* 190–191.

Lovett, M. W., Frijters, J. C., Wolf, M. A., Steinbach, K. A., Sevcik, R. A., & Morris, R. D. (2017). Early intervention for children at risk for reading disabilities: The impact of grade at intervention and individual differences on intervention outcomes. *Journal of Educational Psychology, 109*(7), 889–914.

Maisog, J. M., Einbinder, E. R., Flowers, D. L., Turkeltaub, P. E., & Eden, G. F. (2008). A meta-analysis of functional neuroimaging studies of dyslexia. *Annals of the New York Academy of Sciences, 1145,* 237–259.

Martin, A., Schurz, M., Kronbichler, M., & Richlan, F. (2015). Reading in the brain of children and adults: A meta-analysis of 40 functional magnetic resonance imaging studies. *Human Brain Mapping, 36*(5), 1963–1981.

Meyler, A., Keller, T. A., Cherkassky, V. L., Gabrieli, J. D. E., & Just, M. A. (2008). Modifying the brain activation of poor readers during sentence comprehension with extended remedial instruction: A longitudinal study of neuroplasticity. *Neuropsychologia, 46,* 2580–2592.

Meyler, A., Keller, T. A., Cherkassky, V. L., Lee, D., Hoeft, F., Whitfield-Gabrieli, S., et al. (2007). Brain activation during sentence comprehension among good and poor readers. *Cerebral Cortex, 17*(12), 2780–2787.

Miller, K. J., Leuthardt, E. C., Schalk, G., Rao, R. P. N., Anderson, N. R., Moran, D. W., et al. (2007). Spectral changes in cortical surface potentials during motor movement. *Journal of Neuroscience, 27*(9), 2424–2432.

Millett, D. (2001). Hans Berger: From psychic energy to the EEG. *Perspectives in Biology and Medicine, 44*(4), 522–542.

Mori, S., & Zhang, J. (2006). Principles of diffusion tensor imaging and its applications to basic neuroscience. *Neuron, 51*(5), 527–539.

Nugiel, T., Roe, M. A., Taylor, W. P., Vaughn, S. R., Fletcher, J. M., Juranek, J., et al. (2019). Brain activity in struggling readers before intervention relates to future reading gains. *Cortex, 111,* 286–302.

Odegard, T. N., Ring, J., Smith, S., Biggan, J., & Black, J. (2008). Differentiating the neural response to intervention in children with developmental dyslexia. *Annals of Dyslexia, 58*(1), 1–14.

Orton, S. (1927). Specific reading disability—strephosymbolia. *Journal of the American Medical Association, 90,* 1095–1099.

Ozernov-Palchik, O., Norton, E. S., Wang, Y., Beach, S. D., Zuk, J., Wolf, M., et al. (2019). The relationship between socioeconomic status and white matter microstructure in pre-reading children: A longitudinal investigation. *Human Brain Mapping, 40*(3), 741–754.

Paulesu, E., Danelli, L., & Berlingeri, M. (2014). Reading the dyslexic brain: Multiple dysfunctional routes revealed by a new meta-analysis of PET and fMRI activation studies. *Frontiers in Human Neuroscience, 8,* 830.

Papanicolaou, A. C. (Ed.). (2017). *The Oxford handbook of functional brain imaging in neuropsychology and cognitive neurosciences.* New York: Oxford University Press.

Penfield, W., & Roberts, L. (1959). *Speech and brain mechanisms.* Princeton, NJ: Princeton University Press.

Poeppel, D. (1996). A critical review of PET studies of phonological processing. *Brain and Language, 55,* 317–351.

Power, J. D., Schlaggar, B. L., & Petersen, S. E. (2014). Studying brain organization via spontaneous fMRI signal. *Neuron, 84*(4), 681–696.

Price, C. J., & McCrory, E. (2005). Functional brain imaging studies of skilled reading and developmental dyslexia. In M. J. Snowling & C. Hulme (Eds.), *The science of reading: A handbook* (pp. 473–496). Oxford, UK: Blackwell.

Pugh, K. R., Mencl, W. E., Jenner, A. R., Katz, L., Frost, S. J., Lee, J. R., et al. (2001). Neurobiological studies of reading and reading disability. *Journal of Communication Disorders, 34*(6), 479–492.

Qi, T., Gu, B., Ding, G., Gong, G., Lu, C., Peng, D., et al. (2016). More bilateral, more anterior: Alterations of brain organization in the large-scale structural network in Chinese dyslexia. *NeuroImage, 124*(Pt. A), 63–74.

Raschle, N. M., Zuk, J., & Gaab, N. (2012). Functional characteristics of developmental dyslexia in left-hemispheric posterior brain regions predate reading onset. *Proceedings of the National Academy of Sciences of the USA, 109*(6), 2156–2161.

Rezaie, R., Simos, P. G., Fletcher, J. M., Cirino, P. T., Vaughn, S., & Papanicolaou, A. C. (2011a). Engagement of temporal lobe regions predicts response to educational interventions in adolescent struggling readers. *Developmental Neuropsychology, 36*(7), 869–888.

Rezaie, R., Simos, P. G., Fletcher, J. M., Cirino, P. T., Vaughn, S., & Papanicolaou, A. C. (2011b). Temporo-parietal brain activity as a longitudinal predictor of response to educational interventions among middle school struggling readers. *Journal of the International Neuropsychological Society, 17*(5), 875–885.

Richards, T. L., & Berninger, V. W. (2008). Abnormal fMRI connectivity in children with dyslexia during a phoneme task: Before but not after treatment. *Journal of Neurolinguistics, 21*(4), 294–304.

Richlan, F., Kronbichler, M., & Wimmer, H. (2009). Functional abnormalities in the dyslexic brain: A quantitative meta-analysis of neuroimaging studies. *Human Brain Mapping, 30,* 3299–3308.

Richlan, F., Kronbichler, M., & Wimmer, H. (2013). Structural abnormalities in the dyslexic brain: A meta-analysis of voxel-based morphometry studies. *Human Brain Mapping, 34*(11), 3055–3065.

Roe, M. A., Martinez, J. E., Mumford, J. A., Taylor, W. P., Cirino, P. T., Fletcher, J. M., et al. (2018). Control engagement during sentence and inhibition fMRI tasks in children with reading difficulties. *Cerebral Cortex, 28*(10), 3697–3710.

Schlaggar, B. L., & McCandliss, B. D. (2007). Development of neural systems for reading. *Annual Review of Neuroscience, 30,* 475–503.

Schultz, R. T., Cho, N. K., Staib, L. H., Kier, L. E., Fletcher, J. M., Shaywitz, S. E., et al. (1994). Brain morphology in normal and dyslexic children: The influence of sex and age. *Annals of Neurology, 35,* 732–742.

Seidenberg, M. S. (2005). Connectionist models of word reading. *Current Directions in Psychological Science, 14*(5), 238–242.

Seidenberg, M. S. (2017). *Language at the speed of sight.* New York: Basic Books.

Shaywitz, B. A., Shaywitz, S. E., Blachman, B. A., Pugh, K. R., Fulbright, R. K., Skudlarski, P., et al. (2004). Development of left occipitotemporal systems for skilled reading children after a phonologically-based intervention. *Biological Psychiatry, 55,* 926–933.

Simos, P. G., Fletcher, J. M., Bergman, E., Breier, J. I., Foorman, B. R., Castillo, E. M., et al. (2002). Dyslexia-specific brain activation profile becomes normal following successful remedial training. *Neurology, 58,* 1203–1213.

Simos, P. G., Fletcher, J. M., Sarkari, S., Billingsley, R. L., Denton, C., & Papanicolaou, A. C. (2007a). Altering the brain circuits for reading through intervention: A magnetic source imaging study. *Neuropsychology, 21,* 485–496.

Simos, P. G., Fletcher, J. M., Sarkari, S., Billingsley-Marshall, R., Denton, C., & Papanicolaou, A. C. (2007b). Intensive instruction affects brain magnetic activity associated with reading fluency in children with persistent reading disabilities. *Journal of Learning Disabilities, 40,* 37–48.

Simos, P. G., Rezaie, R., Fletcher, J. M., Juranek, J., Cirino, P. T., Li, Z., et al. (2011). Functional disruption of the brain mechanism for reading: Effects of comorbidity and task difficulty among children with developmental learning problems. *Neuropsychology, 25*(4), 520–534.

Simos, P. G., Rezaie, R., Fletcher, J. M., & Papanicolaou, A. C. (2013). Time-constrained functional connectivity analysis of cortical networks underlying phonological decoding in typically developing school-aged children: A magnetoencephalography study. *Brain and Language, 125*(2), 156–164.

Torgesen, J. K., Alexander, A. W., Wagner, R. K., Rashotte, C. A., Voeller, K. K., & Conway, T. (2001). Intensive remedial instruction for children with severe reading disabilities: Immediate and long-term outcomes from two instructional approaches. *Journal of Learning Disabilities, 34*(1), 33–58.

Vanderauwera, J., Wouters, J., Vandermosten, M., & Ghesquiere, P. (2017). Early dynamics of white matter deficits in children developing dyslexia. *Developmental Cognitive Neuroscience, 27,* 66–77.

Vandermosten, M., Boets, B., Poelmans, H., Sunaert, S., Wouters, J., & Ghesquière, P. (2012). A tractography study in dyslexia: Neuroanatomic correlates of orthographic, phonological and speech processing. *Brain, 135*(Pt. 3), 935–948.

Vaughn, S., Solis, M., Miciak, J., Taylor, W. P., & Fletcher, J. M. (2016). Effects from a randomized control trial comparing researcher and school-implemented treatments with fourth graders with significant reading difficulties. *Journal of Research on Educational Effectiveness, 9*(Suppl. 1), 23–44.

Vogel, A. C., Church, J. A., Power, J. D., Miezin, F. M., Petersen, S. E., & Schlaggar, B. L. (2013). Functional network architecture of reading-related regions across development. *Brain and Language, 125*(2), 231–243.

Vogel, A. C., Petersen, S. E., & Schlaggar, B. L. (2014). The VWFA: It's not just for words anymore. *Frontiers in Human Neuroscience, 8*(88), 1–10.

Wada, J., & Rasmussen, T. (1960). Intracarotid injection of sodium amytal for the lateralization of cerebral speech dominance: Experimental and clinical observations. *Journal of Neurosurgery, 17,* 266–282.

Wang, Y., Mauer, M. V., Raney, T., Peysakhovich, B., Becker, B. L. C., Sliva, D. D., et al. (2017). Development of tract-specific white matter pathways during early reading development in at-risk children and typical controls. *Cerebral Cortex, 27*(4), 2469–2485.

Williams, V. J., Juranek, J., Cirino, P., & Fletcher, J. M. (2018). Cortical thickness and local gyrification in children with developmental dyslexia. *Cerebral Cortex, 28*(3), 963–973.

Wolf, M. A. (2007). *Proust and the squid: The story and science of the reading brain.* New York: HarperCollins.

Yeatman, J. D., Dougherty, R. F., Ben-Shachar, M., & Wandell, B. A. (2012). Development of white matter and reading skills. *Proceedings of the National Academy of Sciences of the USA, 109*(44), E3045–E3053.

CHAPTER 16

Single-Subject Experimental Design

Susan B. Neuman

Although studies of the individual have always had a place in educational and psychological research, investigations involving single subjects have become increasingly popular (Neuman & McCormick, 1995). Traditionally, single-subject experimental research has been useful in clinical applications where the focus has been on the therapeutic value of an intervention for the client. However, applications of single-subject research in areas such as literacy, language education, and cognitive psychology suggest that single-subject designs provide a powerful way of examining interventions, particularly when reporting average differences for groups may have little meaning. Moreover, researchers (Cooper, Heron, & Heward, 2007) are increasingly turning to an analysis of single subjects in conjunction with other research techniques as a way of explicating findings, providing a more integrated and detailed analysis of the impact of interventions.

Why study the individual subject? For one, this approach allows researchers to examine the effects of an experimental treatment or treatments when it is difficult to obtain groups of subjects or when comparability among and between groups is difficult to establish. It can bypass an error often found in group-comparison studies—intersubject variability—because each individual serves as his or her own control. In addition, single-subject designs provide researchers with information on what may be important differences among individuals. For example, although a particular technique might work best for many students, for others an alternative technique may be superior. Furthermore, with replication, researchers can determine whether the intervention is effective for other individuals and in other settings, helping them build important theoretical links in establishing generalizability.

Single-subject experimental design, however, should not be confused with case study methods. Although both study the individual, in a single-subject experiment the investigator deliberately manipulates one or more independent variables. Single-subject experiments are designed to generate functional and causal statements, whereas case studies are designed to provide insight by describing phenomena (see Chapter 2 for a discussion of case studies).

This chapter describes the methodology and the most common procedures, uses, and applications in language and literacy research. Specifically, it addresses the unique questions that may be answered with the methodology and how these questions may be researched and analyzed. Furthermore, examples of literacy studies are woven throughout the descriptions to emphasize how these applications can address key questions, and the strengths and limitations, as well as the important considerations of validity and reliability are highlighted.

FEATURES OF SINGLE-SUBJECT EXPERIMENTAL RESEARCH

Beginning in the 1950s, single-subject experimental research designs came about largely in psychological studies to explore the aftermath of treatments with patients. These studies had to examine ongoing practice instead of waiting for extended posttest periods. Research designs were proposed that allowed researchers to measure changes in behavior for a particular person individually. Although case studies were used extensively at the time, therapists needed a design that could establish a causal relationship, as might be done with experimental research.

Single-subject experimental designs suited this purpose and today are considered to be one of the strongest designs against threats to internal validity that we have in our research arsenal (Kazdin, 2010). This works by having each participant serve as his or her own control. Basically, the participant is exposed to a nontreatment and a treatment phase and performance is measured during each phase.

Six common characteristics make this research design unique to other experimental designs (Alberto & Troutman, 2003). These characteristics, described next, form the fundamental features that set it apart from other approaches.

Baseline and Treatment Conditions

Each single-subject study involves at least one baseline and one treatment condition. The *baseline* refers to a period of time in which the target behavior (dependent variable) is observed and recorded as it occurs, without a special or new intervention. The baseline provides the frame of reference against which all future behavior is compared, and requires more than a single pretest. Because human behaviors can vary, day to day, multiple opportunities must be given for the participant to exhibit a "typical" response; therefore, most researchers recommend incorporating at least three to five data collection points during baseline (see, e.g., Alberto & Troutman, 2003).

For example, a researcher might be interested in examining the effects of an intervention designed to promote fluency. Prior to the intervention, the baseline period would be used to establish the typical fluency rate of the student by administering fluency assessments for several days beforehand. The baseline phase would continue until the researcher is able to achieve the stability of this target behavior—in this case, fluency rate. The treatment condition is a period of time during which the experimental manipulation is introduced and the target behaviors continue to be observed and recorded.

Repeated Measurement

Another distinguishing feature of single-subject experimental research is the repeated and frequent measurement of responses throughout the intervention. This step is different from most experiments, in which the dependent variable is measured only once. Repeated measures are needed to discern a clear pattern of consistency in the behavior over time. They control for the normal variation of behaviors that is expected within short time interventions. This aspect of single-subject design is similar to time-series studies, which investigate groups rather than individuals. If researchers would find that, after a fluency intervention, fluency rates increase and stay at that rate after five or 10 additional trials, then they would have convincing evidence that the treatment was successful.

Single-Variable Rule

In a single-subject study, only one variable is manipulated at a time. This enables researchers to determine the impact of a specific variable on the observed outcomes. Suppose, for example, that a researcher was interested in examining the impact on a student's comprehension performance as a result of a technique called KWL (what do you Know; what do you Want to find out; what would you like to Learn more about) (Ogle, 1986). The researcher would probably establish baseline through multiple assessments of comprehension and then introduce the single treatment of KWL prior to reading the text. The researcher would then continue to assess comprehension in a similar manner as before the intervention began. If scores increased dramatically, the researcher could say with some degree of confidence that it was a result of KWL. In another example, following baseline, a teacher introduces a new core reading series. In the series, the comprehension exercises include previewing, summarizing, reciprocal teaching, and writing. Scores once again go up. However, in this case, the confounding of treatments means that it would be impossible to disentangle which of the treatments caused the effect. Consequently, in single-subject experimental research, only one independent variable usually can be examined at one time.

Internal Validity

Because subjects serve as their own controls in single-subject experimental research, there are fewer standard threats to the internal validity of an investigation than in some other research paradigms. Researchers also build into their studies procedures for assessing the integrity of the independent variable (McCormick, 1990). In some cases, observers are used to judge the integrity of the independent variable during the intervention period. The observer might use a fidelity checklist, noting the critical features of an intervention. This can allow the researcher to measure "drifts" from the planned procedures during the course of the experiment.

In literacy studies, the independent variable or treatment should be a discrete, behavioral treatment that can be conducted in a single session. Multidimensional interventions are not appropriate for single-subject designs. Topics such as examining the impact of "rereading" a text on comprehension or the effects of hearing a story read before reading the story on one's own may lend themselves especially well to single-subject designs. However, topics such as the effects of a new spelling program do not suit this research paradigm. This would likely include an extended intervention over several days with multiple expected outcomes. It would, therefore, be difficult to measure the integrity of the independent variable under such conditions.

Analysis of Data

In single-subject experimental design, conclusions about the effects of an intervention are based on the visual inspection of the data (Kazdin, 2010). At times visual analysis is joined with statistical analysis or combined with other research analyses. There are a number of reasons why the visual inspection of data is particularly compelling in this research design:

- Graphs with repeated measurement of student outcome allow for an ongoing analysis of student performance.
- Unlike traditional experimental research, there are no "objective" measures, such as levels of significance, that indicate the intervention's success. Rather, the researcher makes his or her own decisions about the educational benefits of the intervention based on a visual inspection of the data.

- Conclusions about an intervention's merits can be drawn relatively quickly. For example, if a fluency intervention yields large increases in a student's fluency rate and there is evidence of maintenance, the researcher may decide to discontinue the study and implement the intervention in the instructional program immediately.
- Visual analysis presents a more conservative view of data analysis than other techniques. First, obviously, it is not influenced by sample size. Second, findings that might demonstrate statistical significance in group studies may not be educationally meaningful. Sometimes visual inspection of the data will demonstrate results that tests fail to find statistically. This is especially true with individuals who may not easily be identified in a group (e.g., those with learning disabilities).

To determine the effects of an independent variable, like fluency training, on the dependent variable, fluency rate, for example, the researcher would graph the data collected immediately following each session and visually inspect the differences between the baseline and treatment phases. If there was a clear distinction between baseline and treatment, the researcher would assume a functional relationship. Using a standard A-B-A withdrawal design (described later), for example, the researcher might reverse treatment—take away the intervention—to see whether the data return to baseline. If this occurs, then it is assumed that the intervention is the causal connection in improving the behavior.

External Validity

The most controversial aspect of single-subject experimental design relates to external validity, or the generalizability of the research. How do we know if the results found with one subject may apply to others?

In traditional experimental research, generality of effects is assumed with statistical significance. This term suggests that, given a different sample from the same population, the researcher would likely find the same results, according to certain probability levels ($p < .01$, for example). This statement assumes, therefore, that if the study were replicated, the results would be similar, give or take a margin of error.

The tactics taken by single-subject researchers are different than the traditional experimental paradigm. Some researchers, such as Axelrod and his colleagues, argue that "generalizability" is anathema to single-subject design (Axelrod, 1983). Given that the goal is to conduct a treatment for an individual, and individuals are different, there is no generalizability. "All we can do," Axelrod argues, "is to improve the life of an individual, one by one. If an autistic child no longer engages in self-inflicting activity like banging his head against a wall as a result of an intervention, then this is evidence that the treatment worked—for this child" (S. Axelrod, personal communication, December 14, 1994).

Other single-subject design researchers (Cooper et al., 2007), however, might argue for transferability rather than generalizability. Transferability implies an extension of the effects of the intervention to new populations. For example, a researcher may conduct the same experiment but with different subjects, who may have slightly different characteristics than the subject in the first study. This would provide an extension of their original study. Then they might carry out their intervention in a different context to further examine its transferability. Through repeated replications with different subjects, single-subject experimenters may make important theoretical linkages, establishing the credibility of their intervention to different subjects, different contexts, and different special populations.

EXPERIMENTAL LOGIC
OF SINGLE-SUBJECT EXPERIMENTAL DESIGN

These six features of single-subject experimental design reflect an experimental logic basic to the research paradigm. The design is predicated on three major goals (McCormick, 1995): prediction, verification, and replication. By looking at Figure 16.1, we can see how they work.

Prediction is satisfied through repeated measurement of baseline data until stability is recorded. The logic works like this: If a student shows a consistent level of response throughout the baseline period, then the researcher can *predict* that his or her response will continue to fall within that particular level without additional intervention. Evidence of stability at baseline is foundational to the design. Although there are some variations in baseline 1 in Figure 16.1, it is evident that the measurement shows stability.

Verification is the second basic element in the experimental logic. Procedures for verification will be different across different single-subject designs, but essentially it refers to a requirement that the research must demonstrate that change in a particular score is functionally related to the intervention. For example, in a reversal design, the researcher would show verification by removing the independent variable and then collecting data on the dependent variable. If changes in scores were due to the independent variable, scores should return to baseline levels. This is what has occurred in baseline 2 in the figure. Scores increased as a result of the intervention and then returned to baseline after the independent variable was removed.

Replication serves as the basis for determining the reliability of the results. Repeating phases within experiments may confirm the results. It may also provide assurances that the intervention has consistent effects. In intervention 2 in Figure 16.1, scores return to their upward trend after the intervention is once again initiated.

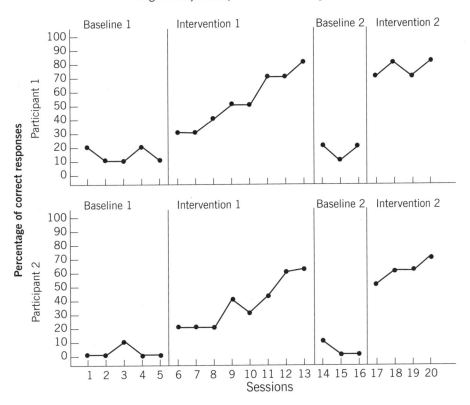

FIGURE 16.1. Example of a single-subject design study.

Requiring evidence of prediction, verification, and replication, therefore, demonstrates that there is a functional relationship between the intervention and the data that are collected. Consequently, the researcher can argue with full assurance for a causal relationship between the independent and dependent variables.

COMMON SINGLE-SUBJECT
EXPERIMENTAL RESEARCH DESIGNS

There is no one particular single-subject design. Rather, there are three common types (Kazdin, 2010) and many, many variations within them. For current purposes, the following designs are discussed:

- A-B-A withdrawal designs.
- Multiple-baseline designs.
- Alternating treatments designs.

A-B-A Withdrawal Designs

In the A-B-A withdrawal family of single-subject design strategies, "A" refers to the no-treatment, or control, phase of the experiment and "B" refers to the treatment phase. To conduct an A-B-A study, the first step would be to state the research problem in a manner that includes operational definitions of our experimental variables. This is very important because precise measurement is critical to examine both stability and variation. Consider a hypothetical example, illustrated in Figure 16.2. Suppose, for instance, that a teacher wanted to assess the impact of a shared book experience on a first-grade student's word-recognition skills. In this hypothetical example, graphed in Figure 16.2, the first baseline phase presents the percentage of target words the child recognized during participation in a reading program where there was regular sustained silent reading intermingled with skill and strategy instruction. This represents "business as usual." During the B phase, the teacher changed instruction to involve daily shared-book experiences, with tests that included the target words, and again recorded results from a word-recognition measure. To determine

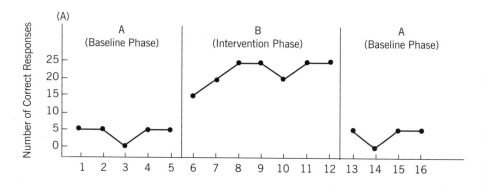

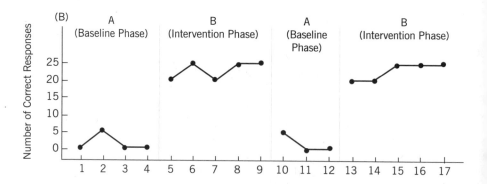

FIGURE 16.2. Example of a reversal design.

whether the student's increased proficiency in this phase was functionally related to the addition of the shared book experience to the program, the shared-book activity was dropped in a second baseline condition. In other words, in this third phase of the experiment, the teacher attempted to verify the prediction that the level of word recognition seen during the first baseline phase would continue if shared-book experiences were not added.

Given that other threats to internal validity are ruled out, the A-B-A design allows reasonable inferences about the effects of treatment. However, some would argue that it is educationally unfeasible to end with a baseline phase. Therefore, most studies would add an additional phase A-B-A-B to demonstrate once again the contribution of the intervention and its educational benefits for the child.

Multiple-Baseline Designs

In the multiple-baseline design, researchers typically vary one of three parameters (subject, behavior, or setting) while keeping the other two constant (Kucera & Axelrod, 1995). The approach takes repeated measures of baseline on two or more dependent variables. Once the baseline is stable, the researcher introduces the independent variable (such as an instructional method), applying it only to the first dependent variable, and continues to repeatedly measure the reader's performance on all the dependent variables. This means that data are collected on those dependent variables still in the baseline condition while at the same time only one independent variable is being manipulated at a time.

Let's take a hypothetical study on reading instruction using this design. Abigail, a fourth grader, has difficulty with reading comprehension, as evidenced by her inability to identify details as well as the main idea and inferencing in a story. The researcher is interested in examining the impact of a strategy designed to encourage Abigail to monitor her use of comprehension by thinking aloud and graphing the number of details she remembers each time she reads a story. Thinking aloud, in this case, is the independent variable. The dependent variables consist of details or literal comprehension, main idea, and inference. For each variable, a score of 0 to 4 was possible, with a total possible score of 12 (calculated by adding all the response skills together).

Prior to the intervention, baseline data were collected on all three dependent variables, as shown in Figure 16.3. Starting in session 5, Abigail is taught to think aloud to find the literal details in the story. As indicated in the figure, Abigail increased her ability to identify details, moving from an average of 1.5 to 2.7 following this intervention. Meanwhile, the other baselines remained stable, indicating a lack of covariation between the dependent variables.

After some improvements in the first dependent variable were observed, beginning in session 9, Abigail is taught to use thinking aloud to focus on

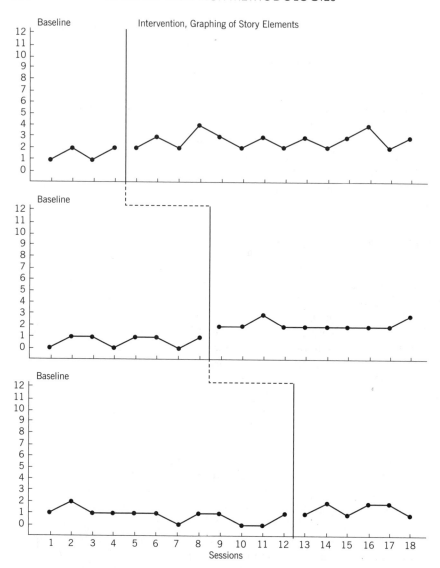

FIGURE 16.3. Example of a multiple-baseline approach.

the main ideas in the story. Then, following a favorable trend in the second dependent variable, the experimental variable is applied to the final condition (inferencing) in addition to the first two. Abigail's ability to identify details and main ideas increases in some sessions following the initiation of the intervention but not in others.

The multiple-baseline design demonstrated that the independent variable of thinking aloud used in this hypothetical study is responsible for some modest improvements in Abigail's ability to identify the main idea. The research design supports this conclusion because, in general, the improvements in Abigail's comprehension occurred only following each intervention, and similar improvements did not occur in the absence of intervention. However, there is considerable overlap in the data points between the baseline and intervention conditions, especially in conditions 1 and 3, in this case, the ability to use inferencing. Therefore, the results of this example indicate that although comprehension was helped somewhat by the use of thinking aloud, it did not appear to be particularly powerful. It is likely, then, that the researcher will turn to other interventions for helping Abigail improve her reading comprehension.

In this case, the multiple-baseline design is well suited for addressing many literacy questions. One caveat, however, should be considered prior to initiating a study with this type of design: Dependent variables need to be functionally independent of one another (so that baselines of still-untreated behaviors remain unaffected) and yet similar enough for each to respond to the same intervention (Kucera & Axelrod, 1995).

Alternating Treatments Design

The final type of single-subject design we consider here is the alternating treatments design. In this design, two or more distinct treatments are introduced, usually following a brief baseline phase. The treatments are then alternated randomly and continued until one treatment proves to be more effective than the other or until it is clear than no method is superior to another. During the entire experiment, the learner's performance for each treatment is plotted on a graph, and the effects of the treatment can be discerned easily by visual analysis. These procedures control for many possible threats to the internal validity of a study such as differential selection of subjects or history effects (Neuman, 1995).

Figure 16.4 provides an example of this design. Suppose a researcher was interested in examining the impact of a technique called previewing, an advanced organizer developed by Graves, Cooke, and LaBerge (1983) on students' comprehension performance compared with a prereading discussion or a no-discussion control condition. In this hypothetical example, assume that after each treatment three students read a passage and then were administered a 10-item comprehension measure. This order of the

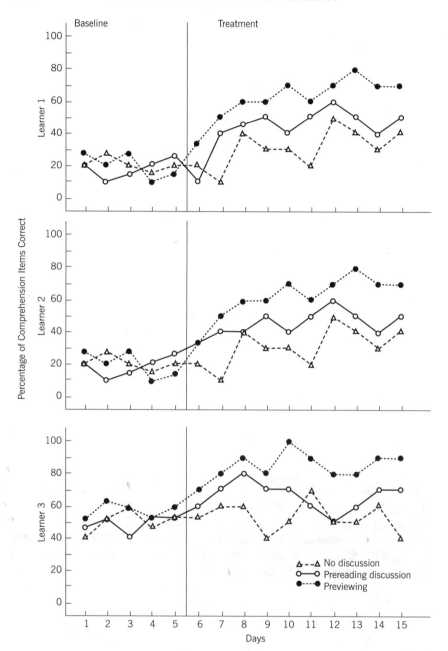

FIGURE 16.4. Example of an alternating treatments approach.

treatments was counterbalanced over a 10-day period, with each treatment applied in random order each day. In other words, each intervention had to "take turns" in terms of when it was applied. As noted in Figure 16.4, the data for each of the three learners, plotted separately for each intervention, clearly indicate that the previewing strategy in this case was more effective than the other treatment or control condition.

The alternating treatments design has several important advantages for research and instruction. It can be used to compare different approaches relatively quickly, allowing for instructional decision making. The graphs are easy to interpret because the data points for each treatment are displayed simultaneously. Furthermore, this design can be used to examine applied questions within the context of instruction, with minimal interference to ongoing classroom activity. These advantages make the alternating treatments design especially useful for teacher-researchers or action researchers in language and literacy.

STANDARDS OF QUALITY IN SINGLE-SUBJECT DESIGN

Single-subject design is a rigorous, scientific methodology if used appropriately. In fact, the federal Institute of Education Sciences What Works Clearinghouse has published a lengthy guide to examining technical aspects of single-case designs (Kratochwill et al., 2010). There are standards of quality. The following quality indicators should be considered when designing studies (Horner et al., 2005):

- Descriptions of participants and settings: Participants need to be described with sufficient detail to allow others to replicate the experiment.
- Independent and dependent variables: Independent and dependent variables must be operationally defined. In the case of the independent variable, researchers need to identify a behavior that can be systematically manipulated and powerful enough to demonstrate immediate effects. In the case of the dependent variable, it is important to use a valid and reliable measure that generates a quantifiable index and can be measured repeatedly over time.
- Baseline: Baseline behaviors must be measured over a sufficient period of time to show stability prior to treatment. Baselines reveal a pattern of responding that are used to predict the pattern of future performance if the independent variable had not been introduced.
- Experimental control: The design must control for common threats to internal validity, such as testing effects, or multiple treatment interference. History sometimes poses a particular problem to the extent that these studies generally occur over time, rendering them more susceptible to intervening events.

- External validity: Experiments should be replicated across participants, settings, or materials.
- Social validity: Social validity is a term coined by single-subject design researchers to refer to the social importance and acceptability of treatment goals, procedures, and outcomes. It is somewhat akin to the notion of effect size, meaning that researchers examine whether the magnitude of change in the dependent variable has practical value and is generally important. Unlike other experiments, however, there is no ballpark definition of what constitutes social importance. Rather, it is determined on a case-by-case basis.

STRENGTHS AND LIMITATIONS

Taken together, single-subject designs can be particularly useful to answer a wide variety of literacy questions (Neuman & McCormick, 1995). These designs may be especially helpful when there is a wide disparity within groups. The personalized evaluation inherent in single-subject designs may present more accurate data on individual differences and may provide further insights on instructional improvements.

The design is ideal for applied settings and clinical practice: to address questions related to practice. It is also cost-effective. It can make causal statements that have traditionally required large sample sizes and extended periods of time. It can provide replications of the experiment across subjects or across settings that may extend its reliability.

However, the design is not without its limitations. Perhaps the greatest limitation for literacy researchers is related to carryover effects. Put simply, a skill once learned cannot be unlearned easily. Results from the previous phase may carry over into the next. This becomes a significant problem, for example, in A-B-A design since the strength of the design is to return to baseline.

Carryover also occurs in other designs, such as multiple-baseline or alternating treatments. In this case, it might look like multiple-treatment interference. Here there is a possibility that one treatment might influence or blend with another. This is a serious problem because it can muddy the waters, making it impossible to attribute the effects of a target behavior to a particular treatment. It may also limit the kinds of questions that can be asked and answered by the designs for literacy researchers.

In addition, treatments themselves must be potentially powerful enough to determine reasonably immediate effects. For example, it would not be wise to examine the effects of sustained silent reading versus strategic instruction on the percentage of time spent reading because it may take multiple sessions before the investigator observes real changes in the dependent variable. Related to this problem, treatments that are developed over a consecutive series of sessions cannot be measured in most of these designs.

For example, if it typically takes a three-step procedure over a 3-day period for a phonics program to improve a student's performance in phonics, then it would be difficult to provide enough repeated measures to examine the effects. Finally, there may be the problem of order effects; that is, the ordering of the intervention or treatment is what accounts for the effect rather than the treatment alone.

Therefore, although these designs can be elegant and efficient for examining the effects of treatment, some constraints need to be considered when employing this design in language and literacy research. Being aware of the constraints, and organizing treatments and procedures accordingly, will enable investigators to use the design to their advantage, answering critical questions in educational research.

EXEMPLARS OF SINGLE-SUBJECT EXPERIMENTAL RESEARCH

I first became aware of this design through a study by Mudre and McCormick (1989) in *Reading Research Quarterly*. In this study, the authors used a multiple-baseline design to examine the effects of parent tutoring on children's comprehension skills. It was an elegant study and provided a clear rationale for why someone might choose to use the single-subject experimental design approach. First, although the children in the study were all underachievers, they exhibited very different reading difficulties. It would have been difficult to define them, given their age differences and reading difficulties, as a group. Second, the parents themselves had different skills; although they might be trained to use strategies to tutor their children, each would do this in a different way depending on their background characteristics and their child's needs. Third, it involved six parents and children. From a single-subject perspective, this would mean a potential of six replications; for a traditional study, it would be considered underpowered.

The authors chose the multiple-baseline approach because they wanted to examine how each strategy might influence readers' use of context, their self-corrections, and their literal comprehension skills. Following an extended baseline period, they began to introduce one tutoring strategy at a time and had parents practice the strategy with the children. At each phase of the treatment, they could compare the strategy taught with the strategies not yet taught. In this way, they could determine whether the experimental variables were responsible for any of the changes seen. For example, during phase 1 of the intervention, parent cuing for self-correction was taught in a workshop, and all parent behaviors (self-correction cues, cues for context use, and praise) were measured for 5 days. A similar strategy was followed with the introduction to new strategies. Following the treatment period, they continued to follow the child's reading, looking first at whether the strategies taught were maintained and whether there might be transfer to a new reading task as a result.

They examined their data through graphic analyses, in combination with *t*-tests for correlated means. Specifically, they looked for indicators of low error rate in reading, use of context, and increases in self-corrections. They reported increases in the use of the desired strategies and continuous improvements for some children more than others.

What were benefits of using this design? The researchers were better able to determine which of the strategies was most effective; they could subsequently individualize instruction to meet the needs of the individual learners, and they could examine immediate effects through the graphing of data. It was ideal for a clinical setting. All of these factors are critically important when we work with children who have special strengths and needs.

Based on my readings of this article and others in special journals, I joined an informal group at the National Reading Conference, led by Sandy McCormick, to learn more about the methodology. Along with my graduate student, we thought that the single-subject design approach might be especially useful to examine parent–child interactions in the home setting. Specifically, our goal was to examine an intervention that might encourage teenage mothers to be more responsive to their child's interactions during literacy and play. Like Mudre and McCormick (1989), we were convinced that a study of individual subjects, given our work with individual differences among teen mothers, would better capture how they might respond to the intervention.

The first and most difficult step in our work (Neuman & Gallagher, 1994) was to operationalize our dependent variables. It made sense to break down our "interactional" goal into specific language interactions that could support children's receptive language. Three behaviors seemed to be critically related to children's language uses: mother's use of labeling (identifying objects); scaffolding (helping to refine the child's approximations to conventional uses); and contingent responsivity (responding to the child's queries with explanations and extensions). Piloting our work, we developed a set of definitions that could act as a codebook for parent–child interactions.

We designed the work as a multiple-baseline single-subject study, introducing each behavior one at a time while we continued to measure all three. First, we visited teen mothers in their homes, recording their language and interactions with their children. Following each visit, we coded and recorded each of the language activities and then plotted them on a graph for visual analysis. Once stability was reached, we introduced a literacy prop box in each home. Based on a theme of a post office, the prop box included a book and play objects related to theme. Every other week, we visited and emphasized one particular skill (e.g., labeling) and then in the subsequent week observed and coded mother–child interaction for that particular behavior as well as the others. Following the treatment, we then gave them a new set of materials and examined their behaviors, hoping that skills learned in one context would transfer to another. Finally, after 6 weeks, we once again observed to examine how these behaviors were maintained over time. Figure 16.5 gives an example from one of our mothers of how the data were graphed throughout the study.

What we found was that all six mother–child dyads clearly revealed changes in the frequency of cues from baseline to intervention. Although the changes differed in magnitude, the intervention produced distinct increases in mothers' uses of labeling, scaffolding, and contingent responsivity. Although scores declined with the transfer to new materials and maintenance, in almost all cases mothers continued to use these strategies to a greater extent than in baseline. Of the three interactional behaviors, cues for contingent responsivity seemed to remain more sustained throughout the study period, indicating mothers' increasing responsivity to their children's literacy initiatives.

We also examined the quality of parent–child interactions by transcribing the data. These data provided a good deal of information on the texture of the interactions that numbers or graphs could not adequately capture. Finally, we examined children's receptive language through the Peabody Picture Vocabulary Test and found dramatic and significant improvements as a result of the intervention (see Table 16.1).

Consequently, we believed that the multiple-baseline design was especially useful for examining our focus question: Does an intervention targeted to improving the quality of parent–child interaction work to enhance children's language development? It allowed us to argue that the intervention "caused" changes in children's language development. At the same time, it highlighted individual variation among our teen mothers. Traditionally, in many group designs, such variation is often not adequately recognized. It also provided a strong case for its effects, given that we had six overall replications.

Using the standards of quality described previously, both studies clearly exemplified these quality features. In both cases, in-depth descriptions of the participants were provided with highly detailed information on the criteria for their selection, their history, and the setting in which the experiment took place. For example, Mudre and McCormick based their work in the reading clinic at the university; Neuman and Gallagher worked in parents' homes.

Independent and dependent variables needed to be discrete, measurable, and clearly defined. In our case, identifying different types of language cues was complex, requiring us to carefully delineate and practice coding how these language cues might look across participants from different cultural perspectives. Since our work was conducted in the natural setting of the home, there was the potential for greater variation than for the cues used in the Mudre and McCormick study.

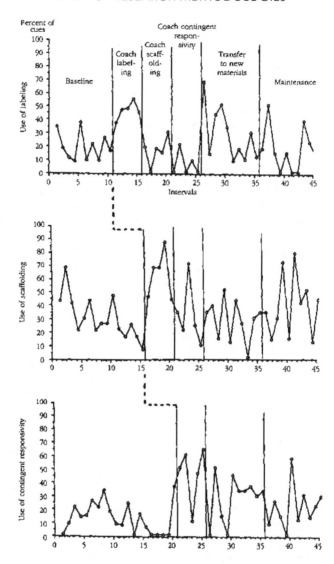

FIGURE 16.5. Example of a multiple-baseline design. From Neuman and Gallagher (1994). Copyright © 1994 International Reading Association. Reprinted by permission.

TABLE 16.1. Pre- and Posttest Mean Percentile Scores, Standard Deviations, and Ranges on the Peabody Picture Vocabulary Test

Variable	N	M	SD	Range
Pretest	6	37.67	19.75	11–60
Posttest	6	74.17*	14.36	60–94

*$p < .01$.

These studies also demonstrated the variance in baselines that is likely to occur in different studies. For example, Mudre and McCormick found stability rather quickly and, therefore, were able to move toward the manipulation of the independent variable, whereas our initial baselines indicated less stability, taking longer before we were able to establish a pattern of response. Therefore, these studies clearly illustrate a central point about baselines: There is no set period of time for establishing baselines; different studies will need different time periods.

Both studies showed a fair amount of experimental control; however, in our study, clearly history might have been a factor in our results. For example, during the 3 months over the course of the study, some families experienced job losses, loss of shelter, and entanglements with law enforcement officials. We attempted to address these issues by carefully documenting these incidents in our participants' lives. Nevertheless, history was a threat to our internal validity.

Generalizability of data is always problematic in studies, regardless of methodology. However, for single-subject design, it has been particularly contentious given the limited sample size and the fact that participants in the research are seldom randomly selected. Extrapolation from the sample to a population constitutes the strongest argument for generalization (Palinscar & DeBruin-Parecki, 1995). The strength of the argument is, to a large extent, a function of the similarities between the participants in the research and those individuals to whom one wishes to generalize. In this case, Mudre and McCormick present an excellent example. Not only do they provide the standard demographic features of their sample, but they also report the sequence of steps they use in the selection process. Furthermore, in addition to the remediation children receive, they describe the nature and focus of all language and literacy instruction in which the children participated. By characterizing the emphases of instruction, the researchers allow the reader to consider how the intervention might be interacting with both the instructional histories and the instruction the children were receiving.

Finally, although both studies do not explicitly report their results in terms of social validity, their efforts to continue to systematically measure their dependent variables through maintenance and examine the transferability of behaviors beyond the interventions allowed for sound evidence for the benefits of the treatment on improving children's achievement.

Single-subject design is also useful to monitor students' progress over time. For example, a study by Reason and Morfidi (2001) measured the progress of eight students on a phonological task, all of whom were learning at a slower rate than others. Examining different teaching conditions using multiple-baseline design, the researchers were able to determine how different teaching approaches might affect the progress of individual students on common phonological measures. Recognizing that struggling readers often have individual strengths and weaknesses that may defy identifying them as a group, the authors highlight the practicality of single-subject design as an alternative methodology to traditional experimental design.

CONCLUSION

In sum, single-subject design methods enable researchers to describe the variability predicted by current theory more precisely than is often possible with either group experiments or thick descriptions. This is important both to better inform practice and to help push our thinking and our theories about literacy development. We must also remember, however, that it is the question that drives the design parameters, not the methodology. Single-subject experimental research may be exquisitely tuned to answer some questions about literacy development and not to others. It may also work in combination with other methods, such as case studies and large-group experimental studies. Furthermore, it provides an efficient strategy for those interested in examining questions in clinical or classroom settings. At the same time, we must also remember that as our questions change, so does our understanding of the problems associated with using research methods for purposes other than those for which they have been traditionally employed.

Single-subject design provides an additional methodological tool to examine critical questions in literacy. In this respect, it provides new ways to inquire, expand theories, and stimulate further explorations in language and literacy development.

REFERENCES

Alberto, P., & Troutman, A. (2003). *Applied behavior analysis for teachers* (6th ed.). Upper Saddle River, NJ: Prentice Hall.

Axelrod, S. (1983). *Behavior modification for the classroom teacher.* New York: McGraw-Hill.

Cooper, J., Heron, T., & Heward, W. (2007). *Applied behavior analysis* (2nd ed.). Upper Saddle River, NJ: Prentice Hall.

Graves, M. F., Cooke, C. L., & LaBerge, M. J. (1983). Effects of previewing difficult short stories on low ability junior high school students' comprehension, recall, and attitudes. *Reading Research Quarterly, 18*, 262–276.

Horner, R., Carr, E., Halle, J., McGee, G., Odom, S., & Wolery, M. (2005). The use of single-subject research to identify evidence-based practice in special education. *Exceptional Children, 71*, 165–179.

Kazdin, A. (2010). *Single-case research designs: Methods for clinical and applied settings.* New York: Oxford University Press.

Kratochwill, T. R., Hitchcock, J., Horner, R. H., Levin, J. R., Odom, S. L., Rindskopf, D. M., et al. (2010). Single-case designs technical documentation. Retrieved from *http://ies.ed.gov/ncee/wwc/pdf/wwc_scd.pdf.*

Kucera, J., & Axelrod, S. (1995). Multiple-baseline designs. In S. B. Neuman & S. McCormick (Eds.), *Single-subject experimental research applications for literacy* (pp. 47–63). Newark, DE: International Reading Association.

McCormick, S. (1990). A case for the use of single-subject methodology in reading research. *Journal of Reading Research, 13*, 69–81.

McCormick, S. (1995). What is single-subject experimental research. In S. B. Neuman & S. McCormick (Eds.), *Single-subject experimental research applications for literacy* (pp. 1–32). Newark, DE: International Reading Association.

Mudre, L. H., & McCormick, S. (1989). Effects of meaning-focused cues on underachieving readers' context use, self-corrections, and literal comprehension. *Reading Research Quarterly, 24*, 89–113.

Neuman, S. B. (1995). Alternating treatments designs. In S. B. Neuman & S. McCormick (Eds.), *Single-subject experimental research applications for literacy* (pp. 64–83). Newark, DE: International Reading Association.

Neuman, S. B., & Gallagher, P. (1994). Joining together in literacy learning: Teenage mothers and children. *Reading Research Quarterly, 29*, 382–401.

Neuman, S. B., & McCormick, S. (Eds.). (1995). *Single-subject experimental research: Applications for literacy.* Newark, DE: International Reading Association.

Ogle, D. (1986). KWL: A teaching model that develops active reading of expository text. *The Reading Teacher, 39*, 564–570.

Palinscar, A. M., & DeBruin-Parecki, A. (1995). Important issues related to single-subject experimental research. In S. B. Neuman & S. McCormick (Eds.), *Single-subject experimental research: Applications for literacy* (pp. 137–152). Newark, DE: International Reading Association.

Reason, R., & Morfidi, E. (2001). Literacy difficulties and single-case experimental design. *Educational Psychology in Practice, 17*, 227–244.

CHAPTER 17

Understanding Literacy Trends through Survey Research

Gwynne Ellen Ash
James F. Baumann
James J. Bason

What are elementary students' attitudes toward reading in school? What do middle school students choose to read in their free time outside school? How do high school teachers accommodate students who struggle to read and understand content area textbooks? How do parents support at home the reading instruction their children receive at school? What content do university teacher educators cover in their courses on elementary reading methods? What teaching experiences and knowledge base about reading do school district administrators have? Answers to questions such as these can be addressed through survey research.

It is the purpose of this chapter to describe how literacy researchers can use surveys to address questions like the preceding about the characteristics of educational groups. We begin with a definition of survey research, followed by a brief history of literacy-related survey research. Next, we describe the types of surveys, and then we address how survey researchers identify populations, draw samples, and make inferences from survey data. We then address the process in which researchers engage when implementing a survey inquiry, followed by a discussion of quality standards for survey research. We conclude by presenting two examples of survey research projects and a summary of the chapter.

WHAT IS SURVEY RESEARCH?

According to the American Statistical Association, the term *survey* "is used most often to describe a method of gathering information from a sample of individuals" (Scheuren, 2004, p. 9). *Survey research* involves a "study in which data are collected from part of a group, for the purpose of describing one or more characteristics of the whole group" (Jaeger, 1997, p. 450). These groups may be persons (e.g., seventh-grade teachers) or broader entities (e.g., a school district). A survey is different from a *census,* which attempts to gather information from an entire population.

Survey research requires systematic methods for collecting information (Groves et al., 2009) in order to generate quantitative descriptions (statistics) of a sample with the purpose of estimating aspects of the broader population (Fowler, 2009). Surveys are popular methods of collecting information from individuals and the preferred means to address research questions when it is most efficient simply to *ask* those who can inform the questions. A survey typically involves the administration of a questionnaire or interview to a relevant group of individuals.

One way to describe surveys involves the degree of organization they entail. In this chapter, we focus on *structured surveys*—that is, research tools that have persons respond to a series of questions. These questions can be answered in face-to-face interviews or through written or electronic media. Structured surveys generate numerical data directly or data that can be categorized and tabulated such that the data can be explored quantitatively through descriptive or inferential statistics. In contrast, researchers can engage in *semistructured interviews* or *qualitative interviews,* in which the interviewer and interviewee engage in more of a conversation than a series of questions and answers. Structured and qualitative interviews address different research questions, and each has its place. Qualitative interviews generate very rich and in-depth data as opposed to structured interviews.

Groves and colleagues (2009) acknowledge that structured surveys are "rather blunt instruments for gathering information," but argue that they also are very "powerful in producing statistical generalizations to large populations" (p. 406). We confine our discussion to structured interviews in this chapter and refer readers to other sources for information about semistructured or qualitative interviews (Gubrium & Holstein, 2002; Rubin & Rubin, 2005; Seidman, 1998).

Finally, it should be understood that surveys are not limited to humans. For example, a researcher might survey objects such as instructional materials or achievement records. Most educational survey research, however, involves questions about the attitudes, knowledge, experiences, and behaviors exhibited by *persons:* teachers, students, administrators, parents, policymakers, or others interested in education. Thus, we focus on survey research that has the potential to address research questions that describe human involvement in literacy education.

A BRIEF HISTORY
OF SURVEY RESEARCH IN LITERACY

The beginnings of survey research can be traced to the late 19th century, with the modern era of sample surveys beginning in earnest in the early 20th century (Weisberg, Krosnick, & Bowen, 1996). The first survey research in literacy occurred in the early 1900s and was tied to what Venezky (1984) referred to as "school surveys," in which U.S. school districts evaluated their entire educational programs, including reading instruction. For example, Venezky described a survey in Cleveland as involving "analyses of the goals of reading instruction, the training of teachers, the methods and materials and time used, and the achievements of students in different components of reading" (p. 18).

Survey research in the social, behavioral, and educational sciences gained widespread acceptance in the 1950s, becoming one of the most popular and efficient methods of collecting information from individuals (Weisberg et al., 1996). In 1961 Austin, Bush, and Huebner described "The Reading Survey" as a "survey method for getting a complete perspective on the reading program" (p. 131), and several significant reading survey studies were conducted during this period. Austin and Morrison (1961) published *The Torch Lighters,* a book describing a mail survey of reading teacher education programs at 74 U.S. colleges and universities, which they replicated 13 years later (Morrison & Austin, 1977). In 2001, Hoffman and Roller reported a modified replication of *The Torch Lighters* research with contemporary teacher educators.

As a follow-up to *The Torch Lighters,* Austin and Morrison asked in 1963, "What guidance do teachers receive *after* they complete their baccalaureate education?" (p. ix). They addressed this question in *The First R* (Austin & Morrison, 1963) by conducting a mail survey of administrators in 1,023 U.S. school districts about the content and conduct of reading instruction and by conducting follow-up, on-site visits in 51 school districts. Barton and Wilder (1964) also reported an extensive study of reading that included face-to-face interviews with leading experts in reading education and mail surveys of university faculty, teachers and principals, and the general public. To provide a contemporary view of elementary reading instruction, Baumann, Hoffman, Duffy-Hester, and Ro (2000) conducted a modified replication of Austin and Morrison's *The First R* research.

Survey research has flourished in the last dozen years. For example, researchers have conducted survey on topics as diverse as the following:

- Students' and teachers' reading habits, interests, attitudes, and motivations for reading (Gambell & Hunter, 2000; Howard & Jin, 2004; Ivey & Broaddus, 2001; Kelley & Decker, 2009; Maynard, Mackay, & Smyth, 2008; McKenna, Kear, & Ellsworth, 1995; Mellard, Patterson, & Prewett, 2007; Mokhtari, Reichard, & Gardner, 2009; Nathanson, Pruslow, & Levitt, 2008).
- Elementary teachers' literacy practices (Ford & Opitz, 2008; Fresch, 2003, 2007).
- Children's early literacy experiences (Al Otaiba, Lewis, Whalon, Dyrlund, & McKenzie, 2009; Hawken, Johnston, & McDonnell, 2005).
- Educators' views on assessments (Hoffman, Assaf, & Paris, 2001; Hoffman, Jenkins, & Dunlap, 2009).
- Teachers' concerns with vocabulary instruction (Berne & Blachowicz, 2008; Hedrick, Harmon, & Wood, 2008; Wood, Vintinner, Hill-Miller, Harmon, & Hedrick, 2009).
- Literacy educators' professional roles and development (Bean, Cassidy, Grumet, Shelton, & Wallis, 2002; Blamey, Meyer, & Walpole, 2008–2009; Commeyras & DeGroff, 1998; Hughes, Cash, Klingner, & Ahwee, 2001).
- Clinical programs (Cuevas, Schumm, Mits-Cash, & Pilonieta, 2006) and reading experts' opinions of trends in the field (Flippo, 1998).

Clearly, educators have used and continue to employ survey research methodology as a means to address a variety of questions about the nature of literacy programs and instruction.

TYPES OF SURVEYS

Surveys come in various forms and can be organized in different ways. The most common way to characterize surveys is by the method of data collection. Survey collection methods include face-to-face surveys, telephone surveys, mail surveys, technology-enhanced surveys, online surveys, and mixed mode surveys. The decision regarding which method to use is typically based on the nature and size of the population under study, the content of the information to be collected, the length of the survey, or the difficulty of the task respondents are asked to complete.

Face-to-Face Surveys

Face-to-face surveys, or structured personal interviews, are preferred by many survey researchers because they afford the most flexibility, allowing a researcher to control the dynamics of the interview process considerably.

Although face-to-face surveys were once the most common type, today telephone, mail, and technology-based surveys are much more common, since they can be conducted for a fraction of the cost of face-to-face surveys (Brooker & Schaefer, 2006). However, several large national surveys still utilize face-to-face methods, among them the National Health Interview Survey (National Center for Health Statistics, 2019) and the General Social Survey (National Opinion Research Center, n.d.).

Advantages of face-to-face surveys include the opportunity for the interviewer to ask for clarification, to ask follow-up or "branched" questions, and to observe and make note of surroundings. In addition, face-to-face surveys tend to produce high response rates. When depth of information and a flexible format are desired and feasible, a face-to-face survey may be the preferred method. When a researcher is interested in a rich, interactive description by a *group* of individuals on a specified topic, a *focus group* may be employed. Given the unique purposes and requirements of focus groups, however, we do not pursue them further in this chapter and refer interested readers to other sources (Greenbaum, 1998; Krueger & Casey, 2008; Stewart, Shamdasani, & Rook, 2006).

Telephone Surveys

When many interviews need to be conducted or the sample of prospective respondents is geographically dispersed, an alternative to face-to-face surveys is a *telephone survey*, which is administering a questionnaire during a phone conversation. Telephone surveys retain some of the advantages of face-to-face surveys—for example, the administrator can explain the purpose of a survey and ask follow-up or branched questions—while providing a more economical way to gather information. In addition, a telephone survey researcher can inquire why an individual chooses to participate in a survey or not. Organizations such as the Harris Poll and the Gallup Poll conduct telephone interviews.

A common approach for identifying telephone numbers is to employ *random digit dialing* (RDD), in which computers randomly generate telephone numbers so that every household in a given area (even those with unlisted numbers) has a known probability of being selected. This can result in highly accurate samples being drawn from specific populations.

The increasing proportion of persons who have replaced their land lines with cell phones (Blumberg & Luke, 2009), however, limits the ability of RDD procedures to produce a generalizable sample given that cell phone numbers are routinely not published. Cell-phone-only households are disproportionately composed of those who are single, are young, and rent their homes (Groves et al., 2009), so telephone samples can be skewed. Additionally, the use of caller ID technology (which can be used to screen calls), and a general increase in refusal rates among persons contacted for telephone surveys, promote the likelihood of a *nonresponse bias* in telephone surveys—that is, the failure to adequately represent the views of those who choose not to participate (Groves, Dillman, Eltinge, & Little, 2002).

Major commercial survey companies have now developed sampling frames of cell-phone-only households, and recent theoretical work (Lavrakas, 2007; Lepkowski et al., 2008) has indicated that conducting surveys with respondents in such households is feasible, although cell phone interviews are more expensive than interviews conducted with landlines. One approach to correcting for bias among cell-phone-only households is to include a subsample of cell-phone-only respondents within a larger RDD survey (Link, Battaglia, Frankel, Osborn, & Mokdad, 2008). In spite of the limitations of telephone surveys, it is generally agreed that they remain a viable and effective way to collect data from large samples of individuals.

Mail Surveys

An alternative to face-to-face or telephone surveys is a *mail survey*, which is distributing a written questionnaire through the postal service. Advantages of mail surveys include relatively low cost, the ability to access a broad sample of potential respondents, and the possibility of obtaining a large number of responses. In addition, there is evidence that mail surveys tend to minimize *social desirability bias* (Tourangeau, Rips, & Rasinski, 2000)—that is, respondents' answering in ways deemed to be socially acceptable or appropriate rather than reflecting their actual attitudes or behaviors—when compared to other survey methods (Hochstim, 1967; Wiseman, 1972).

Mail surveys also have disadvantages. Although they are economical, they may not produce as high a response rate as other types of surveys; one must rely on the respondent to interpret questions properly (i.e., there is no opportunity for clarification); one has no control over the actual administration of the survey; and one cannot determine why persons in the sample choose to participate or not participate.

According to Scheuren (2004), "mail surveys are a powerful, effective, and efficient alternative to their more expensive relatives—the telephone survey and the personal interview" (p. 51). Although mail surveys have limitations just like any type of survey, they have been and remain among the most popular methods employed in literacy survey research (e.g., Austin & Morrison, 1961, 1963; Baumann, Hoffman, et al., 2000; Baumann, Ro, Duffy-Hester, & Hoffman, 2000; Commeyras & DeGroff, 1998; Hoffman et al., 2001; Hoffman & Roller, 2001; Hughes et al., 2001).

Technology-Enhanced Surveys

Technology provides survey researchers a variety of data collection methods. *Computer-assisted telephone interviews* are becoming increasingly common, and they are a way in which technology is enhancing conventional survey procedures. In a computer-assisted telephone interview, the interviewer reads questions from a computer screen and uses a keyboard to enter an interviewee's responses directly, enhancing the speed of obtaining data and the reliability of the data. Similarly, one finds face-to-face surveys being administered by interviewees who use notebook computers to conduct *computer-assisted personal interviews* (Couper et al., 1998). Furthermore, in order to provide greater privacy to respondents in answering sensitive survey items and to assist respondents with poor reading skills, telephone audio-assisted and computer audio-assisted self-interviewing systems are increasingly common methods of data collection (Couper, 2008).

With the advent of computer programs that can recognize speech, telephone surveys can be administered through *interactive voice recognition,* in which a respondent calls a toll-free number and communicates directly by saying prescribed responses. Similarly, using *touch-tone data entry,* interviewees proceed through a prerecorded interview in which they are asked to enter responses through their telephone keypad. These approaches are most useful when factual information is required from the respondent, or when respondent–interviewer interaction is not a necessary requirement for completing an interview (Couper et al., 1998).

Online Surveys

The development of the Internet as a widely used tool for information gathering has opened other possibilities for survey research. *Online surveys* can be distinguished as either *client-side surveys,* which are executed on a respondent's machine, or *server-side surveys,* which are executed on a survey organization's Web server (Couper, 2008; Revilla, Toninelli, Ochoa, & Loewe, 2016). Client-side surveys are typically called *email surveys.*

Email surveys are not used as widely today as the more popular server-side surveys. One primary roadblock in literacy research is that there currently is no known reliable means to access lists of email addresses, so it is difficult to obtain representative samples. Thus, they may not represent broader populations. Client-side surveys are effective for known Internet users for whom email addresses are readily accessible (literacy professors whose email addresses are contained in university directories, teachers within a single district whose email addresses are issued by the district, etc.), but this application requires the creation of specialized sample lists (Hibberts, Johnson, & Hudson, 2012).

Web-based surveys have the advantages of low cost and speed. Although they used to be limited to special populations known to have high rates of Internet access, the widespread use of mobile devices such as tablets and smartphones over the last decade has provided unprecedented access to the Internet; currently in the United States, more than 82% of households now have such access (Ryan, 2018, p. 3). Of the households with access to the Internet, 83% have a cellular data plan, while 82% have broadband Internet access (p. 6). In particular, "younger households (headed by people under age 45), households headed by Blacks or Hispanics, and households with low incomes (under $25,000)" were more likely to use smartphones to access the Internet than to use laptop or desktop computers (p. 3). Even with the growth in Internet access in the United States and throughout the world, online surveys can still create difficulty for researchers related to bias, whether such bias is related to nonresponse, sampling, or other issues (Hibberts et al., 2012).

Social media recruitment for both client- and server-side surveys might have potential to address some of the concerns related to lack of access to emails and the difficulty of building appropriate samples for online surveys (Kosinski, Matz, Gosling, Popov, & Stillwell, 2015). Forgasz, Tan, Leder, and McLeod (2018) used Facebook advertisements to recruit participants (students, parents, and the general public) for three education-focused studies. For minimal cost, Forgasz and colleagues were able to recruit robust samples—in fact, better ones than they were able to create through other recruitment methods.

Social media recruitment poses additional ethical concerns, however, as do online surveys in general. Some issues relate to anonymity and confidentiality (Leung & Unal, 2013), and these might be partially addressed through appropriately designed disclosures of informed consent. However, other issues such as data storage at commercial survey entities are more structural in nature. Nevertheless, with increasing access to the Internet in households, commercially available email lists, and participants through social-media-based recruitment, online survey use will likely continue to increase in the future (Dillman, Smyth, & Christian, 2009). For example, Hutchison, Woodward, and Colwell (2016) used an adaptation of the Survey of Internet Use and Online Reading (Hutchison & Henry, 2010) to survey 1,262 fourth and fifth graders in a large district through a server-side online survey that included the students' demographic data, self-reflections, and performance assessments. Likewise, Fogo, Reisman, and Breakstone (2019) conducted a nationwide online survey in the United States related to disciplinary literacy, looking at teachers' implementation of the Reading Like a Historian curriculum employing the examination of primary source documents.

Mixed Mode Surveys

The *mode* of a survey refers to the manner in which data are collected (Fowler, 2009). Traditionally, surveys involved a single mode, such as gathering data through a face-to-face survey, through the mail, or over the telephone. More recently, however, survey researchers have increasingly used more than one mode in a survey, or a *mixed mode survey* (Dillman et al., 2009).

Researchers employ mixed mode surveys for various reasons, such as to lower costs, to improve timeliness, to reduce coverage error, and to increase response rates (Dillman et al., 2009, Chap. 8). There are several different ways to mix modes. For example, one is to use a Web-based survey for an initial wave of data collection, and then to use a telephone approach to reach nonrespondents to the Web-based method. Another way is to recruit participants by using a telephone method, and then to employ a mail questionnaire for actual data collection.

Although combining data collection approaches does generally increase response rates, there is a risk that respondents may answer survey items differently, depending on the mode utilized (Fowler, 2009). In order to mitigate differential responses to mixed mode surveys, Dillman (2000) suggests using *unimode construction* of survey items. "Unimode construction is writing and presenting of questions to respondents in such a way that assures receipt by respondents of a common mental stimulus, regardless of survey mode" (p. 232). For example, when conducting a telephone interview, interviewers typically do not read the "I don't know" option to respondents; they only code it when it is offered. However, in self-administered modes, such as Web-based or mail surveys, the "I don't know" option is listed so that respondents can choose it should it represent their knowledge or opinion on that item. Unimode construction seeks to prevent these types of differences from affecting survey responses by ensuring that the questions in each mode are received in an identical way, regardless of the mode being used.

TAILORED DESIGN

Most contemporary survey researchers employ some form of the *tailored design method,* which, according to Dillman and colleagues (2009), "involves using multiple motivational features in compatible and mutually supportive ways to encourage high quantity and quality of response to the surveyor's request" (p. 16). A goal of tailored design is to reduce survey errors in coverage, sampling, nonresponse, and measurement (Groves, 2004). A tailored design approach is based on a "social exchange perspective on human behavior . . . which suggests that respondent behavior is motivated by the return that behavior is expected to bring" (Dillman et al., 2009, p. 16). In other words, when a person trusts the group or individuals behind a survey and believes that the costs associated with responding (e.g., time) are outweighed by the potential benefits of the effort to respond, then there is a reasonable likelihood that the person will respond.

When employing a tailored design method, most researchers use a mixed mode survey. For example, consider a university researcher who is interested in surveying state language arts coordinators about their perceptions of a new federal elementary and secondary literacy initiative. A first step might be to use the Internet to search the websites for all 50 states' departments of education. This would elicit the names, email addresses, and postal addresses of the language arts coordinators and language arts senior staff members.

Next, the researcher would send an official-looking email (e.g., using a university logo and signature file) to all language arts coordinators and staff members identified. Within this email, the researcher would explain the purpose of the national survey and indicate that each language arts staff member will soon receive a survey in the mail. The mail survey—professional-looking and printed—would come with a cover letter on the faculty member's university letterhead (or that of a survey research center if there were such a center at the university). For surveys not returned within several weeks, the researcher would send a follow-up email to nonrespondents, inviting them to complete the survey, which this time is attached to the email. This tailored design method, which is intended to promote response rate and minimize survey error, can be used with surveys presented through other media or combinations of media, such as over the telephone or in face-to-face interviews.

POPULATIONS, SAMPLES, AND INFERENCES

When a researcher's question requires responses from a small number of persons—for example, learning about the content area reading practices of subject matter teachers at a specific high school—then it makes sense to interview all individuals. This would involve a census of the entire *population* or surveying all persons who fit a particular classification. A *population parameter* is a value that describes an entire population (e.g., the *mean*, or average, number of years of teaching experienced by the population of all full-time grade 10 English teachers in a specific public school district).

When the population under study is large, however—for instance, when Phi Delta Kappa annually polls Americans about their attitudes toward public schools (Bushaw & McNee, 2009)—a census of the entire population is impractical, costly, or simply not possible. In this situation, other procedures are used to select a subset of the entire population. In fact, most surveys involve a subset of individuals from a population, or *sample*, and most survey researchers wish to gather data on a sample in order to generalize to a broader group (i.e., to estimate a population parameter).

To be able to make generalizations from a sample to a population, a survey researcher must begin by specifying a *sampling frame*, which includes all the members of a given population. Frames, or populations, might be small or large. For example, large populations would include all full-time public school kindergarten teachers in the United States, or all school district superintendents in the 50 states. Examples of smaller populations would be all parents of K–5 students in a small rural school district, or all students who have completed an academic assistance course in reading within the past year at a small state university.

Once a sampling frame is specified, a researcher must determine how to select a *probability sample,* or a subset of the specified population to interview and from which one can make generalizations. Two common types of probability samples are a simple random sample and a stratified random sample. A *simple random sample* is one in which everyone in the sampling frame has an equal chance of being selected through some random process, such as computer random sampling. For example, randomly selecting 1,000 names from all full-time K–5 classroom teachers in the state of Georgia would be a simple random sample.

A *stratified random sample* involves selecting participants from certain subgroups, or *strata,* within a sample. For example, if there were smaller class sizes in the primary grades, there would be proportionally more teachers at those levels. In this situation, a researcher might identify each grade level as a stratum, or subgroup, and then randomly sample each grade level proportionate to its representation in the overall population. The resulting sample would approximate the overall K–5 population better than a simple random sample would.

In probability sampling research, any *sample statistic,* or value that describes the sample such as a sample mean, is not exact; there is some error associated with it. For instance, the average class size of a simple random sample of 1,000 full-time second-grade classroom teachers in Tennessee would be somewhat different from the actual population parameter, should one be able to poll all teachers. If a researcher wishes to use sample statistics to estimate population parameters, the researcher needs to know and report the *sampling error,* or an estimate of the degree of error associated with a sample statistic. This estimate is commonly referred to as the *margin of error* or *margin of sampling error* (Scheuren, 2004, pp. 63–67).

The *margin of sampling error* in a sample statistic is usually reported in plus or minus terms and at some degree of confidence. For example, Baumann, Hoffman, and colleagues (2000) reported that 1,207 responses to their teacher survey resulted in a 2.7% sampling error at the 95% confidence level. This means that any sample statistic they reported for the full sample of teachers would represent the "true" population parameter 95% of the time within plus or minus 2.7% of the reported score.

The margin of sampling error is directly related to sample size. The larger the sample, the smaller the margin of error, the more the sample statistic approximates the population parameter, and the more confidence a consumer can have in the precision of survey results. For example, a simple random sample of 100 would result in about a 10% margin of error, a sample of 500 about 4.5%, and a sample of 1,000 about 3% (Scheuren, 2004, p. 65). A larger sample size is always preferable, but from a cost and efficiency perspective, there often comes a point at which collecting additional cases is not worth the per-case cost. Once sample sizes reach about

1,000, the reduction in sampling error becomes smaller as more and more cases are added, which is why one often finds sample sizes of around 1,000 for public opinion polls.

One final point: The margin of sampling error as we have discussed it refers only to the sampling error. There are other possible errors in survey research, however. These *nonsampling errors* include poorly worded or confusing questions, nonresponse bias, and social desirability bias, to mention a few. Such nonsampling errors cannot be estimated mathematically, so a survey research consumer should be aware of these other sources of error (Fowler, 2009) and read an article critically to determine the degree to which the researcher has attempted to control for, or at least acknowledge, these additional sources.

SURVEY RESEARCH DESIGN PROCESS

Engaging in any scientific inquiry involves a careful, methodical process. Although there is no uniform, agreed-on number of steps in planning and conducting a survey research project, we present a six-step process that captures the essence of recommendations offered by other survey research methodologists (e.g., Jaeger, 1997).

1. *Formulate a research question.* If one accepts the notion that high-quality research begins not with methods but with a carefully framed question (Shulman, 1997), then it follows that the selection of survey research as a method must depend on the formulation of a core research question that is amenable to being answered through a survey. Questions such as those we have used to open this chapter are of the type that would be appropriate for a survey study. Theory should be used to guide the development of the research question, and a thorough literature review of past and current research should be conducted to craft specific research questions.

2. *Devise a measurement strategy.* In this step, a researcher must determine the type of survey and the specific items that will best measure the features of the underlying psychological, behavioral, social, or educational topic or issue under consideration; paying attention to these choices maximizes what is commonly referred to as *construct validity*. Special care also should be taken to ensure that measurement error is minimized. Although it is impossible to eliminate all measurement error, several sources of error can be reduced, including sampling, nonresponse, interviewer, and respondent error. Sampling error is probably the easiest source of error to control. If probability-sampling procedures are used, the range of potential error is known by way of the sampling margin of error. Nonresponse error is more difficult to control. The lower the response rate in a survey, the greater the likelihood that nonresponders may be systematically different from

responders. A researcher needs to obtain additional information about non-respondents in order to determine if responders and nonresponders would have differed in the way they answered survey items. Interviewer error occurs when interviewers fail to follow standardized procedures (e.g., not reading survey questions exactly as written). Training survey interviewers thoroughly minimizes interviewer errors. Finally, respondent errors occur when survey items are unclear; when respondents engage in *satisficing,* or selecting an answer they consider to be reasonable to the researcher (see Krosnick, 1999); or when respondents provide answers to survey questions even when they may not actually have an opinion on the topic (Converse, 1964). A researcher has responsibility for constructing clearly worded items and for being aware of, minimizing, or at least acknowledging respondent error.

   3. *Determine the sampling frame and data collection method.* The next step is to select the appropriate sampling frame, which will be determined in large part by the nature of the research question. If one wishes to seek information from teachers, for example, a researcher must determine which teachers to sample: their position, the grade levels they teach, their subject specialization, the type of schools in which they work (e.g., public vs. private), and the like. A researcher can make generalizations only from the limits of the sampling frame, so identifying the appropriate group to survey is essential. Once the relevant population has been specified, the researcher must determine which method will be used to collect survey data—that is, whether to choose a face-to-face, telephone, mail, technology-enhanced, or mixed mode survey. Again, the research question, as well as pragmatic issues such as research budget and the availability of sampling sources (e.g., professional organization lists, the U.S. Department of Education's Common Core of Data, marketing research lists), will generally guide a researcher in selecting the most suitable survey type.

   4. *Establish sampling methodology and sample size.* The next step in the design process is to determine the method for sampling. If one is surveying a small population, it may be feasible to try to secure responses from all individuals in the population (i.e., to conduct a census). If one is sampling a large population, which is typical in survey research, one must determine whether the sample will be a selective or a probability sample. If it is a *selective sample*—for example, selecting parents who are members of a local parent–teacher organization—one cannot make generalizations to a broader population of parents. There may be times at which a selective sample is appropriate or when it is the only feasible option, but then a researcher must recognize that generalizing to a larger group is not possible. When a researcher employs a *probability* (i.e., random) *sample,* which is the typical standard in survey research, then the researcher should make a decision about sample size with the understanding of what the margin of error will be. Whenever it is economically and pragmatically feasible, a sample should be sufficiently large in order to keep the margin of error reasonably low, so that statements about how a sample may represent the population under study can be made within appropriate confidence limits. When smaller random sample sizes must be selected, a researcher must understand the limits this imposes on generalization and acknowledge these limits in a research report.

5. *Collect and analyze data.* Data collection should be systematic, thorough, and consistent with the accepted procedures for the type of survey employed (Groves et al., 2009, Chap. 5). For example, if a mail survey were used, the researcher would follow a series of phases in distributing, tracking, and monitoring surveys to promote an acceptable response rate and minimize nonresponse bias (Dillman et al., 2009, Chap. 7). Likewise, data analysis procedures should be thoughtful, consistent with the research questions, and systematic. One must establish a data management and analysis plan prior to data collection—ideally, when a study is conceived—so that analyses adequately test research questions. In some cases, simple descriptive statistics such as cross-tabulations will be sufficient and appropriate to answer research questions. In other cases, particularly when a probability sample is obtained, inferential statistics may be appropriate in order to make generalizations from the data. Procedures such as factor or path analyses are sometimes used in analyzing survey data. When inferential statistics are employed, attention should be paid in advance to sample size, to ensure that adequate statistical power will be present for the analysis method to be used (Kraemer & Thiemann, 1987). In short, careful planning at the beginning of the survey process will ensure that analysis requirements are met satisfactorily.

6. *Report findings.* Survey researchers ought to have an intended audience in mind as a study is conceived and planned, and this same audience should be considered and addressed as a report is written. The information contained in the following section on quality standards for survey research and in Table 17.1 can also guide a survey researcher in preparing a research report. Although the form, style, voice, and level of detail may vary, depending on one's audience and intended publication outlet (e.g., a journal devoted strictly to research vs. a journal covering more applied topics), basic standards for reporting an inquiry should be followed. The sixth edition of the *Publication Manual of the American Psychological Association* (American Psychological Association, 2010) is a commonly used standard guide to writing for publication. Strunk and White's (2000) classic "little book," *The Elements of Style,* is always a useful tool for a writer who wishes to be concise and precise.

QUALITY STANDARDS FOR SURVEY RESEARCH

Consumers of survey research should be able to examine key components of a data collection effort to ensure that quality standards have been used, and it is the responsibility of survey researchers to ensure that they provide essential information to allow consumers to effectively evaluate a given survey effort. As a general rule, the methods and procedures reported in a survey should allow replication of the study by other researchers. To accomplish this, the population under study should be clearly defined, and the methods and procedures used to conduct the study should be stated explicitly. This includes how the sample was drawn, the exact questions used in the survey (the survey is often reproduced in an appendix to a report), the number of cases collected during the study, response rate information, the sampling margin of error, and data analysis procedures. Useful information about evaluating response rates, cooperation rates, and refusal rates for a study can be found through the American Association of Public Opinion Research (*www.aapor.org*) and the Council of American Survey Research Organizations (*www.casro.org*). Both of these professional associations provide valuable information on best practices for survey research, formulas to calculate response and refusal rates, and other helpful information to evaluate survey research quality.

As a further aid to evaluate survey research, we reproduce Jaeger's (1997) survey evaluation checklist in Table 17.1. Although Jaeger prepared this as a means to help research consumers evaluate published studies, the checklist is also useful to survey researchers as they conceive of and implement their own studies.

LITERACY SURVEY RESEARCH EXAMPLES

To illustrate the survey research process in literacy, we have selected two examples: the Baumann, Hoffman, and colleagues (2000) national survey of elementary reading instructional practices, and the Mesmer (2006) national survey of primary teachers' uses of and beliefs about beginning reading materials. Table 17.2 contains a condensed version of Jaeger's (1997) survey evaluation criteria and presents a summary of how each literacy survey study compares to these standards.

A Survey of Elementary Reading Instruction Practices

Baumann, Hoffman, and colleagues (2000) conducted a modified replication of Austin and Morrison's 1963 *The First R* study of U.S. public school elementary reading instruction. Noting that debate over the quality and status of elementary reading instruction preoccupied literacy professionals, policymakers, and the general populace in the late 1990s—just as it had

TABLE 17.1. A Short Checklist for Survey Evaluation

1. Does the report contain a list of specific research questions or issues the survey is intended to address?
2. Do the research questions posed by the investigators appropriately and adequately address the topic of the survey; e.g., in a survey on poverty in the United States, does the research include an examination of poverty as a function of race, level of education, and geographic location?
3. Are the research questions posed by the investigators well organized and well structured?
4. Does the report identify the target population to which generalization was desired?
5. Does the report describe available sampling frames?
6. Does the report indicate a close match between the target population and the operational population?
7. Does the report describe the sampling procedures used? Were probability sampling procedures used?
8. Are nonresponse rates reported for the entire survey and for individual questions?
9. Were nonresponse rates low enough to avoid substantial bias errors?
10. Are any analyses of potential sampling bias reported?
11. Are sample sizes sufficient to avoid substantial random errors? Are standard errors of estimate reported?
12. Is the primary mode of data collection (i.e., mailed questionnaires, telephone interviews, face-to-face interviews) consistent with the objectives, complexity, and operational population of the survey?
13. Are survey instruments provided in the report?
14. Are instructions for completing the survey clear and unambiguous?
15. Are questions on instruments clear and unambiguous?
16. Do questions on instruments encourage respondents' honesty in admitting lack of knowledge or uncertainty?
17. Are questions on instruments free from obvious bias, slanting, or "loading"?
18. Was the survey consistent with ethical research practice; e.g., was the anonymity and/or confidentiality of respondents protected?
19. Does the report contain a description of field procedures?
20. Are field procedures adequate and appropriate? Is it likely that major sources of bias error have been avoided?
21. Are data analyses clearly described?
22. Are data analyses appropriate to the purposes of the survey?
23. Did the survey provide answers to the research questions posed by the investigators?
24. Are the researchers' conclusions sound, or are alternative interpretations of findings equally plausible?
25. Does the survey report contain descriptions of deviations from plans for survey implementation and the likely consequences of such deviations?
26. Does the survey report contain an analysis of the quality of the survey?

Note. From Jaeger (1997, pp. 475–476). Copyright © 1997 American Educational Research Association. Reproduced by permission.

LITERACY RESEARCH METHODOLOGIES

TABLE 17.2. Evaluation Summary for the Survey Research Examples

Jaeger's (1997) criteria[a]	Studies critiqued	
	Baumann, Hoffman, et al. (2000)	Mesmer (2006)
Research questions (items 1–3)[b]	• Theoretically and empirically based research question.	• Theoretically and empirically based research question.
Sampling and response rates (items 4–11)	• Probability sample of U.S. elementary teachers, with linked samples for administrators. • Overall survey response rates provided but not item-by-item rates. • Sample margin of error reasonable for primary survey but high for linked surveys.	• Probability sample for members of a professional organization of reading educators, so generalizations limited to this group. • Overall survey response rate provided but not item-by-item rates. • Reasonable sample margin of error reported.
Instrumentation (items 12–18)	• Teacher survey appended to article; administrator surveys available from authors. • Clear instructions for completing survey. • Detailed explanation of survey construction. • Clearly worded questions with no obvious bias in them. • No reliability or validity data provided.	• Survey appended to article. • Clear instructions for completing survey. • Survey construction described. • Clearly worded questions with no obvious bias in them. • No reliability or validity data provided.
Data-gathering procedures (items 19–20)	• Field and data-gathering procedures described in detail.	• Field and data-gathering procedures summarized.
Analyses and conclusions of report (items 21–26)	• Data analyses clearly described and appropriate for purpose of survey. • Descriptive statistics provided in detail and integrated into article narrative. • Thorough discussion of findings. • Limitations acknowledged. • Findings interpreted in relation to both relevant historic and contemporary work.	• Data analyses clearly described and appropriate for purpose of survey. • Descriptive and inferential statistics integrated into article narrative. • Detailed discussion of findings. • Limitations acknowledged. • Plausible interpretations of findings that are connected back to theoretical and research literature.

[a]Adapted from Jaeger's (1997) full survey evaluation checklist presented in Table 17.1.
[b]Numbers correspond to Jaeger's 26 questions presented in Table 17.1.

in the early 1960s (Morrison, 1963)—the authors argued that a contemporary empirical benchmark was needed to address the research question "What is the nature of elementary reading instruction practices today?" (Baumann, Hoffman, et al., 2000, p. 342). Following a search for and reconstruction of original survey instruments, the researchers constructed three forms of a mail survey (classroom teacher, building administrator, and district administrator forms); this survey included multiple-choice, Likert, and open-response items that allowed for querying educators about contemporary issues and permitted cross-decade comparisons.

The primary sample was a probability sample of 3,199 elementary teachers drawn from a national listing of over 900,000 teachers. The researchers used *The First R* procedures as their model: The building and district administrator samples were linked to the teacher sample, with teacher respondents identifying 623 building administrators, who in turn identified 91 district administrators for sampling. Mail surveys were distributed, collected, and analyzed by a university survey research facility. Response rates and sampling errors (at the 95% confidence level) were reported for the teacher (37.7% and 2.7%, respectively), building administrator (25.8% and 7.6%), and district administrator (52.7% and 14.1%) surveys.

Quantitative analyses involved the examination of descriptive statistics and selected cross-tabulations. A random subset of teacher open-response items and all administrator open-response items were analyzed systematically for themes and trends. Results, reported as percentages of respondents, were juxtaposed to *The First R* data by categories, permitting a historic and contemporary look at elementary reading education practices.

Results revealed similarities between teachers of the 1960s and 1990s in that both tended to teach self-contained, heterogeneous classes of students; provided significant time for reading instruction; taught phonics explicitly; were generally not satisfied with their university training in reading instruction; administered required standardized tests; and were challenged by teaching underachieving readers. Differences were noted in the areas of instructional philosophy (a balanced, eclectic view in the 1990s vs. a skill orientation in the 1960s), instructional organization (more whole-class instruction in the 1990s vs. ability grouping in the 1960s), instructional materials (more use of trade books in the 1990s vs. primarily basal readers in the 1960s), early literacy instruction (the reading readiness perspective of the 1960s was supplanted by an emergent literacy orientation), and assessment (use of more nonstandardized, alternative assessments in the 1990s).

The authors noted that several parallel concerns were expressed by teachers of the 1960s and 1990s—most significantly, an urgency to accommodate struggling readers—but they also commented that contemporary teachers and administrators were more likely to modify programs and explore alternative philosophical orientations than were teachers and administrators of the past. They noted that reading instruction of the 1990s was "not some gussied-up version of the good old days"; instead, they found "great energy," "a commitment to children, teaching, and learning," and "a sense of motivated urgency to adopt instructional principles, practices, and philosophies that will accommodate learners of today" (Baumann, Hoffman, et al., 2000, p. 361).

A Survey of Teachers' Opinions of Beginning Reading Materials

Mesmer (2006) also explored elementary reading instruction by investigating kindergarten through third-grade teachers' uses of and beliefs about beginning reading materials. She sought to answer three questions: (1) How do teachers select and use instructional materials? (2) What factors affect teachers' use of materials? (3) What are teachers' perceptions of newer basal reading materials that emphasize decodable texts (instructional selections containing high proportions of words that can be pronounced through phonics skills that have been previously taught to children)?

Mesmer (2006) addressed these questions by conducting a mail survey that included 36 multiple-choice and Likert items and 1 open-response item. The sample consisted of 1,000 teachers randomly selected from of a list of 5,000 members of the International Reading Association who identified themselves as K–3 teachers. Mesmer reported a 38% response rate, with a sampling error of 5.1% at the 95% confidence level. Quantitative analyses involved calculating descriptive statistics and conducting chi-square tests to explore relationships between items. Constant comparative coding was conducted for responses to the open item.

Results revealed that teachers reported using children's literature and leveled texts almost daily; predictable, decodable, and vocabulary-controlled texts were used once or twice a week; and basals and workbooks were used infrequently. Contrary to the assertion that teachers were allowing decodable texts to supplant literature in beginning reading materials, findings revealed that teachers used both types of materials as instructional needs dictated. For example, teachers reported using decodable texts most often when teaching phonics, using literature when teaching comprehension, and using leveled texts when teaching reading fluency.

Findings related to teachers' use of materials demonstrated that their grade-level assignments (K–3), teaching roles (e.g., classroom teachers, reading teachers), and instructional approaches used (e.g., guided reading, 4/6 blocks, direct instruction) did not relate to their selection of instructional texts. Most teachers reported having complete or moderate choice in selecting materials, and they expressed having a balanced and eclectic perspective on reading instruction. Teachers sampled from Texas and California—states that require basal publishers to include decodable text in reading materials—reported using decodable texts more than teachers in other states. These same teachers, however, also reported using literature and leveled texts as frequently as teachers in other states, suggesting that state policies were not limiting them from using other instructional materials.

Mesmer (2006) stated that these K–3 teachers were "doggedly pragmatic," discriminating consumers who selected and used a variety of materials on the basis of their instructional goals, and that "educators need not worry about literature being pushed out of the curriculum" (p. 413). Consistent with findings from prior survey research (Baumann, Hoffman, Moon, & Duffy-Hester, 1998; Baumann, Hoffman, et al., 2000), Mesmer concluded that "teachers appeared to care most about resisting inappropriate uses of materials rather than resisting politically charged mandates, despite the debates in research circles" (p. 413).

SUMMARY

The purpose of this chapter has been to provide an overview of survey research methods employed in literacy research. Survey research is a method for gathering information from a sample of individuals in order to describe characteristics of a larger group. Survey research has been employed in education and social sciences for the past 100 years, with increasing activity in the past decade. Commonly used survey methods involve collecting data through face-to-face, telephone, mail, technology-enhanced, online, and mixed mode surveys. Most surveys involve probability samples from a specified population in order to make generalizations about the broader population. There is a generally accepted and implemented survey research design process that leads researchers from question and hypothesis formulation through sample description and data collection to data analyses and survey reporting. Quality standards can be applied to evaluate published surveys and to guide researchers in designing survey studies. The Baumann, Hoffman, and colleagues (2000) survey of elementary reading instruction practices and the Mesmer (2006) survey of primary teachers' use of beginning reading materials have been presented as examples of literacy education survey research.

REFERENCES

Al Otaiba, S., Lewis, S., Whalon, K., Dyrlund, A., & McKenzie, A. R. (2009). Home literacy environments of young children with Down syndrome: Findings from a web-based survey. *Remedial and Special Education, 31*(2), 96–107.

American Psychological Association. (2010). *Publication manual of the American Psychological Association* (6th ed.). Washington, DC: Author.

Austin, M. C., Bush, C. L., & Huebner, M. H. (1961). *Reading evaluation: Appraisal techniques for school and classroom.* New York: Ronald Press.

Austin, M. C., & Morrison, C., with Kenney, H. J., Morrison, M. B., Gutmann, A. R., & Nystrom, J. W. (1961). *The torch lighters: Tomorrow's teachers of reading.* Cambridge, MA: Harvard Graduate School of Education/Harvard University Press.

Austin, M. C., & Morrison, C., with Morrison, M. B., Sipay, E. R., Gutmann, A. R., Torrant, K. E., & Woodbury, C. A. (1963). *The first R: The Harvard report on reading in elementary schools.* New York: Macmillan.

Barton, A. H., & Wilder, D. E. (1964). Research and practice in the teaching of reading: A progress report. In M. B. Miles (Ed.), *Innovation in education* (pp. 361–398). New York: Teachers College, Columbia University.

Baumann, J. F., Hoffman, J. V., Duffy-Hester, A. M., & Ro, J. M. (2000). The *first R* yesterday and today: U.S. elementary reading instruction practices reported by teachers and administrators. *Reading Research Quarterly, 35,* 338–377.

Baumann, J. F., Hoffman, J. V., Moon, J., & Duffy-Hester, A. M. (1998). Where are teachers' voices in the phonics/whole language debate?: Results from a survey of U.S. elementary classroom teachers. *The Reading Teacher, 51,* 636–650.

Baumann, J. F., Ro, J. M., Duffy-Hester, A. M., & Hoffman, J. V. (2000). Then and now: Perspectives on the status of elementary reading instruction by prominent reading educators. *Reading Research and Instruction, 39,* 236–264.

Bean, R., Cassidy, J., Grumet, J. E., Shelton, D. S., & Wallis, S. R. (2002). What do reading specialists do?: Results from a national survey. *The Reading Teacher, 55,* 736–744.

Berne, J. I., & Blachowicz, C. L. Z. (2008). What reading teachers say about vocabulary instruction: Voices from the classroom. *The Reading Teacher, 62,* 314–323.

Blamey, K. L., Meyer, C. K., & Walpole, S. (2008–2009). Middle and high school literacy coaches: A national survey. *Journal of Adolescent and Adult Literacy, 52,* 310–323.

Blumberg, S. J., & Luke, J. V. (2009). Wireless substitution: Early release of estimates based on data from the National Health Interview Survey, January–June 2008. Retrieved from *www.cdc.gov/nchs/data/nhis/earlyrelease/wireless200905.htm.*

Brooker, R., & Schaefer, T. (2006). *Public opinion in the 21st century: Let the people speak?* Boston: Houghton Mifflin.

Bushaw, B. J., & McNee, J. A. (2009). Americans speak out: Are educators and policy makers listening? The 41st annual Phi Delta Kappa/Gallup Poll of the publics' attitudes toward the public schools. *Kappan, 91*(1), 9–23.

Commeyras, M., & DeGroff, L. (1998). Literacy professionals' perspectives on professional development and pedagogy: A United States survey. *Reading Research Quarterly, 33,* 434–472.

Converse, P. E. (1964). The nature of belief systems in mass publics. In D. E. Apter (Ed.), *Ideology and discontent* (pp. 207–261). New York: Free Press.

Couper, M. P. (2008). *Designing effective web surveys.* Cambridge, UK: Cambridge University Press.

Couper, M. P., Baker, R. P., Bethlehem, J., Clark, C. Z. F., Martin, J., Nicholls, W. L., et al. (1998). *Computer assisted survey information collection.* New York: Wiley.

Cuevas, P., Schumm, J. S., Mits-Cash, M., & Pilonieta, P. (2006). Reading clinics in the U.S.: A national survey of present practice. *Journal of Reading Education, 31*(2), 5–12.

Dillman, D. A. (2000). *Mail and Internet surveys: The tailored design method* (2nd ed.). New York: Wiley.

Dillman, D. A., Smyth, J. D., & Christian, L. M. (2009). *Internet, mail, and mixed-mode surveys: The tailored design method* (3rd ed.). Hoboken, NJ: Wiley.

Flippo, R. F. (1998). Points of agreement: A display of professional unity in our field. *The Reading Teacher, 52,* 30–40.

Fogo, B., Reisman, A., & Breakstone, J. (2019). Teacher adaptation of document-based history curricula: Results of the Reading Like a Historian curriculum-use survey. *Journal of Curriculum Studies, 51*(1), 62–83.

Ford, M. P., & Opitz, M. F. (2008). A national survey of guided reading practices: What we can learn from primary teachers. *Literacy Research and Instruction, 47,* 309–311.

Forgasz, H., Tan, H., Leder, G., & McLeod, A. (2018) Enhancing survey participation: Facebook advertisements for recruitment in educational research. *International Journal of Research and Method in Education, 41*(3), 257–270.

Fowler, F. J. (2009). *Survey research methods* (4th ed.). Thousand Oaks, CA: SAGE.

Fresch, M. J. (2003). A national survey of spelling instruction: Investigating teachers' beliefs and practice. *Journal of Literacy Research, 35,* 819–848.

Fresch, M. J. (2007). Teachers' concerns about spelling instruction: A national survey. *Reading Psychology, 28,* 301–330.

Gambell, T., & Hunter, D. (2000). Surveying gender differences in Canadian school literacy. *Journal of Curriculum Studies, 32*(5), 689–719.

Greenbaum, T. L. (1998). *The handbook of focus group research.* Thousand Oaks, CA: SAGE.

Groves, R. M. (2004). *Survey errors and survey costs.* Hoboken, NJ: Wiley.

Groves, R. M., Dillman, D. A., Eltinge, J. L., & Little, R. J. A. (Eds.). (2002). *Survey nonresponse.* New York: Wiley.

Groves, R. M., Floyd, J. F., Couper, M. P., Lepkowski, J. M., Singer, E., & Tourangeau, R. (2009). *Survey methodology* (2nd ed.). Hoboken, NJ: Wiley.

Gubrium, J. F., & Holstein, J. A. (Eds.). (2002). *Handbook of interview research: Context and method.* Thousand Oaks, CA: SAGE.

Hawken, L. S., Johnston, S. S., & McDonnell, A. P. (2005). Emerging literacy views and practices: Results from a national survey of Head Start preschool teachers. *Topics in Early Childhood Education, 25,* 232–242.

Hedrick, W. B., Harmon, J. M., & Wood, K. (2008). Prominent content vocabulary strategies and what secondary preservice teachers think about them. *Reading Psychology, 29*(5), 443–470.

Hibberts, M., Johnson, R. B., & Hudson, K. (2012). Common survey sampling techniques. In L. Gideon (Ed.), *Handbook of survey methodology for the social sciences* (pp. 53–74). Dordrecht, the Netherlands: Springer.

Hochstim, J. R. (1967). A critical comparison of three strategies of collecting data from households. *Journal of the American Statistical Association, 62,* 976–989.

Hoffman, A. R., Jenkins, J. E., & Dunlap. S. K. (2009). Using DIBELS: A survey of purposes and practices. *Reading Psychology, 30,* 1–6.

Hoffman, J. V., Assaf, L. C., & Paris, S. G. (2001). High-stakes testing in reading: Today in Texas, tomorrow? *The Reading Teacher, 54*, 482–492.

Hoffman, J. V., & Roller, C. M. (2001). The IRA Excellence in Reading Teacher Preparation Commission's report: Current practices in reading teacher education at the undergraduate level in the United States. In C. M. Roller (Ed.), *Learning to teach reading: Setting the research agenda* (pp. 32–79). Newark, DE: International Reading Association.

Howard, V., & Jin, S. (2004). What are they reading?: A survey of the reading habits and library usage patterns of teens in Nova Scotia. *Canadian Journal of Information and Library Science, 28*(4), 25–44.

Hughes, M. T., Cash, M. M., Klingner, J., & Ahwee, S. (2001). Professional development programs in reading: A national survey of district directors. In J. V. Hoffman, D. L. Schallert, C. M. Fairbanks, J. Worthy, & B. Maloch (Eds.), *Fiftieth yearbook of the National Reading Conference* (pp. 275–286). Chicago: National Reading Conference.

Hutchison, A., & Henry, L. A. (2010). Internet use and online literacy among middle grade students at risk of dropping out of school. *Middle Grades Research Journal, 5*(2), 61–75.

Hutchison, A. C., Woodward, L., & Colwell, J. (2016). What are preadolescent readers doing online?: An examination of upper elementary students' reading, writing, and communication in digital spaces. *Reading Research Quarterly, 51*(4), 435–454.

Ivey, G., & Broaddus, K. (2001). "Just plain reading": A survey of what makes students want to read in middle school classrooms. *Reading Research Quarterly, 36*, 350–377.

Jaeger, R. M. (1997). Survey research methods in education. In R. M. Jaeger (Ed.), *Complementary methods for research in education* (2nd ed., pp. 449–476). Washington, DC: American Educational Research Association.

Kelley, M. J., & Decker, E. O. (2009). The current state of motivation to read among middle school students. *Reading Psychology, 30*, 466–485.

Kosinski, M., Matz, S. C., Gosling, S. D., Popov, V., & Stillwell, D. (2015). Facebook as a research tool for the social sciences: Opportunities, challenges, ethical considerations, and practical guidelines. *American Psychologist, 70*(6), 543–556.

Kraemer, H. C., & Thiemann, S. (1987). *How many subjects?: Statistical power analysis in research.* Thousand Oaks, CA: SAGE.

Krosnick, J. A. (1999). Survey research. *Annual Review of Psychology, 50*, 537–567.

Krueger, R. A., & Casey, M. A. (2008). *Focus groups: A practical guide for applied research* (4th ed.). Thousand Oaks, CA: SAGE.

Lavrakas, P. J. (Ed.). (2007). Cell phone numbers and telephone surveying in the U.S. [Special issue]. *Public Opinion Quarterly, 71*(5).

Lepkowski, J. M., Tucker, C., Brick, J. M., de Leeuw, E., Japec, L., Lavrakas, P. J., et al. (2008). *Advances in telephone survey methodology.* Hoboken, NJ: Wiley.

Leung, C., & Unal, Z. (2013). Anonymity and confidentiality in the conduct of online surveys. In C. S. Rhodes & K. Weiss (Eds.), *Ethical issues in literacy research* (pp. 129–138). New York: Routledge.

Link, M. W., Battaglia, M. P., Frankel, M. R., Osborn, L., & Mokdad, A. H. (2008). Comparison of address-based sampling (ABS) versus random-digit dialing (RDD) for general population surveys. *Public Opinion Quarterly,* 72(1), 6–27.

Maynard, S., Mackay, S., & Smith, F. (2008). A survey of young people's reading in England: Borrowing and choosing books. *Journal of Librarianship and Information Science, 40,* 239–253.

McKenna, M. C., Kear, D. J., & Ellsworth, R. A. (1995). Children's attitudes toward reading: A national survey. *Reading Research Quarterly, 30,* 934–956.

Mellard, D., Patterson, M. B., & Prewett, S. (2007). Reading practices among adult education participants. *Reading Research Quarterly, 42,* 188–213.

Mesmer, H. A. E. (2006). Beginning reading materials: A national survey of primary teachers' reported uses and beliefs. *Journal of Literacy Research, 38,* 389–425.

Mokhtari, K., Reichard, C. A., & Gardner, A. (2009). The impact of Internet and television use on the reading habits and practices of college students. *Journal of Adolescent and Adult Literacy, 52,* 609–619.

Morrison, C. (1963). *A critical analysis of reported and recommended reading practices in the elementary schools.* Unpublished doctoral dissertation, Harvard Graduate School of Education, Cambridge, MA.

Morrison, C., & Austin, M. C. (1977). *The torch lighters revisited.* Newark, DE: International Reading Association.

Nathanson, S., Pruslow, J., & Levitt, R. (2008). The reading habits and literacy attitudes of inservice and prospective teachers: Results of a questionnaire study. *Journal of Teacher Education, 59,* 313–321.

National Center for Health Statistics, Centers for Disease Control and Prevention. (2019, January 16). About the National Health Interview Survey. Retrieved from *www.cdc.gov/nchs/nhis/about_nhis.htm#sample_design.*

National Opinion Research Center. (n.d.) General Social Survey. Retrieved from *www.norc.org/Research/Projects/Pages/general-social-survey.aspx.*

Revilla, M., Toninelli, D., Ochoa, C., & Loewe, G. (2016). Do online access panels need to adapt surveys for mobile devices? *Internet Research, 26*(5), 1209–1227.

Rubin, H. J., & Rubin, I. S. (2005). *Qualitative interviewing: The art of hearing data* (2nd ed.). Thousand Oaks, CA: SAGE.

Ryan, C. (2018). *Computer and Internet use in the United States: 2016* (U.S. Census Bureau Report No. ACS 39). Retrieved from *www.census.gov/library/publications/2018/acs/acs-39.html.*

Scheuren, F. (2004). *What is a survey?* Washington, DC: American Statistical Association. Retrieved from *www.unh.edu/institutional-research/sites/default/files/pamphlet.pdf.*

Seidman, I. (1998). *Interviewing as qualitative research: A guide for researchers in education and the social sciences* (2nd ed.). New York: Teachers College Press.

Shulman, L. S. (1997). Disciplines of inquiry in education: A new overview. In R. M. Jaeger (Ed.), *Complementary methods for research in education* (2nd ed., pp. 3–29). Washington, DC: American Educational Research Association.

Stewart, D. W., Shamdasani, P. M., & Rook, D. W. (2006). *Focus groups: Theory and practice* (2nd ed.). Thousand Oaks, CA: SAGE.

Strunk, W., & White, E. B. (2000). *The elements of style* (4th ed.). Boston: Allyn & Bacon.

Tourangeau, R., Rips, L. J., & Rasinski, K. (2000). *The psychology of survey response.* Cambridge, UK: Cambridge University Press.

Venezky, R. L. (1984). The history of reading research. In R. Barr, M. L. Kamil, P. Mosenthal, & P. D. Pearson (Eds.), *Handbook of reading research* (pp. 3–38). New York: Longman.

Weisberg, H. F., Krosnick, J. A., & Bowen, B. D. (1996). *An introduction to survey research, polling, and data analysis.* Thousand Oaks, CA: SAGE.

Wiseman, F. (1972). Methodological bias in public opinion surveys. *Public Opinion Quarterly, 36,* 105–108.

Wood, K., Vintinner, J., Hill-Miller, P., Harmon, J. M., & Hedrick, W. (2009). An investigation of teachers' concerns about vocabulary and the representation of these concerns in content literacy methodology textbooks. *Reading Psychology, 30,* 319–339.

CHAPTER 18

Verbal Protocol Analysis in Literacy

Byeong-Young Cho

This chapter focuses on verbal protocol methodology in inquiries into the nature of reading and literacy. It begins with a definition of verbal protocol analysis and a description of its contributions to our understanding of reading and related phenomena. The chapter examines the current status of verbal protocol research and discusses how perspectives and practices related to verbal protocol analysis have evolved, highlighting the symbiotic nature of methodological advancement and theory building. The chapter then shifts focus to discuss fundamental considerations in verbal protocol study design, and standards for determining the quality of verbal protocol analysis. The chapter concludes with a brief review of two exemplary studies that have used verbal protocol methodology to enhance our knowledge of reading in complex literacy task environments.

WHAT IS VERBAL PROTOCOL ANALYSIS?

Verbal protocol analysis is a system of principles, procedures, and techniques for collecting and interrogating research participants' verbal reports (often called "think-alouds") in order to make inferences about their thoughts, processes, and responses during the execution of a demanding task, such as reading. This operational definition sheds light on some key terms such as *verbal reporting and protocols, task demands, thoughts in the mind,* and *inference making,* which jointly capture the conceptual substance of this unique research method. In what follows, the meanings of these terms and related concepts are clarified so as to unpack the theoretical assumptions behind the use of verbal protocol analysis in reading research.

Verbal Reports and Verbal Protocols

While *verbal reports* and *verbal protocols* differ, they are related both conceptually and methodologically. On the one hand, verbal reports are the spoken language that research participants produce to make their thinking visible to others (in this case, researchers) and to themselves as they do a task (Ericsson & Simon, 1980). In this sense, verbal reports are the rich data collected through research activities for observing task-elicited thinking. Verbal protocols, on the other hand, suggest specific selections of verbal reports—that is, subsets of data meeting the rules or assumptions about the kinds of verbalizations that may provide legitimate evidence related to the focal processes, thoughts, and responses for the specific study (Fox, Ericsson, & Best, 2011). Note that these rules and assumptions of verbal protocols initially must be defined on the basis of existing theoretical models and frameworks. They are then revised and elaborated (or disconfirmed and rejected), as theoretical understandings evolve through complex analyses of verbal protocol data that demonstrate the workings of the focal processes, thoughts, and responses (Pressley & Afflerbach, 1995).

Oftentimes, verbal protocol researchers in reading are concerned about how to induce their readers to generate extensive verbal reports. While having an abundance of data is important, it is equally vital to consider beforehand what constitutes *evidence* that would support research claims to be established through the meticulous analysis of (theoretically justified) verbal protocol data. In a study exploring what experts in history do with multiple sources, for example, the researcher may design a historical inquiry task suited to invite historians to engage in an in-depth textual examination that will allow the researcher to gather rich verbal reports from the historians. Verbal reports, however, are messy. Subsequent analytical procedures must be carried out to discern manifold streams of verbalized thoughts and processes in these messy verbal data, and to locate noticeable consistencies and linkages across multiple data segments (Chi, 1997). In the case of the historical inquiry task, for example, the identification and examination of meaningful verbal protocol data may eventually enable the researcher to offer a unique account of the discipline-specific reasoning as the historians were engaged in to interpret and evaluate varied historical sources (e.g., Leinhardt & Young, 1996; Wineburg, 1998).

It is challenging to anticipate when specific segments of verbal protocol data (i.e., *nodes*), as well as semantic connections across segments (i.e., *links*), will become noticeable. However, as researchers continue to engage deeply with the verbal reports, their understanding of the readers' performance should increase over time, and it should become clearer which lines of the verbal data deserve focused attention and care. Again, the analysis of such verbal protocols—i.e., theory-determined verbal reports—should begin with a thorough examination of the extant models and frameworks that detail the focal reading phenomena for the study, with the goal of continued progress toward updating theoretical understandings with protocol-informed insights.

Thoughts in the Mind

What can we know from verbal protocols? Verbal report data provide a window into the mind, with caveats: The window is narrow, may not be completely transparent, and inevitably constrains what we can see through it. Especially with concurrent verbal reporting (i.e., thinking aloud while performing a task), what is observable from verbal reports is limited by the speaker's working memory during task execution (Crain-Thoreson, Lippman, & McClendon-Magnuson, 1997; Crutcher, 1994; Ericsson & Simon, 1980). For example, research suggests that verbalized thoughts, despite their ephemeral nature, may subsume not only the *information* that is encoded, stored, and retrieved in memory, but the *manipulation* of that information—how it is processed, used, and represented in working memory (Baddeley, 2012). Data analysis must therefore distinguish and determine which strands of verbal protocols match specific kinds of thought (or specific contents of working memory).

Suppose that a reader, Keisha, is thinking out loud while making sense of important words in a text. Keisha is likely to verbalize the words she is tackling, mention aspects of her lexical knowledge and world knowledge that are being activated by the words, and describe how the words she recognizes are related to larger meanings in context. More important, however, are Keisha's comments on the strategies she draws on for both micro- and macro-level text processing, such as identifying key words and integrating their meanings into a summary of her reading. In accord with general theories of reading comprehension (e.g., McNamara & Magliano, 2009; Snow, 2002), verbal protocol data as such may reflect how *text information* and *reader knowledge* are integrated into *mental representations* through *conscious processes*. For the anatomy of reading, numerous moment-by-moment analyses of different components of thinking must be brought together without compromising contextual sensitivity to the settings, conditions, or circumstances of the reader's performance in which all of these components of thinking interact.

The cognitive work of readers and their conscious processes have been of overriding interest to verbal protocol researchers for decades (e.g., Bereiter & Bird, 1985; Bråten & Strømsø, 2003; Gerjets, Kammerer, & Werner, 2011; Olshavsky, 1976–1977; Trabasso & Magliano, 1996). Reading does not, however, involve only cognitive processes. Indeed, a great deal of motivation research has documented that readers' cognitive engagement is deeper and more sustainable when it is fueled by a legitimate reason for reading (Guthrie, Wigfield, & You, 2012). Moreover, a range of individual differences in the beliefs students might bring to reading tasks, such as self-efficacy, agency, and volition, have been shown to contribute to their learning and academic performance in general (Schunk & Bursuck, 2016). Hence engaged reading often evokes emotional and affective responses from readers, which may surface during verbal reporting. If portions of protocol data showing noncognitive activity are disregarded as mere data noise or measurement error, the verbal protocol analysis will be left uninformed about important aspects of reading. Even when the analysis of such protocol data is not an explicit study focus, researchers ought to consider that it could lead to far more sophisticated inferences—for example, about *why* one takes a particular direction in *how* the reader justifies shifts and changes in the pathway to text understanding.

Task Demands

Tasks are another important consideration. Verbal reports are fundamentally task-bound; this distinguishes verbal protocol analysis from the analysis of other kinds of verbal data, such as interviews, speeches, or discourses, for which data generation does not necessarily involve a concurrent situation wherein the participant has to conduct a cognitive task. For this reason, employing tasks with optimal cognitive demands is crucial, particularly in the context of concurrent verbal reporting. Task demands are in general determined by considering the task's components (Doyle, 1983). For instance, to design a reading task for a study focusing on readers' intertextual processing of multiple sources online, the researcher may take into account the *products* expected from the participants upon completion of reading (e.g., responses to test items, written essays), *operations* to be used to generate the product (e.g., information searching, document collection), and *resources* available to facilitate the production process (e.g., task guides, searching tools).

For verbal protocol studies of reading, however, determining task demands also requires a consideration of who (*reader*) reads what (*text*) in what circumstances (*context*). As decades of reading comprehension research have implied (Afflerbach, 2016; McNamara & Magliano, 2009; Pearson & Cervetti, 2015; Snow, 2002), task demands can be calculated and adjusted in terms of the three-way interactions of reader, text, and context-specific attributes. For example, while any task is justified with specific research questions and rationales for the study, two scenarios must be avoided. In the first scenario, highly competent readers work on a simple, familiar, and well-structured text in an easily anticipated context of reading. Such a task cannot provide the necessary quality of verbal reporting because the readers will be unlikely to face novel challenges, unexpected conflicts, or uncertain pathways in meaning making; they will therefore not need to apply much attention or effort, and they will seldom use their full repertoires of skills and knowledge (McNamara, Kintsch, Songer, & Kintsch, 1996). As a result, their verbal reports are likely to be sketchy and may reflect generic thinking and automatized processes at best.

The second scenario to avoid is the opposite one: that in which inexperienced readers with underdeveloped knowledge and skills are asked to process dense texts that they find unfamiliar and complex, in a context they cannot possibly anticipate. This case must be rejected as well in verbal protocol studies because unnerving tasks are problematic in terms of both reader cognition and motivation. It is highly likely that readers face recurrent reading difficulties, without adequate supports and resources, while being repeatedly disoriented in the process of meaning making due to cognitive overload and disengagement (Anderson & Pearson, 1984; Brown, 1980; Sadoski, Goetz, & Rodriguez, 2000). Accordingly, verbal reports will provide little information about the readers' thinking and understanding, as the readers will not have been able to become deeply involved in the task. Furthermore, when the readers' cognitive resources and efforts are largely consumed by task difficulties, verbal reporting is only an additional burden that causes cognitive disruption in their management of the dual task (i.e., reading while verbalizing).

The nature of reading tasks in verbal protocol research should be determined with well-defined research questions, substantiated by detailed theories of reading that support the inquiry. Any methodological choices are justified, first and foremost, with a consideration of the research questions and desirable data sources for the inquiry. On that premise, challenging but achievable tasks can be designed, provided that the researcher anticipates possible reader–text–context interactions that may affect the thoughts, processes, and responses the researcher is seeking to infer from the verbal protocol data.

Inference Making

Verbal protocol analysis requires a process of inference making. *Inference* is a process by which a researcher uses more than one source of information in order to draw a conclusion from good reasoning with legitimate evidence. It is not always easy to make accurate inferences, however, especially when the purpose is to recognize certain patterns and regularities of human thinking in unorganized, messy verbal data. This methodological challenge stems from the fact that the psychological realities of what is verbalized may not be identical (or directly refer) to the psychological realities of what occurs in the mind. In effect, a conceptual distance between language and thought—what is called an *inferential gap* hereafter—has been a central focus of methodological debates on the scientific formality and value of verbal reports as data (e.g., Ericsson & Crutcher, 1991; Ericsson & Simon, 1980; Howe, 1991; Nisbett & Wilson, 1977; Wilson, 1994) and the intertwining of language, cognition, and context involved in verbal protocol analysis (Ericsson & Simon, 1998; Smagorinsky, 1998).

Note that varied forms of verbal reports imply different types of inferential gaps, which require distinct approaches to inference making.

An ongoing discussion (e.g., Afflerbach & Johnston, 1984; Ericsson & Simon, 1998; Fox et al., 2011; Smagorinsky, 1998; Trabasso & Magliano, 1996) has sketched the outlines of how three forms of verbal reports might determine the inferential gaps to be dealt with in verbal protocol analysis (Cho, Woodward, & Afflerbach, 2020). One form is that which accurately mirrors pure thinking processes. If they existed, such *prototype records* would be ideal for thought measurement because they would rarely require inferencing from researchers. To the best of our knowledge, however, it is virtually impossible to collect verbal reports of such a kind, given that verbalization (encoding and producing language) affects thinking in real time.

That said, multiple research syntheses (e.g., Afflerbach, 2000; Fox et al., 2011) have documented that a research participant's verbalized thoughts, while not complete, can represent the thoughts in his or her mind. This is likely to be the case when researchers take proper measures (e.g., enhancement of task understanding, think-aloud pretraining, prompts with minimal interruption) to anticipate and minimize adverse consequences of verbalization on the process of thinking. Verbal reporting done in this manner is more likely to yield *verbal protocols* with a nonsignificant change in the course of thinking and actions. These protocol data are the second form, which invites inferential reasoning based on a researcher's knowledge of the reader, the text, and the context and their interactions situated in the task. As described earlier, verbal protocols indicate the critical part of data for reading inquiries.

Self-explanation is another form. There is always a chance that research participants will become excessively involved in explaining to others (e.g., a researcher) about their reading, and thus unduly waste their given time. Verbal data reported in this manner are likely to contain somewhat "generalized" self-judgments about one's own performance. Such explanations and judgments may be inaccurate, shallow, and hardly revealing about the real-time processes of meaning making during reading. Worse, uncontrolled self-explanation and generalization may considerably distort the course of thinking that would have been enacted without disruptive verbalizations. Although some self-explanation can be helpful (e.g., if the study's focus is on readers' extended reasoning about their performance), it should be noted that the very performance of thinking may be neither adequately carried out under the influences of verbal disruptions nor accurately represented through scattered self-explanations.

Perhaps most difficult to do for research is determining the inferential gaps that exist among what we desire to understand, what data we can acquire, and what we can do with the data (Messick, 1989; Mislevy, Steinberg, & Almond, 2003; Pellegrino, Chudowsky, & Glaser, 2001). Even more challenging is evaluating the proximity and disparity among the construct, observation, and interpretation in order to generate a reliable solution for achieving *integrity of verbal protocols* in relation to proper task design (reducing the gap) and rigorous analytical work (filling the gap) grounded in both theories and data (Afflerbach, 2000; Cho, 2020). As described above, one approach to addressing the issue is to enhance researchers' awareness of different verbal report types, which can help researchers distinguish them even when they appear mixed, and of the distinctive nature of thinking to be inferred from each verbal report type.

In summary, verbal protocol analysis can be better defined when its core terms and their theoretical assumptions are considered. The definition developed throughout this section suggests that researchers must (1) identify theory-informed protocol data from a corpus of readers' verbal reports, (2) examine specific processes of sensemaking underlying the generated verbal protocols, (3) consider factors in determining task demands in reading, and (4) deal with the inferential gap between what is heeded in the mind of the reader and what indeed is verbalized during reading. The effort of taking all these elements into account can create new opportunities to best respond to specific research foci, goals, and questions. The following section shifts to discussing how the verbal protocol research of recent decades has contributed to answering questions about different aspects of reading.

THE LANDSCAPE OF VERBAL PROTOCOL RESEARCH IN READING

The intellectual grounding of verbal protocol analysis is found in the history of knowledge inquiries into language, cognition, reasoning, and learning. For example, William James (1890), well over a century ago, claimed that observation and analysis of *introspection*—one's own investigation and reporting of his or her mind—were the *"first and foremost"* means to *"discover states of consciousness"* in psychological theory construction (p. 185, original emphasis). Questions of whether (and, if so, how reliably) what people say describes what they think, as well as how language and thought inform the process of learning, have been important topics of prolonged debates on cognitive development (Piaget, 1926), language generation (Chomsky, 1968), and contexts of learning (Vygotsky, 1978), just to name a few. Those interested in historical accounts for verbal reporting, or the broader conception of introspection, are recommended to consult seminal works such as those of Boring (1953), Ericsson and Simon (1993, pp. 48–62), and Pressley and Afflerbach (1995, pp. 1–14).

Expanding Boundaries of Verbal Protocol Research

Since Ericsson and Simon's (1980) initial explication of the suitability of verbal report data for scientific studies of thinking, verbal protocol analysis has gained growing popularity in cognitive science and related fields. Verbal protocol studies of reading in this era were informed by theories of text comprehension such as propositional processing, schema activation, and inference generation. One important outcome of this line of work was a compendium of reading comprehension strategies used by expert readers (Pressley & Afflerbach, 1995). Accomplished reading, as has been demonstrated in the verbal protocols of expert readers, was marked by the constructively responsive process embodied as the coordination of goal-directed strategies to make meaning from text.

While verbal protocol studies notably contributed to understanding the cognitive states and structures of expert readers, their aims of using verbal protocols were narrowly conceived to describe somewhat algorithmic processes of expert work. This constrained focus was likely due in part to a prevalent notion of verbal reporting methods as a means of assessing information-processing phenomena (Ericsson & Simon, 1980; Nisbett & Wilson, 1977). This tradition of inquiry seldom addressed participants' feelings, emotions, beliefs, and agency, and the ways in which these socially situated affective processes play out for meaning making. Methodological decisions about verbal protocols were accordingly constrained, as they were bound by the exclusive focus on cognitive processing.

Nonetheless, Pressley and Afflerbach (1995) have relentlessly claimed that reading researchers should not overlook the fact that verbal protocol analysis is a "maturing" methodology (p. 1). As theories and perspectives of reading have evolved, so too have the diversity and richness of knowledge and insights related to verbal reporting and protocol analysis—a situation that highlights the *reciprocity* of theory and methodology in research. Situative perspectives on cognition (e.g., Brown, Collins, & Duguid, 1989; Greeno, 1989), for example, have put forward the idea that acts of reading are contextualized by the particular goals, needs, tasks, and settings as readers perceive to be critical for their work, themselves, and the communities of which they are part. And language activities (including verbal reporting), from cultural and historical perspectives, do mediate various cognitive, emotional, and social responses in the course of reading (Smagorinsky, 1998, 2001). Readers' verbal reports, then, can become an important source of new theoretical insights into complex reader responses that are interwoven with cognitive processes (Afflerbach, 2000; Cho, 2020; Kucan & Beck, 1997). As the idea of theory–methodology reciprocity implies, taking account of alternative perspectives in reading may facilitate a rethinking of verbally reported data in the investigation of underresearched aspects of reading that include, but are not limited to, nuanced cognitive, emotional, and social processes in the sensemaking of text.

Table 18.1 presents some insights into the methodological advances in verbal protocol studies that have been afforded (and constrained) by specific perspectives on reading and readers. Based on changing perspectives on cognition and learning (Greeno, Collins, & Resnick, 1997), the table offers implications for inquiry questions that could be pursued through verbal protocol research in reading, ranging from studies framed by cognitive

TABLE 18.1. A Theoretical–Methodological Landscape of Verbal Protocol Studies in Reading

Underlying perspectives	Methodological advances	Potential theoretical contributions
Information-processing perspectives	Verbal reports count as the only process data source (e.g., no other process data are combined, and outcome data are often missing). Prompts are predetermined by the researcher (e.g., visual signals embedded right at the end of each paragraph in a passage). Artificially crafted text with a limited scope and boundary is given to research participants (mostly, a short written passage or two, or a single text in print). Reading tasks are accompanied by a strict focus on the specific cognitive work involved in the processing of text information (e.g., for the most part, reading goals are given to research participants, and the tasks are optimized to best elicit a cognitive target such as prediction, causal inferencing, or text structure strategy use). Reading is done in an experimental setting in which, by default, contextual factors are assumed to be controlled for.	Creating typologies of information-processing skills in reading (e.g., types of inferences, comprehension strategies, text structure strategies, prior knowledge use). Building expert models of text comprehension and their strategic processing (e.g., to detail the ideal status of reading performance that is achieved at the end point of learning to read). The process of text comprehension done with one single print text in a given context of reading (e.g., summarization, test taking, retelling/text recall). Cognitive factors and individual differences that influence meaning-making processes, such as memory capacities, information processing skills, prior knowledge, goal orientations, inferencing skills, and reacting to processing difficulties.
Cognitive constructivist perspectives	Verbal reports are used as the primary data, in conjunction with collecting and triangulating other complementary data (e.g., eye movements, behavioral observations, pre- and postreading interviews, other complementary process–outcome measures). Prompts are preplanned and spontaneously adjusted, based on the context of investigation (e.g., additional prompts probing reasons for thinking and doing). Reading tasks involve comprehending more than one text with different genres, contents, perspectives, forms and modalities, both in print and digitally, situated within different media contexts (e.g., multitext, hypertext).	Reading strategy use with multiple, digital, and/or alternative texts. Flexibility in the coordination of multiple reading strategies and alternative "fix-it" approaches to reading challenges in various reading contexts (e.g., cognitive flexibility, metacognitive monitoring). Expert readers' processing and managing of novel texts in novel tasks (e.g., disciplinary reading for historical reasoning, scientific argumentation, or literary analysis). Building student models of reading, informed with the processes that are activated and engaged by novice, developing readers (e.g., to inform the assessment and identification of the educational space in

(continued)

TABLE 18.1. *(continued)*

Underlying perspectives	Methodological advances	Potential theoretical contributions
Cognitive constructivist perspectives *(continued)*	Reading tasks impose complex goals, beyond simple information gain from a text (e.g., argumentative essay writing, source selection, text evaluation, problem solving, question generation). Experimental settings are still preferred, but with minimal interruptions of authenticity allowed by the researcher's responsive prompts (e.g., spontaneous verbal reporting without predesignated prompts).	student reading development, to design developmentally suitable curriculum and instruction). Affective responses (e.g., motivation, interest, emotion, engagement) entailed in the task of reading and their interactions with cognitive processing.
Situative–pragmatist perspectives	Data triangulation is the "new normal" to better interpret the meanings of verbal protocols with multiple sources of process data collected with advanced technologies such as screen captures, weblog files, eye tracking, gesture/facial expression recordings). Reading tasks consider a broader spectrum of reading–writing–communicating activities that involve complex reasoning with and about texts (e.g., literacy practices in the context of social networking sites on the Internet). Tasks require use of the meaning constructed from texts, such as critical text sourcing and creative text production. Possibly nonexperimental and more natural settings can be considered, along with a participant's free verbal reporting (with the researcher's close observations and context-responsive prompts).	Self-initiated problem solving and textual decision making in reading (e.g., choices of topics, issues, and problems that ignite learning from texts that are accessed and chosen by readers). Critical engagement processes in identifying and problematizing authentic issues and formulating and investigating compelling questions (e.g., consulting a variety of sources and authorities to examine knowledge claims and the context in which those claims are made, judged, and discussed). Use of social and cultural knowledge when interpreting texts (e.g., embodied knowing through the enaction of reader identities, agencies, and perspectives). Knowledge, beliefs, and experiences, as well as cognitive work, entailed as important resources for sensemaking on a continuum of literacy practices (blurring online–offline boundaries, moving back and forth between different discourse contexts). Building situated models of reading in an authentic context in which readers might find a legitimate and powerful reason for reading (e.g., to inform about the condition, context, or environment in which students are best supported for their participation in reading for empowerment).

traditions to those influenced by more constructive and situative perspectives.

The Current State of Verbal Protocol Research in Reading

What questions have been pursued in contemporary verbal protocol studies in reading? How has the research landscape become more dynamic and complex since the earlier generation of verbal protocol studies? Note first that research questions for any study must be formulated in a way that serves the study's goals and purposes. For example, in an exploratory study venturing into new areas, verbal reporting can be a useful means of collecting information on how a set of yet-to-be-noticed ways of thinking are activated and engaged in a novel task of reading. In a study with theory-building purposes instead, verbal protocols can provide compelling evidence that reveals marked differences between expert and naive reading performance. And verbal reporting and protocol analysis also can be embedded in an intervention study, as a process-oriented measure of student learning, to evaluate whether, and how effectively, a reading intervention supports knowledge transfer (learners' application of procedural knowledge—e.g., how to evaluate the credibility of a text—to an extended task of reading).

Furthermore, research questions for verbal protocol studies of reading must center on examining *specific reader responses*. Again, affordances and constraints in verbal protocol analysis are therefore (re)considered, contingent upon particular theories and perspectives that highlight reading and readers from different angles, and through different lenses. Guided by the notion of theory–method reciprocity in research, the following subsections provide a brief review of empirical work and research questions in the recent verbal protocol literature. The review focuses on *higher-order thinking, epistemic processing, affective response,* and *sociocognitive influence* in reading.

Higher-Order Thinking

A great deal of recent work has adopted protocol analysis techniques to describe the high-level thinking involved in the extended, challenging, and knowledge-demanding tasks of reading done most by student readers at varied developmental stages. One notable trend is a shift in research focus from comprehension of one single text toward more complex situations of processing and using multiple sources for challenging tasks, such as critical learning, source evaluation, or disciplinary reasoning (e.g., Azevedo, Guthrie, & Seibert, 2004; Bråten & Strømsø, 2003; Wineburg, 1998; Wolfe & Goldman, 2005). Examples include proficient high schoolers' intertextual linking of events, people, and ideas from across multiple texts on the Civil War that represent different historical claims and rhetorical styles

(Hartman, 1995); competent adolescents' critical questioning through their navigation in a vast information space to learn about the controversial issue of coal mining (Cho, 2014); and college students' learning of civil law, which requires integrative uses of self-selected texts throughout their coursework (Strømsø & Bråten, 2002).

Noticeably, higher-order reading tasks serve to address challenging study goals and purposes. For instance, research has sought to describe patterns of metacognitive control in online environments (e.g., Coiro & Dobler, 2007) and to identify successful features of Web source integration for disciplinary learning (e.g., Goldman, Braasch, Graesser, Wiley, & Brodowinska, 2012). Other studies have used complex reading tasks to test models for the critical use of multiple sources through the quantification of qualitative verbal data (e.g., Cho, Woodward, Li, & Barlow, 2017). Consequently, opportunities for theoretical advancement have been created in part because verbal protocols contribute to constructing novel accounts of reading as a critical part of today's extended literacies in multisource and multilayered textual environments, such as multiple-documents literacy (Anmarkrud, Bråten, & Strømsø, 2014), digital reading comprehension (Cho & Afflerbach, 2017), disciplinary literacy (Shanahan, Shanahan, & Misischia, 2011), and new literacies of online reading and research (Leu, Kinzer, Coiro, & Cammack, 2004).

Epistemic Processing

An emerging body of verbal protocol research has examined readers' epistemic engagement in various reading contexts. Readers' epistemic responses to texts are guided by their *personal epistemologies,* which refer to individuals' theories of knowledge and knowing. In reading, such epistemic orientations influence perceptions and judgments of texts and authorities. Theory-informed coding schemes (e.g., nature of knowledge and process of knowing) are often employed in examinations of readers' verbal protocols to identify certain types of epistemic beliefs involved in reading (e.g., Ferguson, Bråten, & Strømsø, 2012; Gottlieb & Wineburg, 2012; Mason, Ariasi, & Boldrin, 2011; Trevors, Feyzi-Behnagh, Azevedo, & Bouchet, 2016). A few notable recent studies have reshaped the boundaries of research on epistemic beliefs, going beyond working with typologies. These studies have sought to explore how readers' epistemic cognition—cognitive enaction of epistemic beliefs (e.g., ways a reader counts as knowledge in what situations of reading, processes the reader uses to consult different sources of evidence)—operates in choosing, interrogating, and evaluating texts (e.g., Barzilai & Zohar, 2012; Cho, Woodward, & Li, 2018; Greene, Yu, & Copeland, 2014).

The use of verbal protocols for assessing readers' epistemic processing is undergirded by changing perspectives in research on personal epistemologies (Hammer & Elby, 2004; Hofer, 2004; Sandoval, Greene, &

Bråten, 2016). Personal epistemologies have long been treated as trait-like constructs that are observed with non-task-specific measures such as surveys, questionnaires, and interviews (Hofer & Pintrich, 1997). One criticism of this perspective is that it endorses generic and decontextualized self-report measures, which primarily are intended to gauge fixed mental states of cognition; consequently, less attention has been paid to methodological innovation to better capture how personal epistemologies work in context. A growing desire to understand epistemic cognition in action has drawn increased attention to process-oriented, concurrent measures like verbal reporting as alternatives to the existing non-task-specific, self-report measures (Greene & Azevedo, 2009; Greene, Azevedo, & Torney-Purta, 2008; Greene, Muis, & Pieschl, 2014). Thus, the problem of how to measure cognition has become increasingly informed by changing perspectives on what aspect of cognition to measure, which have in turn led to scientific attempts to theorize reading from a new angle.

Affective Response

The rethinking of verbal protocol analysis may also be of benefit in attempts to understand the influence of reader affect, which may support (or hinder) deep engagement in textual interpretation (Alexander, 2005; Guthrie et al., 2012). It is noteworthy that some studies, albeit very few, have used verbal protocol data to explore the affective processes (e.g., feelings, emotions, interests) entailed as readers are engaged with literary texts (e.g., Eva-Wood, 2004a, 2004b; Wade, Buxton, & Kelly, 1998). For example, Eva-Wood (2004b) has observed that college readers who received *think-and-feel-aloud* (TFA) prompts (e.g., "What feelings do you have as you read . . . ?") engaged with poetry more deeply and intensively than their peers who received generic prompts (e.g., "What are you thinking as you read . . . ?"). The TFA readers' protocols demonstrated patterns of emotional processes, specifically when they were elaborating a speaker's thoughts and feelings; interrogating nuanced uses of words, phrases, and styles; and eventually personalizing text meanings.

Given the paucity of studies on affective engagement in reading, multiple implications can be noted for future verbal protocol studies in this area. First, interrogating verbal reports for affective processes is supported by theories of emotional transactions and relational engagement in literary reading experiences (Miall & Kuiken, 1994; Rosenblatt, 1978). Theory-informed verbal protocol analysis for affective responses could broaden the scope of empirical work on literary reading, which has focused mainly on text comprehension (Kintsch, 1988; Kneepkens & Zwaan, 1994) and has centered on readers' propositional analysis and inference making when they are processing narrative passages (e.g., Long & Bourg, 1996; Magliano, Trabasso, & Graesser, 1999). In addition, this newly recognized methodological affordance may allow a new line of work to experiment with suitable task designs that include authentic texts and reading goals, to better elicit specific aspects of emotional cognition such as personal connections interacting with poetic processing (e.g., Earthman, 1992; Harker, 1994; Peskin, 1998, 2010; Warren, 2011) and literary engagement more broadly (Ivey & Johnston, 2013; Lysaker, Tonge, Gauson, & Miller, 2011). Finally, the field will benefit from research that improves researchers' ability to predict affective influences on cognitive performance, in addressing methodological issues that may come up in the analysis of reader-generated verbal protocol data.

Sociocognitive Influence

In an area somewhat distant from the mainstream work, a few provocative studies have attempted to use verbal protocols as a way of demonstrating nuanced processes of reading as a social practice (e.g., Lewis & Fabos, 2005; Marsh, 2011; Smagorinsky, Cook, & Reed, 2005; Smagorinsky, Daigle, O'Donnell-Allen, & Bynum, 2010). In pioneering work, Smagorinsky and his colleagues (e.g., 2005, 2010) have used verbal protocols to study how individuals enact identities and agency (as well as their socially oriented affect and motivation) when engaging in a continuum of reading–writing activities mediated by challenging disciplinary texts. Lewis and Fabos's (2005) work also deserves attention for its integration of think-aloud techniques into an ethnographic study design. They used verbal report data to construct detailed accounts of students' engagement strategies for reading, writing, and communicating in instant messaging (IM). Retrospective protocols were adapted to observe IM strategies of participating adolescents, who, with the researchers, watched their video-recorded IM sessions, freely talking aloud about what they were noticing.

The idea of "data as a social construction" suggests that researchers be attentive to the social functioning of verbal reporting in research methodologies (Smagorinsky, 1998, 2001). This directly challenges mainstream notions of what can be defined as scientific data (Ericsson & Simon, 1993, 1998), while aligning well with interpretive traditions of inquiry in social sciences research (Denzin & Lincoln, 2008). One implication is that because verbal protocols are always situated in a context of research, the contextual properties of the research and the participants' task performance must be considered in data interpretation. To give an example, in a reading study, the research context determines how the participants' reading was initiated and the conditions in which it was performed; therefore, the researchers must clearly communicate their position with regard to the authenticity of the readers' performance and the circumstances of the reading.

Also, verbal protocol studies in this line could be advantageous in describing how readers position themselves in a literate world and interact with various literacy tools to represent meanings and identities (Smagorinsky, 1998, 2001). This research offers the important insight that verbal reporting methodologies can be used in natural settings (as opposed to traditional approaches using researcher-developed experimental tasks) in which readers as meaning makers think, behave, and feel. This advantage in accessing participants' lifeworld experiences and situated cognition for "on-the-spot problem solving" (Lewis & Fabos, 2005, p. 479) might reposition verbal protocols as a compelling data source that complements other ethnographic data sources (e.g., interviews, participant observations, field notes). This approach serves to better understand the cognitive processes that operate while a person's social responses (e.g., identity processes) are shaping and being shaped by the practice of reading.

To summarize, reading inquiries suggest that verbal protocol analysis has been useful, particularly in exploring new areas of research interests, questions, and goals. Verbal protocol research has constantly challenged and stretched our abilities and wills to test alternative and novel theories of reading and literacy. At the same time, these research studies have contributed to continuing efforts to update verbal protocol methodologies, expanding them to examine readers' cognitive, motivational, affective, and social processes involved in demanding tasks and contexts. Important to note is the reciprocity between verbal reporting methodologies and evolving understandings of reading. This reciprocity is key to explaining the mechanisms in which we revisit existing theories, consider more and newer variables for empirical testing, and propose complementary (and often transformative) approaches to generating new knowledge. Acknowledging the reciprocity, the following section discusses a set of principled knowledge considered in the use of verbal protocol methodologies.

METHODOLOGICAL CONSIDERATIONS FOR VERBAL PROTOCOL RESEARCH

Verbal protocol analysis, like any methodology, has faced criticisms ranging from skepticism about its theoretical bases and assumptions to questions regarding the trustworthiness of its procedures and techniques. As a matter of fact, the rigor of verbal protocol analysis has been improved dialogically in response to these criticisms and to valid calls for empirical testing of both common practices and novel attempts. Some principled practical knowledge that informs research processes for collecting and interrogating verbal protocol data have emerged from this dialogue, as will be discussed in this section.

Principles for Verbal Protocol Study Design

Ericsson and Simon (1993, p. 61) pointed out three main criticisms of verbal reporting and the use of verbal protocol data. These present challenging arguments with respect to the *effect* of verbalization on thinking (i.e., verbal reporting inevitably changes the course of thinking), the *incompleteness* of verbal report data about thinking (i.e., verbal reports cannot capture every single bit of thinking in action), and the *irrelevance* of verbal reports to the thinking under examination (e.g., verbal report data cannot but reflect task-irrelevant behaviors). A well-designed verbal protocol study accounts for these challenges systematically and in a fundamental way. The following subsections outline three matters that must be considered in research design to address these issues: *construct, reactivity,* and *triangulation.*

The Central Role of Theoretical Construct

How adequately and precisely do verbal reports tap into the focal construct as intended, conceptualized, and hypothesized for the study? The problem of construct validity in measurement (Messick, 1989), and, more broadly, the trustworthiness of research methodologies (Creswell & Miller, 2000), can be largely characterized in terms of *construct underrepresentation* and *construct irrelevance.* To begin, the issue of construct underrepresentation is related to the criticism that verbal reports are incomplete. In a study of reading, researchers might face a situation in which verbal protocols fail to provide a complete picture of the construct of reading they seek to observe and examine. Construct underrepresentation occurs not only because participating readers cannot fully describe what they are thinking and doing at every moment, but also because the tasks do not always invite them to activate their full repertoires of knowledge and skills. In addition, construct irrelevance is related to the criticism that verbal protocol studies are prone to producing off-task processes and behaviors. Verbal protocols cannot provide relevant information on the construct of reading when the readers are distracted by problems with ill-designed task features related to settings, procedures, and materials.

The first and most important step researchers can take is to articulate the relevant *theoretical constructs* in concrete terms and in sufficient detail in order to represent the core of readers' performance. A detailed and parsimonious account of the study's theoretical construct provides a guide to all subsequent decisions for the valid task design that elicits the construct-relevant processes. From this guide, three actions follow. First, a *cognitive task analysis* must be done to create maps and charts delineating possible reader responses on the basis of theoretical judgments of their construct (ir)relevance. Next is a *pilot study* to test the suitability of task features (e.g., task goals; products and procedures; operations and resources; and the ways these are structured, sequenced, and introduced to participants). The pilot study traces any misfit between the kind of verbal report data the actual task produces and the results of the prior cognitive task analysis. Last, *alternative explanations* must be developed for any misfit observed in the pilot study and possible causes of construct-irrelevance or construct underrepresentation. Iterative implementation of these research activities may serve to improve the task design by bringing it more fully in line with the theoretical construct.

The Inherent Risk of Reactivity

Another criticism concerns the extent to which verbalization influences thinking. Readers do not only respond to the task of reading, but simultaneously react to what they are saying, and that these reactions might considerably influence the subsequent actions they take to complete the task. Fox and colleagues (2011) described this situation with the term *reactivity*—the mental states of readers being reactive to the forms and contents of their verbalization, which change the course of their thinking to a greater or lesser degree. However, Fox and colleagues' research synthesis documented that no significant differences were found between thinking performance in well-designed verbal protocol tasks and in silent tasks. They also reported that uncontrolled self-explaining behaviors led to significant effects on thinking performance. This result supports the integrity of verbal protocol data for research.

Nonetheless, methodological decisions should be taken to mitigate reactivity effects. First, the *forms of verbal report* that will serve as the primary data sources must be chosen, in accord with the study's goals and questions. Self-explanations, in particular, must be distinguished from verbal protocols, as each form reflects different kinds of reader thinking. At the same time, *modes of verbalization* must be determined: Whether the think-aloud will be concurrent or retrospective; when and how prompts will be given to readers, for what purposes (e.g., reminder, clarification, probing); and what kind of cues will be used to induce retrospective reports (e.g., video-recorded performance, possibly with eye movement traces). Finally, *standardized procedures* for what readers are supposed to do— that is, how the examiners are supposed to guide the readers—must be established to ensure consistency in administration. Creating a checklist in which all instructions and procedures are outlined in order is a useful strategy for training examiners in seamless administration of the verbal protocol procedures.

The Advantage of Triangulation

No single measure of thinking is complete and comprehensive, and therefore an analysis of one single data source cannot yield a full account of reading complexities. Triangulation is becoming standard practice in empirical studies, particularly for interpretive, mixed-method research (Denzin, 1989; Leech & Onwuegbuzie, 2007), and has been claimed to be a most useful strategy for addressing the limitations of verbal report data (Cho, 2020; Magliano & Graesser, 1991; Pressley & Afflerbach, 1995; Veenman, 2005). Note that triangulation is not merely collecting multiple data courses, it is a fundamental approach to observing and constructing a coherent set of evidence to substantiate research claims at the intersection of multiple, complementary data analyses that provide unique insights into the same theoretical construct.

Bråten, Magliano, and Salmerón (2020) have proposed three approaches to triangulation as a means for validating verbal reports. First, readers' *individual differences* are measured and integrated into the analysis of their verbal reports. This approach allows examination of the extent to which the quality and quantity of reading processes inferred from verbal protocol data are correlated with measures of individuals' cognitive and affective characteristics known to influence reader performance (e.g., prior knowledge, reading interests). Demographic factors could be used as covariates to observe differences in verbal reports by different groups (e.g., gender, age, region). A second approach is to include *outcome measures*, built into the study design, to provide a criterion for assessing the utility and effectiveness of the processing (e.g., judgment of cognitive and metacognitive skills in relation to comprehension test scores, written essay qualities, or simply retelling). Finally, *process measures* other than verbal reporting, such as eye-tracking data or logfiles, can enhance the interpretation of reader performance. This approach can demonstrate whether verbal protocols are valid sources of evidence about the specific moment-to-moment processes that are assumed to be used during both reading silently and reading while verbalizing.

Standards for Quality in Verbal Protocol Analysis

Methodological works in the verbal protocol literature tend to focus on the validity and trustworthiness of measurements. Yet verbal protocol analysis is also an intellectual process that demands of readers a series of highly sophisticated inferences and adequate responses to issues that arise in this course. The following subsections discuss the issues, including *contextualized inference, theoretical saturation, evidentiary reasoning*, and *data representation*, informing to create standards for quality in verbal protocol analysis.

Contextualized Inference

Researchers' contextual knowledge is of paramount importance in verbal protocol analysis. Ericsson and Simon (1993) have noted that "context provides a principal source of disambiguation of verbal information" (p. 287). It is almost always the case that the examiners will encounter ambiguous utterances during the interrogation of verbal report data. The ambiguity is caused not only by (para)linguistic challenges (e.g., omitted words and phrases, indiscernible pronunciations, murmuring, and silence) in making sense of speakers' utterances, but by complexities inherent to the underlying thoughts and processes (e.g., are cognitive processes completely distinct from metacognitive processes?). Without developing an acute sense of the context in which these utterances were generated, the examiners are likely to end up relying heavily on their own preferred interpretation (subconsciously, in many cases).

To prevent unintentionally biased practices in coding, data analysis begins with the initial data collection, during which the examiners can make close observations of participants' performance and verbalizations. An important duty of the examiners at the moment is to collect and retain any information that would assist in building their contextual knowledge of the readers' verbal protocols. In addition, the examiners ought to continue engaging in a post hoc process of watching, listening to, and taking memos of recorded verbal reporting sessions—multiple times, if needed—to keep their insights up to date and eventually draw on an overall sense of readers' performance as they proceed to in-depth analysis for data coding. When the study results are reported, the activities done to build contextual knowledge, which might have affected subsequent decisions in the data analysis (e.g., data reduction, ambiguous utterances, noncoded data), should be described as part of the research methods.

Theoretical Saturation

More often than not, it is assumed that verbal protocol research is conducted to support extant theories. In reality, verbal protocol analysis involves iterative processes because researchers confront a theory with data under the ongoing influence of the theory. It is tempting to decide early that one's current theory explains the data well enough, and that the data support the theory. However, it is important to remember that *mutual consistency* of theory and data is neither automatically assured nor easily determined. Rather, verbal reporting not infrequently provides extensive data that cannot be fully explained by any current theories. Yet this situation is not cause for discouragement because encountering unexpected protocol data can lead to the induction of new theories or to grounded theories (Glaser & Strauss, 1967)—the utmost accomplishment of verbal protocol examination.

Practically, the thorough use of coding schemes is an indication that mutual consistency and theoretical saturation are considered an important part of verbal protocol analysis. The coding scheme should constantly evolve, along with the changing models of readers' performance that the researchers are building. Regularities in verbal protocol data that are not explained by any current theory call for a rethinking of the models, the adoption of alternative theories to explain the unexpected patterns, and the reflection of up-to-date knowledge in the evolving coding scheme. Hence, ideally, the latest version of a coding framework demonstrates the theoretical basis and the completeness of the data analysis, at least within the study context. When a verbal protocol study is reported and publicized, the evolving processes and products of coding schemes coupled with exemplary verbal excerpts should be available for audience judgments.

Evidentiary Reasoning

Verbal protocol analysis engages researchers with manifold arguments and reasoning revolving around evidence that may support what they ultimately desire to claim. Two levels of evidentiary reasoning are considered. At the macro level, design of verbal protocol research begins by building an *argument schema* (Toulmin, 1958), which integrates multiple study components into a whole. To illustrate, assertions about the intended construct and related reader responses (*claims*) are closely examined in order to validate research questions. These assertions require compelling evidence and examples from readers' verbal reports (*data*), which are collected with a suitably designed reading task. What constitutes evidence is reasoned on the basis of theoretical constructs (*warrants*), which support the logical reasoning behind the claim–data relationships. Note that the study's warrant will be bolstered by a critical synthesis of related studies (*backing*). Also, validly constructed claims will limit their explanatory power to the very specific conditions accounted for in that study (*qualifiers*), thus opening the possibility of counterclaims and alternative explanations (*rebuttal*).

The researchers employ this macro-level schema as a guide for handling their navigations and movements across nebulous verbal report data in the micro-level analysis. They undertake these *argument moves* (Skalak & Rissland, 1991) through interactions with multiple data points. They justify their coding decisions (*claims*) by negotiating multiple observations of certain regularities and patterns (*evidence*), which are implicit and thus remain hidden in a large pile of unnoticed verbal reports. In addition, theoretical constructs must be locally grounded to support fine-grained, cohesive accounts of interconnected episodes and a noticeably high incidence of a certain form of reader response (*reasoning* or *warranting*). Again, the context of research provides "safeguards" to define the circumstances under which readers' particular thoughts and processes are evoked (*qualifiers*) and to anticipate potential counterclaims to coding decisions (*rebuttals*). These context-specific insights not only enrich the researchers' argument moves, but allow transparent discussion of the study's limitations, unresolved issues, and questions that remain for future research.

Data Representation

Verbal reports are language that represents meaning in abstract forms, and often are coded and analyzed in the form of transcribed written language. The sequential and abstract nature of verbal protocol data makes it difficult for the examiners not only to achieve a holistic view of the entire scope and sequence of verbal information, but to locate and situate significant moments of reader performance within the overall context of verbal reporting. In this respect, data representation (transformation of data in accessible and comprehensible forms) is a necessary and useful method in response to this challenge.

There are two common practices in data representation. The first approach is similar to the narrative style of traditional qualitative research reports, which retain the language forms of the data and display selected "verbal excerpts" that correspond to specific patterns and themes in a linear fashion. The other approach uses numerical forms, especially when the researcher is interested in generalizing quantifiable properties of verbal protocols (e.g., frequencies of the coded incidents; correlations among the codes; and differences in numbers of incidents between different groups designated by characteristics of reader, text, task, goal, or any other significant factor for the study).

In a more innovative way, visual representations may provide a succinct account of the whole context of reader performance inferred from verbal protocol analysis. Two techniques can be suggested (Figure 18.1). One is a sequential display of processing chains (see Figure 18.1, top, for an example of this representational method); the figure represents the order in which four types of focal reading strategies were used by seven high school readers performing two kinds of Internet reading tasks (Cho, 2014). This method provides three benefits by facilitating (1) interrogation of how participants engaged in multiple categories of reading processes (e.g., information location, meaning making, self-monitoring, text evaluation) throughout the course of reading; (2) making sense of the flows of attention allocation, strategy choices, and changes in processing demands; and (3) both qualitative and quantitative comparisons of the participants' self-regulatory patterns according to construct-relevant and task-related variables.

The other is a concept-mapping strategy (see Figure 18.1, bottom, for an example of this method), which represents the meanings that three middle school readers constructed from four historical texts (Cho, 2019). Three advantages of this method are that it facilitates (1) examination of the development of the mental representations (e.g., within-, between-, and cross-textual) constructed in the course of reading by individuals; (2) observation of the intertextual links that readers made as they zigzagged across mental representations; and (3) follow-up analyses, both qualitative and quantitative, to address the complexities of the progression of readers' sensemaking as they moved toward knowing and understanding. Both of these visual representation methods are highly beneficial not only for the intended audience of a study, but for researchers as they strive to keep their analysis sensitive to the contexts of reading within and across individual participants.

1. A sequential analysis of *processing chains*: Seven proficient high school students' reading strategy use to learn from online sources in two different tasks of open website searching and focused website learning (Cho, 2014).

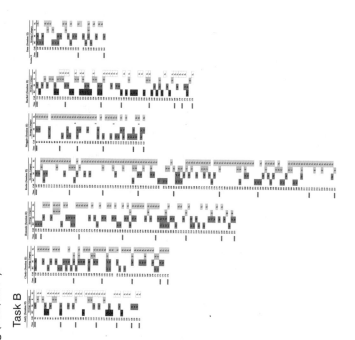

Task B

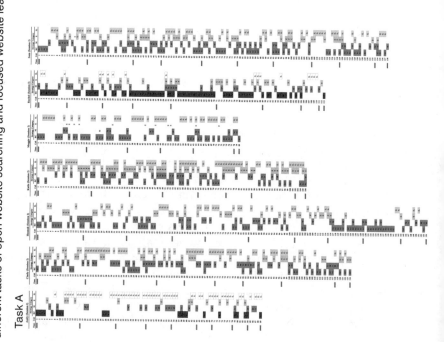

Task A

2. A multilayered analysis of mental representations: Three middle school students' reading for the historical sensemaking of four different texts on a culturally relevant topic in history (Cho, 2019).

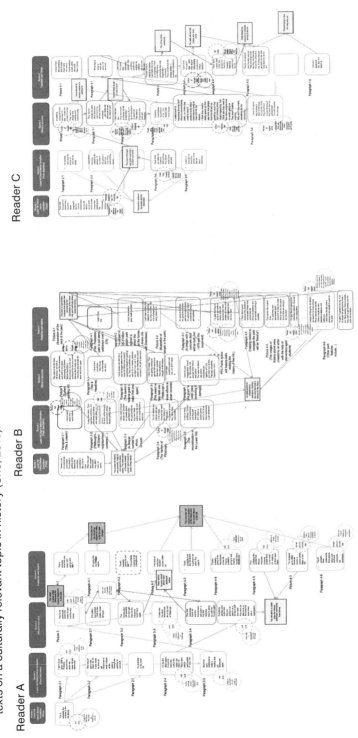

FIGURE 18.1. Data representations resulting from verbal protocol analysis. *Top:* A sequential analysis of *processing chains.* Seven proficient high school students' reading strategy use to learn from online sources in two different tasks of open website searching and focused website learning. Data from Cho (2014). *Bottom:* A multilayered analysis of *mental representations.* Three middle school students' reading for making historical sense of four different texts on a culturally relevant topic in history. Data from Cho (2019).

413

TWO EMPIRICAL STUDIES IN VERBAL PROTOCOL RESEARCH

This section discusses two empirical studies: Hartman's (1995) "Eight Readers Reading" and Goldman and colleagues' (2012) "Comprehending and Learning from Internet Sources." Both studies are exemplary, deserving models for any researcher interested in rigorous and inventive approaches to the use of readers' verbal report data. Moreover, these works demonstrate the reciprocity of evolving literacy theories and verbal reporting methodologies, both of which are critical for understanding complex reading processes and practices in today's extended literacy tasks. Table 18.2 encapsulates how multiple elements of each study reflect the considerations and standards for verbal protocol analysis suggested in the previous section.

Two observations point to the fundamental quality of these two studies: coherence and transparency. Perhaps the most noticeable merit of both studies is their *coherence*, which they demonstrate to be consistently robust across different study components and different research processes. It is particularly worth noting that both studies begin working toward coherence from their initial, thorough examination of "theoretical constructs" and "focal processes, thoughts, and responses" in line with the study goals and questions. Both Hartman (1995) and Goldman's team (2012) seem to have benefited from their theoretical specification of what was aimed to be examined, which provided "blueprints" that allowed them to carry out the subsequent research activities with knowledge and confidence (e.g., participant selection, task design, material preparation, think-aloud procedures, coding schemes, constant comparative analyses, graphical and statistical representations of data). This coherence also provides the audience with a well-designed, macro-level schema with which they are anticipating and navigating across different study components. The coherent argument schema also assists the audience efficiently in comprehending the research activities conducted in phases that build on one another, as well as the rationales for the important decisions involved in those activities. Such levels of study coherence should be integral to the standards for ensuring the quality of verbal protocol analysis.

These compelling works are not free of concerns, due to the common problem of *transparency* in verbal protocol studies. Full transparency requires researchers to provide detailed explanations of their management of verbal protocol data—not only by communicating their confidence in decisions informed by theoretically grounded knowledge, but also by revealing the confusions and conflicts they might have to resolve. Both Hartman (1995) and Goldman's group (2012) provide a great deal of detail about their analytical activities, but some parts of the process are underspecified, such as the researchers' contextual knowledge and argument moves involved in the data analysis. In particular, they are seldom explicit about data deemed "noise and errors," which raises questions of trustworthiness:

TABLE 18.2. Methodological Features of Two Verbal Protocol Studies

Study feature	Hartman (1995)	Goldman et al. (2012)
Overview	*Research questions:* How do readers make intertextual links across multiple passages? *Reader task:* Eight highly proficient high school students read across five passages of different styles that presented different perspectives on the Civil War.	*Research questions:* What are the relationships of sense-making, evaluating, and monitoring processes during reading, and how may these influence online navigation decisions? *Reader task:* Twenty-one undergraduates learned through a Web-based inquiry task about volcanoes, using multiple Internet sources.
Features of study design	Theoretical constructs *Theoretical background:* Cognitive psychology, reading comprehension, semiotics, and literary theories. *Intended construct:* Intertextuality as a cognitive construction in the reader. *Focal processes, thoughts, and responses:* Intertextual linking strategies that readers engaged in across the knowledge sources (the given texts and the texts in readers' memory). *Cognitive task analysis:* Analysis of similar reading tasks in previous studies to determine the conditions of readers, materials, procedures, and data analyses for the present study. *Pilot study:* Twenty-six case studies with different readers and varied texts for trials of think-aloud procedures and protocol analysis approaches.	Theoretical constructs *Theoretical background:* Cognitive science that supports expanded theories of text comprehension (e.g., multiple source comprehension, disciplinary literacy). *Intended construct:* Learning from multiple digital sources in science. *Focal processes, thoughts, and responses:* Cognitive and self-regulatory skills for navigation and selection, evaluation, and integration of information from multiple sources and its representation in the integrated model. *Cognitive task analysis:* Disciplinary reasoning models of science topic, expert explanation, and previous empirical work; no description of the learning task analysis. *Pilot study:* A brief note on pilot testing of verbal reporting and the resulting decision to offer example comments for readers for a training purpose.
	Reactivity in verbal reporting *Verbal data form:* Both during-reading verbal protocol and after-reading self-explanation. *Reporting mode:* Primary concurrent thinking aloud while reading silently, and secondary retrospective reporting cued with researcher queries. *Standardized procedure:* Pretraining, written presentation of task prompt, stop and talk at each reader's discretion, and nonobtrusive reminders.	Reactivity in verbal reporting *Verbal data form:* Concurrent verbal protocol. *Reporting mode:* Thinking aloud during reading. *Standardized procedure:* Material introduction, essay prompt, pretraining (described in detail with the actual materials), thinking aloud while reading aloud (at the end of reading of each sentence and diagram), writing phase, and assessment phase. *(continued)*

TABLE 18.2. *(continued)*

Study feature	Hartman (1995)	Goldman et al. (2012)
	Triangulation	Triangulation
	Individual differences: Verbal skills (as assessed by standardized tests; controlled for participant selection); no information on any follow-up analysis. *Outcome measures:* No explicit information on outcome measures included in the design. *Complementary process measures:* Readers' responses to researcher's queries about their own cognitive processes performed in the reading of the passages.	*Individual differences:* Prior knowledge on the topic (controlled for participant selection); age, number of science courses taken, and rated familiarity to the texts equated between the groups. *Outcome measures:* Pre- and posttests of researcher-designed topic knowledge measures (more and less successful leaners identified from changes in pretest–posttest performance); essay-writing measures for numbers of core concepts, erroneous causes, and conceptual integrations; Web source reliability rankings. *Complementary process measures:* Navigation behaviors from weblog files.
Quality features of protocol analysis	Contextual inference *Contextual information:* No explicit description or discussion of the difficulties and challenges that might have been encountered and addressed during the task implementation. *Contextual knowledge:* No relevant description or discussion found in the study report, except for a discussion of decisions about the unit of analysis.	Contextual inferences *Contextual information:* Gestures were used to identify referents for deictic pronouns; no further explicit description available. *Contextual knowledge:* No relevant description or discussion found in the study report, except for a discussion of decisions about the unit of analysis.
	Theoretical saturation *Coding processes:* A decision-making process about units of analysis (from T-units to TA utterances) discussed; interrater reliability checks conducted by two raters on a subset of data. *Coding framework:* Only top-level categories reported.	Theoretical saturation *Coding processes:* Two phases of coding for processing types and intertextual links; intercoder agreements by two raters. *Coding framework:* A detailed framework for eight coded processes (including descriptions, context-specific examples, and focal text segments being read to which those processes were referenced).

(continued)

TABLE 18.2. *(continued)*

Study feature	Hartman (1995)	Goldman et al. (2012)
	Evidentiary reasoning	Evidentiary reasoning
	Argument schema: A coherent structure demonstrated across claims (findings and implications), data and evidence (verbal protocols), and reasoning (theoretical constructs); a discussion of the possibility of rebuttals due to the contextual limitations of the predetermined text set and task structure; no specific counterclaims discussed; a comment on the qualifier issue with respect to the generalizability of a small case study.	*Argument schema:* A coherent structure demonstrated across claims (findings from processing and case analyses and the general discussion), data and evidence (verbal protocols and other complementary process and outcome data), and reasoning (theoretical constructs); an in-depth discussion of idiosyncratic observations (overall patterns) and alternative explanations.
	Argument moves: No explicit description or discussion with specific examples found in the study report.	*Argument moves:* No descriptions of how codes identified at multiple phases were integrated and how issues and conflicts between the raters were resolved.
	Data representation	Data representation
	Conventional methods: Verbal excerpts, percentages of protocol-revealed linking processes by reader and by text.	*Conventional methods:* Noticeable verbal excerpts and statistical representations for general patterns and group differences.
	Innovative methods: Visually represented with nodes and links, sequential displays of the linking processes and the knowledge sources (their types, directions, and flows) engaged in by readers.	*Innovative methods:* No sequential representation of processing patterns with which group differences could be intuitively detected; no representations of mental models that readers have built in their minds.

For example, what were the rates of noncoded utterances? How were such "non-data" identified and treated? What might the potential impacts have been of reader profiling or pattern recognition in group performance? Was there a mechanism to address researcher bias and, if so, how? Admittedly, the issue of transparency in study reporting is widely observed in the vast verbal protocol literature. However, less-than-ideal practices should not be simply accepted as the norm; rather, each study has a responsibility to notice fundamental problems that might compromise the rigor and trustworthiness of verbal protocol analysis.

The quality of empirical work cannot be judged merely by counting how many checklist items have been ticked. A judgment of a study's methodological rigor is always contingent upon the specific study goals and research questions, which shape how various standards and considerations should be situated and prioritized. Both Hartman (1995) and Goldman and colleagues (2012) have demonstrated high-quality work by undertaking meticulous procedures for collecting and interrogating verbal protocol data, venturing into new areas of research that offer a fundamental knowledge basis for addressing complex problems and issues in demanding literacy tasks and contexts. Hence the studies provide insights and suggestions for future work. Where they have room for improvement, they serve as reminders of the importance of disclosing all relevant information, to allow readers to distinctly see and discuss the nuanced roles of research contexts and researcher decisions behind a study.

SUMMARY

This chapter has described verbal protocol methodology, which has markedly advanced the research in reading and literacy. It has explained the meanings of terms and concepts that are necessary to understand the theoretical and methodological substance of verbal protocol analysis. Conceptual clarity is vital for facilitating shared language use for further conversations, and for thinking through such concepts in ways that can lead to new opportunities for refining research. The chapter also has examined the status of verbal protocol studies and how perspectives and practices of verbal protocol analysis have evolved while expanding the horizons of knowledge in reading and literacy. The discussion has highlighted the symbiotic nature of research and theory building afforded by verbal report data. Informed by a rich history of methodological advancement, the chapter has suggested some important considerations for researchers toward enhancing the rigor and trustworthiness of verbal protocol research. Integrating these considerations into empirical work will help creative researchers achieve both coherence and transparency as they continue to design and test novel approaches, while being aptly critical and unafraid to challenge their own research practices.

REFERENCES

Afflerbach, P. (2000). Verbal reports and protocol analysis. In M. J. Kamil, P. B. Mosenthal, P. D. Pearson, & R. Barr (Eds.), *Handbook of reading research* (Vol. 3, pp. 163–179). Mahwah, NJ: Erlbaum.

Afflerbach, P. (2016). Introduction. In P. Afflerbach (Ed.), *Handbook of individual differences in reading: Reader, text, and context.* New York: Routledge.

Afflerbach, P., & Johnston, P. (1984). On the use of verbal report in reading research. *Journal of Reading Behavior, 16*(4), 307–322.

Alexander, P. A. (2005). The path to competence: A lifespan development of perspective on reading. *Journal of Literacy Research, 37*(4), 413–436.

Anderson, R. C., & Pearson, P. D. (1984). A schema-theoretic view of basic processes in reading. In P. D. Pearson (Ed.), *Handbook of reading research* (pp. 255–291). New York: Longman.

Anmarkrud, O., Bråten, I., & Strømsø, H. I. (2014). Multiple-documents literacy: Strategic processing, source awareness, and argumentation when reading multiple conflicting documents. *Learning and Individual Differences, 30,* 64–76.

Azevedo, R., Guthrie, J. T., & Seibert, D. (2004). The role of self-regulated learning in fostering students' conceptual understanding of complex systems with hypermedia. *Journal of Educational Computing Research, 30*(1–2), 87–111.

Baddeley, A. (2012). Working memory: Theories, models, and controversies. *Annual Review of Psychology, 63,* 1–29.

Barzilai, S., & Zohar, A. (2012). Epistemic thinking in action: Evaluating and integrating online sources. *Cognition and Instruction, 30*(1), 39–85.

Bereiter, C., & Bird, M. (1985). Use of thinking aloud in identification and teaching of reading comprehension strategies. *Cognition and Instruction, 2*(2), 131–156.

Boring, E. G. (1953). A history of introspection. *Psychological Bulletin, 50*(3), 169–189.

Bråten, I., Magliano, J. P., & Salmerón, L. (2020). Concurrent and task-specific self-reports. In D. L. Dinsmore, L. K. Fryer, & M. M. Parkinson (Eds.), *Handbook of strategies and strategic processing: Conceptualization, intervention, measurement, and analysis* (pp. 275–295). New York: Routledge.

Bråten, I., & Strømsø, H. I. (2003). A longitudinal think-aloud study of spontaneous strategic processing during the reading of multiple expository texts. *Reading and Writing: An Interdisciplinary Journal, 16,* 195–218.

Brown, A. L. (1980). Metacognitive development and reading: Theoretical issues in reading comprehension. In R. J. Spiro, B. C. Bruce, & W. F. Brewer (Eds.), *Perspectives from cognitive psychology, linguistics, artificial intelligence, and education* (pp. 453–481). Hillsdale, NJ: Erlbaum.

Brown, J. S., Collins, A., & Duguid, P. (1989). Situated cognition and the culture of learning. *Educational Researcher, 18*(1), 32–42.

Chi, N. T. H. (1997). Quantifying qualitative analyses of verbal data: A practical guide. *Journal of the Learning Sciences, 6*(3), 271–315.

Cho, B.-Y. (2014). Competent adolescent readers' use of Internet reading strategies: A think-aloud study. *Cognition and Instruction, 32*(3), 253–289.

Cho, B.-Y. (2019). *Promoting disciplinary reading and literacy through multisource text inquiries.* Keynote address at the European Conference on Literacy, Copenhagen, Denmark.

Cho, B.-Y. (2020). Examining the process of reading in media text environments. In E. B. Moje, P. Afflerbach, P. Enciso, & N. K. Lesaux (Eds.), *Handbook of reading research* (Vol. 5, pp. 464–486). New York: Routledge.

Cho, B.-Y., & Afflerbach, P. (2017). An evolving perspective of constructively response reading comprehension strategies in multilayered digital text environments. In S. E. Israel (Ed.), *Handbook of research on reading comprehension* (2nd ed., pp. 109–134). New York: Guilford Press.

Cho, B.-Y., Woodward, L., & Afflerbach, P. (2020). Qualitative approaches to the verbal protocol analysis of strategic processing. In D. Dinsmore, L. K. Fryer, & M. M. Parkinson (Eds.), *Handbook of strategies and strategic processing: Conceptualization, intervention, measurement, and analysis* (pp. 373–392). New York: Routledge.

Cho, B.-Y., Woodward, L., & Li, D. (2018). Epistemic processing when adolescents read online: A verbal protocol analysis of more and less successful online readers. *Reading Research Quarterly, 53*(2), 197–221.

Cho, B.-Y., Woodward, L., Li, D., & Barlow, E. (2017). Examining adolescents' strategic processing during online reading with a question-generating task. *American Educational Research Journal, 54*(4), 691–724.

Chomsky, N. (1968). *Language and mind.* New York: Harcourt, Brace & World.

Coiro, J., & Dobler, E. (2007). Exploring the online reading comprehension strategies used by sixth-grade skilled readers to search for and locate information on the Internet. *Reading Research Quarterly, 42*(2), 214–257.

Crain-Thoreson, C., Lippman, M. Z., & McClendon-Magnuson, D. (1997). Windows on comprehension: Reading comprehension processes as revealed by two think-aloud procedures. *Journal of Educational Psychology, 89*(4), 579–591.

Creswell, J. W., & Miller, D. L. (2000). Determining validity in qualitative inquiry. *Theory into Practice, 39*(3), 124–131.

Crutcher, R. J. (1994). Telling what we know: The use of verbal report methodologies in psychological research. *Psychological Science, 5*(5), 241–244.

Denzin, N. K. (1989). *The research act: A theoretical introduction to sociological methods.* Englewood Cliffs, NJ: Prentice-Hall.

Denzin, N. K., & Lincoln, Y. S. (2008). Introduction: The discipline and practice of qualitative research. In N. K. Denzin & Y. S. Lincoln (Eds.), *Strategies of qualitative inquiry* (pp. 1–43). Thousand Oaks, CA: SAGE.

Doyle, W. (1983). Academic work. *Review of Educational Research, 53,* 159–199.

Earthman, E. A. (1992). Creating the virtual work: Readers' processes in understanding literary texts. *Research in the Teaching of English, 26*(4), 381–384.

Ericsson, K. A., & Crutcher, R. J. (1991). Introspection and verbal reports on cognitive processes: Two approaches to the study of thinking: A response to Howe. *New Ideas in Psychology, 9*(1), 57–71.

Ericsson, K. A., & Simon, H. A. (1980). Verbal reports as data. *Psychological Review, 87*(3), 215–251.

Ericsson, K. A., & Simon, H. A. (1993). *Protocol analysis: Verbal reports as data.* Cambridge, MA: MIT Press.

Ericsson, K. A., & Simon, H. A. (1998). How to study thinking in everyday life: Contrasting think-aloud protocols with descriptions and explanations of thinking. *Mind, Culture, and Activity, 5*(3), 178–186.

Eva-Wood, A. L. (2004a). How think-and-feel-aloud instruction influences poetry readers. *Discourse Processes, 38*(2), 173–192.

Eva-Wood, A. L. (2004b). Thinking and feeling poetry: Exploring meanings aloud. *Journal of Educational Psychology, 96*(1), 182–191.

Ferguson, L. E., Bråten, I., & Strømsø, H. I. (2012). Epistemic cognition when students read multiple documents containing conflicting scientific evidence: A think-aloud study. *Learning and Instruction, 22,* 103–120.

Fox, M. C., Ericsson, A., & Best, R. (2011). Do procedures for verbal reporting of thinking have to be reactive?: A meta-analysis and recommendation for best reporting methods. *Psychological Bulletin, 137*(2), 316–344.

Gerjets, P., Kammerer, Y., & Werner, B. (2011). Measuring spontaneous and instructed evaluation processes during Web search: Integrating concurrent thinking-aloud protocols and eye-tracking data. *Learning and Instruction, 21,* 220–231.

Glaser, B. G., & Strauss, A. L. (1967). *The discovery of grounded theory: Strategies for qualitative research.* Chicago: Aldine.

Goldman, S. R., Braasch, J. L. G., Wiley, J., Graesser, A. C., & Brodowinska, K. (2012). Comprehending and learning from Internet sources: Processing patterns of better and poorer learners. *Reading Research Quarterly, 47*(4), 356–381.

Gottlieb, E., & Wineburg, S. (2012). Between Veritas and Communitas: Epistemic switching in the reading of academic and sacred history. *Journal of the Learning Sciences, 21*(1), 84–129.

Greene, J. A., & Azevedo, R. (2007). Adolescents' use of self-regulatory processes and their relation to qualitative mental model shifts while using hypermedia. *Journal of Educational Computing Research, 36*(2), 125–148.

Greene, J. A., Azevedo, R., & Torney-Purta, J. (2008). Modeling epistemic and ontological cognition: Philosophical perspectives and methodological directions. *Educational Psychologist, 43*(3), 142–160.

Greene, J. A., Muis, K. R., & Pieschl, S. (2010). The role of epistemic beliefs in students' self-regulated learning with computer-based learning environments: Conceptual and methodological issues. *Educational Psychologist, 45*(4), 245–257.

Greene, J. A., Yu, S. B., & Copeland, D. Z. (2014). Measuring critical components of digital literacy and their relationships with learning. *Computers and Education, 76*, 55–69.

Greeno, J. G. (1989). Perspectives on thinking. *American Psychologist, 44*(2), 134–141.

Greeno, J. G., Collins, A. M., & Resnick, L. B. (1997). Cognition and learning. In D. C. Berliner & R. C. Calfee (Eds.), *Handbook of educational psychology* (pp. 15–46). New York: Macmillan.

Guthrie, J. T., Wigfield, A., & You, W. (2012). Instructional contexts for engagement and achievement in reading. In S. L. Christenson, A. L. Reschly, & C. Wylie (Eds.), *Handbook of research on student engagement* (pp. 601–634). New York: Springer.

Hammer, D., & Elby, A. (2003). Tapping epistemological resources for learning physics. *Journal of the Learning Sciences, 12*(1), 53–90.

Harker, W. J. (1994). "Plain sense" and "poetic significance": Tenth-grade readers reading two poems. *Poetics, 22*(3), 199–218.

Hartman, D. K. (1995). Eight readers reading: The intertextual links of proficient readers reading multiple passages. *Reading Research Quarterly, 30*(3), 520–561.

Hofer, B. K. (2004). Epistemological understanding as a metacognitive process: Thinking aloud during online searching. *Educational Psychologist, 39*(1), 43–55.

Hofer, B. K., & Pintrich, P. R. (1997). The development of epistemological theories: Beliefs about knowledge and knowing and their relation to learning. *Review of Educational Research, 67*(1), 88–140.

Howe, R. B. K. (1991). Introspection: A reassessment, *New Ideas in Psychology, 9*(1), 25–44.

Ivey, G., & Johnston, P. H. (2013). Engagement with young adult literature: Outcomes and processes. *Reading Research Quarterly, 48*(3), 255–275.

James, W. (1890). *The principles of psychology* (2 vols.). New York: Holt.

Kintsch, W. (1988). The role of knowledge in discourse comprehension: A construction–integration model. *Psychological Review, 95*(2), 163–182.

Kneepkens, E. W. E. M., & Zwaan, R. A. (1994). Emotions and literary text comprehension. *Poetics, 23,* 125–138.

Kucan, L., & Beck, I. (1997). Thinking aloud and reading comprehension research: Inquiry, instruction, and social interaction. *Review of Educational Research, 67*(3), 271–299.

Leech, N. L., & Onwuegbuzie, A. J. (2007). An array of qualitative data analysis tools: A call for data analysis triangulation. *School Psychology Quarterly, 22*(4), 557–584.

Leinhardt, G., & Young, K. M. (1996). Two texts, three readers: Distance and expertise in reading history. *Cognition and Instruction, 14*(4), 441–486.

Leu, D. J., Kinzer, C. K., Coiro, J. L., & Cammack, D. W. (2004). Toward a theory of new literacies emerging from the Internet and other information and communication technologies. In R. B. Ruddell & N. J. Unrau (Eds.), *Theoretical models and processes of reading* (5th ed., 1570–1613). Newark, DE: International Reading Association.

Lewis, C., & Fabos, B. (2005). Instant messaging, literacies, and social identities. *Reading Research Quarterly, 40*(4), 470–501.

Long, D. L., & Bourg, T. (1996). Thinking aloud: Telling a story about a story. *Discourse Processes, 21,* 329–339.

Lysaker, J., Tonge, C., Gauson, D., & Miller, A. (2011). Reading and social imagination: What relationally oriented reading instruction can do for children. *Reading Psychology, 32*(6), 520–566.

Magliano, J. P., & Graesser, A. C. (1991). A three-pronged method for studying inference generation in literary text. *Poetics, 20,* 193–232.

Magliano, J. P., Trabasso, T., & Graesser, A. C. (1999). Strategic processing during comprehension." *Journal of Educational Psychology, 91,* 615–629.

Marsh, J. (2011). Young children's literacy practices in a virtual world: Establishing an online interaction order. *Reading Research Quarterly, 46*(2), 101–108.

Mason, L., Ariasi, N., & Boldrin, A. (2011). Epistemic beliefs in action: Spontaneous reflections about knowledge and knowing during online information searching and their influence on learning. *Learning and Instruction, 21,* 137–151.

McNamara, D. S., Kintsch, E., Songer, N. B., & Kintsch, W. (1996). Are good texts always better?: Interactions of text coherence, background knowledge, and levels of understanding in learning from text. *Cognition and Instruction, 14*(1), 1–43.

McNamara, D. S., & Magliano, J. (2009). Toward a comprehensive model of comprehension. *Psychology of Learning and Motivation, 51,* 297–384.

Messick, S. (1989). Validity. In R. L. Linn (Ed.), *Educational measurement* (3rd ed., pp. 13–103). London: Collier Macmillan.

Miall, D. S., & Kuiken, D. (1994). Foregrounding, defamiliarization, and affect response to literary stories. *Poetics, 22,* 389–407.

Mislevy, R. J., Steinberg, L. S., & Almond, R. G. (2003). On the structure of educational assessments. *Measurement: Interdisciplinary Research and Perspectives, 1*(1), 3–62.

Nisbett, R. E., & Wilson, T. D. (1977). Telling more than we can know: Verbal reports on mental processes. *Psychological Review, 84*(3), 231–259.

Olshavsky, J. E. (1976–1977). Reading as problem solving. *Reading Research Quarterly, 12*(4), 654–674.

Pearson, P. D., & Cervetti, G. N. (2015). Fifty years of reading comprehension theory and practice. In P. D. Pearson & E. H. Hiebert (Eds.), *Research-based practices for teaching Common Core literacy* (pp. 1–24). New York: Teachers College Press.

Pellegrino, J. W., Chudowsky, N., & Glaser, R. (2001). *Knowing what students know: The science and design of educational assessment.* Washington, DC: National Academy Press.

Peskin, J. (1998). Constructing meaning when reading poetry: An expert–novice study. *Cognition and Instruction, 16*(3), 235–263.

Peskin, J. (2010). The development of poetic literacy during the school years. *Discourse Processes, 47,* 77–103.

Piaget, J. (1926). *The language and thought of the child.* New York: Harcourt, Brace.

Pressley, M., & Afflerbach, P. (1995). *Verbal protocols of reading: The nature of constructively responsive reading.* Hillsdale, NJ: Erlbaum.

Rosenblatt, L. M. (1978). *The reader, the text, the poem: The transactional theory of the literary work.* Carbondale: Southern Illinois University Press.

Sadoski, M., Goetz, E. T., & Rodriguez, M. (2000). Engaging texts: Effects of concreteness on comprehensibility, interest, and recall in four text types. *Journal of Educational Psychology, 92*(1), 85–95.

Sandoval, W. A., Greene, J. A., & Bråten, I. (2016). Understanding and promoting thinking about knowledge: Origins, issues, and future directions of research on epistemic cognition. *Review of Research in Education, 40,* 457–496.

Schunk, D. H., & Bursuck, W. D. (2016). Self-efficacy, agency, and volition: Student beliefs and reading motivation. In P. Afflerbach (Ed.), *Handbook of individual differences in reading: Reader, text, and context* (pp. 54–66). New York: Routledge.

Shanahan, C., Shanahan, T., & Misischia, C. (2011). Analysis of expert readers in three disciplines: History, mathematics, and chemistry. *Journal of Literacy Research, 43*(4), 393–429.

Skalak, D., & Rissland, E. (1991). Argument moves in a rule-guided domain. In *Proceedings of the Association for Computing Machinery.* Retrieved September 15, 2019, from *http://users.umiacs.umd.edu/~horty/courses/readings/skalak-rissland-1991-argument-moves.pdf.*

Smagorinsky, P. (1998). Thinking and speech and protocol analysis. *Mind, Culture, and Activity, 5*(3), 157–177.

Smagorinsky, P. (2001). Rethinking protocol analysis from a cultural perspective. *Annual Review of Applied Linguistics, 21,* 233–245.

Smagorinsky, P., Cook, L. S., & Reed, P. M. (2005). The construction of meaning and identity in the composition and reading of an architectural text. *Reading Research Quarterly, 40*(1), 70–88.

Smagorinsky, P., Daigle, E. A., O'Donnell-Allen, C., & Bynum, S. (2010). Bullshit in academic writing: A protocol analysis of a high school senior's process of interpreting *Much Ado about Nothing. Research in the Teaching of English, 44*(4), 368–405.

Snow, C. (2002). *Reading for understanding: Toward a R&D program in reading comprehension.* Santa Monica, CA: RAND.

Strømsø, H. I., & Bråten, I. (2002). Norwegian law students' use of multiple sources while reading expository texts. *Reading Research Quarterly, 37*(2), 208–227.

Toulmin, S. E. (1958). *The uses of argument.* Cambridge, UK: Cambridge University Press.

Trabasso, T., & Magliano, J. P. (1996). Conscious understanding during comprehension. *Discourse Processes, 21,* 255–287.

Trevors, G., Feyzi-Behnagh, R., Azevedo, R., & Bouchet, F. (2016). Self-regulated learning processes vary as a function of epistemic beliefs and contexts: Mixed method evidence from eye tracking and concurrent and retrospective reports. *Learning and Instruction, 42,* 31–46.

Veenman, M. V. J. (2005). The assessment of metacognitive skills: What can be learned from multi-method designs? In C. Artelt & B. Moschner (Eds.), *Lernstrategien und metakognition: Implikationen fur forschung und praxis* (pp. 77–99). Munster, Germany: Waxman.

Vygotsky, L. S. (1978). *Mind in society: The development of higher psychological processes* (M. Cole, V. John-Steiner, S. Scribner, & E. Souberman, Trans.). Cambridge, MA: Harvard University Press.

Wade, S. E., Buxton, W. M., & Kelly, M. (1999). Using think-alouds to examine reader–text interest. *Reading Research Quarterly, 34*(2), 194–216.

Warren, J. E. (2011). "Generic" and "specific" expertise in English: An expert/expert study in poetry interpretation and academic argument. *Cognition and Instruction, 29*(4), 349–374.

Wilson, T. D. (1994), The proper protocol: Validity and completeness of verbal reports, *Psychological Science, 5,* 249–252.

Wineburg, S. (1998). Reading Abraham Lincoln: An expert/expert study in the interpretation of historical texts. *Cognitive Science, 22*(3), 319–346.

Wolfe, M. B. W., & Goldman, S. R. (2005). Relations between adolescents' text processing and reasoning. *Cognition and Instruction, 23,* 467–502.

CHAPTER 19

Considerations of Methodology and Epistemology in Designing Literacy Studies

Sarah J. McCarthey

This chapter builds upon its predecessor in the second edition of this book (Dressman & McCarthey, 2011) by responding to new and revised chapters in this edition and by bringing in current examples, at the same time that it continues to promote a pragmatic approach toward the development of literacy research practices—an approach that makes conscious use of both epistemological concerns and theory across a broad range of ways of doing literacy research. The view of pragmatism derives from the school of philosophy commonly known as American Pragmatism, a school founded in the latter half of the 19th and early 20th centuries by Charles Sanders Peirce, William James, and John Dewey. Its principles include the following:

> A metaphysics that emphasizes processes and relations; a naturalistic and evolutionary understanding of human existence; an analysis of intellectual activity as problem-oriented and as benefiting from historically developed methods; and an emphasis upon the democratic reconstruction of society through educational and other institutions. (Campbell, 1995, p. 14)

In addition, American Pragmatism avoids "ultimate" questions about the nature of reality, such as whether objective truth exists, and instead focuses on what the consequences of acting from a position of positive objectivity or taking a more tentative stance toward an observed phenomenon might be for individuals within a given situation.

By arguing for a pragmatics of literacy research, then, I plan to examine the relations among epistemology, theory, and methodology from a stance grounded in as full a view as possible of the actual conditions in which research is likely to be conducted, rather than in hypothetical conditions removed from the logistical, cultural, historical, and sociopolitical realities of actual schools, homes, and even laboratory settings. Moreover, a pragmatics of literacy research focuses on a broad consideration of the ways in which a research project's epistemological assumptions, methods, and grounding in prior research and/or theory transactionally (Dewey & Bentley, 1949) influence each other, as well as others' likely interpretations and uses of the knowledge generated from the activity of the research.

The chapter also takes into consideration the uses of theory, or *theoretical frames*, in literacy research. I acknowledge that the terms *theory* and *theoretical* have many possible meanings among literacy researchers and have traditionally referred to explanations of specific phenomena grounded in the empirical evidence of research. In this discussion, however, they specifically refer to the more recent practice on the part of researchers employing qualitative methods to apply contemporary social theory—that is, theories originating outside the phenomena on which the researchers are focusing, such as Vygotsky's (1934/1978) theory of the zone of proximal development, Foucauldian theories of language and power (Rabinow, 1984), feminist theories of discourse (e.g., Walkerdine, 1990), or critical race theory (Bell, 1980; Ladson-Billings & Tate, 1995). Although the use of theoretical frames is becoming an increasingly frequent feature of literacy research and has considerable implications for many epistemological and methodological approaches to research, it has received little direct attention or systematic scrutiny as an investigative practice. The use of such external grand narratives may have pragmatic consequences for the ways that knowledge about literacy is both conceptualized and produced (Dressman, 2007, 2008).

The argument proceeds in three sections. First, I provide an introduction to my interest in the topic of technology integration in writing that will ground the discussion of the methodologies and underlying epistemologies. Second, I draw on four chapters in the present book to discuss quasi-experimental, survey, case study, and design-based methods; I consider ways to study the topic of technology integration in writing before considering the underlying epistemologies associated with each approach. In the concluding section, I summarize the arguments and suggest some broad pragmatic principles for the improvement of literacy research as an epistemological, methodological, and theory-building enterprise.

INTEGRATING TECHNOLOGY IN WRITING INSTRUCTION

My interest in the topic of technology integration was born of three issues: (1) studies of policies and practices in writing instruction, (2) research on designing and implementing online tools for writing, and (3) concerns about ways to integrate technology into the teacher education programs I supervise. First, in research I conducted after the implementation of No Child Left Behind in 2002 to understand the effect of policies on teachers' attitudes toward writing (McCarthey, 2008) as well as trends in writing instruction (McCarthey & Mkhize, 2013; McCarthey & Ro, 2011), I was struck by how little technology was used in the elementary classrooms I studied.

Spurred on by my colleagues at the University of Illinois at Urbana–Champaign, Bill Cope and Mary Kalantzis, who developed an online collaborative platform called Scholar (*https://cgscholar.com*), I came to see the potential for online environments to improve students' revision processes, the quality of their feedback, and ultimately their texts. While we found that teachers who used CGScholar increased opportunities for peer-to-peer feedback in their instructional sequences, students expressed interest both in using the tools and providing feedback to one another, and students used self-reviews (Smith, McCarthey, & Magnifico, 2017), we also found that lack of access to computers at home, highly structured writing tasks, and school policies affected students' abilities to take advantage of the online affordances (McCarthey, Magnifico, Woodard, & Kline, 2014). In a follow-up study of a teacher using CGScholar and other digital tools, we found that youth in middle school used technology in more subversive ways in the classroom, but were using a variety of tools at home (e.g., phones) for writing for specific audiences that went unrecognized at school (McCarthey, Kennett, Smith, & West, 2017). While technology acted as a sponsor for writing practices, we found that the ways in which youth took up literate practices often differed from the sanctioned methods and tools (Smith, West, & McCarthey, 2019).

Documenting the challenges of implementing technology in classrooms led me to my third consideration of this topic: How do we model and support the integration of technology into teacher education programs while addressing national and state standards within content areas? I struggled to find studies focused on technology as a professional development tool in writing (McCarthey & Geoghegan, 2016).

The focus on my journey to embrace technology integration highlights the importance of research in this area as questions of technology integration provide opportunities for conducting research from different perspectives. I discuss four of those perspectives in the following section.

FOUR METHODOLOGICAL APPROACHES

Experimental and Quasi-Experimental Designs

In Chapter 9 of this book, Weiland, Shapiro, and Lindsey discuss several methodologies for estimating causal effects. I focus on one of these methodologies: a cluster randomized controlled trial. The hypothetical example of such a trial that I discuss here involves using stratified randomization within six middle school classrooms in two schools, to understand whether an intervention (i.e., the use of a particular online writing environment) is effective in improving the quality of students' texts in a year-long study.

Teachers will be implementing three units (argumentative, informational, and narrative) with the same assignments and routines—drafting, responding through peer review, and revising) in schools. However, the treatment classrooms will be using the online writing program, while the classrooms in the control group will not be using technology for their texts. (In Year 2, the control group will have the opportunity to use computers and the online environment.) Teachers in both conditions have had opportunities to participate in the local version of the National Writing Project the summer before the study, where they wrote daily, gave demonstrations to one another on effective writing practices, and were exposed to some ways to integrate technology into their classrooms. Teachers in the experimental group received specific training on using the online environment; researchers observed the fidelity of the implementation across the experimental classrooms. To measure outcomes, the researchers are using the writing portion of the assessment developed by the Smarter Balanced Assessment Consortium (*www.smarterbalanced.org*). Students in both schools will take the test at the beginning of the year and again at the end of the year.

The epistemological perspective embedded in this example assumes that teachers, students, and writers are like physical objects subject to dynamic laws of behavior. At the level of complex human behavior, these laws may not be the same as those that govern the physical universe; but because variables of human behavior are typically assumed to be normally distributed in the population, there is also assumed to be a regularity (or at least a normative pattern of distribution) to them, which would allow the detection of predictable patterns among them. Patterned predictability in human behavior is the knowledge that experimentalists in literacy research seek, for when a prediction that is planned for comes true more times than chance will allow, then a true pattern—one that may not consider history or culture or individual experience—has been found, and certainty has been obtained, at least for the population as it has been defined. Such knowledge, like knowledge about the laws of planetary movements or genetic heritability, remains true in similar circumstances and is free of the emotional or cultural distortions that characterized belief about the heavens in Ptolemy's time or bloodlines in the Middle Ages. Thus, a fully randomized and procedurally controlled experiment testing the effects of technology integration via the online environment on an objective measure of student achievement should yield reliable information—information that can be used to produce higher student performance in future writing classrooms, and that may be extended (with further experimentation) to other grade levels, student populations, and writing contexts.

The principal strengths of this epistemological perspective are its emphasis on the rationality of knowledge, the clarity of its argument that predictable patterns of human behavior can be known, and the trustworthiness and utilitarian value of knowledge that is considered to have been discovered through its methods. If the previously described experiment yields findings, for example, of higher performance in classrooms with the integration of the online environment, then it would be expected that more classrooms should buy computers, train teachers, and embed this online program in their instruction. Decision making based on what is generalizable beyond its immediate context is clearly the most powerful kind of knowledge, from this perspective.

However, the enactment of such an epistemological perspective also has significant pragmatic limitations. Full control of the experimental context may be practically impossible, or, where possible, may produce a condition so significantly different from the actual school contexts that the experimental context itself becomes a threat to validity. Under quasi-experimental conditions, every compromise in control becomes a possible source of bias, which must be investigated and compensated for through statistical techniques and multiple experiments. Other limitations of the method involve the generalizability of findings and the need to operationally define variables, which may produce an artificial rigidity in the practical application under experimental conditions. In the example above, if the sample does not include enough representation from a particular group, we cannot know whether the results of the experiment hold for these particular groups. Additionally, teachers' own beliefs and facility with the online environment may affect their implementation, despite the training. Although the writing tests developed by Smarter Balanced have been adopted by some states, their validity and reliability have come under fire. For example, White middle-class students have a higher likelihood of scoring higher, due to the match of their background experiences with test items; certain writing constructs are privileged over others; and the use of the computer media favors those students with computer skills over others (Smith & Wheeler, 2019). This raises the question of what other as yet unforeseen variables may inadvertently bias findings whose epistemological foundations and practices provide a rational "guarantee" of their general effectiveness across any and all populations. The defense of truth claims from such studies can become such an overriding preoccupation that experimentalists may attempt to account for more and more variability in their results and design ever more controlled conditions that are increasingly remote from the actual conditions of classrooms and instructional practice. Despite these limitations, controlled experiments continue to be used and provide useful information about aspects of literacy learning and teaching. Like other research methods, experimental designs address certain questions well, while being less effective at illuminating other important issues, particularly with respect to describing the social and organizational complexity of implementing new pedagogical practices.

Survey Research

In Chapter 17, Ash, Baumann, and Bason state that the purpose of survey research is to describe characteristics of a larger group. Let us assume that to study the integration of technology into writing instruction, researchers have decided to conduct a statewide survey to understand teachers' knowledge of technologies for writing, the extent to which they integrate technology, the platforms they use, and factors that influence their use of technology in writing instruction. The researchers have access to a statewide database of teachers, schools, and districts; they are limiting their focus to public middle schools, having determined that middle schoolers are likely to be familiar with technology. Researchers are interested in understanding whether there are differences in the use of technology among teachers in three subject areas in which writing during the school day is likely to occur: language arts, science, and social studies. Thus, they have chosen representative samples of teachers in each of those subjects and have identified the building principals to survey their perceptions of teachers' technology integration in writing. The researchers have decided on an online survey and designed questions in three formats: multiple-choice, Likert scale (1–5), and open-response items in which teachers are asked for examples of technology integration.

In this scenario, the researchers have been careful to consider the issues that often plague surveys as a method: They have considered construct validity to ensure that the questions relate to the topic, have a large sample to increase the number of respondents and reduce sampling errors, and ensured that their statistical methods will be appropriate. They anticipate being able to describe and compare the teachers' responses by subject area.

Undergirding this methodology is the assumption that the responses can be generalized to a larger population. Yet one critique of the method (see Mathiyazhagan & Nandan, 2010) suggests that the results are not necessarily describing a group, but rather a collection of individuals who share only superficial characteristics (e.g., seventh-grade teachers who teach writing as part of the language arts curriculum). The approach assumes an asocial perspective, presuming that the power of the statistical model overrides issues such as student demographics, class size, teachers' years of experience, and teachers' attitudes toward writing and technology. Furthermore, the one-time survey also assumes that teachers' practices and attitudes toward technology integration are static, and that respondents are truthful and consistent in their answers. Additionally, incentives and trust factors affect respondents' motivations (Visser, Krosnick, Lavrakas, & Kim, 2013); thus teachers and administrators may not provide accurate information about their technology integration. Questions such as these arise: What are the incentives for participation by the districts? How much do the respondents trust the confidentiality of their responses? Teachers and administrators who consider the social benefit of responding, such as seeing relevance to their classroom and their own interests in writing and technology, may be more willing to invest the time and effort in completing the survey than others who lack interest in the topic (or feel guilty about not using technology). Despite assurances that online surveys are anonymous, teachers may still not trust that their responses are private and will not be shared with administrators. Surveys presume that the responses teachers give about their practices actually represent what they do in their classroom. This is further complicated by examining the administrators' responses, some of whom may report only on their perceptions of teachers' practices, rather than on classroom observations or more systematic data.

With the goal of describing and comparing populations, survey research is anchored in a positivist view of the world; assumptions include that generalizations can be made across contexts, it is possible to quantify results based on empirical data, and the results are useful for prediction (Kivunji & Kuyini, 2017). However, survey research can straddle the positivist–interpretivist "divide." The added survey items in our example, such as "Give some examples of how you integrate technology," provide an opportunity for respondents to go beyond the closed-ended items and for researchers to identify themes more often associated with interpretivist worldviews. The additional items require interpretation via organizing responses, but they complement the quantifiable items and add the opportunity to consider more contextual aspects, acknowledging that social realities may be multiple and that individual values exist (Kivunji & Kuyini, 2017). The survey described above recognizes that methodologies, while rooted in particular epistemologies such as positivism, are not necessarily exclusive of other worldviews.

Case Studies

In Chapter 2, Compton-Lilly compares case studies and ethnographies, identifying their shared features as well as their differences from one another. Both require assemblages of data sources (such as observations, interviews, field notes, documents, and artifacts), involve thick description of phenomena (Geertz, 1973/2003), and pay attention to cultural practices. The methodologies focus on situated activities within larger contexts for the purposes of meaning construction, with an understanding that subjectivity cannot be avoided and that interpretation is intrinsic to the process. Both are ideal for classrooms and schools, involve storytelling, and can represent the experiences of marginalized people to reveal persistent inequities. In the scenario below, I focus on case studies of two teachers and their classrooms.

To study technology integration in the writing classroom using intrinsic case studies, a researcher is likely to play the role of participant observer in the following scenario: Two seventh-grade teachers in the same middle school (students come from diverse socioeconomic and cultural backgrounds; about 25% of students in each class are emergent bilinguals) have agreed that they will teach three text types (argumentative, informative, and narrative) aligned with the Common Core State Standards in the same order throughout the year; they will use the district-designed rubric as a guide for evaluation. The schedules for completing the units on each genre will be roughly the same in the two classrooms: Students will proceed through drafting, revising, and sharing their texts with the class as audience. In an interview, one teacher reveals that she participated in the National Writing Project the previous summer and has decided to use Google Docs as a platform for students to write, respond, revise, and share their writing for all of the genres. Students will write their first drafts; then they will be divided into groups of four to give feedback on the drafts, using a version of the district rubric that has been adapted by the class. Students will share their final texts with parents at an evening event. In the second classroom, the teacher states that she wants to teach in the "old-fashioned way": Students will prepare handwritten rough drafts; the teacher will use the district rubric; students will edit their work; and the teacher will give individual grades based on the rubric.

Since the teachers are teaching writing at different times during the day, the researcher is able to observe both teachers on a regular basis throughout the school year. In addition to the observations, the researcher interviews each teacher at the beginning and end of each unit, identifies six students from diverse backgrounds in each classroom to interview, and collects all the drafts of the focal students' texts. The researcher is attuned to the cultural practices within each classroom and pays particular attention to how students are using feedback from peers in Google Docs or the teacher's rubrics and grades. During the observations, the researcher is careful to collect demographic characteristics, such as the social class, race, gender, and linguistic background of the class in general and of the focal students in particular. In writing up the study, the researcher will weave these connections and the supporting data together to produce a clear and consistent account of events in both classrooms. The researcher will draw conclusions about the experience of the teacher and students to highlight the differences between the classroom in which technology has been used daily and the more traditionally focused classroom. The narrative will focus on the broader dynamic principles observed in both classes and their likely influences on the writing of the focal students in both classes. The researcher will also attend to the attitudes about writing observed and documented in the interviews with the focal students. Responses to teachers' and students' views of technology use will play a major role in the analyses. The researcher may also analyze the type of feedback students receive, and attend to the types of revisions and the quality of texts students write in each class. Interactions during feedback sessions will be carefully recorded.

The epistemology enacted through a case study such as the foregoing depends on three assumptions about how the human social world is organized, about how knowledge of that world is validated, and about the nature of knowledge about social experience in general. First, in the social world of human experience, people are conceived of not as free-standing individuals but as members of many different normative groups or categories that share a specific history of social, cultural, economic, political, religious, gendered, cognitive, or physical (to name the most prevalent types) experience. This shared experience is also assumed to have created structural conditions that produce behaviors, attitudes, and beliefs that the members themselves and/or outsiders identify as characteristic of that group. To identify an individual in a case study as a member of that group (such as one of the teachers' having participated in the National Writing Project, but not the other), or to describe the setting of the school as urban, or to describe one focal student as Latinx and another as a "struggling" writer—is to invoke, either implicitly or explicitly, powerful norms about experiences and attitudes toward writing, social class, race, language, and disabilities that can have a powerful influence on the sense a researcher gives, and the sense a reader takes, from a case study.

Consequently, a second epistemological assumption is that individuals of a particular group stand in metonymic relation to the groups of which they are a part. For example, to name a student as Latinx is implicitly to generalize one's observations about that student to Latinx students in general; or to name a student as female or male is to suggest that all females or males may share some of the gendered behavior. Thus, although the author of a case study may overtly claim that his or her findings cannot be generalized, the implicit message to readers may be that if an instructional practice (like using Google Docs) works in one setting or with a group of middle school students, it will work in a broad range of middle school settings. The potential contrasting case of the teacher who does not use technology might suggest that all teachers who do not integrate technology via Google Docs into their classrooms are traditionalists (and not open to innovation) by extension. When these two powerful epistemological assumptions are combined with the readability of case study narratives, not only may they encourage the overgeneralization of instructional approaches such as using Google Docs in all settings and with all populations; they may also have the negative practical consequence of reifying stereotypes about the assumed strengths or weaknesses of particular teachers or settings. This may be the most problematic epistemological aspect of case study research. Yet this does not necessarily happen, particularly in studies in which the researcher is careful to make the multiplicity of groups that make up the identity of an individual or setting as a bounded system and their interaction a focus of the analysis and reporting. Exemplary models of case study research such as Compton-Lilly's (2017) following of families over time, and Dyson's (2013) ethnographic case studies of classrooms, provide such extensive details, insights, and examples of specific families and children that the reader understands the particularity of the settings and actors.

A third epistemological assumption of case studies, particularly of those that take a poststructural perspective (e.g., Dressman, Wilder, & Connor, 2005; McCarthey, 1994, 1998, 2004; McCarthey, Woodard, & Kang, 2014), is that the behavior of individuals or groups within particular settings cannot usually be explained as either the additive or integrative result of all the groups to which they belong (e.g., gender, race, religion, linguistic background, and social class together), but rather as the practices and beliefs of these groups as they interact with and contradict one another in ways that challenge rather than uphold stereotypical views. Thus, in Dressman and colleagues' (2005) study, the Latino focal student in the case study is bilingual, has only been in the United States for 2 years, and has been very successful. Analyses of the data demonstrate that prior to coming to the United States, he was a highly proficient reader and writer of Spanish and has been encouraged to maintain his Spanish language proficiency in his home; moreover, transcripts of interviews with the researcher and of his interaction with peers in the classroom show that he has found unexpected connections between his family's experiences in rural Mexico and the experiences of the family in the text read in class. The case goes against the grain of many assumptions about the school experiences of students who are emergent bilinguals. In the McCarthey (1998) study, Rosa was constructed as "shy" by teachers and did not respond in whole-class settings or a small group dominated by a talkative White boy, but she assisted other students in reading and writing tasks in small groups when the group composition changed. While case studies can present trends among teachers' attitudes and the constraints they face in low-income schools, highlighting a particular case can also illustrate the exception to that narrative. For example, the case of Kristen, who taught in a low-income school, showed how she resisted the discourse of "teaching to the test" at the same time she did not follow her colleagues' writers' workshop format, instead developing her own strategy to buck the prevailing narrative (McCarthey, 2008). Likewise, contradictions within a particular teacher's discourses about writing (e.g., Jackson, who combined social practices discourse with creativity and genre discourses) can be highlighted through triangulated data sources and careful analysis (McCarthey et al., 2014).

One of the greatest epistemological strengths of case study research, then, is its capacity to interrupt stereotypical assumptions about groups of students and settings, thus refining the normative findings of experimental and survey research (and accounting for the many exceptional cases that are often not reported in such studies), as well as suggesting new relationships among important social factors.

These epistemological features of case studies have another pragmatic element in common: the ways that case studies are often used to develop theories (in the sense of "grand narratives") about learning and, subsequently, to challenge or support them. Piaget's (1969) work, of course, is a compelling example of the development of theory from case studies; his theory of the development of cognitive structures was derived from his observations of his own three children. Case studies of individual children have also led to the development of theories (in the sense that they are grounded in the empirical evidence) about the ways in which children learn to read and write (e.g., Baghban, 1984; Bissex, 1980; Calkins, 1983). These case studies offer the opportunities to generalize to theory. In addition, some researchers (e.g., Lensmire, 2000; McCarthey, 1994, 2004, 2014) have begun with "grand narratives" such as Bakhtin's (1981) theory of dialogism or Ivanič's (2004) discourses of writing, and have used case studies to support, challenge, or instantiate with data aspects of those theories. Case study research lends itself to both the development and critique of theories because of the potential to examine the particular within the general and vice versa. However, like other methods, the case study approach is effective for examining some questions and not as appropriate for addressing others.

Design-Based Research

Gay Ivey, in Chapter 8, describes design-based research as developing interventions to accomplish specific goals and examining how well they worked. Employing an iterative cycle of intervention–inquiry–revision, researchers use authentic contexts such as classrooms with the goal of change as well as to generate new theories about learning and instruction. While Howell, Butler, and Reinking (2017) have conducted a study similar to the one I am suggesting, design-based research could be used in a new context with a new tool. They asked the question: "How can using digital writing tools within a process orientation be integrated into conventional instruction to help students construct multimodal and conventional arguments?" (p. 186). Because design-based research is adaptive, iterative, and can create possibilities in the local but be taken up across contexts (Ivey, Chapter 8, this volume), the technology integration question can be adapted to a new context while drawing on the previous research.

The proposed study builds on existing literature on computer-assisted collaborative learning (Mercier, Higgins, & da Costa, 2014) and the positive effects of a mapping tool for students to visualize the revision process (Olmanson et al., 2016). The goals will be to test the mapping tool and promote collaboration in the revision process. The research questions begin with this one: How can the use of a cognitive mapping tool and a collaborative revision process using technology help students from diverse backgrounds construct effective texts? The point of the question is to test the tool and build on the knowledge we have about collaborative learning to change classroom norms and to improve students' revision processes. The study will specifically address mitigating inequities within classrooms by assuring that all students have access to Chromebooks both in the classroom and at home. Thus, the researchers in the proposed study will work with the three middle school language arts teachers in a single school to transform their teaching of the revision process using a collaborative process and an innovative tool. The teachers as collaborative partners will meet together with the researchers to discuss and modify the process; students will also have opportunities to provide input into the implementation of the mapping tool. As the researchers and teachers meet, they may be considering the differences in responses among students. For example, how may a teacher's successful implementation of the mapping process for revision in one classroom be inhibiting students' revisions in another?

To what extent does this intervention meet the criteria Ivey has laid out in Chapter 8? First, the intervention will be used within the authentic contexts of the classrooms with specific goals—to improve the revision processes and the quality of the students' texts through the mapping tool and collaboration. It will build on theories of collaborative learning and cognitive mapping to develop new theories about learning to write, and will be potentially transformative due to the combination of the innovative technology with collaboration during a challenging process for teachers to teach and students to learn—revision. Trying out the tool in several classrooms will require adaptations to the particular context and to students' background knowledge and experiences with revision, technology, and collaboration. The software used, the collaborative grouping, and teachers' instructions for revision may all be subject to change. Likewise, understanding how students are using the Chromebooks at home will help answer questions centering around equity; for example, does more access to computers for all students help ameliorate some of the issues identified in previous research, such as the participation gap in which low-income students tend to have less access to the Internet and fewer opportunities for engaging in more sophisticated activities (Greenhow, Walker, & Kim, 2009)? The inclusive methodology and flexibility will include multiple data sources, such as observations of teachers, their instruction around revision, and students; collaborative work groups; interviews with both teachers and students about the mapping tools and revision processes; and collections of students' maps and texts. Team-created rubrics as well as Smarter Balanced writing exam tests may be used to measure text quality; coding schemes to measure collaborative interactions similar to those Mercier (2016) has developed may be used as well.

Ivey points out that design-based research has gained momentum in literacy research in the last decade and is routinely carried out in the learning sciences. As Dressman and I pointed out in our 2011 chapter, the epistemological origins of this methodology are multiple, ranging from design experiments in engineering to neo-Vygotskian research, and we noted that American Pragmatism as articulated by John Dewey (Dewey & Bentley, 1949) is most consistently aligned with design-based research. For Dewey, the world is not made up of discrete objects "bumping into" each other with causal effect; rather, what appear to be discrete objects are actually only temporary assemblages in transactional relation, entities whose encounters with other entities result in changes to both. One may describe and be able to predict the interaction of one entity with another when they are examined in isolation, but the full effects of any interaction are unforeseeable. For example, the earth beneath us appears solid, but is actually a shifting mass of continental plates whose collision in turn affects climate patterns, ocean currents, and biological evolution; a surge in one species' population reduces others and sows the seeds of its own extinction; one nation colonizes another, but then must adapt itself to the mores and practices of its colony; and a single shift in a school's curriculum may produce not only an intended consequence but many others, both positive and negative, as well. Moreover, objective knowledge of phenomena such as plate tectonics, evolution, political science, or instructional theory may or may not allow one to predict the future shape of continents, how or which organisms will evolve, how two cultures will affect each other, or what the full outcome of an educational innovation might be.

From a Pragmatist view, broad, general theoretical knowledge may have its function, but it is to inform, not direct, the development of understanding about a particular situation. The knowledge gained from that particular setting can be adapted and applied to another, but the purpose is not to predict or generalize from the situation. It is from an evaluation of the strengths and the limitations of an epistemology strongly influenced by the tenets of American Pragmatism that its consequences for design-based research as a knowledge-producing activity may best be observed. Philosophers have not named the school founded by Dewey, Charles Sanders Peirce, and William James American Pragmatism out of historical or nationalist impulse, but rather as a way of describing it as something quintessentially and culturally American. Thus, to many Americans (including myself), the focus on problem solving and practicality, as well as the focus on local situations and the inclusion of a broad range of shareholders as well as a broad range of measurements, seem to make so much common sense. What makes common sense seem common, however, is often not a sharing of meanings or ideas, but rather meanings and ideas that are so adaptable and open to interpretation that they can appeal to many different points of view without upsetting the sensibilities of a broad range of constituents.

For example, in its heyday, whole language represented such a common-sense approach to literacy (see Dressman, McCarty, & Benson, 1998, for a discussion of its multiple meanings and implied practices), but its common-sense rationale may also explain why as a practice it was so hard to pin down, and why it was so hard to determine exactly what about its practices were effective and ineffective. Likewise, practices such as process writing, writers' workshop, or peer response may be difficult to describe accurately, with so many stakeholders involved. Not only may such "fuzziness" have an epistemological benefit, but it may also have a rhetorical and political benefit in that it keeps different groups with different interests and different ways of exercising power—that is, teachers, administrators, and researchers— seemingly collaborative and communicative, even though each group may not be aware of the others' actual practices or reasoning. Differences in interpretation of what constitutes a *writers' workshop* or *peer response*, as well as the practices these common terms name, may vary widely across teachers and classrooms, and so any generalization about the effects of the mapping tool or collaboration on text quality within each classroom would be difficult to arrive at. Yet the common use of the same terms by all parties and the political need to appear "collaborative" in the research process may mask these underlying difficulties in the generalizability of findings.

A related attribute of the epistemology enacted by design experiments that seems American and double-edged is the tension or balance between attention to theoretical issues and local circumstances. In Chapter 8, Ivey has described the role of theory in the following way:

> Design-based research is driven by theories not only about how to create conditions to make an intervention work toward a specified goal, but also by theories explaining why an intervention did or did not work. Thus, preliminary theories are placed at risk and potentially tweaked, depending on modifications that proved necessary to make interventions effective for all participants. (p. 145)

While some advocates of design-based research prefer to consider the outcome not as "theories" to explain data, but rather design principles that can guide future interventions, the importance of the iterative process is shared: Conceptual frameworks inform the interventions that are implemented and evaluated, and these prototypes contribute to further theory building (Plomp & Nieveen, 2013).

Although there is much to admire in the iterative model, we may also consider the role of theory in design-based research as an epistemologically pragmatic compromise; that is, the status and existence of theory as an external form of knowledge is acknowledged, but the organic integrity of local conditions prevails. Additionally, naming theory and practice as separate may limit the interaction of one with the other and is distinctly out of character with American Pragmatism; however, its consequence— the development of a rationalized insularity that acts to resist the insights of external criticism that theory can provide—may still be a distinctly American flaw. In other words, the very fluid application of theoretical frameworks within design-based research may result in the legitimization of analyses and conclusions that a more critical and rigorous stance toward one's theory might prevent. In the example of using a technological tool to assist in revision and collaboration, various attractive concepts may lead researchers and teachers to take an uncritical stance in their analysis and interpretation of data to assume that the intervention of the mapping tool in collaborative environments is a very effective way to integrate technology. Considering access to computers at home and school as a theoretical stand-in for reducing inequities may also lead researchers to conclude that other factors, such as race, class, gender, and linguistic background, are not as important as access to innovative tools and instruction. However, the potential for generating theoretical and practical knowledge from design-based research is very promising, especially the opportunities for teacher and student agency in the process.

Through the use of four illustrative hypothetical studies, I have demonstrated the epistemological strengths and weaknesses of particular research methods. Each method can be powerful in illuminating some aspects of literacy teaching and learning but may be limited in its ability to inform us in other ways. For example, experimental designs, despite their limitations to generalize to all populations and their lack of consideration of culture and the individual, can still be used to produce predictable patterns about technology use, instructional practices, and student achievement. Survey data can provide important information about groups of students and administrators, focusing on their self-reported perspectives and practices. Because the method only generates certain types of data, it cannot predict causality or help us understand specific classroom contexts or practices. Case studies have the potential to provide rich data for understanding how individuals and groups experience different types of instructional practices and provide readers with a deep understanding of contexts; yet the patterns in the classrooms studied may differ substantially from patterns in other classrooms and prevent us from using the information in ways that lead to changing practices. Design-based research, because of its pragmatic features, adaptability, and social benefits, can help address questions of what literacy practices work in what settings, but have the same limitations noted for case study research. Underlying each of these methods is a view of knowledge that influences the development of research questions, the data sources, the data collection procedures, and types of analyses. By examining the underlying epistemologies of their methods, researchers can improve the formulation of their questions, procedures, and analyses.

SOCIAL THEORIES AS EPISTEMOLOGICAL RESOURCES

Beyond the epistemological assumptions enacted through the methodologies that literacy researchers use in their investigations, another source of assumptions about how the world is known and what constitutes knowledge has become quite commonplace in the last 30 years, particularly within qualitative methodologies. Unlike traditional reviews of literature, which focus on previous empirical studies related to a research topic, theoretical frames typically make reference to theories and theorists whose perspectives are related to, but removed from the immediate context of, the research setting. For example, while a study of technology use in writing might traditionally rely on previous studies of effective writing instruction and the opportunities and challenges afforded by technology in the classroom, its frame might be derived from one of the four theories about writing and writing instruction identified by Hodges (2017): cognitive processes (e.g., Flower & Hayes, 1981), sociocultural (Bakhtin, 1981; Vygotsky, 1978), sociocognitive (Pajares & Valiante, 2006), or ecological (Bronfenbrenner & Evans, 2000). Or its frame might use theories with a focus on language and power (Bourdieu, 1977; Fairclough, 1989; Gee, 1999) or critical race theory (Bell, 1980; Ladson-Billings & Tate, 1995).

When employed with rigor and thoroughness, theoretical frames represent an important transmethodological innovation in the field of literacy research because they provide additional epistemological resources that can strengthen the truth claims of research findings derived through a broad range of methodological approaches in at least three interrelated ways. First, theoretical frames can help to expand the significance and implications of a research project beyond its immediate practical boundaries, so that the project is comprehensive within, and more relevant to, the context of broader theoretical social-scientific issues. Case studies of the implementations of Google Docs in diverse classrooms considered within the structuralist perspective of Pierre Bourdieu's (1977) *Outline of a Theory of Practice,* for example, might become a study of the ways that space, time, and cultural logic interact within specific material historical conditions. Or critical race theory (Ladson-Billings & Tate, 1995) might explain differences between two teachers' practices in ways of interacting with diverse students during writing. Similarly, an analysis of the collaborative learning interactions in middle school classrooms framed by Vygotsky's (1978) theory of the role of the knowledgeable other might reveal patterns of collaboration that support learning to revise. Bronfenbrenner and Evans's (2000) ecological theory might account for students' differing uses of a mapping tool in relation to the different classroom contexts and the construction of students' texts. A second related benefit is the external source of comparison and contrast for the analysis of data that theoretical frames can provide. Feminist theories of discourse, for example, might be used to account for gender differences in the ways that students collaborate, but they may also provide an occasion for exploring contradictions, when findings do not align with what theory would predict. Moreover, where findings align or do not align with a particular theoretical frame, or where a theoretical frame is used for the first time to account for a particular phenomenon, not only the findings of the study but the theory used is itself expanded or refined or revised. Thus, a third benefit of the use of theoretical frames in literacy research is the opportunity for literacy researchers to contribute to the building of "grand" theories of human social behavior.

However, I also argue that the realization of the epistemological benefits of using social theories in literacy research depends not merely on the use or mention of theory in the report of a study, but more importantly on the quality or nature of that use. In a study of the uses of theoretical frames in literacy research conducted by Dressman (2007), 69 studies published in major literacy research journals that made use of theoretical frames were studied to identify the types, extent, and functions of theory use. Four patterns of use and function were found for the studies, ranging from a *foundational platform* (in which theoretical principles of its frame were alluded to but never fully developed) to a *dialectical scaffold* (in which theory was used analytically both to interrogate and to be interrogated by the study's data, and provided an important "other" point of view against which to compare and contrast findings from the data and, in the process, contribute to the expansion, refinement, or revision of the theoretical frame itself). It would be interesting to conduct a follow-up study of articles published in the years since Dressman's (2007) study appeared, to consider whether researchers are using theory in more *dialectically supported* ways.

CONCLUSION: PROCEED WITH CAUTION

In the pragmatic consideration of epistemology and theory in research methods, I have emphasized the ways in which research is actually conducted within schools, and have attempted to uncover the assumptions behind conducting various types of research. By analyzing the epistemological strengths and weaknesses of each of four research methods, I have noted that different methods are based on different epistemological assumptions, and that this is one reason why they have different strengths and weaknesses. I have also implied that within the epistemological strengths of a particular method lie some of its weaknesses. For example, on closer examination of the generalizability of experimental and quasi-experimental methods, it is nearly impossible to generalize the findings of a study to all groups; furthermore, the predictive nature and rationality of knowledge that is assumed when these methods are used may call for artificial conditions that are almost impossible to create in actual schools, resulting in knowledge that is limited in its utility for classrooms. The self-reported nature of surveys and the focus on describing populations limit their applicability to particular settings. Although case studies are intended to be particularistic and descriptive in their use of narrative as the vehicle for communication, they may have the unintended consequence of encouraging unwarranted generalization. The problem-solving focus within local settings available through design-based research addresses many of the issues created by experimental designs and surveys. Yet the collaborative, adaptable nature of the design makes the findings difficult to replicate; it can also hide the underlying tensions between theory and practice or mask unintended consequences.

Despite the limitations of each, every method has something valuable to contribute to literacy research; yet no one method can cover the range of issues that researchers need to address in such research. Differences in epistemological assumptions among the methods can be viewed as strengths rather than as liabilities because they produce different types of knowledge. Experimental studies can provide some generalizable information with the possibilities of predicting outcomes in a wide range of settings. With a large dataset, surveys can describe a population's perspectives and practices. Case studies provide detailed narratives about particular individuals within a social setting with the power to generate hypotheses. Design-based methods have the capability of solving curricular problems within local settings as information is produced in collaborative relationships.

This investigation of epistemological assumptions among research methods and the use of theory by literacy researchers has three implications for the improvement of research across methodologies. First, I argue for a rigorous skepticism and humility in any approach to conducting research in literacy. Researchers need to be aware of the assumptions underlying the methods they choose and consider the benefits and unintended consequences of their methods, not only from a practical point of view but also from an epistemological perspective. Researchers ought to ask: What are the bases for the claims made? When we focus on these aspects of human interaction, what are we leaving out? What can we learn from this design? What are the limitations of what we can learn? Realizing that each method has a range of strengths and weaknesses, it is important that researchers question their own assumptions as well as those of the designs they choose to employ.

Second, although it may be tempting to suggest that a "mixed methods" approach to studying a phenomenon will ensure that a given topic is well covered, Wilkinson and Staley (2019) point out the many pitfalls that can undermine researchers' intents. Additionally, I argue that the ways in which researchers consider the nature of knowledge may conflict with one another; therefore, simply combining methods may not produce the types of useful data needed to make classrooms better places for our students, but may result in a hodgepodge of information without theoretical grounding. The purposes of the research and the research questions frame the types of data to be collected and analyzed; the results of those analyses need to be represented in different forms such as tables, models, narratives, or themes that are consistent with the epistemological assumptions and research designs. Research questions, sources of data, and types of analyses and interpretations should be aligned with one another and rest on clear, but carefully examined, epistemological assumptions.

Although cautioning against mixing methods, I do recommend *triangulation* (a metaphor from qualitative methods; Stake, 1995) of research methods to improve educational policy and practices. For example, triangulation of research methods would include using multiple methods to study the same general topic, but the actual research questions and designs would differ from one another in scope, type of data collected, and forms of analyses and representations. Triangulation also involves using alternative means of confirming interpretations; therefore, researchers using different tools would check their findings on the same topic with one another. For example, experimentalists could look at survey data from the larger population. Why have design-based researchers not read the classroom narratives that case study researchers have written? Or they might consider investigating the methods that García-Sánchez and Orellana (2019) have developed for involving community members in the research process.

The third implication relates to the use of theory in research methods. Although theoretical alignment can contribute to the readability of a research report, it does not substitute for validity. The benefits of theoretical frames in research reports include expanding the significance and implications of reports, providing opportunities for comparisons and contrasts of data, and building grand theories of social interaction; yet they need to be employed with greater caution than we have done previously. Just as we are suggesting that researchers need to consider and question the epistemologies of their methods, they also need to interrogate the theories they use to make their arguments. Literacy researchers must not only build on the work of others from a variety of perspectives and methods, but also continually engage in dialogue about the assumptions, interpretations, and consequences of their methods.

REFERENCES

Baghban, M. (1984). *Our daughter learns to read and write: A case study from birth to three.* Newark, DE: International Reading Association.

Bakhtin, M. M. (1981). *The dialogic imagination* (M. Holquist, Ed.; C. Emerson & M. Holquist, Trans.). Austin: University of Texas Press.

Bell, D. (1980). *Race, racism, and American law.* Boston: Little, Brown.

Bissex, G. (1980). *Gnyx at wrk.* Cambridge, MA: Harvard University Press.

Bourdieu, P. (1977). *Outline of a theory of practice.* Cambridge, UK: Cambridge University Press.

Bronfenbrenner, U., & Evans, G. W. (2000). Developmental science in the 21st century: Emerging questions, theoretical models, research designs and empirical findings. *Social Development, 9*(1), 115–125.

Calkins, L. (1983). *Lessons from a child: On the teaching and learning of writing.* Exeter, NH: Heinemann.

Campbell, J. (1995). *Understanding John Dewey: Nature and cooperative intelligence.* Chicago: Open Court.

Compton-Lilly, C. (2017). *Reading students' lives: Literacy learning across time.* New York: Routledge.

Dewey, J., & Bentley, A. E. (1949). *Knowing and the known.* Boston: Beacon Press.

Dressman, M. (2007). Theoretically framed: Argument and desire in the production of general knowledge about literacy. *Reading Research Quarterly, 42,* 332–363.

Dressman, M. (2008). *Using social theory in educational research: A practical guide.* London: Routledge.

Dressman, M., & McCarthey, S. J. (2011). Toward a pragmatics of epistemology, methodology, and social theory. In N. K. Duke & M. H. Mallette (Eds.), *Literacy research methodologies* (2nd ed., pp. 441–463). New York: Guilford Press.

Dressman, M., McCarty, L., & Benson, J. (1998). "Whole language" as signifier: Considering the semantic field of school literacy. *Journal of Literacy Research, 30,* 9–52.

Dressman, M., Wilder, P., & Connor, J. C. (2005). Theories of failure and the failure of theories: A cognitive/sociocultural/macrostructural study of eight struggling students. *Research in the Teaching of English, 40,* 8–61.

Dyson, A. H. (2013). *Rewriting the basics: Literacy learning in children's cultures.* New York: Teachers College Press.

Fairclough, N. (1989). *Language and power.* London: Longman.

Flower, L., & Hayes, J. R. (1981). A cognitive process theory of writing. *College Composition and Communication, 32*(4), 365–387.

García-Sánchez, I., & Orellana, M. F. (Eds.). (2019). *Language and cultural practices in communities and schools: Bridging learning from non-dominant groups.* New York: Routledge.

Gee, J. P. (1999). *An introduction to discourse analysis: Theory and method.* New York: Routledge.

Geertz, C. (2003). Thick description: Toward an interpretive theory of culture. In C. Jenks (Ed.) *Culture: Critical concepts in sociology* (pp. 173–196). New York: Routledge. (Original work published 1973)

Greenhow, C., Walker, J. D., & Kim, S. (2009). Millennial learners and net-savvy teens: Examining Internet use among low-income students. *Journal of Computing in Teacher Education, 26*(2), 63–69.

Hodges, T. S. (2017). Theoretically speaking: An examination of four theories and how they support writing in the classroom. *The Clearing House: A Journal of Educational Strategies, Issues and Ideas, 90*(4), 139–146.

Howell, E., Butler, T., & Reinking, R. (2017). Integrating multimodal arguments into high school writing instruction. *Journal of Literacy Research, 49*(2), 181–209.

Ivanič, R. (2004) Discourses of writing and learning to write. *Language and Education, 18*(3), 220–245.

Kivunja, C., & Kuyini, A. B. (2017). Understanding and applying research paradigms in educational contexts. *International Journal of Higher Education, 6*(5), 26–41.

Ladson-Billings, G., & Tate, W. (1995). Toward a critical race theory of education. *Teachers College Record, 97*(1), 47–68.

Lensmire, T. (2000). *Powerful writing, responsible teaching.* New York: Teachers College Press.

Mathiyazhagan, T., & Nandan, D. (2010, July–September). Survey research method. *Media Mimansa,* pp. 34–45.

McCarthey, S. J. (1994). Authors, text, and talk: The internalization of dialogue from social·interaction during writing. *Reading Research Quarterly, 29*(3), 201–231.

McCarthey, S. J. (1998). Constructing multiple subjectivities in classroom learning contexts. *Research in the Teaching of English, 32,* 126–160.

McCarthey, S. J. (2004). Bakhtin's dialogism in a preschooler's talk. *Literacy Teaching and Learning, 8*(2), 27–62.

McCarthey, S. J. (2008). The impact of No Child Left Behind on teachers' writing instruction. *Written Communication, 25,* 462–505.

McCarthey, S. J., & Geoghegan, C. (2016). The role of professional development for enhancing writing instruction. In C. MacArthur, S. Graham, & J. Fitzgerald (Eds.), *Handbook of writing research* (2nd ed., pp. 330–345). New York: Guilford Press.

McCarthey, S. J., Kennett, K., Smith, A., & West, A. (2017). Facilitating students' stances toward technology-enhanced reading and writing in the classroom. *Journal of Literacy and Technology: An International Online Academic Journal, 18*(2), 47–89.

McCarthey, S. J., Magnifico, A., Woodard, R., & Kline, S. (2014). Situating technology—Facilitated feedback and revision: The case of Tom. In K. Pytash & R. Ferdig (Eds.), *Exploring technology for writing and writing instruction* (pp. 152–170). Hershey, PA: Information Science Reference.

McCarthey, S. J., & Mkhize, D. (2013). Teachers' orientations towards writing instruction. *Journal of Writing Research, 4*(4), 300–331.

McCarthey, S. J., & Ro, Y. S. (2011). Approaches to writing instruction. *Pedagogies: An International Journal, 6*(4), 273–295.

McCarthey, S. J., Woodard, R., & Kang, G. (2014). Elementary teachers' negotiating discourses in writing instruction. *Written Communication, 31*(1), 58–90.

Mercier, E. (2016). Teacher orchestration and student learning of mathematics activities in a smart classroom. *International Journal of Smart Technology and Learning, 1*(1), 33–52.

Mercier, E. M., Higgins, S. E., & da Costa, L. (2014). Different leaders: Emergent organizational and intellectual leadership in children's collaborative learning groups. *International Journal of Computer-Supported Collaborative Learning, 9*(4), 397–432.

Olmanson, J., Kennett, K., Magnifico, A., McCarthey, S. J., Searsmith, D., Cope, B., et al. (2016). Visualizing revision; Leveraging student-generated between-draft diagramming data in support of academic writing development. *Technology, Knowledge and Learning, 2*(1), 99–123.

Pajares, F., & Valiante, G. (2006). Self-efficacy beliefs and motivation in writing development. In C. A. MacArthur, S. Graham, & J. Fitzgerald (Eds.), *Handbook of writing research* (pp. 158–170). New York: Guilford Press.

Piaget, J. (1969). *Psychology of intelligence.* Paterson, NJ: Littlefield, Adams.

Plomp, T., & Nieveen, N. (Eds.). (2013). *Educational design research—Part B: Illustrative cases.* Enschede, the Netherlands: SLO.

Rabinow, P. (Ed.). (1984). *The Foucault reader.* New York: Pantheon.

Smith, A., McCarthey, S. J., & Magnifico, A. (2017). Recursive feedback: Evaluative dimensions of e-learning. In B. Cope & M. Kalantzis (Eds.), *E-learning ecologies* (pp. 118–142). New York: Routledge.

Smith, A., West, A., & McCarthey, S. J. (2019). Literacies across sponsorscapes: Mobilizing notions of literacy sponsorship. *Literacy, 54*(2), 22–30.

Smith, K., & Wheeler, K. (2019). Using the Smarter Balanced grade 11 summative assessment in college writing placement. *Assessing Writing, 41,* 76–79.

Stake, R. E. (1995). *The art of case study research.* Thousand Oaks, CA: SAGE.

Visser, P. S., Krosnick, J. A., Lavrakas, P. J., & Kim, N. (2013). Survey research. In H. T. Reis & C. M. Judd (Eds.), *Handbook of research methods in social psychology* (2nd ed., pp. 402–440). New York: Cambridge University Press.

Vygotsky, L. (1978). *Mind in society: The development of higher psychological processes* (M. Cole, V. John-Steiner, S. Scribner, & E. Souberman, Eds. & Trans.). Cambridge, MA: Harvard University Press. (Original work published 1934)

Walkerdine, V. (1990). *Schoolgirl fictions.* New York: Verso.

Wilkinson, I., & Staley, B. (2019). On the pitfalls and promises of using mixed methods in literacy research: Perceptions of reviewers, *Research Papers in Education, 34*(1), 61–83.

CHAPTER 20

Conclusion

Nell K. Duke
Marla H. Mallette

What do we hope you take away from this book? Many things, of course, but we believe that five overarching messages are especially important:

- *Message 1: Many different research methodologies—in fact, each research methodology discussed in this book and others—have valuable contributions to make to the study of literacy.* We believe that each chapter of this book helps to make this point. Each methodology featured includes references to studies that it is hard to deny are important—that have provided new insights, confirmed or disconfirmed previous thinking, moved research forward, and/or influenced classroom practice. Our field would be a lesser place were that type of research unavailable. What we would understand about literacy and literacy learning would be diminished.

Chapters in this book are not, of course, the only source of evidence for the value of many different research methodologies in our understanding of literacy. Perusal of seminal volumes in literacy, such as Volume 5 of the *Handbook of Reading Research* (Moje, Afflerbach, Enciso, & Lesaux, 2020), *The Routledge International Handbook of English, Language and Literacy Teaching* (Wyse, Andrews, & Hoffman, 2010), and *Approaches to Language and Literacy Research: An NCRLL Research in Language and Literacy Series* (Alvermann & Allen, 2005–2010), demonstrates that many different types of research have influenced our understanding across the field. Studies widely cited within literacy include a vast array of different methodologies. Awards bestowed in the field, such as the International Literacy Association Outstanding Dissertation Award, the Dina Feitelson Award, and the Albert J. Harris Award, have been given to studies of a wide range of research methods. And many well-respected literacy scholars have been on record for many years as espousing the value of many different types of research (e.g., Pearson, 2002; Pressley, Duke, & Boling, 2004; Purcell-Gates, 2001; Readence & Barone, 1996; Reinking & Alvermann, 2007; Wilkinson & Bloome, 2008).

• *Message 2: Different types of research are best suited for different types of questions and claims. The match of research methodology to research questions and resulting claims is essential.* This message, too, should be evident in chapter after chapter of this book. Chapter authors discuss the types of questions to which their methodology is well suited and the types of claims that can be made on the basis of that methodology. If you want to understand what goes on in literature circle discussions, you surely will not turn to neuroimaging techniques. If you want to know whether and how neural activity differs for good and poor readers, discourse analysis is not the best choice. If you want to know when and how a reader brings prior knowledge to bear in his or her reading, verbal protocol analysis leaps out as a methodology to use. If your interest is in whether one method of spelling instruction results in better spelling performance than another, experimental research is likely to be the appropriate methodology. This may seem obvious; yet we routinely read studies in which the question asked and/or the claims made do not, in fact, match well the research methodology used. And we encounter rhetoric suggesting that some research methodologies are inherently best, rather than best *for what.* As a field, we must demand that qualifier in discussions of research methodology.

• *Message 3: There are standards of quality for every type of research. There is better- and poorer-quality research of every methodology.* A danger of arguing for the value of many different kinds of research and research perspectives is to imply that "anything goes." We hope that this book has resoundingly countered that implication. For each methodology chapter, authors were asked to identify standards of quality for research using that methodology. Each has done so, and without balking at the task. In the minds of these authors, well known and well respected for their use of their assigned methodology, there are indeed hallmarks of high-quality research. Anything does not go.

We may, in fact, become more discerning of the quality and contribution of a given study when we seriously value many different research methodologies. Suppose, for example, that one is writing a review of literature on emergent literacy development. Assuming that there are limitations of space and reader attention, if one restricts the review primarily or exclusively to case study and ethnographic research, more attention to studies of those methodologies can be given than if the review also includes findings from experimental and correlational studies. One may have to be more selective, then, about the studies of each methodology included. Of course, as we have suggested in Message 2, one's question should be a driving force in determining what studies are afforded attention. But the quality of the work and its contribution can also be discriminating factors. Even in our everyday reading as scholars, the sheer number and range of different types of research that cross our desks mean that we cannot attend to all studies; considerations of quality should help us decide which to attend to more closely.

• *Message 4: Synergy across research methodologies is possible, powerful, and advisable.* What if, starting tomorrow, we conducted nothing but high-quality, exemplary work within each of the research methodologies in this book? What if the standards of quality identified by authors in this volume were instantiated in each and every study? That would be fantastic, but it would not be enough. We need to work not only within but *across* these methods, in what we call *synergy* of research methods.

Among the audience likely to read this book, at least, it seems a platitude to say this—but no number of experiments, in the absence of other types of research, will help us learn what we need to learn about literacy. Similarly, no number of case studies can, in themselves, help us understand everything we want to understand. Our richest and most productive knowledge base will come when different studies involving different research methodologies inform one another—when the whole of what we know in an area is built of many different kinds of parts, each doing what they do best, and together being much more than their sum.

Of course, synergy of research methodologies has occurred. In literacy, we have many examples in which different studies conducted with different methodologies have informed one another and led to greater insight than could have come with one or the other. Elsewhere (Mallette, Duke, Strachan, Waldron, & Watanabe, 2013), we provide detailed examples of such synergies. Here we present two examples only briefly and incompletely. Our intent is not so much to focus on the historical particulars or particulars in content as simply to illustrate that studies conducted with different methodologies informed one another and led to insights that would not have been possible within just one methodology.

One insight made possible, we believe, by research of various methodologies is the insight that teaching children that the speech stream is composed of phonemes can improve their word reading. *Research using technologies* designed to examine the speech stream revealed that phonemes in speech are not separate and distinct, as implied in our written orthography, but rather influence one another. Thus, it may be challenging for children to learn to tease out individual phonemes in words associated with particular letters (e.g., Liberman, Cooper, Shankweiler, & Studdert-Kennedy, 1967). *Research examining children's written text,* particularly their spellings, when they are developing literacy provided an understanding of relationships between the speech stream and orthography (e.g., Chomsky, 1970; Read, 1971). *Correlational studies* revealed relationships between the degree to which children are aware of the speech stream and their achievement and growth in literacy (e.g., Ehri, 1979; Share, Jorm, Maclean, & Matthews, 1984). *Experimental studies* indicated that if children are engaged in activities to become more aware of phonemes in the speech stream, their reading and writing are improved (e.g., Ball & Blachman, 1991; Williams, 1980).

Another insight made possible by studies of various methodologies is that teaching children about text structure improves their comprehension. *Verbal protocols* demonstrated that good readers attend to text structure when they read (see Pressley & Afflerbach, 1995, for a review). *Research comparing good and poor comprehenders* (in a sense, a form of correlational research) found that good comprehenders attend more readily to text structure than poor comprehenders (e.g., Meyer, Brandt, & Bluth, 1980). *Experimental studies* revealed that teaching children to attend to text structure leads to better comprehension (e.g., Armbruster, Anderson, & Ostertag, 1987; Taylor & Beach, 1984). As with the phonemic awareness insight, it is not that each of these studies led independently to the insight, but that they informed and built on one another. The researchers cited research of other methodologies and were clearly influenced by that work. Neither the richness nor the rapidity of identifying the insight could likely have occurred without the synergy of these different research methodologies.

We want to make it clear that although we see the usefulness of mixed research, we are not talking here about mixing methodologies within a study; we mean that different studies, of different methodologies, can inform one another and provide larger insights. Of course, in some cases, mixed methodologies within a study are quite appropriate to a research question or set of questions and have important contributions to make (e.g., Tashakkori & Teddlie, 2003). However, we concur with McCarthey's (Chapter 19, this volume) caution about mixing methods and epistemologies. That is, researchers need to consider the standards of quality, intricacies of design, and need for thoughtful planning of mixed research as described by Onwuegbuzie and Mallette (Chapter 13, this volume). It would not serve the field well simply to mix methodologies if theoretical consistency and methodological rigor are not evidenced throughout the study.

• *Message 5: We must urgently and actively pursue synergy across research methodologies.* Nearly two decades ago, we argued in a commentary in the *Journal of Literacy Research* that the field of literacy is in danger of increasing fragmentation (Duke & Mallette, 2001). In the decades since, this trend has been reversed in some respects but remains in others. For example, in Parsons and colleagues' (2016) extensive examination of content, methodology, and theoretical perspectives of articles published in nine literacy journals between 2009 and 2014, they found that approximately

90% of the published articles in *Scientific Studies of Reading* were quantitative, whereas in *Research in the Teaching of English*, approximately 70% of the published articles were qualitative.

Fragmentation is of particular concern to us when research methodology is confounded with particular areas of study. For example, we find few experimental studies of critical literacy and few case studies in the area of phonemic awareness; yet we believe it is possible to conduct high-quality research in both and see potential contributions to the field in both. For example, we might ask how comprehension achievement differs for children taught with and without critical literacy approaches (our hypothesis would be that one would see higher comprehension achievement among students whose teachers taught with an emphasis on critical literacy). Or we might ask how a child with very strong or very weak phonemic awareness experiences phonemic awareness instruction in school (our interest would be in understanding whether a child whose phonemic awareness is extremely different from that of most peers experiences phonemic awareness instruction differently than intended). Of course, we are not advocating conducting research of every particular kind in every particular area just for the sake of doing it. We argue that particular research methodologies should not be dismissed out of hand as possible contributors to research in a particular area; rather, we should actively seek a variety of questions, and thus methodologies, that could contribute to work in a particular area. We believe that this will be an important step in reversing the trend of fragmentation in the field.

To close, we want to thank again the contributors of this book, whose work individually and collectively has powerfully supported the five messages we have offered here:

- *Message 1:* Many different research methodologies—in fact, each research methodology discussed in this book and others—have valuable contributions to make to the study of literacy.
- *Message 2:* Different types of research are best suited for different types of questions and claims. The match of research methodology to research questions and resulting claims is essential.
- *Message 3:* There are standards of quality for every type of research. There is better- and poorer-quality research of every methodology.
- *Message 4:* Synergy across research methodologies is possible, powerful, and advisable.
- *Message 5:* We must urgently and actively pursue synergy across research methodologies.

We hope that our work, and yours, will do justice to the high bar that our contributors have set.

REFERENCES

Alvermann, D. E., & Allen, J. (Eds.). (2005–2010). *Approaches to language and literacy research: An NCRLL research in language and literacy series.* New York: Teachers College Press.

Armbruster, B. B., Anderson, T. H., & Ostertag, J. (1987). Does text structure/summarization instruction facilitate learning from expository text? *Reading Research Quarterly, 22,* 331–346.

Ball, E. W., & Blachman, B. A. (1991). Does phoneme awareness training in kindergarten make a difference in early word recognition and developmental spelling? *Reading Research Quarterly, 26,* 49–66.

Chomsky, C. (1970). Reading, writing and phonology. *Harvard Educational Review, 40,* 287–309.

Duke, N. K., & Mallette, M. H. (2001). Critical issues: Preparation for new literacy researchers in multi-epistemological, multi-methodological times. *Journal of Literacy Research, 33,* 345–360.

Ehri, L. (1979). *Orthography and the amalgamation of word identities in beginning readers: Final report.* Davis: University of California, Davis.

Liberman, A. M., Cooper, F., Shankweiler, D., & Studdert-Kennedy, M. (1967). Perception of the speech code. *Psychological Review, 74,* 431–461.

Mallette, M. H., Duke, N. K., Strachan, S. L., Waldron, C. H., & Watanabe, L. M. (2013). A quest for synergy in literacy research methodology. In D. E. Alvermann, N. J. Unrau, & R. B. Ruddell (Eds.), *Theoretical models and processes of reading* (6th ed., pp. 91–128). Newark, DE: International Reading Association.

Meyer, B. J. F., Brandt, D. M., & Bluth, G. J. (1980). Use of top-level structure in text: Key for reading comprehension of ninth-grade students. *Reading Research Quarterly, 16,* 72–103.

Moje, E. B., Afflerbach, P., Enciso, P., & Lesaux, N. K. (Eds.). (2020). *Handbook of reading research* (Vol. 5). New York: Routledge.

Parsons, S. A., Gallagher, M. A., & the George Mason University Content Analysis Team. (2016). A content analysis of nine literacy journals, 2009–2014. *Journal of Literacy Research, 48*(4), 476–502.

Pearson, P. D. (2002, May). *Up the down staircase: The role of research in policy and practice.* Paper presented at the annual convention of the International Reading Association, San Francisco, CA.

Pressley, M., & Afflerbach, P. (1995). *Verbal protocols of reading: The nature of constructively responsive reading.* Hillsdale, NJ: Erlbaum.

Pressley, M., Duke, N. K., & Boling, E. C. (2004). The educational science and scientifically-based instruction we need: Lessons from reading research and policy making. *Harvard Educational Review, 74*(1), 30–61.

Purcell-Gates, V. (2001). The role of qualitative and ethnographic research. *Reading Online.* Retrieved from *www.readingonline.org/articles/purcell-gates.*

Read, C. (1971). Preschool children's knowledge of English phonology. *Harvard Educational Review, 41,* 1–34.

Readence, J., & Barone, D. (1996). Expectations and directions for *Reading Research Quarterly*: Broadening the lens. *Reading Research Quarterly, 31,* 8–10.

Reinking, D., & Alvermann, D. E. (2007). Reflections on our editorship. *Reading Research Quarterly, 42,* 460–466.

Share, D. L., Jorm, A. F., Maclean, R., & Matthews, R. (1984). Sources of individual differences in reading acquisition. *Journal of Educational Psychology, 76,* 1309–1324.

Tashakkori, A. M., & Teddlie, C. B. (Eds.). *Handbook of mixed methods in social and behavioral research.* Thousand Oaks, CA: SAGE.

Taylor, B. M., & Beach, R. W. (1984). The effects of text structure instruction on middle-grade students' comprehension and production of expository text. *Reading Research Quarterly, 19,* 134–146.

Wilkinson, I. A. G., & Bloome, D. (2008). Research as principled, pluralistic argument. *Reading Research Quarterly, 43,* 6–8.

Williams, J. P. (1980). Teaching decoding with a special emphasis on phoneme analysis and phoneme blending. *Journal of Educational Psychology, 72,* 1–15.

Wyse, D., Andrews, R., & Hoffman, J. (Eds.). (2010). *The Routledge international handbook of English, language and literacy teaching.* Abingdon, UK: Routledge.

APPENDIX

Alphabetical Listing of the Exemplars

Albers, P. (2007). Visual discourse analysis: An introduction to the analysis of school-generated visual texts. In D. W. Rowe, R. T. Jiménez, D. L. Compton, D. K. Dickinson, Y. Kim, K. M. Leander, et al. (Eds.), *56th yearbook of the National Reading Conference* (pp. 81–95). Oak Creek, WI: National Reading Conference. *(Discourse Analysis)*

Baumann, J. F., Hoffman, J. V., Duffy-Hester, A. M., & Ro, J. M. (2000). *The first R* yesterday and today: U.S. elementary reading instruction practices reported by teachers and administrators. *Reading Research Quarterly, 35,* 338–377. *(Survey Research)*

Beach, R., Enciso, P., Harste, J., Jenkins, C., Raina, S. A., Rogers, R., et al. (2009). Exploring the "critical" in critical content analysis of children's literature. In K. M. Leaner, D. W. Rowe, D. K. Dickinson, M. K. Hundley, R. T. Jamenez, & V. J. Risko (Eds.), *58th yearbook of the National Reading Conference* (pp. 129–143). Oak Creek, WI: National Reading Conference. *(Content Analysis)*

Benge, C., Onwuegbuzie, A. J., Mallette, M. H., & Burgess, M. L. (2010). Doctoral students' perceptions of barriers to reading empirical literature: A mixed analysis. *International Journal of Doctoral Studies, 5,* 55–77. *(Mixed Research)*

Bus, A. G., & van IJzendoorn, M. H. (1999). Phonological awareness and early reading: A meta-analysis of experimental training studies. *Journal of Educational Psychology, 91,* 403–414. *(Meta-Analysis)*

Colwell, J., & Reinking, D. (2016). A formative experiment to align middle-school history instruction with literacy goals. *Teachers College Record, 118*(12), 1–42. *(Design-Based Research)*

Deacon, S. H., Kieffer, M. J., & Laroche, A. (2014). The relation between morphological awareness and reading comprehension: Evidence from mediation and longitudinal models. *Scientific Studies of Reading, 18,* 432–451. *(Correlational Designs: Longitudinal Autoregression)*

Dutro, E., & Haberl, E. (2018). Blurring material and rhetorical walls: Children writing the border/lands in a second-grade classroom. *Journal of Literacy Research, 50*(2), 167–189. *(Content Analysis)*

Dyson, A. H. (2013). *Rewriting the basics: Literacy learning in children's cultures.* New York: Teachers College Press. *(Ethnography and Case Study)*

Gamse, B. C., Jacob, R. T., Horst, M., Boulay, B., & Unlu, F. (2008). *Reading First Impact Study: Final report* (NCEE 2009-4038). Washington, DC: National Center for Education Evaluation and Regional Assistance, Institute of Education Sciences, U.S. Department of Education. *(Causal Effects)*

Gillen, J. (2009). Literacy practices in Schome Park: A virtual literacy ethnography. *Journal of Research in Reading, 32*(1), 57–74. *(Digital Contexts)*

Goldman, S. R., Braasch, J. L. G., Wiley, J., Graesser, A. C., & Brodowinska, K. (2012). Comprehending and learning from Internet sources: Processing patterns of better and poorer learners. *Reading Research Quarterly, 47*(4), 356–381. *(Verbal Protocols)*

Gordon, E., McKibbin, K., Vasudevan, L., & Vinz, R. (2007). Writing out of the unexpected: Narrative inquiry and the weight of small moments. *English Education, 39*(4), 326–351. *(Narrative Approaches)*

Hankins, K. H. (2003). *Teaching through the storm: A journal of hope.* New York: Teachers College Press. *(Narrative Approaches)*

Hartman, D. K. (1995). Eight readers reading: The intertextual links of proficient readers reading multiple passages. *Reading Research Quarterly, 30*(3), 520–561. *(Verbal Protocols)*

Hoffman, J. V., Sailors, M., Duffy, G. G., & Beretvas, N. (2004). The effective elementary classroom literacy environment: Examining the validity of the TEX-IN3 observation system. *Journal of Literacy Research, 36,* 303–334. *(Content Analysis)*

Justice, L. M., McGinty, A. S., Cabell, S. Q., Kilday, C. R., Knighton, K., & Huffman, G. (2010). Language and literacy curriculum supplement for preschoolers who are academically at risk: A feasibility study. *Language, Speech, and Hearing Services in Schools, 41,* 161–178. *(Causal Effects)*

Kieffer, M. J., & Lesaux, N. K. (2008). The role of derivational morphological awareness in the reading comprehension of Spanish-speaking English language learners. *Reading and Writing: An Interdisciplinary Journal, 21,* 783–804. *(Correlational Designs: Correlation and Multiple Regression)*

Kieffer, M. J., & Lesaux, N. K. (2012). Development of morphological awareness and vocabulary knowledge for Spanish-speaking language minority learners: A parallel process latent growth model. *Applied Psycholinguistics, 33,* 23–54. *(Correlational Designs: Longitudinal Growth Modeling)*

Kieffer, M. J., Petscher, Y., Proctor, C. P., & Silverman, R. D. (2016). Is the whole more than the sum of its parts?: Modeling the contributions of language comprehension skills to reading comprehension in the upper elementary grades. *Scientific Studies of Reading, 20,* 436–454. *(Correlational Designs: Latent Variable Modeling)*

Kim, G. M. (2016). Transcultural digital literacies: Cross-border connections and self-representations in an online forum. *Reading Research Quarterly, 51*(2), 199–219. *(Content Analysis)*

Kynard, C. (2010). From Candy Girls to cyber sista-cipher: Narrating Black females' color-consciousness and counterstories in and out of school. *Harvard Educational Review, 80*(1), 30–52. *(Critical Race Methodologies)*

Levesque, K., Kieffer, M. J., & Deacon, S. H. (2017). Morphological awareness and reading comprehension: Examining mediating factors. *Journal of Experimental Child Psychology, 160,* 1–20. *(Correlational Designs: Mediation Analyses)*

Marshall, E. (2004). Stripping for the wolf: Rethinking representations of gender in children's literature. *Reading Research Quarterly, 39*(3), 256–270. *(Content Analysis)*

Mesmer, H. A. E. (2009). Beginning reading materials: A national survey of primary teachers' reported uses and beliefs. *Journal of Literacy Research, 38,* 389–425. *(Survey Research)*

Monaghan, E. J. (1991). Family literacy in early 18th-century Boston: Cotton Mather and his children. *Reading Research Quarterly, 26*(4), 342–370. *(Historical Research)*

Moss, B. (2008). The information text gap: The mismatch between non-narrative text types in basal readers and 2009 NAEP recommended guidelines. *Journal of Literacy Research, 40*(2), 201–219. *(Content Analysis)*

Mudre, L. H., & McCormick, S. (1989). Effects of meaning-focused cues on underachieving readers' context use, self-corrections, and literal comprehension. *Reading Research Quarterly, 24,* 89–113. *(Single-Subject Experimental Design)*

Neuman, S. B., & Gallagher, P. (1994). Joining together in literacy learning: Teenage mothers and children. *Reading Research Quarterly, 29,* 382–401. *(Single-Subject Experimental Design)*

Nugiel, T., Roe, M. A., Taylor, W. P., Vaughn, S. R., Fletcher, J. M., Juranek, J., et al. (2019). Brain activity in struggling readers before intervention relates to future reading gains. *Cortex, 111,* 286–302. *(Neuroimaging)*

Roe, M. A., Martinez, J. E., Mumford, J. A., Taylor, W. P., Cirino, P. T., Fletcher, J. M., et al. (2018). Control engagement during sentence and inhibition fMRI tasks in children with reading difficulties. *Cerebral Cortex, 28*(10), 3697–3710. *(Neuroimaging)*

Steinkuehler, C. (2006). Massively multiplayer online video gaming as participation in a discourse. *Mind, Culture and Activity, 13*(1), 38–52. *(Digital Contexts)*

Steinkuehler, C. (2007). Massively multiplayer online gaming as a constellation of literacy practices. *E-Learning and Digital Media, 4*(3), 297–318. *(Digital Contexts)*

Strong, J. Z. (2019). *Effects of a text structure intervention for reading and writing: A mixed methods experiment.* Unpublished doctoral dissertation, University of Delaware, Newark, DE. *(Instrument Development)*

Wohlwend, K. (2012). The boys who would be princesses: Playing with gender identity intertexts in Disney Princess transmedia. *Gender and Education, 24*(6), 593–610. *(Discourse Analysis)*

Yoshikawa, H., Leyva, D., Snow, C. E., Treviño, E., Barata, M., Weiland, C., et al. (2015). Experimental impacts of a teacher professional development program in Chile on preschool classroom quality and child outcomes. *Developmental Psychology, 51,* 309–322. *(Causal Effects)*

Index

Page numbers in *italic* indicate a figure or a table